RESEARCH HANDBOO
PRO-ENVIRONMENTA

Research Handbook on Employee Pro-Environmental Behaviour

Edited by

Victoria K. Wells

Professor of Sustainable and Ethical Management, The York Management School, University of York, UK

Diana Gregory-Smith

Reader (Associate Professor) in Marketing, Newcastle University Business School, Newcastle University, UK

Danae Manika

Professor of Marketing, Newcastle University Business School, Newcastle University, UK

Edward Elgar
PUBLISHING

Cheltenham, UK • Northampton, MA, USA

Published by
Edward Elgar Publishing Limited
The Lypiatts
15 Lansdown Road
Cheltenham
Glos GL50 2JA
UK

Edward Elgar Publishing, Inc.
William Pratt House
9 Dewey Court
Northampton
Massachusetts 01060
USA

Paperback edition 2020

A catalogue record for this book
is available from the British Library

Library of Congress Control Number: 2018931774

This book is available electronically in the **Elgar**online
Business subject collection
DOI 10.4337/9781786432834

ISBN 978 1 78643 282 7 (cased)
ISBN 978 1 78643 283 4 (eBook)
ISBN 978 1 83910 443 5 (paperback)

Typeset by Servis Filmsetting Ltd, Stockport, Cheshire
Printed and bound by CPI Group (UK) Ltd, Croydon CR0 4YY

Contents

v

Contributors

Bilal Afsar is an Assistant Professor in the department of Management Sciences at Hazara University, Mansehra, Pakistan. He did his PhD from Asian Institute of Technology, Thailand. His research interests include environmental management, organisational psychology, leadership and innovation management.

Neal M. Ashkanasy OAM is Professor of Management in The University of Queensland (UQ) Business School at The University of Queensland, Australia. He studies emotion in organisations, leadership, culture, and ethical behaviour. He has published in journals such as the *Academy of Management Journal* and the *Academy of Management Review*, the *Journal of Management*, and the *Journal of Applied Psychology*. He served as Editor-in-Chief of the *Journal of Organizational Behavior*, Associate Editor for the *Academy of Management Review*, and is currently Associate Editor for *Emotion Review* and Series Editor for *Research on Emotion in Organizations*. He is a Fellow of several learned societies, including the Society for Industrial and Organizational Psychology (SIOP) and APS.

Wayne Binney was previously Associate Professor of Marketing at Deakin University, Melbourne. He remains an active marketing researcher in consumer behaviour, sustainability and social marketing.

Megan J. Bissing-Olson completed her PhD in the School of Psychology at The University of Queensland. Her research examines within-person variability in environmental behaviour in relation to affective experience.

Frances Bowen is Head of the School of Business and Management, and Professor of Innovation Studies at Queen Mary University of London, UK. She previously served as Deputy Head of the School and Director of Research at the School. She specialises in corporate strategy and environmental governance. Originally from Wales, she returned to the UK in 2011 after eight years at the Haskayne School of Business, University of Calgary (Canada). There she had served as Associate Dean (Research) and as Director of the International Resource Industries and Sustainability Centre (IRIS). She has been a Visiting Fellow at the Smith School of Enterprise and the Environment at the University of Oxford (2009), and held an ESRC Knowledge Exchange Fellowship at Defra in 2013–14. Professor Bowen is often asked to provide advice on regulating for a sustainable economy to companies and to regulatory bodies such as the Environment Agency, the Department for Environment, Food and Rural Affairs (Defra), the National Audit Office and the Department for Business, Innovation and Skills (BIS).

Peter Bradley is Senior Lecturer in Economics at the University of the West of England (UWE). He was previously at Surrey University and joined the Centre for Environmental Strategy (CES) in 2006 as an EPSRC research fellow looking at the industrial and social ecology of urban resource flows. Peter has a BSc degree in Environmental Science specialising in environmental chemistry (University of Plymouth), an MSc in Economic Management and Policy (University of Strathclyde) and a PhD in Ecological Economics (University of Surrey). Peter is a member of the British Institute of Energy Economics and the International Society for Ecological Economics.

Linda Brennan is a Professor based in the School of Media and Communication at RMIT University in Melbourne. In the lead up to becoming a full time academic, Dr. Brennan had an active consulting practice in marketing and strategic research. Her clients include government, not for profit and educational institutions. Her research interests are social and government marketing and especially the influence of marketing communications and advertising on behaviour.

John Callewaert, PhD is the Emerging Opportunities Programme Director at the Graham Sustainability Institute and a Lecturer in the College of Literature, Science, and the Arts at the University of Michigan. As Emerging Opportunities Programme Director at the Graham Institute, John is responsible for designing, implementing, and overseeing a wide range of activities which support translational knowledge efforts involving subject matter experts, decision makers, and key stakeholders in outlining viable pathways towards sustainability solutions. Dr. Callewaert came to the Graham Institute in 2009 after serving for two years as the Director of the University of Michigan-Flint Office of Research. From 2000–2007, Callewaert was the founding director of the Institute for Community and Environment at Colby-Sawyer College and an Associate Professor of Social Sciences and Education. Between 1984 and 1987 he served as an agricultural volunteer with Peace Corps Nepal, working on improving seed supplies in remote hill villages. Dr. Callewaert serves as an associate editor for the *Journal of Environmental Studies and Sciences* and as an advisory board member for The Integrated Assessment Society and the Association for the Advancement of Sustainability in Higher Education.

Yu Ha Cheung is Associate Head and Senior Lecturer in the Department of Management and Director of the Master of Human Resources Management Programme at Hong Kong Baptist University. She received her PhD degree in Business Administration from the University of Missouri – Columbia, USA. She has taught in the US, Hong Kong and Mainland China. Her research interests include developmental relationships, career development, workplace green behaviour and cross-cultural management.

Cristina E. Ciocirlan, PhD is the 2015 recipient of a US Fulbright Scholar Award in the UK, to study environmental behaviours in organisations at Durham University. She worked with local and international banks and consulted with small and medium-sized businesses. As a graduate student, she received full scholarships to study in Prague, the Czech Republic, Budapest, Hungary and Colchester, UK. She presented several papers at national and state conferences (two of which won 'The Best Paper Award') and published her research in peer-reviewed journals. Her research interests focus on environmental management, managerial decision-making, and family business management. Ciocirlan teaches courses in Management and Organisational Behaviour, Human Resource Management, and other management courses at Elizabethtown College, Pennsylvania, USA.

Matthew C. Davis is a Lecturer (Assistant Professor) at Leeds University Business School, UK, a Chartered Psychologist and an Associate Fellow of the British Psychological Society. Matthew's research centres on how people interact with their environments, the impact of different office designs and the topic of environmental sustainability. His expertise lies in the area of organisational and environmental psychology. Matthew has worked with partners such as Rolls-Royce, Marks and Spencer, Arup Consulting and British Gas. He has published his research in international journals and high-quality edited books. Matthew has been quoted in various UK, US and international newspapers and magazines.

Stephan Dilchert is an Associate Professor of Management at the Zicklin School of Business at Baruch College, City University of New York. His research focuses on the role of personality, intelligence, and other individual differences variables in personnel decisions. He is particularly interested in how these characteristics relate to creativity, counter-productive behaviours, and pro-environmental behaviours amongst employees. He co-edited a volume on *Managing Human Resources for Environmental Sustainability* for the SIOP Professional Practice Series (with Susan Jackson and Deniz S. Ones), and co-chaired the 2011 SIOP

Theme Track on Environmental Sustainability and the 2012 SIOP Leading Edge Consortium on the same topic. His work on creativity was recognised with the Meredith P. Crawford Fellowship from the Human Resources Research Organization and the S. Rains Wallace Award from the Society for Industrial and Organizational Psychology. Dr. Dilchert currently serves as Editor-in-Chief of the *International Journal of Selection and Assessment*. In addition to a PhD in industrial and organisational psychology from the University of Minnesota, he holds SHRM-SCP certification from the Society for Human Resource Management as well as SPHR certification from the Human Resources Certification Institute.

Cleber Dutra is an Associate Professor and a visiting Research Fellow in sustainability management at the Technische Universität Berlin (Germany). His main areas of interest include innovation, sustainability, multi-organisational programmes, resource efficiency, pro-environmental/ sustainable behaviour, and CSR.

Paul C. Endrejat has studied Psychology at the University of Potsdam and the Universiteit Utrecht and is currently working as a Research Associate at the Department of Industrial, Organizational and Social Psychology at Technische Universität Braunschweig. His main research foci are innovation processes in teams, Design Thinking, and increasing energy-conversation behaviours within organisations. These various research topics are tied together by a strong interest in interaction analytical research methods and Motivational Interviewing. Concurrently, he works as a trainer in the faculty's graduate programme and as a consultant for various change management projects in the industrial sector.

Shane Fudge is an Associate in Energy Policy at the University of Exeter. Projects that Shane has been involved in since beginning work in the area of sustainability include: RESOLVE (research group on lifestyles, values and environment); BARENERGY (barriers and opportunities to changing consumer behaviour at EU level); UNLOC (understanding local and community governance of energy); CRISP (creating innovative sustainability pathways); and REDUCE (reshaping energy demand of users by communication). He has also been involved in consultancy work, the latest one commissioned by AMDEA into the relationship between technology and behavioural practices around household energy use.

Birgitta Gatersleben is Reader in Environmental Psychology at the University of Surrey where she leads the Environmental Psychology Research Centre and the MSc in Environmental Psychology. Her research focuses on understanding and promoting sustainable lifestyles and experiences with the natural environment.

Diana Gregory-Smith is a Senior Lecturer (Associate Professor) in Marketing at the Birmingham Business School, University of Birmingham. Her main research interest lies in the area of consumer psychology, particularly applied to ethical and sustainable consumption. Her second research area is social marketing, with a particular emphasis on health and environmental behaviour amongst consumers and employees. Diana has published in several subject-specific and interdisciplinary journals such as *Journal of Business Ethics, Psychology & Marketing, Journal of Marketing Management, Journal of Marketing Communications, Sustainability, Journal of Sustainable Tourism, Tourism Management, Studies in Higher Education*, amongst others.

Amelie V. Güntner is currently working as a Research Associate at the Department of Industrial, Organizational and Social Psychology at Technische Universität Braunschweig. Beforehand, she studied Psychology at the SRH University Heidelberg and the Vrije Universiteit Amsterdam. In her research, Amelie Güntner looks at the interactional dynamics in the context of change management projects. In doing so, she focuses on the micro behaviours in change-related conversations, for example, as those between change agents and change recipients, to derive implications for successful change communication. In this regard, she uses the communication approach of Motivational Interviewing to provide energy managers with a training that supports them in their daily communication with energy users.

Regina Hahn is an Associate Professor of Organization Development and Corporate Management at the Hochschule Niederrhein (HSNR), University of Applied Sciences, Germany. Her research examines sustainability management, corporate social responsibility, and change management, specifically from a micro-level perspective. Her work has been published in internationally renowned journals such as *Organization & Environment* and the *Journal of Business Ethics*, amongst others. Regina holds a PhD in management from Heinrich-Heine-University Düsseldorf, Germany. Before starting her university career she worked for several years as an internal consultant for a large industrial conglomerate.

Simone Kauffeld is Professor at the Institute for Psychology and the Department of Industrial, Organizational and Social Psychology. She is also a co-founder of the 4A-Side Corporation and Vice President at the TU Braunschweig for teaching, studies and further education. Since 2007, she has been Head of Department for Industrial, Organizational, and Social Psychology at the Technical University of Braunschweig. Besides her university career, she has also worked as an industrial consultant for several change management projects. As a co-founder of the 4A-Side Corporation she offers a research-based consultation for further education, communications skills, and teams and leadership development.

Rachael M. Klein is a Senior Manager and Team Lead of Client Analytics at Korn Ferry, where she designs, executes and consults on workforce analytics projects in support of leadership selection and development, talent management and organisational strategy. She received her PhD in industrial/organisational psychology from the University of Minnesota. Her research interests related to corporate social responsibility include measuring and promoting environmental sustainability within organisations. Her dissertation, 'Employee Motives for Engaging in Environmentally Sustainable Behaviors: A Multi-Study Analysis', was focused on the creation of a taxonomy of motives for and barriers to green and ungreen behaviour and the development of an Environmental Sustainability Motives Scale to assess these motives and barriers. Klein's research was supported by a National Science Foundation Graduate Research Fellowship and has been published in the *Journal of Applied Psychology* and in edited volumes related to sustainability (including the SIOP Professional Practices series volume *Managing Human Resources for Sustainability*). She was a member of the planning committee for the 2011 SIOP Theme Track on Environmental Sustainability and has reviewed journal articles related to environmental sustainability.

Florian E. Klonek studied Psychology and Computer Sciences at the Free University Berlin and the University of Sydney. Upon completing his studies, he started working as a Research Associate for the Department of Industrial/Organizational and Social Psychology at TU Braunschweig, Germany. In April 2016, he finished his PhD in which he investigated a socio-interactional intervention (i.e., motivational interviewing) within a large university change management project. Florian Klonek is currently a postdoctoral researcher at the Centre of Transformative Work Design at the University of Western Australia. In his research, he bridges methodological approaches from different disciplines, including psycholinguistics, change management and computer science, to better understand interactional dynamics in a variety of organisational and social settings. His research interests include team dynamics, leader–follower interactions, training transfer and effective career guidance.

Matthew Leach is a Professor of Energy and Environmental Systems at the Centre for Environment and Sustainability, University of Surrey. He initially trained for and became a Mechanical Engineer and now has an MSc in Environmental Technology from Imperial College and a PhD from Imperial in Energy Policy. His research focuses on techno-economic and environmental analyses for improvements in the built environment through energy efficiency and integration of low carbon energy supply. Matthew also leads on a university-level research theme on 'Urban Living'.

Alicia S. M. Leung is an Associate Professor of Management at the Hong Kong Baptist University. She received her PhD degree in Management Learning from the University of Lancaster, UK. She is active in researching and writing materials about Asian organisations and management issues. Her research interests lie in the areas of gender differences, business ethics, workplace incivility, and corporate social responsibility. She is currently the director of the Master of Science in Strategic Human Resources Programme.

Simon Lockrey is currently a Research Fellow in the Industrial Design programme at RMIT University, and Director of global urban gardening brand Glowpear. Simon has worked on hundreds of commercial design and engineering projects for organisations such as Breville, Dyson, Whirlpool and Nestle, generating many millions of dollars in income and intellectual property. His academic research projects relate to life cycle assessment (LCA), co-design, emerging technology, energy efficiency and sustainability strategy.

Danae Manika is Professor of Marketing at Newcastle University Business School, Newcastle University. Using a multi-disciplinary approach, blending the lines between marketing, psychology, and advertising, her research aims to answer a fundamental marketing research question: 'How to diminish the knowledge-behaviour gap?' Particularly, her research focuses on behaviour change and takes an information processing approach, which identifies, classifies and examines cognitive and affective factors that influence individuals'/consumers'/employees' decisions and choices after exposure to campaigns/messages/interventions; and translate knowledge acquisition to behaviour change/formation. She often uses health and environmental social issues as the venue for understanding the knowledge-behaviour gap. This research on health and environmental behaviour change has direct implications for social marketing and behavioural interventions that motivate health and environmental action, respectively. Her research has been published in journals, such as *Psychology & Marketing, Journal of Business Ethics, Journal of Marketing Management, Computers in Human Behavior, Technological Forecasting and Social Change, Information Technology & People, Journal of Health*

Communication, International Journal of Advertising, Journal of Marketing Communications, and *Tourism Management* amongst others.

Robert W. Marans, PhD is Research Professor at the University of Michigan's Institute for Social Research and Professor Emeritus of Architecture and Urban Planning in the university's Taubman College of Architecture and Urban Planning. For more than three decades, he has conducted evaluative studies and research dealing with various aspects of communities, neighbourhoods, housing, and parks and recreational facilities. His research has focused on user requirements and the manner in which attributes of the physical and sociocultural environments influence individual and group behaviour and the quality of community life. Dr. Marans' most recent book, *Investigating Quality of Urban Life: Theory, Methods, and Empirical Research* was published by Springer (2011). His current research considers the impact of the built and natural environments on quality of life, the role of neighbourhood in the health of Detroit residents, and issues of sustainability and energy conservation in buildings and institutional settings.

Niamh Murtagh is a Senior Research Fellow at the Bartlett School of Construction and Project Management, University College London. Her research area is sustainable behaviour, including energy, transport and recycling, with a particular focus on sustainable behaviour within construction.

Thomas A. Norton is a Management Consultant based in London. He completed his MPsych/PhD degrees at The University of Queensland, Australia. His research focuses on organisational culture and climate, and employee green behaviour. He has published his research in the journals *Industrial and Organizational Psychology, Organization & Environment, Journal of Environmental Psychology,* and *Journal of Organizational Behavior,* and contributed a chapter to the book *The Psychology of Green Organizations.*

Deniz S. Ones is the Hellervik Professor of Industrial Psychology, a Distinguished McKnight Professor, and a Distinguished Teaching Professor at the University of Minnesota. She has received numerous prestigious awards for her research on individual differences, amongst them the 1998 Ernest J. McCormick Award for Distinguished Early Career Contributions from the Society for Industrial and Organizational Psychology (SIOP), as well as the 2003 Cattell Early Career Research Award from the Society for Multivariate Experimental Psychology. Ones also received the Award for Professional Contributions and Service to Testing from the Association of Test Publishers. She is a Fellow of the

Association for Psychological Science and the American Psychological Association (Divisions 5 and 14), for which she also chaired the Committee on Psychological Testing and Assessment. She co-edited the first (2001) and second (2018) editions of the bestselling, multi-volume *SAGE Handbook of Industrial, Work, and Organizational Psychology*. She has served as Editor-in-Chief of the *International Journal of Selection and Assessment* and Associate Editor of the *Journal of Personnel Psychology*. She also co-edited a volume on *Managing Human Resources for Environmental Sustainability* for the SIOP Professional Practice Series (with Susan Jackson and Stephan Dilchert) and co-chaired the 2011 SIOP Theme Track on Environmental Sustainability and the 2012 SIOP Leading Edge Consortium on the same topic.

Felix Ostertag, PhD is a Postdoctoral Research Fellow and Lecturer at the Department of Sustainability Management at the University of Hohenheim, Stuttgart. Furthermore, he will serve as a Visiting Professor at the University of Strasbourg in 2018. His research examines voluntary pro-environmental behaviour in the workplace, holistic value creation of social enterprises, and workplace outcomes that relate to meaningfulness of relationships, gratitude, and well-being. His work has been recognised, for instance, by the FGF with the Best Sustainable- and Social-Entrepreneurship Research Award 2013. Currently, he holds a DAAD (German Academic Exchange Service) Fellowship to conduct cross-cultural research at the Southwestern University of Finance and Economics in Chengdu, China, the EM Strasbourg Business School (University of Strasbourg), France, and Ca' Foscari University of Venice, Italy.

Pascal Paillé is a full Professor at Laval University, Quebec, Canada. His research focuses on greening organisations by putting the focus at the employee level. His research concerns both green human resource management and employee pro-environmental behaviours. His research has been published in the *Journal of Business Ethics, Journal of Business Research, International Journal of Human Resource Management, Journal of Environmental Psychology, Business, Strategy and the Environment, Journal of Applied Business Research*, amongst others.

Stacey L. Parker joined the School of Psychology, The University of Queensland (UQ), Australia, as a Lecturer in Organisational Psychology in 2013. This was following a postdoctoral research position in the Business School of Queensland University of Technology. She completed her PhD in occupational health psychology at UQ Psychology in 2012. Her research focuses on employee stress and motivation, particularly what individuals and organisations can do to manage stress and improve performance. Through this work she aims to help organisations and their employees devise new strategies to work healthier while still being productive. Stacey is an organisational psychologist who consults, to both private and public organisations, on issues like recruitment and selection, training and development, workload management, and operational safety. She also serves on the editorial board for the *Journal of Occupational Health Psychology*.

Angela Ruepert is Postdoctoral Researcher in Environmental Psychology at the University of Groningen. Her research is focused on understanding the factors that influence pro-environmental behaviour at the workplace. She is interested in how personal values and contextual factors, such as corporate environmental responsibility, which can strengthen people's focus on benefiting the environment, interact and, as such, encourage pro-environmental behaviour at work.

Sally V. Russell is an Associate Professor in the Sustainability Research Institute at the University of Leeds, UK. She leads the research group 'Businesses and Organisations for Sustainable Societies' and is the programme leader of the BA Environment and Business. Her research focuses broadly on behaviour change for sustainability with a particular emphasis on how emotional reactions to environmental issues affect subsequent behaviour and decision-making – both within and outside organisations. Her work has been published in journals including: *Water Resources Research*, the *Journal of Environmental Management*, *Business Strategy and the Environment*, *Frontiers in Psychology*, and the *Journal of Organisational Change Management*. She currently serves on the editorial boards of *Business, Strategy and Environment*, *Journal of Organizational Behavior*, and *Journal of Management & Organization*.

Imad Shah is currently working in the Institute of Management Studies at University of Peshawar. He did his PhD in entrepreneurship from University of Essex, UK.

Asad Shahjehan is serving as an Assistant Professor in the department of Management Sciences at Hazara University, Mansehra, Pakistan. His areas of interest are organisational behaviour and employee psychology.

Warren Staples, PhD is a Lecturer in management in the School of Management at RMIT University. His research interests are the practice of corporate social responsibility/sustainability, public management, public procurement, and corporate governance.

Linda Steg is Professor of Environmental Psychology at the University of Groningen. Her research focuses on understanding factors influencing environmental behaviour, the effects and acceptability of strategies aimed to encourage pro-environmental behaviour, and how and why acting pro-environmentally affects well-being. She is particularly interested in the human dimensions of a sustainable energy transition.

Terry Tudor is an Associate Professor in waste management at the University of Northampton (UK). His main areas of interest include sustainable waste management in both organisations and households, pro-environmental behaviour and resilience.

David Uzzell is Professor of Environmental Psychology at the University of Surrey. His research interests include critical psychological approaches to changing consumption and production practices in the context of climate change, including research on the role of organised labour in sustainable production, and the psychological benefits of the greening of offices.

Caroline Verfuerth is a PhD student at the Sheffield University Management School and part of the Critical Research in Marketing and Society (CReiMS) research cluster. Her PhD research focuses on spillover effects from behaviour change interventions in organisations to pro-environmental behaviours at home, with a particular focus on sustainable diets. She has previously gained an MSc in Environmental Psychology from the Otto-von-Guericke-University Magdeburg and a BSc in Psychology from the University of Hamburg, Germany. Caroline is also a co-founder of the British Environmental Psychology Society (BrEPS).

Karli Verghese is Principal Research Fellow and Associate Professor in the Industrial Design programme at RMIT University. Her research projects have included the development of decision support tools for packaging, resource efficiency, food waste, eco-design and one currently being developed for Australia's Antarctic research station (Casey). Research themes include the role of packaging, packaging sustainability, food loss/waste across supply chains, resource efficiency, waste management, and life cycle assessment.

Victoria K. Wells is Professor of Sustainable and Ethical Management at The York Management School, York University (UK). Her research interests lie in the application of behavioural psychology to consumers, foraging ecology models of consumer behaviour and environmental behaviour, psychology and social marketing with a particular focus on employee behaviour. Prior to joining academia she worked in Marketing Communications as an Account Executive. She has published in a wide range of journals including *Tourism Management, Journal of Business Research, Journal of Marketing Management, Marketing Theory, Service Industries Journal, Journal of Business Ethics* and *Psychology and Marketing*, amongst others.

Brenton M. Wiernik is an Assistant Professor of Industrial–Organizational Psychology at the University of South Florida. His research focuses on the measurement and application of individual differences, including vocational interests, personality traits and cognitive abilities, for understanding how individuals develop and change throughout their working lives. He studies how individual differences impact employee responses to changing work demands, such as changing needs to promote environmental sustainability through work behaviour. Wiernik also actively works to develop new quantitative methods for psychometric assessment and meta-analysis. His work has appeared in journals such as the *Journal of Vocational Behavior, Career Development International, Annual Review of Organizational Psychology and Organizational Behavior, Multivariate Behavioral Research, Industrial and Organizational Psychology*, and the *Journal of Managerial Psychology*, as well as numerous edited scholarly books. Wiernik was the lead editor of *Managing Expatriates: Success Factors in Private and Public Domains* and serves on editorial boards of the *Journal of Environmental Psychology*, the *Journal of Managerial Psychology*, and the *International Journal of Selection and Assessment*.

Lei Yang is a PhD candidate with particular interests in pro-environmental behaviours in the School of Business and Management at Queen Mary University of London, UK. She holds a Master's Degree in Business (Behavioural Science) from the University of Warwick, and a BA (Hons) in International Business Management from the University of Nottingham Ningbo China.

Hannes Zacher is Professor of Work and Organisational Psychology at the Institute of Psychology, University of Leipzig. In his research programme, he investigates ageing at work, career development and occupational well-being; proactivity, innovation, leadership, and entrepreneurship; and green organisational climate and employee green behaviour.

1. Introduction to the *Research Handbook on Employee Pro-Environmental Behaviour*

Victoria K. Wells, Diana Gregory-Smith and Danae Manika

It is generally accepted that it is important to study pro-environmental behaviour in various contexts (Steg and Vlek 2009) and the majority of the work in this area has taken place in the home by examining and encouraging sustainable consumption (Reisch and Thøgersen 2017). However, pro-environmental behaviour is also important within organisational environments as highlighted by interest in the field of corporate social responsibility (Aguinis and Glavas 2012), corporate environmental responsibility (CER) and corporate ecological responsiveness (Bansal and Roth 2000). Over the last few years there has also been increasing attention on the pro- or anti-environmental behaviours of employees (Lo et al. 2012; Lamm et al. 2013; Robertson and Barling 2015). It is vital to understand this area as individual employees' behaviour contributes significantly to an organisation's environmental performance and employees spend a considerable amount of their day at work. However, in 2009 Davis and Challenger calculated that only about 2 per cent of studies on pro-environmental behaviour were based in the workplace, and of these, most focused on waste and few were theoretically based. The field has grown and developed significantly since 2009 with work on employee pro-environmental behaviour often using a range of theories and models, either developed in general social psychology or specifically from broad pro-environmental studies to assess employee environmental behaviour, often by adapting them to the organisational context. This *Handbook* provides a snapshot in time of a now rapidly developing field.

Recent advances in the examination of employee environmental behaviour have more carefully delineated and categorised the many types of pro- and anti-environmental behaviours that employees can enact in an organisational context (see Chapter 2 in particular). However, there still remains much debate about the terminology used and the focus of these studies. Even within this *Handbook* many different terms for employee pro-environmental behaviour are used, including employee green behaviours (EGB), employee environmental commitment, voluntary pro-environmental behaviour of employees (VPBE), organisational citizenship behaviours for the environment (OCBE) and green workplace behaviour. These different terminologies reflect the different disciplines from which they come (many of which are represented here) and whether they focus on voluntary behaviour or those prescribed as part of a job role or both. They also highlight the current discussion about direct (direct gestures to enhance the environment – e.g., conserving water) or indirect (motivating other staff to engage in direct gestures) (Homburg and Stolberg 2006) pro-environmental behaviours. These discussions are still ongoing and are reflected throughout the chapters included in this *Handbook*.

Over the last ten years, there has been increasing interest in the area of employee pro-environmental behaviour, which has largely focused on the antecedents and consequences of employee pro-environmental behaviour. This work is highlighted in Part II of the *Handbook*. However, increasingly, research is also utilising technological approaches to gain a greater understanding of employees' behaviour and produce effective interventions and campaigns with real-world significance (see Parts III and IV of the *Handbook*).

The *Handbook* contains a mix of empirical, theoretical and discussion chapters from a range of backgrounds including organisational psychology, human resource management (HRM) and social marketing. The chapters provide a range of different methods, from interviews and focus groups, to longitudinal surveys and diary methods. The *Handbook* also contains work from across the globe, with studies from the USA and Europe as well as Asia and Australia highlighting the global reach and appeal of this area of study.

The *Handbook* chapters are split into six parts covering a broad range of topics. The first part (What is employee pro-environmental behaviour?) includes two chapters. Both chapters attempt to clarify what green behaviour in organisations is and what it looks like, first from the employee perspective and second from the HRM perspective.

The first chapter (Chapter 2) presents and discusses the Green Five taxonomy. This chapter builds on the recurring theme, already discussed above, regarding the problem of multiple definitions and taxonomies of green or pro-environmental behaviours in the workplace. The chapter proposes that many definitions currently utilised in the area are too narrow, and too focused on the three Rs (reduce, reuse, recycle). To overcome this, the chapter develops the Green Five taxonomy to demonstrate the full range of behaviours. As the authors note, this can include all dimensions of job performance, including core technical performance (e.g., mutual fund managers choosing investments based on companies' environmental performance, tractor operators driving more slowly to reduce fuel usage), counterproductive work behaviours (ignoring sustainable purchasing policies), communication (writing sustainability reports), effort/initiative (going out of one's way to act sustainably), hierarchical leadership (supporting subordinates' green ideas), and others. They also highlight Campbell and Wiernik's (2015) study, which described EGB as a compound performance domain – a collection of performance behaviours spanning multiple substantive performance dimensions which are united by a common goal – rather than a separate performance dimension unto themselves. The taxonomy contains 17 behavioural categories with five meta-categories, each with similar functional goals and common psychological underpinnings. They also highlight the cross-cultural validity of the taxonomy, at least across Europe and the USA. The chapter finishes by presenting implications for HRM practice.

The second chapter in this part (Chapter 3) concentrates on Green HRM (GHRM) and distinguishes it from sustainable HRM. The chapter comments that many organisations have a haphazard approach to environmental management, and engage in 'random acts of greenness', or a set of disparate green initiatives, with mixed effects (Makower and Pike 2008). By contrast, a coherent, strategic approach to sustainability via GHRM being performed in a consistent and integrative fashion is necessary. GHRM elements such as recruitment, job design, training and development, performance measurement and green orientation and onboarding are presented and discussed. The chapter also discusses how green education in firms is delivered. Overall the chapter seeks to show what GHRM does and does not look like and concludes by highlighting the importance of encouraging participation in green issues and making links to corporate social responsibility (CSR) programmes.

The second part of the *Handbook* contains chapters that focus on a diverse range of antecedents and consequences of green employee behaviour. This part contains nine chapters and is by far the biggest section in the *Handbook*. This reflects the breadth of literature in the broad area of employee environmental behaviour, with a particular focus on antecedents of green employee behaviour.

The first chapter in this part (Chapter 4) examines a range of individual factors that can promote or inhibit environmentally relevant employee behaviours. The chapter examines the influence of attitudes, knowledge, demographics and stable individual differences via meta-analyses and their relationship with employee green behaviours. They highlight the importance of intentions, habits and motives as well as the values of conscientiousness, openness and agreeableness on employee green behaviours. From these, the authors make suggestions for HRM practice and suggestions for interventions. They also note the need to align these interventions with broader organisational environmental goals.

The second chapter in this part (Chapter 5) concentrates on the voluntary pro-environmental behaviour of employees (VPBE) and their role in corporate greening. It discusses the characteristics of VPBEs and examines their theoretical determinants via the Theory of Planned Behaviour (TPB) and Norm Activation Model (NAM). In doing so, this chapter highlights the role of attitudes, social and personal norms, perceived organisational support and affective commitment. It also assesses a range of different interventions including one on one conversations, interventions via e-mail and also via newsletters. Overall, the chapter also draws attention to the often-neglected role of habit (also noted in Chapter 3) in establishing a pro-environmental organisational climate.

The third chapter in this part (Chapter 6) highlights the role of values and context as antecedents of pro-environmental behaviour at the workplace. Situated in the domain of CER, the chapter highlights the need to engage employees in multiple pro-environmental behaviours. It highlights the extent to which employees are focused on the environment as an important determinant of pro-environmental behaviour and why employees would be willing and likely to behave pro-environmentally at work, even though it may be somewhat costly, effortful or inconvenient. Additionally, they note the role of values (in particular biospheric values) identity and norms via the values–identity–personal norms (VIP) model. They suggest that values provide a stable basis for, and determine the strength of, people's focus on benefiting the environment while contextual factors may further strengthen people's focus on benefiting the environment by making these values accessible or by additionally steering people's focus towards environmental aspects. They note that while values are important, without an enabling context where employees can act upon their values, they will not change their behaviour for the better. The results of their empirical studies highlight that contextual factors may particularly encourage pro-environmental actions amongst those with relatively weak biospheric values.

The fourth chapter in this part (Chapter 7) examines individual differences in the performance of behaviour and, in particular, it focuses on within-person variability of behaviour and change over time. In this way, it examines the temporal patterns in behaviour and how an individual's behaviour may change, or be inconsistent, across a day, a week, a month, a year and so on. In particular, the chapter focuses on the role of positive affect as an antecedent of this temporal variability and presents a conceptual framework to guide future research. The chapter additionally highlights daily diary studies as a useful methodology for conducting research with an extensive longitudinal design.

The fifth chapter in this part (Chapter 8) examines employee pro-environmental behaviour and its determinates in Hong Kong. In particular, it focuses on, via an empirical study, three factors affecting employees' engagement in green behaviours. These factors are job characteristics (especially autonomy at work), management involvement (in particular management expectations) and employee intrinsic motivation. The authors highlight that, in the Hong Kong context, intrinsic motivation is the most important determinant but management expectations are also key. Overall, they suggest that developing environmental education of employees is crucial to encouraging engagement with environmental practices.

The sixth chapter in this part (Chapter 9) examines the role of the 'caring manager' or 'caring leader'. The chapter builds on Gilligan's ethics of care and applies this to the employee environmental behaviour perspective. The chapter examines the role of support from managers in supporting employees to be more environmentally friendly and suggests that employees are more likely to perform responsible environmental behaviour when they are supported by their manager. The authors also highlight the potential for managers to help employees overcome burden, constraints and tensions. Their key message is that managers must support employees if they want to support the environment.

The seventh chapter in this part (Chapter 10) examines further the role of the leader on employees' environmental behaviour. The chapter highlights that leaders facilitate pro-environmental behaviour change within organisations and that the employees' immediate manager is likely to have the most immediate effect on employees' behaviour. The authors examine and discuss the potential effects of a range of leadership styles, including transformational leadership, environmental leadership, green entrepreneurial leadership and spiritual leadership. They also discuss the potential impact of leadership development initiatives.

The eighth chapter in this part (Chapter 11) builds on earlier chapters by focusing on organisations and, particularly, how managers can encourage their employees to be green at work and build a green culture. They utilise the concept of complex adaptive systems (those that adapt to their environment through the interaction of multiple, interdependent elements) to examine the range of methods, interventions and incentives that organisations use to encourage employee pro-environmental behaviour. These include leader modelling (transformational leadership), incentives schemes (financial/non-financial), the organisational environment (infrastructure) and recruitment and training. The authors also examine the consequences or outcomes of employee green behaviours and highlight environmental performance and cost savings as key. In using the complex systems approach, they highlight the reciprocity cycle of influence between employees and the organisation as a whole and highlight the importance of involving front-line employees in any developments. They also describe this as a dynamic learning process, where there is experiential and vicarious learning resulting in system level cultural change.

The final chapter in this part (Chapter 12) examines symbolic motives of pro-environmental behaviour for both employees and, more broadly, organisations. The chapter highlights that green employee behaviours can be superficial, improvised and symbolic in nature, rather than based on true environmentalism. The framework presented in the chapter highlights that organisations are motivated to engage in PEB due to legitimation restrictions, the need for competitiveness, stakeholder pressures, and ecological responsibility. Alternatively, employees are motivated to engage in PEB due to normative and symbolic reasons, job requirements and ecological responsibility. The authors highlight three key motivations – appropriateness, competitiveness, and status, that operate at both organisational and employee levels.

The third part of the *Handbook* contains three chapters which, to a greater or lesser extent, focus on interventions that encourage pro-environmental behaviour amongst employees or target organisational green behaviour change. While interventions and their implications have been discussed briefly in some of the previous chapters above, the chapters in this part particularly focus on discussing interventions and their elements in detail.

The first chapter in this part (Chapter 13) looks at the role of self-determination theory (SDT) and participatory action research to raise employees' motivation by concentrating on three elements: relatedness, autonomy and control. To do this, the authors use participatory interventions (PI) as a method of involving employees in the planning and decision process for pro-environmental behaviours, which are implemented in their workplace. As the authors note, participation is the process during which employees gain influence regarding information-processing, decision-making, or problem-solving (Wagner 1994). In this regard, a PI is not done *for* or *on*, but *with* employees (Heron and Reason 2001). The chapter puts forward a range of tools that can be used to empower employees, which include reflective listening, force field analysis and action planning.

The second chapter in this part (Chapter 14) also looks at a potential way to build up employees' motivation, in this case towards energy-saving behaviour. Via socio-motivational and micro-interactional perspectives, which build on change management research, they propose motivational interviewing to potentially help energy managers (change agents) to discuss energy saving with employees. Motivational interviewing is defined as a 'collaborative conversation style for strengthening a person's own motivation and commitment to change' (Miller and Rollnick 2013: 12) and originates from clinical psychology.

The final chapter in this part (Chapter 15) highlights the resource-based challenges and structural influences that employees face. Via structuration theory, the 'Nine Ps' framework (Brennan et al. 2015) and Life Cycle Analysis (LCA) this chapter seeks ways in which employees' environmental behaviours can be improved. Structuration is the reciprocal relationship between people, their actions, and the social structures in which they act. The authors use two case studies (Uniting Agewell and eco-design) to illustrate their approach and suggest that with a thoughtful design, both organisations and stakeholders can co-create behavioural infrastructures to provide agency to participants that enhance environmental outcomes.

The fourth part of the book focuses on behavioural feedback through technology, a growing area of interest, and here reflected in two real-world field trials. The first chapter in this part (Chapter 16) seeks to overcome problems of earlier feedback studies (proving monthly feedback, aggregated by building) by providing feedback targeted to the individual and close to the behaviour. For the field trial (supported by focus groups) the researchers installed energy monitoring devices at each work desk to provide individual energy feedback. Additionally, the authors measured attitudes, values and self-identity as well as self-reported behaviour. A clear finding from the field trail is that self-reported behaviour was not related to energy use, before or after the intervention, highlighting that self-reported behaviour is unlikely to be accurate and that actual energy behaviour should be collected where possible. Technological advances make this increasingly feasible and practical for energy behaviours. They also suggest that automation, such as powering down PCs when not used for a period of time, may be more effective than behaviour change (Staddon et al. 2016). The study also highlights potential ethical issues regarding energy surveillance.

The second chapter (Chapter 17) in this part examined energy feedback, in the form of a smart metering intervention alongside the emergence and diffusion of social norms. The authors used an energy footprint tool (MyEcoFootprint) over the course of a 7-month intervention supplemented by the collection of survey data. The authors suggest that after norms emerge, they are then diffused and this in turn translates into behaviour.

The fifth part of the book focuses on contextual issues in employee environmental behaviour or behaviour change in particular contexts. The first of these chapters (Chapter 18) seeks to examine the key characteristics of environmental behaviour change in large organisations where the complexity of the change may be much larger or more significant. The authors note that given the complex nature of large organisations and the number of influencing factors, organisational change is unlikely to be linear and there will be several challenges which will need to be overcome. These challenges can include the role of managers, organisational culture and identity. The authors highlight a need for a participatory approach (supporting the work in Chapter 13), which seeks to involve staff in the process, explains what is happening and why; this is therefore more likely to engage them. In turn, greater engagement and ownership of the process might lead to a greater chance of success.

The second chapter in this part (Chapter 19) provides an overview of the Sustainability Cultural Indicators Program (SCIP), a multi-year project designed to measure and track the culture of sustainability on the University of Michigan's (U-M) Ann Arbor campus. The chapter focuses on organisational transformation to create and maintain a culture of sustainability in a university context. The chapter contains an analysis of results from 2012 to 2015, providing longitudinal data and highlighting the important role that institutional support plays.

The final part of the *Handbook* contains one chapter. This final chapter (Chapter 20) is focused on spillover behaviour and extends the study of employee environmental behaviour to examine its potential effects on home behaviours and behaviours away from the workplace and vice versa. The authors discuss the concept of 'spillover' and its various conceptualisations in pro-environmental behaviour research, along with a summary of current literature on the spillover of environmentally friendly behaviours in various contexts. Different methodological approaches (quantitative, qualitative and mixed) used in past studies that investigated spillover effects, both between behaviours and between settings, are critically discussed. The chapter concludes with practical implications for social marketing campaigns and behaviour change programmes that promote pro-environmental behaviours in organisations.

Each of the chapters contained within the *Handbook* highlights both practical recommendations for managers and future research directions. It is clear that much empirical work in the area of employee environmental behaviour, with a number of exceptions (some of which can be seen in this *Handbook*), uses quantitative methodologies, cross-sectional, convenience samples, self-reported data, and is conducted in single national contexts. It is well known that self-reported data may not be a reliable indicator of actual behaviour (see Chapter 16) and we encourage researchers in this area to measure actual behaviour change and to embrace the fast-moving technological advancements in this field to allow this. The field would also benefit from embracing the potential inter-disciplinary nature of the area more fully, using more interpretive methods over a longer time span and analysing cross-cultural differences. This should examine all aspects of this behaviour via a broad multi-level perspective such as that put forward by Norton et al. (2015).

Much of the research in the area is still focused on examining potential antecedents of employee pro-environmental behaviour and the future research directions highlight further advances in this field (in this *Handbook* suggestions include: cognitive abilities, vocational interests, employee assessment systems, contextual factors, values, and effects of different leadership styles for example) as well as suggestions to integrate these and examine potential moderating and mediating effects. This work is being rigorously done but is yet to reveal a clear path of relevance for practitioners who want to know what works, and how to develop environmental behaviour on the ground effectively. So, we encourage researchers to build on the work in Parts III and IV of the *Handbook* to develop real-world interventions and campaigns and to test the effectiveness of interventions so practitioners can be sure that what they are using will actually work.

REFERENCES

Aguinis, H. and A. Glavas (2012), 'What we know and don't know about corporate social responsibility: A review and research agenda', *Journal of Management*, 38(4), 932–68.
Bansal, P. and K. Roth (2000), 'Why companies go green: A model of ecological responsiveness', *Academy of Management Journal*, 43(4), 717–36.
Brennan, L., W. Binney, J. Hall and M. Hall (2015), 'Whose Job is that? Saving the biosphere starts at work', *Journal of Nonprofit & Public Sector Marketing*, 27(3), 307–30.
Campbell, J.P. and B.M. Wiernik (2015), 'The modeling and assessment of work performance', *Annual Review of Organisational Psychology and Organisational Behavior*, 2, 47–74.
Davis, G. and R. Challenger (2009), 'Climate change – warming to the task', *The Psychologist*, 22, 112–15.
Heron, J. and P. Reason (2001), 'The practice of co-operative inquiry: Research "with" rather than "on" people', in P. Reason and H. Bradbury (eds), *Handbook of Action Research: Participative Inquiry and Practice*, London: Sage, pp. 144–54.
Homburg, A. and A. Stolberg (2006), 'Explaining pro-environmental behavior with a cognitive theory of stress', *Journal of Environmental Psychology*, 26(1), 1–14.
Lamm, E., J. Tosti-Kharas and E.G. Williams (2013), 'Read this article, but don't print it: Organizational citizenship behavior toward the environment', *Group & Organization Management*, 38(2), 163–97.
Lo, S.H., G-J.Y. Peters and G. Kok (2012), 'A review of determinants of and interventions for proenvironmental behaviors in organizations', *Journal of Applied Social Psychology*, 42(12), 2933–67.
Makower, J. and C. Pike (2008), *Strategies for the Green Economy: Opportunities and Challenges in the New World of Business*, Irvine, CA: McGraw-Hill.
Miller, W.R. and S. Rollnick (2013), *Motivational Interviewing. Helping People Change* (3rd edn), New York: Guilford Press.
Norton, T.A., S.L. Parker, H. Zacher and N.M. Ashkanasy (2015), 'Employee green behavior: A theoretical framework, multilevel review, and future research agenda', *Organization & Environment*, 28(1), 103–25.

Reisch, L.A. and J. Thøgersen (2017), *Handbook of Research on Sustainable Consumption*, Cheltenham, UK and Northampton, MA, USA: Edward Elgar Publishing.

Robertson, J.L. and J. Barling (2015), *The Psychology of Green Organisations*, Oxford: Oxford University Press.

Staddon, S.C., C. Cycil, M. Goulden, C. Leygue and A. Spence (2016), 'Intervening to change behaviour and save energy in the workplace: A systematic review of available evidence', *Energy Research and Social Science*, 17, 30–51.

Steg, L. and C. Vlek (2009), 'Encouraging pro-environmental behaviour: An integrative review and research agenda', *Journal of Environmental Psychology*, 29, 309–17.

Wagner, J.A. (1994), 'Participation's effects on performance and satisfaction: A reconsideration of research evidence', *Academy of Management Review*, 19(2), 312–30.

PART I

WHAT IS EMPLOYEE PRO-ENVIRONMENTAL BEHAVIOUR?

2. Multiple domains and categories of employee green behaviours: more than conservation

Deniz S. Ones, Brenton M. Wiernik,*
Stephan Dilchert and Rachael M. Klein

Amidst ongoing deterioration of the global ecosystem (IPCC 2015), organisations are increasingly concerned with ensuring that their operations contribute to, or at least do not detract from, environmental sustainability (Jabbour and Santos 2006). Organisations seek to enhance their environmental performance both out of general concern for ensuring global welfare, as well as out of recognition that environmental deterioration threatens access to the natural resources necessary for their operations (Holme et al. 2000). To this end, organisations around the globe have implemented a variety of pro-environmental initiatives to improve their environmental performance (D'Mello et al. 2011), and numerous methods for tracking organisational environmental impacts have been proposed (Dilchert and Ones 2012).

While assessment of environmental performance at the organisational (and higher; Roy and Goll 2014; Wiernik 2012) levels is critical, it is important to recognise that organisational performance is a function of individual employees within the organisation performing relevant behaviours. Unfortunately, organisational practice, lay conceptualisations, and even scholarly research in this area often thinks too narrowly about the nature of these behaviours. For many individuals, pro-environmental behaviours begin and end with the '3 Rs' – reduce, reuse, recycle. Similarly, many studies and organisational interventions focus narrowly on single pro-environmental behaviours, such as turning off lights and electronics, purchasing eco-friendly products, or participating in environmental volunteering projects (e.g., Carrico and Riemer 2011; Goldstein et al. 2008; McDonald 2011; Vyvyan et al. 2007; Xu et al. 2017). This narrow focus often hampers progress towards environmental goals, as any single behaviour can have only limited beneficial impact (Kaiser et al. 2007). Scholarship that does not explicitly recognise and model different types of workplace behaviours that serve or detract from environmental sustainability goals results in a research literature that is theoretically fragmented, empirically incomplete, and inefficient for applied practice purposes.

13

To effectively promote employee pro-environmental behaviour and appropriately research the antecedents and consequences of different types of green behaviours, there is a need for clear conceptual definitions of employee green behaviours and an organising taxonomy of the diverse array of behaviours that can be performed. This is the aim of this chapter. In the sections below, we define employee green behaviours and describe how they fit into general models of job performance. Then, we describe a comprehensive taxonomy of employee green behaviours. Next, we discuss the features of available measures of employee green behaviours. Finally, we discuss how considering the full array of employee green behaviours can enhance organisational human resource management (HRM) practices that promote environmental sustainability.

2.1   DEFINING EMPLOYEE GREEN BEHAVIOURS

Employee green behaviours (EGB) are 'scalable actions and behaviours that employees engage in that are linked with and contribute to or detract from environmental sustainability' (Ones and Dilchert 2012: 87). There are several important features of this definition. First, the focus is on the environmental performance of individual employees. While organisation-, department-, or group-level environmental performance may be of interest, it is the actions of individuals within these larger units that drive environmental benefit and harm. Within a single organisation or team, employees can vary widely in their environmentally relevant behaviours, so understanding the nature and antecedents of individual-level employee green behaviours is necessary to change larger unit environmental performance.

Second, the definition focuses on employee environmental behaviours, not outcomes. By focusing on what employees actually do, EGB exclude environmental outcomes that are outside individual control. An employee's environmental footprint is impacted not only by their own actions, but also by their co-workers (e.g., other department members demanding on-site meetings), the organisation (e.g., supplying energy-inefficient computers), and external stakeholders (e.g., government regulations). As is the case for other domains of job performance, managing employee environmental performance requires addressing the behaviours employees themselves can change (Campbell and Wiernik 2015).

Third, EGB are scalable or measurable. Employee environmental performance can be rated in terms of its overall degree of beneficial or harmful impact on the environment, and individual employee green behaviours can be scaled in terms of their importance for environmental sustainability goals, their difficulty to perform, and other features. Different employees have quantitatively different impacts on the environment; evaluating employee environmental performance requires assessing their behaviours.

Fourth, the definition encompasses both positive green behaviours that benefit the environment and negative ungreen behaviours that actively harm the environment. Employees can both engage in (or refrain from) green behaviours (e.g., create sustainable products, recycle) and engage in (or refrain from) ungreen behaviours (e.g., pollute, end a green volunteering programme). Refraining from positive environmental behaviours is not the same as actively harming the environment. Both green and ungreen behaviours impact the environment, and both promoting green behaviours and inhibiting ungreen behaviours is necessary for effective environmental performance. Inclusion of both beneficial and harmful behaviours is one reason we prefer the label 'employee green behaviours' over 'employee pro-environmental behaviours', as the latter neglects the critical negative behavioural repertoire associated with this behavioural domain. Ungreen behaviours have also been termed 'counterproductive sustainability behaviours (CSB)' (Dilchert 2018).

A notable feature explicitly not a part of the definition of EGB is whether they are voluntary or extra-role. Some proposed definitions of employee pro-environmental behaviours specify that these behaviours are discretionary (e.g., Boiral 2009). This stricture is unnecessary. While some employee green behaviours may be voluntary (e.g., using public transport to commute), others may be required by the organisation (e.g., following waste disposal protocols). For some jobs, employee green behaviours may even be part of an employee's formal job role (e.g., technicians installing solar panels; Dierdorff et al. 2009, 2013). For some categories of EGB (particularly *Avoiding harm*, see below), we have observed that 22–73 per cent of positive employee green behaviours reported in our US critical incident studies were explicitly required by the organisation (cf. 2–33 per cent for critical incidents reported in Europe; Wiernik et al. 2013). Somewhat alarmingly, many organisations also require negative, environmentally harmful ungreen behaviours (i.e., 15–31 per cent of *Avoiding harm*, *Transforming*, and *Conserving* behaviours in our US critical incidents studies and 18–60 per cent of these behaviours in our European database). Many organisations require their employees to use procedures that harm the environment, to forego reusing materials, to use harmful waste disposal procedures, etc. By limiting their investigations to only voluntary green behaviours, researchers ignore these critical areas of employee impact on the natural environment.

Compared to pro-environmental behaviours performed in non-work settings ('individual behaviours contributing to environmental sustainability'; Mesmer-Magnus et al. 2012: 160), employee green behaviours have several distinctive features. First, because they are performed in work settings, EGB are often subject to social norms, power dynamics, and role expectations not present in private non-work settings (cf. Stern 2000), and EGB may be impelled by motives (e.g., concern with organisational reputation) not present in other settings (Klein 2014; see Wiernik et al. 2018, Chapter 4, this volume). Second, whereas non-work pro-environmental behaviours are based on individual volitional choice (excepting limitations based on socio-economic availability of green options), as noted above, EGB are subject to a degree of organisational oversight and may be explicitly required or prohibited. Indeed, EGB are best conceptualised as part of the general employee job performance construct domain – that is, as all those employee job performance behaviours that impact the natural environment. The structure of EGB largely parallels the structure of general job performance, and green behaviours are part of all job performance dimensions. We discuss how EGB fit into broader job performance models in the following sections.

2.1.1   Employee Green Behaviours as Job Performance

The above discussion of whether employee green behaviours must be voluntary raises the question of how this construct domain fits into general models of job performance (Campbell and Wiernik 2015; Viswesvaran and Ones 2000; cf. Norton et al. 2015). Are EGB an entirely new dimension of job performance, or do they fit into one or more broader performance constructs? Some researchers argue that employee green behaviours should be conceptualised as a facet of contextual performance/organisational citizenship behaviour ('performance that supports the social and psychological environment in which [technical] performance takes place'; Organ 1997: 95; cf. Motowidlo 2000). For example, Lamm et al. (2013: 165) defined organisational citizenship behaviour for the environment (OCB-E) as 'voluntary behaviour not specified in official job descriptions that, through the combined efforts of individual employees, help to make the organisation and/or society more sustainable' (see also Boiral 2009; Boiral and Paillé 2012). These definitions mirror early definitions of general OCB by requiring that green behaviours be voluntary, extra-role, and unrewarded; these features are unnecessary, as employee green behaviours are simply workplace behaviours which impact the natural environment (these features have also been abandoned as part of the definition of OCB; Organ 1997). Moreover, employee green behaviours and OCB have different structures (Borman and Motowidlo 1997; LePine et al. 2002; Ones and Dilchert 2012; Podsakoff et al. 2000), and employee green behaviours are not limited to behaviours typically considered to be part of the OCB domain (e.g., helping, persistence, volunteering). In fact, depending on the nature of the job, EGB can be part of all dimensions of job performance, including core technical performance (e.g., mutual fund managers choosing investments based on companies' environmental performance, tractor operators driving more slowly to reduce fuel usage), counterproductive work behaviours (ignoring sustainable purchasing policies), communication (writing sustainability reports), effort/initiative (going out of one's way to act sustainably), hierarchical leadership (supporting subordinates' green ideas), and others. Campbell and Wiernik (2015) described EGB as a compound performance domain – a collection of performance behaviours spanning multiple substantive performance dimensions that are united by a common goal – rather than a separate performance dimension unto themselves. Similarly, we suggest that different types of employee green behaviours can be thought of as calling upon multiple behavioural performance domains.

2.2   THE GREEN FIVE TAXONOMY OF EMPLOYEE GREEN BEHAVIOURS

Most research on employee green behaviours (and on pro-environmental behaviours generally; see Kaiser 1998) focuses on predicting single behaviours and often conceptualises EGB as being limited to reducing resource use, reusing materials, and recycling. Construct valid, generalisable research on employee green behaviours and effective organisational management of employee environmental performance require considering a wider range of environmentally relevant employee behaviours. Organisational environmental sustainability research and practice need a taxonomy that spans the full range of employee green behaviours to guide conceptualisation, measurement, and intervention.

The Green Five taxonomy, introduced by Ones and Dilchert (2012), comprehensively describes the diversity of environmentally relevant behaviours employees perform at work. It is a content-based taxonomy that groups environmental behaviours based on the similarity of the behaviours being performed, their common functional goals, and shared purported psychological underpinnings. The taxonomy is hierarchically organised, with overall environmental performance at the apex, five broad meta-categories below it, and increasingly narrow subcategories below them. Categories at each hierarchical level of the taxonomy include both positive and negative (green and ungreen) employee behaviours. The Green Five taxonomy is illustrated in Figure 2.1. In the sections below,

Employee Green Behaviours

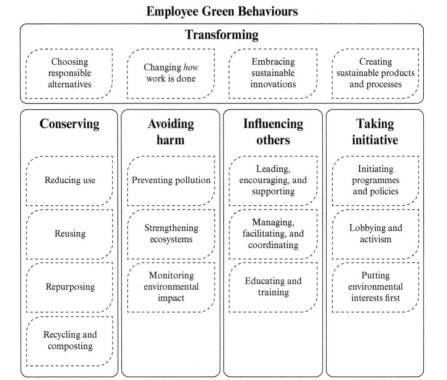

Figure 2.1   Meta-categories and subcategories of employee green behaviours in the Green Five taxonomy

we review the research that led to the development of the Green Five taxonomy, describe the content of each behavioural category, and discuss applications and ongoing research on the structure of employee green behaviours.

2.2.1   Development of the Green Five Taxonomy

The Green Five taxonomy was developed in stages. In the initial development stage, 1,299 critical incidents were gathered from 274 interviews with individuals holding 189 different types of jobs in 157 organisations across 20 US industries. Employees were asked to describe behaviours they had observed co-workers perform that had a (positive or negative) impact on the environment. The content of each critical incident was analysed and sorted by multiple raters (cf. Anderson and Wilson 1997), leading to a working taxonomy of green behavioural categories. We tested the sufficiency of these emerging behavioural categories by collecting a new confirmatory sample of 773 critical incidents, which was gathered from 133 interviews with individuals holding 97 job types in 92 organisations across 16 US industries. We also generated hypothetical employee green behaviours (i.e., behaviours that, while they may be performed by employees in some jobs, were not described in any of the critical incidents samples) to attempt to identify behaviours that did not fit into the emerging taxonomy. All of the new behavioural critical incidents and all hypothetical employee green behaviours were sorted into one or more of the identified green behaviour categories, indicating that the taxonomy comprehensively and unambiguously spanned the green behaviour domain. We then examined the cross-cultural applicability of the taxonomy by gathering 1,002 additional critical incidents from 208 interviews with employees holding 86 different job types in 70 organisations across 15 industries in 14 European countries (Belgium, Bulgaria, Czech Republic, Denmark, England, Finland, France, Germany, Greece, Ireland, Italy, Norway, Sweden, and Turkey; Hill et al. 2011).

The resulting taxonomy consists of 17[1] functionally distinguishable behavioural categories with relatively homogeneous content. These 17 categories are organised under five broad meta-categories (the Green Five). The current working Green Five taxonomy is illustrated in Figure 2.1. Next, we describe each meta-category and its subcategories, as well as their functional cores (the aim or goal the behaviours are intended to bring about) and common psychological underpinnings.

2.2.2   Transforming[2]

The behaviours in this meta-category are aimed at adapting and changing work products and processes to make them more sustainable. Example behaviours in this meta-category include commuting by bicycle rather than driving, purchasing locally produced goods, changing the order that tasks are done to generate less waste, and using a tablet computer rather than printouts to process paperwork. Job-specific examples include many forms of green technical performance, such as a researcher investigating new agricultural plants that require fewer pesticides, an architect designing a low-impact building, a store owner moving refrigerated items closer together to reduce cooling needs, and a procurement agent choosing sources based on their sustainability records.

The psychological core of *Transforming* behaviours is adaptability and openness to change. The four *Transforming* subcategories vary in the degree to which they require creative and innovative effort and ability from employees versus merely adopting existing sustainable solutions. At the high end, *Creating sustainable products and processes* involves generating novel ideas and new, innovative solutions that are more sustainable. This subcategory might also be called *Eco-innovation*. The second subcategory, *Embracing sustainable innovations*, involves implementing emerging innovative ideas and applying them to one's specific situation (e.g., adapting a work procedure to use a new more sustainable technology). Its negative pole involves active hostility to innovative solutions and clinging to established, less sustainable procedures. The final two subcategories involve adopting more well-established green options. *Choosing responsible alternatives* involves choosing the most sustainable option (e.g., for equipment, raw materials, supplies, or energy) out of available alternatives. *Changing how work is done* involves optimising existing processes to improve their environmental impact. These subcategories still require openness to change, but they require less innovation and creative effort from employees.

Transforming behaviours are the foundation of employee green behaviours; to some degree, all green behaviours require changing one's behaviour and adapting to new ways of doing things (Maloney and Ward 1973). For this reason, in Figure 2.1, *Transforming* behaviours are shown at the top of the taxonomy, spanning other categories of employee green behaviour. Based on factor analyses, *Transforming* behaviours tend to be the best indicators of the general factor of employee green behaviours (Wiernik et al. 2016b).

2.2.3 Conserving

This meta-category includes behaviours aimed at avoiding wastefulness and thus preserving resources. It encompasses behaviours traditionally described as the '3Rs' (reduce, reuse, recycle). About half of all behavioural incidents we have gathered through our research fall into the *Conserving* meta-category. *Conserving* includes preservation of a wide variety of resources – water, energy, gas, other natural resources, supplies, raw materials, etc. *Conserving* behaviours may target diverse resources, but they are united in their common functional goal for avoiding wastefulness and their psychological underpinnings of frugality, thrift, and responsibility. Scales including only items assessing reducing use of water, energy, gas, and supplies and recycling of glass, paper, metal, and oil may target many resources, but they capture a very narrow range of environmentally relevant behaviours (see the distinction between environmental behaviours and outcomes, in section 2.1).

The *Conserving* subcategories range in their degree of effectiveness for resource preservation. *Reducing use* of resources is the most responsible way to conserve because it minimises initial environmental impact. *Reusing* and *Repurposing* are also effective for reducing impact, as they involve using the same materials multiple times, rather than disposing of them after a single use, either for the same function (*Reusing*) or for purposes other than those originally intended (*Repurposing*). Finally, *Recycling* conserves the least resources and only mitigates impact because it requires additional energy, raw materials (including fuel for transportation), and processing before resources can be recovered for further use. *Recycling* also includes composting organic waste which, while better than landfill, is less effective than if such waste can be repurposed or never produced in the first place. Hence, from a resource conservation point of view, *Reducing use* is the most desirable and *Recycling* the least desirable option among *Conserving* subcategories.

2.2.4   Avoiding Harm

This meta-category includes behaviours aimed at avoidance and inhibition of negative environmental behaviour, reducing impact, and mitigating/ restoring environmental damage. The negative pole of this meta-category includes behaviours that harm the environment by diminishing the health of the Earth's ecosystems and disrupting natural biological, chemical, and physical processes that help the planet recover from distress. The most common behaviours in this category are polluting or, at the positive end, proactively *Preventing pollution*. In our critical incidents databases, most behaviours in this meta-category were negative. The other two *Avoiding harm* subcategories support the primary function of avoiding environmental damage. *Monitoring environmental impact* involves assessing behaviours, processes, and outcomes to anticipate the potential for long-term harm (e.g., calculating one's carbon footprint, assessing water quality around manufacturing sites). *Strengthening ecosystems* includes actions aimed at repairing or recovering from existing environmental damages, either at small scales (e.g., cleaning up litter, purchasing carbon offsets, using plants to filter toxins from the air) or at large scales (e.g., mine reclamation, mitigating an oil spill, planting trees to replenish logged areas, stopping fishing to allow a fishery to recover).

The psychological core of most *Avoiding harm* behaviours at the positive end is cautiousness, self-control, and responsibility (versus carelessness and irresponsibility at the negative pole). Behaviours associated with proactively avoiding harm or repairing existing environmental damage also involve altruism, particularly if they involve repairing harm caused by others or are motivated out of concern for the welfare of future generations.

2.2.5   Influencing Others

This meta-category focuses on behaviours aimed at spreading sustainability behaviours to other individuals. *Influencing others* behaviours enhance sustainability by exploiting economies of scale; one individual's pro-environmental behaviours can cause others to act more sustainably. *Influencing others* is an inherently social category, so its psychological underpinnings are extraversion, agreeableness, and interpersonal skill. Specific behaviours in this meta-category correspond to general job performance behaviours related to leadership, management, and communication and are structured accordingly (see Campbell and Wiernik 2015). *Leading, encouraging, and supporting* (or simply, *Green leadership*) includes interpersonal influence behaviours that encourage, support, incentivise, empower, motivate, and guide others to behave more environmentally responsibly, as well as behaviours that model effective environmental performance for others. *Managing, facilitating, and coordinating* (or simply, *Green management*) includes behaviours that help make others' green behaviours easier or more effective, such as making opportunities for green behaviours accessible, providing sufficient resources to enable green behaviours, coordinating green behaviours across individuals, units, or organisations, and organising plans or procedures for green behaviours. *Educating and training* involves behaviours aimed at enhancing others' environmentally relevant declarative and procedural knowledge. It includes short-term training on environmentally responsible procedures and behaviours, awareness-raising interventions, and larger-scale environmental education and outreach activities. This subcategory also includes providing individuals with feedback on their environmental performance. All of these behaviours can be directed towards subordinates, co-workers, and superiors, as well as individuals outside the organisation, such as clients, industry and strategic partners, suppliers, community members, and other stakeholders.

2.2.6   Taking Initiative

The last Green Five meta-category includes behaviours that are proactive, entrepreneurial, and involve a certain level of personal risk or sacrifice. It is analogous to general job performance behaviours related to initiative and effort (Campbell and Wiernik 2015), as well as proactive performance constructs (e.g., personal initiative, voice, taking charge; Thomas et al. 2010). This meta-category includes behaviours that break the mould, take risks, and go against societal expectations. These behaviours also require willingness to forego certain benefits and to suffer potential negative consequences (e.g., financial loss, discomfort, social consequences) because of their performance. *Taking initiative* behaviours serve the function of rejecting the (unsustainable) status quo and proactively changing the context for a more sustainable future. The psychological core of *Taking initiative* is proactivity (Fuller and Marler 2009; Thomas et al. 2010). Unlike *Influencing others*, behaviours included in *Taking initiative* may or may not be social in nature, and they can be directed at *Avoiding harm*, *Transforming*, or *Conserving*. The distinguishing feature of *Taking initiative* is the exceptional effort, personal sacrifice, and proactivity involved in performing them (cf. the *Effort, persistence, initiative* factor in the job performance model by Campbell and Wiernik 2015).

The entrepreneurial aspect of this meta-category is manifested in its subcategory *Initiating programmes and policies*. The programmes and policies that employees might initiate can address any aspect of environmental sustainability or domain of employee green behaviours (e.g., initiating a new organisational recycling programme, forming a Green Team to plan sustainability programmes, instituting a sustainable purchasing policy). The key feature that distinguishes behaviours in this subcategory from merely being behaviours in their targeted categories is that initiating behaviours involve effort on the part of the actor to change the status to a new more sustainable reality. Initiating a programme or policy involves creating or developing a new venture and thus requires some degree of risk-taking and willingness to sacrifice (money, resources, and/or effort, for example).

Another *Taking initiative* subcategory is *Lobbying and activism* (these might also be called *Green voice behaviours*; Thomas et al. 2010). These behaviours involve advocating for environmental causes, including to supervisors, organisational decision makers, governments, and other power-holding individuals and institutions. Again, risk is involved as *Lobbying and activism* behaviours are intended to change the status quo towards increased sustainability, without necessarily considering all possible outcomes to employees themselves. Overcoming organisational inertia and standing out requires courage.

The final *Taking initiative* subcategory is *Putting environmental interests first*. This subcategory involves sacrificing one's own interests (personal, comfort, convenience, financial, social, etc.) in the name of environmental sustainability. For example, this subcategory includes turning down profitable but harmful projects and commuting via public transport despite it taking longer than driving.

Table 2.1 provides examples of positive and negative behaviours for each of the categories described above.

Table 2.1   Example behaviours in each Green Five content category

Employee green behaviour category	Example positive behaviour	Example negative behaviour
*Transforming**		
Choosing responsible alternatives	Purchasing eco-friendly cleaning chemicals; Purchasing energy-efficient equipment	Using raw materials from unsustainable sources
Changing how work is done	Changing shipping routes to be more efficient; Using public transit to commute	Changing to a less sustainable work procedure; Implementing a procedure with known environmental costs in place of an eco-friendly procedure
Creating sustainable products and processes	Removing toxic chemicals from a manufacturing process; Creating a mutual fund investing in environmentally responsible companies	Ignoring environmental considerations when designing new products
Embracing sustainable innovations	Installing a green roof to reduce cooling needs; Using virtual rather than in-person meetings	Insisting on computer printouts when paperless options are available
Conserving		
Reducing use	Printing double sided; Turning off lights when unneeded	Leaving a machine running when not in use; Using resources wastefully
Reusing	Washing plastic lab equipment rather than discarding; Using durable, rather than disposable products and/or equipment	Using single-use products when durable alternatives are available
Repurposing	Diverting cooking oil to make biodiesel; Collecting rainwater for industrial use	Sending expiring food to a landfill rather than giving to local farmers requesting it for animal feed
Recycling and composting	Recycling cans, bottles, paper; Composting food waste	Throwing away carpet scraps rather than using available recycling processes
Avoiding harm		
Preventing pollution	Installing a collection system to prevent water contamination; Scrubbing emissions before release	Contaminating soil by dumping harmful chemicals; Improperly disposing of paint, oil, or other hazardous substances

Table 2.1 (continued)

Employee green behaviour category	Example positive behaviour	Example negative behaviour
Strengthening ecosystems	Maintaining wildlife areas around work facilities; Cleaning up litter around local area	Clear-cutting unnecessarily; Growing pesticide-dependent crops
Monitoring environmental impact	Preparing a company emissions and resource use report; Calculating the lifecycle carbon cost of a product	Failing to follow up on cleanup effort after a negative environmental event
Influencing others		
Leading, encouraging, and supporting**	Providing incentives for biking or using public transit commute; Modelling effective green behaviours	Mocking a co-worker who takes food waste home to compost
Managing, facilitating, and coordinating**	Making recycling bins accessible to all employees; Arranging an employee carpool network	Creating unnecessary bureaucratic obstacles for green behaviours
Educating and training	Training employees in proper chemical handling; Providing feedback on green performance	Instructing employees to discard unused materials
Taking initiative		
Initiating programmes and policies	Creating a new sustainable purchasing policy; Forming a Green Team to plan sustainability programmes	Stopping a successful environmental programme
Lobbying and activism	Pushing organisation to disclose environmental record; Advocating for environmental issues to supervisor	Advocating for programmes or policies that are environmentally harmful
Putting environmental interests first	Turning down an environmentally harmful project; Not using an air conditioner on hot days	Prioritising one's comfort or convenience over environmental concerns

Notes: * Ones and Dilchert (2012) called this meta-category 'Working sustainably'; ** Ones and Dilchert (2012) grouped these behaviours under one subcategory, we separate them based on the conceptual distinction between leadership and management performance (cf. Campbell and Wiernik 2015).

2.2.7   Notable Features and Sufficiency of the Green Five Taxonomy

The Green Five is a content-based taxonomy – behaviours are clustered according to their common functional goals and psychological underpinnings. The 17 subcategories and five meta-categories described are conceptually distinguishable and are useful for evaluating the comprehensiveness of green behaviour assessments and interventions and for targeting feedback to improve specific areas of environmental performance. The Green Five taxonomy should not be interpreted as a latent factor structure, neither formative nor reflective. Employee green behaviours in different meta-categories are expected to be intercorrelated. There is a strong general factor of employee environmental performance, whether assessed by self-reports, supervisor reports, or objective measures (Ones and Dilchert 2013; Wiernik et al. 2016b), and specific behavioural subcategories across the Green Five meta-categories may correlate if they share common antecedents, hurdles, or motives. That said, in a study of 643 employed adults, Wiernik et al. (2016b) applied item response theory-based factor analyses to the 85-item Multidimensional Employee Green Behaviour Scale (designed to comprehensively sample behaviours from all 17 specific Green Five categories, see Table 2.2) and found that empirical green behaviour factors generally resembled the Green Five meta-categories (cf. Dilchert et al. 2017, who replicated these results in a sample of 681 employed adults).

Conceptually, many specific behaviours belong to multiple Green Five meta-categories and subcategories. For example, helping a co-worker plan a public transport commute belongs to both the *Leading, encouraging, and supporting* and the *Changing how work is done* subcategories. Similarly, organising a new programme to clean up litter in the local community belongs to both *Initiating programmes and policies* and *Strengthening ecosystems*. This is not a problem (cf. Norton et al. 2015); it simply reflects that individual green behaviours can serve multiple functional goals and are determined by multiple individual and situational antecedents. Forcing behaviours to belong exclusively to single categories and failing to acknowledge substantial factor cross-loadings ignores important features of these complex behaviours (cf. Boiral and Paillé 2012).

Compared to other proposed organisational schemes for employee green behaviours, the Green Five taxonomy has several advantages. Norton et al. (2015) proposed a division of EGB into voluntary versus required green behaviours. Their required (or task-related) EGB category reflects EGB performed as part of employees' core technical job duties and purportedly includes behaviours related to adhering to organisational environmental policies, changing methods of work, choosing responsible alternatives, and creating sustainable products and processes (p. 105). By contrast, voluntary (or proactive) EGB involve personal initiative that exceeds organisational environmental expectations and purportedly includes prioritising environmental interests, initiating environmental programmes and policies, lobbying and activism, and encouraging others. This characterisation is inappropriate. Behaviours in each of the sub-categories of the Green Five may or may not be required by organisations or job roles. The Norton et al. (2015) taxonomy conflates motive (requirement versus others) with behavioural content. This distinction parallels early conceptualisations of organisational citizenship behaviour that emphasised voluntariness over specific behavioural content; OCB researchers eventually recognised that OCB may or may not be required and rewarded and that a focus on the actual behaviours of interest (helping, persistence, etc.) is more fruitful (Organ 1997; Rotundo and Sackett 2002). Emphasis on whether a green behaviour is required or not distracts from a focus on its behavioural content and the diversity of other motives and antecedents that may impel it.

Boiral and Paillé (2012) proposed a three-factor model of employee green behaviours. They argue that employee green behaviours should be conceptualised as 'organisational citizenship behaviours directed toward the environment', so their model is designed to closely parallel the lower-order factors of general OCB (Borman and Motowidlo 1997; Podsakoff et al. 2000). Their model includes factors called 'eco-helping' (supporting co-workers in performing sustainable behaviours), 'eco-civic engagement' (participating in organisational pro-environmental events, keeping apprised of organisational pro-environmental initiatives), and 'eco-initiatives' (proposing new sustainable ideas, volunteering to carry out green tasks). As noted above, there is no reason to expect that employee green behaviours and OCB have the same structure, and green behaviours can be a part of all dimensions of job performance (not only OCB). Because Boiral and Paillé's model imposes the OCB structure onto the green behaviour domain, it focuses almost exclusively on behaviours related to *Influencing others* and *Taking initiative*, excluding the large majority of employee green behaviours performed in most workplaces (Ones and Dilchert 2012).

2.3   MEASURING EMPLOYEE GREEN BEHAVIOURS

To address concerns with low reliability, weak predictability, and poor construct coverage of single-item measures, in the past eight years several research teams have developed multi-behaviour measures of employee green behaviours. We reviewed the literature on employee green behaviours to identify available measures. We searched the Web of Science Social Science Citation Index and Google Scholar for the terms 'employee green behaviour', 'work* green behaviour', 'employee pro-environmental behaviour', 'work* pro-environmental behaviour', and 'organisational citizenship behaviour for the environment'. Additionally, over the past decade, we have actively searched for, read, and compiled articles and scales assessing employee green behaviours; we reviewed our research libraries for relevant scales and added these to our review. Altogether, we identified 25 multi-item scales. Single-item measures, measures designed for non-work (versus workplace) use (e.g., Kaiser 1998; Stern et al. 1999), and measures based on objective counts (e.g., mass of recycled material, kWh of energy used) were excluded. Features of these scales (e.g., scale names, authors) are shown in Table 2.2.

We content-analysed each of these scales to determine the number of items assessing each Green Five meta-category. The first two authors read the items on each scale and classified each according to the Green Five meta-category it primarily targeted. Interrater agreement was 95 per cent; disagreements were resolved through discussion.

Authors of most EGB measures described them in general terms and intended them to capture the green behaviour domain broadly. Despite their broad descriptions, however, the item content of most scales is very narrow. Most scales include items from only one or two of the Green Five meta-categories. For example, many scales included only items assessing recycling/reducing use (*Conserving*) and sustainable product choices (*Transforming*) behaviours. Scales conceptualised as 'organisational citizenship behaviour for the environment', consistent with general OCB's focus on interpersonal support and personal initiative, typically focused almost exclusively on *Influencing others* and *Taking initiative* behaviours, ignoring the more technical dimensions of EGB (*Conserving*, *Avoiding harm*) that make up the majority of behaviours (Ones and Dilchert 2012) with the greatest impact (Stern 2000) in this domain.

Many scales included multiple vague, general EGB items without specific behavioural content (e.g., 'I adequately completed assigned duties in environmentally friendly ways'; Bissing-Olson et al. 2013; 'I undertake environmental actions that contribute positively to the image of my organisation'; Boiral and Paillé 2012; 'Perform environmental tasks that are not required by my company'; Graves et al. 2013). These types of items are likely to have the same deficiencies as measures of general job performance that use vague statements about 'accomplishing work goals' or 'completing assigned tasks effectively', including increased

Table 2.2 Content analysis of employee green behaviours measures: mapping of items to the Green Five

Scale	Subscales	Green Five meta-categories					
		T	C	AH	IO	TI	Gen.
Measures intended to comprehensively assess EGB							
Organisational Citizenship Behaviour for the Environment (Boiral and Paillé 2012)	Eco-helping; Eco-civic engagement; Eco-initiatives			1	4	1	4
Organisational Citizenship Behaviour towards the Environment (Lamm et al. 2013)			12				
Organisational Citizenship Behaviour Directed towards the Environment (Temminck et al. 2015)		2		1		4	
Pro-Environmental Behaviour at the Work-place Scale (Homburg and Stolberg 2006)	Direct environmental behaviour; Indirect environmental behaviour				2	1	2
Environmental Management Practices Scale (Montabon et al. 2007)		1		1	1	1	
Employee Environmental Behaviours (Chou 2014)		2	5				
Employee Pro-environmental Behaviours (Graves et al. 2013)		3	2	1	4	1	2
Pro-Environmental Behaviours at Work Scale (Nag 2012)	Pro-Environmental Behaviours; Pro-Environmental Behaviours at a Cost to Self	2	5			1	
Workplace Pro-Environmental Behaviours (Robertson and Barling 2013)			5			1	
Workplace Environmentally Friendly Behaviours (Manika et al. 2015)	Recycling; Energy saving; Printing reduction		14				1

Table 2.2 (continued)

Scale	Subscales	Green Five meta-categories					
		T	C	AH	IO	TI	Gen.
Workplace Green Behaviours (Kim et al. 2014)	Voluntary WGB; Green Advocacy	1	5		3		
Daily Employee Green Behaviour (Bissing-Olson et al. 2013; Norton et al. 2014)	Task-related EGB; Proactive EGB; Helping EGB; Counterproductive EGB		1		3	3	5
Daily Employee Green Behaviour Scale (Norton et al. 2017)			5				
Daily Employee Green Behaviour Scale – Alternative (Norton et al. 2017)							3
Employee Green Behaviours (Norton 2016)	Task-related EGB; Proactive EGB	15	8	2	2	4	1
Employee Green Behaviour Norms Scale (McConnaughy 2014)	Working Sustainably; Conserving; Avoiding harm; Influencing others; Taking initiative	6	8	3	4	6	
Brief Employee Green Behaviour Scale (Ones and Dilchert 2009)		4	3	3	3	2	
Multidimensional Employee Green Behaviour Scale (Wiernik et al. 2016b)	Transforming; Conserving; Avoiding harm; Influencing others; Taking initiative	25	20	17	11	12	
Short Employee Green Behaviour Scale (Wiernik et al. 2016a)	Transforming; Conserving; Avoiding harm; Influencing others; Taking initiative	10	6	4	2	3	

Measures targeting specific EGB categories

Innovative Environmental Management Scale (Cantor et al. 2012)	2			1
Conservation Behaviour Scale (Carrico and Riemer 2011)			6	
Environmentally Specific Transformational Leadership (Robertson and Barling 2013)		7		
Electricity Saving Behaviour Scale (Zhang et al. 2013)	1		5	2
Energy-Saving Behaviours (Scherbaum et al. 2008)			6	6
Sustainability Behaviour Support Behaviourally Anchored Rating Scale (Ramus and Steger 2000)		6		

Support for innovation; Competence building; Communication; Information dissemination; Management of goals/responsibilities; Rewards/ recognition

Notes: T = Transforming; C = Conserving; AH = Avoiding harm; IO = Influencing others; TI = Taking initiative; Gen. = general employee green behaviours whose specific behavioural content could not be determined (e.g., 'I undertake environmental actions that contribute positively to the image of my organisation'; Boiral and Paillé 2012); values are the number of items tapping each meta-category.

rater-specific error, idiosyncratic rater definitions of 'environmentally friendly' and implicit theories of green behaviour, and inconsistent use of rating scales (Campbell and Wiernik 2015; Hoffman et al. 2012). While these general evaluative items may have some uses (such as for repeated measures in experience-sampling research designs), for most research and applications, more concretely specified items will yield greater reliability and interpretability for both respondents and assessment users.

Across EGB measures, *Avoiding harm* behaviours (preventing pollution, monitoring impact, restoring damaged ecosystems) were particularly poorly represented. Scales also almost exclusively measured positive green behaviours; negative (ungreen) behaviours were almost entirely absent from existing measures. Only a small number of scales included sufficient items from each of the Green Five meta-categories to truly comprehensively cover the employee green behaviour construct space. These include scales by Norton (2016) and McConnaughy (2014), several scales by Ones and colleagues (Ones and Dilchert 2009; Wiernik et al. 2016b, 2016a), and a scale by Graves et al. (2013; though this scale had weak coverage of *Avoiding harm*).

We identified a small number of scales designed to measure specific narrow dimensions of employee green behaviours. As focused measures, we would expect their items to cluster into one or a few Green Five categories. Such measures can be useful when researchers are interested in the unique nomological network of specific green behaviour domains or when organisations are particularly concerned with promoting a specific class of green behaviour (e.g., environmental innovation, green leadership, waste reduction). Some of these scales provide good coverage of their target behavioural domain (e.g., the Ramus and Steger 2000 scale assesses a wide range of green leadership behaviours). However, other scales are so narrowly defined that their items are essentially identical (e.g., the Carrico and Riemer 2011 scale contains six items asking about turning off lights and equipment when not in use), leading to inflated reliability estimates and narrow construct coverage (a phenomenon referred to as a 'bloated specific' factor; Cattell 1978).

In future research and application, scale developers must be more deliberate in their choices about how to measure employee green behaviours. A scale can be comprehensive or focused in its coverage, depending on measurement needs, but researchers must describe the content and meaning of their scales accurately. If a scale contains exclusively *Conserving* or *Influencing others* behaviours, it is not a measure of employee green behaviours broadly. If a specific category of green behaviour (e.g., *Conserving*) is of interest, it is perfectly fine to focus on that category and assess it reliably, but conclusions must be limited in their scope accordingly. If the goal is to measure employee green behaviours comprehensively, scale developers must ensure that items representing each Green Five meta-category (and ideally each subcategory) are included. Based on our review of available scales, those scales that were developed using the Green Five taxonomy (i.e., McConnaughy 2014; Ones and Dilchert 2009; Wiernik et al. 2016a, 2016b) provide the most comprehensive and balanced coverage of the full range of employee green behaviours. We recommend that researchers seeking to measure employee green behaviour broadly use these scales (or other rigorously developed scales based on the Green Five taxonomy). Importantly, if researchers aim to report subscale scores in addition to overall environmental performance, they must ensure that sufficient items are included for each dimension to ensure reliability (cf. Gignac and Watkins 2013). For either of these measurement aims, vague items asking about undifferentiated 'environmentally friendly behaviours' have limited divergent validity or utility for feedback and decision-making, so they generally should be avoided.

One promising area for future research and practice is to develop employee green behaviour measures that are tailored to fit specific jobs, industries, or organisations. Each of the reviewed scales was designed to be widely applicable across work contexts. Such measures are useful and permit commensurate measurement across studies, but they also often consist primarily of relatively low difficulty, everyday behaviours in a domain (cf. Bennett and Robinson 2000). By developing measures for more specific employee populations (e.g., supply chain managers, wind turbine technicians, architects, lawyers, researchers), researchers will be better able to capture these behaviours with higher fidelity in each context.

2.4   IMPLICATIONS FOR HRM PRACTICE

The behavioural taxonomy described in this chapter has implications for organisational human resource management practices that address environmental sustainability. The taxonomy should be used to inform the behaviours that organisations choose to target with HRM programmes and help to organise and evaluate programmes' design and effectiveness. For any pro-environmental HRM programme, practitioners must specify which specific employee green behaviours they wish to impact. Then, potential programmes can be evaluated for whether they will be effective for promoting (or inhibiting) behaviours in these categories. If the goal of an HRM programme is to target employee environmental performance broadly, the Green Five taxonomy can similarly be used to evaluate whether the full range of green behaviours has been covered and to identify areas where further attention may be needed.

The full range of HRM tools can be used to promote effective environmental performance in each Green Five category. Most organisations rely on motivational interventions designed to raise environmental awareness and concern, but interventions can be more effective if they are deeply embedded into organisational HRM practice. For example, job design can incorporate EGB into employee role responsibilities. Ergonomics can be used to place recycling and compost bins in locations convenient to employees. Organisational pro-environmental initiatives can be used in recruitment and green competencies added to job descriptions to attract applicants likely to be strong environmental performers. Hiring systems can be designed to assess green competencies and predict on-the-job green behaviours. Environmental values can be incorporated into organisational socialisation processes, and employees can be trained on sustainable methods for performing their core work tasks. For performance management, organisations can set environmental performance goals for each employee and incorporate green behaviours into performance evaluation systems. Organisations can further design sustainability-focused career paths and incorporate sustainability into their portfolio of skill requirements for leadership and executive development and advancement.

For all environmental initiatives, HRM practitioners should gather data and conduct surveys to assess employees' attitudes and responses to organisational environmental messages and to evaluate the effectiveness of the initiatives. Environmental sustainability can be incorporated into all areas of HRM practice, and these practices should be designed to address the full range of green behaviours that can be performed by employees in all jobs, industries, and organisational levels. By addressing the diversity of employee green behaviours beyond traditional notions of conservation and the 3Rs, organisations can advance their own strategic environmental goals and promote the long-term sustainability of the planet on which they operate.

NOTES

* This work was supported by the Belgian American Educational Foundation through a fellowship to B. M. Wiernik.
1. Ones and Dilchert's (2012) original taxonomy contained 16 subcategories. Subsequent research suggested that the Encouraging and Supporting Others should be divided into separate subcategories corresponding to environmental management and environmental leadership (cf. Campbell and Wiernik 2015). These behaviours have somewhat divergent antecedents, consequences, and feedback needs, but empirically they are strongly correlated.
2. In Ones and Dilchert's (2012) original taxonomy, this meta-category was called

'Working sustainably'. This label was ambiguous, so it was changed to 'Transforming' to better reflect the meaning of the construct. Its behavioural content is unchanged.

REFERENCES

Anderson, L. and S. Wilson (1997), 'Critical incident technique', in D. L. Whetzel and G. R. Wheaton (eds), *Applied Measurement Methods in Industrial Psychology*, Palo Alto, CA: Davies-Black Publishing, pp.89–112.

Bennett, R. J. and S. L. Robinson (2000), 'Development of a measure of workplace deviance', *Journal of Applied Psychology*, **85** (3), 349–60.

Bissing-Olson, M. J., A. Iyer, K. S. Fielding and H. Zacher (2013), 'Relationships between daily affect and pro-environmental behavior at work: The moderating role of pro-environmental attitude', *Journal of Organisational Behavior*, **34** (2), 156–75.

Boiral, O. (2009), 'Greening the corporation through organisational citizenship behaviors', *Journal of Business Ethics*, **87** (2), 221–36.

Boiral, O. and P. Paillé (2012), 'Organisational citizenship behaviour for the environment: Measurement and validation', *Journal of Business Ethics*, **109** (4), 431–45.

Borman, W. C. and S. J. Motowidlo (1997), 'Task performance and contextual performance: the meaning for personnel selection research', *Human Performance*, **10**, 99–109.

Campbell, J. P. and B. M. Wiernik (2015), 'The modeling and assessment of work performance', *Annual Review of Organisational Psychology and Organisational Behavior*, **2**, 47–74.

Cantor, D. E., P. C. Morrow and F. Montabon (2012), 'Engagement in environmental behaviors among supply chain management employees: An organisational support theoretical perspective', *Journal of Supply Chain Management*, **48** (3), 33–51.

Carrico, A. R. and M. Riemer (2011), 'Motivating energy conservation in the workplace: An evaluation of the use of group-level feedback and peer education', *Journal of Environmental Psychology*, **31** (1), 1–13.

Cattell, R. B. (1978), *The Scientific Use of Factor Analysis in Behavioral and Life Sciences*, Boston, MA: Springer US.

Chou, C.-J. (2014), 'Hotels' environmental policies and employee personal environmental beliefs: Interactions and outcomes', *Tourism Management*, **40**, 436–46.

Dierdorff, E. C., J. J. Norton, D. W. Drewes, C. M. Kroustalis, D. Rivkin and P. Lewis (2009), *Greening of the World of Work: Implications for O*NET-SOC and New and Emerging Occupations*, Raleigh, NC: National Center for O*NET Development, accessed 17 May 2015 at http://www.ctdol.state.ct.us/wia/memos/2009/ONET-GreeningOfWorld.pdf.

Dierdorff, E. C., J. J. Norton, C. M. Gregory, D. Rivkin and P. Lewis (2013), 'O*NET's national perspective on the greening of the world of work', in A. H. Huffman and S. R. Klein (eds), *Green Organisations: Driving Change with I-O Psychology*, New York: Routledge, pp.348–78.

Dilchert, S. (2018), 'Counterproductive sustainability behaviors and their relationship to personality traits', *International Journal of Selection and Assessment*, **26** (1), 49–56.

Dilchert, S. and D. S. Ones (2012), 'Measuring and improving environmental sustainability', in S. E. Jackson, D. S. Ones, and S. Dilchert (eds), *Managing Human Resources for Environmental Sustainability*, San Francisco, CA: Jossey-Bass/Wiley, pp.187–221.

Dilchert, S., B. K. Mercado and D. S. Ones (2017), *Facet- and Factor-Level Relationships between Personality & Multidimensional Green Work Behaviors*, Poster presented at the European Association of Work and Organisational Psychology conference, Dublin, Ireland, May.

D'Mello, S., D. S. Ones, R. M. Klein, B. M. Wiernik and S. Dilchert (2011), *Green Company Rankings and Reporting of Pro-Environmental Efforts in Organisations*, Poster presented at the annual conference of the Society for Industrial and Organisational Psychology, Chicago, IL, April.

Fuller, J. B., Jr. and L. E. Marler (2009), 'Change driven by nature: A meta-analytic review of the proactive personality literature', *Journal of Vocational Behavior*, **75** (3), 329–45.

Gignac, G. E. and M. W. Watkins (2013), 'Bifactor modeling and the estimation of model-based reliability in the WAIS-IV', *Multivariate Behavioral Research*, **48** (5), 639–62.

Goldstein, N. J., R. B. Cialdini and V. Griskevicius (2008), 'A room with a viewpoint: Using social norms to motivate environmental conservation in hotels', *Journal of Consumer Research*, **35** (3), 472–82.

Graves, L. M., J. Sarkis and Q. Zhu (2013), 'How transformational leadership and employee motivation combine to predict employee proenvironmental behaviors in China', *Journal of Environmental Psychology*, **35**, 81–91.

Hill, L., D. S. Ones, S. Dilchert, B. M. Wiernik, R. M. Klein and S. D'Mello (2011), *Employee Green Behaviors in Europe: A Cross-Cultural Taxonomic Investigation*, Paper presented at the annual conference of the Society for Industrial and Organisational Psychology, Chicago, IL, April.

Hoffman, B. J., C. A. Gorman, C. A. Blair, J. P. Meriac, B. Overstreet and E. K. Atchley (2012), 'Evidence for the effectiveness of an alternative multisource performance rating methodology', *Personnel Psychology*, **65** (3), 531–63.

Holme, R. and P. Watts (2000), *Corporate Social Responsibility: Making Good Business Sense*, Conches-Geneva, Switzerland: World Business Council for Sustainable Development.

Homburg, A. and A. Stolberg (2006), 'Explaining pro-environmental behavior with a cognitive theory of stress', *Journal of Environmental Psychology*, **26** (1), 1–14.

IPCC (2015), *Climate Change 2014: Mitigation of Climate Change. Contribution of Working Group III to the Fifth Assessment Report of the Intergovernmental Panel on Climate Change*, New York: Cambridge University Press, accessed 17 May 2015 at http://www.ipcc.ch/report/ar5/wg3/.

Jabbour, C. J. C. and F. C. A. Santos (2006), 'The evolution of environmental management within organisations: Toward a common taxonomy', *Environmental Quality Management*, **16** (2), 43–59.

Kaiser, F. G. (1998), 'A general measure of ecological behavior', *Journal of Applied Social Psychology*, **28** (5), 395–422.

Kaiser, F. G., P. W. Schultz and H. Scheuthle (2007), 'The theory of planned behavior without compatibility? Beyond method bias and past trivial associations', *Journal of Applied Social Psychology*, **37** (7), 1522–44.

Kim, A., Y. Kim, K. Han, S. E. Jackson and R. E. Ployhart (2014), 'Multilevel influences on voluntary workplace green behavior: Individual differences, leader behavior, and coworker advocacy', *Journal of Management*, **43** (5), 1335–58.

Klein, R. M. (2014), *Employee Motives for Engaging in Environmentally Sustainable Behaviors: A Multi-Study Analysis*, Doctoral dissertation, Minneapolis, MN: University of Minnesota, accessed at http://hdl.handle.net/11299/191323.

Lamm, E., J. Tosti-Kharas and E. G. Williams (2013), 'Read this article, but don't print it: Organisational citizenship behavior toward the environment', *Group & Organisation Management*, **38** (2), 163–97.

LePine, J. A., A. Erez and D. E. Johnson (2002), 'The nature and dimensionality of organisational citizenship behavior: A critical review and meta-analysis', *Journal of Applied Psychology*, **87** (1), 52–65.

Maloney, M. P. and M. P. Ward (1973), 'Ecology: Let's hear from the people: An objective scale for the measurement of ecological attitudes and knowledge', *American Psychologist*, **28** (7), 583–6.

Manika, D., V. K. Wells, D. Gregory-Smith and M. Gentry (2015), 'The impact of individual attitudinal and organisational variables on workplace environmentally friendly behaviours', *Journal of Business Ethics*, **126** (4), 663–84.

McConnaughy, J. (2014), *Development of an Employee Green Behavior Descriptive Norms Scale*, Master's thesis, San Bernardino, CA: California State University, San Bernardino, accessed 17 May 2015 at http://scholarworks.lib.csusb.edu/etd/83.

McDonald, S. (2011), 'Green behaviour: Differences in recycling behaviour between the home and the workplace', in D. Bartlett (ed.), *Going Green: The Psychology of Sustainability in the Workplace*, Leicester: British Psychological Society, pp. 59–64.

Mesmer-Magnus, J., C. Viswesvaran and B. M. Wiernik (2012), 'The role of commitment in bridging the gap between organisational sustainability and environmental sustainability', in S. E. Jackson, D. S. Ones, and S. Dilchert (eds), *Managing Human Resources for Environmental Sustainability*, San Francisco, CA: Jossey-Bass/Wiley, pp. 155–86.

Montabon, F., R. Sroufe and R. Narasimhan (2007), 'An examination of corporate reporting, environmental management practices and firm performance', *Journal of Operations Management*, **25** (5), 998–1014.

Motowidlo, S. J. (2000), 'Some basic issues related to contextual performance and organisational citizenship behavior in human resource management', *Human Resource Management Review*, **10** (1), 115–26.

Nag, M. (2012), *Pro-Environmental Behaviors in the Workplace: Is Concern for the Environment Enough?*, Doctoral dissertation, College Park, MD: University of Maryland, accessed at http://hdl.handle.net/1903/13837.

Norton, T. (2016), *A Multilevel Perspective on Employee Green Behaviour*, Doctoral dissertation, Brisbane, Australia: University of Queensland, accessed at https://doi.org/10.14264/uql.2016.285.

Norton, T. A., S. L. Parker, H. Zacher and N. M. Ashkanasy (2015), 'Employee green behavior: A theoretical framework, multilevel review, and future research agenda', *Organisation & Environment*, **28** (1), 103–25.

Norton, T. A., H. Zacher, S. L. Parker and N. M. Ashkanasy (2014), *A Daily Diary Study on Predictors of Workplace Pro-Environmental Behaviors*, Paper presented at the International Congress for Applied Psychology, Paris, France, July.

Norton, T. A., H. Zacher, S. L. Parker and N. M. Ashkanasy (2017), 'Bridging the gap between green behavioral intentions and employee green behavior: The role of green psychological climate', *Journal of Organisational Behavior*, **38** (7), 996–1015.

Ones, D. S. and S. Dilchert (2009), *Green Behaviors of Workers: A Taxonomy for the Green Economy*, Paper presented at the annual meeting of the Academy of Management, Chicago, IL, August.

Ones, D. S. and S. Dilchert (2012), 'Employee green behaviors', in S. E. Jackson, D. S. Ones, and S. Dilchert (eds), *Managing Human Resources for Environmental Sustainability*, San Francisco, CA: Jossey-Bass/Wiley, pp. 85–116.

Ones, D. S. and S. Dilchert (2013), 'Measuring, understanding, and influencing employee green behaviors', in A. H. Huffman and S. R. Klein (eds), *Green Organisations: Driving Change with I-O Psychology*, New York: Routledge, pp. 115–48.

Organ, D. W. (1997), 'Organisational citizenship behavior: It's construct clean-up time', *Human Performance*, **10** (2), 85–97.

Podsakoff, P. M., S. B. MacKenzie, J. B. Paine and D. G. Bachrach (2000), 'Organisational citizenship behaviors: A critical review of the theoretical and empirical literature and suggestions for future research', *Journal of Management*, **26** (3), 513–63.

Ramus, C. A. and U. Steger (2000), 'The roles of supervisory support behaviors and environmental policy in employee "ecoinitiatives" at leading-edge European companies', *Academy of Management Journal*, **43** (4), 605–26.

Robertson, J. L. and J. Barling (2013), 'Greening organisations through leaders' influence on employees' pro-environmental behaviors', *Journal of Organisational Behavior*, **34** (2), 176–94.

Rotundo, M. and P. R. Sackett (2002), 'The relative importance of task, citizenship, and counterproductive performance to global ratings of job performance: A policy-capturing approach', *Journal of Applied Psychology*, **87** (1), 66–80.

Roy, A. and I. Goll (2014), 'Predictors of various facets of sustainability of nations: The role of cultural and economic factors', *International Business Review*, **23** (5), 849–61.

Scherbaum, C. A., P. M. Popovich and S. Finlinson (2008), 'Exploring individual-level factors related to employee energy-conservation behaviors at work', *Journal of Applied Social Psychology*, **38** (3), 818–35.

Stern, P. C. (2000), 'Toward a coherent theory of environmentally significant behavior', *Journal of Social Issues*, **56** (3), 407–24.

Stern, P. C., T. Dietz, T. Abel, G. A. Guagnano and L. Kalof (1999), 'A value-belief-norm theory of support for social movements: The case of environmentalism', *Human Ecology Review*, **6** (2), 81–98.

Temminck, E., K. Mearns and L. Fruhen (2015), 'Motivating employees towards sustainable behaviour', *Business Strategy and the Environment*, **24** (6), 402–12.

Thomas, J. P., D. S. Whitman and C. Viswesvaran (2010), 'Employee proactivity in organisations: A comparative meta-analysis of emergent proactive constructs', *Journal of Occupational and Organisational Psychology*, **83** (2), 275–300.

Viswesvaran, C. and D. S. Ones (2000), 'Perspectives on models of job performance', *International Journal of Selection and Assessment*, **8** (4), 216–26.

Vyvyan, V., C. Ng and M. Brimble (2007), 'Socially responsible investing: The green attitudes and grey choices of Australian investors', *Corporate Governance*, **15** (2), 370–81.

Wiernik, B. M. (2012), *Measuring National Sustainability: Making Sense of a Multidimensional Construct*, Paper presented at the annual conference of the Society for Industrial and Organisational Psychology, San Diego, CA, April.

Wiernik, B. M., S. Dilchert and D. S. Ones (2013), 'Organisational environmental policies and employee behavior: comparing European and U.S. samples', in G. Hertel, C. Binnewies, S. Krumm, H. Holling, and M. Kleinmann (eds), *Imagine the Future World: How Do We Want to Work Tomorrow?* Abstract Proceedings of the 16th EAWOP Congress 2013, Münster, Germany: Münstersche Informations- und Archivsystem multimedialer Inhalte, p. 502.

Wiernik, B. M., S. Dilchert and D. S. Ones (2016a), 'Age and employee green behaviors: A meta-analysis', *Frontiers in Psychology*, 7, 194.

Wiernik, B. M., S. Dilchert, D. S. Ones and R. M. Klein (2016b), *Item Factor Analysis of Employee Green Behaviors*, Poster presented at the annual conference of the Society for Industrial and Organisational Psychology, Anaheim, CA, April.

Wiernik, B. M., D. S. Ones, S. Dilchert and R. M. Klein (2018), 'Individual antecedents of pro-environmental behaviors: Implications for employee green behaviours', in V. K. Wells, D. Gregory-Smith, and D. Manika (eds), *Research Handbook on Employee Pro-Environmental Behaviour*, Cheltenham, UK and Northampton, MA, USA: Edward Elgar Publishing, pp. 63–82.

Xu, X., A. Maki, C. Chen, B. Dong and J. K. Day (2017), 'Investigating willingness to save energy and communication about energy use in the American workplace with the attitude-behavior-context model', *Energy Research & Social Science*, **32**, 13–22.

Zhang, Y., Z. Wang and G. Zhou (2013), 'Antecedents of employee electricity saving behavior in organisations: An empirical study based on norm activation model', *Energy Policy*, **62**, 1120–27.

3. Green human resources management
Cristina E. Ciocirlan

3.1 INTRODUCTION

Academics and practitioners agree that, in the future, the source of sustainable competitive advantage will come from the social and environmental stewardship that goes beyond compliance with the law or profit maximisation (Epstein and Buhovac 2014; Sroufe et al. 2010). Thus, 'leading and facilitating sustainability initiatives and creating a sustainability culture are the critical tasks confronting human resources professionals now' (Sroufe et al. 2010: 35).

Renwick et al.'s (2008) paper entitled *Green HRM: A Review, Process Model and Research Agenda*, represents one of the early conceptualisations of GHRM.[1] By 2011, the field of green human resources management (GHRM) had become a small, but growing, subset of human resource management (HRM) (Jackson et al. 2011). Since then, the field has grown exponentially, as evidenced by the rising number of articles and books, special issues of several top management and HR journals, as well as by the increased interest from professional organisations such as the Academy of Management, the Chartered Institute of Personnel and Development (CIPD) in the UK, and the Society for Human Resource Management (SHRM) in the US, and globally. The field has attracted both theoretical and empirical attention (CIPD 2009; Dumont et al. 2015; Milliman 2013; Renwick et al. 2016).

While the term 'sustainability' is often used interchangeably with terms such as 'environmental' or 'green', the term 'green HRM' should not be confused with 'sustainable HRM'. The latter has been defined as 'a new approach to the employment relationship considering corporate and societal goals of ecological, social, human and economic sustainability' (Ehnert et al. 2013: 19). Essentially, GHRM is a subset of sustainable HRM (Cohen et al. 2012; Ehnert et al. 2013).

GHRM was defined in the literature as a set of practices that adapt traditional HR functions to integrate environmental concerns, values, and attitudes: recruiting and selecting employees according to environmental criteria, designing jobs that incorporate environmental tasks and methods, providing environmental training and development, offering opportunities to participate in the setting of sustainability goals and in the process of implementation of environmental programmes via individual and group decision-making avenues, measuring performance according to environmental criteria, and offering rewards based on environmental performance (Jabbour and Santos 2008a; Renwick et al. 2013). To be effective, GHRM activities must be integrated with each other and with other organisational practices, in a systemic fashion (Jackson et al. 2012; Renwick et al. 2013).

Increasingly, GHRM has a strategic role in building and maintaining a sustainable competitive advantage. HR is uniquely positioned within the organisation to communicate the social purpose of the organisation; it can bring together internal and external stakeholders and partner with other organisations to help assess the environmental impact of its operations, and align its core activities using recruiting, and selection, training and development, performance evaluation and compensation to support a sustainable strategy (Cohen et al. 2012; Jackson et al. 2012; Renwick et al. 2016). While GHRM has made significant advances in functional areas, HR professionals face significant challenges in performing a strategic role related to communication of sustainability goals, alignment of HR activities with environmental sustainability, and employee involvement in green initiatives (Renwick et al. 2016).

Several theories are applied in the GHRM field, in diverse contexts. For instance, ability-motivation-opportunity (AMO) framework was applied to describe several functional areas of green HR (Renwick et al. 2013), and to map the antecedents of green HRM innovation in the manufacturing sector of Malaysia (Rajiani et al. 2016); signalling theory was applied in green recruiting (Gully et al. 2013; Guerci et al. 2016a); paradox theory was applied to describe the complexity that Italian companies face when implementing GHRM practices (Guerci and Carollo 2016); and the theory of normative conduct (TNC) was applied to assess the role of employee perceptions of green work climate in determining engagement in discretionary green behaviours (Norton et al. 2014). Most empirical studies use quantitative methodologies, cross-sectional, convenience samples, and self-reported data, and are conducted in single national contexts. More research, particularly interdisciplinary, using cross-cultural samples, qualitative and mixed research methods, and a longitudinal time span, is needed to advance the field (Dögl and Holtbrügge 2014; Guerci et al. 2016a; Jackson et al. 2012; Renwick et al. 2013; Subramanian et al. 2016).

The purpose of this chapter is to review recent literature on green HRM, outline directions for future research, and discuss implications for practitioners. In particular, I will discuss the functional activities of green recruiting and selection, green orientation and onboarding, green training and development, green leadership and culture, employee involvement and participation in sustainability, green performance evaluation, green compensation, and green talent management. These functional green activities are the most developed in the extant literature; they also hold the most promise for the future of GHRM as a discipline (Renwick et al. 2016). I will also discuss the strategic role of GHRM in building and maintaining a competitive advantage. While, often, decision makers may be motivated by ecocentric values and goals, the anthropocentric mindset is still deeply ingrained in the current paradigm of thinking and business decision-making models; further, the resource-based view (RBV) of the firm and its adaptations are still the dominant theories guiding the practice of management, although theories based on ecological knowledge and the natural resource views of the firm are gaining ground in academic circles (Borland et al. 2016; Pogutz and Winn 2016). Therefore, practitioners could make a business case for sustainability by demonstrating the strategic role of GHRM in organisations.

This chapter has four further sections. The first section will discuss how the functional activities of HR are transformed by integrating environmental criteria, goals, and values into traditional policies and processes. The next section will discuss the strategic role of GHRM in ensuring a competitive advantage. The next section discusses recommendations for future research, and the last section provides implications for practitioners.

3.2   FUNCTIONAL ACTIVITIES OF GREEN HRM

In GHRM, the traditional HR functions of recruiting, orientation and onboarding, training and development, performance evaluation, compensation, and talent management are adapted to incorporate environmental goals, values, and criteria. They will be described in the sub-sections below.

3.2.1   Green Recruiting and Selection

Green recruiting represents activities such as targeting and attracting green candidates (Gully et al. 2013; Rose 2014). Job candidates are increasingly interested in environmental issues and in a survey of over 3,000 postgraduate students, 93 per cent of respondents said that social/ environmental issues 'are important to a business's long-term success'. The three most important issues they identified for business to get right in the next ten years were the following: climate and energy, sustainable product development/marketing, and resource conservation. Further, 83 per cent of respondents agreed with the statement 'I would take a 15 per cent pay cut to have a job that seeks to make a social or environmental difference in the world' and 71 per cent agreed with the statement 'I would take a 15 per cent pay cut to have a job in a company committed to corporate and environmental responsibility' (Net Impact 2014).

While some literature points to a gap between environmental attitudes and behaviours (Echegaray and Hansstein 2017; Redondo and Puelles 2016), the attention and concern of the general public for environmental phenomena, such as climate change, are on the rise. Specifically, university graduates and future job applicants are concerned about environmental issues (Kim and Wolinsky-Nahmias 2014; Wachholz et al. 2014). Moreover, due to demographic trends and skill gaps, significant talent shortages are projected, both in developed and developing economies (Cappelli 2015; Melguizo and Perea 2016). Given these trends, the reputation of employers and the quality of an employer's brand are becoming increasingly important in attracting good candidates (Dögl and Holtbrügge 2014).

Studies based on signalling theory suggest that, to attract talented candidates who exhibit green values and attitudes, organisations must focus on building and maintaining their reputation as a green employer of choice (Guerci et al. 2016a; Jackson et al. 2011). Environmental activities and products are used as signals to potential employees that the company cares about environmental responsibility. These signals arouse pride in job seekers of being potentially associated with that company and communicate to green candidates that the company enjoys a competitive advantage over other employers; they also create a perception, in job seekers' minds, that a value fit exists with that organisation (Dögl and Holtbrügge 2014; Guerci et al. 2016a; Jones et al. 2014; Williamson et al. 2003; Willness and Jones 2013). Indeed, the reputation of a company as a green employer had positive effects on attracting job applicants in an Italian sample (Guerci et al. 2016a).

Targeting and recruiting green candidates must be coupled with selection processes that use valid and reliable environmental criteria in decision-making. Many companies select employees whose jobs entail the display of environmental attitudes and the execution of green tasks (Ones and Dilchert 2013). Screening devices could be incorporated in the hiring process to select candidates with stable internal traits, green attitudes, and motivations. For instance, behavioural interview questions could uncover relevant environmental values (Liebowitz 2010). Regardless of the selection device used, HR managers should ensure that these devices are job-related and reliable (Fodchuk 2007; Ciocirlan 2016).

3.2.2   Green Orientation and Onboarding

The socialisation of new employees into company culture starts with orientation and onboarding. Information about environmental philosophy, values, programmes, and ongoing projects would help communicate to new employees that their first impressions obtained via interviews and initial interaction with the company were valid. An effective orientation programme would also reinforce in employees' minds the idea that the company seriously cares about environmental issues (Jabbour 2013). For example, organisations such as Clif Bar, Toyota Motor Sales USA, and the Port of Houston designed new employee orientation programmes that include information about ongoing environmental projects and environmental policies that need to be followed (Liebowitz 2010). Platforms such as web conferences, or a company intranet could be used to deliver effective green orientation programmes (Ulus and Hatipoglu 2016).

3.2.3   Green Training and Development (T&D)

Perhaps of all the GHRM activities, green T&D has been studied most extensively in the literature. Scholars are interested in studying both the content and process of environmental training and development. According to an extensive literature review, goals of environmental training programmes in organisations included enhancing awareness of environmental issues in organisations, enhancing skills in order to reduce the environmental impact of activities, strengthening another HR practice, improving environmental performance of the organisation, and improving overall organisational performance (Jabbour 2013). The literature on green T&D is generally concerned with the content, process, and evaluation of T&D programmes. The following sub-sections reflect this categorisation.

Content
Performing a task in a green manner requires knowledge of green processes and products. For example, in order to conduct environmental accounting, or triple bottom-line accounting, employees must have knowledge of life cycle costing and environmental activity-based costing (Livesey and Kearins 2002). In the food packaging industry, new employees receive training in health and safety, clean production, safe use and disposal of chemicals, drills to learn the proper way to treat chemicals and spills, and handling of hazardous waste (Dumont et al. 2015). Other technical green management practices might include life cycle assessment, environmental auditing, and environmental impact analyses (Teixeira et al. 2012), energy

saving methods (Cohen et al. 2012), or waste reduction methods (e.g., Mohawk Industries) (Weinstein 2008).

Some companies offer green training to comply with international standards, such as ISO 14001 or ISO 150015. These standards require designing and planning environmental training, training for third parties, delivery, and evaluation of environmental training programmes (Teixeira et al. 2012). Others view green T&D as a pillar of green culture development, with the goal to enhance employee awareness of environmental issues and improve the overall sustainability of the organisation (Cohen et al. 2012; Muros et al. 2012).

Process

Apart from *what* is taught, the GHRM literature also considers *how* green education is delivered. Many companies conduct green training in-house, through corporate universities. Some of the innovative training practices include the following: monthly workshops that include third parties, annual events with all the subsidiaries to exchange environment practices, environmental training of manufacturing cells, attending international fairs, offering awards with an ecological theme, internal contests, and corporate campaigns involving planting trees (Teixeira et al. 2012).

Mirroring the growth of digital technology, many companies (e.g., Caribou Coffee) offer online educational programmes (Muros et al. 2012). Platforms such as cloud software, virtual teams, e-reading, and online learning have great potential in delivering green education (Rose 2014). In a study of UK organisations, raising awareness to environmental issues internally, through seminars and posters, was more popular than other forms of training, probably because of their lower costs (Zibarras and Coan 2015).

Giving employees the opportunity to leave for extended periods of time allows for meaningful reflection and learning about environmental issues. For instance, many global organisations (e.g., PricewaterhouseCoopers) send their employees to developing countries to learn about issues related to global sustainable development. Others (e.g., Patagonia) encourage employees to take sabbaticals with an environmental theme (Bauer et al. 2012).

However, scholars argue that most green T&D models adopted by organisations today are ineffective; they consist of a potpourri of disparate tools and stem from an anthropological paradigm, which emphasises humans' dominance over nature and assumes a zero-sum relationship between economic and environmental goals. They propose the replacement of these outdated learning models with ecocentric models of education, which focus on the systemic nature of the interaction between humans and the natural environment and a focus on the triple bottom line (TBL). The Eastern philosophy, centred on the harmony of body, mind, spirit, and nature, is offered as an alternative paradigm (Rose 2014). Organisations should envisage green education as a long-term investment, along with corporate profitability goals. Green education should emphasise creativity and imagination and should prompt employees to seek profit maximisation without negatively impacting resource and energy efficiency (Rose 2014; Shrivastava 2010).

Apart from *what* is included in green training and *how* it is conducted in organisations today, there is a great variation regarding *who* gets the training as well. Some companies (e.g. Caribou Coffee) educate not only their employees, but also their customers (Muros et al. 2012). Further, some companies only offer green training for green jobs, while others offer green training to all employees, regardless of job characteristics (Guerci and Carollo 2016).

Evaluation of training
Researchers and practitioners are also interested in evaluation models. How effective is the training? How do we know whether it is effective or not? Most companies evaluate the effectiveness of training programmes through exams and tests administered at the end of the training sessions. Less frequently, some companies also collect data on employee satisfaction with training, in order to improve the effectiveness of the training process in the future (Teixeira et al. 2012).

Evidence indicates that green training has a positive effect upon pollution reduction, while employee training and communication has a positive impact upon successful implementation of ISO 14001 (Jabbour and Santos 2008b). Green training also mediates the relationship between customer pressures and environmental performance. For example, in a study of 74 Italian service and manufacturing companies, Guerci et al. (2016b) found that companies used green training to respond to customer pressures and improve their environmental performance. However, green training did not mediate the relationship between regulatory pressures and environmental performance, suggesting that companies respond to regulatory pressures through other mechanisms. Often, green T&D may simply enhance awareness about environmental issues, and consequently, end up changing attitudes. Activities such as informing employees on the overall organisational expenses with electricity, or the consequences of non-green actions, and explaining relevant green behaviours could be important in changing attitudes (Chou 2014). In a Brazilian sample, the most proactive company in green management had an integrated approach to green awareness, which suggests that green activities often reinforce one another: the more a company offered environmental training to employees and managers, the more it engaged in more sophisticated green management practices and vice versa (Teixeira et al. 2012).

3.2.4   Green Leadership and Culture

The importance of executive support for environmental actions and initiatives cannot be overstated, as employees look to organisational leaders to figure out what is important and hold executives accountable for their actions (DuBois et al. 2013; Dumont et al. 2015; Liebowitz 2010; Ones and Dilchert 2013; Sheehan et al. 2014; Zibarras and Coan 2015). When senior managers are supportive of green practices, the organisations engage in effective environmental programmes (Zibarras and Ballinger 2011). Many organisations (e.g., The Hershey Company) create formal structures around environmental values by appointing a Sustainability coordinator or a Chief Sustainability Officer (Ones and Dilchert 2013), or assign environmental responsibility to a designated C-level position.

Organisational leaders have a strategic role in the cultural integration of green values. Muster and Schrader (2011) adapted Edgar Schein's classic definition of organisational culture to say that a green culture 'can be understood as a pattern of shared basic assumptions [. . .] about the environment and environmental issues' (pp. 142–143). To create an authentic green culture, leaders might first start with a clear communication of, and commitment to, environmental goals and policies (Zibarras and Coan 2015). Evidence shows that, when employees are aware of a published corporate environmental policy and of a clear policy to reduce fossil fuel consumption, they are more likely to design and implement eco-initiatives in their area of activity (Ramus and Steger 2000). Second, leaders should adopt a whole systems approach to GHRM, where all organisational levels would be involved in designing, implementing, and supporting sustainability efforts. Only through such a systemic, holistic approach, would sustainability-thinking be embedded in the mindset of all employees and result in employees 'owning' sustainability (DuBois et al. 2013). Third, leaders must essentially be transformational: they must put the interests of the organisation above their own, and act in consistence with stated ecocentric beliefs and values (Bolino and Turnley 2003; Egri and Herman 2000).

3.2.5   Employee Involvement and Participation

Employee participation refers to 'the range of mechanisms used to involve the workforce in decisions at all levels of the organization, whether undertaken directly with employees, or indirectly through their representatives' (Wilkinson et al. 2010: 11–12). Direct participation may occur through avenues such as suggestion programmes, team meetings, employee surveys, quality circles, conferences, company intranet, or self-autonomous teams. Using these platforms, employees are encouraged to participate and exchange opinions regarding environmental protection efforts (Dumont et al. 2015; Guerci and Carollo 2016). Representative participation may occur via work councils, unions, health and safety committees, or joint committees (Markey et al. 2016). In a study of 700 Australian organisations, the most common method of employee participation in emission reduction programmes was direct participation, specifically via team meetings (Markey et al. 2016).

Evidence shows that, when employees are involved in a meaningful way in decision-making regarding the implementation of environmental management programmes, such as the ISO 14001 standards or carbon emission reduction programmes, they feel that they have a stake in the successful implementation of these programmes. Thus, they will put forth more effort into them and will be genuinely engaged in their implementation (Boiral 2009; Daily and Huang 2001; Markey et al. 2016; Perez et al. 2009). At Caribou Coffee, employee engagement was positively correlated with engagement in environmental behaviours (Ones and Dilchert 2013). Creating participation structures such as town hall meetings and employee suggestion programmes would enable employees to develop ideas to reduce waste and increase efficiency (Liebowitz 2010). Further, employees who hold green values and attitudes are less likely to complain about the extra effort and inconvenience required by the adoption of pollution-reduction technologies (Boiral 2009).

Higher employee involvement in environmental programmes has benefits not only for organisational environmental performance, but also for typical areas of concerns for HR, such as engagement and turnover. Studying two Australian organisations, Benn et al. (2015) found that employee involvement in green initiatives was positively associated with higher overall employee engagement, and negatively correlated with turnover. In an Italian study, employee involvement practices mediated the relationship between customer pressure and environmental performance (Guerci et al. 2016b).

3.2.6 Green Performance Evaluation

An important focus of the green performance management literature is developing valid and reliable indicators to measure green performance. These indicators measure how resources needed for one's job have been obtained, how they were used, and how much waste was generated. Other indicators include efficiency of machines, amount of machine downtime due to employee idleness or machine breakdowns, and printing costs (Dumont et al. 2015). Another important area of research is how information about resource usage and efficiency is used and entered into an integrated information system that measures the impact of employees' jobs on the natural environment. Such a comprehensive system helps organisations learn and continuously improve the process of greening jobs (Rose 2014).

Coupled with measurement, periodic communication of green targets and green behaviours is necessary. In a qualitative study of energy conservation behaviours in organisations, many organisations lacked proper communication regarding energy-saving initiatives, which in turn contributed to a low perception of self-efficacy among employees. Employees were not aware of the benefits of specific energy-saving behaviours and which behaviours were under their control. Participants also quoted a lack of feedback on personal behaviour. Being aware of how much one prints, for instance, was quoted as a determinant of printing reduction behaviour (Lo et al. 2012).

3.2.7   Green Compensation and Reward Management

To communicate the importance of environmental programmes to senior executives, some companies, such as 3M, Bristol-Myers Squibb, Procter and Gamble, and Sunoco, include social and environmental criteria when evaluating and rewarding executive performance (Berrone and Gomez-Mejia 2009b; Guerci and Carollo 2016). For instance, the SC Johnson Company awards bonuses to managers who achieve their Greenlist™ goals (Liebowitz 2010).[2] While on the surface, linking executive compensation to green criteria seems a natural way to enhance environmental performance, literature is mixed. Some studies found that tying compensation to the implementation of environmental programmes had a positive effect on the adoption of environmental strategies by companies (Guerci et al. 2016b; King and Lenox 2004; Russo and Harrison 2005). Other studies found that higher salaries were actually related to lower social responsibility (McGuire et al. 2003), and short-term compensation had a negative effect on corporate social performance, while long-term compensation had a positive effect on corporate social performance (Deckop et al. 2006). Companies with a strong environmental reputation actually offered a lower total compensation to their executives (Stanwick and Stanwick 2001).

While tying executive compensation to environmental and social initiatives is becoming a widespread practice, there are several concerns with this approach. First, the positive and direct link between environmental initiatives and economic results has not been demonstrated. Second, different stakeholder groups have mixed beliefs regarding corporate social responsibility (CSR): some may favour CSR programmes, others do not. For instance, employees may not approve of environmental initiatives if such initiatives threaten their job security. Third, research in behavioural economics and psychology shows that offering extrinsic rewards for a behaviour that requires creativity and innovation might destroy intrinsic motivations to perform that behaviour (Pink 2009). Executives might have already been motivated to engage in social and environmental practices to begin with, spurred by promises of positive self-image, fairness, or pure altruism. Paying them to implement CSR programmes might distort these otherwise noble motivations. Fourth, social-based compensation might encourage risky and opportunistic behaviour by executives. Since the effectiveness of many social and environmental programmes is difficult to evaluate, executives may manipulate their reporting and value (Berrone and Gomez-Mejia 2009a).

Given the issues associated with compensation, scholars recommend that organisations use non-financial incentives, such as extra vacation days, counting volunteer time as part of employees' regular working time, offering paid time off on the annual Earth Day,[3] offering a bicycle for employees who bike to work, charity gift certificates, and offering telecommuting options. Companies such as Eaton Corporation, Evo Gear, Husky, and many organisations designated by Fortune as 'best places to work' offer these non-monetary incentives (Berrone and Gomez-Mejia 2009a; Boiral 2009). Other creative non-monetary rewards include the following: employee of the month awards for best green performance, planting a tree for each employee, providing opportunities for employees to attend a global wildlife event (Guerci and Carollo 2016) and tying key performance indicators (KPIs) to a compensation system that rewards outstanding performance in the environmental area (Dumont et al. 2015).

Other opportunities include offering prizes for green innovations (Chou 2014). For instance, 3M offers the Most Hazardous Waste Prevented Award Programme, the 'Pollution Prevention Pays' (3Ps) programme (EPA 2016), Dow Chemicals offers the 'Waste Reduction Always Pays' programme (Laden and Gray 2016), and FedExKinko offers an 'Environmental Branch of the Year' award (Esty and Winston 2006). Some companies reward suggestions that are practical and applicable (Guerci and Carollo 2016); others reward suggestions that actually get implemented with an additional bonus (Dumont et al. 2015). As expected, individual, team, and organisational incentives for green performance are more common in large, rather than small, organisations (Zibarras and Coan 2015).

3.2.8   Green Talent Management

A talent management approach to GHRM involves pursuing green HR and strategic activities in an integrated fashion: recruiting and selecting green candidates must be followed by green orientation, training, and performance evaluation that includes environmental criteria. Employees must be encouraged to engage in green behaviours, provide suggestions for eco-initiatives and be rewarded for these suggestions. Organisational leaders would communicate and exemplify a green mission and vision, which will lead to building a green culture and strengthening the employer's green reputation. Thus, green HR activities must be interconnected and must support one another. They cannot be executed in a disparate and disconnected fashion (Jackson et al. 2011; Renwick et al. 2016).

For instance, financial decisions related to green HR activities must be considered together: since selection and training processes are closely linked, companies may realise that focusing on green credentials in the selection process may reduce their investment in green training afterwards (Guerci and Carollo 2016). In a Chinese manufacturing study, strategic HR activities had a positive impact on greening organisational culture only when managers were convinced that their company had a clear policy to encourage environmental awareness, the company believed in environmental preservation, and made a strong effort to educate employees in the importance of protecting the environment (Paillé et al. 2014). Johnson and Miller (2012) describe how the Aveda Corporation aligns all of its functional HR activities with its environmental mission and goals. In a qualitative study based on case studies of nine Brazilian companies, Teixeira et al. (2012) found that companies that exhibited a proactive green management were also characterised by a green organisational culture and teamwork and top management support of environmental issues, and performed technical green management practices, such as life cycle assessment, environmental auditing, and environmental impact analyses. In a study of 1,230 Chinese employees, green competencies were positively correlated with green behaviours and other variables. Thus, HR managers should integrate green competencies, such as ecological knowledge and skills, in their employee selection processes (Subramanian et al. 2016).

Further, a talent management approach to GHRM involves a continuous process of revising and refining policies and practices. Information on green behaviours could be collected via surveys and interviews, and used to measure the effectiveness of sustainability policies related to ethical climate, organisational support, or company mission (e.g., Procter & Gamble) (Biga et al. 2012).

In sum, green talent management provides a coherent platform to integrate the functional green HR activities described above. The functional green HR activities should not be performed in a vacuum; rather, green hiring, orientation and onboarding, T&D, performance evaluation, and compensation only contribute to an organisation's environmental performance if they are connected to each other. The next section explains how green HRM can create and maintain a competitive advantage for organisations.

3.3   THE STRATEGIC ROLE OF GHRM

GHRM can provide a source of competitive advantage, provided that several conditions exist. First, organisations must be responsive to internal and external pressures to transform their cultural practices. Internal pressures often come from employees situated at different organisational levels (Ciocirlan 2016). According to surveys, employees consider 'work itself' as very important to their motivation, and 'meaningfulness' as very important to their job satisfaction (SHRM 2014). Both prioritising environmental objectives and encouraging employees to evaluate the environmental impact of their jobs are likely to enhance meaningfulness and job satisfaction of employees. Other variables, such as the use of cross-functional environmental teams, and sharing experiences in environmental management, are positively correlated with the strategic integration of environmental concerns (Jabbour et al. 2010).

Along with internal pressures, external stakeholder pressures are also important. In an Italian sample of manufacturing and service firms, customer and regulatory pressure had a direct and positive effect on firms' environmental performance. In particular, customer pressure had a positive and significant effect on the adoption of green hiring practices, green training and involvement, and green performance management and compensation. Regulatory pressure had a positive and significant effect on green hiring, but not on the other green practices. Regarding the relative strength of the two types of pressure, customer pressure had a larger effect than regulatory pressure on the adoption of GHRM practices, probably due to the economic motivation attached to the former (Guerci et al. 2016b).

Second, green HRM should be performed in a consistent and integrative fashion. Many organisations have a haphazard approach to environmental management, and engage in 'random acts of greenness', or a set of disparate green initiatives with mixed effects (Makower 2008). By contrast, a coherent, strategic approach to sustainability is necessary. In a cluster analysis, such a coherent approach made a difference between leader and laggard firms (Sroufe et al. 2010). In organisations that have achieved environmental integration, the involvement of top management was continuous, and environmental management was perceived as a source of competitive advantage (Jabbour et al. 2010).

Third, HR managers must exhibit critical strategic roles and competencies, identified as important in adopting GHRM practices. In a study of Malaysian manufacturing and service companies, Yong and Mohd-Yusoff (2016) found that two strategic roles of HR professionals, strategic positioner and change champion, had a direct and positive effect on the adoption of green HR practices, such as green job analysis, green recruiting, green training, and green rewards and compensation systems.

3.4   DIRECTIONS FOR FUTURE RESEARCH

The field of GHRM has benefitted from a great deal of attention in the past few years. However, more research is necessary in each of the functional areas of green HR, as well as the strategic role of green HR (Renwick et al. 2016; Jackson et al. 2012).

In the area of recruitment, studies using signalling theory made tremendous advances in our understanding of the process of green reputation-building and its role in targeting and attracting green employers (Dögl and Holtbrügge 2014; Guerci et al. 2016a; Jackson et al. 2011; Jones et al. 2014; Willness and Jones 2013). However, we still do not have a good understanding of the process by which candidates form a perception of an organisation's environmental performance and values. In terms of timing, we do not know at what stage of the perception-forming process that information about environmental practices is most visible and significant in influencing the decision of a green candidate to choose their employer (Jackson et al. 2011).

Most studies on green recruiting use cross-sectional data and small samples, based on self-reported data (Dögl and Holtbrügge 2014). To identify the antecedents of green reputation and the complex relationships between green reputation and employee commitment, more longitudinal studies, drawing from large samples, and studies based on objective data, are necessary. Further, more literature is necessary to identify the factors that determine a candidate's interest in a certain employer, in particular, the impact of different sources of information about a company on candidate attraction. Cross-country analyses and studies that involve samples other than graduate students might be beneficial (Guerci et al. 2016a).

With respect to training, a disproportionate number of studies focus on the manufacturing sector (Jabbour 2013). This is surprising, especially since the service sector has an increasing contribution to the economy, both in developed and developing economies. More research is necessary in training methods used in organisations functioning in the service sector, such as healthcare or tourism (Chenven and Copeland 2013; Kim and Choi 2013; Pinzone et al. 2016). In terms of national context, the extensive literature review conducted by Jabbour (2013) reveals that most environmental training literature focuses on practices in the developed world, and many studies are conceptual, rather than empirical. Further, the influence of national cultures on the shaping of green organisational cultures is an interesting area of research, particularly for global companies with multiple subsidiaries around the world (Jackson et al. 2011). More research on understanding environmental practices in developing countries, as well as more comparative research on the practices used in different national contexts is necessary. Regarding the research methodology to address environmental training, more articles using qualitative and mixed methods are necessary to paint a complete picture of environmental practices in organisations (Guerci and Carollo 2016; Jabbour 2013).

Most of the literature on motivating green employees focuses on extrinsic motivation tactics, such as setting green targets, goals and responsibilities, rewarding environmental suggestions, providing financial/ tax incentives, monthly managerial bonuses, public recognition, paid vacations, gift certificates, incorporating green performance indicators in performance appraisals, and so on (Renwick et al. 2013). Fewer studies address the intrinsic motivation of green employees. The concept of green job design as such an intrinsic mechanism is largely underdeveloped in the GHRM literature. The job characteristic model (JCM) of job design developed by Hackman and Oldham (1980) could be adapted to show how designing jobs around employees' green values and tasks will enhance these employees' level of intrinsic motivation (Ciocirlan 2016).

Apart from contributions from organisational behaviour or management disciplines, more interdisciplinary research is needed to grow the budding field of GHRM (Renwick et al. 2016). Transforming workplace behaviours requires changing habits and ways of thinking about work, organisations, and sustainability. Recent advances in the field of neuroscience explain how brain pathways are created to form automatic behaviours, or habits. Changing these automatic behaviours requires analysing the three components of a habit: its cue, reward, and routine (Duhigg 2014; Lehrer 2009). Transforming behaviours and attitudes to incorporate green values might benefit from cross-disciplinary studies, situated at the intersection of neuroscience, organisational learning, and organisational performance.

Green HR could also learn from other well-established disciplines, such as Organisational Development (OD). OD, as a systematic and planned change philosophy, has the potential of transforming the culture of an organisation and enhancing its capabilities (Stolz 2014). Practices such as survey feedback, socio-technical systems, action research, and employee involvement processes, which are the backbone of OD, would be very helpful in increasing their organisation's readiness to change (Rose 2014). Since valid measures of green organisational cultures still need to be refined (Jackson et al. 2011), GHRM could tap into the extensive literature on organisational culture developed in OD.

Discussions on how best to achieve behaviour transformation and green cultures in organisations are inherently related to how sustainability is taught in business schools across the world. Job candidates, and thus, future employees, are often trained in business schools, in graduate and postgraduate programmes. As long as business education teaches students that work and life should be treated in a separate manner, that humans are rightly dominant over nature, and that organisational problems must be solved with a rational and analytical mindset, any mention of passion and emotion towards sustainability is likely to encounter ridicule and embarrassment (Shrivastava 2010). By contrast, the ideal approach to business education is a holistic one, which integrates the cognitive, spiritual, emotional, and physical aspects of the managerial work. Value-centred models of business education, such as *Giving Voice to Values (GVV)*, pioneered by The Aspen Institute, USA, or *Sustainability through Student Empowerment*, developed at Antwerp Management School, Belgium, are such examples of holistic education. Future research might examine how such holistic pedagogy might affect attitudes and behaviours of job candidates, and subsequently, of future employees.

3.5   IMPLICATIONS FOR PRACTITIONERS

Practitioners who aim at transforming their organisational cultures and enhance environmental performance should start with the process of green recruiting and selection. Building a reputation as 'green employer of choice' should be a priority in attracting green candidates. There are several avenues by which organisations can communicate to job candidates aspects of their brand as a green employer: using the company website or social media to post information about environmental programmes (Guerci et al. 2016a); word of mouth from current employees to their network of family and friends; and discussing environmental values, environmental records, policies, and practices with job seekers and new employees (Guerci and Carollo 2016; Jabbour 2013; Willness and Jones

2013). Organisations could enhance their green recruiting efforts directly, by targeting universities that offer programmes in sustainability, and indirectly, by recruiting a diverse workforce: diversity is positively correlated with innovation and creativity, two elements absolutely necessary in sustainability (Liebowitz 2010).

To ensure that green HR activities are consistent with one another, organisations should use competency models in hiring, selection, and T&D performance evaluation (Rose 2014; Subramanian et al. 2016). These competency models would specify abilities to understand stakeholders' expectations regarding environmental responsibility and skills, knowledge about CSR and environmental sustainability, using computer technologies to communicate such information, persuasion skills, supporting line managers' efforts in culture change, amongst others (Cosby 2014; DuBois et al. 2013; Subramanian et al. 2016).

Managers can also use several recommendations to 'green' the cultures of their organisations. The importance of leadership to creating a green culture has been well documented in the literature (Boiral 2009; Boiral et al. 2009). Green development practices aimed at teaching transformational leadership behaviours and sustainability should be developed. Further, changing the organisational structure to allow for a more egalitarian and participative process of decision-making, allowing employees the autonomy and freedom to set social and environmental goals, can increase employee commitment to environmental programmes (Berrone and Gomez-Mejia 2009a; Daily and Huang 2001). Policies such as 3M's or Google's 20 per cent of time policy might be beneficial for sustainable innovation, as employees could use this time to develop green products or processes.

While performing GHRM activities is more common and feasible in large organisations (Zibarras and Coan 2015), their use in small companies should not be prohibitive. Organisations such as the Small Business Administration in the US, CIPD in the UK, and SHRM, globally, provide recruiting information and screening tools that could be adapted by small companies for green recruiting and selection. Further, many European governments offer financial support for environmental training, and other GHRM activities (Guerci and Carollo 2016). The US and other governments might follow European models, in order to facilitate the planning and execution of GHRM activities in organisations. Regulators could lower taxes on compensation related to environmental performance (Guerci et al. 2016b). Managers of small firms could make a business case for implementing GHRM in their organisations. Evidence shows that the tangible (financial) and intangible benefits (building goodwill and preempting legislation) of GHRM activities exceed their costs (O'Donohue and Torugsa 2016).

GHRM policies are not without risks. For example, green work–life interventions might be perceived as an instance of unwarranted meddling of corporations into employees' private lives. Employees might also feel that they are expected, or forced, to participate in green behaviours at work and in their private lives. To appease these concerns, it is imperative that organisations clearly communicate the voluntary nature of the green work–life interventions (Muster and Schrader 2011). Further, engaging in voluntary green behaviours at work, while good for the organisation and its reputation, might bear personal career, health, and family costs, especially if the organisational culture does not appreciate or reward these behaviours (Sonenshein et al. 2014). As stewards for ensuring the health and wellness of employees, HR managers have an important role in minimising these risks.

NOTES

1. The terms green HRM and GHRM are used interchangeably throughout the chapter.
2. Greenlist™ is a database that ranks ingredients based on their level of greenness, or their impact on the environment (Liebowitz 2010).
3. Engaging in optional initiatives outside of the organisation spurs green behaviours within the organisation, because they communicate to employees that caring for the environment is an important organisational value (Boiral 2009).

REFERENCES

Bauer, T.N., B. Erdogan, and S. Taylor (2012), 'Creating and maintaining environmentally sustainable organizations: Recruitment and onboarding', *Business Administration Faculty Publications and Presentations, Paper 28.*

Benn, S., S.T.T. Teo, and A. Martin (2015), 'Employee participation and engagement in working for the environment', *Personnel Review*, **44**, 492–510.

Berrone, P., and L.R. Gomez-Mejia (2009a), 'The pros and cons of rewarding social responsibility at the top', *Human Resource Management,* **48** (6), 959–971.

Berrone, P., and L.R. Gomez-Mejia (2009b), 'Environmental performance and executive compensation: An integrated agency-institutional perspective', *Academy of Management Journal*, **52** (1), 103–126.

Biga, A., S. Dilchert, A.S. McCance, R.E. Gibby, and A.D. Oudersluys (2012), 'Environmental sustainability and organization sensing at Procter & Gamble', in S.E. Jackson, D.S. Ones, and S. Dilchert (eds), *Managing Human Resources for Environmental Sustainability* (vol. 32), San Francisco, CA: John Wiley and Sons, pp. 362–374.

Boiral, O. (2009), 'Greening the corporation through organizational citizenship behaviors', *Journal of Business Ethics*, **87** (2), 221–236.

Boiral, O., M. Cayer, and C.M. Baron (2009), 'The action logics of environmental leadership: A developmental perspective', *Journal of Business Ethics*, **85** (4), 479–499.

Bolino, M.C., and W.H. Turnley (2003), 'Going the extra mile: Cultivating and managing employee citizenship behavior', *The Academy of Management Executive*, **17** (3), 60–71.

Borland, H., V. Ambrosini, A. Lindgreen, and J. Vanhamme (2016), 'Building theory at the intersection of ecological sustainability and strategic management', *Journal of Business Ethics*, **135**, 293–307.

Cappelli, P.H. (2015), 'Skill gaps, skill shortages, and skill mismatches: Evidence and arguments for the United States', *ILR Review*, 0019793914564961.

Chartered Institute of Personnel and Development (CIPD) (2009), *Shared Purpose and Sustainable Organisation Performance*, London: CIPD.

Chenven, L., and D. Copeland (2013), 'Front-line worker engagement: Greening health care, improving worker and patient health, and building better jobs', *New Solutions: A Journal of Environmental and Occupational Health Policy*, **23** (2), 327–345.

Chou, C.J. (2014), 'Hotels' environmental policies and employee personal environmental beliefs: Interactions and outcomes', *Tourism Management*, **40**, 436–446.

Ciocirlan, C.E. (2016), 'Environmental workplace behaviors: Definition matters', *Organization and Environment*, **30** (1), 51–70.

Cohen, E., S. Taylor, and M. Muller-Camen (2012), *HRM's Role in Corporate Social and Environmental Sustainability*, Alexandria, VA: SHRM Foundation.

Cosby, D.M. (2014), 'Sustainability program leadership for human resource development professionals: A competency model', *Journal of Organizational Culture, Communication and Conflict*, **18** (2), 79–86.

Daily, B.F., and S.C. Huang (2001), 'Achieving sustainability through attention to human resource factors in environmental management', *International Journal of Operations and Production Management*, **21** (12), 1539–1552.

Deckop, J.R., K.K. Merriman, and S. Gupta (2006), 'The effects of CEO pay structure on corporate social performance', *Journal of Management*, **32** (3), 329–342.

Dögl, C., and D. Holtbrügge (2014), 'Corporate environmental responsibility, employer reputation and employee commitment: an empirical study in developed and emerging economies', *International Journal of Human Resource Management*, **25** (12), 1739–1762.

DuBois, C.L., M.N. Astakhova, and D.A. DuBois (2013), 'Motivating behavior change to support organizational environmental sustainability goals', in A.H. Huffman, and S.R. Klein (eds), *Green Organizations: Driving Change with IO Psychology*, New York: Routledge, pp. 186–207.

Duhigg, C. (2014), *The Power of Habit: Why We Do What We Do in Life and Business*, St. Louis, MO: Turtleback Books.

Dumont, J., J. Shen, and X. Deng (2015), 'Green HRM practices: A case study', *Journal of International Management Studies*, **15** (2), 15–22.

Echegaray, F. and F.V. Hansstein (2017), 'Assessing the intention-behavior gap in electronic waste recycling: The case of Brazil', *Journal of Cleaner Production*, **142**, 180–190.

Egri, C.P., and S. Herman (2000), 'Leadership in the North American environmental sector: Values, leadership styles, and contexts of environmental leaders and their organizations', *Academy of Management Journal*, **43** (4), 571–604.

Ehnert, I., W. Harry, and K.J. Zink (2013), 'Sustainability and HRM: An introduction to the field', in I. Ehnert, W. Harry, and K.J. Zink (eds), *Sustainability and Human Resource Management: Developing Sustainable Business Organizations*, Heidelberg: Springer Science and Business Media, pp. 3–32.

Environmental Protection Agency (EPA) (2016), *From 'Pollution Prevention Pays' to Sustainability at 3M*, accessed 27 December 2016 at www.epa.gov/lean/3m-lean-six-sigma-and-sustainability.

Epstein, M.J., and A.R. Buhovac (2014), *Making Sustainability Work: Best Practices in Managing and Measuring Corporate Social, Environmental, and Economic Impacts*, San Francisco, CA: Berrett-Koehler Publishers.

Esty, D.C., and A.S. Winston (2006), *Green to Gold*, New Haven, CT: Yale University Press.

Fodchuk, K.M. (2007), 'Work environments that negate counterproductive behaviors and foster organizational citizenship: Research-based recommendations for managers', *The Psychologist-Manager Journal*, **10** (1), 27–46.

Guerci, M., and L. Carollo (2016), 'A paradox view on green human resource management: Insights from the Italian context', *The International Journal of Human Resource Management*, **27** (2), 212–238.

Guerci, M., A. Longoni, and D. Luzzini (2016b), 'Translating stakeholder pressures into environmental performance – the mediating role of green HRM practices', *The International Journal of Human Resource Management*, **27** (2), 262–289.

Guerci, M., F. Montanari, A. Scapolan, and A. Epifanio (2016a), 'Green and nongreen recruitment practices for attracting job applicants: Exploring independent and interactive effects', *International Journal of Human Resource Management*, **27** (2), 129–150.

Gully, S.M., J.M. Phillips, W.G. Castellano, K. Han, and A. Kim (2013), 'A mediated moderation model of recruiting socially and environmentally responsible job applicants', *Personnel Psychology*, **66**, 935–973.

Hackman, J.R., and G.R. Oldham (1980), *Work Redesign*, Reading, MA: Addison-Wesley.

Jabbour, C.J.C. (2013), 'Environmental training in organisations: From a literature review to a framework for future research', *Resources, Conservation and Recycling*, **74**, 144–155.

Jabbour, C.J.C., and F.C.A. Santos (2008a), 'The central role of human resource management in the search for sustainable organizations', *International Journal of Human Resource Management*, **19** (12), 2133–2155.

Jabbour, C.J.C., and F.C.A. Santos (2008b), 'Relationships between human resource dimensions and environmental management in companies: Proposal of a model', *Journal of Cleaner Production*, **16**, 51–58.

Jabbour, C.J.C., F.C.A. Santos, and M.S. Nagano (2010), 'Contributions of HRM throughout the stages of environmental management: Methodological triangulation applied to companies in Brazil', *The International Journal of Human Resource Management*, **21** (7), 1049–1089.

Jackson, S.E., D.S. Ones, and S. Dilchert (2012), *Managing Human Resources for Environmental Sustainability* (vol. 32), San Francisco, CA: John Wiley and Sons.

Jackson, S.E., D.W.S. Renwick, C.J.C. Jabbour, and M. Muller-Camen (2011), 'State-of-the-art and future directions for green human resource management: Introduction to the special issue', *German Journal of Research in Human Resource Management*, **25** (2), 99–116.

Johnson, H., and K. Miller (2012), 'HR initiatives for environmental mission alignment at Aveda corporation', in S.E. Jackson, D.S. Ones, and S. Dilchert (eds), *Managing Human Resources for Environmental Sustainability* (vol. 32), San Francisco, CA: John Wiley and Sons, pp. 309–318.

Jones, D.A., C.R. Willness, and S. Madey (2014), 'Why are job seekers attracted by corporate social performance? Experimental and field tests of three signal-based mechanisms', *Academy of Management Journal*, **57** (2), 383–404.

Kim, S.H., and Y. Choi (2013), 'Hotel employees' perception of green practices', *International Journal of Hospitality and Tourism Administration*, **14** (2), 157–178.

Kim, S.Y., and Y. Wolinsky-Nahmias (2014), 'Cross-national public opinion on climate change: The effects of affluence and vulnerability', *Global Environmental Politics*, **14** (1), 79–106.

King, A.A., and M.J. Lenox (2004), 'Prospects for developing absorptive capacity through internal information provision', *Strategic Management Journal*, **25** (4), 331–345.

Laden, F., and G.M. Gray (2016), 'Toxics use reduction: pro and con', *RISK: Health, Safety and Environment*, **4** (3), 4.

Lehrer, J. (2009), *How We Decide*, Boston, MA: Houghton Mifflin Harcourt.

Liebowitz, J. (2010), 'The role of HR in achieving a sustainability culture', *Journal of Sustainable Development*, **3** (4), 50–57.

Livesey, S.M., and K. Kearins (2002), 'Transparent and caring corporations? A study of sustainability reports by The Body Shop and Royal Dutch/Shell', *Organization and Environment*, **15** (3), 233–258.

Lo, S.H., G.J.Y. Peters, and G. Kok (2012), 'Energy-related behaviors in office buildings: A qualitative study on individual and organisational determinants', *Applied Psychology*, **61** (2), 227–249.

Makower, J. (with C. Pike) (2008), *Strategies for the Green Economy: Opportunities and Challenges in the New World of Business*, Irvine, CA: McGraw-Hill.

Markey, R., J. McIvor, and C.F. Wright (2016), 'Employee participation and carbon emissions reduction in Australian workplaces', *The International Journal of Human Resource Management*, **27** (2), 173–191.

McGuire, J., S. Dow, and K. Argheyd (2003), 'CEO incentives and corporate social performance', *Journal of Business Ethics*, **45** (4), 341–359.

Melguizo, Á., and J. Perea (2016), 'Mind the skills gap! Regional and industry patterns in emerging economies', *OECD Development Centre Working Papers*, No. 329, Paris: OECD.

Milliman, J. (2013), 'Leading-edge Green Human Resource practices: Vital components to advancing environmental sustainability', *Environmental Quality Management*, **23**, 31–45.

Muros, J.P., K. Impelman, and L. Hollweg (2012), 'Sustainability in coffee sourcing and implications for employee engagement at Caribou Coffee', in S.E. Jackson, D.S. Ones, and S. Dilchert (eds), *Managing Human Resources for Environmental Sustainability* (vol. 32), San Francisco: John Wiley and Sons, pp. 375–404.

Muster, V., and U. Schrader (2011), 'Green work-life balance: A new perspective for green HRM', *German Journal of Human Resource Management: Zeitschrift für Personalforschung*, **25** (2), 140–156.

Net Impact (2014), *Business as Unusual: The Social and Environmental Impact Guide to Graduate Programs – For Students by Students*, San Francisco, CA: Net Impact.

O'Donohue, W., and N. Torugsa (2016), 'The moderating effect of "Green" HRM on the association between proactive environmental management and financial performance in small firms', *The International Journal of Human Resource Management*, **27** (2), 239–261.

Ones, D., and S. Dilchert (2013), 'Measuring, understanding, and influencing employee green behaviors', in A.H. Huffman, and S.R. Klein (eds), *Green Organizations: Driving Change with I.O. Psychology*, New York: Routledge, pp. 115–148.

Paillé, P., Y. Chen, O. Boiral, and J. Jin (2014), 'The impact of human resource management on environmental performance: An employee-level study', *Journal of Business Ethics*, **121** (3), 451–466.

Perez, O., Y. Amichai-Hamburger, and T. Shterental (2009), 'The dynamic of corporate self-regulation: ISO 14001, environmental commitment, and organizational citizenship behavior', *Law and Society Review*, **43** (3), 593–630.

Pink, D. (2009), *Drive: The Surprising Truth About What Motivates Us*, New York: Riverhead Books.

Pinzone, M., M. Guerci, E. Lettieri, and T. Redman (2016), 'Progressing in the change journey towards sustainability in healthcare: The role of "Green" HRM', *Journal of Cleaner Production*, **122**, 201–211.

Pogutz, S., and M.I. Winn (2016), 'Cultivating ecological knowledge for corporate sustainability: Barilla's innovative approach to sustainable farming', *Business Strategy and the Environment*, **25** (6), 435–448.

Rajiani, I., H. Musa, and B. Hardjono (2016), 'Ability, motivation and opportunity as determinants of green human resource management innovation', *Research Journal of Business Management*, **10** (1–3), 51–57.

Ramus, C.A., and U. Steger (2000), 'The roles of supervisory support behaviors and environmental policy in employee "ecoinitiatives" at leading-edge European companies', *Academy of Management Journal*, **43** (4), 605–626.

Redondo, I., and M. Puelles (2016), 'The connection between environmental attitude–behavior gap and other individual inconsistencies: A call for strengthening self-control', *International Research in Geographical and Environmental Education*, 1–14.

Renwick, D.W., C.J. Jabbour, M. Muller-Camen, T. Redman, and A. Wilkinson (2016), 'Contemporary developments in green (environmental) HRM scholarship', *The International Journal of Human Resource Management*, **27** (2), 114–128.

Renwick, D.W., T. Redman, and S. Maguire (2008, April), 'Green HRM: A review, process model, and research agenda', *Discussion Paper No 2008.01*, University of Sheffield Management School, UK.

Renwick, D.W., T. Redman, and S. Maguire (2013), 'Green human resource management: A review and research agenda', *International Journal of Management Reviews*, **15** (1), 1–14.

Rose, K. (2014), 'Adopting industrial organizational psychology for eco sustainability', *Procedia Environmental Sciences*, **20**, 533–542.

Russo, M.V., and N.S. Harrison (2005), 'Organizational design and environmental performance: Clues from the electronics industry', *Academy of Management Journal*, **48** (4), 582–593.

Sheehan, M., T.N. Garavan, and R. Carbery (2014), 'Sustainability, corporate social responsibility and HRD', *European Journal of Training and Development*, **38** (5), 370–386.

Shrivastava, P. (2010), 'Pedagogy of passion for sustainability', *Academy of Management Learning and Education*, **9** (3), 443–455.

SHRM (2014), *Employee Job Satisfaction and Engagement: The Road to Economic Recovery. A Research Report*, Alexandria, VA: SHRM.

Sonenshein, S., K. DeCelles, and J. Dutton (2014), 'It's not easy being green: Self-evaluations and their role in explaining support of environmental issues', *Academy of Management Journal*, **57**, 17–37.

Sroufe, R., J. Liebowitz, and N. Sivasubramaniam (2010), 'Are you a leader or a laggard? HR's role in creating a sustainability culture', *People and Strategy*, **33** (1), 34–42.

Stanwick, P.A., and S.D. Stanwick (2001), 'CEO compensation: Does it pay to be green?', *Business Strategy and the Environment*, **10** (3), 176–182.

Stolz, I. (2014), 'The role of OD practitioners in developing corporations' capacity to practice corporate citizenship: A sociomaterial case study', *European Journal of Training and Development*, **38** (5), 436–455.

Subramanian, N., M.D. Abdulrahman, L. Wu, and P. Nath (2016), 'Green competence framework: Evidence from China', *The International Journal of Human Resource Management*, **27** (2), 151–172.

Teixeira, A.A., C.J.C. Jabbour, and A.B.L. de Sousa Jabbour (2012), 'Relationship between green management and environmental training in companies located in Brazil: A theoretical framework and case studies', *International Journal of Production Economics*, **140** (1), 318–329.

Ulus, M., and B. Hatipoglu (2016), 'Human aspect as a critical factor for organization sustainability in the tourism industry', *Sustainability*, **8** (3), 232.

Wachholz, S., N. Artz, and D. Chene (2014), 'Warming to the idea: University students' knowledge and attitudes about climate change', *International Journal of Sustainability in Higher Education*, **15** (2), 128–141.

Weinstein, M. (2008, March/April), 'It's not easy being green', *Training*, 20–25.

Wilkinson, A., P. Gollan, M. Marchington, and D. Lewin (2010), 'Conceptualizing employee participation in organizations', in A. Wilkinson, P. Gollan, M. Marchington, and D. Lewin (eds), *The Oxford Handbook of Participation in Organizations*, Oxford: Oxford University Press.

Williamson, I.O., D. Lepak, and J.E. King (2003), 'The effect of company recruitment web site orientation on individuals' perceptions of organizational attractiveness', *Journal of Vocational Behavior*, **63**, 242–263.

Willness, C.R., and D.A. Jones (2013), 'Corporate environmental sustainability and employee recruitment: Leveraging "green" business practices to attract talent', in A.H. Huffman, and S.R. Klein (eds), *Green Organizations: Driving Change with IO Psychology*, New York: Routledge, pp. 231–250.

Yong, J.Y., and Y. Mohd-Yusoff (2016), 'Studying the influence of strategic human resource competencies on the adoption of green human resource management practices', *Industrial and Commercial Training*, **48** (8), 416–422.

Zibarras, L., and C. Ballinger (2011), 'Promoting environmental behavior in the workplace: A survey of UK organizations', in D. Bartlett (ed.), *Going Green: The Psychology of Sustainability in the Workplace*, Leicester: The British Psychological Society, pp. 84–90.

Zibarras, L.D., and P. Coan (2015), 'HRM practices used to promote pro-environmental behavior: A UK survey', *The International Journal of Human Resource Management*, **26** (16), 2121–2142.

PART II

ANTECEDENTS AND CONSEQUENCES OF EMPLOYEE PRO-ENVIRONMENTAL BEHAVIOUR

4. Individual antecedents of pro-environmental behaviours: implications for employee green behaviours

Brenton M. Wiernik,* Deniz S. Ones,
Stephan Dilchert and Rachael M. Klein

Environmental degradation is ultimately driven by harmful actions performed by individuals (Stern 2000). Achieving environmental sustainability thus requires changing individuals' behaviour to be more environmentally responsible (Maloney and Ward 1973). As organisations aim to improve their institutional environmental performance, they must improve the individual environmental performance of each of their employees. Effective management of employee environmental performance, however, requires understanding why employees perform positive and negative green behaviours and how these drivers can be leveraged most effectively using human resource management (HRM) tools. In this chapter, we review research on the individual-level factors that promote and inhibit environmentally relevant employee behaviours. We examine research on knowledge-based and attitudinal drivers of pro-environmental behaviours, as well as the influence of demographic characteristics and stable psychological individual differences. Finally, we discuss research on the effectiveness of alternative types of behavioural interventions aimed at improving individuals' contributions to environmental sustainability and how organisations can leverage individual antecedents to enhance employee green performance.

Like all work performance behaviours, employee green behaviours (defined as "scalable actions and behaviours that employees engage in that are linked with and contribute to or detract from environmental sustainability"; Ones and Dilchert 2012: 87) are directly determined by three individual factors – declarative knowledge, procedural knowledge and skill, and volitional choices (motivation) of where, at what level, and how long to direct one's effort (McCloy et al. 1994). Other individual characteristics, such as values, attitudes, personality traits, as well as organisational interventions, contribute to employee green behaviours either by providing employees with the knowledge and skill needed to perform the relevant behaviours or by influencing their choices about where and how to direct their effort. In each section below, we consider how the constructs reviewed may impact each of the three direct determinants of employee green behaviours.

To date, most research in this domain has focused on non-work pro-environmental behaviours (PEB), rather than employee green behaviours (EGB). In our review, we draw on this broader pro-environmental behaviour literature while also highlighting available evidence specifically for work settings. Throughout this chapter, we focus on meta-analytic estimates of relations between antecedents and employee green behaviours. Compared to primary studies, meta-analyses can correct for the influences of sampling error, measurement error, range restriction, and other artefacts, leading to more accurate, less biased estimates of construct relations (Schmidt and Hunter 2015). Ideally, meta-analyses should correct for measurement error and range restriction; failure to do so downwardly biases relations and leads to overly pessimistic conclusions about the impact of antecedents on individual behaviour (Ones et al. 2017b; Schmidt and Hunter 2015). Unfortunately, most pro-environmental behaviour meta-analyses have failed to correct for measurement error and none have corrected for range restriction (see Tables 4.1–4.3). As a result, the effect sizes reported in this chapter are downwardly biased. When meta-analyses for specific antecedents are unavailable, we provide narrative reviews of the available evidence.

4.1   ENVIRONMENTAL AWARENESS, KNOWLEDGE, AND SKILL

Much research and practice on improving individual environmental performance in organisational, educational, and general life settings has focused on efforts to increase individuals' environmental awareness, knowledge, and skill (Cherian and Jacob 2012; Kollmuss and Agyeman 2002; Osbaldiston and Schott 2012; Renwick et al. 2013; Steg and Vlek 2009; Unsworth et al. 2013; Young et al. 2015; Yun et al. 2013). Awareness of environmental problems and knowledge of how to solve them are key enabling capabilities for employee green behaviours (see Environmental Motives, Section 4.3). Without awareness that environmental problems exist, individuals are unlikely to act in ways to ameliorate them (Hansla et al. 2008). However, mere awareness is insufficient – individuals must also understand how their own behaviours contribute to environmental problems (Stern et al. 1999) and the actions they can take to ameliorate them (Hines et al. 1987). "It is important to know that something needs to be done, but it is even more important to know what and how to do it" (Dilchert and Ones 2012: 195).

Table 4.1 summarises the results of five meta-analyses reporting relations of PEB with environmental knowledge, awareness, and attitudinal antecedents. The table shows bar charts scaled to magnitudes of the unreliability-corrected correlations to permit graphical comparison of the relative strength of different antecedents of PEB. Meta-analytic evidence supports a moderate relation between environmental awareness and pro-environmental behaviours. In the most recent and largest meta-analysis, Klöckner (2013) found uncorrected correlations of $r = .22$ between awareness of environmental problems and PEB (cf. corrected $\rho = .30$; Hines et al. 1987). Few studies have examined awareness/knowledge–green behaviour relations in work settings (Norton et al. 2015), but given the magnitude of relations between job knowledge and performance (Hunter and Hunter 1984) and knowledge and skills' roles as direct determinants of job performance (McCloy et al. 1994), we expect these relations to be substantial. Available evidence suggests that these relations may be even stronger in work settings than in non-work settings. For example, Amenumey (2015) observed a strong relation between employee environmental knowledge and EGB ($r_c = .54$, corrected for unreliability) for 480 Ghanaian textile workers. This strong relation suggests that training programmes designed to increase employee environmental knowledge may be highly effective for promoting EGB (Renwick et al. 2013).

Awareness, knowledge, and skill are necessary but insufficient conditions for employee green behaviours. Employees cannot act sustainably if they do not know how, but knowledge itself does not imply that employees are motivated to choose to perform green behaviours. The gap between environmental awareness and action has been long-observed (Littledyke 2008), and most recent psychological research on pro-environmental behaviours has focused on factors that influence environmental motivation, including environmental attitudes and motives, stable individual differences, and demographic characteristics.

4.2   ENVIRONMENTAL ATTITUDES

Researchers have examined the impact of environmental attitudes on PEB for over 40 years. Following Hines et al.'s (1987) seminal meta-analysis, three theoretical models connecting environmental attitudes to behaviour have been heavily researched.

Schwartz's (1977) Norm Activation Model (NAM) proposes that PEB are primarily driven by prosocial motives (e.g., concern for other people, concern for future generations, concern for other species and the planet as a whole). An individual's set of personal/moral norms that guides their

Table 4.1   *Meta-analytic relations of pro-environmental behaviour with environmental awareness, knowledge and attitudes*

Variable	k	N	r	ρ	Comparison	Source
Awareness	**24**	**13,215**	**.22**			Klöckner (2013)
Awareness	18	8,276	.19			Bamberg & Möser (2007)
Awareness/knowledge	17			.30		Hines et al. (1987)
Awareness/knowledge	3	1,557		.38		Han & Hansen (2012)
Personal responsibility	**10**	**4,217**	**.10**			Klöckner (2013)
Personal responsibility	6	1,866	.24			Bamberg & Möser (2007)
Personal responsibility	6			.33		Hines et al. (1987)
General env. concern	**42**			**.34**		Hines et al. (1987)
Env. concern (NEP)	5	3,499	.09			Klöckner (2013)
Behavioural attitudes	**30**	**14,053**	**.36**			Klöckner (2013)
Behavioural attitudes	17	6,751	.42			Bamberg & Möser (2007)
Behavioural attitudes	9			.38		Hines et al. (1987)
Attitudes/concern	3	2,787		.58		Han & Hansen (2012)
PBC	**32**	**15,020**	**.40**			Klöckner (2013)
PBC	18	8,029	.30			Bamberg & Möser (2007)
PBC	4	2,450		.38		Han & Hansen (2012)
Social norms	**31**	**14,170**	**.24**			Klöckner (2013)
Social norms	18	7,325	.31			Bamberg & Möser (2007)
Social norms	3	1,903		.53		Han & Hansen (2012)
Personal/moral norms	**29**	**14,451**	**.32**			Klöckner (2013)
Personal/moral norms	11	6,840	.39			Bamberg & Möser (2007)
Guilt	5	323	.30			Bamberg & Möser (2007)
Personal/moral norms	3	2,130		.70		Han & Hansen (2012)
Habit	**10**	**7,747**	**.46**			Klöckner (2013)
Intention	**26**	**12,945**	**.55**			Klöckner (2013)
Intention	15	5,654	.52			Bamberg & Möser (2007)
Intention	12	4,253	.54			Schwenk & Möser (2009)
Intention	6			.49		Hines et al. (1987)
Intention	3	1,918		.46		Han & Hansen (2012)

Note: r = observed mean correlation; ρ = unreliability-corrected correlation; Comparison bars show the relative magnitudes of corrected correlations (ρ) across antecedents (when ρ not reported, observed r was corrected using a reliability of .85 for both variables to estimate bar length); NEP = New Environmental Paradigm scale (Dunlap and Van Liere 1978); Env. = environmental; PBC = perceived behavioural control; blank cells indicate information not reported; Han and Hansen (2012) correlations are limited to sustainable food choices.

prosocial (including environmental) behaviour is posited to develop in response to their awareness of environmental problems, their acceptance of personal responsibility for contributing to those problems, and the support from members of the individual's social network (social norms). Stern et al.'s (1999) Values-Beliefs-Norms model (VBN) is similar, but proposes a strict causal sequence among these variables that has not been supported by meta-analytic tests (Klöckner 2013).

In contrast, Ajzen's (1991) Theory of Planned Behaviour (TPB) is a rational decision-making model that proposes that individuals perform PEB (among other behaviours) in order to maximise their self-interests. TPB posits that pro-environmental behaviours are directly determined by individuals' conscious behavioural intentions, which in turn are driven by their attitudes towards those behaviours (whether they believe they will realise positive benefits from the behaviour), their feelings that they will be able to enact the behaviour if attempted (expectancy or perceived behavioural control), and interpersonal pressure from valued others (social norms).

Several authors have proposed integrative models that combine the propositions of NAM and TPB, as well as research on the influence of unconscious behavioural habits (Ouellette and Wood 1998; Triandis 1979), to predict pro-environmental behaviour (Bamberg and Schmidt 2003; Kaiser 2006; Klöckner and Blöbaum 2010). These combined models integrating the effects of values, rational decisions, and unconscious habits are more effective for predicting PEB than any individual model (Klöckner 2013; cf. Bamberg and Möser 2007; Han and Hansen 2012).

The synthesised meta-analytic results in Table 4.1 show that behavioural intentions, habits, and perceived behavioural control have the strongest relations with pro-environmental behaviour ($r = .55, .46, .40$, respectively; Klöckner 2013). General environmental concern, cost–benefit attitudes towards specific behaviours (Behavioural Attitudes in Table 4.1), ascriptions of personal responsibility for solving environmental problems, and personal and social norms all show weaker relations with PEB. Meta-analytic structural equations models suggest that intentions and habits are the only direct determinants of PEB, with the other constructs in these models having only indirect effects through these two variables (Bamberg and Möser 2007; Han and Hansen 2012; Klöckner 2013). Habits and intentions show the strongest zero-order observed correlations with PEB, supporting their proximal primacy to these behaviours.

These exact theoretical models have not often been tested in work settings. However, analogous constructs are common in many studies. For example, green psychological climate is similar to perceived behavioural control (Norton et al. 2014) and employee environmental commitment is similar to behavioural intentions (Mesmer-Magnus et al. 2012); these constructs appear to show analogous relations with employee green behaviours as with non-work PEB (Graves et al. 2013; Norton et al. 2017). Studies have also found similar effects of environmental attitudes (Norton et al. 2014), social norms (Kim et al. 2014; Paillé et al. 2016), habits (Marans and Lee 1993; Wiernik et al. 2014), and personal norms (Flannery and May 2000; Scherbaum et al. 2008) on employee green behaviours as on non-work PEB.

Together, meta-analytic tests of general PEB models and results from recent primary studies in work contexts support intentions and habits as major drivers of green behaviour. These results suggest that organisational interventions that encourage employee green intentions (e.g., environmental goal setting, environmental commitment) and facilitate the development of green habits (e.g., making green behaviours convenient, installing green behavioural prompts, organised green behaviour drives) may be effective for enhancing employee environmental performance.

4.3   ENVIRONMENTAL MOTIVES

Research supports the power of psychosocial attitudinal constructs for predicting environmental behaviours, both in general life and workplace settings. However, these constructs cannot fully account for individual differences in environmental performance (all of these constructs together accounted for only 36 per cent of the variance in PEB; Klöckner 2013). Thus, there is room for additional personal and environmental factors to incrementally contribute to understanding employee green behaviour. One reason psychosocial models of green behaviour may fail to fully account for green behaviour is that these models focus almost exclusively on environmental sustainability as the driving motive behind environmental behaviour. This perspective fails to consider that green behaviour is a complex, multidimensional, and multiply determined construct. Individuals may perform green behaviours for many different reasons, and the same behaviours can simultaneously serve multiple psychological functions.

Klein (2014) conducted a series of qualitative and quantitative studies examining the motives individuals report for their employee green behaviours. These studies identified 18 distinct functional motives grouped into four conceptual categories. *Prosocial motives* drive environmental performance to benefit entities other than oneself; this category includes performing green behaviours to benefit the environment, for altruistic reasons, or out of a sense of social responsibility. Constructs such as altruistic and biospheric environmental concern (Schultz 2001) and connectedness to nature (Brugger et al. 2011; Kaiser et al. 2013) also belong to this category. *Enabling capabilities* are conditions that increase employees' capacity to perform green behaviours or the ease of doing so. The absence of enabling capabilities prevents employees from engaging in positive environmental actions. This category includes knowledge and skill for performing green behaviours, availability of sustainable options, convenience of green behaviours, and one's habits or personal preferences. *Extrinsic motives* involve engaging in green behaviours to receive some form of personal benefit to oneself, such as to receive health or safety benefits or due to financial considerations. Schultz's (2001) egoistic environmental concern also belongs to this category. Hartig et al. (2007) also suggested that individuals may engage with nature and perform PEB to receive psychological recuperative benefits. Finally, *image motives* reflect desires to perform green behaviours to enhance one's own or the organisation's reputation, out of pressure from organisational or cultural norms, or because such behaviours are required. Klein (2014) found that prosocial motives and enabling capabilities showed stronger relations with EGB than did extrinsic or image motives.

It is important to remember that each of the motives described above can both motivate and inhibit employee green behaviours. For example, financial motives may drive resource conservation behaviours out of a desire to reduce supply costs, but they may also inhibit green purchasing if sustainable products are more expensive than alternatives. Similarly, many motives can impact both positive (green) and negative (ungreen) behaviours. For example, while procedural skill can enable proper disposal of hazardous chemicals, without proper training employees may learn incorrect procedures and falsely believe that their behaviour is environmentally beneficial. Different categories of employee green behaviours (Ones and Dilchert 2012; see Ones et al. 2018, Chapter 2, this volume) are likely to be associated with distinct characteristic patterns of motives. Organisations must carefully consider what motives underlie the green behaviours they seek to promote (or discourage) and how these psychological levers can best be moved to drive environmental performance.

4.4   STABLE INDIVIDUAL DIFFERENCES

Compared to psychosocial constructs, much less research has examined the influence of stable psychological individual differences, such as cognitive abilities, personality traits, and interests and values, on green behaviours (Norton et al. 2015; Ones and Dilchert 2013). A consequence of this disparity is that research on employee green behaviours remains largely disconnected from broader research on the dispositional drivers of job performance and behaviour in general. Behaviour is a function of the person, the situation, and the interactions between the two (e.g., job niche finding). The inordinate theoretical focus in pro-environmental behaviour research on situational variables and the absence of strong research on dispositional drivers of green behaviour is a serious conceptual and explanatory deficiency. Practically, for workplace applications, the separation of employee green behaviour research from research on other performance domains makes it difficult for organisations to determine whether staffing, training, and management efforts to promote employee green behaviours may have adverse consequences for other job performance areas (or, conversely, whether the same HRM techniques can enhance employee performance across domains; Dilchert and Ones 2011). Nonetheless, there have been a handful of investigations reporting quantitative summaries of relations between pro-environmental behaviours and values, self-efficacy, and time orientations. These are summarised in Table 4.2.

Meta-analyses have shown that non-materialistic values (low importance attached to the acquisition of wealth and material goods; Hurst et al. 2013), future time perspective (tendency to have highly meaningful mental representations of future events that impel behaviour, including tendencies towards planning and achievement of future goals; Milfont et al. 2012), and general self-efficacy (Hines et al. 1987) are each substantially related to general life PEB (see Table 4.2). The magnitudes of these relations are in the moderate range.

More recently, studies have begun to examine the influence of the Big Five personality traits on pro-environmental behaviour in work and non-work settings. Across studies, countries, and demographic groups, Conscientiousness, Openness, and Agreeableness are consistently associated with pro-environmental behaviours, including resource conservation and natural preservation (Wiseman and Bogner 2003), electricity reduction (Milfont and Sibley 2012), recycling and responsible waste management (Swami et al. 2011), green purchasing (Fraj and Martinez 2006; Luchs and Mooradian 2012), and green behaviours measured generally (Brick and Lewis 2016; Hilbig et al. 2013; Kvasova 2015; Markowitz et al. 2012). Extraversion and Emotional Stability show less consistent relations across studies and types of pro-environmental behaviour. Similarly, in workplace settings, employee green behaviours are moderately positively related to Conscientiousness, Agreeableness, and Openness (Dilchert and Ones 2011; Kim et al. 2014). Individuals who are responsible, empathetic, and who place value in beauty, ideas, and novel experiences appear to tend

Table 4.2   *Meta-analytic relations of pro-environmental behaviour with stable individual differences and demographic characteristics*

Variable	k	N	r	ρ	Comparison	Source
Self-transcendence values	4	4,011	.06			Klöckner (2013)
Self-enhancement values	3	3,274	.01			Klöckner (2013)
Non-materialism values†	9	2,667	.24	.32		Hurst et al. (2013)
Self-efficacy/ILOC	15			.37		Hines et al. (1987)
Future time perspective	13	5,261	.26			Milfont et al. (2012)
Past/present time persp.	4	3,875	.06			Milfont et al. (2012)
Educational level	11			.19		Hines et al. (1987)
Income	10			.16		Hines et al. (1987)
Gender	4			.08		Hines et al. (1987)
Age						
Employee green beh.	**22**	**4,676**	**.09**	**.10**		Wiernik et al. (2016)
Conserving	22	4,676	.10	.12		Wiernik et al. (2016)
Avoiding harm	22	4,676	.10	.12		Wiernik et al. (2016)
Transforming	22	4,676	.04	.05		Wiernik et al. (2016)
Influencing others	22	4,676	.09	.12		Wiernik et al. (2016)
Taking initiative	22	4,676	.04	.05		Wiernik et al. (2016)
Non-work PEB	**182**	**50,185**	**.04**	**.05**		Wiernik et al. (2013)
Conserving	18	9,646	.10	.12		Wiernik et al. (2013)
Before 1995	6	2,288	−.09	−.11		Wiernik et al. (2013)
1995 & later	12	7,358	.15	.18		Wiernik et al. (2013)
Avoiding harm	5	4,037	.12	.17		Wiernik et al. (2013)
Responsible purch.	7	8,357	−.10	−.10		Wiernik et al. (2013)
Influencing others	2	687	.01	.01		Wiernik et al. (2013)
Political behaviours	2	4,279	.03	.03		Wiernik et al. (2013)
Engaging with nature	4	3,912	.15	.20		Wiernik et al. (2013)
Non-work PEB	10			−.15		Hines et al. (1987)

Note: r = observed mean correlation; ρ = unreliability-corrected correlation; Comparison bars show the relative magnitudes of corrected correlations (ρ) across antecedents (when ρ not reported, observed r was corrected using a reliability of .85 for both variables [demographics not corrected] to estimate bar length); ILOC = internal locus of control; persp. = perspective; † includes correlations with intentions and behaviour; beh. = behaviour; PEB = pro-environmental behaviour; purch. = purchasing; blank cells indicate information not reported.

to act in environmentally responsible ways. However, given the centrality of the Big Five constructs to personality theory and application (Hough and Connelly 2013; Stanek and Ones 2018), much more research on these relations is needed.

Similarly, research is needed on the contributions of other dispositional constructs, such as cognitive abilities (Ones et al. 2017a) and vocational interests (Hansen and Wiernik 2018), to employee green behaviours. The relevance of cognitive abilities is likely to arise from individuals' facility with acquiring more environmental knowledge and their capacity to strategically reason about the long-term consequences of human behaviours on the ecology of this planet. It would be interesting to examine whether the sizeable awareness/knowledge–PEB relations summarised in Table 4.1 can be explained by individual differences in cognitive ability. Similarly, the sizeable relation for future time orientation should be examined after controlling for cognitive ability.

Research is also needed on how employee assessment systems can be designed to predict employee green behaviours – how can interviews, test batteries, situational judgement tests, and other methods be constructed to identify employees who are likely to share organisational environmental values and be effective environmental performers (Campbell 2013)?

4.5   DEMOGRAPHIC CHARACTERISTICS

A large body of research has examined differences in pro-environmental behaviour across gender, education, age, and socio-economic groups (Klein et al. 2012). Sociological and social psychological theories of green behaviour often posit that differences in resources, power, and access across demographic groups leads to strong differences in environmental performance. Such beliefs are also reflected in popular press stereotypes of environmentally conscious "eco-consumers" – such individuals are typically portrayed as young, female, well-educated, and affluent. Meta-analytic evidence shows little support for such characterisations (Klein 2014).

Table 4.2 also presents meta-analytic findings for demographic differences. As shown in Table 4.2, education and income are only weakly related to pro-environmental behaviour (Hines et al. 1987). General education does not necessarily lead to greater pro-environmental knowledge, skill, or motivation. Hines et al.'s (1987) meta-analysis suggested that gender is unrelated to PEB, but more recent studies have suggested that women do tend to perform somewhat more sustainable behaviours in non-work (Klein et al. 2011a; Luchs and Mooradian 2012) and work settings (Klein et al. 2011b).

Age shows more complex relations with pro-environmental behaviour. Wiernik et al.'s (2013) meta-analysis of age–green behaviour relations outside the workplace found that, contrary to stereotypes of younger individuals as more eco-friendly consumers, older individuals tended to spend more time engaging with nature (e.g., outdoor recreation) and to perform more Avoiding Harm and Conservation behaviours. These relations likely reflect that levels of the personality traits Conscientiousness and Agreeableness, which are strongly related to PEB, also increase with age. Similarly, in a cross-cultural meta-analysis of employee green behaviours, Wiernik et al. (2016) also found small positive linear relations of age with Conserving and Avoiding Harm employee green behaviours. They also found curvilinear relations of age with Transforming and Influencing Others behaviours. Transforming behaviours increased in frequency until age 55, then began to decrease again; the authors interpreted this relation as indicating that employees nearing retirement are unlikely to be willing to dramatically change their work habits and procedures to be more sustainable. Influencing Others behaviours did not change in frequency between 18 and 45, but then increased rapidly until age 55, when they levelled off again. This relation likely reflects that this life stage is when employees tend to transition into supervisory roles where they have more power to perform environmental leadership, management, and instructional behaviours. Importantly, while these patterns of change are theoretically interesting and support models of pro-environmental behaviour emphasising the importance of habit and behavioural control, it is important to remember that even the strongest age–employee green behaviour relations remain small in terms of absolute magnitude.

4.6   INTERVENTIONS

Finally, much research has focused on designing, implementing, and evaluating various interventions to promote positive environmental behaviours and discourage negative environmental behaviours. These interventions have targeted a variety of psychosocial mechanisms to enhance individuals' environmental knowledge and procedural skill for green behaviours and motivation to act in more sustainable ways. Osbaldiston and Schott (2012) reported a comprehensive meta-analysis of research on environmental interventions conducted across all life settings. Their results are summarised in Table 4.3.

Pro-environmental behaviour interventions can be grouped into four categories based on the psychological mechanisms targeted to promote behaviour. *Salience interventions* increase motivation for green behaviour by drawing individuals' attention to sustainable options and making performing green behaviours easier. These interventions include making green behaviours convenient (e.g., placing recycling bins in employee offices), providing prompts (e.g., popup reminders to follow sustainable purchasing guidelines), appealing to individuals' sense of responsibility

Table 4.3   Meta-analytic effects of interventions on pro-environmental behaviour

Type of intervention	k	N	r	d	Comparison	Source
Convenience/salience						
Increasing ease	19		.24	.49		Osbaldiston & Schott (2012)
Prompts	44		.30	.62		Osbaldiston & Schott (2012)
Information						
Justifications	44		.21	.43		Osbaldiston & Schott (2012)
Instructions	5		.15	.31		Osbaldiston & Schott (2012)
Monitoring/incentives						
Feedback	6		.15	.31		Osbaldiston & Schott (2012)
Rewards	36		.22	.46		Osbaldiston & Schott (2012)
Psychosocial processes						
Social modelling	26		.30	.63		Osbaldiston & Schott (2012)
Cognitive dissonance	13		.42	.93		Osbaldiston & Schott (2012)
Commitment	32		.20	.40		Osbaldiston & Schott (2012)
Goal setting	15		.33	.69		Osbaldiston & Schott (2012)

Note: r = observed mean correlation; d = observed mean Cohen's d value; Comparison bars show the relative magnitudes of estimated corrected correlations (ρ) across interventions, correcting observed r using a reliability of .85 for PEB [intervention reliability not corrected] to estimate bar length; blank cells indicate information not reported; all interventions targeted a single behavioural criterion (e.g., recycling).

(e.g., "Only you can prevent forest fires"), or making green behaviours required. *Informational interventions* enhance individuals' environmental knowledge and green behavioural skill. These interventions range in depth and complexity from simple justifications (why individuals should perform green behaviours), to instructions (the procedural steps to follow), to providing comprehensive environmental education. *Monitoring and feedback interventions* involve tracking individual environmental performance and providing tailored feedback, penalties, and rewards. Finally, *psychosocial interventions* leverage social psychological and perceptual processes, particularly those emphasised by NAM and TPB, to influence employees' green behavioural choices. These interventions can include asking employees to formally state environmental commitments and set specific green behavioural goals, embedding models or social norms of effective green behaviour in employees' work environments, or promoting employee self-efficacy for performing green behaviours. One form of psychosocial intervention that appears to be particularly effective is asking individuals to evaluate whether their environmentally significant behaviours match their espoused environmental values. The cognitive dissonance generated when individuals realise that their behaviours do not support their values can lead individuals to change to more concordant, sustainable alternatives.

In non-work contexts, each of these types of interventions individually can effectively enhance green behaviours to some degree, but the most effective interventions combine several approaches to target pro-environmental behaviours using multiple psychological mechanisms (Osbaldiston and Schott 2012). Research on workplace pro-environmental interventions is in its infancy. Semmel et al. (2012) conducted a preliminary meta-analysis of this literature, but found that available research examined too wide a range of specific employee green behaviours and used too varied a set of interventions to draw conclusions about the efficacy of any particular intervention–behaviour combination. More systematic research on the effectiveness of specific interventions for specific employee green behaviours is needed.

4.7   IMPLICATIONS FOR HRM PRACTICE

Industrial–organisational psychologists and HRM practitioners can leverage the range of individual antecedents of employee green behaviours to enhance employee environmental performance in many ways. Broadly, green HRM practices fall into one of two camps – practitioners can seek to bring more environmentally responsible individuals into their organisations or they can enhance the environmental performance of existing employees. The diversity of tools practitioners can use to promote green behaviours is illustrated in Figure 4.1.

These tools include far more than the skill training and motivational practices most commonly employed to enhance green performance (Norton et al. 2015; Temminck et al. 2015; Young et al. 2015). For example, ergonomics and workplace design can be used to reduce environmental barriers to green behaviours, such as by placing compost bins in convenient locations or by providing a centralised system for equipment sharing. Job design can be used to embed green tasks into employees' core responsibilities.

Green HRM goals can also be integrated into staffing systems. Organisational pro-environmental initiatives and green job tasks can be used to attract environmentally conscious applicants, and targeted recruitment of populations with pre-existing green skills (e.g., environmental student groups) can reduce training needs. These practices may also contribute to better applicant reactions and higher offer acceptance rates (Jones et al. 2014). Selection systems can be designed to assess green competencies and the psychological characteristics (personality

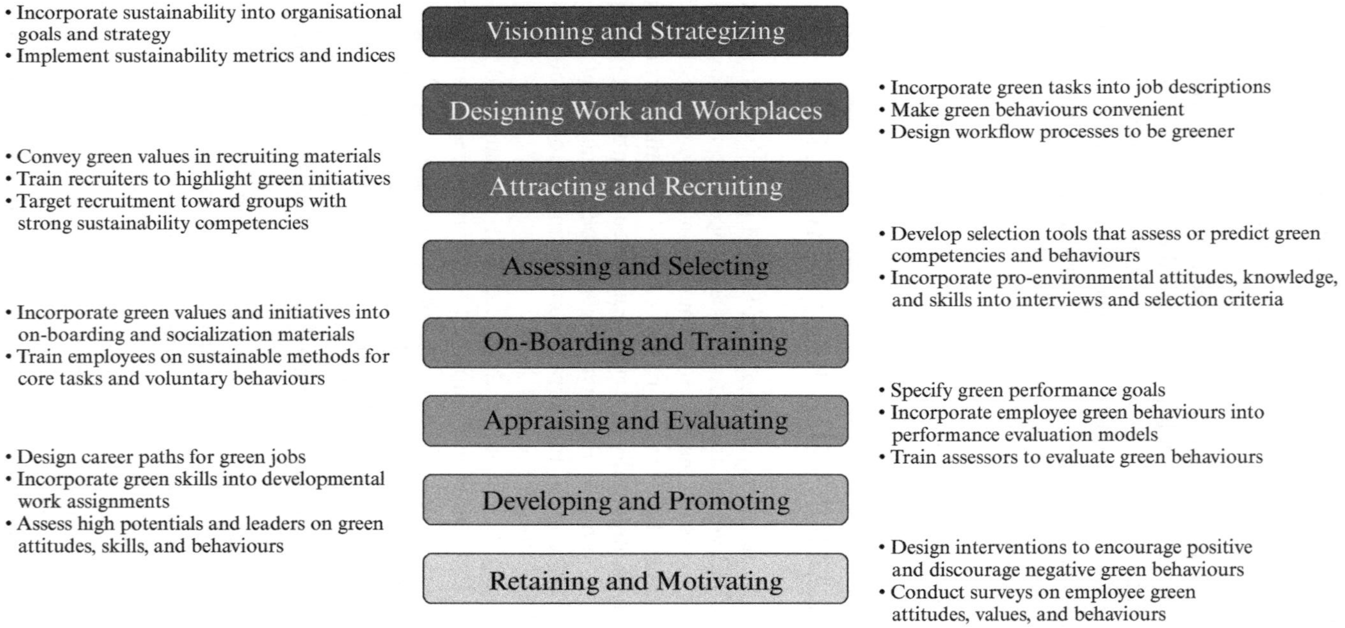

Source: Adapted from Muros (2012) and reprinted from Dilchert et al. (2017), © 2016 SAGE Publications. Reprinted with permission.

Figure 4.1 How HRM practices can be used to promote environmental sustainability

traits, values, interests, environmental commitment) that predict effective environmental performance. Onboarding and socialisation programmes can be used to instil organisational environmental values in new hires.

Practitioners can similarly enhance green behaviours using employee development and management systems. Organisations can set employee environmental goals and incorporate green criteria into performance management reviews. Organisations can further design sustainability-focused career paths and incorporate green competencies into skill requirements for leadership and executive development and advancement. Organisational sensing, engagement surveys, and benchmarking can be used to gauge employee acceptance of organisational pro-environmental initiatives and internationalisation of organisational sustainability goals.

All of these efforts will be most effective if they are aligned with broader organisational environmental goals and if sustainability is deeply embedded into the organisation's business strategy (Baumgartner and Ebner 2010; Mesmer-Magnus et al. 2012). Whatever approaches are used, it is important for organisational practitioners to remember that employee green behaviours and environmental motives are both complex, multidimensional constructs. Different categories of employee green behaviours may be more responsive to different motives and amenable to change through different HRM practices. Practitioners must carefully consider which motives and other personal characteristics underlie each behaviour they wish to target and develop their HRM practices accordingly. Employee green behaviours are a vital component of all jobs that must be encouraged to promote organisational environmental performance and global environmental sustainability. By embedding environmental values into core business strategies and using the full array of HRM techniques, organisations can enhance both their own success and the well-being of the planet.

NOTE

*   This work was supported by the Belgian American Educational Foundation through a fellowship to B. M. Wiernik.

REFERENCES

Ajzen, I. (1991), 'The theory of planned behavior', *Organisational Behavior and Human Decision Processes*, **50** (2), 179–211.
Amenumey, F. (2015), *Variables That Impact Environmental Sustainability Behaviors of Employees in the Textile Manufacturing Industry in Ghana*, Doctoral dissertation,

Minneapolis, MN: University of Minnesota, accessed at http://hdl.handle.net/11299/174881.

Bamberg, S. and G. Möser (2007), 'Twenty years after Hines, Hungerford, and Tomera: A new meta-analysis of psycho-social determinants of pro-environmental behavior', *Journal of Environmental Psychology*, **27** (1), 14–25.

Bamberg, S. and P. Schmidt (2003), 'Incentives, morality, or habit? Predicting students' car use for university routes with the models of Ajzen, Schwartz, and Triandis', *Environment and Behavior*, **35** (2), 264–85.

Baumgartner, R. J. and D. Ebner (2010), 'Corporate sustainability strategies: Sustainability profiles and maturity levels', *Sustainable Development*, **18** (2), 76–89.

Brick, C. and G. J. Lewis (2016), 'Unearthing the "green" personality: Core traits predict environmentally friendly behavior', *Environment and Behavior*, **48** (5), 635–58.

Brugger, A., F. Kaiser and N. Roczen (2011), 'One for all? Connectedness to nature, inclusion of nature, environmental identity, and implicit association with nature', *European Psychologist*, **16** (4), 324–33.

Campbell, J. P. (2013), 'Assessment in industrial and organisational psychology: An overview', in K. F. Geisinger, B. A. Bracken, J. F. Carlson, J.-I. C. Hansen, N. R. Kuncel, S. P. Reise, and M. C. Rodriguez (eds), *APA Handbook of Testing and Assessment in Psychology*, vol. 1, Washington, DC: American Psychological Association, pp. 355–95.

Cherian, J. P. and J. Jacob (2012), 'A study of green HR practices and its effective implementation in the organisation: A review', *International Journal of Business and Management*, **7** (21), 25.

Dilchert, S. and D. S. Ones (2011), *Personality and Its Relationship to Sustainable and Unsustainable Workplace Behaviors*, Paper presented at the annual conference of the Society for Industrial and Organisational Psychology, Chicago, IL, April.

Dilchert, S. and D. S. Ones (2012), 'Measuring and improving environmental sustainability', in S. E. Jackson, D. S. Ones, and S. Dilchert (eds), *Managing Human Resources for Environmental Sustainability*, San Francisco, CA: Jossey-Bass/Wiley, pp. 187–221.

Dilchert, S., B. M. Wiernik and D. S. Ones (2017), 'Sustainability: Implications for organisations', in S. G. Rogelberg (ed.), *The SAGE Encyclopedia of Industrial and Organisational Psychology*, 2nd edn, vol. 4, Thousand Oaks, CA: Sage, pp. 1570–74.

Dunlap, R. E. and K. D. Van Liere (1978), 'The "new environmental paradigm"', *The Journal of Environmental Education*, **9** (4), 10–19.

Flannery, B. L. and D. R. May (2000), 'Environmental ethical decision making in the U.S. metal-finishing industry', *Academy of Management Journal*, **43** (4), 642–62.

Fraj, E. and E. Martinez (2006), 'Influence of personality on ecological consumer behaviour', *Journal of Consumer Behaviour*, **5** (3), 167–81.

Graves, L. M., J. Sarkis and Q. Zhu (2013), 'How transformational leadership and employee motivation combine to predict employee proenvironmental behaviors in China', *Journal of Environmental Psychology*, **35**, 81–91.

Han, Y. and H. Hansen (2012), 'Determinants of sustainable food consumption: A meta-analysis using a traditional and a structura equation modelling approach', *International Journal of Psychological Studies*, **4** (1), 22.

Hansen, J.-I. C. and B. M. Wiernik (2018), 'Work preferences: Vocational interests and values', in D. S. Ones, N. Anderson, C. Viswesvaran, and H. K. Sinangil (eds), *The SAGE Handbook of Industrial, Work and Organisational Psychology*, 2nd edn, vol. 1, London, UK: Sage, pp. 404–48.

Hansla, A., A. Gamble, A. Juliusson and T. Gärling (2008), 'The relationships between awareness of consequences, environmental concern, and value orientations', *Journal of Environmental Psychology*, **28** (1), 1–9.

Hartig, T., F. Kaiser and E. Strumse (2007), 'Psychological restoration in nature as a source of motivation for ecological behaviour', *Environmental Conservation*, **34** (4), 291–9.

Hilbig, B. E., I. Zettler, M. Moshagen and T. Heydasch (2013), 'Tracing the path from personality – via cooperativeness – to conservation', *European Journal of Personality*, **27** (4), 319–27.

Hines, J. M., H. R. Hungerford and A. N. Tomera (1987), 'Analysis and synthesis of research on responsible environmental behavior: A meta-analysis', *Journal of Environmental Education*, **18** (2), 1–8.

Hough, L. M. and B. S. Connelly (2013), 'Personality measurement and use in industrial and organisational psychology', in K. F. Geisinger, B. A. Bracken, J. F. Carlson, J.-I. C. Hansen, N. R. Kuncel, S. P. Reise, and M. C. Rodriguez (eds), *APA Handbook of Testing and Assessment in Psychology*, vol. 1, Washington, DC: American Psychological Association, pp. 501–31.

Hunter, J. E. and R. F. Hunter (1984), 'Validity and utility of alternative predictors of job performance', *Psychological Bulletin*, **96** (1), 72–98.

Hurst, M., H. Dittmar, R. Bond and T. Kasser (2013), 'The relationship between materialistic values and environmental attitudes and behaviors: A meta-analysis', *Journal of Environmental Psychology*, **36**, 257–69.

Jones, D. A., C. R. Willness and S. Madey (2014), 'Why are job seekers attracted by corporate social performance? Experimental and field tests of three signal-based mechanisms', *Academy of Management Journal*, **57** (2), 383–404.

Kaiser, F. (2006), 'A moral extension of the theory of planned behavior: Norms and anticipated feelings of regret in conservationism', *Personality and Individual Differences*, **41** (1), 71–81.

Kaiser, F., T. Hartig, A. Brugger and C. Duvier (2013), 'Environmental protection and nature as distinct attitudinal objects: An application of the Campbell paradigm', *Environment and Behavior*, **45** (3), 369–98.

Kim, A., Y. Kim, K. Han, S. E. Jackson and R. E. Ployhart (2014), 'Multilevel influences on voluntary workplace green behavior: Individual differences, leader behavior, and coworker advocacy', *Journal of Management*, **43** (5), 1335–58.

Klein, R. M. (2014), *Employee Motives for Engaging in Environmentally Sustainable Behaviors: A Multi-Study Analysis*, Doctoral dissertation, Minneapolis, MN: University of Minnesota, accessed at http://hdl.handle.net/11299/191323.

Klein, R. M., S. D'Mello and B. M. Wiernik (2012), 'Demographic characteristics and employee sustainability', in S. E. Jackson, D. S. Ones, and S. Dilchert (eds), *Managing Human Resources for Environmental Sustainability*, San Francisco, CA: Jossey-Bass/Wiley, pp. 117–54.

Klein, R. M., D. S. Ones and S. Dilchert (2011a), *Meta-Analysis of Gender Differences in Environmental Knowledge, Concern, and Behavior*, Paper presented at the annual conference of the Society for Industrial and Organisational Psychology, Chicago, IL, April.

Klein, R. M., D. S. Ones, S. Dilchert and A. Biga (2011b), *Meta-Analysis of Gender Differences in Green Workplace Behaviors across Cultural Regions*, Poster presented at the annual conference of the Society for Industrial and Organisational Psychology, Chicago, IL, April.

Klöckner, C. A. (2013), 'A comprehensive model of the psychology of environmental behaviour: A meta-analysis', *Global Environmental Change*, **23** (5), 1028–38.

Klöckner, C. A. and A. Blöbaum (2010), 'A comprehensive action determination model: Toward a broader understanding of ecological behaviour using the example of travel mode choice', *Journal of Environmental Psychology*, **30** (4), 574–86.

Kollmuss, A. and J. Agyeman (2002), 'Mind the gap: Why do people act environmentally and what are the barriers to pro-environmental behavior?', *Environmental Education Research*, **8** (3), 239–60.

Kvasova, O. (2015), 'The Big Five personality traits as antecedents of eco-friendly tourist behavior', *Personality and Individual Differences*, **83**, 111–16.

Littledyke, M. (2008), 'Science education for environmental awareness: Approaches to integrating cognitive and affective domains', *Environmental Education Research*, **14** (1), 1–17.

Luchs, M. G. and T. A. Mooradian (2012), 'Sex, personality, and sustainable consumer behaviour: Elucidating the gender effect', *Journal of Consumer Policy*, **35** (1), 127–44.

Maloney, M. P. and M. P. Ward (1973), 'Ecology: Let's hear from the people: An objective scale for the measurement of ecological attitudes and knowledge', *American Psychologist*, **28** (7), 583–6.

Marans, R. W. and Y.-J. Lee (1993), 'Linking recycling behavior to waste management planning: A case study of office workers in Taiwan', *Landscape and Urban Planning*, **26** (1), 203–14.

Markowitz, E. M., L. R. Goldberg, M. C. Ashton and K. Lee (2012), 'Profiling the "pro-environmental individual": A personality perspective', *Journal of Personality*, **80** (1), 81–111.

McCloy, R. A., J. P. Campbell and R. Cudeck (1994), 'A confirmatory test of a model of performance determinants', *Journal of Applied Psychology*, **79** (4), 493–505.

Mesmer-Magnus, J., C. Viswesvaran and B. M. Wiernik (2012), 'The role of commitment in bridging the gap between organisational sustainability and environmental sustainability', in S. E. Jackson, D. S. Ones, and S. Dilchert (eds), *Managing Human Resources for Environmental Sustainability*, San Francisco, CA: Jossey-Bass/Wiley, pp. 155–86.

Milfont, T. L. and C. G. Sibley (2012), 'The big five personality traits and environmental engagement: Associations at the individual and societal level', *Journal of Environmental Psychology*, **32** (2), 187–95.

Milfont, T. L., J. Wilson and P. Diniz (2012), 'Time perspective and environmental engagement: A meta-analysis', *International Journal of Psychology*, **47** (5), 325–34.

Muros, J. P. (2012), 'Going after the green: Expanding industrial–organisational practice to include environmental sustainability', *Industrial and Organisational Psychology*, **5** (4), 467–72.

Norton, T. A., S. L. Parker, H. Zacher and N. M. Ashkanasy (2015), 'Employee green behavior: A theoretical framework, multilevel review, and future research agenda', *Organisation & Environment*, **28** (1), 103–25.

Norton, T. A., H. Zacher and N. M. Ashkanasy (2014), 'Organisational sustainability policies and employee green behaviour: The mediating role of work climate perceptions', *Journal of Environmental Psychology*, **38**, 49–54.

Norton, T. A., H. Zacher, S. L. Parker and N. M. Ashkanasy (2017), 'Bridging the gap between green behavioral intentions and employee green behavior: The role of green psychological climate', *Journal of Organisational Behavior*, **38** (7), 996–1015.

Ones, D. S. and S. Dilchert (2012), 'Employee green behaviors', in S. E. Jackson, D. S. Ones, and S. Dilchert (eds), *Managing Human Resources for Environmental Sustainability*, San Francisco, CA: Jossey-Bass/Wiley, pp. 85–116.

Ones, D. S. and S. Dilchert (2013), 'Measuring, understanding, and influencing employee green behaviors', in A. H. Huffman and S. R. Klein (eds), *Green Organisations: Driving Change with I-O Psychology*, New York: Routledge, pp. 115–48.

Ones, D. S., S. Dilchert, C. Viswesvaran and J. F. Salgado (2017a), 'Cognitive ability: Measurement and validity for employee selection', in J. L. Farr and N. T. Tippins (eds), *Handbook of Employee Selection*, 2nd edn, New York: Routledge, pp. 251–76.

Ones, D. S., C. Viswesvaran and F. L. Schmidt (2017b), 'Realizing the full potential of psychometric meta-analysis for a cumulative science and practice of human resource management', *Human Resource Management Review*, **27** (1), 201–15.

Ones, D. S., B. M. Wiernik, S. Dilchert and R. M. Klein (2018), 'Multiple domains and categories of employee green behaviors: More than conservation', in V. K. Wells, D. Gregory-Smith, and D. Manika (eds), *Research Handbook on Employee Pro-Environmental Behaviour*, Cheltenham, UK and Northampton, MA, USA: Edward Elgar Publishing, pp. 13–38.

Osbaldiston, R. and J. P. Schott (2012), 'Environmental sustainability and behavioral science: Meta-analysis of proenvironmental behavior experiments', *Environment and Behavior*, **44** (2), 257–99.

Ouellette, J. A. and W. Wood (1998), 'Habit and intention in everyday life: The multiple processes by which past behavior predicts future behavior', *Psychological Bulletin*, **124** (1), 54–74.

Paillé, P., J. H. Mejía-Morelos, A. Marché-Paillé, C. C. Chen and Y. Chen (2016), 'Corporate greening, exchange process among co-workers, and ethics of care: An empirical study on the determinants of pro-environmental behaviors at coworkers-level', *Journal of Business Ethics*, **136** (3), 655–73.

Renwick, D. W. S., T. Redman and S. Maguire (2013), 'Green human resource management: A review and research agenda', *International Journal of Management Reviews*, **15** (1), 1–14.

Scherbaum, C. A., P. M. Popovich and S. Finlinson (2008), 'Exploring individual-level factors related to employee energy-conservation behaviors at work', *Journal of Applied Social Psychology*, **38** (3), 818–35.

Schmidt, F. L. and J. E. Hunter (2015), *Methods of Meta-Analysis: Correcting Error and Bias in Research Findings*, 3rd edn, Thousand Oaks, CA: Sage.

Schultz, P. W. (2001), 'The structure of environmental concern: Concern for self, other people, and the biosphere', *Journal of Environmental Psychology*, **21** (4), 327–39.

Schwartz, S. H. (1977), 'Normative influences on altruism', in L. Berkowitz (ed.), *Advances in Experimental Social Psychology*, vol. 10, New York: Academic Press, pp. 221–79.

Schwenk, G. and G. Möser (2009), 'Intention and behavior: A Bayesian meta-analysis with focus on the Ajzen–Fishbein Model in the field of environmental behavior', *Quality & Quantity*, **43** (5), 743–55, accessed at. https://doi.org/10/fv57q3.

Semmel, S., R. M. Klein, D. S. Ones, S. Dilchert and B. M. Wiernik (2012), *A Meta-Analytic Review of Interventions Aimed at Greening Our Workforce*, Poster presented at the annual conference of the Society for Industrial and Organisational Psychology, San Diego, CA, April.

Stanek, K. C. and D. S. Ones (2018), 'Taxonomies and compendia of cognitive ability and personality measures relevant to industrial, work, and organizational psychology', in D. S. Ones, N. Anderson, C. Viswesvaran, and H. K. Sinangil (eds), *The SAGE Handbook of Industrial, Work and Organisational Psychology*, 2nd edn, vol. 1, London, UK: Sage, pp. 366–407.

Steg, L. and C. Vlek (2009), 'Encouraging pro-environmental behaviour: An integrative review and research agenda', *Journal of Environmental Psychology*, **29** (3), 309–17.

Stern, P. C. (2000), 'Toward a coherent theory of environmentally significant behavior', *Journal of Social Issues*, **56** (3), 407–24.

Stern, P. C., T. Dietz, T. Abel, G. A. Guagnano and L. Kalof (1999), 'A value-belief-norm theory of support for social movements: The case of environmentalism', *Human Ecology Review*, **6** (2), 81–98.

Swami, V., T. Chamorro-Premuzic, R. Snelgar and A. Furnham (2011), 'Personality, individual differences, and demographic antecedents of self-reported household waste management behaviours', *Journal of Environmental Psychology*, **31** (1), 21–6.

Temminck, E., K. Mearns and L. Fruhen (2015), 'Motivating employees towards sustainable behaviour', *Business Strategy and the Environment*, **24** (6), 402–12.

Triandis, H. C. (1979), 'Values, attitudes, and interpersonal behavior', *Nebraska Symposium on Motivation*, **27**, 195–259.

Unsworth, K. L., A. Dmitrieva and E. Adriasola (2013), 'Changing behaviour: Increasing the effectiveness of workplace interventions in creating pro-environmental behaviour change', *Journal of Organisational Behavior*, **34** (2), 211–29.

Wiernik, B. M., S. Dilchert and D. S. Ones (2016), 'Age and employee green behaviors: A meta-analysis', *Frontiers in Psychology*, **7**, 194.

Wiernik, B. M., R. M. Klein, D. S. Ones and S. Otto (2014), *Pro-Environmental Behaviors in Work and Non-Work Settings*, Paper presented at the International Congress for Applied Psychology, Paris, France, July.

Wiernik, B. M., D. S. Ones and S. Dilchert (2013), 'Age and environmental sustainability: A meta-analysis', *Journal of Managerial Psychology*, **28** (7/8), 826–56.

Wiseman, M. and F. X. Bogner (2003), 'A higher-order model of ecological values and its relationship to personality', *Personality and Individual Differences*, **34** (5), 783–94.

Young, W., M. Davis, I. M. McNeill, B. Malhotra, S. Russell, K. Unsworth and C. W. Clegg

(2015), 'Changing behaviour: Successful environmental programmes in the workplace', *Business Strategy and the Environment*, **24** (8), 689–703.
Yun, R., P. Scupelli, A. Aziz and V. Loftness (2013), 'Sustainability in the workplace: Nine intervention techniques for behavior change', in S. Berkovsky and J. Freyne (eds), *Persuasive Technology*, Germany: Springer Berlin Heidelberg, pp. 253–65.

5. Disentangling voluntary pro-environmental behaviour of employees (VPBE) – fostering research through an integrated theoretical model

Regina Hahn and Felix Ostertag

5.1 INTRODUCTION AND RESEARCH FOCUS

The relevance of corporations for sustainable development is widely accepted, as is the relevance of environmental sustainability for corporations. With corporate environmental initiatives on the increase (Lo et al. 2012) there is also a significant amount of research on corporate environmental initiatives, performance, and standards (for an overview see Bansal and Gao 2006). Most of this research focuses on the *organisational* level (Lo et al. 2012), neglecting the origin of organisational performance: *individual* behaviour. Pro-environmental behaviour (PEB) of employees contributes significantly to corporate sustainability (Temminck et al. 2015) and hence to the conservation of the environment. In current research, however, PEB of employees is not sufficiently taken into account (Blok et al. 2015). Considering that pro-environmental actions in employees' everyday working lives usually occur as discretionary behaviour, especially *voluntary pro-environmental behaviour of employees* (VPBE) there are calls for further investigation (Lülfs and Hahn 2013). The exploration of PEB of employees and particularly VPBE should thus be a cornerstone of the research on corporate environmental behaviour.

Against this background, this chapter aims to provide an overview of existing concepts, models, and research streams from different fields such as environmental psychology or Organisational Citizenship Behaviour for the Environment (OCBE) to explain VPBE. The aim is to illustrate the origin of different antecedents of VPBE to help scholars better understand their theoretical grounding, explain connections between different models and determinants, and present the current status of research on different sources of PEB and VPBE. By building a solid theoretical grounding this chapter aims at being a fruitful starting point for further research on PEB in the workplace, particularly focusing on VPBE.

In the following, we will start with an overview of key characteristics of PEB that need to be kept in mind when interpreting results on possible determinants and causalities. We deem this necessary because many studies on PEB fail to explicitly define the term (Poortinga et al. 2004) and those that do vary in their perception of what constitutes PEB. The main part of this chapter then focuses on the illustration of determinants of VPBE. An explanation of VPBE, however, is not enough to change current practices. An enhancement of VPBE in everyday working practices needs behavioural interventions that both stimulate an employee's motivation and simultaneously consider the external environment (i.e., the workplace) in which the behaviour in question may occur. Therefore, we provide recommendations for practitioners on how to foster VPBE by means of intervention techniques that shape boundary conditions and nudge employees towards the desired behaviours. The chapter ends with a conclusion and an outlook.

5.2   CHARACTERISTICS AND CONCEPTUAL FOUNDATIONS OF VPBE

Pro-environmental behaviours are multi-dimensional (e.g., Bratt et al. 2015; Larson et al. 2015) and versatile in their appearance. When analysing general PEB, researchers use a variety of labels such as "green behaviour", "conservation behaviour", "organisational citizenship behaviour directed towards the environment (OCBE)", "sustainable behaviour", "environmentally friendly/responsible behaviour" or "environmentally responsible behaviour" (for an overview see, e.g., Dilchert and Ones 2012). The diverse and inconsistent use of terms has led to a cluttered conception of PEB. However, conceptual heterogeneity issues are not limited to research on general PEB but are also true for pro-environmental research in the business context (e.g., Blok et al. 2015; Ciocirlan 2016). Thus, this section aims to determine the scope of VPBE by clarifying domains, characteristics, and theoretical foundations.

Several researchers have identified different domains of PEB which might be helpful for a more thorough understanding of the term. Larson et al. (2015), for example, differentiate between conservation lifestyle behaviours (e.g., household actions in the private sphere), social environmentalism (e.g., peer interactions and group membership), environmental citizenship (e.g., civic engagement in the policy arena), and land stewardship (e.g., support for wildlife and habitat conservation). Specifically for PEB *of employees*, Ones and Dilchert (2012a) see five major behavioural categories: Working sustainably (behaviours employees engage in to enhance the environmental sustainability of work products and processes), avoiding harm (involving avoidance and inhibition of negative environmental behaviours), conserving (avoiding wastefulness and thus preserving resources), influencing others (employee behaviours aimed at spreading sustainability behaviours to other individuals), and taking initiative (proactive, entrepreneurial behaviours that go against societal expectations). In spite of different categorisations, several studies show that some of the PEB categories described in the literature are substantially correlated so that "[t]here appears to be a psychological construct core to pro-environmental behaviors" (Dilchert and Ones 2012: 191). Based on this assumption, we see the following specific characteristics of VPBE.

First, VPBE can be directly or indirectly targeted towards the environment. In a direct way, it addresses environmental concerns, such as energy issues (e.g., in the form of energy savings), waste issues (e.g., in the form of recycling residues or separating trash), resource issues (e.g., in the form of saving packaging materials, paper, or water), and emission issues (e.g., using less-polluting modes of transportation, finding sources of contaminant emissions). In an indirect way, VPBE does not lead to environmental improvements right away. Rather, it acts as an enabler for such improvements. Examples include making suggestions for improving environmental practices of the company, identifying technical malfunctions that may have significant environmental impacts, or questioning ecologically harmful corporate practices.

Second, VPBE is discretionary individual behaviour that is *not* organisationally prescribed or mandatory, namely, behaviour that is not explicitly included in formal role descriptions, role expectations or job requirements but nevertheless takes place within the organisational context and hence – as will be shown in the following – is subject to organisational circumstances. However, such voluntary behaviour can of course still be connected to the employees' job (e.g., switching off the lights in the office when going to lunch). The criterion for the behaviour we consider here is that it implies a choice situation for the individual.

In quest of the conceptual origins of VPBE that might help to identify possible determinants, two dominant research streams emerge: Organisational Citizenship Behaviour for the Environment (OCBE) and environmental psychology. Organ (1997: 91) characterises Organisational Citizenship Behaviour (OCB) as "contributions to the maintenance and enhancement of the social and psychological context that supports task performance." This concept is strongly connected to related terms such as contextual performance, pro-social behaviour and extra-role behaviour (e.g., Borman and Motowidlo 1993; Van Scotter et al. 2000), all of which refer to some form of voluntary employee behaviour beyond organisational tasks. Recently, OCBE emerged (e.g., Tosti-Kharas et al. 2016;

Paillé et al. 2013; Lamm et al. 2013; Boiral 2009; Daily et al. 2009) linking OCB to the natural environment (for differences between OCB and OCBE see Lülfs and Hahn 2014; Lamm et al. 2013). OCBE is understood as "discretionary acts by employees within the organisation not rewarded or required that are directed toward environmental improvement" (Daily et al. 2009: 246). Scholars differentiate several forms of OCBE, that is, eco-initiatives (a form of discretionary behaviour involving suggestions for improving environmental practices), eco-helping (voluntary willingness to help colleagues better integrate environmental concerns in the workplace) and eco-civic engagement (voluntary participation in the environmental programmes and activities of the organisation) (Boiral and Paillé 2012; Paillé et al. 2013). As it originates from industrial and organisational psychology, research on OCBE mainly focuses on *organisational* determinants within the working context. Frequently analysed determinants include perceived organisational support, employee commitment to the organisation, and organisational commitment (e.g., Temminck et al. 2015; Lamm et al. 2013; Tosti-Kharas et al. 2016; Paillé and Boiral 2013).

In contrast, the understanding of VPBE derived from environmental and conservation psychology traditionally focuses on *individual* determinants, transferring results from private-sphere PEB to PEB in the workplace. Against this theoretical background, PEB is often understood as "actions contributing to environmental conservation, or human activity intended to protect natural resources, or at least reduce environmental deterioration" (Juárez-Nájera et al. 2010: 687). Accordingly, Ones and Dilchert (2012a: 87) define PEB in the workplace as "scalable actions and behaviours that employees engage in that are linked with and contribute to or detract from environmental sustainability." Empirical studies that stem from environmental psychology commonly address internal factors such as values, attitudes, beliefs, and norms (e.g., Scherbaum et al. 2008; Wall et al. 2007; Nordlund and Garvil 2013).

Despite the different emphases to approach PEB of employees, a notable number of contributions (e.g., Blok et al. 2015; Lülfs and Hahn 2013; Lülfs and Hahn 2014; Lo et al. 2012; Gadenne et al. 2009; Tudor et al. 2008; Andersson et al. 2005; Cordano and Frieze 2000) theoretically and empirically link ideas from environmental psychology to the corporate context. A stronger link between research on PEB within companies and research on OCBE with its pronounced focus on organisational determinants, hence, seems promising for the explanation of VPBE and will be reviewed in the following section.

5.3 A REVIEW ON THEORIES AND DETERMINANTS OF VPBE

Determinants of PEB in general mostly stem from three theoretical models: the Theory of Planned Behaviour (TPB) (Ajzen 1991), the Norm-Activation Model (NAM) (Schwartz and Howard 1981) and the Value-Belief-Norm Theory (VBN) (Stern et al. 1999). The TPB explains rational, goal-oriented behaviour, whereas the NAM and the VBN are models that explain behaviour from a moral perspective. The suitability of solely moral or rational models to predict work-related voluntary PEB is questionable and therefore scholars encourage the combination of all three theories (Paillé and Mejía-Morelos 2014). Thus, in accordance with the antecedents of general PEB identified by the meta-analysis of Bamberg and Möser (2007), there is consensus that an explanation of PEB of employees needs at least both rational and moral determinants (e.g., Lo et al. 2014). However, relying on only major social psychological theories may result in too narrow a focus to explain PEB in the workplace (Ones and Dilchert 2012b). Moreover, such an approach would be limited with regard to identifying effective interventions that promote VPBE (Unsworth et al. 2013). The integration of additional affective antecedents and employees' perceptions of their organisational conditions is thus a promising avenue to better understand the emergence of VPBE (e.g., Afsar et al. 2016; Lamm et al. 2013; Paillé et al. 2016; Temminck et al. 2015). Since VPBE is not only performed once but rather on a daily basis, incorporating past behaviour alongside social and emotional factors also seems reasonable and would do justice to Triandis' (1977) Theory of Interpersonal Behaviour as well as Perugini and Bagozzi's (2001) Model of Goal-directed Behaviour. Several studies indicate that, besides intentions, the automatic activation of habitual behaviours by situational cues might play a crucial role for promoting voluntary pro-environmental behaviour (e.g., Bamberg and Schmidt 2003; Carrus et al. 2008) and VPBE (e.g., Holland et al. 2006). Hence an integrated modelling approach that considers the advantages and disadvantages of various behavioural roots is likely to provide the best insights into the diverse antecedents of VPBE (see Table 5.1).

The TPB is a suitable starting point to explain PEB in the workplace (Blok et al. 2015). The psychological literature on everyday PEB has long built upon the TPB, which proposes that behaviour is directly determined by behavioural intention (which itself is an outcome of attitude towards the behaviour, subjective norms, and perceived behavioural control). The TPB has proven successful in explaining several types of private PEB, including household recycling (Tang et al. 2011), travel mode

88

Table 5.1 Behavioural roots of VPBE and the need for synthesis

Behavioural Root	Advantages	Disadvantages	Additional Challenges for VPBE
Moral considerations (e.g., Norm Activation Theory, Value–Belief-Norm Theory)	Consideration of value orientations and personal norms	Underestimates the role of intentions and neglects the context of decisions	
Rational decision-making (e.g., Theory of Planned Behaviour)	Cognition of situational framework conditions; intentions as a direct predictor of rational behaviour	Neglects emotions, moral obligations, and repetitive nature of behaviour	Relation to the environment + Corporate context
Habits (e.g., Theory of Interpersonal Behaviour)	Consideration of past behaviour and routine behaviour patterns; habits as a boundary condition to rational behaviour	Neglects situational constraints and facilitating conditions +	
Emotions and affects	Consideration of commitment, passion, and feelings	Lacks rational foundation of decision-making	

Need for an integrated modelling approach

choice (Harland et al. 1999; Heath and Gifford 2002; Bamberg and Schmidt 2003), waste composting (Taylor and Todd 1995; Mannetti et al. 2004), and general PEB (Kaiser et al. 1999). Applications of the TPB to voluntary PEB within the business context have become more frequent in recent years (e.g., Hurtz and Williams 2009; Martin-Peña et al. 2010). Researchers agree that internal (individual) as well as external (corporate) factors explain PEB in the corporate context (e.g., Blok et al. 2015; Lamm et al. 2013; Lo et al. 2012). Determinants from the TPB and the NAM are therefore often complemented by additional organisational variables like organisational climate and commitment for the organisation. These will be illustrated subsequently.

While few empirical studies have tested the entire TPB framework (see Warburton and Terry 2000; Hurtz and Williams 2009, for notable exceptions), several studies indicate that the inclusion of behavioural intention can help to explain PEB in companies (e.g., Tudor et al. 2007; Martin-Peña et al. 2010). Several other studies build on this assumption to identify further determinants (e.g., Cordano and Frieze 2000; Flannery and May 2000; Ramus and Killmer 2007; Scherbaum et al. 2008; Cordano et al. 2010; Vazquez Brust and Liston-Heyes 2010). Studies on the relationship between intention and behaviour in general provide mixed results but several meta-analyses reveal that intentions are reliably associated with behaviour (Armitage and Conner 2001; Milne et al. 2000; Sheeran 2002) and directly influence the behaviour in question (Webb and Sheeran 2006). When turning specifically to PEB, Schwenk and Möser (2009) show that the correlation between intention and behaviour is above average compared to other kinds of behaviour. Following this line of argument, we assume that intentions are a direct predictor of VPBE.

Proposition 1: Employees' pro-environmental intentions positively influence their voluntary pro-environmental behaviour at work (#1 in Figure 5.1*).*

The TPB posits that one predictor of behavioural intentions is attitude towards the respective behaviour. Attitudes refer to a person's overall assessment of the advantages and disadvantages of performing a given behaviour (e.g., "energy-saving would be beneficial to me or the organisation"). Attitude has been identified as playing an important role in the explanation of PEB in the business context (e.g., Cordano and Frieze 2000; Cummings 2008; Flannery and May 2000; Gadenne et al. 2009; Papagiannakis and Lioukas 2012; Tudor et al. 2007; Lo et al. 2012). Environmental attitudes do not necessarily translate to PEB or practices; that is to say, attitudes have an indirect influence on behaviour (Gadenne et al. 2009). In this sense, attitudes have an influence on behavioural intentions to perform PEB within companies (e.g., Cordano and Frieze 2000; Flannery and May 2000; Tudor et al. 2007; Cordano et al. 2010). The question of which behavioural attitudes need to be measured depends on which behaviour is being studied. We posit that general attitudes towards the environment ("green attitude" or "eco-attitude") will probably not be a strong predictor of intentions to carry out voluntary PEB in the workplace. Instead, specific attitudes towards the behaviour under study are likely to be a stronger predictor. Several studies measuring a specific (positive or negative) attitude, including towards organic viticulture (Cordano et al. 2010), towards pollution prevention as a waste management goal (Cordano and Frieze 2000), towards conservation and pollution (Gadenne et al. 2009), towards recycling (Tudor et al. 2007), and towards key contemporary environmental management issues (Cummings 2008) indicate that attitudes are strong predictors of PEB in the business sphere. Even if it is widely acknowledged that employees' attitudes towards environmental issues are indeed a relevant aspect of sustainable behaviour, attitude itself has no direct influence on behaviour; rather, its influence is an indirect one (Buchan 2005; Carpenter and Reimers 2005; Ervin et al. 2013; Gadenne et al. 2009). We, therefore, postulate that attitudes towards voluntary pro-environmental behaviour influence the formation of the intention to behave sustainably.

Proposition 2: Employees' attitudes towards voluntary pro-environmental behaviour positively influence their pro-environmental intentions at work (#2 in Figure 5.1*).*

A determinant which is included in the TPB as well as in the NAM, is social norms[1] (although the latter posits that they are eventually incorporated into personal norms). Social norms express the motive to behave in accordance with the expectations of relevant others and thus reflect the influence of perceived general normative pressure. In the literature on environmental psychology, the importance of social norms for PEB is thoroughly documented (for a review, see Biel and Thøgersen 2007). Research suggests that social norms are also relevant in the business context (e.g., Carpenter and Reimers 2005; Cohen et al. 2010; Cordano and Frieze 2000; Lo et al. 2012; Papagiannakis and Lioukas 2012; Ramus and Killmer 2007; Vazquez Brust and Liston-Heyes 2010). Of particular interest for voluntary PEB are co-workers' pro-environmental expectations (e.g., Norton et al. 2014). Behaviour in companies is easily observed by one's peers in the workplace, and there is regular social contact with one another (Carrico and Riemer 2011); therefore, co-workers are an important reference for employees.

Leaders seem to be another important source of perceived normative pressure (Blok et al. 2015; Ramus and Steger 2000; Zutshi and Sohal 2003). Several studies highlight the importance of supervisors and "environmental leadership" for PEB and corporate greening (e.g., Lo et al. 2012; Bansal and Roth 2000; Egri and Herman 2000; Robertson and Barling 2013). Leaders function as "relevant others" for employees and hence provide them with social norms (Daily et al. 2009). As such, they inform employees about the expectations of others. In addition, supervisors and leaders encourage ecological initiatives in the workplace and can, for example, deliver motivational appeals in one-on-one conversations, by email, or through newsletters (Carrico and Riemer 2011).

However, research in environmental psychology suggests that social norms do not have a *direct* influence on intention as posited by the TPB. Instead, when *personal* norms are included in models to explain PEB, the direct influence of social norms is reduced (Thøgersen 1999, 2006; Klöckner and Blöbaum 2010; Klöckner and Oppedal 2011). Based on Cialdini et al.'s (1990) Focus Theory of Normative Conduct and in line with the environmental norm taxonomy developed by Thøgersen (2006), we assume that injunctive social norms in particular (i.e., norms that reflect beliefs about what behaviour others approve), as opposed to descriptive social norms (i.e., norms that represent beliefs about other people's behaviour) (e.g., Karlin et al. 2014; Norton et al. 2014), can influence VPBE indirectly via personal norms as long as they become internalised.

Proposition 3: Employees' injunctive social norms concerning the environment positively influence their personal environmental norms at work (#3 in Figure 5.1*).*

Building on this assumption, we will now discuss the relevance of personal norms for the explanation of voluntary pro-environmental behaviour. According to the NAM, personal norms are internalised social norms, because social norms influence personal norms through personal interaction (i.e., an individual learns from shared expectations in social interactions) (Schwartz 1977). Therefore, personal norms are considered a stable reference to the personal value system. In the environmental domain several studies indicate that the personal norm (as the central determinant of the NAM) is indeed suitable for predicting PEB in the business context (e.g., Andersson et al. 2005; Papagiannakis and Lioukas 2012; Scherbaum et al. 2008). However, personal norms have no direct impact on PEB (Bamberg and Möser 2007). They are considered a reference for the individual to generate intentions in decision-making situations. Therefore, they have an indirect impact on behaviour via intentional processes.

Proposition 4: Employees' personal environmental norms positively influence their pro-environmental intentions at work (#4 in Figure 5.1*).*

A personal norm is activated when three fundamental prerequisites are met. The individual must (a) be aware that it is necessary to act in the given situation to solve a problem, (b) recognise that his/her own action is linked with the problem, and (c) recognise his/her ability to act himself/herself to change the situation (Schwartz 1973). Awareness is aroused by employees' emotions, which generate interest in the topic and focus the employee's attention (Howard-Grenville 2006) on relevant environmental issues. Tudor et al. (2008) show that the level of awareness is an indirect predictor of sustainable waste management behaviour. Gadenne et al. (2009) show that environmental awareness is a predictor of environmental practices in small and medium enterprises. We hence posit that awareness indirectly determines voluntary pro-environmental intentions by influencing the personal norm, which itself is a reference for the individual to generate intentions for voluntary PEB.

Proposition 5: Employees' general awareness of consequences for the environment positively influences their personal environmental norms at work (#5 in Figure 5.1*).*

According to the TPB, one determinant of pro-environmental intentions is perceived behavioural control. Perceived behavioural control is understood as an individual's perceived ease or difficulty of performing a particular behaviour (Ajzen 1991). The TPB postulates that individuals estimate their ability to perform a given behaviour before actually executing it. In addition, people are more likely to develop an intention to perform a behaviour over which they perceive a high level of control than a behaviour over which they perceive little control. Research on voluntary PEB in the private sphere has shown that perceived behavioural control seems to be an important determinant of PEB (Harland et al. 1999). Recent studies indicate that perceived behavioural control is also relevant for various workplace-related VPBEs, such as energy-saving in the office, commuting-mode choice, and general pro-environmental behaviour of employees (e.g., Blok et al. 2015; Lo et al. 2014; Wall et al. 2007). We presume that this behavioural influence occurs in two different ways: first, perceived behavioural control may influence the intention of VPBE, and second, if perceived behavioural control not only reflects perceived but rather actual barriers to perform VPBE, then it is presumably also directly linked to the contemplable behaviour.

Proposition 6: Employees' perceived behavioural control to act pro-environmentally positively influences their pro-environmental intentions at work (#6 in Figure 5.1*).*

Proposition 7: Employees' perceived behavioural control to act pro-environmentally positively influences their voluntary pro-environmental behaviour at work (#7 in Figure 5.1*).*

In the corporate context, perceived behavioural control is determined by organisational circumstances. In this regard, research on OCBE shows the importance of perceived organisational support (Paillé and Boiral 2013; Paillé et al. 2013). Perceived organisational support represents an individual's perception of the organisation's willingness to reciprocate hard work with rewards and support in future endeavours (Lamm et al. 2013). Regarding PEB, this means that employees engage in PEB in the workplace if they perceive that their organisation cares about the environment and appreciates individual environmental efforts (e.g., Norton et al. 2014; Temminck et al. 2015). If the organisation is actually trying to improve its environmental performance, the individual perception of the organisational environmental efforts likely leads to a reduction of perceived behavioural barriers. We hence suggest that perceived organisational support in general and particularly when appreciating employees' environmental efforts, influences the perceived behavioural control of employees.

Proposition 8: Employees' perceived organisational support for the environment positively influences their perceived behavioural control to act pro-environmentally at work (#8 in Figure 5.1*).*

Furthermore, perceived organisational support for the environment is likely to have another indirect effect on employees' PEB. Extra-role behaviours of employees are usually guided by their cognition of and alignment to organisational norms (Chatman 1989). Thus, regarding PEB, perceived organisational pro-environmental efforts might represent a normative motivational force (Ramus and Killmer 2007) that stimulates the willingness of employees to align their behaviour with the organisations' pro-environmental expectations. Although empirical evidence in regard to VPBE is scarce, Ramus and Steger (2000) being a notable exception, we suggest that perceived organisational support for the environment influences VPBE via the formation of social norms.

Proposition 9: Employees' perceived organisational support for the environment positively influences their injunctive social norms concerning the environment (#9 in Figure 5.1*).*

According to Allen and Meyer (1990) affective organisational commitment emphasises an individual's emotional attachment to, involvement in, as well as identification with, an organisation. As shown by the meta-analysis of Riketta (2002), affective commitment is strongly related to extra-role behaviour and might therefore be considered a determinant of VPBE as well. A majority of empirical studies indicate that affective commitment mediates the relationship between perceived organisational support and PEB of employees (e.g., Paillé and Boiral 2013; Temminck et al. 2015). However, if we particularly consider perceived organisational support for the environment, the relationship might not be as straightforward as mentioned before (Lamm et al. 2013). In the following we briefly outline that affective commitment rather acts as a moderator when it comes to explain VPBE by means of perceived organisational support for the environment.

Generally, if an organisation appreciates environmental efforts and employees are affectively committed to their organisation, it seems reasonable that their striving for a congruent behaviour (i.e., pro-environmental behaviour) is enhanced (Daily et al. 2009). Higher levels of affective commitment might therefore motivate employees to follow the organisational environmental norms and perform in accordance to them (Vlachos et al. 2016). Furthermore, as a result of missing identification with an organisation, the emergence of social norms that originate from an emphasis of organisational pro-environmental values might even be weakened. This is because employees that only show low levels of affective commitment do not care about their organisation (Temminck et al. 2015) and instead prioritise other values (e.g., Unsworth et al. 2013). We hence suggest that employees' affective organisational commitment moderates the relationship between perceived organisational appreciation of environmental efforts and social norms.

Proposition 10: Employees' affective organisational commitment positively moderates the relationship between perceived organisational support for the environment and injunctive social norms concerning the environment (#10 in Figure 5.1*).*

Voluntary PEB is frequently performed as if it is a kind of daily, routine behaviour within a stable context, the work environment. These are important antecedents of habit formation (Limayem et al. 2007). We hence posit that voluntary PEB eventually ceases to be rational and purposive and instead can be characterised as habitual. This view is supported by research in environmental psychology (Warburton and Terry 2000; Stern 2000; Bamberg and Schmidt 2003; Gregory and Di Leo 2003; Klöckner and Matthies 2004; Verplanken and Wood 2006). Verplanken et al. (2008), for example, show that habitual drivers are central to travel mode choice and Carrus et al. (2008) point to the relevance of past behaviour regarding intentions to recycle and use public transportation. Habits have not received extensive attention in the literature on PEB *within companies* (for notable exceptions, see Lo et al. 2012; Ramus and Killmer 2007). Nevertheless, we think that they play an essential role in VPBE. They need to be thoroughly understood in order to explain such behaviour in companies and to possibly aim to achieve gradual changes in habits over time.

According to Limayem et al. (2007) there are three major views on how to connect habit and intention: (1) habit as a predictor of intention; (2) habit as a direct predictor of behaviour; (3) habit as a moderator between intention and behaviour. The literature on environmental psychology shows strong support for the third view. Aarts et al. (1998: 1369), for example, show that habit sets "a boundary condition for the applicability of the theories of reasoned or planned behaviour in predicting and explaining repeated behaviours". In the same vein, the empirical research of Verplanken and colleagues (e.g., Verplanken et al. 1997; Verplanken et al. 2008) supports the conclusion that habit has a moderator effect on the relationship between intention and behaviour; thus, the stronger the habit, the smaller the effect of intention on behaviour. In line with this research, habits might be a moderating factor for the relationship between intention and VPBE.

Proposition 11: Employees' pro-environmental habits moderate the relationship between pro-environmental intentions and voluntary pro-environmental behaviour at work (#11 in Figure 5.1*).*

5.4   RECOMMENDATIONS FOR PRACTITIONERS

As discussed, voluntary PEB of employees is behaviour that is not *formally* rewarded or supported. Thus, it cannot be directly linked to corporate reward systems. Every corporate measure that is directed at voluntary PEB questions its non-obligatory form. However, as proposed by the literature on OCB, the degree to which discretionary behaviours

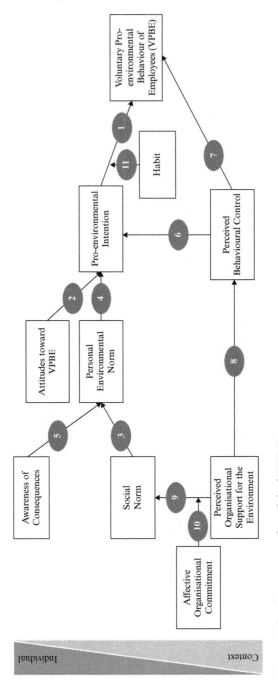

Figure 5.1   An integrated model of VPBE

Table 5.2   Selected measures and instruments to enhance VPBE

Targeted Determinant	Measure to Enhance VPBE	Exemplary Instrument
Personal environmental norm	• Ongoing education on environmental issues • Selection of environmentally conscious employees • Enhancement of employee self-commitment	• Internal bulletins, emails • Assessment centre, aptitude tests, job interviews • Objective agreements
Awareness of consequences	• Information and peer education	• Internal bulletins, environmental reports, dissemination of the organisation's environmental policy, publication of environmental performance statistics
Perceived organisational support for the environment and perceived behavioural control	• Formal corporate greening programmes • Supervisory support • Environmental leadership	• Sustainability goals and strategy, environmental management systems • Motivational appeals in one-on-one conversations, by email, through newsletters • Provision of training and learning opportunities
Social norm	• Supervisors as role models (acting and giving feedback) • Pro-environmental climate	• Provision of training and learning opportunities • Green company days
Habits	• Strong situational changes	• For example, forcing employees to use public transport instead of providing company cars

are mandatory or rewarded should be viewed as a continuum and not in a monolithic manner (Organ et al. 2006). As such, VPBE could be indirectly encouraged (see Table 5.2 for an overview of selected measures).

Our model indicates some connections to the management of corporate greening. The first one, however, is rather disappointing from a managerial point-of-view. We have argued that a central determinant of VPBE is the personal norm, which seems to support the fact that it is difficult for the company to influence VPBE. Personal norms can only be influenced in the long-term as they are learned from shared expectations in social interactions. In this context, corporate influence is rather limited. Thus, apart from ongoing education, the initial choice of environmentally conscious employees can be regarded as an elemental part of "green human resource management" (Bauer et al. 2012). Moreover, strategies focusing on self-commitment can also be an option to influence an employee's personal norms.

Instead of influencing the "content" of personal norms, their mere "activation" could possibly be easier for managers to target. To activate personal norms, a substantial awareness of both environmental problems and of their consequences (in terms of the environmental impact of behaviour) is necessary. Information and peer education, for example, have the potential to increase this awareness by enhancing an employee's knowledge about environmental problems, about the company's impact on the natural environment, and about individual opportunities to influence this impact (Lülfs and Hahn 2014). Boiral (2009) lists the following potential ways of enhancing employees' knowledge about environmental problems: internal bulletins, environmental reports, dissemination of the organisation's environmental policy, and publication of environmental performance statistics. Nevertheless, environmental awareness might be even more difficult to raise among non-managerial employees compared with managers, because the former are usually less involved in planning and implementing environmental strategies (Schmit et al. 2012) and might thus have a narrower perception of the (potential) environmental impact of the company.

Another practical implication of our model is that it might be promising for companies to further strengthen their formal corporate greening programmes even if they are not targeted towards voluntary behaviours. They could have an influence on perceived behavioural aspects such as perceived behavioural control and perceived organisational support for the environment and thus can at least act as a distal predictor of VPBE. What becomes even more evident here is that pseudo-activities or forms of "greenwashing" do not work as motivation for VPBE since employees are usually in the position to better evaluate their employers' true engagement towards the environment than external stakeholders. In the worst case, this could even backfire if employees recognise that the efforts are just a pretence, which would have an indirect negative influence on VPBE. Similar considerations apply for supervisory support. Several studies highlight the importance of supervisors and "environmental leadership" for corporate greening (e.g., Bansal and Roth 2000; Egri and Herman 2000).

Our model helps to explain how supervisors can support VPBE. First, we state that VPBE is only indirectly appreciated. This makes supervisors an even more important factor as they are the ones that encourage ecological initiatives in the workplace and can, for example, deliver motivational appeals in one-on-one conversations, by email, or through newsletters (Carrico and Riemer 2011). Second, supervisors can act as role models for pro-environmental behaviour (Robertson and Barling 2013) and increase their employee's desire to gain approval by performing VPBEs (Graves et al. 2013). They function as "relevant others" for employees and hence provide them with social norms (Daily et al. 2009). As such, they inform employees about the expectations of others. And third, if supervisors visibly support environmental initiatives undertaken by employees, the social norm can become effective, which means that if co-workers carry out VPBE, this could encourage others to follow (e.g., Norton et al. 2014). In other words, in pursuit of symbolical rewards such as social recognition and prestige, both central elements within the Social Exchange Theory (Cropanzano and Mitchell 2005), peer pressure might induce individuals to act pro-environmentally just because it is congruent to the expectations of a relevant group (e.g., Schultz et al. 1995). In sum, establishing a pro-environmental organisational climate is likely to benefit the emergence of VPBEs. Such a climate reflects a set of shared perceptions regarding pro-environmental policies, procedures, and practices that an organisation appreciates and expects (Norton et al. 2012). A strong pro-environmental climate is able to create social norms (Norton et al. 2014) and encourages employees to behave consistently with the organisation's environmental goals (James et al. 2008) by lowering behavioural barriers.

Finally, habitual processes are often neglected not only in the analysis of VPBE but also in its practical implications. Nevertheless, we propose that habitual processes moderate the influence of intentions on VPBE. Yet, even habits can be modified (Hunecke et al. 2001), for example, by strong changes of situations (e.g., forcing employees to use public transport instead of providing company cars), since habits are generated by success-fully performing stable behavioural patterns in stable situations (Klöckner and Matthies 2004).

5.5   CONCLUSIONS AND OUTLOOK

This chapter aimed to provide an overview of existing concepts, models, and research streams for the explanation of voluntary PEB of employees. Our explanation of origin, connections, and current research status of important determinants of PEB from environmental psychology and OCBE offers a valuable starting point for further empirical studies on PEB and VPBE. For such studies, the following issues should be taken into consideration: As argued throughout the chapter, a deeper link between research on PEB and research on OCBE might be fruitful for both research streams. OCBE might profit from results on individual employees' norms, values, and the contribution of the TPB to environmental behaviours. Research on PEB can be complemented by organisational determinants to paint a holistic picture of PEB. An empirical testing of such a holistic framework seems to be eligible.

NOTE

1. In his Theory of Planned Behaviour Ajzen (1991) makes use of the term subjective norms instead of social norms. He argues that subjective norms are a composite construct consisting of a person's normative belief of the other's approval of a certain behaviour and the person's motivation to comply with the other's expectations. According to Thøgersen's (2006) norm taxonomy such a conceptualisation of subjective norms reflects a subset of injunctive norms that should rather be termed subjective social norms. Thus, for consistency and readability purposes, we use the term *social norms* whenever we refer to either Ajzen's (1991) concept of subjective norms or other comparable forms of social norms.

REFERENCES

Aarts, H., B. Verplanken and A. Knippenberg (1998), 'Predicting behavior from actions in the past: Repeated decision making or a matter of habit?', *Journal of Applied Social Psychology*, **28**(15), 1355–1374.

Afsar, B., Y. Badir and U. S. Kiani (2016), 'Linking spiritual leadership and employee pro-environmental behavior: The influence of workplace spirituality, intrinsic motivation, and environmental passion', *Journal of Environmental Psychology*, **45**, 79–88.

Ajzen, I. (1991), 'The theory of planned behavior', *Organizational Behavior and Human Decision Processes*, **50**(2), 179–211.

Allen, N. J. and J. P. Meyer (1990), 'The measurement and antecedents of affective, continuance and normative commitment to the organization', *Journal of Occupational Psychology*, **63**(1), 1–18.

Andersson, L., S. Shivarajan and G. Blau (2005), 'Enacting ecological sustainability in the MNC: A test of an adapted value-belief-norm framework', *Journal of Business Ethics*, **59**(3), 295–305.

Armitage, C. J. and M. Conner (2001), 'Efficacy of the theory of planned behaviour: A meta-analytic review', *British Journal of Social Psychology*, **40**(4), 471–499.

Bamberg, S. and G. Möser (2007), 'Twenty years after Hines, Hungerford, and Tomera: A new meta-analysis of psychosocial determinants of pro-environmental behaviour', *Journal of Environmental Psychology*, **27**(1), 14–25.

Bamberg, S. and P. Schmidt (2003), 'Incentives, morality, or habit? Predicting students' car use for university routes with the models of Ajzen, Schwartz, and Triandis', *Environment and Behavior*, **35**(2), 264–285.

Bansal, P. and J. J. Gao (2006), 'Building the future by looking to the past—Examining research published on organizations and environment', *Organization & Environment*, **19**(4), 458–478.

Bansal, P. and K. Roth (2000), 'Why companies go green: A model of ecological responsiveness', *The Academy of Management Journal*, **43**(4), 717–736.

Bauer, T. N., B. Erdogan and S. Taylor (2012), 'Creating and maintaining environmentally sustainable organizations: Recruitment and on-boarding', in Susan E. Jackson, Deniz S. Ones and Stephan Dilchert (eds), *Managing Human Resources for Environmental Sustainability*, San Francisco, CA: Jossey-Bass, pp. 222–240.

Biel, A. and J. Thøgersen (2007), 'Activation of social norms in social dilemmas: A review of the evidence and reflections on the implications for environmental behaviour', *Journal of Economic Psychology*, **28**(1), 93–112.

Blok, V., R. Wesselink, O. Studynka and R. Kemp (2015), 'Encouraging sustainability in the workplace: A survey on the pro-environmental behaviour of university employees', *Journal of Cleaner Production*, **106**, 55–67.

Boiral, O. (2009), 'Greening the corporation through organizational citizenship behaviors', *Journal of Business Ethics*, **87**(2), 221–236.

Boiral, O. and P. Paillé (2012), 'Organizational citizenship behaviour for the environment: Measurement and validation', *Journal of Business Ethics*, **109**(4), 431–445.

Borman, W. C. and S. J. Motowidlo (1993), 'Expanding the criterion domain to include elements of contextual performance', in Neal Schmitt and Walter C. Borman (eds), *Personnel Selection in Organizations*, San Francisco, CA: Jossey-Bass, pp. 71–98.

Bratt, C., P. C. Stern, E. Matthies and V. Nenseth (2015), 'Home, car use, and vacation: The structure of environmentally significant individual behavior', *Environment and Behavior*, **47**(4), 436–473.

Buchan, H. F. (2005), 'Ethical decision making in the public accounting profession: An extension of Ajzen's theory of planned behavior', *Journal of Business Ethics*, **61**(2), 165–181.

Carpenter, T. D. and J. L. Reimers (2005), 'Unethical and fraudulent financial reporting: Applying the theory of planned behavior', *Journal of Business Ethics*, **60**(2), 115–129.

Carrico, A. R. and M. Riemer (2011), 'Motivating energy conservation in the workplace: An evaluation of the use of group-level feedback and peer education', *Journal of Environmental Psychology*, **31**(1), 1–13.

Carrus, G., P. Passafaro and M. Bonnes (2008), 'Emotions, habits and rational choices in ecological behaviours: The case of recycling and use of public transportation', *Journal of Environmental Psychology*, **28**(1), 51–62.

Chatman, J. A. (1989), 'Improving interactional organizational research: A model of person-organization fit', *Academy of Management Review*, **14**(3), 333–349.

Cialdini, R. B., R. R. Reno and C. A. Kallgren (1990), 'A focus theory of normative conduct: Recycling the concept of norms to reduce littering in public places', *Journal of Personality and Social Psychology*, **58**(6), 1015–1026.

Ciocirlan, C. E. (2016), 'Environmental workplace behaviors: Definition matters', *Organization & Environment*, **30**(1), 51–70.

Cohen, J., Y. Ding, C. Lesage and H. Stolowy (2010), 'Corporate fraud and managers' behavior: Evidence from the press', *Journal of Business Ethics*, **95**(2), 271–315.

Cordano, M. and I. H. Frieze (2000), 'Pollution reduction preferences of US environmental managers: Applying Ajzen's theory of planned behavior', *The Academy of Management Journal*, **43**(4), 627–641.

Cordano, M., R. S. Marshall and M. Silverman (2010), 'How do small and medium enterprises go "green"? A study of environmental management programs in the US wine industry', *Journal of Business Ethics*, **92**(3), 463–478.

Cropanzano, R. and M. S. Mitchell (2005), 'Social exchange theory: An interdisciplinary review', *Journal of Management*, **31**(6), 874–900.

Cummings, L. S. (2008), 'Managerial attitudes toward environmental management within Australia, the People's Republic of China and Indonesia', *Business Strategy and the Environment*, **17**(1), 16–29.

Daily, B. F., J. W. Bishop and N. Govindarajulu (2009), 'A conceptual model for organizational citizenship behaviour directed toward the environment', *Business & Society*, **48**(2), 243–256.

Dilchert, S. and D. S. Ones (2012), 'Measuring and improving environmental sustainability', in Susan E. Jackson, Deniz S. Ones and Stephan Dilchert (eds), *Managing Human Resources for Environmental Sustainability*, San Francisco, CA: Jossey-Bass, pp. 187–221.

Egri, C. P. and S. Herman (2000), 'Leadership in the North American environmental sector: Values, leadership styles, and contexts of environmental leaders and their organizations', *Academy of Management Journal*, **43**(4), 571–604.

Ervin, D., J. Wu, M. Khanna, C. Jones and T. Wirkkala (2013), 'Motivations and barriers to corporate environmental management', *Business Strategy and the Environment*, **22**(6), 390–409.

Flannery, B. L. and D. R. May (2000), 'Environmental ethical decision making in the US metal-finishing industry', *The Academy of Management Journal*, **43**(4), 642–662.

Gadenne, D. L., J. Kennedy and C. McKeiver (2009), 'An empirical study of environmental awareness and practices in SMEs', *Journal of Business Ethics*, **84**(1), 45–63.

Graves, L. M., J. Sarkis and Q. Zhu (2013), 'How transformational leadership and employee motivation combine to predict employee proenvironmental behaviors in China', *Journal of Environmental Psychology*, **35**, 81–91.

Gregory, G. D. and M. Di Leo (2003), 'Repeated behavior and environmental psychology: The role of personal involvement and habit formation in explaining water consumption', *Journal of Applied Social Psychology*, **33**(6), 1261–1296.

Harland, P., H. Staats and H. A. M. Wilke (1999), 'Explaining proenvironmental intention and behavior by personal norms and the theory of planned behavior', *Journal of Applied Social Psychology*, **29**(12), 2505–2528.

Heath, Y. and R. Gifford (2002), 'Extending the theory of planned behavior: Predicting the use of public transportation', *Journal of Applied Social Psychology*, **32**(10), 2154–2189.

Holland, R. W., H. Aarts and D. Langendam (2006), 'Breaking and creating habits on the working floor: A field-experiment on the power of implementation intentions', *Journal of Experimental Social Psychology*, **42**(6), 776–783.

Howard-Grenville, J. A. (2006), 'Inside the black box: How organizational culture and subcultures inform interpretations and actions on environmental issues', *Organization & Environment*, **19**(1), 46–73.

Hunecke, M., A. Blöbaum, E. Matthies and R. Hoger (2001), 'Responsibility and environment: Ecological norm orientation and external factors in the domain of travel mode choice behavior', *Environment and Behavior*, **33**(6), 830–852.

Hurtz, G. M. and K. J. Williams (2009), 'Attitudinal and motivational antecedents of participation in voluntary employee development activities', *Journal of Applied Psychology*, **94**(3), 635–653.

James, L. R., C. C. Choi, C.-H. E. Ko, P. K. McNeil, M. K. Minton, M. A. Wright and K.-I. Kim (2008), 'Organizational and psychological climate: A review of theory and research', *European Journal of Work and Organizational Psychology*, **17**(1), 5–32.

Juárez-Nájera, M., J. G. Rivera-Martínez and W. A. Hafkamp (2010), 'An explorative socio-psychological model for determining sustainable behavior: Pilot study in German and Mexican Universities', *Journal of Cleaner Production*, **18**(7), 686–694.

Kaiser, F. G., M. Ranney, T. Hartig and P. A. Bowler (1999), 'Ecological behavior, environmental attitude, and feelings of responsibility for the environment', *European Psychologist*, **4**(2), 59–74.

Karlin, B., N. Davis, A. Sanguinetti, K. Gamble, D. Kirkby and D. Stokols (2014), 'Dimensions of conservation: Exploring differences among energy behaviors', *Environment and Behavior*, **46**(4), 423–452.

Klöckner, C. A. and A. Blöbaum (2010), 'A comprehensive action determination model: Toward a broader understanding of ecological behaviour using the example of travel mode choice', *Journal of Environmental Psychology*, **30**(4), 574–586.

Klöckner, C. A. and E. Matthies (2004), 'How habits interfere with norm-directed behaviour: A normative decision-making model for travel mode choice', *Journal of Environmental Psychology*, **24**(3), 319–327.

Klöckner, C. A. and I. O. Oppedal (2011), 'General vs. domain specific recycling behaviour – Applying a multilevel comprehensive action determination model to recycling in Norwegian student homes', *Resources, Conservation and Recycling*, **55**(4), 463–471.

Lamm, E., J. Tosti-Kharas and E. G. Williams (2013), 'Read this article, but don't print it: Organizational citizenship behavior toward the environment', *Group & Organization Management*, **38**(2), 163–197.

Larson, L. R., R. C. Stedman, C. B. Cooper and D. J. Decker (2015), 'Understanding the multi-dimensional structure of pro-environmental behavior', *Journal of Environmental Psychology*, **43**, 112–124.

Limayem, M., S. G. Hirt and C. M. K. Cheung (2007), 'How habit limits the predictive power of intention: The case of information system continuance', *MIS Quarterly*, **31**(4), 705–737.

Lo, S. H., G.-J. Y. Peters and G. Kok (2012), 'Energy-related behaviors in office buildings: A qualitative study on individual and organisational determinants', *Applied Psychology*, **61**(2), 227–249.

Lo, S. H., G.-J. Y. Peters, G. J. P. van Breukelen and G. Kok (2014), 'Only reasoned action? An interorganizational study of energy-saving behaviors in office buildings', *Energy Efficiency*, **7**(5), 761–775.

Lülfs, R. and R. Hahn (2013), 'Corporate greening beyond formal programs, initiatives, and systems: A conceptual model for voluntary pro-environmental behavior of employees', *European Management Review*, **10**(2), 83–98.

Lülfs, R. and R. Hahn (2014), 'Sustainable behavior in the business sphere: A comprehensive overview of the explanatory power of psychological models', *Organization & Environment*, **27**(1), 43–64.

Mannetti, L., A. Pierro and S. Livi (2004), 'Recycling: Planned and self-expressive behaviour', *Journal of Environmental Psychology*, **24**(2), 227–236.

Martin-Peña, M. L., E. Díaz-Garrido and J. M. Sánchez López (2010), 'Relation between management's behavioural intentions toward the environment and environmental actions', *Journal of Environmental Planning and Management*, **53**(3), 297–315.

Milne, S., P. Sheeran and S. Orbell (2000), 'Prediction and intervention in health-related behavior: A meta-analytic review of protection motivation theory', *Journal of Applied Social Psychology*, **30**(1), 106–143.

Nordlund, A. M. and J. Garvil (2013), 'Effects of values, problem awareness, and personal norm on willingness to reduce personal car use', *Journal of Environmental Psychology*, **23**(4), 339–347.

Norton, T. A., H. Zacher and N. M. Ashkanasy (2012), 'On the importance of pro-environmental organizational climate for employee green behavior', *Industrial and Organizational Psychology*, **5**(4), 497–500.

Norton, T. A., H. Zacher and N. M. Ashkanasy (2014), 'Organisational sustainability policies and employee green behaviour: The mediating role of work climate perceptions', *Journal of Environmental Psychology*, **38**, 49–54.

Ones, D. S. and S. Dilchert (2012a), 'Employee green behaviors', in Susan E. Jackson, Deniz S. Ones and Stephan Dilchert (eds), *Managing Human Resources for Environmental Sustainability*, San Francisco, CA: Jossey-Bass, pp. 85–116.

Ones, D. S. and S. Dilchert (2012b), 'Environmental sustainability at work: A call to action', *Industrial and Organizational Psychology*, **5**(4), 444–466.

Organ, D. W. (1997), 'Organizational citizenship behavior: It's construct clean-up time', *Human Performance*, **10**(2), 85–97.

Organ, D. W., P. M. Podsakoff and S. B. MacKenzie (2006), *Organizational Citizenship Behavior: Its Nature, Antecedents, and Consequences*, Thousand Oaks, CA: Sage Publications.

Paillé, P. and O. Boiral (2013), 'Pro-environmental behavior at work: Construct validity and determinants', *Journal of Environmental Psychology*, **36**, 118–128.

Paillé, P. and J. H. Mejía-Morelos (2014), 'Antecedents of pro-environmental behaviours at work: The moderating influence of psychological contract breach', *Journal of Environmental Psychology*, **34**, 124–131.

Paillé, P., O. Boiral and Y. Chen (2013), 'Linking environmental management practices and organizational citizenship behaviour for the environment: A social exchange perspective', *International Journal of Human Resource Management*, **24**(18), 3552–3575.

Paillé, P., J. H. Mejía-Morelos, A. Marché-Paillé, C. C. Chen and Y. Chen (2016), 'Corporate greening, exchange process among co-workers, and ethics of care: An empirical study on the determinants of pro-environmental behaviors at coworkers-level', *Journal of Business Ethics*, **136**(3), 655–673.

Papagiannakis, G. and S. Lioukas (2012), 'Values, attitudes and perceptions of managers as predictors of corporate environmental responsiveness', *Journal of Environmental Management*, **100**, 41–51.

Perugini, M. and R. P. Bagozzi (2001), 'The role of desires and anticipated emotions in goal-directed behaviours: Broadening and deepening the theory of planned behaviour', *British Journal of Social Psychology*, **40**(1), 79–98.

Poortinga, W., L. Steg and C. Vlek (2004), 'Values, environmental concern, and environmental behavior: A study into household energy use', *Environment and Behavior*, **36**(1), 70–93.

Ramus, C. A. and A. B. C. Killmer (2007), 'Corporate greening through prosocial extrarole behaviours – a conceptual framework for employee motivation', *Business Strategy and the Environment*, **16**(8), 554–570.

Ramus, C. A. and U. Steger (2000), 'The roles of supervisory support behaviors and environmental policy in employee "ecoinitiatives" at leading-edge European companies', *Academy of Management Journal*, **43**(4), 605–626.

Riketta, M. (2002), 'Attitudinal organizational commitment and job performance: A meta-analysis', *Journal of Organizational Behavior*, **23**, 257–266.

Robertson, J. L. and J. Barling (2013), 'Greening organizations through leaders' influence on employees' pro-environmental behaviors', *Journal of Organizational Behavior*, **34**(2), 176–194.

Scherbaum, C. A., P. M. Popovich and S. Finlinson (2008), 'Exploring individual-level factors related to employee energy-conservation behaviors at work', *Journal of Applied Social Psychology*, **38**(3), 818–835.

Schmit, M. J., S. Fegley, E. Esen, J. Schramm and A. Tomassetti (2012), 'Human resource management efforts for environmental sustainability', in Susan E. Jackson, Deniz S. Ones and Stephan Dilchert (eds), *Managing Human Resources for Environmental Sustainability*, San Francisco, CA: Jossey-Bass, pp. 61–83.

Schultz, P. W., S. Oskamp and T. Mainieri (1995), 'Who recycles and when? A review of personal and situational factors', *Journal of Environmental Psychology*, **15**(2), 105–121.

Schwartz, S. H. (1973), 'Normative explanations of helping behaviour: A critique, proposal and empirical test', *Journal of Experimental Social Psychology*, **9**, 349–364.

Schwartz, S. H. (1977), 'Normative influences on altruism', *Advances in Experimental Social Psychology*, **10**, 221–280.

Schwartz, S. H. and J. A. Howard (1981), 'A normative decision-making model of altruism', in J. Philippe Rushton and Richard M. Sorrentino (eds), *Altruism and Helping Behavior*, Hillsdale, NJ: Lawrence Erlbaum Associates, pp. 89–211.

Schwenk, G. and G. Möser (2009), 'Intention and behavior: A Bayesian meta-analysis with focus on the Ajzen–Fishbein Model in the field of environmental behavior', *Quality & Quantity*, **43**(5), 743–755.

Sheeran, P. (2002), 'Intention-behavior relations: A conceptual and empirical review', in Wolfgang Stroebe and Miles Hewstone (eds), *European Review of Social Psychology*, Chichester: Psychology Press, pp. 1–36.

Stern, P. C. (2000), 'New environmental theories: Toward a coherent theory of environmentally significant behavior', *Journal of Social Issues*, **56**(3), 407–424.

Stern, P. C., T. Dietz, T. Abel, G. A. Guagnano and L. Kalof (1999), 'A value-belief-norm theory of support for social movements: The case of environmentalism', *Human Ecological Review*, **6**(2), 81–97.

Tang, Z., X. Chen and J. Luo (2011), 'Determining sociopsychological drivers for rural household recycling behaviour in developing countries: A case study from Wugan, Hunan, China', *Environment and Behavior*, **43**(6), 848–877.

Taylor, S. and P. Todd (1995), 'An integrated model of waste management behavior: A test of household recycling and composting intentions', *Environment and Behavior*, **27**(5), 603–630.

Temminck, E., K. Mearns and L. Fruhen (2015), 'Motivating employees towards sustainable behaviour', *Business Strategy and the Environment*, **24**(6), 402–412.

Thøgersen, J. (1999), 'The ethical consumer. Moral norms and packaging choice', *Journal of Consumer Policy*, **22**(4), 439–460.

Thøgersen, J. (2006), 'Norms for environmentally responsible behaviour: An extended taxonomy', *Journal of Environmental Psychology*, **26**(4), 247–261.

Tosti-Kharas, J., E. Lamm and T. E. Thomas (2016), 'Organization or environment? Disentangling employees rationales behind organizational citizenship behavior for the environment', *Organization & Environment*, Online First, DOI: 10.1177/1086026616668381.

Triandis, H. C. (1977), *Interpersonal Behavior*, Monterey, CA: Brooks/Cole Publications.

Tudor, T. L., S. W. Barr and A. W. Gilg (2007), 'Linking intended behaviour and actions: A case study of healthcare waste management in the Cornwall NHS', *Resources, Conservation and Recycling*, **51**(1), 1–23.

Tudor, T. L., S. W. Barr and A. W. Gilg (2008), 'A novel conceptual framework for examining environmental behaviour in large organizations: A case study of the Cornwall national health service (NHS) in the United Kingdom', *Environment and Behavior*, **40**(3), 426–450.

Unsworth, K. L., A. Dmitrieva and E. Adriasola (2013), 'Changing behaviour: Increasing the effectiveness of workplace interventions in creating pro-environmental behaviour change', *Journal of Organizational Behavior*, **34**(2), 211–229.

Van Scotter, J., S. J. Motowidlo and T. C. Cross (2000), 'Effects of task performance and contextual performance on systemic rewards', *Journal of Applied Psychology*, **85**(4), 526–535.

Vazquez Brust, D. A. and C. Liston-Heyes (2010), 'Environmental management intentions: An empirical investigation of Argentina's polluting firms', *Journal of Environmental Management*, **91**(5), 1111–1122.

Verplanken, B. and W. Wood (2006), 'Interventions to break and create consumer habits', *Journal of Public Policy & Marketing*, **25**(1), 90–103.

Verplanken, B., H. Aarts and A. van Knippenberg (1997), 'Habit, information acquisition, and the process of making travel mode choices', *European Journal of Social Psychology*, **27**(5), 539–560.

Verplanken, B., I. Walker, A. Davis and M. Jurasek (2008), 'Context change and travel mode choice: Combining the habit discontinuity and self-activation hypotheses', *Journal of Environmental Psychology*, **28**(2), 121–127.

Vlachos, P. A., N. G. Panagopoulos and A. A. Rapp (2016), 'Employee judgments of and behaviors toward corporate social responsibility: A multi-study investigation of direct, cascading, and moderating effects', *Journal of Organizational Behavior*, **35**(7), 990–1017.

Wall, R., P. Devine-Wright and G. A. Mill (2007), 'Comparing and combining theories to explain proenvironmental intentions: The case of commuting-mode choice', *Environment and Behavior*, **39**(6), 731–753.

Warburton, J. and D. J. Terry (2000), 'Volunteer decision-making by older people: A test of a revised theory of planned behavior', *Basic and Applied Social Psychology*, **22**(3), 245–257.

Webb, T. L. and P. Sheeran (2006), 'Does changing behavioural intentions engender behavior change? A meta-analysis of the experimental evidence', *Psychological Bulletin*, **132**(2), 249–268.

Zutshi, A. and A. S. Sohal (2003), 'Stakeholder involvement in the EMS adoption process', *Business Process Management Journal*, **9**(2), 133–148.

6. Environmental considerations as a basis for employee pro-environmental behaviour
Angela Ruepert and Linda Steg

6.1 INTRODUCTION

The world is facing serious environmental problems due to greenhouse gas emissions and pollution (Du Nann Winter and Koger 2004; Steg and Vlek 2009; Vlek and Steg 2007). Organisations contribute to such environmental problems by using natural resources, raw materials and energy (Robertson and Barling 2015). Many organisations recognise their responsibility in mitigating environmental problems and explicitly aim to realise corporate environmental responsibility (CER). CER implies that organisations have the goal to enhance their environmental performance (Dahlsrud 2008), to reduce their environmental impact. Importantly, genuine CER not only implies that pro-environmental goals are explicit in the mission of the organisation, but also that adequate strategies have been implemented to realise these goals, that environmental performance outcomes are monitored, and that additional actions are taken where needed (Steg et al. 2003). To enhance their environmental performance, organisations not only need to reduce the environmental impact of their production and organisational processes, but also encourage pro-environmental behaviour among their employees (Dixon et al. 2015). Pro-environmental behaviour can be defined as behaviour that harms the environment as little as possible or even benefits it. Encouraging pro-environmental behaviour at the workplace is thus key for CER, and ultimately in reducing environmental problems.

Until now, studies on pro-environmental behaviour have typically focused on factors influencing private or household pro-environmental behaviour, while less is known about pro-environmental behaviour at work. Studies on private and household pro-environmental behaviour yielded important insights in factors encouraging such behaviour, as we will explain below. Yet, the question remains if similar factors would also influence pro-environmental behaviour at work.

Encouraging pro-environmental behaviour at work (as well as in the private sphere) can be challenging, as many pro-environmental behaviours imply a conflict between individual benefits in the short-term and long-term benefits for the environment (De Groot and Steg 2009; Nordlund and Garvill 2002). For example, taking public transportation instead of the car to work is often considered to be less comfortable (Redman et al. 2013), and switching off the computer when leaving the office for a longer time can be perceived as more time consuming and less convenient than leaving it on. In the current chapter, we will discuss why employees may be willing and likely to behave pro-environmentally, even though it may be somewhat costly, effortful or inconvenient. Considering the scope of environmental problems, it is important that people do not only engage in single pro-environmental behaviours, but that they consistently engage in many different pro-environmental behaviours. Therefore, it seems specifically relevant to consider generic factors influencing pro-environmental actions that are likely to influence many different behaviours over and again, in different contexts. Such generic factors could influence behaviours at work in a similar way, and via similar processes, as behaviour at home.

Even though behaving pro-environmentally is somewhat costly or bothersome, research on pro-environmental behaviour in the private sphere has shown that many people are willing and motivated to engage in pro-environmental behaviours (Abrahamse et al. 2007; Harland et al. 2007; Steg et al. 2014a). They are more motivated and willing to engage in pro-environmental behaviour when they are focused on doing the right thing and benefiting the environment, rather than merely on the convenience and financial costs related to pro-environmental behaviours (Lindenberg and Steg 2007; Lindenberg 2012; Steg et al. 2014a). Hence, a key question is which factors determine the extent to which people focus on benefiting the environment and to what extent this in turn influences people's willingness to engage in pro-environmental behaviour at work. The Integrated Framework for Encouraging Pro-environmental Behaviour (IFEP; Steg et al. 2014a) proposes that the extent to which people are focused on the environment depends on the values people strongly endorse and on contextual factors that make them focus on value-relevant consequences. Values provide a stable basis for, and determine the a priori strength of, people's focus on benefiting the environment, while contextual factors may further strengthen people's focus on benefiting the environment by making these values accessible or by additionally steering people's focus towards environmental aspects.

In this chapter, we will first discuss which values are important for employee pro-environmental behaviour, and explain that particularly biospheric values (i.e., valuing nature and the environment) are a consistent predictor of pro-environmental actions. Subsequently, we will discuss the process through which biospheric values influence pro-environmental behaviour at work. Next, we will discuss how contextual factors can influence the likelihood that people act upon different values, thereby influencing the likelihood that people engage in pro-environmental behaviour at work.

6.2   WHICH VALUES ARE IMPORTANT TO UNDERSTAND PRO-ENVIRONMENTAL BEHAVIOUR AT WORK?

Values are defined as 'desirable goals, varying in importance, that serve as guiding principles in people's lives' (Schwartz 1992: 21). Values reflect the general goals people strive for in their lives that may affect various beliefs, norms and actions in different contexts. Values determine what people attend to, how people evaluate various aspects of a situation and what choices are being made. Values are abstract and general and remain relatively stable over time (Stern 2000). People differ in the extent to which they endorse different values and this affects which consequences they consider when making choices, how they evaluate different options and which choices they make. Notably, people seem to particularly attend to and consider consequences of choices that have important implications for their core values (Perlaviciute and Steg 2015; Steg et al. 2014a; Stern et al. 1995). Depending on the consequences for their core values, they will form an overall evaluation of a behavioural option. When a behavioural option has positive consequences for their core values, they will evaluate it positively, while options that are expected to have negative consequences for their core values will be evaluated negatively. Next, based on this overall evaluation, other consequences of choices that do not have important implications for their core values, may also then be evaluated positively or negatively (Perlaviciute and Steg 2015).

Four types of values are particularly relevant to understand environmental behaviour: egoistic, hedonic, altruistic and biospheric values (e.g., De Groot and Steg 2008; Steg et al. 2014b). People with strong egoistic values will particularly consider the individual costs and benefits of behavioural choices. People with strong hedonic values particularly consider pleasure and effort when making choices. Both egoistic and hedonic values reflect self-enhancement values, making it more likely that people consider how choices will impact on them personally and act in their self-interest. Egoistic and hedonic values oftentimes inhibit pro-environmental actions, especially when such actions are somewhat costly and effortful. People with strong altruistic values are especially concerned about the welfare of other people and society, while people with strong biospheric values particularly consider consequences for nature and the environment. Both altruistic and biospheric values reflect self-transcendent values, and make people particularly consider collective consequences of actions. Altruistic and particularly biospheric values generally promote pro-environmental actions.

Research has shown that biospheric values that reflect a key concern with nature and the environment are the most important and consistent predictor of different types of pro-environmental behaviours (e.g., De Groot and Steg 2008; Dietz et al. 2005; Honkanen and Verplanken 2004; Stern et al. 1999). People who strongly endorse biospheric values are more likely to focus on and consider what implications different behavioural options have for the environment. The stronger their biospheric values, the more motivated people are to act in a way that benefits (or causes the least damage to) the environment. Importantly, because values are considered to be relatively stable over time and to transcend situations (Stern 2000), biospheric values would be an important predictor of different types of pro-environmental behaviours in different contexts, not only at home but also at work.

6.3 THE PROCESS THROUGH WHICH BIOSPHERIC VALUES INFLUENCE EMPLOYEE PRO-ENVIRONMENTAL BEHAVIOUR

Because values reflect the abstract and general goals people strive for in life, they mainly predict pro-environmental behaviour indirectly. An important route through which biospheric values promote pro-environmental behaviour is via environmental self-identity. Environmental self-identity reflects the extent to which an individual sees him or herself as a type of person who acts pro-environmentally (Van der Werff et al. 2013a). Research on environmental behaviour in the private sphere has shown that the stronger a person sees taking care of nature and the environment as a guiding principle in his or her life (i.e., has strong biospheric values), the more likely this person is to see him or herself as a person who acts pro-environmentally (i.e., has strong environment self-identity; Mannetti et al. 2004; Van der Werff et al. 2013a; Van der Werff et al. 2013b; Van der Werff et al. 2014a). People with a strong environmental self-identity are more likely to engage in pro-environmental behaviour because they are motivated to be, or appear to be, consistent and thus to act in line with how they see themselves (Van der Werff et al. 2013a). Research on environmental behaviour in the private sphere revealed that environmental self-identity affects pro-environmental behaviour by strengthening personal norms to act pro-environmentally (Van der Werff et al. 2013b). Personal norms reflect self-expectations and are experienced as feelings of moral obligation to engage in the relevant behaviour (Schwartz 1977). Individuals with strong personal norms to act pro-environmentally feel morally obliged to behave accordingly, because doing so makes them feel good, while not doing so would make them feel bad (e.g., guilty; Scherbaum et al. 2008; Van der Werff et al. 2013b).

Personal norms may be conceptualised at the general level, such as personal norms to engage in pro-environmental behaviour in general, or at a specific level, for example the personal norm to recycle or the personal norm to reduce household energy use (Carrus et al. 2008; Steg et al. 2011). Studies revealed that strong general, as well as specific, environmental personal norms encourage different pro-environmental behaviours, such as turning off the tap while brushing one's teeth (Harland et al. 2007), willingness to pay higher prices for environmentally friendly food (Wiidegren 1998), intention to participate in actions to reduce emissions of particulate matter (Steg and De Groot 2010), reductions in car use (Nordlund and Garvill 2003), participation in smart energy projects (Van der Werff and Steg 2016), as well as pro-environmental actions in general (e.g., Nordlund and Garvill 2002; Van der Werff et al. 2013b). Yet, it seems that people are most likely to act upon their personal norms when this behaviour is not too costly and when they do not perceive significant barriers for doing so (Bamberg and Schmidt 2003; Steg and Vlek 2009). It seems that people are willing to incur some personal costs (e.g., in the sense of money, time or effort) and act upon their personal norms to benefit the environment, but if the context seriously constrains such behaviours and the behavioural costs are too high, individuals may not act upon their personal norms (Thøgersen 1996). When the context seriously constrains pro-environmental behaviour or when the behavioural costs are rather high, people can reduce unpleasant feelings by not acting upon personal norms via self-serving denial. For example, they can deny the seriousness of environmental problems, reject their liability for these problems, deny their personal ability or competence to perform the necessary actions, or indicate that individual pro-environmental actions are not effective in reducing environmental problems (Lindenberg and Steg 2007).

In sum, biospheric values are likely to affect pro-environmental behaviour at work by influencing environmental self-identity and personal norms to act pro-environmentally. This is captured in the values–identity–personal norms model (VIP model) to explain pro-environmental behaviour at work. Notably, the VIP model proposes that people with relatively strong biospheric values are more likely to have a stronger environmental

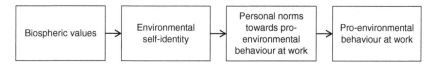

Figure 6.1   Values–Identity–Personal (VIP) norms model to explain
how environmental considerations predict pro-environmental
behaviour at work

self-identity, thus seeing themselves more as the type of person who acts pro-environmentally (Van der Werff et al. 2013a). Next, the VIP model proposes that people are motivated to behave in line with their environmental self-identity, because they feel morally obliged to do so, as reflected in strong personal norms to act pro-environmentally at work, which will in turn encourage pro-environmental actions (see Figure 6.1).

6.3.1   Illustration – Testing the VIP Model to Predict Employee Pro-environmental Behaviour

Studies have mostly tested parts of the VIP model and focused on pro-environmental behaviour in the private sphere. A recent study tested the full VIP model to explain employee pro-environmental behaviour (Ruepert et al. 2016).

Method

A questionnaire study was conducted among a sample of employees from four large-scale organisations in different European countries, including two state organisations (a municipality in the Netherlands and a university in Spain), and two service providers in the field of natural resources (a public water and wastewater service provider in Romania and an energy supplier in Italy).

Biospheric values were measured by a 16-item value scale reflecting biospheric, altruistic, egoistic and hedonic values (Steg et al. 2014b). Participants rated the importance of each value as a guiding principle in their life on a scale from −1 (opposed to my values) to 7 (of supreme importance). Biospheric values were represented by four items (*Respecting the earth*: harmony with other species; *Unity with nature*: fitting into nature; *Protecting the environment*: preserving nature; *Preventing pollution*: protecting natural resources). Mean score of the four biospheric values items was computed ($M = 5.3$, $SD = 1.34$); the resulting biospheric values scale showed high internal consistency ($\alpha = .87$).

Environmental self-identity was measured by a three-item scale: 'Acting pro-environmentally is an important part of who I am', 'I am the type of person who acts pro-environmentally' and 'I see myself as a pro-environmental person' (Van der Werff et al. 2014a). Scores on these items could range from 1 (totally disagree) to 7 (totally agree). Mean scores on these items were computed ($M = 5.3$, $SD = 1.27$); the internal consistency of the resulting environmental self-identity scale was high ($\alpha = .91$).

Personal norms to engage in pro-environmental behaviour at work were measured with four items: 'I feel guilty if I do not act pro-environmentally at work', 'I feel morally obliged to act pro-environmentally at work', 'I feel proud when I act pro-environmentally at work', and 'I would violate my principles if I would not act pro-environmentally at work' (adapted from Steg and De Groot 2010). Items were scored on a scale ranging from 1 (totally disagree) to 7 (totally agree). Mean scores of these items were computed ($M = 5.1$, $SD = 1.34$); the internal consistency of the personal norms scale was high ($\alpha = .84$).

Pro-environmental behaviour at work was measured by asking how often employees engaged in different environmental behaviour. Based on interviews with key people in the case studies, behaviours over which employees would have control to some extent were identified. An impact-oriented measure of environmental behaviour was employed (cf. Gatersleben 2012), by assessing energy use and the environmental impact of behaviour via a methodology developed by environmental scientists of the Centre of Energy and Environmental Sciences of the University of Groningen (IVEM), which has been successfully used in earlier studies (e.g., Abrahamse and Steg 2011; Gatersleben et al. 2002). Two types of self-reported behaviours, which are generally believed to have a positive impact on the environment (i.e., waste prevention and recycling) and two types of self-reported behaviours with a negative impact (i.e., energy use at the workplace and energy use related to transport) were included.

Waste prevention was measured with the following two items, with scores ranging from 1 (never) to 7 (always): 'At work how often do you read emails from the computer screen rather than printing them?', and 'At work how often do you use as little paper as possible when printing (e.g., 2 pages per paper, two-sided etc.)?'. Environmental scientists of the IVEM assessed that using as little paper as possible benefits the environment on average 7.3 times as much than reading emails from the computer screen instead of printing them. Therefore, the environmental impact of these behaviours was assessed by weighing the scores on the item on using as little paper as possible 7.3 times more than the scores on the item on reading from the computer screen instead of printing before aggregating the scores on both scales. Data were transformed so that scores on waste prevention could range from 1 (never) to 7 (always) ($M = 5.8$, $SD = 1.29$).

Recycling was measured with one item: 'How often do you separate your paper from the regular garbage at work?'. Therefore, there was no need to transform the data to assess environmental impact. Scores on this item ranged from 1 (never) to 7 (always) ($M = 5.8$, $SD = 1.84$).

Energy use at the workplace was assessed on the basis of four items, of which one item was an open-ended question ('How many hours a day are the lights on at your workspace?') and three items were scored on a scale ranging from 1 (never) to 7 (always) ('How often do you have the lights on at your workspace when there is no one in there?', 'How often do you switch the lights off in your workspace when you go home and nobody is left in your workspace?', and 'At work how often do you switch your computer off when you go home?'). Environmental scientists from IVEM assessed energy use at the workplace on the basis of these four items ($M = 25.5$ MJ, $SD = 4.52$).

Energy use related to transport was assessed by four items, of which one item was an open-ended question ('How many kilometres per week do you on average travel for work by car (business trips)?') and three items were scored on a scale ranging from 1 (never) to 7 (always): 'When you travel for work (business trips), how often do you travel by car?', 'When you commute or drive for work purposes (business trips), how often do you drive in an energy efficient way (looking ahead and anticipating on traffic, brake and accelerate quietly, and change to a higher gear as soon as possible)?', and 'When you drive for work (business trips), how often do you carpool rather than drive alone?'. Environmental scientists from IVEM assessed energy use related to transport with these four items ($M = 153.4$ MJ, $SD = 427.69$).

Results

The first part of the VIP model was supported: stronger biospheric values were associated with a stronger environmental self-identity ($R^2 = .34$; $F(1,530) = 273.73$, $\beta = .58$, $p < .001$). In turn, the more employees see themselves as the kind of person who acts pro-environmentally, the stronger their personal norm to act pro-environmentally at work ($R^2 = .63$; $F(1,519) = 883.57$, $\beta = .79$, $p < .001$). Moreover, as expected, environmental self-identity mediated the relationship between biospheric values and personal norms to behave pro-environmentally at work. The mean indirect effect from the bootstrap analysis with 1000 resamples derived from the full sample was positive and significant (a x b = .39). The bias-corrected bootstrap estimate of the indirect effect had a 95 per cent confidence interval ranging from .33 to .45. In the indirect path, a unit increase in biospheric values increased environmental self-identity by a = .51. Holding biospheric values constant, a unit increase in environmental

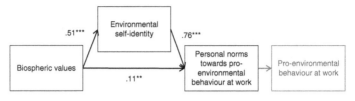

Notes: ** p < .01; *** p < .001.

*Figure 6.2   The influence of biospheric values on personal norms towards
pro-environmental behaviour at work*

self-identity increased personal norms to behave pro-environmentally
at work by b = .76. The direct effect (c = .50) of biospheric values
on personal norms to behave pro-environmentally at work was also
positive and significant (*p* < .001). Holding environmental self-identity
constant, a unit increase in biospheric values increased personal norms
by c = .11. This implies that biospheric values affected personal norms
to act pro-environmentally at work both directly as well as indirectly via
environmental self-identity (see Figure 6.2).

Next, the effect of personal norms on the different behaviours was
tested. As expected, personal norms towards pro-environmental behaviour
at work was positively related to different pro-environmental behaviours
at work (see Figure 6.3), but the relationships were rather weak; the
explained variance ranged from 1 per cent to 4 per cent. More specifically,
regression analysis revealed that stronger personal norms to behave pro-
environmentally at work were associated with more waste prevention at
work (β = .29, *p* < .001), more recycling (β = .20, *p* < .001), and lower
energy use at the workplace (β = −.15, *p* < .01). Interestingly, stronger
personal norms to behave pro-environmentally at work were associated

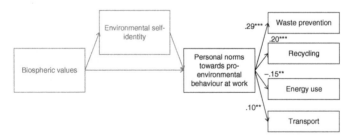

Notes: ** p < .01; *** p < .001.

*Figure 6.3   The influence of personal norms to behave pro-environmentally
at work on different types of environmental behaviour at work*

with a higher transport-related energy use ($\beta = .10$, $p = .03$). A possible explanation is that employees have limited control over the distance they need to travel for work purposes. When the distance driven for work purposes was excluded from the environmental impact of behaviour related to transport scale, stronger personal norms to act pro-environmentally at work were related to less energy use related to transport ($\beta = .20$, $p < .001$).

Discussion

Results revealed that employees with relatively strong biospheric values indeed have a stronger environmental self-identity, which in turn strengthened their feelings of moral obligation to behave pro-environmentally at work. These findings suggest that biospheric values are an important source of feelings of moral obligation to behave pro-environmentally at work, and that employees with relatively strong biospheric values seem to accept the importance of engaging in pro-environmental actions at the workplace. This implies that, in contrast to what some scholars have argued (Bolderdijk et al. 2013; Maio et al. 2001), employees seem to see pro-environmental behaviour at work as their personal responsibility.

The results of this study further showed that when employees have strong personal norms to behave pro-environmentally at work, they are somewhat more likely to use less energy at the workplace, to engage in energy-saving behaviour related to transport, to engage in waste prevention behaviour, and to recycle more. However, the relationships between personal norms and these environmental behaviours at work were not very strong. One reason for this relatively weak relationship may be that employees perceived significant barriers to engage in the behaviours included in the study, inhibiting them to act upon their personal norms. Indeed, as indicated above, research on pro-environmental behaviour at home has shown that personal norms are not always very predictive of behaviour; personal norms seem to be less strongly related to relatively costly behaviour (Bamberg and Schmidt 2003; Steg and Vlek 2009).

6.4 UNDER WHICH CONDITIONS DO ENVIRONMENTAL CONSIDERATIONS INFLUENCE EMPLOYEE PRO-ENVIRONMENTAL BEHAVIOUR?

The weak relationship between personal norms and pro-environmental behaviour at work suggests that the organisational context may inhibit some types of pro-environmental behaviour at work. These results point to a first important role of the context in influencing pro-environmental actions at work: pro-environmental actions are more likely when the context enables people to act upon their values. When behaviour is too costly, acting on biospheric values may threaten the fulfilment of other values, such as egoistic or hedonic values, that are important to people as well. Even those with strong biospheric values may not act pro-environmentally when the behaviour is very inconvenient or highly effortful.

Yet, contextual factors may not only affect pro-environmental behaviour at work by inhibiting or facilitating such behaviour; they may also affect the extent to which people are focused on benefiting the environment and thus the likelihood of pro-environmental behaviour at work. An example of such a contextual factor is the organisation's mission and the strategies that have been implemented to accomplish that mission. When an organisation mainly aims to generate profits, employees may be more likely to be focused on implications of behaviour for their egoistic values and they may be less focused on benefiting the environment. In contrast, when an organisation explicitly aims to reduce its environmental impact and aims to realise Corporate Environmental Responsibility (CER), the likelihood that employees are focused on benefiting the environment may increase, thus increasing the likelihood of pro-environmental actions at work. Another example is the task people are working on. Certain tasks can make people focus more on benefiting the environment and could thus influence the likelihood that people engage in pro-environmental behaviour. For example, when people are working on a project aimed at making the office building more energy efficient, they may be more focused on benefiting the environment in general than when they are working on a project aimed at reducing the production costs. Contextual factors can thus make people focus more on the environment and less on other considerations, thereby increasing the likelihood of pro-environmental behaviour.

Such contextual factors may not only affect the likelihood that people act upon the values they endorse, but they may also influence people differently depending on the extent to which they endorse different values. This would explain why people do not always act consistently across situations and do not always have stable preferences. Two lines of reasoning suggest that the effects of contextual factors, such as the organisation's ambition to realise CER, depends on the extent to which people endorse biospheric values, but they differ in whether effects of contextual factors on behaviour would be most significant for those with relatively strong versus weak biospheric values.

The literature on value activation would suggest that biospheric values will particularly encourage pro-environmental actions when these values are activated by contextual factors (such as CER), thereby reminding people of what they find important in life (i.e., the quality of nature and the environment; Hahnel et al. 2014; Verplanken and Holland 2002). Following this line of reasoning, contextual factors that make people focus on benefiting the environment are likely to particularly encourage pro-environmental actions among those who strongly value the environment in the first place, that is, people who strongly endorse biospheric values. In a similar vein, scholars have proposed that contextual factors that reduce people's focus on doing the right thing for the environment particularly affect those with relatively weak biospheric values (Steg et al. 2014a; Verplanken and Holland 2002). Such contextual factors, such as an organisation's ambition to increase profits, can remind those with relatively weak biospheric values that the quality of nature and the environment is not an important goal in their life, thereby reducing the likelihood that they will engage in pro-environmental behaviour.

Alternatively, it has been argued that people with strong biospheric values are a priori more strongly focused on doing the right thing for the environment and therefore can counteract influences of value-incongruent contextual factors (Kleingeld 2015; Steg et al. 2014a). Following this reasoning, contextual factors that strengthen people's focus on benefiting the environment would particularly encourage pro-environmental actions among those with relatively weak biospheric values, who are a priori less likely to focus on the environmental consequences of their choices. In other words, there is more potential for strengthening their focus on benefiting the environment and their motivation to behave pro-environmentally compared to those with relatively strong biospheric values. People with stronger biospheric values are a priori more strongly focused on benefiting the environment and therefore more likely to act pro-environmentally in many different situations. As such, strong biospheric values can serve as a buffer against the weakening effect of contextual factors that could make people less focused on benefiting the environment (Steg et al. 2014a). Recent research on the effect of the organisation's mission and strategies to accomplish that mission on pro-environmental behaviour at work has supported the latter reasoning (Ruepert et al. 2017).

6.4.1   Illustration – Testing the Influence of Contextual Factors and Biospheric Values on Pro-environmental Behaviour of Employees

This study examined to what extent the organisation's mission, and strategies to accomplish that mission (a contextual factor), affects pro-environmental behaviour at work, and whether this effect depends on the extent to which employees endorse biospheric value. The authors hypothesised that believing that an organisation has the ambition to realise CER

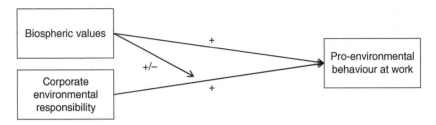

Figure 6.4   Theoretical model on the influence of CER and employees'
biospheric values on pro-environmental behaviour at work

(versus profit-making) will increase the likelihood that employees focus on benefiting the environment, in turn increasing the likelihood that they act pro-environmentally at work. Next, it was hypothesised that people are more likely to act pro-environmentally at work when they strongly endorse biospheric values. The authors further explored the interaction between CER (versus profit-making) and biospheric values on the likelihood of pro-environmental behaviour at work (see Figure 6.4).

Method
A questionnaire study was conducted among employees of a municipality in the Netherlands. The study measured biospheric values, perceptions of CER and pro-environmental behaviour.

Biospheric values strength was measured by a questionnaire consisting of 16 items representing four types of values: biospheric, altruistic, egoistic and hedonic values (Steg et al. 2014b). Participants rated the importance of each value as a guiding principle in their life on a scale from -1 (opposed to my values) to 7 (of supreme importance). Biospheric values were represented by four items (*Respecting the earth*: harmony with other species; *Unity with nature*: fitting into nature; *Protecting the environment*: preserving nature; *Preventing pollution*: protecting natural resources). The biospheric values scale showed high internal consistency ($\alpha = .98$). Therefore the mean score on these items was computed ($M = 4.8$, $SD = 1.41$).

Believing that the organisations aims to realise CER was measured with three items: 'My organisation has the goal to minimalise its impact on the environment', 'My organisation has implemented policy and procedures to minimalise its impact on the environment' and 'My organisation has stated in its mission to implement sustainable (pro-environmental) policy'. Answers were provided on a scale ranging from 1 (strongly disagree) to 7 (strongly agree). These three items showed high internal consistency ($\alpha = .82$). Therefore, the mean scores were computed ($M = 4.8$, $SD = 1.32$).

Pro-environmental behaviour was measured by asking the respondents to make several investment decisions in which they had to weigh environmental benefits against financial or convenience costs. Participants were asked to make five different hypothetical investment decisions. All investment decisions were made on a scale varying from 1 (much harm to the environment, but low [financial or convenience] costs) to 5 (little harm to the environment, but high [financial or convenience] costs). In two investment decisions, the pro-environmental option involved costs for the organisation, while in three investment decisions the pro-environmental option involved personal costs (financial or convenience) for the participant him- or herself. Mean scores across the five investment decisions were computed ($M = 3.7$, $SD = .66$, $\alpha = .71$).

Besides, self-reported environmental behaviour at work was measured, following the impact-oriented definition. Two types of pro-environmental behaviours related to waste handling were included: waste prevention ($M = 5.1$, $SD = 1.28$) and recycling ($M = 6.5$, $SD = .96$), and two energy-use behaviours: energy use at the workplace ($M = 30.4$ MJ, $SD = 8.19$) and energy use related to transport ($M = 45.1$ MJ, $SD = 96.84$).

Results
First, as expected, results showed that employees made pro-environmental investment decisions when they believed their organisation aims to realise CER ($\beta = .12$, $t(275) = 2.16$, $p < .05$). Also, the more the employees believed their organisation aims to realise CER, the lower their energy use at the workplace ($\beta = -.15$, $t(241) = -2.40$, $p < .05$), and the more they recycled ($\beta = .12$, $t(275) = 2.01$, $p < .05$). Believing that the organisation has the ambition to realise CER was not significantly related to energy use related to transport ($\beta = -.04$, $t(244) = -.64$, $p = .52$) and waste prevention ($\beta = .04$, $t(275) = .66$, $p = .51$).

Second, as expected, stronger biospheric values were related to more pro-environmental behaviour. More specifically, stronger biospheric values were related to more pro-environmental investment decisions ($\beta = .44$, $t(275) = 8.26$, $p < .001$), lower energy use at the workplace ($\beta = -.24$, $t(241) = -2.82$, $p < .001$) and more recycling ($\beta = .21$, $t(275) = 3.57$, $p < .001$). Biospheric values strength was not significant related to energy use related to transport ($\beta = .04$, $t(244) = .55$, $p = .59$) and waste prevention ($\beta = .09$, $t(275) = 1.43$, $p = .15$).

More interestingly, a significant interaction effect was found between believing that the organisation aims to realise CER and biospheric values on different pro-environmental behaviours. The results showed that especially people with relatively weak biospheric values were more likely to act pro-environmentally at work when they believed that the

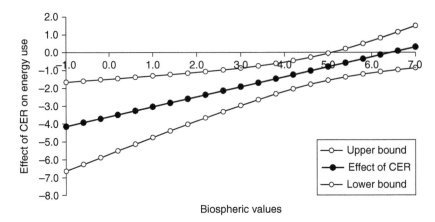

Figure 6.5   *The effect of believing that the organisation aims to realise CER on energy use at the workplace for different strengths of biospheric values*

organisation in which they worked cared for the environment and aimed to realise CER. This was true for pro-environmental investment deci-sions ($\beta = -.11$, $t(273) = -2.12$, $p < .05$), energy use at the workplace ($\beta =.17$, $t(239) = 2.67$, $p < .01$; see Figure 6.5), and waste prevention ($\beta = -.15$, $t(273) = -2.54$, $p < .05$). In contrast, believing that the organisa-tion aims to realise CER did not significantly affect the likelihood of pro-environmental behaviour among those with relatively strong bio-spheric values, as they were more likely to behave pro-environmentally anyway, irrespective of their perception of the organisation's ambition to realise CER.

Discussion

It was shown that people with relatively weak biospheric values are more strongly motivated to act pro-environmentally at work when contextual factors make them focused on doing the right thing for the environment, that is, when they thought their organisation was committed to realise CER. In contrast, people with relatively strong biospheric values seemed a priori more likely to be focused on benefiting the environment, and to behave pro-environmentally irrespective of whether they thought their organisation was committed to realise CER (Ruepert et al. 2017). This means that contextual factors that make people focused on benefiting the environment may encourage pro-environmental actions of people, particularly when they are not strongly motivated to do so a priori, on the basis of their biospheric values.

6.5   DISCUSSION AND RESEARCH AGENDA

The results above suggest that contextual factors particularly encourage pro-environmental actions among those with relatively weak biospheric values. In contrast, people with relatively strong biospheric values seem to behave pro-environmentally irrespective of the presence of contextual factors that may strengthen their focus on benefiting the environment. These findings seem to be in contrast with literature on value activation that suggests that contextual factors especially affect the pro-environmental actions of those with relatively strong biospheric values. An explanation for these seemingly contradictory findings may be that in most studies respondents strongly endorsed biospheric values, meaning that these studies included only a few people with very weak biospheric values. Hence, it may be that contextual factors that can make people focus on benefiting the environment particularly affected behaviour among those with moderately strong biospheric values as compared to rather strong biospheric values. The question remains how relevant contextual factors would affect those with rather weak biospheric values. Future research can investigate whether there may be a curvilinear relationship between biospheric value strength and contextual factors on pro-environmental behaviour at work. When people strongly endorse biospheric values, they may be motivated to benefit the environment and engage in pro-environmental behaviour in many different situations, even in the absence of contextual factors that would strengthen their focus on benefiting the environment, as reflected in our results. Yet, when biospheric values are very weak, meaning that people do not (or hardly) care about nature and the environment, contextual factors that can make people focus on benefiting the environment may not encourage pro-environmental behaviour at work because these contextual factors do not match their important values. Yet, when biospheric values are moderately strong, people may a priori not be strongly focused on benefiting the environment, but in the presence of the right contextual factors their focus on benefiting the environment may be strengthened, increasing the likelihood that they will engage in pro-environmental actions. Future research is needed to examine the conditions under which contextual factors affect pro-environmental behaviour among those with relatively strong, moderate and weak biospheric values.

Another factor that may be relevant in this respect is the costliness of the behaviour. It could be that when acting pro-environmentally is rather costly, people with relatively strong biospheric values may also not be likely to act pro-environmentally, because doing so would threaten the fulfilment of their hedonic or egoistic values, which may also be important to them. Yet, it may be that in such cases contextual factors that increase the likelihood that people are focused on benefiting the environment encourage pro-environmental behaviour among those with relatively strong biospheric values, because such contextual factors may weaken their focus on the behavioural costs. Yet, when acting pro-environmentally is rather costly, people with relatively weak biospheric values may not act pro-environmentally, even in the presence of contextual factors that can strengthen their focus on benefiting the environment, because such contextual factors will not succeed in substantially changing their focus on the costs involved in the behaviour. Future research is needed to examine the effects of biospheric values and contextual factors on low and high cost pro-environmental behaviour, to provide further insight into how biospheric values and contextual factors interact in influencing pro-environmental behaviour.

6.6   PRACTICAL RECOMMENDATIONS

In this chapter, we discussed a conceptual framework aimed to understand and predict environmental behaviour at work. Our reasoning has some important practical implications for ways to encourage various types of pro-environmental behaviour at work. First, our research shows that organisational factors such as CER promote pro-environmental actions at work. Notably, CER particularly increased the likelihood of such actions among workers with relatively weak biospheric values. This implies that organisational leaders can play a key role in encouraging pro-environmental actions among their employees. There are many possible ways to communicate the organisation's commitment to CER, for example by clearly demonstrating the ambitions to realise CER, not only in words but also in daily practice. Also, people's focus on benefiting the environment can be enhanced by shaping tasks and roles. More generally, any contextual factor that makes people focus on the appropriateness of pro-environmental behaviour could potentially encourage pro-environmental behaviour at work. Accordingly, interventions can be focused on creating a supporting context to empower and enable employees to act pro-environmentally at work; future studies are needed to test the effects of different contextual factors.

Our research suggests that when people have strong personal norms to behave pro-environmentally at work, they are somewhat more likely to engage in different types of pro-environmental actions at work. Yet, relationships between personal norms and environmental behaviour at work are not always very strong. A key issue to consider here is how employees can be empowered to act upon their (strong) personal norms to act pro-environmentally at work. Probably, employees face barriers to act upon their feelings of moral obligation to behave pro-environmentally at work. This again suggests that it is crucial to consider the context in which decisions are made in a different way as well, and to create a work context that enables employees to act upon their personal norms. Various interventions can be employed to enable and facilitate pro-environmental behaviour at work that communicate, demonstrate and facilitate the relevant actions.

Employees feel more strongly morally obliged to behave pro-environmentally at work when they strongly endorse biospheric values and have a strong environmental self-identity. This implies that personal norms can be (further) strengthened by targeting people's biospheric values and environmental self-identity. Earlier in this chapter we discussed value activation, but also that values are relatively stable over time. With regard to environmental self-identity, research suggests that environmental self-identity can be strengthened by making people aware of their previous pro-environmental actions, as environmental self-identity not only depends on the level of endorsement of biospheric values, but also on people's past environmental actions (Van der Werff et al. 2014b). When people realise they have acted pro-environmentally, their environmental self-identity will be strengthened, which increases the likelihood of pro-environmental actions as they aim to be consistent. In contrast, when they realise they did not act pro-environmentally, their environmental self-identity will be weakened, reducing the likelihood of pro-environmental actions in the future. This suggests that the environmental self-identity of employees could be strengthened when they are made aware of their voluntary engagement in pro-environmental behaviour at work, which clearly signals they are a pro-environmental person. Some organisations tend to employ external incentives or sanctions to encourage pro-environmental behaviour, such as penalties for not conforming to environmental policies, or reimbursing travel costs only when employees use pro-environmental means of transport. When employing such external incentives, employees may be less likely to attribute their pro-environmental actions at work to their own volition and their self. As a consequence, their environmental self-identity may not be strengthened.

6.7   SUMMARY

In this chapter, we discussed why employees would be willing and likely to behave pro-environmentally at work, even though it may be somewhat costly, effortful or inconvenient. Based on the IFEP, we proposed that employees are more likely to engage in pro-environmental behaviour at work when they are focused on benefiting the environment, which depends on the values people strongly endorse and the contextual factors. We proposed that employees are particularly more likely to act pro-environmentally at work when they strongly endorse biospheric values. Biospheric values encourage pro-environmental behaviour at work via a similar process to pro-environmental behaviour in the private sphere: they strengthen environmental self-identity and personal norms to act pro-environmentally at work, which motivates employees to act accordingly. Besides, contextual factors affect the likelihood that people act upon their values and personal norms to engage in pro-environmental behaviour at work. First, contextual factors may directly affect behaviour, as they may inhibit and facilitate such choices. Examples are the availability of recycling bins, the quality of public transport options to commute, or the need to drive long distances for work purposes. Second, contextual factors can affect pro-environmental actions indirectly, by affecting the extent to which people focus on benefiting the environment. We discussed how the influence of contextual factors on pro-environmental behaviour depends on the extent to which people endorse biospheric values. Notably, we indicated that contextual factors, such as CER, can especially encourage those with relatively weak biospheric values to behave more pro-environmentally at work. We hope this chapter encourages researchers to systematically study the conditions under which pro-environmental behaviour at work will be promoted, and particularly examine the role of values and contextual factors in this respect. This can inform the design of policies aimed at increasing pro-environmental behaviour among employees, and as such improve the environmental performance of organisations.

REFERENCES

Abrahamse, W. and L. Steg (2011), 'Factors related to household energy use and intention to reduce it: The role of psychological and socio-demographic variables', *Human Ecology Review*, **18**(1), 30–40.

Abrahamse, W., L. Steg, C. Vlek and T. Rothengatter (2007), 'The effect of tailored information, goal setting, and tailored feedback on household energy use, energy-related behaviors, and behavioral antecedents', *Journal of Environmental Psychology*, **27**(4), 265–276.

Bamberg, S. and P. Schmidt (2003), 'Incentives, morality, or habit? Predicting students' car use for university routes with the models of Ajzen, Schwartz and Triandis', *Environment and Behavior*, **35**(2), 264–285.

Bolderdijk, J. W., L. Steg and T. Postmes (2013), 'Fostering support for work floor energy conservation policies: Accounting for privacy concerns', *Journal of Organisational Behavior*, **34**(2), 195–210.

Carrus, G., P. Passafaro and M. Bonnes (2008), 'Emotions, habits and rational choices in ecological behaviours: The case of recycling and use of public transportation', *Journal of Environmental Psychology*, **28**(1), 51–62.

Dahlsrud, A. (2008), 'How corporate social responsibility is defined: An analysis of 37 definitions', *Corporate Social Responsibility and Environmental Management*, **15**(1), 1–13.

De Groot, J. I. M. and L. Steg (2008), 'Value orientations to explain beliefs related to environmental significant behavior: How to measure egoistic, altruistic, and biospheric value orientations', *Environment and Behavior*, **40**(3), 330–354.

De Groot, J. I. M. and L. Steg (2009), 'Mean or green: Which values can promote stable pro-environmental behavior?', *Conservation Letters*, **2**(2), 61–66.

Dietz, T., A. Fitzgerald and R. Schwom (2005), 'Environmental values', *Annual Review of Environmental Resources*, **30**, 355–372.

Dixon, G. N., M. B. Deline, K. McComas, L. Chambliss and M. Hoffmann (2015), 'Using comparative feedback to influence workplace energy conservation a case study of a university campaign', *Environment and Behavior*, **47**(6), 667–693.

Du Nann Winter, D. and S. M. Koger (2004), *The Psychology of Environmental Problems*, Mahwah, NJ: Lawrence Erlbaum.

Gatersleben, B. (2012), 'Measuring pro-environmental behaviour', in L. Steg, A. E. Van den Berg and J. I. M. De Groot (eds), *Environmental Psychology. An Introduction*, Oxford: John Wiley and Sons, pp. 132–140.

Gatersleben, B., L. Steg and C. Vlek (2002), 'Measurement and determinants of environmentally significant consumer behavior', *Environment and Behavior*, **34**(3), 335–362.

Hahnel, U. J. J., C. Ortmann, L. Korcaj and H. Spada (2014), 'What is green worth to you? Activating environmental values lowers price sensitivity towards electric vehicles', *Journal of Environmental Psychology*, **40**, 306–319.

Harland, P., H. Staats and H. A. M. Wilke (2007), 'Situational and personality factors as direct or personal norm mediated predictors of pro-environmental behavior: Questions derived from norm-activation theory', *Basic and Applied Social Psychology*, **29**(4), 323–334.

Honkanen, P. and B. Verplanken (2004), 'Understanding attitudes towards genetically modified food: The role of values and attitude strength', *Journal of Consumer Policy*, **27**(4), 401–420.

Kleingeld, P. (2015), 'Consistent egoists and situation managers: Two problems for situationism', *Philosophical Explorations*, **18**(3), 344–361.

Lindenberg, S. (2012), 'How cues in the environment affect normative behavior', in L. Steg, A. E. Van den Berg and J. I. M. De Groot (eds), *Environmental Psychology: An Introduction*, Oxford: Wiley Publishers, pp. 119–128.

Lindenberg, S. and L. Steg (2007), 'Normative, gain and hedonic goal frames guiding environmental behavior', *Journal of Social Issues*, **63**(1), 117–137.

Maio, G. R., J. M. Olson, L. Allen and M. M. Bernard (2001), 'Addressing discrepancies between values and behavior: The motivating effect of reasons', *Journal of Experimental Social Psychology*, **37**(2), 104–117.

Mannetti, L., A. Pierro and S. Livi (2004), 'Recycling: Planned and self-expressive behaviour', *Journal of Environmental Psychology*, **24**(2), 227–236.

Nordlund, A. M. and J. Garvill (2002), 'Value structures behind proenvironmental behavior', *Environment and Behavior*, **34**(6), 740–756.

Nordlund, A. M. and J. Garvill (2003), 'Effects of values, problem awareness, and personal norm on willingness to reduce personal car use', *Journal of Environmental Psychology*, **23**(4), 339–347.

Perlaviciute, G. and L. Steg (2015), 'The influence of values on evaluations of energy alternatives', *Renewable Energy*, **77**, 259–267.

Redman, L., M. Friman, T. Gärling and T. Hartig (2013), 'Quality attributes of public transport that attract car users: A research review', *Transport Policy*, **25**, 119–127.

Robertson, J. L. and J. Barling (2015), 'Introduction', in J. L. Robertson and J. Barling (eds), *The Psychology of Green Organisations*, New York: Oxford University Press, pp. 3–11.

Ruepert, A. M., K. Keizer and L. Steg (2017), 'The relationship between corporate environmental responsibility, employees' biospheric values and pro-environmental behaviour at work', *Journal of Environmental Psychology*, **54**, 65–78.

Ruepert, A. M., K. Keizer, L. Steg, F. Maricchiolo, G. Carrus, A. Dumitru, . . . D. Moza (2016), 'Environmental considerations in the organisational context: A pathway to pro-environmental behaviour at work', *Energy Research and Social Science*, **17**, 59–70.

Scherbaum, C. A., P. M. Popovich and S. Finlinson (2008), 'Exploring individual-level factors related to employee energy-conservation behaviors at work', *Journal of Applied Social Psychology*, **38**(3), 818–835.

Schwartz, S. H. (1977), 'Normative influences on altruism', in L. Berkowitz (ed.), *Advances in Experimental Social Psychology* (10th edn), New York: Academic Press, pp. 221–279.

Schwartz, S. H. (1992), 'Universals in the content and structure of values: Theoretical advances and empirical tests in 20 countries', in M. Zanna (ed.), *Advances in Experimental Social Psychology*, Hillsdale, NJ: Academic Press, pp. 1–65.

Steg, L. and J. I. M. De Groot (2010), 'Explaining prosocial intentions: Testing causal relationships in the norm activation model', *British Journal of Social Psychology*, **49**(4), 725–743.

Steg, L. and C. Vlek (2009), 'Encouraging pro-environmental behaviour: An integrative review and research agenda', *Journal of Environmental Psychology*, **29**(3), 309–317.

Steg, L., J. W. Bolderdijk, K. Keizer and G. Perlaviciute (2014a), 'An integrated framework for encouraging pro-environmental behaviour: The role of values, situational factors and goals', *Journal of Environmental Psychology*, **38**, 104–115.

Steg, L., J. I. M. De Groot, L. Dreijerink, W. Abrahams and F. Siero (2011), 'General antecedents of personal norms, policy acceptability, and intentions: The role of values, worldviews, and environmental concern', *Society and Natural Resources*, **24**(4), 349–367.

Steg, L., G. Perlaviciute, E. Van der Werff and J. Lurvink (2014b), 'The significance of hedonic values for environmentally relevant attitudes, preferences, and actions', *Environment and Behavior*, **46**(2), 163–192.

Steg, L., C. Vlek, S. Lindenberg, T. Groot, H. Moll, T. S. Uiterkamp and A. Van Witteloostuijn (2003), 'Towards a comprehensive model of sustainable corporate performance. Second interim report of the Dutch SCP project', University of Groningen, Groningen 2003.

Stern, P. C. (2000), 'Toward a coherent theory of environmentally significant behavior', *Journal of Social Issues*, **56**(3), 407–424.

Stern, P. C., T. Dietz, T. D. Abel, G. A. Guagnano and L. Kalof (1999), 'A value-belief-norm theory of support for social movements: The case of environmentalism', *Human Ecology Review*, **6**(2), 81–97.

Stern, P. C., L. Kalof, T. Dietz and G. A. Guagnano (1995), 'Values, beliefs, and proenvironmental action: Attitude formation toward emergent attitude objects', *Journal of Applied Social Psychology*, **25**(18), 1611–1636.

Thøgersen, J. (1996), 'Recycling and morality a critical review of the literature', *Environment and Behavior*, **28**(4), 536–558.

Van der Werff, E. and L. Steg (2016), 'The psychology of participation and interest in smart energy systems: Comparing the value-belief-norm theory and the value-identity-personal norm model', *Energy Research & Social Science*, **22**, 107–114.

Van der Werff, E., L. Steg and K. Keizer (2013a), 'The value of environmental self-identity: The relationship between biospheric values, environmental self-identity and environmental preferences, intentions and behaviour', *Journal of Environmental Psychology*, **34**, 55–63.

Van der Werff, E., L. Steg and K. Keizer (2013b), 'It is a moral issue: The relationship between environmental self-identity, obligation-based intrinsic motivation and pro-environmental behaviour', *Global Environmental Change*, **23**(5), 1258–1265.

Van der Werff, E., L. Steg and K. Keizer (2014a), 'I am what I am, by looking past the present the influence of biospheric values and past behavior on environmental self-identity', *Environment and Behavior*, **46**(5), 626–657.

Van der Werff, E., L. Steg and K. Keizer (2014b), 'Follow the signal: When past pro-environmental actions signal who you are', *Journal of Environmental Psychology*, **40**, 273–282.

Verplanken, B. and R. W. Holland (2002), 'Motivated decision making: Effects of activation and self-centrality of values on choices and behavior', *Journal of Personality and Social Psychology*, **82**(3), 434–447.

Vlek, C. and L. Steg (2007), 'Human behavior and environmental sustainability: Problems, driving forces, and research topics', *Journal of Social Issues*, **63**(1), 1–19.

Wiidegren, Ö. (1998), 'The new environmental paradigm and personal norms', *Environment and Behavior*, **30**(1), 75–100.

7. Between- and within-person variability in employee pro-environmental behaviour
Hannes Zacher and Megan J. Bissing-Olson

7.1 INTRODUCTION

Over the past few years, organisational scholars and practitioners have become increasingly interested in employees' pro-environmental behaviour, its predictors, and how to enhance it to achieve environmental sustainability goals (e.g., Norton et al. 2014; Paillé and Boiral 2013; Unsworth et al. 2013; for a review, see Norton et al. 2015a; Kim et al. 2014; Robertson and Barling 2013). Ones and Dilchert (2012a) define employee pro-environmental (or "green") behaviour as behaviour in the work context that contributes to, or detracts from, environmental sustainability. As is the case with all forms of work behaviour (Dalal et al. 2014), employees differ from each other in the general (or average) proficiency with which they carry out pro-environmental behaviour at work. For example, one employee might be generally more inclined than another to engage in workplace behaviours such as recycling, conserving energy and water, and avoiding waste. Moreover, the extent to which each employee shows pro-environmental behaviour can vary and change over time. For instance, the behaviour of both employees may vary from one workday to the next.

It is now very common in the organisational literature for researchers to not only focus on between-person differences in work behaviour, but also on within-person variability and change in behaviour over time. For example, research has demonstrated within-person variability in task performance (Chi et al. 2015), organisational citizenship behaviour (Dalal et al. 2009), and innovative performance (Zacher and Wilden 2014). However, an interest in within-person variability in employee pro-environmental behaviour has only recently emerged (Bissing-Olson et al. 2012, 2015). In a comprehensive review on employee pro-environmental behaviour, Norton and colleagues (2015a: 118) observed "a surprising lack of research at the within-person level" and stated that, "To progress the field, researchers clearly need to develop models that include this level of analysis and account for dynamic fluctuations in employee green behaviour". If researchers only conceptualise and measure employee pro-environmental behaviour in terms of average or "general" behaviour, a number of interesting and important questions remain unanswered (Bissing-Olson 2016), including: How strongly does employees' pro-environmental behaviour vary over time, for instance from day to day? Are there certain temporal patterns that describe when employees engage in pro-environmental behaviour (e.g., at the beginning of the week or workday)? How do daily work experiences and events influence employees' ability, motivation, and opportunity to show pro-environmental behaviour? Are there between-person differences in the within-person relationships between experiences, events, and behaviour?

The main goal of this chapter is to highlight the scientific and practical importance of distinguishing between between-person differences in average levels of employee pro-environmental behaviour on the one hand, and within-person variability and change in employee pro-environmental behaviour on the other. To this end, we first explain what is meant by between-person differences and within-person variability and change in employee pro-environmental behaviour. Second, we describe two quantitative daily diary studies that examined both between-person differences and within-person variability in employee pro-environmental behaviour. Third, we present a conceptual framework and examples to guide future systematic investigations of predictors of between- and within-person variability in employee pro-environmental behaviour. Fourth, we describe different research designs and analytical strategies to investigate between- and within-person variability in employee pro-environmental behaviour. We conclude the chapter by discussing implications for organisational practice.

7.2   WHAT IS MEANT BY BETWEEN- AND WITHIN-PERSON VARIABILITY?

Research taking a between-person perspective typically focuses on the extent to which employees differ in their general or average levels of pro-environmental behaviour at work. Thus, studies using between-person designs (e.g., cross-sectional survey studies, between-person experiments) aim to explain variability between employees (or groups of employees). This idea is illustrated in Figure 7.1 using the grey, straight horizontal lines labelled "Average level of behaviour of Employee . . . across days." These average levels represent general levels of pro-environmental behaviour over time, for example, how often, overall, employees A, B, and C showed pro-environmental behaviour over the past week. Studies taking a between-person perspective typically ask employees to mentally aggregate

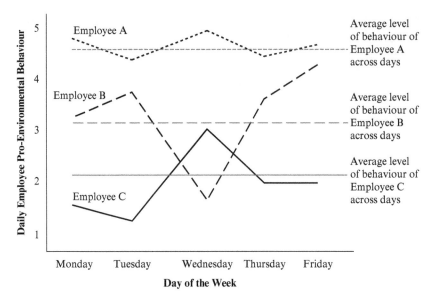

*Figure 7.1   Differences between employees, and variability within
employees, in employee pro-environmental behaviour over time*

the extent to which they engage in pro-environmental behaviour over time. Oftentimes, items in these studies do not specify the time interval, but measure the extent to which employees show pro-environmental behaviour in general. For instance, Norton et al. (2014) asked participants to respond to broad statements such as "I fulfil responsibilities specified in my job description in environmentally friendly ways" and "I take initiative to act in environmentally friendly ways at work." Although employee pro-environmental behaviour occurs to varying levels (or does not occur at all) on a daily basis, some research points toward a relatively high temporal stability in pro-environmental behaviour over longer periods of time (i.e., two years), suggesting that the general tendency to behave in pro-environmental ways might stem from a stable underlying prosocial personality trait (Kaiser and Byrka 2011).

Most existing studies on employee pro-environmental behaviour have focused on these differences in general levels of pro-environmental behaviour by adopting a between-person perspective and using cross-sectional designs. For example, in three studies, Paillé and Boiral (2013) examined between-person differences in organisational citizenship behaviour for the environment (i.e., eco-helping, eco-civic engagement, and eco-initiatives). Consistent with assumptions based on social exchange theory, they

showed that employees who feel more supported by their organisation are generally more willing to engage in such behaviours. Another
example is a study by Kim et al. (2014), which showed that between-
person differences in conscientiousness and moral reflectiveness were
associated with employee pro-environmental behaviour. Also taking a
between-person perspective, Norton et al. (2014) investigated relationships between perceived organisational sustainability policies, green work
climate perceptions, and employee pro-environmental behaviour. They
found that between-person differences in perceived sustainability policies
were associated with between-person differences in green work climate
perceptions. Climate perceptions, in turn, explained between-person variation in employee pro-environmental behaviour. Finally, Robertson and
Barling (2013) developed and tested a model, according to which leaders
with higher levels of environmentally specific transformational leadership
behaviour and pro-environmental behaviour should have subordinates
with higher pro-environmental passion and behaviour. Between-person
data from 139 leader-subordinate dyads supported the proposed model.
In summary, research that takes a between-person perspective investigates
how between-person differences in certain person or context attributes are
associated with between-person differences in employee pro-environmental behaviour. It is important to note that, as between-person designs focus
on differences between individuals, they do not allow conclusions to be
drawn about within-person variability and change in behaviour over time.

 In contrast, research adopting a within-person perspective focuses on
the extent to which individual employees' pro-environmental behaviour
fluctuates or changes over different periods of time, such as hours, days,
weeks, months, or years. These dynamics are illustrated in Figure 7.1
for three employees whose levels of pro-environmental behaviour vary
intraindividually across one work week. The line for each employee
represents the extent of day-to-day fluctuation (or stability) in pro-
environmental behaviour. Because behavioural fluctuation over time
is the focus of within-person research, such research is also a form
of longitudinal research (Wang et al. 2017; Ployhart and Vandenberg
2010). Longitudinal research requires that employee pro-environmental
behaviour is assessed multiple times across a meaningful time period with
meaningful intervals between measurement occasions (Wang et al. 2017).
Methods for conducting such research have been described as "intensive
longitudinal methods".

 Within-person designs allow researchers to explain the total variance
in measures of pro-environmental behaviour using predictors at both the
between- and within-person levels. It is important to note, however, that
even when using within-person designs, predictors at the between-person

level (e.g., demographic variables, personality characteristics) can only explain differences between employees in *average* levels of pro-environmental behaviour. Only predictors that vary within persons over time can explain within-person variation in employee pro-environmental behaviour. Moreover, within-person designs allow for the investigation of how between-person differences relate to the level of within-person variability and change over time. In other words, do employees differ in the extent to which their pro-environmental behaviour fluctuates over time? For instance, employees with a less positive pro-environmental attitude may report a stronger increase in their pro-environmental behaviour after an intervention than employees with a more positive pro-environmental attitude, because the latter group of employees already engages in high levels of pro-environmental behaviour (i.e., there is not much room for improvement).

It is important to distinguish within-person variability in pro-environmental behaviour from within-person change. While both rely on intensive longitudinal designs and measurement, within-person studies focusing only on intraindividual variability (see diary studies discussed in the next section) are not able to draw conclusions about intraindividual change. In contrast, within-person studies focusing on intraindividual change can describe how and possibly explain why pro-environmental behaviour changes within employees over a certain period of time (in addition to capturing intraindividual variability).

Within-person designs may also facilitate the discovery of complexities and seeming contradictions in the relationships between employee pro-environmental behaviour and other variables that between-person designs cannot detect (Bissing-Olson 2016). For instance, the within-person relationships between employees' experiences of daily positive affect (e.g., feeling excited, happy) and daily pro-environmental behaviour at work might be positive, whereas the between-person relationship between aggregated levels of daily positive affect and pro-environmental behaviour might be negative (Figure 7.2). This hypothetical situation represents an example of Simpson's paradox (Wagner 1982), which occurs when separate groups of data (e.g., multiple data points for individual) show a different trend than the aggregated data. A prominent example from the organisational psychology literature is research by Vancouver et al. (2001), who challenged the notion that self-efficacy is always positively related to job performance, as found in most between-person studies (Stajkovic and Luthans 1998). Indeed, using a within-person design, Vancouver and colleagues (2001) showed that when participants experienced a level of self-efficacy higher than their person average, they were overconfident and, thus, showed lower performance.

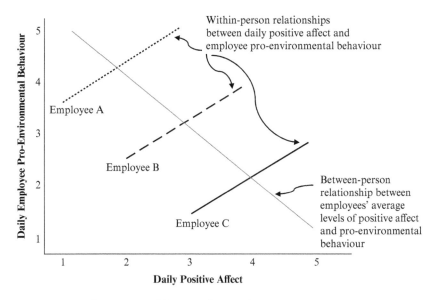

Figure 7.2   Illustration of Simpson's paradox

To briefly summarise, up to this point we have clarified what is meant by between- and within-person variability in pro-environmental behaviour and discussed some consequences of this distinction. Next, we describe two studies that investigated employee pro-environmental behaviour from a within-person perspective.

7.3   REVIEW OF EMPIRICAL STUDIES ON BETWEEN- AND WITHIN-PERSON VARIABILITY IN EMPLOYEE PRO-ENVIRONMENTAL BEHAVIOUR

As noted earlier, so far only very few studies in the organisational literature have examined both between- and within-person variability in pro-environmental behaviour. The only two daily diary studies available focus on explaining intraindividual variability but not intraindividual change. The first study was conducted by Bissing-Olson et al. (2013). Based on Fredrickson's (2003) broaden-and-build theory, the researchers suggested that three predictors would explain variability in employees' daily task-related pro-environmental behaviour (i.e., the extent to which required work tasks are completed in environmentally friendly ways). On the one hand, they hypothesised that within-person variability in daily low-arousal positive affect (e.g., the experience of emotions such as contentment) and high-arousal positive affect (e.g., the experience of emotions such as excitement) would explain daily task-related pro-environmental behaviour. On the other hand, they assumed that between-person differences in pro-environmental attitude would positively relate to aggregate scores of daily task-related pro-environmental behaviour at the between-person level.

Furthermore, Bissing-Olson and colleagues (2013) proposed that within-person variability in daily high arousal positive affect and between-person differences in pro-environmental attitude would explain variability in employees' engagement in daily proactive pro-environmental behaviour (i.e., the extent to which employees show personal initiative when acting in environmentally friendly ways at work). They also hypothesised that between-person differences in pro-environmental attitude would moderate the hypothesised within-person relationships between daily positive affect and pro-environmental behaviour, such that relationships are stronger when pro-environmental attitude is less positive and weaker when pro-environmental attitude is more positive. The rationale for these moderation hypotheses was that the level of pro-environmental behaviour of employees with a more positive pro-environmental attitude is less dependent on daily motivation in the form of positive affect.

To test their hypotheses, Bissing-Olson and colleagues (2013) collected baseline survey data as well as daily survey data across ten workdays from 56 employees working in small businesses. Results of multi-level analyses revealed that 71 per cent of the total variance in daily task-related pro-environmental behaviour resided between individuals, whereas 29 per cent of the total variance resided at the within-person level. This means that more than two-thirds of the total variance could potentially be explained by between-person predictors such as pro-environmental attitude, and less than one-third of the total variance could potentially be explained by within-person predictors such as daily affect. These findings suggested that multi-level analyses of data were justified. Results further showed that, consistent with hypotheses, daily low-arousal positive affect and pro-environmental attitude were positively related to daily task-related pro-environmental behaviour. In addition, daily high-arousal positive affect positively predicted daily proactive (but not task-related) pro-environmental behaviour among employees with a less positive pro-environmental attitude, but not among employees with a more positive pro-environmental attitude.

More recently, Norton et al. (2017b) proposed that there would be a positive association between two between-person constructs, "corporate environmental strategy" (i.e., employees' knowledge and awareness of their organisation's environmental strategy) and "green psychological climate" (i.e., employees' perceptions and interpretations of organisational policies, practices, and procedures related to environmental sustainability). Moreover, they suggested that green psychological climate would moderate the positive relationship between employees' daily green behavioural intentions and their pro-environmental behaviour on the following day. Specifically, they argued that the relationship would be stronger when green psychological climate is more positive, because a positive green psychological climate provides employees with cues on how to better translate their intentions into behaviour. Daily pro-environmental behaviour was operationalised using questions about employees' daily engagement in behaviours such as recycling, saving water and energy, and avoiding waste.

Norton and colleagues (2017b) tested their hypotheses using baseline and daily survey data collected from 74 employees across ten workdays. For green behavioural intentions, multi-level analyses indicated that 66 per cent of the total variance resided at the between-person level and 34 per cent of the total variance resided at the within-person level. Similarly, for employee pro-environmental behaviour, 73 per cent of the total variance resided at the between-person level and 27 per cent of the total variance resided at the within-person level. Interestingly, these proportions of between- and within-person variability in employee pro-environmental behaviour are very similar to those reported by Bissing-Olson and colleagues (2013). Thus, it appears that a large proportion of pro-environmental behaviour is relatively stable over short periods of time (i.e., two weeks), whereas approximately one-third of the total variance in behaviour depends on within-person factors.

Consistent with hypotheses, results of Norton et al.'s (2017b) study further showed that corporate environmental strategy was positively related to the green psychological climate at the between-person level. Green psychological climate moderated the within-person relationship between green behavioural intentions and next-day employee green behaviour. Specifically, the within-person relationship was positive when employees perceived a more positive green psychological climate, and it was weak and non-significant when employees perceived a less positive green psychological climate. Additional tests showed that corporate environmental strategy had a significant indirect effect on next-day green behaviour through the interaction between daily intentions and the green psychological climate. Overall, these findings suggest that organisations should ensure that their employees have strong behavioural intentions to engage in pro-environmental behaviour, and that organisations should communicate a corporate environmental strategy that employees perceive in terms of a favourable green psychological climate.

7.4   CONCEPTUAL FRAMEWORK OF BETWEEN- AND WITHIN-PERSON PREDICTORS OF PRO-ENVIRONMENTAL BEHAVIOUR

In their literature review, Norton and colleagues (2015a) put forward an integrative multi-level model of predictors and outcomes of employee pro-environmental behaviour. In addition to context factors (i.e., institutional, organisational, leader, and team characteristics), they suggested that stable interindividual differences (e.g., pro-environmental attitude, personality) and dynamic intraindividual states (e.g., affect, intentions, motivation) predict pro-environmental behaviour via different motivational states. In this section, we extend Norton and colleagues' (2015a) model by proposing a systematic conceptual framework to guide future research on predictors of between- and within-person variability in employee pro-environmental behaviour (Table 7.1; see also Bissing-Olson 2016). Our framework organises predictors of employee pro-environmental behaviour along two central dimensions: predictor category (person vs. context), and temporal characteristics of predictor (stable vs. dynamic). While the temporal characteristics dimension is represented by two categories in Table 7.1, we note that this dimension is continuous, in that the temporal stability of predictors can vary between highly stable over time to highly dynamic over time.

Furthermore, as noted earlier, only between-person factors can explain variability in employee pro-environmental behaviour measured at the between-person level, and only within-person factors can explain variability and change in employee pro-environmental behaviour measured at the within-person level. However, between-person factors can predict within-person scores that are aggregated (averaged) to the between-person level. For instance, high levels of daily pro-environmental behaviour that are very stable over longer periods of time indicate that an employee has habitualised her or his pro-environmental behaviour (Klöckner and Matthies 2004). Such habitual (or automatic) behaviour might be predicted by stable between-person differences in, for instance, personality or values. Moreover, person and context factors as well as more stable and more dynamic predictors may interact in predicting employee pro-environmental behaviour.

Next, we discuss some possible predictors in each of the four quadrants in Table 7.1, followed by a discussion of possible interactions among predictors.

Table 7.1 Predictors of employee pro-environmental behaviour

Predictor Category	Temporal Characteristics of Predictors	
	Stable	Dynamic
Person	Demographic variables Personality characteristics Attitudes, norms, and values	Affect Motivation Perceived control

Context	Laws and regulations
	Human resource management
	  practices
	Organisational culture and climate
	Job characteristics
		Work events
		Time pressure
		Interpersonal interactions
		  (e.g., leadership and
		  support)

7.4.1 Stable Person Predictors

Predictors of employee pro-environmental behaviour that are on the more stable end of the temporal variability continuum include demographic characteristics, personality characteristics, attitudes, norms, and values (Table 7.1). With regard to demographic characteristics, research has shown that older workers show higher levels of pro-environmental behaviour than younger workers (Norton et al. 2017a; Wiernik et al. 2016). Of course, age is a variable that also changes relatively slowly within persons over time; however, most research examines age using between-person designs due to practical difficulties associated with long-term longitudinal designs (e.g., costs). In a meta-analysis including 4,676 workers from 22 samples, Wiernik and colleagues (2016) found that age was weakly positively related to pro-environmental behaviours, suggesting that older workers engage in these behaviours somewhat more frequently than younger workers. In terms of personality characteristics as predictors, Kim et al. (2014) found that conscientiousness and moral reflectiveness were positively associated with voluntary pro-environmental behaviour in a sample of 325 office workers. Finally, with regard to attitudes, norms, and values, Norton et al. (2014) found positive relationships between individual employees' green work climate perceptions and their task-related and proactive pro-environmental behaviour.

Future research is needed that not only examines between-person relationships between stable predictors and general pro-environmental behaviour, but also relationships between these predictors and the degree of temporal variability in pro-environmental behaviours. For example, it may be possible that employees with a less positive pro-environmental attitude vary more in their daily levels of pro-environmental behaviour than employees with a more positive pro-environmental attitude, because the former group of employees is more susceptible to environmental cues and internal states and pressures. In contrast, people with a more positive pro-environmental attitude may vary little in their pro-environmental behaviour because they are more aware of and responsive to opportunities to engage in this behaviour and because for them pro-environmental behaviour has become habitual (Bissing-Olson 2016).

7.4.2   Dynamic Person Predictors

Predictors of pro-environmental behaviour that fall into the more dynamic end of the temporal variability continuum include employee affect, motivation, and perceived control (Table 7.1). As described earlier, Bissing-Olson et al. (2013) found that daily experiences of positive affect are associated with daily pro-environmental behaviour. In a more recent study outside the work context, the same authors showed that dynamic experiences of pride about pro-environmental behaviour were positively, and dynamic experiences of guilt about pro-environmental environmental behaviour were negatively associated with actual engagement in pro-environmental behaviour (Bissing-Olson et al. 2016). With regard to motivation, Norton et al. (2017b) showed that workers' daily intentions to engage in pro-environmental behaviour were positively associated with engagement in pro-environmental behaviour on the next day, but only when workers perceived a positive pro-environmental climate in their organisation.

Currently, there is no research that considers the related concepts of self-efficacy and perceived control as dynamic predictors of pro-environmental behaviour (Bissing-Olson 2016). Intentions, self-efficacy, and perceived control are concepts from the theory of planned behaviour, which is frequently used as a theoretical framework in the environmental literature (Greaves et al. 2013; Cordano and Frieze 2000; Ajzen 1991). For instance, on some days employees may feel more confident with regard to carrying out certain tasks in environmentally friendly ways than on other days. Similarly, they might find it easier to engage in pro-environmental behaviour in some work situations or contexts than in others (Blumberg and Pringle 1982). While they may feel in control about behaviours such as recycling and reducing energy and waste in their office, engaging in these behaviours may not be possible when they are on a business trip or working from home.

7.4.3 Stable Context Predictors

Turning to potential context predictors of pro-environmental behaviour, we suggest that laws and regulations, human resource management practices, organisational culture and climate, and job characteristics are at the more stable end of the temporal variability continuum (Table 7.1). So far, hardly any research has examined effects of institutional factors, such as laws and regulations, on employee green behaviour (Norton et al. 2015a). The reason for this may be that such research requires an even broader multi-level perspective that includes the organisational or country levels. Similarly, the existing research on organisational culture and climate as predictors of employee pro-environmental behaviour is theoretical or focuses on between-person differences in perceived culture and climate instead of comparisons between organisations (Norton et al. 2015b; Norton et al. 2012).

With regard to human resource management, Paillé et al. (2014) conducted a study in which data was collected from top management team members, chief executive officers, and frontline workers. They found that employee organisational citizenship behaviour for the environment fully mediates the association between human resource management practices and environmental firm performance. Finally, further research is needed on job characteristics as predictors of employee pro-environmental behaviour. For example, five characteristics suggested by the job characteristics model (Hackman and Oldham 1976) – job autonomy, skill variety, task identity, task significance, and feedback – might relate differentially to employee engagement in pro-environmental behaviours (Bissing-Olson et al. 2015). Research on such context-related factors is important because affect, motivation, and perceived control might not always translate into action by themselves, but their effects may be dependent on the job situation (Kollmuss and Agyeman 2002).

7.4.4 Dynamic Context Predictors

Context predictors of employee pro-environmental behaviour that fall onto the more dynamic end of the temporal variability continuum include work events, time pressure, and interpersonal interactions (Table 7.1). So far, no research exists on daily work events and time pressure as predictors of pro-environmental behaviour. However, affective events theory suggests that positive and negative emotional events at work can lead to either affect- or judgment-driven behaviours (Weiss and Cropanzano 1996). Thus, it may be possible that certain pro-environmental behaviours, such as organisational citizenship behaviour for the environment (Boiral and Paillé 2012), are triggered or constrained by emotional work events. Similarly, time pressure at work may lead employees to prioritise task accomplishment over voluntary behaviours that promote the environment. With regard to interpersonal interactions, research at the between-person level has shown that leadership behaviour and social support are associated with employee pro-environmental behaviour (Robertson and Barling 2013; Kim et al. 2014; Ramus and Steger 2000). However, leadership behaviours and social support are, similar to employee pro-environmental behaviour, dynamic variables that may vary from one day to the next. Thus, future research should examine them using within-person designs.

7.4.5 Interactions Among Predictors

As already hinted at above, it seems important to examine interactions between person and context, as well as stable and dynamic predictors of employee pro-environmental behaviour. Simply stated, work behaviour is a function of ability, motivation, and opportunity (Blumberg and Pringle 1982). Thus, contextual factors may strengthen or constrain the effects of person predictors on pro-environmental behaviour. So far, to the best of our knowledge, no research has examined interactions of person and context factors on employee pro-environmental behaviour. In contrast, some researchers have examined interactions between stable and dynamic person predictors. In multi-level models, stable between-person factors may not only predict average within-person outcomes, they can also inter-act with dynamic within-person predictors in predicting within-person outcomes. In other words, stable between-person factors may influence the direction and strength of within-person associations. Studies that have focused on such interactions include one by Bissing-Olson et al. (2013) that examined interactions between daily positive affect and employees' pro-environmental attitude (a between-person factor) in predicting daily task-related and proactive pro-environmental behaviour, and one study by Norton et al. (2017b) that investigated the between-person variable green psychological climate as a moderator of the within-person relation-ship between daily green behavioural intentions and next-day employee pro-environmental behaviour.

7.5 RESEARCH DESIGNS AND ANALYTICAL STRATEGIES

Generally, researchers distinguish between active and passive methods for studying daily experiences and behaviour (Bissing-Olson 2016; Mehl and Conner 2012; Conner and Lehman 2012). Active methods entail that participants self-report their experiences (e.g., moods, thoughts) and behaviour (e.g., energy use) to the researcher. Advantages of active methods are that researchers can tap experiences and behaviour that are only accessible to, and observable by, participants themselves; disadvantages of active methods are that self-reports may be subject to various reporting biases (e.g., self-enhancement bias).

Specific active methods include experience sampling, daily diaries, and event sampling. In experience sampling studies, participants provide reports multiple times throughout the day, at variable or fixed time intervals (Beal 2015; Bolger and Laurenceau 2013; Fisher and To 2012). Variable time-based strategies entail that participants provide reports between four and ten times a day at semi-random times. Fixed time-based strategies also require reports multiple times throughout the day, but the reporting times are on a fixed schedule known to participants. Variable and fixed time-based strategies can be used for studying phenomena that are continuous and ongoing (e.g., awareness of environmental issues) or that are likely to be affected by retrospective memory bias (e.g., actual engagement in pro-environmental behaviour).

In daily diary studies, participants typically report on their experiences and behaviour once or twice a day at fixed times (Gunthert and Wenze 2012; Nezlek 2012; Ohly et al. 2010). Quantitative surveys in diary studies can be administered through paper and pencil booklets, handheld electronic devices, smartphone apps, or links to online surveys via email (Green et al. 2006). There are several useful tutorials on diary studies in the general psychology literature (Bolger et al. 2003; Mehl and Conner 2012; Nezlek 2012; Hektner et al. 2007), and in the organisational literature (Ohly et al. 2010; Fisher and To 2012; Beal 2012, 2015; Beal and Weiss 2003).

In event-based sampling studies, participants report on their experiences and behaviour only after a predefined event occurs, such as criticism from a customer (Moskowitz and Sadikaj 2012; Reis and Gable 2000). Event-based sampling involves collecting data on relatively rare or discrete events (e.g., travel mode decisions). Whereas experience sampling studies have the advantage of assessing ongoing experiences and thus reducing memory biases, daily diaries are less burdensome to participants and thus have higher compliance and lower attrition rates. However, diary measures must be very brief to limit participation time and effort, which may decrease their reliability and validity. The advantage of event sampling is that researchers can measure infrequent and discrete events and related processes; they also reduce retrospective biases.

Passive methods infer or measure experiences and behaviour through the use of devices such as electronically activated recorders (i.e., auditory sampling), pedometers (i.e., physical activity), and GPS (i.e., physical location). The main advantage of passive methods is that participants do not have to fill out surveys; however, participants need to continuously wear the devices, which may be expensive. Such a continuous sampling strategy allows passively capturing ongoing experience, such as ambient noise or physiological experience (e.g., skin conductance as a measure of arousal or stress). Using this method, data is collected constantly, without gaps from the beginning to the end of the data collection period. Specific passive methods are acoustic sampling and passive telemetrics. Acoustic sampling involves taking acoustic samples from participants' immediate environment, such as conversations or ambient noise (Mehl and Robbins 2012). Passive telemetrics is an unobtrusive technology that makes use of sensors to transmit physiological, behavioural, and environmental data (Goodwin 2012). While acoustic sampling and passive telemetrics allow naturalistic observation of a range of objective phenomena, they may also create a rather high evaluation apprehension due to privacy intrusions.

To analyse data collected via the study designs described above, researchers need to use multi-level methods such as random coefficient modelling in software packages such as hierarchical linear modelling (Raudenbush and Bryk 2002) or Mplus (Muthén and Muthén 2012). These packages allow for the separation of the total variance in pro-environmental behaviour and its predictors into their between-person and within-person components. It is important to note, however, that within-person studies do not necessarily allow researchers to draw conclusions about the causal nature of relationships. To address this issue, researchers could make use of lagged within-person designs (i.e., controlling for previous assessments of the dependent variable) or latent change score methodology (McArdle 2009; Liu et al. 2016; Wang et al. 2017), control for relevant confounding variables, or combine the within-person methodology with an experimental approach. The latter approach involves manipulation of the independent variable and the random assignment of participants to experimental and control groups.

In summary, there are many advantages to within-person designs using experience sampling, daily diaries, event sampling, or passive methods. As Mehl and Conner (2012) point out, they "allow researchers to study experience, behaviour, environments, and physiology of individuals in their *natural settings*, in (close to) *real time*, and on *repeated* occasions" (p. xix). While there are issues to consider with regard to design, measurement, and analysis, within-person designs are ideal for addressing research questions relating to variability, change, duration, co-occurrence, temporal patterns, as well as interactions between person and context, and interactions between dynamic and stable characteristics (Augustine and Larsen 2012).

7.6 RECOMMENDATIONS FOR PRACTITIONERS

The distinction between between- and within-person variability in employee pro-environmental behaviour has implications for organisational practice. When pro-environmental behaviour is conceptualised and analysed using a between-person perspective, knowledge of interindividual differences that predict general or average forms of pro-environmental behaviour may be used in personnel selection. Accordingly, researchers with a background in personnel selection have emphasised the importance of between-person differences in employee pro-environmental behaviour (Ones and Dilchert 2012b). Companies that are interested in hiring employees that frequently display pro-environmental behaviour can incorporate relevant predictors in their selection test batteries. For instance, research by Kim et al. (2014) suggests that companies could select for conscientiousness and moral reflectiveness to hire employees that are likely to engage in voluntary pro-environmental behaviour. A disadvantage of this between-person approach is that it focuses on average behaviour at a single point in time and thus neglects potential within-person variation in behaviour over time (Bissing-Olson et al. 2012). However, future research could shed light on person and context predictors of the extent of within-person variability in pro-environmental behaviour, so that companies can select those employees that show high levels and little variation in their behaviour over time.

A within-person perspective on pro-environmental behaviour can further provide practitioners with a better understanding of when and under which conditions employees are more likely to engage in pro-environmental behaviour on a daily basis. For example, organisations could attempt to enhance employees' daily positive affect, daily pro-environmental intentions, and their perceptions of green organisational climate to improve daily pro-environmental behaviour (Bissing-Olson et al. 2013; Norton et al. 2017b). It is important for practitioners to understand that pro-environmental behaviour may vary within employees from one day to the next, and that both stable between-person factors and more dynamic within-person factors are associated with such variability. They can then take steps to both increase employees' general levels of pro-environmental behaviour as well as to reduce within-person variability in behaviour to achieve consistently high environmental performance.

7.7   CONCLUSION

In this chapter, we explained what is meant by between- and within-person variability in employee pro-environmental behaviour, reviewed two recent daily diary studies that adopted a within-person perspective, put forward a conceptual framework and examples of predictors of pro-environmental behaviour, and summarised implications for future research and practice. In contrast to the single "snapshots" of pro-environmental behaviour that traditional cross-sectional designs have captured, within-person designs and intensive longitudinal methods provide researchers with more detailed and dynamic "films" of pro-environmental behaviour. Moreover, a multi-level perspective allows researchers to investigate the extent to which person- and context-related, dynamic and stable predictors, and interactions among these predictors explain the total variability in pro-environmental behaviour over time.

REFERENCES

Ajzen, I. (1991), 'The theory of planned behavior', *Organisational Behavior and Human Decision Processes*, **50**, 179–211.

Augustine, A. A. and R. J. Larsen (2012), 'Emotion research', in M. R. Mehl and T. S. Conner (eds), *Handbook of Research Methods for Studying Daily Life*. New York: Guilford Press.

Beal, D. J. (2012), 'Industrial/organisational psychology', in M. R. Mehl and T. S. Conner (eds), *Handbook of Research Methods for Studying Daily Life*. New York: Guilford Press.

Beal, D. J. (2015), 'ESM 2.0: State of the art and future potential of experience sampling methods in organisational research', *Annual Review of Organisational Psychology and Organisational Behavior*, **2**, 383–407.

Beal, D. J. and H. M. Weiss (2003), 'Methods of ecological momentary assessment in organisational research', *Organisational Research Methods*, **6**, 440–464.

Bissing-Olson, M. J. (2016), 'Affect and pro-environmental behavior in everyday life'. Doctoral Dissertation, The University of Queensland.

Bissing-Olson, M. J., K. S. Fielding and A. Iyer (2015), 'Diary methods and workplace pro-environmental behaviors', in J. L. Robertson and J. Barling (eds), *The Psychology of Green Organisations*. New York: Oxford University Press.

Bissing-Olson, M. J., K. S. Fielding and A. Iyer (2016), 'Experiences of pride, not guilt, predict pro-environmental behavior when pro-environmental descriptive norms are more positive', *Journal of Environmental Psychology*, **45**, 145–153.

Bissing-Olson, M. J., A. Iyer, K. S. Fielding and H. Zacher (2013), 'Relationships between daily affect and pro-environmental behavior at work: The moderating role of pro-environmental attitude', *Journal of Organisational Behavior*, **34**, 156–175.

Bissing-Olson, M. J., H. Zacher, K. S. Fielding and A. Iyer (2012), 'An intraindividual perspective on pro-environmental behaviors at work', *Industrial and Organisational Psychology: Perspectives on Science and Practice*, **5**, 500–502.

Blumberg, M. and C. D. Pringle (1982), 'The missing opportunity in organisational research: Some implications for a theory of work performance', *Academy of Management Review*, **7**, 560–569.

Boiral, O. and P. Paillé (2012), 'Organisational citizenship behaviour for the environment: Measurement and validation', *Journal of Business Ethics*, **109**, 431–445.

Bolger, N. and J. P. Laurenceau (2013), *Intensive Longitudinal Methods: An Introduction to Diary and Experience Sampling Research*. New York, Guilford Press.

Bolger, N., A. Davis and E. Rafaeli (2003), 'Diary methods: Capturing life as it is lived', *Annual Review of Psychology*, **54**, 579–616.

Chi, N. W., H. T. Chang and H. L. Huang (2015), 'Can personality traits and daily positive mood buffer the harmful effects of daily negative mood on task performance and service sabotage? A self-control perspective', *Organisational Behavior and Human Decision Processes*, **131**, 1–15.

Conner, T. S. and B. J. Lehman (2012), 'Getting started: Launching a study in daily life', in M. R. Mehl and T. S. Conner (eds), *Handbook of Research Methods for Studying Daily Life*. New York: Guilford Press, pp. 89–107.

Cordano, M. and I. H. Frieze (2000), 'Pollution reduction preferences of U.S. environmental managers: Applying Ajzen's Theory of Planned Behavior', *Academy of Management Journal*, **43**, 627–641.

Dalal, R. S., D. P. Bhave and J. Fiset (2014), 'Within-person variability in job performance: A theoretical review and research agenda', *Journal of Management*, **40**, 1396–1436.

Dalal, R. S., H. Lam, H. M. Weiss, E. R. Welch and C. L. Hulin (2009), 'A within-person approach to work behavior and performance: Concurrent and lagged citizenship-counterproductivity associations, and dynamic relationships with affect and overall job performance', *Academy of Management Journal*, **52**, 1051–1066.

Fisher, C. D. and M. L. To (2012), 'Using experience sampling methodology in organisational behavior', *Journal of Organisational Behavior*, **33**, 865–877.

Fredrickson, B. L. (2003), 'Positive emotions and upward spirals in organisations', in K. S. Cameron, J. E. Dutton and R. E. Quinn (eds), *Positive Organisational Scholarship*. San Francisco, CA: Berrett-Koehler.

Goodwin, M. S. (2012), 'Passive telemetric monitoring: Novel methods for real-world behavioral assessment', in M. R. Mehl and T. S. Conner (eds), *Handbook of Research Methods for Studying Daily Life*. New York: Guilford Press.

Greaves, M., L. D. Zibarras and C. Stride (2013), 'Using the theory of planned behavior to explore environmental behavioral intentions in the workplace', *Journal of Environmental Psychology*, **34**, 109–120.

Green, A. S., E. Rafaeli, N. Bolger, P. E. Shrout and H. T. Reis (2006), 'Paper or plastic? Data equivalence in paper and electronic diaries', *Psychological Methods*, **11**, 87–105.

Gunthert, K. C. and S. J. Wenze (2012), 'Daily diary methods', in M. R. Mehl and T. S. Conner (eds), *Handbook of Research Methods for Studying Daily Life*. New York: Guilford Press.

Hackman, J. R. and G. R. Oldham (1976), 'Motivation through the design of work: Test of a theory', *Organisational Behavior and Human Performance*, **16**, 250–279.

Hektner, J. M., J. A. Schmidt and M. Csikszentmihalyi (2007), *Experience Sampling Method: Measuring the Quality of Everyday Life*. Thousand Oaks, CA: Sage.

Kaiser, F. G. and K. Byrka (2011), 'Environmentalism as a trait: Gauging people's prosocial personality in terms of environmental engagement', *International Journal of Psychology*, **46**, 71–79.

Kim, A., Y. Kim, K. Han, S. E. Jackson and R. E. Ployhart (2014), 'Multilevel influences on voluntary workplace green behavior: Individual differences, leader behavior, and coworker advocacy', *Journal of Management*, **43**(5), 1335–1358.

Klöckner, C. A. and E. Matthies (2004), 'How habits interfere with norm-directed behaviour: A normative decision-making model for travel mode choice', *Journal of Environmental Psychology*, **24**, 319–327.

Kollmuss, A. and J. Agyeman (2002), 'Mind the gap: Why do people act environmentally and what are the barriers to pro-environmental behavior?', *Environmental Education Research*, **8**, 239–260.

Liu, Y., S. Mo, Y. Song and M. Wang (2016), 'Longitudinal analysis in occupational health psychology: A review and tutorial of three longitudinal modeling techniques', *Applied Psychology: An International Review*, **65**, 379–411.

McArdle, J. J. (2009), 'Latent variable modeling of differences and changes with longitudinal data', *Annual Review of Psychology*, **60**, 577–605.

Mehl, M. R. and T. S. Conner (2012), *Handbook of Research Methods for Studying Daily Life*. New York: Guilford Press.

Mehl, M. R. and M. L. Robbins (2012), 'Naturalistic observation sampling: The electronically activated ear (EAR)', in M. R. Mehl and T. S. Conner (eds), *Handbook of Research Methods for Studying Daily Life*. New York: Guilford Press.

Moskowitz, D. S. and G. Sadikaj (2012), 'Event-contingent sampling', in M. R. Mehl and T. S. Conner (eds), *Handbook of Research Methods for Studying Daily Life*. New York: Guilford Press.

Muthén, L. K. and B. O. Muthén (2012), *Mplus Version 7*. Los Angeles, CA: Muthén and Muthén.

Nezlek, J. B. (2012), *Diary Methods*. Thousand Oaks, CA: Sage.

Norton, T. A., S. L. Parker and N. M. Ashkanasy (2017a), 'Employee green behavior and aging', in N. A. Pachana (ed.), *Encyclopedia of Geropsychology*. Singapore: Springer.

Norton, T. A., S. L. Parker, H. Zacher and N. M. Ashkanasy (2015a), 'Employee green behavior: A theoretical framework, multilevel review, and future research agenda', *Organisation and Environment*, **28**, 103–125.

Norton, T. A., H. Zacher and N. M. Ashkanasy (2012), 'On the importance of pro-environmental organisational climate for employee green behavior', *Industrial and Organisational Psychology: Perspectives on Science and Practice*, **5**, 497–500.

Norton, T. A., H. Zacher and N. M. Ashkanasy (2014), 'Organisational sustainability policies and employee green behaviour: The mediating role of work climate perceptions', *Journal of Environmental Psychology*, **38**, 49–54.

Norton, T. A., H. Zacher and N. M. Ashkanasy (2015b), 'Pro-environmental organisational culture and climate', in J. L. Robertson and J. Barling (eds), *The Psychology of Green Organisations*. New York: Oxford University Press.

Norton, T. A., H. Zacher, S. L. Parker and N. M. Ashkanasy (2017b), 'Bridging the gap between green behavioral intentions and employee green behavior: The role of green psychological climate', *Journal of Organisational Behavior*, doi: 10.1002/job.2178.

Ohly, S., S. Sonnentag, C. Niessen and D. Zapf (2010), 'Diary studies in organisational research: An introduction and some practical recommendations', *Journal of Personnel Psychology*, **9**, 79–93.

Ones, D. S. and S. Dilchert (2012a), 'Employee green behaviors', in S. E. Jackson, D. S. Ones and S. Dilchert (eds), *Managing HR for Environmental Sustainability*. San Francisco, CA: Jossey-Bass/Wiley.

Ones, D. S. and S. Dilchert (2012b), 'Environmental sustainability at work: A call to action', *Industrial and Organisational Psychology: Perspectives on Science and Practice*, **5**, 444–466.

Paillé, P. and O. Boiral (2013), 'Pro-environmental behavior at work: Construct validity and determinants', *Journal of Environmental Psychology*, **36**, 118–128.

Paillé, P., Y. Chen, O. Boiral and J. Jin (2014), 'The impact of human resource management on environmental performance: An employee-level study', *Journal of Business Ethics*, **121**, 451–466.

Ployhart, R. E. and R. J. Vandenberg (2010), 'Longitudinal research: The theory, design, and analysis of change', *Journal of Management*, **36**, 94–120.

Ramus, C. A. and U. Steger (2000), 'The roles of supervisory support behaviors and environmental policy in employee "ecoinitiatives" at leading-edge European companies', *Academy of Management Journal*, **43**, 605–626.

Raudenbush, S. W. and A. S. Bryk (2002), *Hierarchical Linear Models: Applications and Data Analysis Methods*. Thousand Oaks, CA: Sage.

Reis, H. T. and S. L. Gable (2000), 'Event-sampling and other methods for studying everyday experience', in H. T. Reis and C. M. Judd (eds), *Handbook of Research Methods in Social and Personality Psychology*. New York: Cambridge University Press.

Robertson, J. L. and J. Barling (2013), 'Greening organisations through leaders' influence on employees' pro-environmental behaviors', *Journal of Organisational Behavior*, **34**, 176–194.

Stajkovic, A. D. and F. Luthans (1998), 'Self-efficacy and work-related performance: A meta-analysis', *Psychological Bulletin*, **124**, 240–261.

Unsworth, K. L., A. Dmitrieva and E. Adriasola (2013), 'Changing behaviour: Increasing the effectiveness of workplace interventions in creating pro-environmental behaviour change', *Journal of Organisational Behavior*, **34**, 211–229.

Vancouver, J. B., C. M. Thompson and A. A. Williams (2001), 'The changing signs in the relationships among self-efficacy, personal goals, and performance', *Journal of Applied Psychology*, **86**, 605–620.

Wagner, C. H. (1982), 'Simpson's paradox in real life', *The American Statistician*, **36**, 46–48.

Wang, M., D. J. Beal, D. Chan, D. A. Newman, J. B. Vancouver and R. J. Vandenberg (2017), 'Longitudinal research: A panel discussion on conceptual issues, research design, and statistical techniques', *Work, Aging and Retirement*, **3**, 1–24.

Weiss, H. M. and R. Cropanzano (1996), 'Affective events theory: A theoretical discussion of the structure, causes and consequences of affective experiences at work', *Research in Organisational Behavior*, **18**, 1–74.

Wiernik, B. M., S. Dilchert and D. S. Ones (2016), 'Age and employee green behaviors: A meta-analysis', *Frontiers in Psychology*, **7**, 194.

Zacher, H. and R. G. Wilden (2014), 'A daily diary study on ambidextrous leadership and self-reported employee innovation', *Journal of Occupational and Organisational Psychology*, **87**, 813–820.

8. Workplace green behaviour of managerial and professional employees in Hong Kong
Yu Ha Cheung and Alicia S. M. Leung

8.1 INTRODUCTION

In response to social expectations, public policies, statutory regulations, pressures from media and non-government organisations, many multi-national corporations, either in compliance to statutory requirements or on a voluntary basis, have invested internally and externally to meet their stakeholders' expectations on environmental sustainability issues. As one of the pillars of corporate sustainability, organisations worldwide have increasingly embraced the necessity of achieving environmental sustainability. Porter and van der Linde (1995) suggested that being green serves as a new source of competitive advantage for companies. There is evidence showing that companies' green behaviours are being rewarded in the form of a better corporate image, cost reductions, increased market performance and competitiveness, and higher stock-market premiums (Ambec and Lanoie 2008; Cetindamar and Husoy 2007; Fussler et al. 2004; Griffin and Mahon 1997; Jo et al. 2015).

While the organisation-level study of environmental sustainability has received substantial attention, the investigation of individual-level green behaviour in the workplace remains limited (Scherbaum et al. 2008). Organisations' actions have been regarded as the largest direct source of many environmental problems, and they are taking measures to alleviate the problems as ways to be socially responsible. Among the measures taken, the most common initiative is encouraging employees to behave in an environmentally friendly manner or act green in the workplace (Society for Human Resource Management 2009). Indeed, the aggregate of the green actions of each individual employee taken in the workplace should have a significant impact on the environment in a positive way (Stern 2000).

In general, green behaviour refers to behaviour which aims to reduce resources and energy consumption, cutting waste and gas emissions, and increasing the use of renewable, recyclable, and non-toxic substances and materials in private, public, and work contexts (Kollmuss and Agyeman

2002; Stern 2000). Researchers have suggested individuals' engagement in green behaviour is influenced by personal characteristics and situational factors (e.g., Black et al. 1985; Kim et al. 2017; Steg and Vlek 2009). Given that "the determinants of individual behaviour within organisations are likely to be different from those of political or household behaviours" (Stern 2000: 410), it is important to explore how both personal and situation factors affect employees' engagement in green behaviour in the workplace.

In this chapter, we aim to examine some proximal predictors of employee green behaviour in the workplace. Although the importance of workplace green behaviour is becoming increasingly well recognised, we know little about the factors affecting employees' engagement in green behaviour. More specifically, we examine the relationships of job characteristics (autonomy at work), management involvement (i.e., management expectations on employees' engagement in green behaviour and formal green initiatives including committees) and employee intrinsic motivation to green behaviour (intrinsic motivation). Understanding the impact of these factors is essential in helping us to develop a theoretical framework for investigating workplace green behaviour and developing strategies to foster workplace green behaviour.

8.2   WORKPLACE GREEN BEHAVIOUR

Green behaviour has been defined in a number of ways, such as pro-environmental behaviour (Kollmuss and Agyeman 2002), environmentally friendly behaviour (Bamberg 2002), environmental behaviour (Berger 1997), eco-friendly behaviour (Ohtomo and Hirose 2007), environmental significant behaviour (Stern 2000), environmentally conscious behaviour (Lee and Holden 1999), environmentally responsible behaviour (Caltabiano and Caltabiano 1995), or low-carbon behaviour. Kollmuss and Agyeman (2002: 240) defined pro-environmental behaviour as "behaviour that consciously seeks to minimise the negative impact of one's actions on the natural and built world". Individual-level green behaviour can take place in the public sphere, private sphere, and within organisations and the factors influencing individuals' engagement in green behaviour is thought to vary across situations (Stern 2000).

Acting green requires engagement from organisation members of all levels. The implementation of environmental management systems (e.g., ISO 14001), development of pro-environmental strategies, and adoption of eco-friendly technologies, work processes and practices are dependent on management (Jo et al. 2015; Sharma 2000). However, it is widely recognised that employees' engagement in workplace green behaviours is an indispensable force in reducing pollution caused by organisations (Boiral 2005). The successful implementation of green initiatives, either for compliance of statutory or regulatory requirements and societal expectations, requires the collective actions of all organisational members, not merely senior management. Interestingly, acting green in the workplace is not normally specified in job descriptions and employees are not obligated to behave green. Unless explicitly specified, in a sense workplace green behaviour can be regarded as a form of extra-role behaviour or organisational citizenship behaviour (Boiral 2009; Kim et al. 2017). This poses additional challenges for management to implement green initiatives.

In terms of the human resources input for pursuing environmental sustainability, Pfeffer (2010) stresses the importance of managing employees and orchestrating their efforts to conserve resources and minimise waste in operations in order to reduce the burden imposed on the environment. Encouraging employees to engage in workplace green behaviour is an indispensable element in achieving environmental sustainability in addition to redesigning work or production processes, purchasing eco-friendly machinery, equipment, and materials, and building eco-friendly infrastructure. Unlike the installation of hardware and redesign of work processes, which can be a one-off effort, continuous support and persistent efforts from employees in engaging in various forms of pro-environmental behaviours are necessary in order to yield significant positive results.

8.3   HONG KONG'S GREEN EFFORTS

Early efforts to act green have been mainly from the Hong Kong Government as the business community and the general public were not familiar with the concept of acting green (Chan and Yam 1995). The establishment of the Environmental Protection Department (EPD) in 1986 marked the Hong Kong Government's commitment to protecting the environment. The early EPD's primary functions were limited to environmental law enforcement and environmental politics implementation. After a 2005 restructuring, the EPD was housed under the Environment Bureau created in 2007 to oversee the formation and implementation of policies which relate to the city's environmental protection and sustainable development, such as air and noise pollution, energy and water consumption, waste management, natural conservation, and international cooperation in environmental protection issues. Over the years, the EPD has grown from a department with 283 staff in 1987 to more than 1,839 staff in 2015 (www.epd.gov.hk).

Engagement from the business community and the general public to act green is the key to combating environmental problems. In the White Paper "Pollution in Hong Kong – A Time to Act" released in 1989, it indicated that regulatory efforts and education would be the main means to protect the environment. In 1990, the Private Sector Committee on Environment was set up to encourage participation from the business community and to facilitate government-and-business cooperation in tackling environmental problems. The Environmental Campaign Committee was also formed in the same year to promote public awareness of and participation in environmental protection issues. Despite a range of policies, schemes, and initiatives, acting green is mainly a matter of compliance to laws and regulations and/or a corporate social responsibility action for the business community. It has been suggested that the enforcement of environmental related laws and regulations was inadequate because companies were not required to disclose compliance information (Ho et al. 1994; Ng 2000).

In terms of disclosure, Hong Kong companies appeared to be less willing to disclose information related to environment and energy use but more willing to disclose information about community involvement and fair business practices (Gao et al. 2005). The efforts in pushing and pulling the business community to act green have been greatly strengthened by the new reporting requirement implemented by the Hong Kong Stock Exchange (HKEx) in 2016. Listed companies in Hong Kong are required to disclose policies, compliance, and performance data on various environmental and social aspects in their annual or Environmental, Social, and Governance (ESG) reports submitted to the Hong Kong Stock Exchange. At present, the environment part includes three aspects: emission (6 KPIs), use of resources (5 KPIs), and environmental impacts and management (1 KPI) (Hong Kong Stock Exchange 2015).

For the green efforts exerted by small and medium-sized enterprises (SMEs), it appears that they are less willing and capable of engaging in green initiatives beyond the regulatory requirements than large companies. Studer and colleagues reported that most SMEs in Hong Kong considered voluntary environmental activities (e.g., environmental support programmes and award schemes) as costly and unnecessary activities, such that these activities exerted limited impact in uplifting SMEs' environmental performance in Hong Kong (Studer et al. 2006; Studer et al. 2008). In addition to costs and resources, insufficient knowledge appears to be another challenge for SMEs to act green, such as in green procurement (Ho et al. 2010). Unlike large companies, which have the financial, technical, and human resources to institutionalise green efforts, such as by obtaining ISO 14001 certification, SMEs are less privileged in these aspects. Their employees are likely the major contributor to SMEs' green efforts.

Obtaining various green certifications and green/eco labels from pro-environmental groups, local and international institutions are a useful means for many Hong Kong companies and public organisations to show their green commitment and achievements, e.g., ISO 14001 certification, WWF Hong Kong's Low Carbon Operation Programme, Hong Kong Green Organisation Certification, and Hong Kong Green Mark Certification. To recognise and reward the green contributions of the business community and public organisations, a number of election or competition campaigns are organised annually by various pro-environmental groups, federations of industries and trades, corporations, and the EPD, e.g., Hong Kong Green Awards, Hong Kong Awards for Environmental Excellence, Hong Kong Green Innovations Award, Sustainable Business Award, Hang Seng Pan Pearl River Delta Environment Awards, and BOCHK Corporate Environmental Leadership Awards, etc. As 98 per cent of the Hong Kong companies are SMEs and they employ about 46 per cent of the workforce in the private sector, their engagement in environmentally friendly behaviour has a great impact on the city's sustainable development. In recognition of the SMEs' contributions, many awards have a sub-category for SMEs. Thus, motivating employees to act green is an important sustainability topic for organisations of all sizes in Hong Kong.

8.4   FACTORS AFFECTING WORKPLACE GREEN BEHAVIOUR

Researchers have suggested a number of individual and organisational factors influencing employees' green behaviours in the workplace. Daily et al. (2009) theorised that employees' environmental concern, organisational commitment, perceived supervisory support for environmental efforts, and perceived corporate social performance are key determinants of their engagement in green behaviours. Using a health service organisation in the UK as an illustration, Tudor et al. (2007) suggested that employees' beliefs about the severity and benefit of waste management are important predictors for their waste management behaviours. Scherbaum et al. (2008) found that individuals' environmental worldviews and environmental personal norms affected employees' energy-conservation behaviours and behavioural intentions.

Although a formal environmental management system (EMS) can provide an integrated solution for organisations to function pro-environmentally, the actions of senior management also play an important role in affecting employees' engagement in workplace green behaviour. For instance, Daily and her colleagues found that management support was directly related to the environmental performance of the organisation as perceived by employees (Daily et al. 2007). As an extra-role behaviour, we also expect that job characteristics are likely to affect workplace green behaviour. Indeed, Parker and Wall (1998) found that job characteristics have a stronger relationship with extra-role behaviour than with in-role behaviour.

Researchers have stressed the importance of taking an integrative approach in investigating green behaviour at the individual-level. In his discussion of the barriers to act pro-environmentally, Blake (1999) identified three types of barriers: individuality, responsibility, and practicality. Individuality referred to attitude and personality; responsibility referred to the perceived control of the situation or felt responsibility to the situation; and practicality referred to social and institutional constraints to act in an environmentally friendly manner. In addition to the proposition of taking an integrative approach in examining factors that encourage pro-environmental behaviour, Steg and Vlek (2009) also highlighted the importance of studying the proximal antecedents. The purpose of this study is to examine how some proximal personal, organisational and job characteristics are related to commitment in workplace green behaviour of managerial and professional employees in Hong Kong.

8.4.1 Autonomy at Work

According to Hackman and Oldham (1980), employees who perceive higher levels of autonomy at work are more likely to believe their work output is a function of their own efforts and decisions, which in turn makes them feel more responsible for their work. With higher levels of autonomy at work, employees not only have more control over how to perform their in-role duties, but are also empowered to take new initiatives other than their immediate tasks (Frese et al. 1996). In other words, autonomy at work provided by management is likely to influence employees' perception about the feasibility of modifying their work practices and routines to become more pro-environmental.

Hypothesis 1: Autonomy at work will be positively related to engagement in workplace green behaviour.

8.4.2   Management Involvement

As environmentally conscious employees may not necessarily act green due to social pressure or practicality (Ohtomo and Hirose 2007), we expect that management involvement plays a crucial role in affecting employees' green behaviour in the workplace. This is because management expectations have a powerful effect on employees' workplace behaviour. When management expresses their wish to create a green workplace, whether it is done through internal promotion, changes in work and production process and procedures, use of more energy efficient machinery, or establishment of a formal committee or positions for promoting and implementing environmentally friendly initiatives, it shows a clear signal to employees about the expectations of acting green.

More importantly, management involvement legitimises the idea of "being green" as an indispensable element of achieving corporate sustainability and also as a means of fulfilling corporate social responsibility (Greening and Gray 1994). As a result of this legitimisation, the managerial and professional employees will be more likely to frame green initiatives as an opportunity rather than a threat and support the green initiatives (Sharma 2000).

Bamberg (2002) suggested that individuals who have an implementation plan are more likely to act green. Management green involvement is likely to prompt employees' intention to act pro-environmentally and encourage those who have already had the intention or plan to act accordingly. Thus, management involvement is a positive force for employee's engagement in workplace green behaviour.

Hypothesis 2: Management expectations will be positively related to engagement in workplace green behaviour.

Hypothesis 3: Having a committee or designated personnel for green initiatives in the organisation will be positively related to engagement in workplace green behaviour.

8.4.3   Intrinsic Motivation

Similar to green actions in the non-work context, employees' engagement in green behaviour in the workplace is presumably due to their genuine concern about the well-being of nature and human habitats (Bamberg 2003). As a form of extra-role behaviour with an implication of changing some work processes and behaviour in the workplace in favour of protecting the environment, employees need to take charge of their actions (Morrison and Phelps 1999). Intrinsic motivation is an important determinant of green behaviour because of its function in directing attention and regulating effort, especially when persistence of effort is required (Kanfer 1990). Being persistent is essential to tackling long-term problems such as conservation and pollution because it requires behaviour change and adopting new habits and routines. There has been emerging evidence indicating that intrinsically motivated employees are more likely to sustain their green efforts because they feel good about their actions (van der Linden 2015).

When employees are intrinsically driven to act green, they are more driven to acquire information and learn how to create a green workplace and devote time and effort to engage in green behaviour. Moreover, being intrinsically motivated, employees are more capable of seeking out opportunities to act in an environmentally friendly manner in the workplace (Hostager et al. 1998). Therefore, they are more likely to advocate for the cause and be innovative in their green actions – acting as green champions in organisations. Conversely, the green efforts of employees who are only extrinsically motivated may only be temporary. Using data from students of Princeton University who participated in a nationwide campus energy competition initiative, van der Linden (2015) found that energy consumption was significantly lower during the competition (extrinsic motivation) but bounced back to the before-competition level.

Hypothesis 4: Intrinsic motivation will be positively related to workplace green behaviour.

8.5 METHOD

We invited 337 full-time employees enrolled in the postgraduate programmes of a local university in Hong Kong to complete a 2-wave online survey. An invitation email with a link to the Time 1 online survey was sent to each potential participant. The purpose of the survey was explained, confidentiality of the responses and voluntary participation were emphasised in the invitation email. To encourage participation, we offered a HK$50 supermarket coupon (£5) as an incentive for completing the 2-wave survey. Three weeks after the completion of the Time 1 survey, the Time 2 online survey link was emailed to the respondents. A reminder email was sent one week after each wave of invitation email. We received 215 responses at Time 1 and 199 of matched responses at Time 2, representing 59.05 per cent of the initial sample. A listwise deletion reduced the sample size to 194 because of missing data. In this sample, 75.8 per cent of the respondents were female and 47.5 per cent were in the age range of 26 to 30. In terms of the nature of their employment organisations, 63.9 per cent were private companies and 47.9 per cent were small to medium organisations (fewer than 1,000 employees).

8.5.1 Measures

Data about all predictors (autonomy at work, management expectations, and intrinsic motivation), except committee/green personnel, were collected in Time 1. Data about workplace green behaviour was collected in Time 2. Table 8.1 contains the measures included in the study.

8.6 RESULTS

We conducted a confirmatory factor analysis to test construct distinctiveness (see Table 8.2). The results showed that a seven-factor model fit the data well (χ^2 = 417.16, df = 254; Comparative Fit Index (CFI) = .94; Tucker-Lewis Index (TLI) = .92; Root Mean Square Error of Approximation (RMSEA) = .06). Descriptive statistics and zero-order intercorrelations of the variables are presented in Table 8.3. Zero-order correlations indicate that intrinsic motivation and management expectations were significantly correlated with engagement in general green behavivour and low-carbon office practices. We tested our hypotheses using hierarchical regression analyses and the result is shown in Table 8.4.

Autonomy at work significantly predicted champion green behaviour (β = .17, $p \leq .05$) and was only marginally related to electricity use (β = .15, $p \leq .10$). Thus, Hypothesis 1 received partial support. Hypothesis 2 received some support as management expectations significantly predicted conventional green behaviour (β = .17, $p \leq .05$), paper use (β = .30, $p \leq .001$), and electricity use (β = .16, $p \leq .05$) but not champion green behaviour. Hypothesis 3 suggested that having a committee or designated personnel for green initiatives in the organisation would be positively related to engagement in workplace green behaviour. However, our results did not support this hypothesis. Hypothesis 4 suggested that intrinsic motivation was positively related to workplace green behaviour and it was fully supported. As shown in Table 8.3, intrinsic motivation significantly predicted champion green behaviour (β = .38, $p \leq .001$), conventional green behaviour (β = .27, $p \leq .001$), paper use (β = .24, $p \leq .001$), and electricity use (β = .19, $p \leq .01$).

Table 8.1　Variables and measures

Predictors

Intrinsic motivation
- 4 items; α = .91
- adapted from Tierney et al.'s (1999) intrinsic motivation scale
- measure employee enjoyment for activities related to generating new ideas for environmentally friendly work processes and products
- 5-point Likert scale (1 = "Strongly disagree" to 5 = "Strongly agree")
- Sample item: "I enjoy coming up with new ideas for environmentally friendly work processes or products"

Management expectations
- 4 items; α = .93
- measure management expectations on engaging in environmentally friendly behaviour, implementing environmentally friendly work processes and practices, deriving environmentally friendly work procedures and production processes, and procurement of environmentally friendly products
- 5-point Likert scale (1 = "Strongly disagree" to 5 = "Strongly agree")
- Sample item: "All units or departments are expected to procure environmentally friendly products"

Committee/Green personnel
- whether the organisation has "a committee or a designated person responsible for promoting and implementing environmentally friendly policies and practices"
- "Yes" = 1; "No" = 2

Autonomy at work
- 3 items; α = .87
- measure employees' perception of autonomy in designing and arranging their work
- Spreitzer's (1995) self-determination sub-dimension of psychological empowerment
- 5-point Likert scale (1 = "Strongly disagree" to 5 = "Strongly agree")
- Sample item: "I have significant autonomy in determining how I do my work"

Workplace Green Behaviour

General green behaviour
1. Champion green behaviour
- 4 items; α = .89
- adapted from Scott and Bruce's (1994) entrepreneurial behaviour to reflect employees' initiatives taken in pursuit of green ideas and practices
- Sample item: "Promote and champion environmentally friendly ideas and practices to others"

Table 8.1   (continued)

Workplace Green Behaviour

2. Conventional green behaviour
   - 3 items; α = .72
   - Sample item: "Follow environmentally friendly work processes and practices recommended by others"
   - 5-point Likert scale (1 = "Not at all like me" to 5 = "Very much like me")

Low-carbon office practices
   - Based on the 5 performance areas of WWF Hong Kong's Low Carbon Office Operation Programme: lighting, computer and office equipment, paper use, printing and photocopying, and heat ventilation and air conditioning (HVAC)

1. Paper use
   - 3 items; α = .66
   - Sample item: "I copy double-sided"

2. Electricity use
   - 4 items; α = .75
   - adopted from Scherbaum et al.'s (2008) energy conservation behaviour
   - Sample item: "I turn off the air conditioning when I leave my work area"
   - 5-point Likert scale (1 = "Never" to 5 = "Always")

Control Variables
   - Age
   - Gender
   - Self-esteem (Rosenberg's (1965) 10-item scale; α = .79)
   - Felt responsibility for change (Morrison and Phelp's (1999) 5-item scale; α = .70)
   - Organisation size
   - Country-origin of the organisation (i.e., Local or Non-local)
   - Organisation type (i.e., Private or Public)

8.7   DISCUSSION

Our study provides some initial evidence showing the relative impacts of some proximal predictors of employees' engagement in workplace green behaviour. Among the predictors, intrinsic motivation was the most robust predictor for all four types of workplace green behaviour. This result is consistent with recent propositions raised by scholars (e.g., van der Linden 2015).

Autonomy at work appeared to have a stronger effect on champion green behaviour than the conventional type of green behaviour. Champion green behaviour is comparatively more complex and cognitively demanding.

Table 8.2   Rotated factor analysis of workplace green behaviour

Items	Factor 1	Factor 2	Factor 3	Factor 4
General Green Behaviour[a]				
Search out environmentally friendly technologies, processes, techniques, and/or products.	**.795**	.110	.100	.281
Promote and champion environmentally friendly ideas and practices to others.	**.774**	.090	.106	.288
Develop plans and schedules for the implementation of environmentally friendly ideas.	**.901**	.110	.055	.019
Investigate and secure resources needed to implement environmentally friendly ideas and practices.	**.847**	.116	.023	.157
Follow environmentally friendly work processes and practices recommended by others.	.419	−.050	.087	**.692**
Consume products made by renewable or recycled materials.	.415	.117	.185	**.515**
Adopt work habits that save energy and natural resources.	.251	.114	.094	**.743**
Low-carbon Office Practices[b]				
I copy double-sided.	.095	.111	**.878**	.094
I print double-sided.	.133	−.059	**.880**	.043
I recycle used paper.	−.089	.290	**.565**	.350
I turn off the computer when I finish using it.	−.097	**.519**	−.054	.415
I turn off the lights when I leave a room that is unoccupied.	.005	**.804**	.028	.142
I turn off the screen when I am not using my computer.	.140	**.658**	.137	.059
I turn off the air conditioning when I leave my work area.	.249	**.777**	.071	−.050
I keep the thermostat at the temperature recommended by the government.	.226	.397	.361	−.207

Notes: Loadings of the items for each factor are bolded.
a Respondents were asked to indicate how accurately each statement describes their involvement in green behaviour in general, using a 5-point Likert scale (1 = "Not at all like me" to 5 = "Very much like me").
b Respondents were asked to indicate how often they engage in each behaviour using a 5-point Likert scale (1 = "Never" to 5 = "Always").

Table 8.3 *Descriptive statistics and zero-order correlations of variables*

Variables	Mean	s.d.	1	2	3	4	5	6	7	8	9	10	11	12	13	14
1. Age[a]	2.52	1.26														
2. Gender[b]	.76	.43	.01													
3. Self-esteem	3.62	.48	.21**	.00												
4. Felt responsibility	3.45	.57	.29***	.01	.29***											
5. Organisation size[c]	4.46	1.96	.08	-.18*	.09	-.01										
6. Local[d]	.71	.46	-.15*	-.07	-.08	-.24***	-.03									
7. Private[e]	.64	.48	.03	.25***	.03	.21**	-.16*	-.41***								
8. Autonomy	3.57	.81	.13	.07	.33***	.35***	-.08	-.28***	.14							
9. Management expectations	3.42	.78	.04	.01	.15*	.15*	.15*	-.09	.07	.15*						
10. Committee/Green Personnel	.40	.49	.06	-.10	.07	.03	.31***	-.05	-.06	.00	.21**					
11. Intrinsic motivation	3.87	.68	.14*	.01	.16*	.28***	.08	-.09	.01	.27***	.25***	-.07				
12. Champion GB	2.94	.77	-.02	-.15*	.01	.21**	.03	.03	-.01	.16*	.13	-.02	.42***			
13. Conventional GB	3.56	.59	-.09	-.07	.14*	.02	-.01	-.03	-.01	.10	.19*	.06	.27***	.56**		
14. Paper use	4.34	.68	-.01	.07	.12	.05	.02	.09	.01	.03	.29***	-.02	.28***	.23***	.31***	
15. Electricity use	4.22	.74	.08	.10	.08	.08	-.11	.03	.05	.16*	.16*	-.02	.23***	.29***	.28***	.25***

Notes:

n = 194

a 1 = 25 or younger, 2 = 26–30, 3 = 31–35, 4 = 36–40, 5 = 41–45, 6 = 46–50, 7 = 51–55, 8 = 56 or older

b 1 = female, 2 = male

c 1 = 1–50 employees, 2 = 51–99 employees, 3 = 100–499 employees, 4 = 500–999 employees, 5 = 1000–4999 employees, 6 = 5000–9999 employees, 7 = 10,000–49,000 employees, 8 = 50,000 or more employees

d 1 = local organisation, 0 = non-local organisation

e 1 = private organisation, 0 = public organisation

*p ≤ .05 **p ≤ 0.01 ***p ≤ 0.001

Table 8.4 Hierarchical regression for workplace green behaviour

Variables	General Green Behaviour				Low-carbon Office Practices			
	Champion Green Behaviour		Conventional Green Behaviour		Paper use		Electricity use	
	β	ΔR^2	β	ΔR^2	β	ΔR^2	β	ΔR^2
Control variables		.08		.04		.04		.04
Age[a]	−.08		−.13†		−.03		.07	
Gender[b]	.15*		.07		.08		.07	
Self-esteem	−.05		.17*		.12		.07	
Felt responsibility	.26***		.00		.04		.05	
Organisation size[c]	.02		−.03		.04		−.10	
Local[d]	.07		−.06		.13		.07	
Private[e]	.01		−.03		.04		.03	
Job Characteristic		.02*		.00		.00		.02†
Autonomy at work	.17*		.07		.01		.15†	
Management Involvement		.01		.03†		.08***		.02†
Management expectations	.11		.17*		.30***		.16*	
Committee/Personnel	−.07		.03		−.08		−.01	
Individual Motivation		.12***		.06***		.05***		.03**
Intrinsic motivation	.38***		.27***		.24***		.19**	
R^2		.24***		.14**		.16***		.11*

Notes:
n = 194 Standardised coefficients are reported
a 1 = 25 or younger, 2 = 26–30, 3 = 31–35, 4 = 36–40, 5 = 41–45, 6 = 46–50, 7 = 51–55, 8 = 56 or older
b 1 = female, 2 = male
c 1 = 1–50 employees, 2 = 51–99 employees, 3 = 100–499 employees, 4 = 500–999 employees, 5 = 1000–4999 employees, 6 = 5000–9999 employees, 7 = 10,000–49,000 employees, 8 = 50,000 or more employees
d 1 = local organisation, 0 = non-local organisation
e 1 = private organisation, 0 = public organisation
† p ≤ .10 *p ≤ .05 **p ≤ 0.01 ***p ≤ 0.001

Employees need to put in extra effort to identify problems, search for relevant information, and generate innovative alternatives and solutions (Zhang and Bartol 2010). Thus, employees will engage in more champion green behaviour only if they have a relatively high degree of control and freedom to do their work.

In examining the links between management involvement and workplace green behaviour, our results indicated that management expectations are a key determinant. Although it was positively linked to conventional green behaviour, paper use, and electricity use, interestingly, it was not related to champion green behaviour. This may imply that employees will behave pro-environmentally as a demonstration of their compliance with management expectations.

Organisations often introduce steering committees, task forces, or designated staff to manage green initiatives as a strategic response to institutional pressures (Child and Tsai 2005; DiMaggio and Powell 1983). Contrary to our expectation, having a committee or designated personnel responsible for implementation of green initiatives was not significantly related to any forms of workplace green behaviour. This may be explained by the fact that a committee or designated personnel play a symbolic role. The lack of authority and resources of these institutional arrangements hamper their functionality. Therefore, our results suggested that symbolic institutional arrangements may not be an effective intervention in affecting employees' workplace green behaviour.

8.8   MANAGERIAL IMPLICATIONS

One of the key findings in this study is the lack of a relationship between having a committee or designated personnel and workplace green behaviour. About 40 per cent of the respondents reported the existence of such arrangements in their organisations, especially large ones. If employees see them as a symbolic gesture or a necessary component for accreditation or certification, their functions and effectiveness may be impaired. The good news is that, even without these institutional arrangements, employees can be motivated by the green involvement of the management. This is particularly encouraging for the SMEs.

Our results suggest that management expectations are an important determinant of workplace green behaviour. Organisations should enhance their communication with employees to increase their understanding of the organisation's expectations. Moreover, these communications should be explicit and not symbolic. Walking one's talk is essential to show management's determination of acting green. Talking and acting towards green initiatives is likely to communicate a clear and strong message to employees about management's seriousness and commitment to act responsibly towards environmental sustainability. Talking without acting is likely to arouse negative responses from employees (Walker and Wan 2012). Moreover, since the respondents in our study are managerial and professional employees, they are likely to serve as role models for their subordinates and other co-workers because of their status (Kim et al. 2017). Thus, gaining the "buy-in" from these employees is especially important.

Organisations should also explore a wide range of measures to encourage their employees to act green. As our results indicate, having a committee or designated staff to manage environmentally friendly initiatives has little impact on influencing their workplace green behaviour. Since the respondents in our study were well-educated, managerial or professional employees, they are more likely to gain access to strategic information and knowledge. Therefore, in addition to establishing a structure, developing concrete strategies and providing information and resources, empowering employees may be more effective in changing workplace behaviour of environmental concerns (Steg and Vlek 2009).

Top management can take several basic steps in developing environmental education, such as providing information and knowledge about environmental issues and skills in environmental action strategies, in order to raise employees' awareness about the importance of acting green (Hines et al. 1986–87). As our results showed that enhancing employees' intrinsic motivation to act green is particularly important, management should explore means to increase the employees' intrinsic motivation. For instance, in addition to providing environmental education, organisations can provide opportunities for employees to be involved in green activities. These activities can either be conducted internally as staff interests or recreation programmes, or as collaborative programmes organised in partnership with external green groups, such as WWF, Friends of the Earth, Green Power, and World Green Organisation, etc. The primary goal of encouraging employees to participate in these activities is to help employees internalise the value of going green and develop green habits through employee engagement.

8.9   LIMITATIONS AND FUTURE RESEARCH

One limitation of the current research is our self-reported data. Although common method variance is an issue, we believe the problem was reduced as the data of predictors and dependent variables were collected at different times, separated by a three-week period. As our samples were well-educated, full-time managerial and professional employees, we are not certain the results could be generalised to less-educated, non-managerial and non-professional employees. Future research should expand the diversity of the sample in their studies.

In this study, we only explored one motivation variable – how intrinsic motivation was linked to workplace green behaviour. Future research should explore how other motives may be related to workplace green behaviour, such as altruistic motives or status motives. For altruistic motives, individuals would engage in workplace green behaviour in order to be a good citizen of the organisation or the community. There is substantive evidence supporting the connection of altruism and environmental issues in various domains (e.g., Schultz and Zelezny 1998). For status motives, engagement in workplace green behaviour can build a pro-environmental reputation with work groups or organisations (Semmann et al. 2005). An experimental study found that status motives were associated with purchase intentions of products, regardless of whether they are visible or non-visible to others (Griskevicius et al. 2010).

Although we hypothesised and found that the expectations of management on employees' green behaviour was significant, we did not examine the impacts of their actual actions other than setting up a committee or having a designated person to implement green initiatives. Future research may consider exploring how different forms of management green actions may be related to employees' workplace green behaviour, either positively or negatively. For instance, positive reinforcement, such as awards or expression of gratitude, may encourage employees to act pro-environmentally. Geller (2002) pointed out that rewards are effective in motivating green behaviour because of the positive affect and attitudes elicited from their behavioural change. From a series of experiments, Grant and Gino (2010) found that expression of thanks doubled the likelihood of further helping and increased the frequency of helping actions and time spent on helping.

As noted by Steg and Vlek (2009), examining the effectiveness of various interventions in promoting green behaviour is another important topic for future research. They proposed two strategies (i.e., informational and structural strategies) to reward green behaviour and punish environmentally unfriendly behaviour. Informational strategies include provision of information, persuasion, social support and role models, and participation. Structural strategies include availability of products and services, regulatory requirements, and pricing. Future research may explore the application of these two strategies and evaluate their effectiveness in organisational settings.

REFERENCES

Ambec, S. and P. Lanoie (2008), 'Does it pay to be green? A systematic overview', *Academy of Management Perspectives*, **22** (4), 45–62.

Bamberg, S. (2002), 'Effects of implementation inventions on the actual performance of new environmentally friendly behaviors – results of two field experiments', *Journal of Environmental Psychology*, **22** (4), 399–411.

Bamberg, S. (2003), 'How does environmental concern influence specific environmental related behaviors? A new answer to an old question', *Journal of Environmental Psychology*, **23** (1), 21–32.

Berger, I. (1997), 'The demographics of recycling and the structure of environmental behavior', *Environment and Behavior*, **29** (4), 515–531.

Black, J., P. Stern and J. Elworth (1985), 'Personal and contextual influences on household energy adaptations', *Journal of Applied Psychology*, **70** (1), 3–21.

Blake, J. (1999), 'Overcoming the "value-action gap" in environmental policy: Tensions between national policy and local experience', *Local Environment*, **4** (3), 257–278.

Boiral, O. (2005), 'The impact of operator involvement in pollution reduction: Case studies in Canadian chemical companies', *Business Strategy and the Environment*, **14** (6), 339–360.

Boiral, O. (2009), 'Greening the corporation through organizational citizenship behaviors', *Journal of Business Ethics*, **87** (2), 221–236.

Caltabiano, N. and M. Caltabiano (1995), 'Assessing environmentally responsible behaviour', *Psychological Reports*, **76** (3 Supp.), 1080–1082.

Cetindamar, D. and K. Husoy (2007), 'Corporate social responsibility practices and environmentally responsible behavior: The case of the United Nations Global Compact', *Journal of Business Ethics*, **76** (2), 163–176.

Chan, R. and E. Yam (1995), 'Green movement in a newly industrializing area: A survey on attitudes and behavior of the Hong Kong citizens', *Journal of Community and Applied Social Psychology*, **5** (4), 273–284.

Child, J. and T. Tsai (2005), 'The dynamic between firms' environmental strategies and institutional constraints in emerging economies: Evidence from China and Taiwan', *Journal of Management Studies*, **42** (1), 95–125.

Daily, B., J. Bishop and N. Govindarajulu (2009), 'A conceptual model for organizational citizenship behavior directed toward the environment', *Business and Society*, **48** (2), 243–256.

Daily, B., J. Bishop and R. Steiner (2007), 'The mediating role of EMS teamwork as it pertains to HR Factors and perceived environmental performance', *Journal of Applied Business Research*, **23** (1), 95–109.

DiMaggio, P. and W. Powell (1983), 'The iron cage revisited: Institutional isomorphism and collective rationality in organizational fields', *American Sociological Review*, **48** (2), 147–160.

Frese, M., W. Kring, A. Soose and J. Zempel (1996), 'Personal initiative at work: Differences between East and West Germany', *Academy of Management Journal*, **39** (1), 37–63.

Fussler, C., A. Cramer and S. Van der Vegt (2004), *Raising the Bar: Creating Value with the United Nations Global Compact*, Sheffield: Greenleaf Publishing.

Gao, S., S. Heravi and J. Xiao (2005), 'Determinants of corporate social and environmental reporting in Hong Kong: A research note', *Accounting Forum*, **29** (2), 233–242.

Geller, E. Scott (2002), 'The challenges of increasing proenvironmental behavior', in Robert Bechtel and Arza Churchman (eds), *Handbook of Environmental Psychology*, New York: Wiley, pp. 525–540.

Grant, A. and F. Gino (2010), 'A little thanks goes a long way: Explaining why gratitude expressions motivate prosocial behavior', *Journal of Personality and Social Psychology*, **98** (6), 946–955.

Greening, D. and B. Gray (1994), 'Testing a model of organizational response to social and political issues', *Academy of Management Journal*, **37** (3), 467–498.

Griffin, J. and J. Mahon (1997), 'The corporate social performance and corporate financial performance debate: Twenty-five years of incomparable research', *Business and Society*, **36** (1), 5–31.

Griskevicius, V., J. Tybur and B. Van den Bergh (2010), 'Going green to be seen: Status, reputation, and conspicuous conservation', *Journal of Personality and Social Psychology*, **98** (3), 392–404.

Hackman, J. Richard and Greg Oldham (1980), *Work Redesign*, Reading, MS: Addison-Wesley.

Hines, J., H. Hungerford and A. Tomera (1986–87), 'Analysis and synthesis of research on responsible pro-environmental behavior: A meta-analysis', *The Journal of Environmental Education*, **18** (2), 1–8.

Ho, L., N. Dickinson and G. Chan (2010), 'Green procurement in the Asian public sector and the Hong Kong private sector', *Natural Resources Forum*, **34** (1), 24–38.

Ho, S., P. Ng and A. Ng (1994), 'A study of environmental reporting in Hong Kong', *Hong Kong Accountant*, **5** (1), 62–65.

Hong Kong Stock Exchange (2015), Main Board Rules 13.91, Appendix 27 Environmental, Social and Governance Reporting Guide, accessed 11 January 2017 at http://en-rules.hkex.com.hk/net_file_store/new_rulebooks/h/k/HKEX4476_3841_VER10.pdf.

Hostager, T., T. Neil, R. Decker and R. Lorentz (1998), 'Seeing environmental opportunities: Effects of intrapreneurial ability, efficacy, motivation and desirability', *Journal of Organizational Change Management*, **11** (1), 11–25.

Jo, H., H. Kim and K. Park (2015), 'Corporate environmental responsibility and firm performance in the financial services sector', *Journal of Business Ethics*, **131** (2), 257–284.

Kanfer, Ruth (1990), 'Motivation theory and organizational psychology', in Marvin Dunnette and Leaetha Hough (eds), *Handbook of Industrial and Organizational Psychology* (2nd edn), vol. 1, Palo Alto, CA: Consulting Psychologists Press, pp. 75–170.

Kim, A., Y. Kim, K. Han, S. Jackson and R. Ployhart (2017), 'Multilevel influences on voluntary workplace green behavior individual differences, leader behavior, and coworker advocacy', *Journal of Management*, **43** (5), 1335–1358.

Kollmuss, A. and J. Agyeman (2002), 'Mind the gap: Why do people act environmentally and what are the barriers to pro-environmental behavior?', *Environmental Education Research*, **8** (3), 239–260.

Lee, J. and S. Holden (1999), 'Understanding the determinants of environmentally conscious behavior', *Psychology and Marketing*, **16** (5), 373–392.

Morrison, E. and C. Phelps (1999), 'Taking charge: Extra-role efforts to initiate workplace change', *Academy of Management Journal*, **42** (4), 403–419.

Ng, A. (2000), 'Going green: More cause than concern', *Australian CPA*, **70** (7), 64–65.

Ohtomo, S. and Y. Hirose (2007), 'The dual-process of reactive and intentional decision-making involved in eco-friendly behaviour', *Journal of Environmental Psychology*, **27** (2), 117–125.

Parker, S. and T. Wall (1998), *Job and Work Design: Organizing Work to Promote Well-being and Effectiveness*, Thousand Oaks, CA: Sage.

Pfeffer, J. (2010), 'Building sustainable organizations: The human factor', *Academy of Management Perspectives*, February 2010, 37–48.

Porter, M. and C. van der Linde (1995), 'Toward a new conception of the environment-competitiveness relationship', *Journal of Economic Perspectives*, **9** (4), 97–118.

Rosenberg, M. (1965), *Society and the Adolescent Self-image*, Princeton, NJ: Princeton University Press.

Scherbaum, C., P. Popovich and S. Finlinson (2008), 'Exploring individual-level factors related to employee energy-conservation behaviors at work', *Journal of Applied Social Psychology*, **38** (3), 818–835.

Schultz, P. and L. Zelezny (1998), 'Values and pro-environmental behavior: A five-country survey', *Journal of Cross-Cultural Psychology*, **29** (4), 540–558.

Scott, S. and R. Bruce (1994), 'Determinants of innovative behavior: A path model of individual innovation in the workplace', *Academy of Management Journal*, **37** (3), 580–607.

Semmann, D., H. Krambeck and M. Milinski (2005), 'Reputation is valuable within and outside one's own social group', *Behavioral Ecology and Sociology*, **57** (6), 611–616.

Sharma, S. (2000), 'Managerial interpretations and organizational context as predictors of corporate choice of environmental strategy', *Academy of Management Journal*, **43** (4), 681–697.

Society for Human Resource Management (2009), SHRM Poll: Green Initiatives, What Has Changed in One Year?, accessed 10 January 2017 at www.shrm.org/Research/SurveyFindings/Articles/Pages/GreenInitiativesduringfinanciallychallengingtimes-SHRMPoll.aspx.

Spreitzer, G. (1995), 'Psychological empowerment in the workplace: Dimensions, measurement, and validation', *Academy of Management Journal*, **38** (5), 1442–1465.

Steg, L. and C. Vlek (2009), 'Encouraging pro-environmental behaviour: An integrative review and research agenda', *Journal of Environmental Psychology*, **29** (3), 309–317.

Stern, P. (2000), 'Toward a coherent theory of environmentally significant behavior', *Journal of Social Issues*, **56** (3), 407–424.

Studer, S., R. Welford and P. Hills (2006), 'Engaging Hong Kong business in environmental change: Drivers and Barriers', *Business Strategy and the Environment*, **15** (6), 416–431.

Studer, S., S. Tsang, R. Welford and P. Hills (2008), 'SMEs and voluntary environmental initiatives: A study of stakeholders' perspectives in Hong Kong', *Journal of Environmental Planning and Management*, **51** (2), 285–301.

Tierney, P., S. Farmer and G. Graen (1999), 'An examination of leadership and employee creativity: The relevance of traits and relationships', *Personnel Psychology*, **52** (3), 591–620.

Tudor, T., S. Barr and A. Gilg (2007), 'Linking intended behavior and actions: A case study of healthcare waste management in the Cornwall NHS', *Resources, Conservation and Recycling*, **51** (1), 1–23.

van der Linden, S. (2015), 'Intrinsic motivation and pro-environmental behaviour', *Nature Climate Change*, **5** (7), 612–613.

Walker, K. and F. Wan (2012), 'The harm of symbolic actions and green-washing: Corporate actions and communications on environmental performance and their financial implications', *Journal of Business Ethics*, **109** (2), 227–242.

Zhang, X. and K. Bartol (2010), 'Linking empowering leadership and employee creativity: The influence of psychological empowerment, intrinsic motivation, and creative process engagement', *Academy of Management Journal*, **53** (1), 107–128.

9. Dare to care in environmental sustainability context: how managers can encourage employee pro-environmental behaviour
Pascal Paillé

9.1 INTRODUCTION

Over the last twenty years the ethics of care has become a framework of interest to examine to what extent the introduction of principles of care, feminism morality, and other virtues (e.g., sensitivity, compassion, empathy and so on) may contribute to shape a more sustainable workplace (Burton and Dunn 1996; Gabriel 2015; Hamington and Sander-Staudt 2011; Kroth and Keeler 2009; Lawrence and Maitlis 2012; Liedtka 1996; Simola 2003; Simola 2012; Simola et al. 2010; Solomon 1992). Since the earliest works in the area (Mayeroff 1971; Noddings 1984), the ethical care perspective has widened its scope by progressively integrating numerous fields of research (Engster 2011), and by entailing a wide range of concerns from the person to globalisation (Held 2006).

Despite this burgeoning literature, scant research has addressed the topic of sustainability through the lens of an ethics of care. This topic still remains very marginal in management theory, and even more in the human resource management literature. Yet care ethicists have repeatedly insisted on the necessity to challenge established management knowledge (Solomon 1998). If the protection of the natural environment (as the cared-for) is the ultimate objective for a better society (Becker 2012), the organisational members (as caregivers) are a means to this end. For this to be done, in accordance with Liedtka (1996), employees should be at the centre of management's attention in order to develop a caring community within the organisation.

Sama et al. (2004) have proposed that responsiveness should be stimulated at the organisational level (i.e., senior management), and should be widespread among all members to create a community of care practice toward the natural environment. Paillé et al. (2016) put the focus at the colleague-level, and reported that experiencing social exchange among peers shapes a work context which fosters the willingness to help colleagues who want to care about the natural environment. A missing piece of the current literature is the role that can be played by immediate managers in such a community of caring practice. Accordingly, this chapter discusses and rethinks the role of the manager for the achievement of sustainability. The chapter is organised as follows. In the first section, although I recognise that the ethical care perspective is deeper and implies a wide range of other issues, I propose to give some benchmarks on the main aspects of the ethics of care on which we will focus. In the next section, my intention is to put environmental sustainability on the map to better understand how managers may contribute to sustainability at their own level by adopting care principles that help achieve a better society. I continue by highlighting the responsibility of corporations for supporting managers to enact caring activities in the context of environmental sustainability.

9.2 ETHICS OF CARE: THEORETICAL FOUNDATIONS

9.2.1 The Origin of Ethics of Care

It is now well established that with the publication of *In a Different Voice* in the early 1980s, Gilligan has widely contributed to the emergence of a new approach to ethics based on care. In her book, Gilligan (1982) criticised the findings of a study undertaken by Kohlberg on moral development levels. According to Kohlberg (1969), moral development is a process that entails three distinct stages reflecting the preconventional, conventional, and postconventional moral development levels. At the preconventional level the individual is oriented toward himself, and his moral conscientiousness is not well fixed. At the conventional level, he or she orients toward others; his or her morality takes into account both laws and social norms. At the postconventional level, the morality of the individual moves from others to humankind. His or her morality is aligned with abstract principles of fairness. Hawk (2011) stated that one of the key arguments advanced by Gilligan against Kohlberg was the temptation of Kohlberg to generalise his conclusions while the data were highly contextualised (i.e., Harvard University male students). In her work, as an alternative to Kohlberg's theory, Gilligan sought to show that men and women deal with moral issues on different bases. Her conclusion is that women tend to adopt a moral reasoning which takes into account relationships with others, whereas men are more prone to rely on abstraction in their moral reasoning (Held 2006).

Essentially, Gilligan (1982) laid the foundations of an ethics of care. Subsequent works have contributed to grow and strengthen her initial propositions (Fisher and Tronto 1990; Held 2006; Noddings 1984; Tronto 1993). However, Gilligan neglected an essay entitled *On Caring*, published ten years before by Mayeroff (1971), in which the key basic principle on caring was established as follows, "to help another person grow is at least to help him to care for something or someone apart from himself, and it involves encouraging and assisting him to find and create areas of his own in which he is able to care" (p. 13). What is particularly illuminating in this quotation is the proposition that caring is not merely involved within a particular relatedness (for example, between a mother and her child), but may also be regarded in a broader perspective by taking into account a wide range of concerns tied into everyday life (this point will be discussed in section 9.3 regarding the environment). Tronto (1993) argued that more often than not, care ethicists have studied caring by prioritising interpersonal relationships, at the expense of other areas of interest. In this regard, recent works and developments have extended care by adopting a more globalising perspective demonstrating the relevance of issues such as labour, market, international affairs, and so on (Held 2006).

This extension of the scope of caring has introduced new domains in which care may take place. As such, this extension contributes to the resurfacing circles metaphor shaped by Noddings (1984). She distinguished between natural caring and ethical caring. Natural caring concerns relatedness, that is, the persons loved by caregivers (family members, friends, and so on) and are located in the inner circle. Ethical caring concerns relationships, that is, all others with whom caregivers may be bound (neighbours, organisational members, and so on), that are located in an external circle. A last and third circle outside the first two encompasses what Hawk (2011) has labelled as "the rest of the world" (p. 8). Care ethicists differently interpret how the degree of closeness entailed by these circles affects the provision of care. For example, points of discussion concern the duties of those who are able to care for someone or something. For example, Engster (2005) stated that lack of resources is one major limitation and, given this obstacle, the caregiver is more prone to prioritise the cared-for, who can effectively receive care. Additionally, Slote (2007) advanced that empathy helps to overcome obstacles that stem from spatial and/or temporal distance. This suggests that the moral obligations to care are not necessarily triggered by the closeness between the caregiver and the cared-for. This means that the cared-for located within the inner circle have no more privileges than those located in an outside circle, but the difference is explained by the ability of the caregiver to deliver the provision of care in a concrete manner.

9.2.2 The Care Process

The provision of care is a practice underlined by a set of virtues (Held 2006), that are articulated in an ongoing process (Fisher and Tronto 1990; Mayeroff 1971; Noddings 1984; Tronto 1993). This process articulates several phases of caring (similar to care attention – see Solomon 1998), taking care of, caregiving, and care-receiving. Without these virtues the aims of caring cannot be successfully achieved (Engster 2005). According to Tronto (1993) phases and virtues are intertwined.

The care activity starts with *attentiveness*, implying that the caregiver is able to recognise that someone is in need (Tronto 1993). From the standpoint of the caregiver, attentiveness assumes a minimum of knowledge about his or her abilities (Mayeroff 1971) and the situation in which the need takes place (Puka 2011) as well as empathy at some level (Engster 2005; Slote 2007). The second virtue is *responsiveness*. Once the caregiver has understood the nature of the need of the cared-for, the former becomes aware of the necessity to engage in caring in an appropriate way to fulfil the need of the latter (Engster 2005). In so doing, the caregiver makes the critical move to meet the need of the cared-for (Sander-Staudt 2011). *Respect* is the third virtue of care. In the context of care provision, respect means that the caregiver treats the cared-for while avoiding any form of judgement (Engster 2005). These three virtues are typically agreed by most care ethicist researchers such as, among others, Engster (2005), Fisher and Tronto (1990), Tronto (1993) and Sander-Staudt (2011). Two last virtues are also considered. Responsibility "generates the felt desire to fill the unmet need" (Hawk 2011: 14), and the competence to properly deliver the care that is based on adequate and sufficient resources (Tronto 1993). As an end point, while Fisher and Tronto (1990), and Tronto (1993) have connected attentiveness and responsiveness with caring about and care-receiving, respectively, Tronto (1993) and Hawk (2011) have tied responsibility to taking care of, and finally Tronto (1993) has linked competence to caregiving.

9.3 ETHICS OF CARE IN THE CONTEXT OF ENVIRONMENTAL SUSTAINABILITY

9.3.1 The Place of the Environment in the Care Ethical Perspective

Since the middle of the 2000s, the ethical care perspective has moved beyond its historical roots (incarnated by the relationships mother–child) to explore how care may be theorised in a more global perspective (see

Held 2006). However, as I explained in the general introduction, until now very little work has been undertaken to apply the ethical care perspective in the context of environmental sustainability. In the next sections, I propose to what extent the above developments give us the appropriate benchmarks we need to describe and explore caring about the natural environment within organisational settings.

Although most care ethicists have in reality never neglected the topic of the natural environment as a possible "cared-for", in a care ethics perspective they have merely suggested the environment as a topic of interest. Mayeroff (1971) introduced the possibility that individuals may care for an idea. He also proposed that caring for an idea is not so different from caring for a person, since according to his assumption in both cases the same pattern is at work. We should recognise that in his work Mayeroff has not specifically mentioned the environment as a possible cared-for. As such, in his essay, the connection between the care activity and the natural environment is not really obvious. But by starting from his point of view we can adopt a broader sense and speculate that, for a given person, caring for an idea might correspond to caring for the environment if, for this person, sustainability is an important idea, or cause, that needs to be promoted or defended. Although Noddings (1984) also believes that it is possible to care for an idea, she introduces a slight difference between people and ideas. She proposes examining ideas as a form of aesthetic caring she places beyond natural caring.

Noddings (1984) has been criticised for having limited her purpose about care activity in the motherhood relationship. However, she was among the first, and perhaps the only one at the time she wrote her essay, to develop some propositions on how the natural environment can be examined within the lens of an ethical care perspective. Noddings (1984) stated that for a human being caring for the natural environment is not the same as caring for the environment to preserve the beauty of the landscape. She claimed that behaving ethically is to protect nature for human beings, and proposed that caring for nature falls into the aesthetic domain of care, rather than the ethical domain.

Although Noddings (1984) did not deny that individuals may feel obligated to take care of nature, for her the status of cared-for cannot be granted to the natural environment, since this "cared-for" does not have the ability to contribute to the relationship. Nature cannot reciprocate. As such, in her perspective, care for the environment falls into aesthetic caring. Interestingly, when care ethicists have expanded the boundaries of care activity, the connecting point between ethics of care and environmental sustainability has become more explicit. A good example is offered by Fisher and Tronto (1990), in which they proposed that caring is an "activity that includes everything that we do to maintain, continue, and repair our 'world' so that we can live in it as well as possible. That world includes our bodies, ourselves, and our environment" (p. 40). Later, Tronto (1993) specifies that the act of care, although typically oriented toward people, can also be delivered to objects, or to the natural environment.[1] In this regard, repairing environmental damage or avoiding it in the first place assumes that individuals are aware that something should be done.

9.3.2   Extending the Scope: Moving Care Toward the Environment

Individuals may care about the environment by trying to repair environmental damage at their own level in many ways on a voluntary basis; they can minimise the consumption of energy at home (e.g., Webb et al. 2014), or they can defend the cause of the environment by engaging in activism (e.g., Dono et al. 2010). However, contrary to public or private settings, in organisational settings it could be more difficult for individuals to repair environmental damage on a voluntary basis, since they may often face a number of possible internal obstacles at organisational, managerial or individual levels (Raineri and Paillé 2016). Of course, despite these barriers employees are able to perform small gestures in a free manner, such as commuting by using public transportation (Steg and Vlek 2009). Even so, acts performed by individuals seem intuitively less significant than environmental politics undertaken by their firm (Huffman and Klein 2013).

Detrimental effects of climate change on biodiversity (Heller and Zavaleta 2009), as well as recent examples of events such as the BP oil spill (Penday et al. 2013) support a sense of necessity to care about the environment not only for our contemporaries but also for the next generations. In this regard, Held (2006) has extended the scope of care. As a concluding remark, she encompassed sustainability within the new topics that need to be addressed, by arguing that "taking responsibility for global environmental well-being would become among the central concerns of a caring global policy" (p. 166). Consistent with Held and some others (e.g., Hawk 2011), it can be proposed that when individuals care about the environment, they contribute at their own level to mitigate damage to the environment. In addition, caring about the natural environment in the short term is also adopting a care disposition toward future generations in order to reduce, as much as possible, the harmful consequences generated by previous and current generations (Becker 2012).

Held's (2006) quotation above leads to the following question: if the best expression of an act of care is the care delivered by an individual (the caregiver) to one another (the cared-for), and if the natural environment cannot be regarded as a cared-for, to what extent can an act of caring be lavished on the environment within an organisational context? As a starting point, it is noted by Noddings (1984) that "there is no true ethical relation between humans and plants because the relation is logically one-sided and there is no other consciousness to receive the caring" (p. 170). But she emphasised that one person may be offended by another when the latter acts with carelessness toward the natural environment. For example, if I do my best to sort my waste into the appropriate bins, I would be shocked if I see that other people have neglected to do the same (e.g., I find food in the recycling bin). This means that to best understand how caring can be expressed in the context of environmental sustainability, the act of caring should be decentralised and reintroduced in the relationship among persons. This also means that the ongoing process of caring described above may help us to formalise how individuals may take care of the environment.

9.4   THE CARING MANAGER IN THE CONTEXT OF ENVIRONMENTAL SUSTAINABILITY

9.4.1   Dealing with Tensions in Organisational Settings

Very little work has used the lens of an ethics of care to examine how managers might give support to his or her subordinates to help them achieve sustainability in the organisational context. According to Hawk (2011), "caring, at minimum, involves meeting the basic needs of individuals" and "developing their capabilities" (p. 25). Care activity begins with the first stage of "caring about" and the underlying virtue of attentiveness. The need expressed by the cared-for should be perceived and understood by the caregiver. Prior research shows that employees tend to adopt responsible behaviour at work when they perceive that their manager helps them to meet their needs toward the natural environment (Gkorezis 2015). Other research has reported that support provided by the leader may be affected by the employees' belief that they do not have sufficient capabilities to behave eco-friendly (Paillé et al. 2013).

In this regard, research suggests that managers have no obligation to support subordinates even if these latters feel the need to protect the environment. In an empirical qualitative study undertaken among managers in automotive industries, Fineman (1997) reported that managers have their own agenda, and often feel free to espouse or not environmental concerns even when these are acknowledged as important issues that ought to be incorporated as an element of firm strategy. Fineman (1997) has discussed part of his findings in light of Kohlberg's theory of moral development. His interpretation is that, overall, managers tend to focus their moral judgement only at the conventional level, and rarely move beyond this (i.e., to the postconventional level). Finally, Fineman (1997) also suggested that "moral conduct requires more than the application of certain ethical rules" (p. 36). Regarding the context of environmental sustainability, the ethics of care proposes ethical guidelines for shaping moral conduct based on a "feminine" perspective, drawing upon a set of virtues: interdependence, cooperation, solidarity, empowerment, compassion and so forth (see among others, Liedtka 1996; Solomon 1998; Wicks et al. 1994). As such, the ethical care perspective has a different take on the kind of situation reported by Fineman in his investigation. Caring managers are those who give priority to their relationships with other people, and more particularly with their subordinates, opting for a managerial approach that emphasises feminine virtues.

Care ethicists have strongly emphasised the importance of these feminine virtues for helping a person in need (Wicks et al. 1994). Although this aspect is central in the ethics of care, Solomon (1998) suggested that the context must be taken into account to appreciate caregiving, and is especially important within organisational contexts in which caregiving takes place. Literature on management and, more particularly, literature on human resource management, typically focuses on the employees' needs that serve the organisational interests first (Liedtka 1996). In this way, research in this area has sought to give attention to the basic needs that are more likely to trigger employee motivation toward their job (e.g., Gagné and Deci 2005).

However, care ethicists argued that within a caring organisation, profit should be the mean and individuals the end (Liedtka 1996). In this regard, Sander-Staudt (2011) argued that "developing care as a basic motive in business agents, and empowering business agents already in possession of caring empathy can help move corporations beyond the basic goal of profit generation" (p. 274). Additionally, as reminded more recently by Hawk (2011) "most care ethicists have been clear about not suborning the needs and the development of the one caring to the one cared-for" (p. 22). This means that the manager as an organisational representative should move beyond the needs merely tied to their job by encompassing as much as possible needs that are important for the employee even when these needs are less valued by the corporation in the short run. Consistent with this, Solomon (1998) argued that caring for "an employee or a manager in the organisation inevitably includes a certain concern for the person" (p. 525). From the stance of the caring manager, meeting his or her subordinates' needs can be achieved by giving them appropriate support. If the employees' needs are related to environmental concerns, this means that the caring manager should give appropriate support to help them in this area.

9.4.2 Abilities of the Caring Manager

According to Gabriel (2015), in organisational settings, support given by the leader is perhaps the best expression of the caring leader. This idea is consistent with the previous propositions by Kroth and Keeler (2009) when they modelled caring relationships between managers and subordinates (the Recursive Model of Manager–Employee Caring) based on perceived support given by the organisation, from which derives the concept of perceived supervisor support (Rhoades and Eisenberger 2002). Research in environmental sustainability has documented both theoretically (Daily et al. 2009; Lülfs and Hahn 2013; Ramus and Killmer 2007) and empirically (Cantor et al. 2012; Paillé and Boiral 2013; Ramus 2001; Ramus and Steger 2000) how support given by the leader contributes to fostering the employees' willingness to adopt attitudes and behaviours in the workplace that harm the natural environment as little as possible.

Managerial support for the environment refers to "the employee's belief that the supervisor provides subordinates with the resources and feedback needed to participate in environmental initiatives" (Cantor et al. 2012: 35). The general argument is that employees perform responsible environmental behaviour when they are supported by their manager. Although scarce, some findings give support to this argument (Cantor et al. 2012; Ramus and Steger 2000). However, even if a manager gives support to his or her subordinates, it is not sufficient in itself to consider that the former acts as a caring manager. In this regard, Gabriel (2015) has recently offered some interesting insights that can help formalise the way in which a manager acts as a caring leader in the specific context of environmental sustainability.

A caring manager should demonstrate a set of distinctive abilities. For example, according to Gabriel (2015) caring managers should be connected with their subordinates, and as such "they must be willing to give their time, advice, recognition and support generously and demonstrate that they are genuinely concerned for the realisation of a mission or a project" (p. 9). When a manager cares for his or her subordinates, he or she may contribute by sustaining an idea or a cause that is important for employees. In accordance with the core principles and feminine virtues conveyed by the ethical care perspective, we can appreciate the role of the manager by considering that individuals may also have a particular relationship with the natural environment. Thus, a caring manager helps his or her subordinates to nurture a relation with the natural environment, when he or she contributes to empower his or her subordinates by enabling them to give, in their work, the same priority to issues related to the environment as other tasks. In this case, he or she may contribute to help subordinates to develop their commitment toward the natural environment. Mesmer-Magnus et al. (2012) have defined employee environmental commitment "as the extent to which an individual is dedicated to environmental sustainability and is willing to engage in pro-environmental behaviors" (p. 170). They have speculated a strong link between employee environmental commitment and responsible behaviour toward the environment when top management and line managers are engaged with environmental sustainability and demonstrate supportive actions for the environmental cause.

Noddings (1984) has suggested that a caring relationship requires "a form of responsiveness or reciprocity on the part of the cared-for" (p. 150). Care ethicists give a lot of importance to the responsiveness displayed by the cared-for, since without the emergence of this care virtue the care activity cannot really be achieved (Engster 2005). Once they receive support from their managers, subordinates act as caregivers. As a cause that needs to be defended, the environment becomes the "cared-for." In this regard, care ethicists conceived care as a concrete act (Palmer and Stoll 2011), because care is "a form of labour" that assumes relatedness between the caregiver and the cared-for (Held 2006). That relation exists through virtues conveyed by the care process (see above). Subordinates can express their responsiveness toward the environment by performing sustainable actions in their job. The green Human Resource Management (green HRM) literature indicates that employees may adopt a wide range of friendly behaviours toward the environment, such as avoiding harm, working sustainably, influencing others, taking eco-initiatives, and conserving (Ones and Dilchert 2012). This means that in organisational settings, the provision of care for the environment can be expressed by employees in very different ways. Conserving is perhaps the most cogent act of caring for the environment, since related sustainable intentions are typically associated with concrete gestures or individual actions by which it is possible for employees to adopt an ethical position toward the environment. They can turn-off their computer before leaving their office, they can use their own cup for coffee, they can take the stairs instead of the lift, and so on. Conserving is about avoiding wastefulness, and reflects the individuals' proneness to reduce use, reuse and recycle. For example, when individuals are affected by deforestation, and concerned by the deleterious effects on local ecosystems in Amazonia, although several thousand kilometres away, they engage in a concrete act to care for the environment when they reduce paper use at work. In addition, although it could sometimes be difficult to avoid printing, individuals may nonetheless try to reduce paper consumption by printing double-sided. These examples are consistent with an ethical care perspective in the global context (Held 2006).

9.5   THE CORPORATION RESPONSIBILITY, THE CARING MANAGERS AND ENVIRONMENTAL SUSTAINABILITY

9.5.1   Helping the Manager Supply the Provision of Care

According to care ethicists, the corporation has a responsibility to supply sufficient resources to their employees to allow them to engage in care activity at work (e.g., Engster 2011; Liedtka 1996; Solomon 1998). However, from the caregiver standpoint a "want to care" is not sufficient in itself (Mayeroff 1971). To fulfil the needs of the cared-for, the caregiver should be able to deliver the care with appropriate means. In the words of Fisher and Tronto (1990), these means refer to the ability factors of time, material resources, knowledge and skills. However, as explained above, in organisational settings a lack of resources is often described as one of the internal obstacles that impede organisational members engaging in environmentally friendly behaviours (Zibarras and Ballinger 2011).

Nevertheless, care ethicists have claimed repeatedly that lack of ability is not itself a sufficient reason to allow a person to disengage from his or her moral obligations to care about someone or something. The same idea may be applied to managers. By shaping the moral judgment of the managers, these abilities give them the ethical guidelines to behave in the appropriate way. This means that the manager should overcome his or her own beliefs regarding environmental sustainability. Whatever his or her conviction about the necessity, or not, to protect the environment, the manager has the moral duty to help his or her subordinates to develop and maintain their environmental capabilities. In this regard, in accordance with the ethical care perspective, the caring manager's actions toward his or her subordinates are underpinned by the care virtue of respect.

Care ethicists have stressed that caring is helping individuals to meet their basic human capabilities (e.g., Hawk 2011). This means that caregivers should have the capacities to properly deliver care. However, typically, caregivers may face important obstacles to supplying adequate care that are a lack of means "to engage in intensive care for another" (e.g., Engster 2005). Lack of resources is even more stringent within organisations. Consistent with this, Theobald and Cooper (2011) have claimed that, often, organisational members have to do more with less resource. Hence, despite his or her benevolence, or his or her desire to fulfil basic needs of subordinates, managers may face scarcity of available resource. In such a shrinking resources context, it may be difficult to engage in a caring activity.

Care ethicists (Tronto 1993) have stated that burden is one important aspect that emerges from, and is embedded in, care activity. Turning back to the metaphor of concentric circles (Noddings 1984), it is helpful to appreciate how the employee's willingness to engage in caring activity toward the environment may be affected by burden. Whereas caring is natural in the inner circle (e.g., family members), it is ethical in a second circle (e.g., organisational members), and aesthetic in the furthest circle (e.g., the natural environment). If the caregiver is unable to provide care in an adequate manner because of lack of resources in terms of time and/or skills, he or she is likely to become burdened, especially when the provision of care is delivered beyond natural caring. Natural caring is significantly less impacted by burden than ethical or aesthetical caring. But, in our view, when corporations try to become greener, they are more concerned about ethical and aesthetic forms of care. Although corporations may face internal tensions, they have the responsibility to allocate appropriate resources to allow employees to do their core tasks well (McWilliams and Siegel 2001), but there is no obligation to provide them with resources for the provision of care. Even so, corporations should introduce care into the job design of each of their employees (Solomon 1998).

9.5.2   Sustaining the Manager to Overcome Internal Tensions

Therefore, if taking care of the natural environment is not part of the job, it may be difficult for individuals without appropriate resources to engage in environmentally friendly behaviour as long as they have not fulfilled their job requirements. Therefore, in this kind of situation, employees may face resource depletion limiting their engagement in protecting the natural environment. They may feel burdened if, to take care of the environment, they must tap into resources (e.g., time) that were only assigned to their job duties. In the context of burden, individuals often deal with their capacity to perform a behaviour under their own judgment of autonomy (Boudewyns 2013). Ease or difficulty of engaging in conserving behaviour in the workplace (i.e., reducing, reusing or recycling) can be explained by internal or external sources of control (Hornik et al. 1995). While internal sources of control refer to an individual's knowledge, skills and abilities, external sources of control are perceived as aids or hindrances in the work environment, such as available facilities or cooperation with other people (Kraft et al. 2005). For example, Tudor et al. (2007) reported that lack of time may affect healthcare employees' willingness to engage in sustainable waste management actions in their job. However, lack of time becomes non-significant when employees consider waste management as an important issue and when they habitually reuse materials. Based on these findings, it can be assumed that in certain circumstances the perception of easiness may moderate the relationship between employee environmental commitment and his or her propensity to adopt conserving behaviours in their job.

Finally, corporations also have an important role to play in the context of environmental sustainability, especially when employees experience lack of resources to do what they expect to be good for the natural environment. As we suggested above, numerous reasons may lead a manager to disregard the reality of environmental issues. However, he or she should manage their staff by overcoming his or her own beliefs. In accordance with Engster (2011), "a caring firm should foster a work environment that allows workers to exercise their basic capabilities for reason, imagination, communication, and sociability, and avoid assigning mind-numbing or back-breaking work that erodes workers' basic capabilities" (p. 102). Whatever the reasons for his or her disinterest (see Gifford 2011), as an organisational member and as a corporation representative in the mind of employees, the manager has the moral duty to support his or her subordinates for whom the protection of the natural environment is an important need. In addition, the manager has a great responsibility to avoid making his or her subordinates feel burdened, when they are unable to find the resources to allow them to care adequately for the environment. Therefore, the caring manager should manage beyond his or her own constraints to help his or her subordinates to fulfil their basic needs relating to the environment. Consistent with Solomon (1998) this can be achieved by integrating care as a part of job description not as a requirement to follow (i.e., what management scholars label in-role behaviour), but as a possibility derived from a community of practices within the organisation (Sama et al. 2004).

9.6   CONCLUSION

Sama et al. (2004) have claimed that the natural environment needs caring attentiveness through a community of practice based on dialogue among organisational members. In accordance with Lawrence and Maitlis (2012) the enactment of an ethical care perspective can be achieved by promoting exchanges among organisational members based on narrative practices (i.e., constructing histories of sparkling moments, contextualising struggles and constructing polyphonic future oriented stories). Finally, and perhaps more important regarding our purpose, a recurrent plea among care ethicists is about the lack of resources hampering caregivers' engagement in care activity. In this regard, lack of time is often noted by environmental scholars (e.g., Tudor et al. 2007), as well as care ethicists (e.g., Engster 2005) as a major obstacle that impedes individuals in engaging in pro-environmental behaviour, or in caring activity. Thus, a care-based management approach should try to avoid workers feeling burdened by an overload of tasks in their job by giving them sufficient time to engage in caregiving.

NOTE

1. In this regard, in the endnote she indicates the closeness between an ethic of care and the ecofeminism ethical perspective. Although the ethic of care and ecofeminism share the same objective by stressing how to achieve a more sustainable world, discussions about the status of "caring" have engendered some disputes among these feminist ethicists. This topic is out of the scope of the present chapter. Interested readers may refer to the paper of MacGregor (2004).

REFERENCES

Becker, U. C. (2012), *Sustainability Ethics and Sustainability Research*, Heidelberg: Springer.
Boudewyns, V. (2013), 'A meta-analytical test of perceived behavioral control interactions in the Theory of Planned Behavior,' Unpublished Doctoral dissertation, University of Maryland.
Burton, B. and C. Dunn (1996), 'Feminist ethics as a moral grounding for stakeholder theory', *Business Ethics Quarterly*, **6**, 133–147.
Cantor, D. E., P. C. Morrow and F. Montabon (2012), 'Engagement in environmental behaviors among supply chain management employees: An organisational support theoretical perspective', *Journal of Supply Chain Management*, **48**, 33–51.
Daily, B. F., J. W. Bishop and N. Govindarajulu (2009), 'A conceptual model for organisational citizenship behavior directed toward the environment', *Business and Society*, **48** (2), 243–256.
Dono, J., J. Webb and B. Richardson (2010), 'The relationship between environmental activism, pro-environmental behaviour and social identity', *Journal of Environmental Psychology*, **30** (2), 178–186.
Engster, D. (2005), 'Rethinking care theory: The practice of caring and the obligation to care', *Hypatia*, **20** (3), 50–74.
Engster, D. (2011), 'Care ethics and stakeholder theory', in M. Hamington and M. Sander-Staudt (eds), *Applying Care Ethics to Business*, New York: Springer, pp. 93–110.
Fineman, S. (1997), 'Constructing the green manager', *British Journal of Management*, **8** (1), 31–38.
Fisher, B. and J. Tronto (1990), 'Toward a feminist theory of caring', in E. Abel and M. Nelson (eds), *Circles of Care: Work and Identity in Women's Lives*, Albany, NY: State University of New York Press, pp. 35–62.

Gabriel, Y. (2015), 'The caring leader – What followers expect of their leaders and why?', *Leadership*, **11** (3), 316–334.

Gagné, M. and E. L. Deci (2005), 'Self-determination theory and work motivation', *Journal of Organisational Behavior*, **26** (4), 331–362.

Gifford, R. (2011), 'The dragons of inaction: Psychological barriers that limit climate change mitigation and adaptation', *American Psychologist*, **66**, 290–302.

Gilligan, C. (1982), *In a Different Voice*, Cambridge, MA: Harvard University Press.

Gkorezis, P. (2015), 'Supervisor support and pro-environmental behavior: The mediating role of LMX', *Management Decision*, **53** (5), 1045–1060.

Hamington, M. and M. Sander-Staudt (2011), *Applying Care Ethics to Business*, New York: Springer.

Hawk, T. (2011), 'An ethic of care: A relational ethic for the relational characteristics of organisations', in M. Hamington and M. Sander-Staudt (eds), *Applying Care Ethics to Business*, New York: Springer, pp. 3–34.

Held, V. (2006), *The Ethics of Care: Personal, Political, and Global*, Oxford: Oxford University Press.

Heller, N. E. and E. S. Zavaleta (2009), 'Biodiversity management in the face of climate change: A review of 22 years of recommendations', *Biological Conservation*, **142** (1), 14–32.

Hornik, J., J. Cherian, M. Madansky and C. Narayana (1995), 'Determinants of recycling behavior: A synthesis of research results', *The Journal of Socio-Economics*, **24**, 105–127.

Huffman, A. H. and S. R. Klein (2013), 'I-O psychology and environmental sustainability in organisations: A natural partnership', in A. H. Huffman and S. R. Klein (eds), *Green Organisations Driving Change with I-O Psychology*, New York: Routledge, pp. 3–16.

Kohlberg, L. (1969), *Stages in the Development of Moral Thought and Action*, New York: Holt Rinehart and Winston.

Kraft, P., J. Rise, S. Sutton and E. Røysamb (2005), 'Perceived difficulty in the theory of planned behaviour: Perceived behavioural control or affective attitude?', *British Journal of Social Psychology*, **44**, 479–496.

Kroth, M. and C. Keeler (2009), 'Caring as a managerial strategy', *Human Resource Development Review*, **8** (4), 506–531.

Lawrence, T. B. and S. Maitlis (2012), 'Care and possibility: Enacting an ethic of care through narrative practice', *Academy of Management Review*, **37** (4), 641–663.

Liedtka, J. (1996), 'Feminist morality and competitive reality: A place for an ethic of care', *Business Ethics Quarterly*, **6**, 179–200.

Lülfs, R. and R. Hahn (2013), 'Corporate greening beyond formal programs, initiatives, and systems: A conceptual model for voluntary proenvironmental behavior of employees', *European Management Review*, **10**, 83–98.

MacGregor, S. (2004), 'From care to citizenship: Calling ecofeminism back to politics', *Ethics and the Environment*, **9** (1), 56–84.

Mayeroff, M. (1971), *On Caring*, New York: Harper and Row.

McWilliams, A. and D. Siegel (2001), 'Corporate social responsibility: A theory of the firm perspective', *Academy of Management Review*, **26** (1), 117–127.

Mesmer-Magnus, J., C. Viwsevara and B. M. Wiernik (2012), 'The role of commitment in bridging the gap between organisational sustainability and environmental sustainability', in S. E. Jackson, D. S. Ones, and S. Dilchert (eds), *Managing Human Resource for Environmental Sustainability*, San Francisco, CA: Jossey-Bass, pp. 155–186.

Noddings, N. (1984), *Caring: A Feminine Approach to Ethics and Moral Education*, Berkeley, CA: University of California Press.

Ones, D. and S. Dilchert (2012), 'Environmental sustainability at work: A call to action', *Industrial and Organisational Psychology*, **5**, 444–466.

Paillé, P. and O. Boiral (2013), 'Pro-environmental behavior at work: Construct validity and determinants', *Journal of Environmental Psychology*, **36**, 118–128.

Paillé, P., O. Boiral and Y. Chen (2013), 'Linking environmental management practices and organisational citizenship behavior for the environment: A social exchange perspective', *International Journal of Human Resource Management*, **24** (18), 3552–3575.

Paillé, P., J. H. Mejía-Morelos, A. Marché-Paillé, C. C. Chen, and Y. Chen (2016), 'Corporate greening, exchange process among co-workers, and ethics of care: An empirical study on the determinants of pro-environmental behaviors at co-workers-level', *Journal of Business Ethics*, **136** (3), 655–673.

Palmer, D. E. and M. L. Stoll (2011), 'Moving toward a more caring stakeholder theory: Global business ethics in dialogue with the feminist ethics of care', in M. Hamington and M. Sander-Staudt (eds), *Applying Care Ethics to Business*, New York: Springer, pp. 111–127.

Penday, N., D. E. Rupp and M. A. Thornton (2013), 'The morality of corporate environmental sustainability: A psychological and philosophical perspective', in A. H. Huffman and S. R. Klein (eds), *Green Organisations Driving Change with I-O Psychology*, New York: Routledge, pp. 69–92.

Puka, B. (2011), 'Taking care of business: Caring in competitive corporate structures', in M. Hamington and M. Sander-Staudt (eds), *Applying Care Ethics to Business*, New York: Springer, pp. 175–200.

Raineri, N. and P. Paillé (2016), 'Linking corporate policy and supervisory support with environmental citizenship behaviors: The role of employee environmental beliefs and commitment', *Journal of Business Ethics*, **137** (1), 129–148.

Ramus, C. (2001), 'Organisational support for employees: Encouraging creative ideas for environmental sustainability', *California Management Review*, **43**, 85–105.

Ramus, C. and U. Steger (2000), 'The roles of supervisory support behaviors and environmental policy in employee eco-initiatives at leading-edge European companies', *Academy of Management Journal*, **43**, 605–626.

Ramus, C. A. and A. B. Killmer (2007), 'Corporate greening through prosocial extrarole behaviours – a conceptual framework for employee motivation', *Business Strategy and the Environment*, **16** (8), 554–570.

Rhoades, L. and R. Eisenberger (2002), 'Perceived organisational support: A review of the literature', *Journal of Applied Psychology*, **84** (4), 698–714.

Sama, L. M., S. A. Welcomer and V. W. Gede (2004), 'Who speaks for the trees? Invoking an ethic of care to give voice to the silent stakeholder', in S. Sharma and M. Starik (eds), *Stakeholders, the Environment and Society*, Cheltenham, UK and Northampton, MA, USA: Edward Elgar Publishing, pp. 140–165.

Sander-Staudt, M. (2011), 'Care as a corporate virtue', in M. Hamington and M. Sander-Staudt (eds), *Applying Care Ethics to Business*, New York: Springer, pp. 259–278.

Simola, S. (2003), 'Ethics of justice and care in corporate crisis management', *Journal of Business Ethics*, **46**, 351–361.

Simola, S. (2012), 'Exploring "embodied care" in relation to social sustainability', *Journal of Business Ethics*, **107** (4), 473–484.

Simola, S. K., J. Barling and N. Turner (2010), 'Transformational leadership and leader moral orientation: Contrasting an ethic of justice and an ethic of care', *The Leadership Quarterly*, **21** (1), 179–188.

Slote, M. (2007), *The Ethics of Care and Empathy*, New York: Routledge.

Solomon, R. C. (1992), 'Corporate roles, personal virtues: An Aristotelean approach to business ethics', *Business Ethics Quarterly*, **2** (3), 317–339.

Solomon, R. C. (1998), 'The moral psychology of business: Care and compassion in the corporation', *Business Ethics Quarterly*, **8** (3), 515–533.

Steg, L. and C. Vlek (2009), 'Encouraging pro-environmental behaviour: An integrative review and research agenda', *Journal of Environmental Psychology*, **29**, 309–317.

Theobald, T. and C. Cooper (2011), *Doing the Right Thing: The Importance of Wellbeing in the Workplace*, London: Palgrave Macmillan.

Tronto, J. C. (1993), *Moral Boundaries: A Political Argument for an Ethic of Care*, New York: Routledge.

Tudor, T. L., S. W. Barr and A. W. Gilg (2007), 'Linking intended behaviour and actions: A case study of healthcare waste management in the Cornwall NHS', *Resources, Conservation and Recycling*, **51**, 1–23.

Webb, T. L., Y. Benn and B. P. Chang (2014), 'Antecedents and consequences of monitoring domestic electricity consumption', *Journal of Environmental Psychology*, **40**, 228–238.

Wicks, A. C., D. R. Gilbert, and R. E. Freeman (1994), 'A feminist reinterpretation of the stakeholder concept', *Business Ethics Quarterly*, **4**, 475–497.

Zibarras, L. and C. Ballinger (2011), 'Promoting environmental behaviour in the workplace: A survey of UK organisations', in D. Bartlett (ed.), *Going Green: The Psychology of Sustainability in the Workplace*, Leicester: British Psychological Society, pp. 84–90.

10. Leadership and employee pro-environmental behaviours

Bilal Afsar, Asad Shahjehan and Imad Shah

> Our environment, the world in which we live and work, is a mirror of our
> attitudes and expectations.
>
> Earl Nightingale

10.1 INTRODUCTION

In an increasingly environmentally conscious world, organisations have
an ethical and moral obligation to protect the environment and encourage
employees to display pro-environmental behaviour (PEB). The success of
corporate environmental initiatives depends, not just on environmental
management systems and technological innovations, but also on the
willingness of individual employees to engage in the pro-environmental
behaviours that preserve or restore the quality of the natural environment (Boiral 2009; Daily et al. 2009; Jabbour and Santos 2008a, 2008b).
Corresponding to an ever growing need to develop new leadership models
that accentuate environment, sustainability, and social responsibility,
without sacrificing profits (Fry and Slocum 2008), more and more managers are coming to realise that they should encourage PEBs among their
employees and strive proactively to improve their environmental responsibility (Aguilera et al. 2007). Pro-environmental behaviour at the workplace entails that employees help in improving the corporation's green
image among its stakeholders due to its non-obligatory, discretionary, and
volunteering nature (De Groot and Steg 2009).

Employee PEBs are important – while they may seem trivial, just
like other forms of collective action they can have a significant impact.
Furthermore, just because an organisational decision has been made or
new technology has been introduced, does not mean that the employees
themselves will change their behaviour. Rather, a great deal of organisational and psychological research has shown that personal characteristics
(e.g., environmental values) and contextual factors (e.g., leadership) are
central in changing employee environmental behaviour (e.g., Stern 2000;
Robertson and Barling 2013). While much environmental research has

focused on environmental attitudes and values, a review by Young and colleagues (2015) of changes in actual environmental performance indicators showed that attitude change was not necessary. Given these findings and the imbalance in research, we focus on the effect of a workplace contextual factor (i.e., leadership) on employee PEB.

Organisational leaders can motivate followers to engage in PEBs (e.g., using less electricity or water, reusing materials, consuming less, using public transport to get to work, etc.) and to engender PEBs among employees. The role of leaders is paramount and although employees' PEBs are critical to the success of organisational environmental initiatives, there is little understanding of the leadership mechanisms that foster these behaviours. However, within the literature, the positive impact of leadership on environmental behaviour and performance is widely acknowledged (Barling et al. 2002; Ramus and Steger 2000; Robertson and Barling 2013).

Streams of conceptual development and empirical research consider various leadership styles in facilitating PEB change. These include research on corporate ecological responsiveness (Bansal and Roth 2000) and corporate social responsibility (Waldman et al. 2006); however, scholars have noted the need for more research that examines leaders' facilitation of PEB change within organisations (Robertson and Barling 2013). Most recently, researchers have begun to respond to calls for organisations to be more environmentally responsible, and have extended the leadership literature to investigate whether and how leaders might influence individuals' PEBs (Barling 2014). In considering the impact of leadership on the employee's PEBs, we focus specifically on the role of the employee's immediate manager. Although leadership provided by top management is important (e.g., Banerjee et al. 2003), the employee's immediate manager is an important representative of the organisation to them (Eisenberger et al. 2001), and is likely to have a critical impact on his/her environmental attitudes and behaviours (Andersson et al. 2005; Daily et al. 2009; Ramus and Steger 2000).

As PEB is a voluntary behaviour, not every leadership style is likely to be equally effective (Kuenzi and Schminke 2009). Several leadership types have been linked to positive environmental initiatives (e.g., spiritual leadership (Afsar et al. 2016); transactional leadership (Egri and Herman 2000); ethical leadership (Metcalf and Benn 2013); participatory leadership (Harman 1981)). The purpose of this chapter is to examine the effects of various leadership styles (transformational, transactional, environmental, environmental transformational, green entrepreneurial, and spiritual leadership) on employees' PEBs. We will also discuss which of the leaders' behaviours are critical to motivate an employee to engage in PEB.

10.2   TRANSACTIONAL AND TRANSFORMATIONAL LEADERSHIP

Transactional leadership is solely based on the principle of exchange between leader and follower by providing necessary incentives (e.g., reward) or disincentives (e.g., punishment) to followers in order to generate desired task outcomes (Bass 1985; Burns 1978). This style of leadership is found to be effective for obligatory tasks through extrinsic motivation but when it comes to voluntary behaviours such as PEB, the effectiveness decreases considerably. According to Bass (1999) transactional leaders motivate employees to fulfill expectations regarding job performance (i.e., required behaviours), while transformational leaders motivate followers to exceed expectations (e.g., citizenship behaviour). Thus, transactional leaders may be effective for motivating employees to perform required PEB, while transformational leaders might be more effective at motivating employees to engage in voluntary PEB. Our emphasis is on voluntary PEB because leaders motivate their followers to display environmentally friendly organisational citizenship behaviours. Since the majority of the employees' PEBs are discretionary and voluntary behaviours, a transactional leadership style might not be effective. In contrast, the perspective of the charismatic and transformational leadership focuses on how leaders evoke extraordinary performance from their followers. For example, charismatic leaders have the ability to obtain outstanding outcomes by articulating a vision and sense of mission, showing determination and confidence in followers, and communicating high performance expectations (House and Shamir 1993; Klein and House 1995). Such leaders help to improve the intrinsic motivation of followers by engaging in activities that give a sense of pleasure and meaning to them.

Transformational leadership involves four behaviours: idealised influence (sharing of ethical values to act as role models), inspirational motivation (elevating employees' motivation), intellectual stimulation (helping employees think about issues in new and innovative ways), and individualised consideration (demonstrating concern for individuals' needs) to inspire subordinates to achieve extraordinary outcomes and develop their own leadership abilities (Bass 1998; Bass and Riggio 2006). Each of these behaviours offers important insights into the nature and challenge of environmental leadership. For example, Portugal and Yukl (1994) highlight "articulating an appealing vision with environmental elements (inspirational motivation), changing perceptions about environmental issues (intellectual stimulation), and taking symbolic actions to demonstrate personal commitment to environmental issues" (idealised influence; p. 274) as relevant behaviours for environmental leadership.

Similarly, Graves and Sarkis (2011) point to the importance of these leadership behaviours to environmental leadership, but extend their focus to include individualised consideration (e.g., recognising each individual's ability to address environmental problems and provide tailored learning opportunities based on these abilities) as an important component.

Judge and Piccolo (2004, p. 755) suggested that transformational leaders articulate an appealing organisational mission and focus on higher order intrinsic needs. According to Dvir et al. (2002), transformational leaders ensure that individuals challenge the status quo and are stimulated intellectually by transcending their own self-gain for a higher collective gain.

Transformational leaders develop energising goals, vision and values; and inspire followers to pursue entrepreneurial intentions to influence their creative behaviours. In line with the social exchange perspective (Blau 1964), a leader's individualised consideration encourages employees to reciprocate. Giving inspirational motivation to employees to transform existing systems and plan new ways to address environmental problems helps them to display eco-friendly behaviours. Transformational leaders with an idealised influence exhibit optimism and excitement about novel perspectives and this "championing role" might enhance eco-innovation through intellectual stimulation (Afsar et al. 2016).

Transformational leaders provide a personal as well as collective value system, access to resources and information, effective communication, self-confidence and inner direction. When followers' individual needs and expectations are considered, they tend to reciprocate by exploring new opportunities with a better focus on important organisational issues and processes.

Transformational leadership positively influences organisations' and individuals' environmental performance. Based on a case study of eight ISO 14001 certified factories involving interviews with the environmental manager and the human resource manager of each company, Ángel del Brío et al. (2008) concluded that managers' transformational leadership behaviours are critical in factories' environmental performance. In a different survey-based study, business students who scored high on transformational leadership were supportive of environmentally sustainable business practices (Ng and Burke 2010). Gilstrap and Gilstrap (2012) used qualitative interviews with 40 U.S.-based ecopreneurs to investigate their perceptions about the essential characteristics of ecopreneurs and ecopreneurial leadership. The study found strong resonance between ecopreneurs' descriptions and elements of the transformational leadership construct: encouraging positive motivation, creating new visions for organisations, and inducing new behaviour on the part of organisational members.

According to empirical evidence from a study conducted by Robertson and Barling (2013), the greening of organisations can be enhanced through leaders' influence and application of environmentally specific situational as well as transformational leadership styles. From the results of their quantitative study, they draw the conclusion that leaders' environmental transformational leadership was associated with subordinates' harmonious passion for the environment through behavioural modelling. Moreover, according to Judge and Piccolo (2004), transactional leadership has become the most widely studied of all leadership theories and has been shown to influence diverse behaviours. Some authors have also found transactional leadership, if consistently and influentially applied, to influence environmental sustainability within organisations (Robertson and Barling 2013). It was, however, found within the literature that this type of leadership should be carefully trained and organisations should encourage the implementation of leadership development initiatives with the aim of influencing behaviours and employees to respond and change accordingly (Bandura 1977), hence contributing to the greening of organisations.

Transformational leadership is effective to enhance PEBs as compared to transactional leadership. Followers of a transformational leader often show desire to engage in PEBs when they experience a supportive and non-controlling work environment where personal and organisational transformations and changes are promoted. Moreover, articulation and alignment of followers' personal value systems with the interests of the organisation may increase followers' understanding and commitment toward attainment of collective values such as PEBs.

10.3   ENVIRONMENTAL LEADERSHIP

Environmental leadership is defined as "the ability to influence individuals and mobilise organisations to realise a vision of long-term ecological sustainability" (Egri and Herman 2000: 2). This definition dominated the environmental management literature until Gallagher (2012) argued for an urgent need to confront environmental issues. She defined environmental leadership as "a process by which Earth's inhabitants apply interpersonal influence and engage in collective action to protect the planet's natural resources and its inhabitants from further harm" (p. 5).

Environmental leadership is generally considered a prerequisite to corporate greening (Boiral 2009; Egri and Herman 2000; Flannery and May 1994). Environmental leaders attribute higher importance to self-transcendence values (benevolence and universalism) than to self-enhancement values (achievement, hedonism, and power). They are more likely to exhibit a transformational/new leadership style than either a transactional/traditional leadership style or a laissez-faire leadership style.

Through enactment of the four transformational leadership behaviours, environmentally specific transformational leaders use their relationship with subordinates to intentionally influence and encourage their subordinates to engage in workplace pro-environmental behaviours. In manifesting idealised influence, environmental leaders are guided by and demonstrate their moral commitment to the natural environment. In doing so, they serve as role models who share their environmental values and choose to do what is right by taking actions that serve to protect the environment. Environmental leaders motivate employees through passion and optimism to overcome psychological setbacks and external obstacles, and to go beyond what is good for themselves by engaging in behaviours that benefit the natural environment (Galeazzo et al. 2012: 214). They encourage subordinates to think about environmental issues in new and innovative ways, question long-held assumptions about their own and their organisation's environmental practices, and address environmental problems in an innovative manner. Environmental leaders establish close individualised relationships with followers within which they help each employee to develop his or her skills and abilities to protect the natural environment. To do so, leaders transmit their environmental values, model their environmental behaviours, and raise questions about environmental assumptions and priorities.

Research findings consistently point to the significance of values that extend beyond self-interest in predicting individual PEBs (Steg and Vlek 2009). To a large extent, environmental leaders hold similar values. The importance of values to environmental leadership is well recognised in theoretical work, and findings from both qualitative and quantitative research have identified various values that environmental leaders typically hold (e.g., Egri and Herman 2000; Shrivastava 1994). For example, Egri and Herman (2000) found that environmental leaders were more open to change, self-transcendent and eco-centric.

Drawing from the theory of reasoned action (Ajzen and Fishbein 1977) and the theory of planned behaviour (Ajzen 1985, 1987, 1991, 2002), individuals' attitudes towards a specific behaviour are positively associated with their behavioural intentions to engage in that behaviour. In the context of environmental leadership, managers' intentions to formulate, engage in, and implement corporate environmental initiatives increase as their attitudes towards the natural environment become more favourable. Supporting this assertion, empirical data from several studies across a variety of industries have demonstrated that pro-environmental attitudes are indeed antecedents of managers' PEB intentions (e.g., Cordano and

Frieze 2000; Cordano et al. 2010; Flannery and May 1994, 2000; Marshall et al. 2005). So pro-environmental leaders are more likely to (a) hold personal values that go beyond self-interest, (b) have favourable attitudes toward the natural environment, (c) perceive social pressure (in the form of subjective and descriptive norms) to support environmental initiatives, and (d) view environmental issues as opportunities for their organisations – as Reed Markham says, "Successful leaders see the opportunities in every difficulty rather than the difficulty in every opportunity."

Environmental leaders are expected to move from the dominant social paradigm (DSP), characterised by overconfidence in industrial advancement, economic growth, and technological progress, to a new environmental paradigm (NEP), characterised by an emphasis on environmental protection and recognition of the limitations of industrial growth due to natural resources depletion (Boiral 2009; Egri and Herman 2000). According to Metcalf and Benn (2013, p. 369), the complexity of sustainability issues requires "leaders of extraordinary abilities" to manage such complexity, something that can hardly be taken for granted inside organisations and certainly requires more investigation. Environmental leadership is thus generally associated with various managerial practices: implementation of an environmental management system (e.g., Robinson and Clegg 1998), promotion of a proactive environmental strategy (e.g., Boiral et al. 2014), stakeholder management (e.g., Berman et al. 1999; Buysse and Verbeke 2003), and reporting practices (e.g., Jose and Lee 2007), amongst others.

Leaders' supportive behaviours do matter in the context of influencing workplace PEBs. Ramus and Killmer (2007) consider both general and environmentally specific (Ramus and Steger 2000) supervisory supportive behaviours as a dominant factor that influences employee's environmental initiatives. Likewise, Daily et al. (2009) drew on the norm of reciprocity and social exchange theory to posit that supervisors' support for environmental initiatives is positively related to employees' environmental organisational citizenship behaviours (OCBE; discretionary PEBs that are not explicitly recognised by the formal reward system; Boiral 2009). Ramus (2002) identified six types of supervisory supportive behaviours exhibited by leaders in firms with a record of supporting employees' environmental initiatives. These behaviours include innovation (fostering employees' initiatives, ideas, and learning), competence-building (supporting training and education initiatives), communication (encouraging employees to bring forth their ideas and critiques), information dissemination (sharing corporate information), rewards and recognition (praising and rewarding employees in an effort to support and reinforce desired behaviours), and management of goals and responsibilities (disseminating performance goals and responsibilities by using quantitative and qualitative measures).

Environmental commitment of leaders can help them to perform actions such as recycling behaviours, turning off lights when leaving the office, and using reusable water bottles and coffee cups (Lamm et al. 2013). Since followers always try to be like their leaders, so these actions motivate them to engage in PEBs. Leading by example is critical, as studies have consistently shown that managers' commitment to the environment is too often superficial, ceremonial and more focused on appearances than substance (Boiral 2007; Boiral and Roy 2007; Springett 2003; Yin and Schmeidler 2009). As highlighted by Metcalf and Benn (2013), environmental actions must be driven by the leaders' integrity and coherence between the professed values and the displayed behaviours. People buy into their leaders first and then into their vision (Maxwell 2007: 274). The leader's credibility and character are the traits that are never compromised by followers. So if they observe any action or behaviour as not genuine and honest, they would stop believing their leader's words and hence would result in deterioration of positive behaviour such as PEB.

Two decades ago, Portugal and Yukl (1994) argued that environmental leadership would become more important in the twenty-first century than it was in the previous century; emerging research on environmental leadership suggests that they were correct. Characteristics of environmental leadership include mobilising people and resources to pursue a more environmentally sustainable future. The values of environmental leaders are eco-centric, open to change, have a need for a fit between personal and professional values and actions, and are self-transcendent – which are the most notable motivators of pro-environmental behaviour and action to address climate change.

10.4   ENVIRONMENTAL TRANSFORMATIONAL LEADERSHIP

Environmentally specific transformational leadership encourages behaviours that would promote moral commitment to preserve the natural environment and an environmentally sustainable planet (Graves et al. 2013). By displaying strong passion for the environment and collective good of the planet beyond personal interests, leaders inculcate inspirational motivation in their followers to enact environmentally friendly behaviours. They have the conviction to think about future generations, and their actions are reciprocated by employees who try to contribute positively to protect the environment. These leaders also remain open to employees' suggestions and ideas about eco-innovation and enhancing the environmental performance of the organisations (intellectual stimulation). Another important dimension of transformational leadership is individualised consideration and when it is integrated in environmental leadership, close relationships are established between leaders and followers. Leaders transmit their own values and behaviours about the environment and followers share with confidence and ease their concerns, priorities, and ideas for the environment.

Environmentally specific transformational leaders articulate a vision with an emphasis on environmental performance and motivate employees intrinsically (through discussions, trainings, and informal rewards and compensation) as well as extrinsically (through formal and monetary rewards) to display PEBs. Since each employee attaches different importance to the environment on the basis of his/her own values, preferences, perceptions, knowledge and awareness, it is the transformational leader who can assess the development needs of each individual and accordingly provides learning opportunities.

Environmental transformational leadership also enhances an individual's autonomous and external motivation to perform behaviours for the collective good (Graves et al. 2013). These linkages have been explained with the help of self-determination theory (Deci and Ryan 1985, 2002; Ryan et al. 2013), a broad theory of human growth and development that focuses on the interplay between the active, growth-oriented individual and the social environment. According to self-determination theory (SDT), an individual's behaviour is determined by the type of motivation he/she possesses. We will discuss two important types of motivations found to be highly relevant in the context of PEB (autonomous and controlled motivation). When an individual engages in a behaviour that is consistent with his/her values and self-concept and provides a sense of pleasure, joy, meaning, and fulfillment, it is referred to as identified or autonomous motivation (Deci and Ryan 2000; Judge and Piccolo 2004).

Daily et al. (2009) argued that environmental transformational leaders present a vision of a sustainable future, talk about the importance of environmental sustainability, and provide support and confidence to employees to achieve environmentally friendly objectives. They motivate employees to have higher-order values by talking frequently about the need and importance of PEBs. The ideological explanation of environmental goals along with an emphasis on how these goals would make the world a better place to live in, in the present as well as in the future, may help employees to shape their behaviours in accordance with these goals. Employees may think of becoming a part of this higher-order value and hence may incorporate it into their identities and meaningfulness (Bono and Judge 2003; Jung and Avolio 2000). For example, their actions would mean a healthy environment, a safer planet to live in, and a better place to be a part of – all of which would make their behaviours more meaningful.

There are employees in the organisation who are committed to the planet and environmental sustainability; their engagement in PEBs is rooted in identified or autonomous motivation. Employees who are intrinsically motivated to perform PEBs find such behaviours interesting, pleasurable, and full of fun (e.g., saving electricity for the sake of saving earth gives meaning and fulfillment, or proposing an idea to promote eco-friendliness provides pleasure). When an employee engages in an action because of a belief that he/she must or should do it, controlled or external motivation is the underlying mechanism operating in such employees (Deci and Ryan 2000; Gagné and Deci 2005). Individuals act under the influence of external contingencies such as the threat of punishment, being part of an environmentally friendly culture, pay and rewards, approval from supervisors and co-workers, etc. Employees who are motivated externally to perform PEBs do so because they want to obtain extrinsic rewards and approval from supervisors, peers, and subordinates, perform PEBs explicitly mentioned as a part of their job, such as environmental management system requirements and green corporation strategies, or to avoid inconvenience. They want to be considered responsible and good in the eyes of others instead of bad and attempting to protect their image. Introjected motivations stem from a feeling of being left out in a negative sense and social aloofness caused due to any behaviour that is not acceptable by the majority in the organisation. Like transformational leadership scholars, SDT researchers stress the effect of leadership on employee motivation (Baard et al. 2004; Otis and Pelletier 2005). Leader behaviours that support employee autonomy (e.g., encouraging initiative, giving employees some choice of tasks, providing flexibility, and informational feedback) encourage autonomous motivation. In examining employee motivation to engage in PEBs, we focus on autonomous motivation, as well as the external motivation component of controlled motivation. Organisations that use environmental management systems and reward programmes may provide external motivation to employees to perform PEBs (Andersson et al. 2005; Ramus 2002).

Transformational leaders may make use of external rewards and motivation besides internal rewards and motivation (Bono and Judge 2003). In fact, Judge and Piccolo (2004) posit that transformational leaders do motivate followers who meet expectations through external rewards, monetary benefits, and performance-based rewards. Thus, environmental transformational leaders may utilise these performance-based rewards to motivate employees' PEBs. Further, some of the elements of environmental transformational leadership may enhance external motivation. For instance, the environmental transformational leader's focus on developing employees' capabilities may facilitate external motivation by increasing competence. Employees who feel competent to perform PEBs may be more motivated by the presence of external rewards because they believe they can perform the behaviours required to attain them. They may also be motivated to engage in PEBs to win over the approval of their leaders.

10.5 GREEN ENTREPRENEURIAL LEADERSHIP

Dean and McMullen (2007) combined the idea of green (e.g., environmental protection, sustainable development) with entrepreneurship. They define that environmental entrepreneurship is the process of discovering, evaluating, and exploiting economic opportunities that are present in environmentally relevant market failures. It appears that the environment-related opportunities can't be exploited without the influence of leaders to mobilise both their followers and company (Egri and Herman 2000). As a result, leadership happens to be a core component in the entrepreneurial process and the two aspects can't be separated. According to the rationale mentioned above, a green entrepreneur should also play a role as a green leader to realise the vision of long-term ecological sustainability by discovering and exploiting the opportunities coming from environmental issues.

According to the literature, two of the most important characteristics of an entrepreneurial leader are proactiveness and vision. When ecological sustainability and pro-environmental vision is integrated with entrepreneurial leadership, the concept of green entrepreneurial leadership emerges. Thus, a green entrepreneurial leader communicates high environmental performance expectations by articulating green vision. Employees become motivated to achieve high performance because they are given the confidence and trust to implement their own proactive eco-friendly initiatives (Klein and House 1995). Green entrepreneurial leadership is committed to serve stakeholders, the community, and the environment in an environmentally friendly manner. In essence, green entrepreneurial leaders act as role models by displaying discretionary eco-initiatives to add value and social welfare and demonstrate normatively appropriate conducts on communication, reinforcement, and decision-making (Brown et al. 2005). Environment-related opportunities can't be discovered and exploited if the leader inclines to avoid challenging the status quo and taking actions to realise this. Hence, a green entrepreneurial leader might possess a proactive personality. Leaders' behaviours can also facilitate the implementation of more formal environmental practices by demonstrating the degree of their personal commitment in this area and their willingness to be a source of support in the organisation's effort to become greener.

10.6   IMPORTANCE OF LEADERS' PERSONAL VALUES

> You can't lead anyone else further than you have gone yourself.
>
> Gene Mauch

Research based on social psychology has shown that beliefs and values play an important role in explaining behaviours, including those related to general environmental issues (Ajzen 1991; Daily et al. 2009; Lülfs and Hahn 2013). Similarly, in the literature on environmental management, personal values have been considered as one of the main drivers of managers' commitment to, and actions for, corporate greening (Balmer et al. 2007; Bansal and Roth 2000; Cordano and Frieze 2000; Williams and Schaefer 2013).

Leading by example is a mechanism through which leaders transmit their values to their followers (Dragoni 2005; Yaffe and Kark 2011) and thereby elicit desirable behaviours from followers. In this regard, leaders' PEB can be instrumental in eliciting the same behaviour from their followers. When an organisation introduces formal sustainability programmes, leaders' green behaviours signal the importance of environmental stewardship (Russo and Harrison 2005; Starik and Rands 1995) and encourage employees to engage in activities such as environmentally ethical decision-making and eco-innovation (Flannery and May 2000; Ramus and Steger 2000). The cost and time that they require may also be perceived as a constraint to OCBEs. Moreover, important environmental aspects are often quite technical, notably in industrial organisations. As a result, managers may feel that they lack the competencies and information to adopt appropriate OCBEs, except for very simple and mostly symbolic actions, such as using scrap paper for notes or minimising printing. The perception that OCBEs can be adopted easily is therefore assumed to be a strong predictor of such behaviours. With the hope of establishing strong relationships with their leaders (Aguilera et al. 2007), employees may strive to express similar values, for leader–follower value congruence promotes a higher quality of leader–follower relationships (Krishnan 2002).

Leaders embody their values in their behaviour. Leading by example is a mechanism through which leaders transmit their values to their followers (Dragoni 2005; Yaffe and Kark 2011) and thereby elicit desirable behaviours from followers. In this regard, leaders' own PEBs can be instrumental in eliciting the same behaviour from their followers. When an organisation introduces formal sustainability programmes, leaders' green behaviours signal the importance of environmental stewardship (Russo and Harrison 2005; Starik and Rands 1995) and encourage employees to engage in activities such as environmentally ethical decision-making and eco-innovation (Flannery and May 2000; Ramus and Steger 2000).

Having higher status and power, leaders serve as role models (Bass 1985); for followers in the work group, they are essential sources of information pertaining to important and appropriate behaviour (Mayer et al. 2007). As such, the behaviour of a leader can influence the motivation and behaviour of followers (Derue et al. 2011), including the discretionary pro-social behaviours of followers (Ilies et al. 2007). With the hope of establishing strong relationships with their leaders (Aguilera et al. 2007), employees may strive to express similar values, for leader–follower value congruence promotes higher quality of leader–follower relationships (Krishnan 2002). When employees observe others around them engaging in particular patterns of behaviour, they are likely to engage in such behaviours out of a desire to fit in, establish, and strengthen their social relationships. Thus, the relational motive is a primary psychological function that may motivate employees to respond to direct and indirect social cues indicating that PEB is desirable and valued by others.

10.7   SPIRITUAL LEADERSHIP

Organisations nowadays can be viewed as spiritual entities due to the fact that people spend a lot of time at their workplaces and hence their spiritual identities are embedded in their organisations (Benefiel 2005). The question of concern is which leadership approach is most suitable to foster employees' PEB. The most rational leadership theory can be the one that causes the individual to genuinely think about the nature and environment as an integrated part of the self. This integration can be best explained by spiritual leadership which creates a strong association between spirituality and environmentalism (Shrivastava 1994).

Pro-environmental behaviour at work is a type of pro-social behaviour; it is not obligatory; it relates to a genuine concern for the planet; it can only be displayed when an individual thinks of future generations, nature, and humankind (Paillé and Boiral 2013; Scherbaum et al. 2008). Fry and Slocum (2008) advocated that, in order to maximise the triple bottom line (people through employee well-being, planet through environmental responsibility, sustainability and corporate social responsibility, and profit through financial performance and revenue growth), the most effective style of management is through spiritual leadership. Spiritual leaders develop values of hope and faith, and altruistic love in a compelling transcendent vision of positively serving community, future generations, and nature, by increasing intrinsic motivation and a sense of membership and being understood and appreciated among followers (Fry and Slocum 2008).

Egri and Herman (2000) commented that the characteristics of a spiritual leader such as his/her eco-centric approach, concern to preserve nature, striving to preserve the environment for future generations, and strong intention to serve humankind through high morals and ethics, made them ideal to motivate employees to engage in PEBs. The focus of spiritual leadership is on collective social influence processes at the workplace, enabling employees to experience transcendence and find meaning and purpose in life (sense of calling), to enmesh in a network of social connections (sense of membership), and to align their personal spiritualities with organisational spiritualities (value alignment). De Groot and Steg (2008) suggested that individuals with environmental values, such as personal inclination towards preserving the planet and eco-centric philosophy, were more committed to display PEB. Spiritual leadership addresses individual values through sense of calling and membership and thus may induce stronger environmental values into them. In turn, the level of autonomous motivation to engage in PEB increases when the individuals are imbued with stronger environmental values.

Pro-environmental behaviour is a complex behaviour because it involves a pro-social dimension of work, and it is extremely difficult for managers to convince or motivate an employee to display such behaviour through traditional leadership styles or approaches (Paillé and Boiral 2013). Probably the most effective way to trigger PEB is to arouse a sense of deeper meaning in life, a sense of community, and a care for nature and the planet among employees, and convincing them that what they do today has a long-term consequence on society and future generations.

According to Fairholm (1996), spiritual leaders lead people through intellectual discourse and dialogue, encourage self-directed free moral choice tasks for the betterment of society, and give meaning and purpose to them about their work roles. These behaviours are conceptually highly relevant to trigger PEB. For instance, spiritual leadership promotes employees' experience of transcendence through the work process to go beyond their own self-interests for the good of others and society. There is an evident connection of spirituality with nature, environment, and humankind (Taylor 2001). Pandey and Gupta (2008) proposed that personal spirituality impacts one's environmental considerations. Shrivastava (2010) suggested that the emotional and spiritual development of an individual is indispensable for his/her behaviour to save the environment and to display eco-centrism.

Crossman (2010) notes that spiritual leadership embraces spiritual values and synergises the spirit with the environment of the individuals.

Therefore, it is suggested that spiritual leadership is one of the most effective leadership approaches when it comes to influence employees to display PEB. Hernandez (2008) suggested that spiritual leadership simultaneously integrates the three vital Ps (Profit, People, and Planet). They not only take care of the Planet (through stewardship, Confucianism, encouragement of moral values) and the People (by empowering them and sharing power and responsibility) but also the Profit (through transformation of employees to feel self-worthy of achieving goals). Spiritual leaders implement stewardship and servanthood concepts that focus on sustainability through intergenerational reciprocity, community benefits, and nature preservation (Karakas 2010). Spiritual leadership cultivates environmental morality which would help to preserve nature and hence humankind (Fairholm 1996). Spiritual leaders preach to their followers to display a strong commitment to a sustainable environment, so as to pass on a better world to future generations.

Afsar et al. (2016) found that there is a positive relationship between spiritual leadership and workplace spirituality and this effect becomes stronger when the subordinates' perceptions of organisational support and care are higher. Workplace spirituality leads to an increase in an employee's intrinsic motivation as well as environmental passion. Moreover, a greater level of environmental awareness has been found to strengthen the relationship between workplace spirituality and environmental passion. Both intrinsic motivation and environmental passion, in turn, increase the display of PEB by employees. Educating employees about environmental problems and conveying to them the importance of being environmentally responsible may help to increase PEB. Managers should understand that a leadership approach, such as spiritual leadership, that can lift the heart and engage the soul, instead of just being impeccably logical, is the way forward to trigger followers' PEBs. Followers have varying spiritual values, aspirations, and energies, so leaders may integrate personal spirituality with organisational spirituality and requirements by providing organisational support and care.

Table 10.1 summarises and outlines the main effect of each leadership style on employee pro-environmental behaviour.

10.8   MANAGERIAL IMPLICATIONS

Research suggests that leadership does matter when it comes to motivating employees to display PEBs. Environmental leaders are most likely to exhibit a transformational leadership style. Therefore, organisations should try to arrange training programmes to teach managers how to

Table 10.1   Summary of the leadership styles and their effect on pro-environmental behaviour

Leadership style	Effect on Pro-environmental Behaviour	References
Charismatic Leadership	. . . one of the organisations helped by charismatic leadership reduced its energy consumption by 50%.	(Young et al. 2015)
Ethical Leadership	Leadership can be useful here because previous studies have reported the positive association between ethical leadership and pro-environmental behaviour.	(Gkorezis and Petridou 2017)
Laissez-faire Leadership	The manager avoids involvement in environmental issues; he/she does not make decisions on environmental issues or respond to questions on environmental issues.	(Bass 1985 1999)
Transactional Leadership	. . . consists of behaviours such as assigning responsibility for environmental goals and tasks, monitoring for mistakes or problems, and administering rewards and punishments and is also likely to be positively linked to Pro-Environmental Behaviours.	(Unsworth et al. 2013)
Transformational Leadership	. . . environmentally specific transformational leadership was associated with subordinates' harmonious passion for the environment, and indirectly associated with subordinates' workplace pro-environmental behaviours.	(Robertson and Barling 2013)
Responsible Leadership	. . . is the art or ability to mobilise stakeholders inside and outside the corporation to achieve business goals related to environmental sustainability.	(Jang et al. 2017)
Spiritual Leadership	Organisational leaders who exhibit spiritual leadership and help to build a spiritual working environment may encourage employees to act in pro-environmental ways, such as having concern for the environmental and social impact of the business as well as taking responsibility for those impacts.	(Afsar et al. 2016)

be effective in promoting employees' PEBs. Given that transformational leadership (e.g., Barling et al. 1996; Dvir et al. 2002) and safety-specific transformational leadership (e.g., Mullen and Kelloway 2009) can be explicitly trained, leadership development initiatives might beneficially emphasise how leadership can be expressed to influence the greening of organisations. Organisations might benefit from creating climates (e.g., organisational pro-environmental climate; Russell and Griffiths 2008) that encourage and reward leaders (and employees) for enacting environmentally friendly behaviours.

It is practically important for leaders to understand what fosters PEB among employees. Leaders should try to initiate socialisation and training programmes to bring their subordinates closer. This can be applied to a recruitment strategy by selecting those employees who prefer environmental and collective goals and aspirations over individual goals and aspirations. Leaders should articulate a green vision to inspire employees, recognise their efforts and give autonomy in job-related activities, clarify goals through collaboration and clearly specify tasks, responsibilities, and rewards, understand their needs and demands, build trust and confidence among employees to try out new ideas. It is important to recognise that not only the motivational issue of "what do you want" is important for employees to engage in PEBs, but that the self-identity issue of "who you are" also plays an important role in stimulating employees' PEB.

Pro-environmental behaviour may be boosted if an employee has positive emotions towards environmental activism, sustainability, and protection. Leaders can change the workplace environment to include more positive environmentally related cues, which should help in activating employees' green goals. For example, an intervention designed to increase stairwalking rather than elevator use should provide cues, not only near the stairs and elevator, but also in employees' offices and cubicles. When these positive environmental cues are available, it will lead to greater employee pro-environmental behaviour. Educating employees about environmental problems and conveying to them the importance of being environmentally responsible may help to increase pro-environmental behaviour. Leaders influence their followers' workplace pro-environmental behaviours when they (i) share their values (idealised influence), (ii) convince followers that they can achieve at levels previously considered almost impossible (inspirational motivation), (iii) help employees think about issues in new and innovative ways (intellectual stimulation), and (iv) establish a relationship with their employees (individualised consideration) through which they can exert an influence on pro-environmental behaviours (Afsar et al. 2016).

Managers should understand that a leadership approach, such as spiritual leadership, that can lift the heart and engage the soul instead of just being impeccably logical, is the way forward to trigger followers' pro-environmental behaviours. Followers have varying spiritual values, aspirations, and energies, so managers may integrate personal spirituality with organisational spirituality and requirements by providing organisational support and care. Wider employee participation in environmental management, rather than restricting involvement to managers and specialists, is often seen as crucial to successful outcomes (Hanna et al. 2000; Remmen and Lorentzen 2000).

Leaders should provide extensive training to employees in business practices that are environmentally friendly. Leaders might be able to increase their employees' daily pro-environmental behaviour through the promotion of pro-environmental attitudes. Although employees may have pre-existing environmental attitudes that they bring to the workplace, creating an organisational climate that supports environmental protection might also promote positive environmental attitudes amongst employees (Russell and Griffiths 2008).

10.9   FUTURE RESEARCH

Despite receiving initial scholarly interest and empirical support, research investigating the effects of leadership on employees' PEBs is still in its infancy. Given this, the potential for future research in this area is virtually unlimited, and we conclude this chapter by exploring several avenues for future research. Although a growing body of research suggests that different leadership behaviours matter in the context of corporate environmental issues, there is no research suggesting that leaders who enact specific leadership behaviours are more successful in influencing individuals' PEBs. Ramus and Killmer (2007) contend that supervisors' support may be the key factor in employees' motivation to engage in pro-environmental initiatives. Future research should examine whether some potential moderators, such as green mindfulness and green self-efficacy, explain the relationship between leaders' supporting behaviours and employees' PEBs. Like other areas (e.g., occupational health and safety), research has focused on the effects of general and target-specific leadership behaviours on specific targeted outcomes. Although both have been shown to exert positive effects, research now needs to understand which is more effective. More specific to this chapter, research should examine which leadership style evokes higher levels of employees' workplace PEBs and investigate why one might exert greater effects.

The potential mediators that could further explain the effect of leadership styles on pro-environmental behaviours might be organisational pro-environmental climate (Norton et al. 2013; Russell and Griffiths 2008), and green human resource management (HRM) practices (Afsar et al. 2016). Previous research on occupational health and safety demonstrates that leaders play a large role in shaping group members' safety climate perceptions, which in turn affect their safety-related behaviours (e.g., Neal and Griffin 2004; Zohar 1980; Zohar and Luria 2005). Extending this to an environmental context may suggest that environmental leadership behaviours are important in determining employees' pro-environmental climate perceptions. Another potential mediating variable that can be explored in detail is intrinsic motivation and its effect on PEBs. With respect to moderating variables, future research could examine both individual difference variables and organisational contextual variables. For example, future research could investigate whether employees' materialistic values (Richins and Dawson 1992) affect the relationship between leadership behaviours and employees' environmental performance, whether pressure from stakeholders to be socially responsible has an effect on this relationship, or whether the implementation of an environmental management system and/or green HRM practices (see Renwick et al. 2013 for a review) strengthens this relationship. Another practical avenue of research might be to investigate the influence of different leadership attributes, such as charisma (Shamir et al. 1994), on PEB and environmental sustainability.

Employee PEBs are important – while they may seem trivial, just like other forms of collective action they can have a significant impact. Leaders play an important role in motivating employees to engage in PEBs. However, there is no single leadership style that can help organisations to enhance the PEBs of employees. Among leadership styles that managers can adopt, transformational leadership, environmental leadership, environmental transformational leadership, spiritual leadership, and green entrepreneurial leadership are the most effective ones. The main emphasis of these leadership styles is to increase intrinsic motivation of employees so that they start caring about the environment and feel it purposeful to contribute towards protecting the environment. Still the research on the effect of leadership style on employees' PEB is in its infancy, and future research should try to explore the psychological mechanisms through which leaders motivate employees to engage in PEBs.

REFERENCES

Afsar, B., Y. Badir and U. S. Kiani (2016), 'Linking spiritual leadership and employee pro-environmental behavior: The influence of workplace spirituality, intrinsic motivation, and environmental passion', *Journal of Environmental Psychology*, **45**, 79–88.

Aguilera, R. V., D. E. Rupp, C. A. Williams and J. Ganapathi (2007), 'Putting the S back in corporate social responsibility: A multilevel theory of social change in organisations', *Academy of Management Review*, **32**(3), 836–863.

Ajzen, I. (1985), 'From intentions to actions: A theory of planned behavior', in J. Kuhl and J. Beckman (eds), *Action Control: From Cognition to Behavior*. Heidelberg: Springer, pp. 11–39.

Ajzen, I. (1987), 'Attitudes, traits, and actions: Dispositional prediction of behavior in personality and social psychology', *Advances in Experimental Social Psychology*, **20**, 1–63.

Ajzen, I. (1991), 'The theory of planned behavior', *Organisational Behavior and Human Decision Processes*, **50**(2), 179–211.

Ajzen, I. (2002), 'Constructing a TPB questionnaire: Conceptual and methodological considerations', Working Paper, University of Massachusetts, Amherst, September 2002a, available online at http://www-unix.oit.umass.edu/~aizen/pdf/tpb.measurement.pdf.

Ajzen, I. and M. Fishbein (1977), 'Attitude-behavior relations: A theoretical analysis and review of empirical research', *Psychological Bulletin*, **84**(5), 888–918.

Andersson, L., S. Shivarajan and G. Blau (2005), 'Enacting ecological sustainability in the MNC: A test of an adapted value-belief-norm framework', *Journal of Business Ethics*, **59**(3), 295–305.

Ángel del Brío, J., B. Junquera and M. Ordiz (2008), 'Human resources in advanced environmental approaches: A case analysis', *International Journal of Production Research*, **46**(21), 6029–6053.

Baard, P. P., E. L. Deci and R. M. Ryan (2004), 'Intrinsic need satisfaction: A motivational basis of performance and well-being in two work settings', *Journal of Applied Social Psychology*, **34**(10), 2045–2068.

Balmer, J. M., K. Fukukawa and E. R. Gray (2007), 'The nature and management of ethical corporate identity: A commentary on corporate identity, corporate social responsibility and ethics', *Journal of Business Ethics*, **76**(1), 7–15.

Bandura, A. (1977), 'Self-efficacy: Toward a unifying theory of behavioral change', *Psychological Review*, **84**(2), 191.

Banerjee, S. B., E. S. Iyer and R. K. Kashyap (2003), 'Corporate environmentalism: Antecedents and influence of industry type', *Journal of Marketing*, **67**(2), 106–122.

Bansal, P. and K. Roth (2000), 'Why companies go green: A model of ecological responsiveness', *Academy of Management Journal*, **43**(4), 717–736.

Barling, J. (2014), *The Science of Leadership: Lessons from Research for Organisational Leaders*. New York: Oxford University Press.

Barling, J., C. Loughlin and E. K. Kelloway (2002), 'Development and test of a model linking safety-specific transformational leadership and occupational safety', *Journal of Applied Psychology*, **87**(3), 488.

Barling, J., T. Weber and E. K. Kelloway (1996), 'Effects of transformational leadership training on attitudinal and financial outcomes: A field experiment', *Journal of Applied Psychology*, **81**(6), 827.

Bass, B. M. (1985), *Leadership and Performance Beyond Expectations*. New York: Free Press.

Bass, B. M. (1998), *Transformational Leadership: Industrial, Military, and Educational Impact*. Mahwah, NJ: Lawrence Erlbaum Associates.

Bass, B. M. (1999), 'Two decades of research and development in transformational leadership', *European Journal of Work and Organisational Psychology*, **8**(1), 9–32.

Bass, B. M. and R. E. Riggio (2006), *Transformational Leadership* (2nd edn). New York: Psychology Press.

Benefiel, M. (2005), 'The second half of the journey: Spiritual leadership for organisational transformation', *The Leadership Quarterly*, **16**(5), 723–747.

Berman, S. L., A. C. Wicks, S. Kotha and T. M. Jones (1999), 'Does stakeholder orientation matter? The relationship between stakeholder management models and firm financial performance', *Academy of Management Journal*, **42**(5), 488–506.

Blau, P. M. (1964), *Exchange and Power in Social Life*. New York: Wiley.

Boiral, O. (2007), 'Corporate greening through ISO 14001: A rational myth?', *Organisation Science*, **18**(1), 127–146.

Boiral, O. (2009), 'Greening the corporation through organisational citizenship behaviors', *Journal of Business Ethics*, **87**(2), 221–236.

Boiral, O., C. Baron and O. Gunnlaugson (2014), 'Environmental leadership and consciousness development: A case study among Canadian SMEs', *Journal of Business Ethics*, **123**(3), 363–383.

Boiral, O. and M.-J. Roy (2007), 'ISO 9000: Integration rationales and organisational impacts', *International Journal of Operations and Production Management*, **27**(2), 226–247.

Bono, J. E. and T. A. Judge (2003), 'Self-concordance at work: Toward understanding the motivational effects of transformational leaders', *Academy of Management Journal*, **46**(5), 554–571.

Brown, M. E., L. K. Treviño and D. A. Harrison (2005), 'Ethical leadership: A social learning perspective for construct development and testing', *Organisational Behavior and Human Decision Processes*, **97**(2), 117–134.

Burns, J. M. (1978), *Leadership*. New York: Harper and Row.

Buysse, K. and A. Verbeke (2003), 'Proactive environmental strategies: A stakeholder management perspective', *Strategic Management Journal*, **24**(5), 453–470.

Cordano, M. and I. H. Frieze (2000), 'Pollution reduction preferences of US environmental managers: Applying Ajzen's theory of planned behavior', *Academy of Management Journal*, **43**(4), 627–641.

Cordano, M., R. S. Marshall and M. Silverman (2010), 'How do small and medium enterprises go "green"? A study of environmental management programs in the US wine industry', *Journal of Business Ethics*, **92**(3), 463–478.

Crossman, J. (2010), 'Conceptualising spiritual leadership in secular organisational contexts and its relation to transformational, servant and environmental leadership', *Leadership and Organisation Development Journal*, **31**(7), 596–608.

Daily, B. F., J. W. Bishop and N. Govindarajulu (2009), 'A conceptual model for organisational citizenship behavior directed toward the environment', *Business and Society*, **48**(2), 243–256.

De Groot, J. I. and L. Steg (2008), 'Value orientations to explain beliefs related to environmental significant behavior how to measure egoistic, altruistic, and biospheric value orientations', *Environment and Behavior*, **40**(3), 330–354.

De Groot, J. I. and L. Steg (2009), 'Mean or green: Which values can promote stable pro-environmental behavior?', *Conservation Letters*, **2**(2), 61–66.

Dean, T. J. and J. S. McMullen (2007), 'Toward a theory of sustainable entrepreneurship: Reducing environmental degradation through entrepreneurial action', *Journal of Business Venturing*, **22**(1), 50–76.

Deci, E. L. and R. M. Ryan (1985), 'The general causality orientations scale: Self-determination in personality', *Journal of Research in Personality*, **19**(2), 109–134.

Deci, E. L. and R. M. Ryan (2000), 'The "what" and "why" of goal pursuits: Human needs and the self-determination of behavior', *Psychological Inquiry*, **11**(4), 227–268.

Deci, E. L. and R. M. Ryan (2002), *Handbook of Self-determination Research*. Rochester, NY: University Rochester Press.

Derue, D. S., J. D. Nahrgang, N. Wellman and S. E. Humphrey (2011), 'Trait and behavioral theories of leadership: An integration and meta-analytic test of their relative validity', *Personnel Psychology*, **64**(1), 7–52.

Dragoni, L. (2005), 'Understanding the emergence of state goal orientation in organisational work groups: The role of leadership and multilevel climate perceptions', *Journal of Applied Psychology*, **90**(6), 1084.

Dvir, T., D. Eden, B. J. Avolio and B. Shamir (2002), 'Impact of transformational leadership on follower development and performance: A field experiment', *Academy of Management Journal*, **45**(4), 735–744.

Egri, C. P. and S. Herman (2000), 'Leadership in the North American environmental sector: Values, leadership styles, and contexts of environmental leaders and their organisations', *Academy of Management Journal*, **43**(4), 571–604.

Eisenberger, R., S. Armeli, B. Rexwinkel, P. D. Lynch and L. Rhoades (2001), 'Reciprocation of perceived organisational support', *Journal of Applied Psychology*, **86**(1), 42.

Fairholm, G. W. (1996), 'Spiritual leadership: Fulfilling whole-self needs at work', *Leadership and Organisation Development Journal*, **17**(5), 11–17.

Flannery, B. L. and D. R. May (1994), 'Prominent factors influencing environmental activities: Application of the environmental leadership model (ELM)', *The Leadership Quarterly*, **5**(3), 201–221.

Flannery, B. L. and D. R. May (2000), 'Environmental ethical decision making in the US metal-finishing industry', *Academy of Management Journal*, **43**(4), 642–662.

Fry, L. W. and J. W. Slocum (2008), 'Maximizing the triple bottom line through spiritual leadership', *Organisational Dynamics*, **37**(1), 86–96.

Gagné, M. and E. L. Deci (2005), 'Self-determination theory and work motivation', *Journal of Organisational Behavior*, **26**(4), 331–362.

Gallagher, D. R. (2012), *Environmental Leadership: A Reference Handbook*. Los Angeles, CA: Sage Publications.

Gilstrap, C. A. and C. M. Gilstrap (2012), 'Ecopreneurial leaders and transformational leadership', *Environmental Leadership: A Reference Handbook*, **1**, 172–180.

Gkorezis, P. and E. Petridou (2017), 'Corporate social responsibility and pro-environmental behaviour: Organisational identification as a mediator', *European Journal of International Management*, **11**(1), 1–18.

Graves, L. M., J. Sarkis and Q. Zhu (2013), 'How transformational leadership and employee motivation combine to predict employee proenvironmental behaviors in China', *Journal of Environmental Psychology*, **35**, 81–91.

Hanna, M. D., W. R. Newman and P. Johnson (2000), 'Linking operational and environmental improvement through employee involvement', *International Journal of Operations and Production Management*, **20**(2), 148–165.

Harman, W. W. (1981), 'Two contrasting concepts of participatory leadership', *Theory Into Practice*, **20**(4), 225–228.

Hernandez, M. (2008), 'Promoting stewardship behavior in organisations: A leadership model', *Journal of Business Ethics*, **80**(1), 121–128.

House, R. J. and B. Shamir (1993), 'Toward the integration of transformational, charismatic, and visionary theories', in M. M. Chemers and R. Ayman (eds), *Leadership Theory and Research: Perspectives and Directions*. San Diego, CA: Academic Press, pp. 81–107.

Ilies, R., J. D. Nahrgang and F. P. Morgeson (2007), 'Leader-member exchange and citizenship behaviors: A meta-analysis', *Journal of Applied Psychology*, **92**, 269–77.

Jabbour, C. J. C. and F. C. A. Santos (2008a), 'The central role of human resource management in the search for sustainable organisations', *The International Journal of Human Resource Management*, **19**(12), 2133–2154.

Jabbour, C. J. C. and F. C. A. Santos (2008b), 'Relationships between human resource dimensions and environmental management in companies: Proposal of a model', *Journal of Cleaner Production*, **16**(1), 51–58.

Jang, Y. J., T. Zheng and R. Bosselman (2017), 'Top managers' environmental values, leadership, and stakeholder engagement in promoting environmental sustainability in the restaurant industry', *International Journal of Hospitality Management*, **63**, 101–111.

Jose, A. and S.-M. Lee (2007), 'Environmental reporting of global corporations: A content analysis based on website disclosures', *Journal of Business Ethics*, **72**(4), 307–321.

Judge, T. A. and R. F. Piccolo (2004), 'Transformational and transactional leadership: A meta-analytic test of their relative validity', *Journal of Applied Psychology*, **89**(5), 755.

Jung, D. I. and B. J. Avolio (2000), 'Opening the black box: An experimental investigation of the mediating effects of trust and value congruence on transformational and transactional leadership', *Journal of Organisational Behavior*, **21**(8), 949–964.

Karakas, F. (2010), 'Spirituality and performance in organisations: A literature review', *Journal of Business Ethics*, **94**(1), 89–106.

Klein, K. J. and R. J. House (1995), 'On fire: Charismatic leadership and levels of analysis', *The Leadership Quarterly*, **6**(2), 183–198.

Krishnan, V. R. (2002), 'Transformational leadership and value system congruence', *International Journal of Value-Based Management*, **15**(1), 19–33.

Kuenzi, M. and M. Schminke (2009), 'Assembling fragments into a lens: A review, critique, and proposed research agenda for the organisational work climate literature', *Journal of Management*, **35**(3), 634–717.

Lamm, E., J. Tosti-Kharas and E. G. Williams (2013), 'Read this article, but don't print it: Organisational citizenship behavior toward the environment', *Group and Organisation Management*, **38**(2), 163–197.

Lülfs, R. and R. Hahn (2013), 'Corporate greening beyond formal programs, initiatives, and systems: A conceptual model for voluntary pro-environmental behavior of employees', *European Management Review*, **10**(2), 83–98.

Marshall, R. S., M. Cordano and M. Silverman (2005), 'Exploring individual and institutional drivers of proactive environmentalism in the US wine industry', *Business Strategy and the Environment*, **14**(2), 92.

Mayer, D., L. Nishii, B. Schneider and H. Goldstein (2007), 'The precursors and products of justice climates: Group leader antecedents and employee attitudinal consequences', *Personnel Psychology*, **60**(4), 929–963.

Metcalf, L. and S. Benn (2013), 'Leadership for sustainability: An evolution of leadership ability', *Journal of Business Ethics*, **112**(3), 369–384.

Mullen, J. E. and E. K. Kelloway (2009), 'Safety leadership: A longitudinal study of the effects of transformational leadership on safety outcomes', *Journal of Occupational and Organisational Psychology*, **82**(2), 253–272.

Neal, A. and M. A. Griffin (2004), 'Safety climate and safety at work', in M. R. Frone and J. Barling (eds), *The Psychology of Workplace Safety*. Washington, DC: American Psychological Association, pp. 15–34.

Ng, E. S. and R. J. Burke (2010), 'Predictor of business students' attitudes toward sustainable business practices', *Journal of Business Ethics*, **95**(4), 603–615.

Norton, T., H. Zacher and N. Ashkanasy (2013), 'The mediating role of pro-environmental psychological climate on the relationships between green organisational policies and employee behaviours', Paper presented at the IOP 2013: 10th Industrial and Organisational Psychology Conference.

Otis, N. and L. G. Pelletier (2005), 'A motivational model of daily hassles, physical symptoms, and future work intentions among police officers', *Journal of Applied Social Psychology*, **35**(10), 2193–2214.

Paillé, P. and O. Boiral (2013), 'Pro-environmental behavior at work: Construct validity and determinants', *Journal of Environmental Psychology*, **36**, 118–128.

Pandey, A. and R. K. Gupta (2008), 'Spirituality in management a review of contemporary and traditional thoughts and agenda for research', *Global Business Review*, **9**(1), 65–83.

Portugal, E. and G. Yukl (1994), 'Perspectives on environmental leadership', *The Leadership Quarterly*, **5**(3–4), 271–276.

Ramus, C. A. (2002), 'Encouraging innovative environmental actions: What companies and managers must do', *Journal of World Business*, **37**(2), 151–164.

Ramus, C. A. and A. B. Killmer (2007), 'Corporate greening through prosocial extrarole behaviours: A conceptual framework for employee motivation', *Business Strategy and the Environment*, **16**(8), 554–570.

Ramus, C. A. and U. Steger (2000), 'The roles of supervisory support behaviors and environmental policy in employee "Ecoinitiatives" at leading-edge European companies', *Academy of Management Journal*, **43**(4), 605–626.

Remmen, A. and B. Lorentzen (2000), 'Employee participation and cleaner technology: Learning processes in environmental teams', *Journal of Cleaner Production*, **8**(5), 365–373.

Renwick, D. W., T. Redman and S. Maguire (2013), 'Green human resource management: A review and research agenda', *International Journal of Management Reviews*, **15**(1), 1–14.

Richins, M. L. and S. Dawson (1992), 'A consumer values orientation for materialism and its measurement: Scale development and validation', *Journal of Cconsumer Research*, **19**(3), 303–316.

Robertson, J. L. and J. Barling (2013), 'Greening organisations through leaders' influence on employees' pro-environmental behaviors', *Journal of Organisational Behavior*, **34**(2), 176–194.

Robinson, D. and A. Clegg (1998), 'Environmental leadership and competitive advantage through environmental management system standards', *Eco-Management and Auditing*, **5**(1), 6–14.

Russell, S. and A. Griffiths (2008), 'The role of emotions in driving workplace pro-environmental behaviors', in W. J. Zerbe, C. E. Härtel and N. M. Ashkanasy (eds), *Emotions, Ethics and Decision-Making*. Bingley: Emerald Group Publishing Limited, pp. 83–107.

Russo, M. V. and N. S. Harrison (2005), 'Organisational design and environmental performance: Clues from the electronics industry', *Academy of Management Journal*, **48**(4), 582–593.

Ryan, R. M., V. Huta and E. L. Deci (2013), 'Living well: A self-determination theory perspective on eudaimonia', in A. Delle Fave (ed.), *The Exploration of Happiness*. Netherlands: Springer, pp. 117–139.

Scherbaum, C. A., P. M. Popovich and S. Finlinson (2008), 'Exploring individual-level factors related to employee energy conservation behaviors at work', *Journal of Applied Social Psychology*, **38**(3), 818–835.

Shamir, B., M. B. Arthur and R. J. House (1994), 'The rhetoric of charismatic leadership: A theoretical extension, a case study, and implications for research', *The Leadership Quarterly*, **5**(1), 25–42.

Shrivastava, P. (1994), 'Ecocentric leadership in the 21st century', *The Leadership Quarterly*, **5**(3–4), 223–226.

Shrivastava, P. (2010), 'Pedagogy of passion for sustainability', *Academy of Management Learning and Education*, **9**(3), 443–455.

Springett, D. (2003), 'Business conceptions of sustainable development: A perspective from critical theory', *Business Strategy and the Environment*, **12**(2), 71.

Starik, M. and G. P. Rands (1995), 'Weaving an integrated web: Multilevel and multisystem perspectives of ecologically sustainable organisations', *Academy of Management Review*, **20**(4), 908–935.

Steg, L. and C. Vlek (2009), 'Encouraging pro-environmental behaviour: An integrative review and research agenda', *Journal of Environmental Psychology*, **29**(3), 309–317.

Stern, P. C. (2000), 'New environmental theories: Toward a coherent theory of environmentally significant behavior', *Journal of Social Issues*, **56**(3), 407–424.

Taylor, B. (2001), 'Earth and nature-based spirituality (part I): From deep ecology to radical environmentalism', *Religion*, **31**(2), 175–193.

Unsworth, K. L., A. Dmitrieva and E. Adriasola (2013), 'Environmental Leadership', Symposium to the Division of: Organizations and the Natural Environment (ONE), Organizational Behavior (OB) and Managerial and Organizational Cognition (MOC), available at https://www.researchgate.net/profile/Kerrie_Unsworth/publication/291359898_Environmental_Leadership/links/573431f808ae9ace840746b7/Environmental-Leadership.pdf.

Waldman, D. A., D. S. Siegel and M. Javidan (2006), 'Components of CEO transformational leadership and corporate social responsibility', *Journal of Management Studies*, **43**(8), 1703–1725.

Williams, S. and A. Schaefer (2013), 'Small and medium-sized enterprises and sustainability:

Managers' values and engagement with environmental and climate change issues', *Business Strategy and the Environment*, **22**(3), 173–186.

Yaffe, T. and R. Kark (2011), 'Leading by example: The case of leader OCB', *Journal of Applied Psychology*, **96**(4), 806.

Yin, H. and P. J. Schmeidler (2009), 'Why do standardized ISO 14001 environmental management systems lead to heterogeneous environmental outcomes?', *Business Strategy and the Environment*, **18**(7), 469–486.

Young, W., M. Davis, I. M. McNeill, B. Malhotra, S. Russell, K. Unsworth and C. W. Clegg (2015), 'Changing behaviour: Successful environmental programmes in the workplace', *Business Strategy and the Environment*, **24**(8), 689–703.

Zohar, D. (1980), 'Safety climate in industrial organisations: Theoretical and applied implications', *Journal of Applied Psychology*, **65**(1), 96.

Zohar, D. and G. Luria (2005), 'A multilevel model of safety climate: Cross-level relationships between organisation and group-level climates', *Journal of Applied Psychology*, **90**(4), 616.

11. A virtuous cycle: how green companies grow green employees (and vice versa)

Thomas A. Norton, Stacey L. Parker, Matthew C. Davis, Sally V. Russell and Neal M. Ashkanasy

Stakeholders increasingly evaluate contemporary organisations in terms of their environmental sustainability (Szekely and Knirsch 2005). In view of this it is unsurprising to find that: institutional forces put pressure on organisations to aspire to environmental sustainability (Kiron et al. 2015); policymakers promulgate environmental regulations (e.g., Zhu and Sarkis 2007); rival companies turn environmental performance into competitive advantage (e.g., Montabon et al. 2007); and consumers expect that the products and services they procure are provided with due consideration to the natural environment (Choi and Ng 2011). Moreover, breaching environmental responsibilities has significant implications for even the largest organisations, as shown in the case of Volkswagen shares which lost 40 per cent of their value as a direct consequence of circumventing emissions tests (Mooney 2016). As a result, pro-environmental or "green" behaviour is becoming an important component in the spectrum of workplace behaviours (Ones and Dilchert 2012). Importantly, and as Alt and Spitzeck (2016) point out, employee engagement in green behaviour at work helps drive an organisation's environmental performance. It seems that, much like innovation and safety-related behaviours, facilitating green behaviours is an imperative for businesses looking to succeed in the 21st century (Elkington 1997).

To address this issue, we will begin this chapter by defining employee green behaviour and providing an outline of the top-down processes organisations use to encourage their employees to be environmentally friendly at work. We will next describe the evidence showing organisation-level outcomes of green behaviour at work and argue that organisations act as complex adaptive systems, before discussing the potential for EGB-promoting organisational policies to effect broader cultural change in organisations. Finally, we will provide recommendations to practitioners to facilitate the greening of organisations.

11.1 EMPLOYEE GREEN BEHAVIOUR

In the broadest sense, employee green behaviour (EGB) refers to individual actions at work that have an effect (positive or negative) on the natural environment. Beyond this general description, however, a confusing plethora of overlapping concepts abound (see Ones and Dilchert 2012). The majority of these to date emphasise two central characteristics of green behaviour: that such behaviours are positive and lie outside of formal organisational roles (i.e., they are extra-role). By extra-role green behaviour, we mean behaviours performed with the intention of helping (or more likely minimising harm to) the environment, that are not expected, required, nor rewarded by an organisation. This sub-class of EGB aligns closely with the concept of organisational citizenship behaviour (OCB; see Podsakoff et al. 2000). This is reflected in the fact that researchers explicitly recognise OCBs directed towards the environment (see Boiral and Paillé 2012).

More recently, however, environmental sustainability has come to be manifest in formal expectations and requirements for EGB (Ones and Dilchert 2012). To this end, many organisations dedicate roles to manage their environmental performance, such as Environmental Manager or Chief Sustainability Officer (Schmit et al. 2012). In view of this, conceptualising EGB as a type of voluntary citizenship-type behaviour neglects a growing prevalence of EGBs (Ones and Dilchert 2012) that are not entirely volitional, and thus provides an incomplete picture.

This is not simply a conceptual issue however. For example, Motowidlo and Van Scotter (1994) demonstrated clear empirical differences in antecedents for required versus voluntary behaviours at work. Moreover, such distinctions are found in the specific context of EGB. Thus, in a review of the literature, Norton et al. (2015a) identified, across multiple organisational levels, distinct predictors for required and voluntary EGBs. For example, Bissing-Olson et al. (2013) found distinct relationships between activated positive affect (e.g., feeling excited) and proactive EGB, and unactivated positive affect (e.g., feeling calm) and task-related EGB. Similarly, Norton et al. (2014) found distinct relationships between injunctive organisational norms and task-related EGB, and descriptive norms and proactive EGB. In this chapter, therefore, we consider EGB as reflecting employee-level behaviours, either in-role or extra-role, performed with the intention of helping the natural environment. So the question now arises as to what role organisations play in promoting EGBs. We discuss this next.

11.2   THE ROLE OF ORGANISATIONS IN PROMOTING EGB

Research has shown (e.g., Davis and Coan 2015; Norton et al. 2015a; Osbaldiston and Schott 2012; Russell et al. 2016; Unsworth 2015) that organisations employ a wide range of methods, interventions and initiatives to encourage environmental cultures and EGB in practice. Whilst some aspects of behaviour change are likely to be led and driven by employees themselves or initiated by outside actors or regulations, the literature in this field provides an indication as to levers and approaches that organisations can take themselves to promote EGB in the workplace. In the following, we highlight some of the approaches that have received support in changing EGB, including leader modelling, introducing incentive schemes, improving the organisational environment, and recruiting and training environmentally aware employees. Programmes that feature combinations of these approaches are especially effective.

11.2.1   Leader Modelling

Yukl (2013) points out that leaders influence key organisational outcomes, including financial performance, culture and employee retention. Ones and Dilchert (2012) emphasise the influence of leaders on the adoption of EGBs. In this regard, Ramus and Steger (2000) specify that employees are aware of their leaders' and managers' pro-environmental actions and these in turn influence the performance of subordinates' behaviours. In other words, consistent with classical behavioural modelling theory (Bandura 1997), leaders are in a position to communicate and to role model the EGBs they want their employees to adopt, and to emphasise the importance of performing these behaviours.

The importance of leaders setting such an example was demonstrated by Cairns et al. (2010) who found leaders influence environmentally friendly travel planning amongst employees. Charismatic leadership and the display of personal commitment towards environmental issues has been credited with driving reductions in energy consumption within schools (Schelly et al. 2011). Similarly, Robertson and Barling (2013) found that environmentally specific transformational leadership influences both employees' environmental passion and green behaviour. In another study, Graves et al. (2013) found that transformational leaders help to motivate staff to engage in EGB. It seems, therefore, that leaders have the opportunity to support, stimulate and role model desired green behaviours, which is the key to achieving broader change in organisational culture (Davis and Coan 2015; Schwartz et al. 2010; Russell et al. 2016; Young et al. 2015).

11.2.2 Incentive Schemes

A second factor that has been shown to influence the adoption of EGBs in organisational settings is deployment of incentive schemes. In this regard, incentives have been used to support pro-environmental behaviour change and may offer a means of engaging staff who do not hold pro-environmental attitudes or who perceive changing their behaviour to be too great an effort (Kollmuss and Agyeman 2002). Financial incentives in particular have been used effectively within the construction industry to reward employees for reducing material waste onsite (Chen et al. 2002; Li et al. 2003). In more recent work, Cox et al. (2012) found that a combination of financial incentives and time off serve to encourage employees to make sustainable travel choices.

Other studies have demonstrated the power of non-monetary incentives. For example, Handgraaf et al. (2013) found non-financial rewards to be more effective in achieving energy reductions than financial incentives. This is consistent with self-determination theory, where behaviour enacted for autonomous reasons (i.e., I want to do it), rather than controlled reasons (i.e., I am doing it for rewards), is initiated more often, with better persistence, and with better quality performance outcomes (Gagné and Deci 2005). Non-financial rewards may take the form of public praise and recognition, environmental gifts or experiences (e.g., Davis et al. 2014). It is likely that the efficacy of the reward will be contingent upon the context, organisational culture and effort required to perform the desired EGB.

11.2.3 The Organisational Environment

The third major factor affecting employees' likelihood of engaging in EGBs is the physical environment that organisations design for their employees, including the supporting infrastructure (Young et al. 2015). Adjustments to buildings and infrastructure can be used to make EGB more convenient, reduce barriers to action and spur uptake. For example, Wu et al. (2013) found that the availability of recycling and composting bins is related to the performance of recycling behaviours. Along similar lines, other studies (Brothers et al. 1994; Ludwig et al. 1998) have demonstrated that simply increasing the proximity of recycling bins to workers increases recycling rates.

Conversely, making undesirable behaviours less convenient may nudge workers towards acting green. For example, Van Houten et al. (1981) show that adjusting the timing of lifts/elevators to make them a slower alternative to stairs leads to increased use of stairwells. Organisations can also provide facilities to support greener transport choices, for example, the provision of showers, lockers, changing rooms, bike facilities and shuttle buses (Cairns et al. 2010). Signs and prompts can also be placed at key decision-making points or close to places where green behaviours take place, e.g., around recycling bins, near light switches and devices, to prompt employees to make an environmental choice/enact EGB (e.g., Austin et al. 1993; Russell et al. 2016; Schelly et al. 2011; van Nieuw-Amerongen et al. 2011).

11.2.4 Recruitment and Training

Additional strategies that can be adopted to promote EGB is to attract and to train more environmentally minded employees (Davis and Coan 2015). Human Resource Management processes in major firms are increasingly being used to signal organisations' sustainability credentials and to appeal to younger workers' interest in working for responsible companies (Ehnert 2009; Renwick et al. 2013).

Changes in recruitment, coupled with increased environment-focused training and induction (increasingly common in the US and UK; Renwick et al. 2013), seem to help organisations to develop a workforce with higher environmental knowledge and awareness. In this regard, Cantor et al. (2012) found that provision of training in specific environmental processes or issues produces positive impacts on energy and waste behaviours (see also Jones et al. 2012) in addition to supporting pro-environmental innovations in processes (Rothenberg 2003). Training may help employees to avoid inefficient use of technologies or buildings (e.g., heating and ventilation systems, copiers, etc.) and to achieve environmental savings (Davis et al. 2014).

11.2.5 Combinations

While we have outlined each of these approaches separately, research suggests that it is often a combination of approaches that are most effective. For example, Russell et al. (2016) found that the combination of modelling behaviour by organisational leaders, signs and prompts, and communication is an effective means to reduce employees' energy use. There is also evidence to suggest that the more targeted the interventions can be to the specific behaviour, the more effective they are likely to be (Abrahamse et al. 2005).

11.3   ORGANISATIONAL-LEVEL ENVIRONMENTAL SUSTAINABILITY

To date, the predominant question in the literature has been: How do we increase green behaviour at work? As a consequence of focusing on the antecedents of EGB, there has been very limited focus on the outcomes of EGB (Norton et al. 2015a); in other words: How does EGB contribute to organisational environmental performance? Scholars researching this question typically use environmental performance and cost saving as dependent variables. While the evidence addressing this question is still emerging, early indications are positive (for a review, see Norton et al. 2015a).

Consistent with the prevalent literature, we have thus far described EGB and the ways that organisations might choose to encourage such behaviour among individual employees. The conclusion from this discussion is that organisations should seek to encourage EGB by creating the perception that such behaviour is valued (e.g., leader endorsement, incentives), and by facilitating performance through the physical environment (e.g., providing opportunities and removing barriers). While some may argue that EGB has inherent value (Goldstein et al. 2008), more sceptical readers might question why EGB, as an employee-level contribution, matters in the context of organisation-level environmental performance. Indeed, the return on investment of operating in an environmentally friendly way is an important feature in building a business case for environmental sustainability (Finster and Hernke 2014).

To resolve this conundrum, we now provide an account of the evidence linking EGB and organisation-level outcomes. Indeed, we argue specifically that even ostensibly minor EGBs can have disproportionately large impacts on the environmental behaviour of an organisation as a whole. In support of this idea, we consider an organisation as a complex adaptive system (Anderson 1999), in which there is a reciprocating cycle of influence between employees and the organisation as a whole. In such a system, employees have dual agency, wherein they react to an organisational context that they help to create (Frank and Fahrbach 1999). Through this reasoning, and with insights from the literature on organisational culture, we propose that EGBs might be a particularly important ingredient in the recipe for green organisations.

In the organisational psychology literature, EGB is typically seen as an outcome of organisation- and individual-level factors and processes (Norton et al. 2015a). There are, however, examples of research that look at the outcomes of processes that include EGB. For example, there is convincing evidence that corporate environmental management practices do have a positive effect on the financial performance of firms (see Albertini 2013, for a meta-analysis). This relationship appears to be stronger when companies develop more complex strategies (e.g., continuous environmental innovations in manufacturing processes and/or product-focused innovations to services/products with marketing to green consumers). Indeed, although many companies adopt a green strategy that involves investing in technological advancements (e.g., aimed at reducing waste/pollution), such technological improvements will only take us so far; in the future we need to look to operator involvement (i.e., EGB) for the next wave of financial return (Boiral 2005). In this way EGB constitutes a mechanism, through which top-down processes, such as those we described earlier in this chapter, achieve their intended outcomes.

The literature contains a suite of studies examining the contribution of EGB to organisational environmental performance. In this regard, Boiral et al. (2015) found managers' self-report EGBs are positively related to perceptions of environmental performance in comparison to competitors. Similarly, Chen et al. (2015) found a positive relationship between front-line employees' self-report environmental involvement and a measure of environmental performance using data from CEOs and external stakeholders. Finally, Paillé et al. (2014) found that the relationship between strategic human resource management (top management team data) and environmental performance (CEO data) was wholly explained by EGB (employee data). Thus, EGB appears to be positively related with subjective, but in some cases multi-source, measures of environmental performance.

Other researchers have focused on specific components of environmental performance, such as energy use and waste reduction. In one such intervention study, discussed earlier, Van Houten and his colleagues (1981) found that by making environmentally harmful behaviour (e.g., use of an elevator) more inconvenient, they could reduce employees' engagement in this behaviour and subsequently save costs. More recently, Carrico and Riemer (2011) conducted an intervention study aimed at motivating energy conservation at a US University. Through quite simple interventions (i.e., monthly group-based feedback via email and peer educators), office workers were encouraged to reduce energy use. These interventions were compared to an information-only control condition that simply educated employees about how and why to conserve energy. Results over a four-month period indicated that feedback and peer education resulted in 7 per cent and 4 per cent reductions in energy use, whereas sites where the control condition was implemented actually had an increase in energy use of 4 per cent.

Another facet of environmental performance involves reducing waste.

To this end, researchers have incentivised waste reduction in the construction industry using reward schemes (Chen et al. 2002; Li et al. 2003; Tam and Tam 2008). Tam and Tam (2008) rewarded employees with 30 per cent of the costs saved through their EGB. This resulted in a 23 per cent reduction in construction costs, and approximately HKD500,000 rewarded to employees. In another study, Chen and his colleagues (2002) compared workers involved in a similar scheme with a control group. The incentivised group saved approximately HKD1,500,000 over three months. A caveat of these findings is that, particularly in the construction industry, employees might take shortcuts and produce low-quality work in an effort to reduce waste (Chen et al. 2002).

In a related study, Boiral (2005) observed significant pollution reduction and costs savings, often exceeding managers' expectations, through the involvement of employees in environmental management planning. As shown in case studies, involving front-line employees who are better placed to understand the practicalities of environmental management practices led to more proactive and preventative solutions. Boiral (2005) did note that there were difficulties in precisely measuring the influence of human factors in this process, owing to a lack of environmental data, the interdependence between human and technical factors, and temporal factors (e.g., necessary delays in seeing the results of changes). Nonetheless, despite these difficulties, Boiral found that the role of the employee was far from negligible (and potentially more important than improvements garnered from technological advancements alone).

Other researchers have attempted to examine relationships between EGB and an organisation's competitive advantage. Extending on Boiral's (2005) call for more research on the human factors involved in environmental management, del Brio et al. (2007) conducted a large-scale survey study of factory workers in Spain (i.e., 110 different factories). They found that employee involvement in environmental activity was a critical factor significantly associated with employees' perceptions of environmental competitive advantage (as was senior leadership on green issues). In a further study, Casler et al. (2010) describe the contribution of EGB to the competitive advantage of a microbrewery. In particular, employee recommendations regarding environmental opportunities helped create substantial waste and energy reduction, cost savings, as well as new revenue streams.

Based on the foregoing discussion, it is clear that empirical support exists to support the proposition that EGB makes a positive contribution to an organisation's environmental performance – and potentially to an improved competitive edge. In organisations, however, behaviour does not occur in a vacuum (King et al. 2010). It is observed by, and communicated to, other employees, and has the potential to influence subsequent behaviour. Although typical conceptualisations might place it at, or towards, the end of one causal chain, it might be just as suitably placed at the start of another. This view is particularly appropriate when considering organisations as complex systems, where employees have dual agency.

11.3.1   Complex Adaptive Systems

Baumann (2015) defines complex adaptive systems as those that adapt to their environment through the interaction of multiple, interdependent elements. Eidelson (1997) notes that organisations meet this definition to the extent that they comprise heterogeneous employees interacting with one another, and responding to their environment without full central control. Moreover, organisations adapt in response to changes in the external environment (Carlisle and McMillan 2006; Schneider and Somers 2006). The natural state of organisations is dynamic insofar as elements within the system change as new information becomes available (Dooley 1997). This is consistent with Schein's (1992) definition of organisational culture as reflecting a company's learned ability to solve problems of internal integration and external adaptation. In this way, an organisation is in effect "path-dependent" (i.e., the organisation's present state is an evolutionary progression from its initial state via a series of intermediary states; see Schneider and Somers 2006; Sterman and Wittenberg 1999).

A key characteristic of complex systems is that behaviour at the system (i.e., organisational) level emerges from the interaction of individual elements (i.e., employees) adhering to a hierarchy of local rules from general to specific (Eidelson 1997; Holland 1989; Schneider and Somers 2006). In other words, order at the system level emerges from individual interactions at lower levels, rather than from a centralised control (Anderson 1999; Eidelson 1997). Take for example the response of birds on the fringe of a flock to the sight of a predator. As these birds respond to this change in their environment and instinctively move away from the threat, others adhere to local rules regarding separation, alignment, and cohesion (e.g., Hildenbrandt et al. 2010; Reynolds 1987), to the effect that the whole flock moves away from the predator. Thus, the behaviour of a few individuals in response to their environment can, in the right circumstances, change the behaviour of the system as a whole (Anderson 1999). Thus, it is vital for organisations to capitalise on the potential of individual-level EGB (which typically has negligible environmental impact; see Paillé et al. 2014) to influence system-level activity with more easily demonstrable environmental outcomes.

11.3.2 Behaviour in Complex Adaptive Systems

In complex adaptive systems, individuals make behavioural decisions in response to their perception of the environment at a particular point in time using local rules. Local rules are formed over time, and comprise past perceptions, behaviours and consequences (Anderson 1999), and exist in a hierarchy from general to specific (Holland 1989). Individuals can use specific rules (e.g., "print in draft mode except for final client copy") in familiar situations, while reverting to more general rules (e.g., "conserve resources where possible") to guide activity in unfamiliar situations (Anderson 1999; Holland 1989). Individuals modify rules for future use based on the consequences they receive via feedback loops (Eidelson 1997).

Feedback loops are patterns of self-organisation that emerge when elements of a system (e.g., employees) create new information (e.g., behaviour and its consequences), which they then use to modify future behaviour (Bateson 1972). Because these elements in complex adaptive systems are interconnected, feedback loops also exist between individuals, thus allowing the system to self-organise (Sterman and Wittenberg 1999). In psychology, this is analogous to vicarious learning, whereby an individual learns via observing the consequences of others' behaviour (Bandura 1977). Thus, through experiential and vicarious learning, interactions among individuals produce local rules that guide behaviour within the system. To the extent that feedback loops connect the various individuals within that system (e.g., organisation), these rules spread throughout the system, and adherence to them produces emergent behaviour at the system level (Baumann 2015; Schneider and Somers 2006).

We can see then that behaviour in a complex adaptive system is a dynamic learning process. In much the same way, although from a different perspective, Schein (1990) defines organisational culture as representing the learning shared throughout a company. In both cases, past experiences are shared via feedback loops, and inform the rules that guide future activity. From a cultural perspective, these rules reflect fundamental assumptions about the world, and constitute the beliefs and values shared among employees. This suggests that individual behaviour, such as EGB, might constitute a mechanism that develops, maintains and adapts an organisational culture towards environmental sustainability (Linnenluecke and Griffiths 2010; Norton et al. 2015b). To understand this fully, we need to consider behaviour in the context of organisational culture.

Schein's (1992) "iceberg" model of culture includes three levels: (1) a fixed set of fundamental assumptions about the world that informs (2) more malleable beliefs and values, which are demonstrated through (3) tangible artefacts and behaviours (which in turn often reflect assumptions at Level 1). Note, in particular, that Schein sees behaviour as a form of cultural artefact. Hatch's (1993) dynamic model builds on Schein's work. In addition to assumptions, beliefs and values, and artefacts, the Hatch model includes symbols, which she defines as artefacts that take on additional symbolic meaning in the way they are used by organisational members. For example, while the use of renewable energy at Sierra Nevada Brewing Co. is an artefact of the company's green culture (Norton et al. 2015b), employees using a solar-powered beer trailer to showcase their beers and solar technology might have additional symbolic meaning (Sierra Nevada Brewing Co. 2015). In Hatch's view, then, some behaviours and artefacts in effect constitute cultural symbols.

11.3.3   Behaviours as Mechanisms for Culture Change in a Complex System

The most significant contribution of Hatch's (1993) model is that it considers the relationships between the structural components of culture (i.e., assumptions, beliefs and values, artefacts, symbols). As a structural model of organisational culture and a dynamic model of culture change, Hatch's model provides a conceptual framework for both top-down and bottom-up processes, thus making it compatible with the idea that organisations are complex adaptive systems, in which employees have dual agency and create the environment that influences their activity. An important implication of the relationships in Hatch's model is that they permit changes to beliefs and values as a result of changes at more tangible levels. For example, if redesigning products to be more environmentally friendly is seen as an effective way to behave at work, it can reshape the beliefs and values within the organisation, and examples of green products might even take on additional meaning to become symbols that encourage employees to reinterpret their fundamental assumptions about the organisation.

According to Frank and Fahrbach (1999), such culture change occurs at two levels. First, individual attitudes towards EGB would have to change to the point that it is seen as an effective way to respond to external pressures on the system (e.g., regulatory, normative and socio-cultural pressure around environmental sustainability; Scott 1995). Via feedback loops, positive consequences also help to inform local rules that shape behaviour such that, when a similar situation is encountered in the future, employees behave in a way that is likely to produce positive outcomes (Anderson 1999). If the consequences of EGB, for example, are negligible, neutral or negative, employees are unlikely to modify existing local rules to include them. Formal elements, such as incentive programmes (e.g., Tam and Tam 2008; Handgraaf et al. 2013) are an effective way to provide or amplify the positive consequences of EGB, and increase the likelihood that local rules are modified for their inclusion.

Second, attitudes towards EGB need to be distributed throughout the system (Frank and Fahrbach 1999) through feedback loops. As we described earlier, the self-organisation of local rules is a process of experiential and vicarious learning. Where individuals do not interact via feedback loops (i.e., because such loops do not exist), however, the process of vicarious learning is impeded. In cases where individuals are not directly connected by feedback loops (e.g., if they do not interact and exchange information about their experiences with one another), where one employee could learn from the experiences of another, new connections might be required (Anderson 1999). Communication can establish such new connections – with the effect of increasing the density of interactions in the system (Dooley 1997). Organisations in which information is shared freely might facilitate quick adaptation to changes in external conditions (Caldwell and O'Reilly 1995).

From this perspective, therefore, there are two conditions under which EGB might lead to broader, system-level (i.e., cultural) change. First, employees need to be encouraged to modify the local rules that guide their behaviour through feedback and learning (i.e., through seeing the benefits of EGB). The form and effectiveness of such feedback would be moderated by individual factors, such as environmental attitudes (Bamberg 2003) and/or motivation towards the environment (Pelletier et al. 1998). Second, interconnections between employees are needed to facilitate the modification of local rules being distributed throughout the system. Under such conditions it is possible that the net result would be changes to the local rules that extend to the system-level (i.e., beliefs and values), and consequently the emergent behaviour of the system itself (Frank and Fahrbach 1999). Mitleton-Kelly (2011) provides an example of such a change in a case study of two hospitals. Hospital X empowered employees to explore and implement new ideas, whereas in Hospital Y new ideas had to be approved before they could be tested. Teams in Hospital X discussed the new ideas and their outcomes openly with other groups, and initiated cross-team projects. The outcome of this knowledge-sharing and collaboration was emergent change throughout Hospital X (Mitleton-Kelly 2011).

11.4 RECOMMENDATIONS FOR PRACTITIONERS

To effect system-level green behaviour, practitioners should seek to (1) create a workplace environment conducive to EGB, (2) directly encourage EGB, and (3) facilitate the dissemination of information about EGB throughout the system. In the first regard, management need to do more than simply incorporate EGB into organisational policies and procedures. Norton and his colleagues (2014) found employees' perceptions of whether or not their organisation genuinely values environmental sustainability fully explained any effect a policy towards sustainability had on EGB. Accordingly, EGB needs to be expressly included in the organisation's values and reflected in tangible artefacts, such as environmentally friendly products and services, and employee recruitment and training practices (see Bratton and Bratton 2015; Jackson et al. 2012). In the end, by creating a workplace environment that supports environmental sustainability, employees can start to create basic (i.e., global) rules that incorporate green values and influence activity within the system (Eidelson 1997), and come to reinterpret their fundamental assumptions about the nature of the world.

From here, practitioners should engage with employees directly to encourage EGB and develop more specific rules. A general theme emerging from research in this area is that empowering employees is an important factor in encouraging EGB. For example, Lingard et al. (2001) demonstrate the benefits of participative goal setting towards environmental targets. Moreover, and at a general level, complex adaptive systems require exploration and exploitation of new ideas (e.g., Mitleton-Kelly 2011). Taken together, these points imply that organisations provide employees with the freedom to experiment with new behaviours and practices. In this regard, practitioners should seek to provide opportunities (e.g., green competitions) and resources (e.g., hybrid company vehicles), and remove constraints (e.g., lack of information about how to be green at work) to EGB.

However, given the dynamic and complex nature of organisations, which sometimes appear to border on chaos (Guastello 2013), managers need to be especially clear about the goals they set for their employees to meet contemporary environmental standards. From this perspective, practitioners should look to shape and direct EGB within their own organisations. They can do so by modelling appropriate behaviours and manipulating incentive schemes. For example, Sierra Nevada Brewing Co.'s Green Machine programme incentivises employees to use alternative transport for work-related travel (Sierra Nevada Brewing Co. 2015). Similarly, encouraging leaders within the company to role model EGB is an important signal for employees both in terms of demonstrating espoused values and providing clear examples of desired behaviour (Robertson and Barling 2013; Russell and McIntosh 2011). Consistent with the research evidence (Russell et al. 2016), managers should seek to develop integrated policies that incorporate elements of all the different approaches to encouraging employees to engage in EGBs.

Finally, practitioners should facilitate the dissemination of insights and learning drawn from EGB throughout the organisation to allow system-level rules to emerge. From this perspective, the question becomes: How can I maximise the utility of each instance of EGB to influence the system as a whole? To do so, managers should not only provide feedback to employees engaging in EGB (e.g., in performance appraisals; Boiral 2005; Zibarras and Coan 2015) in the interests of experiential learning, but also strive to increase the density of feedback loops between different elements (e.g., employees, teams) in the system to promote vicarious learning. Using the example of Hospital X (Mitleton-Kelly 2011), encouraging cross-team collaboration and knowledge sharing through open discussions helped system-level changes emerge from local changes to behaviour. Similarly, Sierra Nevada Brewing Co. operates an employee-led quality circle (Lagrosen 2013), which provides a forum where members from across the company meet to discuss and problem-solve issues, including environmental performance (Casler et al. 2010).

11.5   CONCLUSIONS

In this chapter, we have provided an overview of how organisational factors influence EGB, and how these behaviours also contribute to organisation-level outcomes. In this way, we describe how EGB can have a bottom-up effect on the organisation itself through emergent behaviour from the perspective of complex adaptive systems, thus creating a virtuous cycle. By facilitating employees' modification of local rules guiding behaviour to include EGB, organisations might be able to enhance the effectiveness of their formal structures and develop a positive culture towards environmental sustainability. To this end, we provide recommendations for practitioners in this area. We believe looking at EGB from the perspective of complex adaptive systems is an interesting and valuable contribution to this area because it empowers individuals to think globally and act locally in response to a dire challenge (Espinosa and Porter 2011). The scale of the environmental challenges that loom large over the next decades requires widespread action. By explaining the potential for individual-level behaviour to lead to emergent behaviour at the organisational, institutional and societal level, a complex adaptive systems approach highlights the personal responsibility we all share.

REFERENCES

Abrahamse, W., L. Steg, C. Vlek and T. Rothengatter (2005), 'A review of intervention studies aimed at household energy conservation', *Journal of Environmental Psychology*, **25**, 273–91.

Albertini, E. (2013), 'Does environmental management improve financial performance? A meta-analytic review', *Organization and Environment*, **26**, 431–57.

Alt, E. and H. Spitzeck (2016), 'Improving environmental performance through unit-level organizational citizenship behaviors for the environment: A capability perspective', *Journal of Environmental Management*, **182**, 48–58.

Anderson, P. (1999), 'Complexity theory and organization science', *Organization Science*, **10**, 216–32.

Austin, J., D. B. Hatfield, A. C. Grindle and J. S. Bailey (1993), 'Increasing recycling in office environments: The effects of specific, informative cues', *Journal of Applied Behavior Analysis*, **26**, 247–53.

Bamberg, S. (2003), 'How does environmental concern influence specific environmentally related behaviors? A new answer to an old question', *Journal of Environmental Psychology*, **23** (1), 21–32.

Bandura, A. (1977), 'Self-efficacy: Toward a unifying theory of behavioral change', *Psychological Review*, **84**, 191–215.

Bandura, Albert (1997), *Self-efficacy: The Exercise of Control*, New York: W. H. Freeman and Company.

Bateson, Gregory (1972), *Steps to an Ecology of Mind*, Chicago, IL: University Press.

Baumann, O. (2015), 'Models of complex adaptive systems in strategy and organization research', *Mind and Society*, **14**, 169–83.

Bissing-Olson, M. J., A. Iyer, K. S. Fielding and H. Zacher (2013), 'Relationships between daily affect and pro-environmental behavior at work: The moderating role of pro-environmental attitude', *Journal of Organizational Behavior*, **34**, 156–75.

Boiral, O. (2005), 'The impact of operator involvement in pollution reduction: Case studies in Canadian chemical companies', *Business Strategy and the Environment*, **14**, 339–60.

Boiral, O. and P. Paillé (2012), 'Organizational citizenship behaviour for the environment: Measurement and validation', *Journal of Business Ethics*, **109**, 431–45.

Boiral, O., D. Talbot and P. Paillé (2015), 'Leading by example: A model of organizational citizenship behavior for the environment', *Business Strategy and the Environment*, **24**, 532–50.

Bratton, A. and J. Bratton (2015), 'Human resource approaches', in Jennifer L. Robertson and Julian Barling (eds), *The Psychology of Green Organizations*, New York: Oxford University Press, pp. 274–95.

Brothers, K. J., P. J. Krantz and L. E. McClannahan (1994), 'Office paper recycling: A function of container proximity', *Journal of Applied Behavior Analysis*, **27**, 153–60.

Cairns, S., C. Newson and A. Davis (2010), 'Understanding successful workplace travel initiatives in the UK', *Transportation Research Part A: Policy and Practice*, **44**, 473–94.

Caldwell, D. and C. O'Reilly (1995), 'Promoting team-based innovation in organizations: The role of normative influence', paper presented at the Fifty-Fourth Annual Meeting of the Academy of Management, Vancouver, BC.

Cantor, D. E., P. C. Morrow and F. Montabon (2012), 'Engagement in environmental behaviors among supply chain management employees: An organizational support theoretical perspective', *Journal of Supply Chain Management*, **48**, 33–51.

Carlisle, Y. and E. McMillan (2006), 'Innovation in organizations from a complex adaptive systems perspective', *Emergence: Complexity and Organization*, **8**, 2–9.

Carrico, A. R. and M. Riemer (2011), 'Motivating energy conservation in the workplace: An evaluation of the use of group-level feedback and peer education', *Journal of Environmental Psychology*, **31**, 1–13.

Casler, A., M. J. Gundlach, B. Persons and S. Zivnuska (2010), 'Sierra Nevada Brewing Company's thirty-year journey toward sustainability', *People and Strategy*, **33**, 44–51.

Chen, Y., G. Tang, J. Jin, J. Li and P. Paillé (2015), 'Linking market orientation and environmental performance: The influence of environmental strategy, employee's environmental involvement, and environmental product quality', *Journal of Business Ethics*, **127**, 479–500.

Chen, Z., H. Li and C. T. C. Wong (2002), 'An application of bar-code system for reducing construction wastes', *Automation in Construction*, **11**, 521–33.

Choi, S. and A. Ng (2011), 'Environmental and economic dimensions of sustainability and price effects on consumer responses', *Journal of Business Ethics*, **104**, 269–82.

Cox, A., T. Higgins, R. Gloster, B. Foley and A. Darnton (2012), 'The impact of workplace initiatives on low carbon behaviours', accessed 6 December 2016 at www.gov.scot/Resource/0039/00390309.pdf.

Davis, M. C., R. Challenger, D. N. W. Jayewardene and C. W. Clegg (2014), 'Advancing socio-technical systems thinking: A call for bravery', *Applied Ergonomics*, **45**, 171–80.

Davis, M. C. and P. Coan (2015), 'Organizational Change', in Jennifer L. Robertson and Julian Barling (eds), *The Psychology of Green Organizations*, New York: Oxford University Press, pp. 244–74.

del Brio, J. A., E. Fernandez and B. Junquera (2007), 'Management and employee involvement in achieving an environmental action-based competitive advantage: An empirical study', *The International Journal of Human Resource Management*, **18**, 491–522.

Dooley, K. J. (1997), 'A complex adaptive systems model of organization change', *Non-linear Dynamics, Psychology, and Life Sciences*, **1**, 69–97.

Ehnert, Ina (2009), *Sustainable Human Resource Management*, London: Springer.

Eidelson, R. J. (1997), 'Complex adaptive systems in the behavioral and social sciences', *Review of General Psychology*, **1**, 42–71.

Elkington, John (1997), *Cannibals With Forks: The Triple-bottom Line of 21st Century Business*, Oxford: Capstone.

Espinosa, A. and T. Porter (2011), 'Sustainability, complexity and learning: Insights from complex systems approaches', *The Learning Organization*, **18**, 73–86.

Finster, M. P. and M. T. Hernke (2014), 'Benefits organizations pursue when seeking competitive advantage by improving environmental performance', *Journal of Industrial Ecology*, **18**, 652–62.

Frank, K. A. and K. Fahrbach (1999), 'Organization culture as a complex system: Balance and information in models of influence and selection', *Organization Science*, **10**, 253–77.

Gagné, M. and E. L. Deci (2005), 'Self-determination theory and work motivation', *Journal of Organizational Behavior*, **26**, 331–62.

Goldstein, N. J., R. B. Cialdini and V. Griskevicius (2008), 'A Room with a viewpoint: Using social norms to motivate environmental conservation in hotels', *Journal of Consumer Research*, **35**, 472–82.

Graves, L. M., J. Sarkis and Q. Zhu (2013), 'How transformational leadership and employee motivation combine to predict employee proenvironmental behaviors in China', *Journal of Environmental Psychology*, **35**, 81–91.

Guastello, Stephen J. (2013), *Chaos, Catastrophe, and Human Affairs: Applications of Nonlinear Dynamics to Work, Organizations, and Social Evolution*, New York: Psychology Press.

Handgraaf, M. J. J., M. A. Van Lidth de Jeude and K. C. Appelt (2013), 'Public praise vs. private pay: Effects of rewards on energy conservation in the workplace', *Ecological Economics*, **86**, 86–92.

Hatch, M. J. (1993), 'The dynamics of organizational culture', *Academy of Management Review*, **18**, 657–93.

Hildenbrandt, H., C. Carere and C. K. Hemelrijk (2010), 'Self-organized aerial displays of thousands of starlings: A model', *Behavioral Ecology*, **21**, 1349–59.

Holland, John H. (1989), *Induction: Processes of Inference, Learning, and Discovery*, Cambridge, MA: MIT Press.

Jackson, Susan E., Deniz S. Ones and Stephan Dilchert (eds) (2012), *Managing Human Resources for Environmental Sustainability*, San Francisco, CA: Jossey-Bass.

Jones, J., J. Jackson, T. Tudor and M. Bates (2012), 'Strategies to enhance waste minimization and energy conservation within organizations: A case study from the UK construction sector', *Waste Management and Research: The Journal of the International Solid Wastes and Public Cleansing Association*, **30**, 981–90.

King, B. G., T. Felin and D. A. Whetten (2010), 'Perspective-finding the organization in organizational theory: A meta-theory of the organization as a social actor', *Organization Science*, **21**, 290–305.

Kiron, D., N. Kruschwitz, K. Haanaes, M. Reeves, S.-J. Fuisz-Kehrbach and G. Kell (2015), 'Joining forces: Collaboration and leadership for sustainability', *MIT Sloan Management Review*, **56**. Accessed 4 December 2016 at http://sloanreview.mit.edu/projects/joining-forces.

Kollmuss, A. and J. Agyeman (2002), 'Mind the Gap: Why do people act environmentally and what are the barriers to pro-environmental behavior?', *Environmental Education Research*, **8**, 239–60.

Lagrosen, Stephan (2013), 'Quality circles', in Eric H. Kessler (ed.), *Encyclopedia of Management Theory*, vol. 1, pp. 645–6.

Li, H., Z. Chen and C. T. C. Wong (2003), 'Barcode technology for an incentive reward program to reduce construction wastes', *Computer-Aided Civil and Infrastructure Engineering*, **18**, 313–24.

Lingard, H., G. Gilbert and P. Graham (2001), 'Improving solid waste reduction and recycling performance using goal setting and feedback', *Construction Management and Economics*, **19**, 809–17.

Linnenluecke, M. K. and A. Griffiths (2010), 'Corporate sustainability and organizational culture', *Journal of World Business*, **45**, 357–66.

Ludwig, T. D., T. W. Gray and A. Rowell (1998), 'Increasing recycling in academic buildings: A systematic replication', *Journal of Applied Behavior Analysis*, **31**, 683–86.

Mitleton-Kelly, E. (2011), 'A complexity theory approach to sustainability: A longitudinal study in two London NHS hospitals', *The Learning Organization*, **18**, 45–53.

Montabon, F., R. Sroufe and R. Narasimhan (2007), 'An examination of corporate reporting, environmental management practices and firm performance', *Journal of Operations Management*, **2**, 988–1014.

Mooney, A. (2016, 9 October), 'Investment lessons to learn from the VW scandal', *Financial Times*. Accessed 5 December 2016 at https://www.ft.com/content/84258efa-7128-11e6-a0c9-1365ce54b926.

Motowidlo, S. J. and J. R. Van Scotter (1994), 'Evidence that task performance should be distinguished from contextual performance', *Journal of Applied Psychology*, **79**, 475–80.

Norton, T. A., S. L. Parker, H. Zacher and N. M. Ashkanasy (2015a), 'Employee green behavior: A theoretical framework, multilevel review, and future research agenda', *Organization and Environment*, **28**, 103–25.

Norton, T. A., H. Zacher and N. M. Ashkanasy (2014), 'Organisational sustainability policies and employee green behaviour: The mediating role of work climate perceptions', *Journal of Environmental Psychology*, **38**, 49–54.

Norton, T. A., H. Zacher and N. M. Ashkanasy (2015b), 'Pro-environmental organizational culture and climate', in Jennifer L. Robertson and Julian Barling (eds), *The Psychology of Green Organizations*, Oxford: Oxford University Press, pp. 322–48.

Ones, D. S. and S. Dilchert (2012), 'Environmental sustainability at work: A call to action', *Industrial and Organizational Psychology: Perspectives on Science and Practice*, **5**, 444–66.

Osbaldiston, R. and J. P. Schott (2012), 'Environmental sustainability and behavioral science: Meta-analysis of proenvironmental behavior experiments', *Environment and Behavior*, **44**, 257–99.

Paillé, P., Y. Chen, O. Boiral and J. Jin (2014), 'The impact of human resource management on environmental performance: An employee-level study', *Journal of Business Ethics*, **121**, 451–66.

Pelletier, L. G., K. M. Tuson, I. Green-Demers, K. Noels and A. M. Beaton (1998), 'Why are you doing things for the environment? The motivation toward the environment scale', *Journal of Applied Social Psychology*, **28**, 437–68.

Podsakoff, P. M., S. B. MacKenzie, J. B. Paine and D. G. Bachrach (2000), 'Organizational citizenship behaviors: A critical review of the theoretical and empirical literature and suggestions for future research', *Journal of Management*, **26**, 513–63.

Ramus, C. A. and U. Steger (2000), 'The roles of supervisory support behaviors and environmental policy in employee "ecoinitiatives" at leading-edge European companies', *Academy of Management Journal*, **43**, 605–26.

Renwick, D. W. S., T. Redman and S. Maguire (2013), 'Green human resource management: A review and research agenda', *International Journal of Management Reviews*, **15**, 1–14.

Reynolds, C. W. (1987), 'Flocks, herds and schools: A distributed behavioural model', *Proceedings of the Fourteenth Annual Conference on Computer Graphics and Interactive Techniques*, New York: Association for Computing Machinery, pp. 25–34.

Robertson, J. L. and J. Barling (2013), 'Greening organizations through leaders' influence on employees' pro-environmental behaviors', *Journal of Organizational Behavior*, **34**, 176–94.

Rothenberg, S. (2003), 'Knowledge content and worker participation in environmental management at NUMMI', *Journal of Management Studies*, **40**, 1783–802.

Russell, S. V. and M. McIntosh (2011), 'Changing organizational culture for sustainability', in Neal M. Ashkanasy, Celeste P. M. Wilderom and Mark F. Peterson (eds), *Handbook of Organizational Culture and Climate* (2nd edn), Thousand Oaks, CA: Sage, pp. 393–411.

Russell, S. V., A. Evans, K. S. Fielding and C. Hill (2016), 'Turn it off: An action research study of top management influence on energy conservation in the workplace', *Frontiers in Psychology*, **7**, 1–10.

Schein, Edgar H. (1985), *Organizational Culture and Leadership*, San Francisco, CA: Jossey-Bass.

Schein, E. H. (1990), 'Organizational Culture', *American Psychologist*, **45**, 109–19.

Schein, E. H. (1992), *Organizational Culture and Leadership* (2nd edn), San Francisco: Jossey-Bass.

Schelly, C., J. E. Cross, W. S. Franzen, P. Hall and S. Reeve (2011), 'Reducing energy consumption and creating a conservation culture in organizations: A case study of one public school district', *Environment and Behavior*, **43**, 316–43.

Schmit, Mark J., S. Fegley, E. Esen, J. Schramm and A. Tomassetti (2012), 'Human resource management efforts for environmental sustainability: A survey or organizations', in Susan E. Jackson, Deniz S. Ones and Stephan Dilchert (eds), *Managing Human Resources for Environmental Sustainability*, San Francisco, CA: Jossey-Bass, pp. 61–79.

Schneider, M. and M. Somers (2006), 'Organizations as complex adaptive systems: Implications of complexity theory for leadership research', *Leadership Quarterly*, **17**, 351–65.

Schwartz, T., M. Betz, L. Ramirez and G. Stevens (2010), 'Sustainable energy practices at work: Understanding the role of workers in energy conservation', *Proceedings of the Sixth Nordic Conference on Human-Computer Interaction*, Reykjavik, pp. 452–62.

Scott, William R. (1995), *Institutions and Organizations*, Thousand Oaks, CA: Sage.

Sierra Nevada Brewing Co. (2015), *Biennial Sustainability Report*, accessed 6 December 2016 at http://www.sierranevada.com/brewery/about-us/sustainability.

Sterman, J. D. and J. Wittenberg (1999), 'Path dependence, competition, and succession in the dynamics of scientific revolution', *Organization Science*, **10**, 322–41.

Szekely, F. and M. Knirsch (2005), 'Responsible leadership and corporate social responsibility: Metrics for sustainable performance', *European Management Journal*, **23**, 628–47.

Tam, V. W. Y. and C. M. Tam (2008), 'Waste reduction through incentives: A case study', *Building Research and Information*, **36**, 37–43.

Unsworth, K. L. (2015), 'Green me up Scotty: Psychological interventions to increase pro-environmental behaviors', in Jennifer L. Robertson and Julian Barling (eds), *The Psychology of Green Organizations*, New York: Oxford University Press, pp. 215–43.

Van Houten, R., P. A. Nau and M. Merrigan (1981), 'Reducing elevator energy use: A comparison of posted feedback and reduced elevator convenience', *Journal of Applied Behavior Analysis*, **14**, 377–87.

van Nieuw-Amerongen, M. E., S. P. J. Kremers, N. K. de Vries and G. Kok (2011), 'The use of prompts, increased accessibility, visibility, and aesthetics of the stairwell to promote stair use in a university building', *Environment and Behavior*, **43**, 131–9.

Wu, D. W.-L., A. DiGiacomo and A. Kingstone (2013), 'A sustainable building promotes pro-environmental behavior: An observational study on food disposal', *PloS One*.

Young, W., M. Davis, I. M. McNeill, B. Malhotra, S. V. Russell, K. Unsworth and C. W. Clegg (2015), 'Changing behaviour: Successful environmental programmes in the workplace', *Business Strategy and the Environment*, **24**, 689–703.

Yukl, Gary A. (2013), *Leadership in Organizations*, 8th edn, New York: Pearson Education.

Zhu, Q. and J. Sarkis (2007), 'The moderating effects of institutional pressures on emergent green supply chain practices and performance', *International Journal of Production Research*, **45**, 4333–55.

Zibarras, L. D. and P. Coan (2015), 'HRM practices used to promote proenvironmental behavior: A UK survey', *International Journal of Human Resource Management*, **26**, 2121–42.

12. Organisational and employee symbolic environmental behaviours: an integrated multi-level framework
Lei Yang, Danae Manika and Frances Bowen

12.1 INTRODUCTION

A large body of research that has recently emerged in literature and practice shows that organisations do not substantially perform pro-environmental behaviours (PEB). Some organisations have also been exposed by others (e.g. external individuals or organisations) to engage in symbolic environmental-related activities (e.g. *greenwashing*) rather than true environmentalism. At the individual level, the symbolic motive is also the latest development in the environmental psychology literature. Even though both organisational- and individual-level research of PEB has recognised the existence of symbolism embedded in ecological activities, scholars have not yet examined how symbolic reasons for PEB can be classified and examined through an integrated multi-level perspective. The focus of this chapter is therefore to establish a multi-level framework in the sense of explaining symbolic PEB at both organisational and employee levels.

An example of corporate *greenwashing* behaviour is the Volkswagen (VW) emissions scandal in September 2015. Before the scandal, the company claimed that they had adopted a common-rail fuel injection system in their vehicles, which had better fuel atomisation, air/fuel ratio control and emissions control (Jääskeläinen and Khair 2015). The so-called low-emission VW vehicles allowed the company to obtain green car subsidies and tax exemptions in the USA. However, the United States Environmental Protection Agency (EPA) found that VW cars were cheating emissions tests through a "defeat device". The device was able to automatically adjust performance when tested and concealed the fact that the engine emitted nitrogen oxide pollutants up to 40 times above the USA pollution standards (Hotten 2015).

Greenwashing is a deliberate information management strategy in which firms can selectively reveal positive information about their environmental performance while hiding facts of less favourable activities (Lyon and Maxwell 2011). Yet this idea of naïve *greenwashing* is less applicable today with the pervasion of social media and smart technologies. This calls for a broader consideration of corporate greening, which is nowadays redirected from *greenwashing* to *symbolic corporate environmentalism* (Bowen 2014). Symbolic corporate environmentalism refers to "the shared meanings and representations surrounding changes made by managers within firms that they describe as primarily for environmental reasons" (Bowen 2014: 31). As suggested by the symbolic corporate environmentalism construct, all organisational environmental behaviours contain both symbolic and material components (Forbes and Jermier 2012). For instance, building a green factory contains a material component of a clean energy usage system and a symbolic component such as showcasing an image of taking environmental responsibility through certification.

Bowen (2014) further explained that a green practice might result in either symbolic or substantive performance or both. Symbolic performance refers to the extent to which behaviour is appreciated and generates positive social evaluations. Substantive performance represents the impact of organisational activities on the natural environment in terms of minimising ecological damage. *Greenwashing* is the most widely acknowledged type of organisational behaviour that is merely symbolic, but it does not account for substantially benefiting the environment. Thus, the term *symbolic environmentalism* is a wider concept, which includes *greenwashing* but also encompasses substantive performance, and is the focus of this chapter.

The phenomenon of symbolic environmentalism however is not merely restricted to corporations. Employees sometimes also engage in symbolic environmentalism in the workplace. Boiral (2007) uncovered the ceremonial aspect of employees' ecological activities under the pressure of ISO 14001, which is one of the most famous environmental management systems among organisations. There are deviations of employees' work behaviours from standard prescriptions proposed by ISO 14001, but these deviations are reduced as much as possible during auditing.

> Just like students who go over their notes before a final exam, the managers and employees consulted – sometimes for the first time – ISO 14001 documentation; they read the procedures, updated their knowledge, and attempted to ensure that the system would be in order at the time of the audit. (Boiral 2007: 138)

In other words, green employee behaviours can also be superficial, improvised, and symbolic in nature, rather than based on true environmentalism.

Thus, symbolic environmentalism can take place across two levels: the corporate/organisation level and the employee/individual level. The motives behind symbolic corporate environmentalism have been analysed in prior literature through conventional and critical perspectives (which are discussed later in this chapter). However, the reasons behind symbolic employee environmentalism have not been the subject of much investigation. Hence, the aim of this chapter is to explore this gap in the literature and uncover the drivers of, and mechanisms underlying, the symbolism of environmental activities across organisational and employee levels via an integrated multi-level framework. Multi-level frameworks help to specify relationships among theoretical constructs at different levels (Randel 2002) and can benefit researchers and practitioners to advance their understanding of environmental symbolism by exploring the commonalities and differences across the two levels.

This chapter first defines pro-environmental behaviour at both organisational and employee levels. Second, the reasons why organisations and employees engage in pro-environmental behaviours are discussed based on theoretical foundations at each level. Third, the chapter discusses the drivers of symbolic environmental behaviour at each level and presents an integrated multi-level framework of symbolic environmental behaviour. The framework summarises the drivers of environmental symbolism by organisations and employees. The chapter concludes with practical implications and areas for further research. By identifying the reasons why organisations and employees engage in environmental activities symbolically through an integrated perspective, this chapter opens a new perspective of examining the performance of green behaviours within different contexts. It also provides valuable insights for government, organisations, managers, and employees to confront the symbolic component of their environmental behaviours as well as to reconsider, adjust, or restructure interventions of pro-environmental behaviours. Eventually it helps to promote true environmentalism among organisations and employees in the long run.

12.2 DEFINING PRO-ENVIRONMENTAL BEHAVIOUR AT BOTH ORGANISATIONAL AND EMPLOYEE LEVELS

Since the 1970s, there has been a rise in environmental behaviour studies with an emphasis on understanding human responses to environmental issues, as a way to advance environmental protection practice (Kazdin 2009). *Pro-environmental behaviour* is defined as an action that intentionally seeks to minimise negative behavioural impacts on the natural and built world (Kollmuss and Agyeman 2002; Steg et al. 2012; Stern 2000). In other words, PEB is a type of environmental behaviour that has a positive impact on "the availability of materials or energy" and can alter "the structure and dynamics of ecosystems or the biosphere" in a beneficial way (Stern 2000: 408).

PEB is also referred to as conservation behaviour (Macey and Brown 1983), responsible environmental behaviour (Kollmuss and Agyeman 2002), ecological behaviour (Tilikidou and Delistavrou 2008), green behaviour (Norton et al. 2015), environmentally significant behaviour (Stern 2000), environmentally friendly behaviour, environmentally sustainable behaviour, and responsible environmental behaviour (Osbaldiston and Schott 2012), among other terms. It is a multi-level construct that comprises individual/employee, organisational, institutional, and social-cultural levels, although scholars rarely examine more than one level at a time. In this chapter, we focus on two levels: organisational and individual/employee levels.

Corporate sustainability or corporate greening in the management literature is normally a general designation of PEB at the organisational level. Organisational PEB (O-PEB) is defined as firm practices that aim to reduce negative environmental impacts. These practices are mostly devoted to obtaining environmental credibility, to cope with stakeholders' expectations of environmental accountability (Buysse and Verbeke 2003), and to adapt to the trend of competitions over environmental-related resources (Hart 1995). In management studies, examples of O-PEB are the adoption of an environmental management system (e.g. ISO 14001), the establishment of environmental policies, the formulation or adjustment of environmental strategy (reactive or proactive), the encouragement and implementation of environmental innovation (product-focused or process-focused), and the promotion of employees' initiatives and participations in environmental programmes, among others. Organisational activities are widely acknowledged as a source of environmental problems (Whiteman et al. 2013), which is why O-PEB has received significant attention in academic literature and the popular press.

At the individual level, there are contextual differences between PEB in the household and in the workplace. For example, a major difference between the workplace and the household contexts is economic constraints: employees are less sensitive to costs of electricity, water, and other spending in the workplace than individuals in their home. This chapter will focus on the workplace context, and employees' PEB, which is important to the success of organisational greening (Anderson and Bateman 2000; Boiral and Paillé 2012; Ones and Dilchert 2012b; Ramus and Killmer 2007). Employees' PEB (E-PEB) will be used as the term from here onwards to refer to individual-level PEB at the workplace. E-PEB is defined as employees' measurable actions that are linked with environmental sustainability (Ones and Dilchert 2012a), and are intentional and fully under the control of employees (Mesmer-Magnus et al. 2012). Examples of E-PEB are complying with organisational pro-environmental policies in the workplace, and engaging in green practices at the workplace such as recycling, water saving, energy saving, printing reduction, and pro-environmental commuting behaviours (Manika et al. 2015) among others.

In the literature, E-PEB has been analysed based on two main research streams (Robertson and Barling 2015). One is established from the perspective of environmental management, which normally regards employee behaviours as part of environmental practices and organisational change processes (Boiral 2009; Robertson and Barling 2015), while another stream is generated from the organisational psychology literature, which stresses individual-level and voluntary behaviour in the workplace on the strength of socio-psychological models (Boiral and Paillé 2012; Ones and Dilchert 2012a; Robertson and Barling 2015). This chapter will explain E-PEB mainly based on the second stream of research, because it examines the psychological and motivational aspect of employee green actions, paves the way for understanding the drivers of symbolic E-PEB, and aims to identify common features shared with O-PEB literature.

Based on the discussion above, Table 12.1 summarises the definitions of the constructs: PEB, O-PEB and E-PEB. This chapter will contribute to understanding the drivers of O-PEB and E-PEB separately before merging them into the multi-level framework proposed here. The following section presents a summary of the theoretical foundations of PEB at each level.

Table 12.1   Definitions of PEB, O-PEB, and E-PEB constructs

Construct	Definition
Pro-environmental behaviour (PEB)	An action that intentionally seeks to minimise negative behavioural impacts on the natural and built world (Kollmuss and Agyeman 2002; Steg et al. 2012; Stern 2000).
Organisational pro-environmental behaviour (O-PEB)	Firm practices that aim to reduce negative environmental impacts.
Employee pro-environmental behaviour (E-PEB)	Employees' measurable actions linked to environmental sustainability (Ones and Dilchert 2012a), which are intentional and fully under the control of employees (Mesmer-Magnus et al. 2012).

12.3   DRIVERS OF ORGANISATIONAL AND EMPLOYEE PRO-ENVIRONMENTAL BEHAVIOURS

12.3.1   Theoretical Foundations and Motives of O-PEB

The corporate greening literature is built on three theoretical streams: institutional theory, stakeholder theory, and the resource-based view. In addition, environmental behaviour in the management literature is often embedded in studies of corporate social responsibility (CSR), as green behaviours can be part of corporations' socially responsible activities. This section summarises these theoretical foundations at the organisational level to explain the motives of O-PEB.

Institutional theory and O-PEB

Institutions, as described by Jepperson (1991: 149) are "socially constructed, routine-reproduced, program or rule systems". Institutions consist of cognitive, normative, and regulative pillars that are fundamental to the stability and meaningfulness of social actions (Scott 1995). Three pillars of the institutional environment are embodied in strategies and activities that organisations use to materialise meaningfulness, appropriateness, and legitimacy.

Suchman (1995: 574) explains that "legitimacy is a generalised perception or assumption that the actions of an entity are desirable, proper, or appropriate within some socially constructed system of norms, values, beliefs, and definitions." According to Scott (1995), the three pillars of institutions relate to different bases for legitimacy: the cognitive one emphasises sources of legitimacy from adopting a common framework of reference; the normative one stresses a moral base for legitimacy; and the regulative one focuses on the conformity to rules and legal requirements. Organisations can acquire legitimacy from the institutional environment if their actions accord with regulatory, normative, and cognitive standards. In addition, it is argued that organisational legitimacy and reputation are closely interrelated because legitimacy is an essential although not a sufficient condition to attain a positive reputation (Doh et al. 2010; King and Whetten 2008).

Legitimate organisations are the kind that meet social expectations and, therefore, are accepted, valued, and considered as right, appropriate, and good (Aldrich and Fiol 2007; Doh et al. 2010). Driven by the need for achieving legitimacy, institutional theory informs us why organisations act on their social responsibilities (including O-PEB). When the external environment has institutionalised a normative demand for corporate social responsibility, companies are more likely to engage in socially responsible activities (Campbell 2007). Also, Galaskiewicz (1991) proposed that normative or cultural institutions offer incentives to motivate organisational socially responsible behaviours.

Stakeholder theory and O-PEB
Stakeholder theory is another widely applied theory to explain O-PEB. A "stakeholder" is defined as any individual or group that has an impact on the firm's performance or is influenced by the firm's business objectives and activities (Freeman 2010). Scholars have made a distinction between primary and secondary stakeholders. Shareholders, employees, suppliers, customers, and public agencies are primary stakeholders as they have formal and direct relationships with the firm, while interest groups and the media are secondary stakeholders as they do not have formal associations with the organisation (Buysse and Verbeke 2003; Clarkson 1995).

Stakeholder theory suggests that corporations are expected to not only concentrate on shareholders' value creation, but also expand their considerations of various interests of salient stakeholders, such as customer satisfaction, regulatory compliance, good corporate citizenship, and environmental responsibilities (Buysse and Verbeke 2003). This is because each interest group has its own "stake" to make an impact on a company's ecological responsiveness. For instance, consumers may choose to purchase or not to purchase, boycott or even bring a lawsuit towards companies without good environmental records (García-de-Frutos et al. 2016). Competitors may try to lobby for stricter or weaker environmental regulations, or increase pressures for ecological responsiveness through environmental leadership and innovations. Investors may promote green management by investing/withholding or withdrawing investment by shareholder activism. Supply chain pressure, employment issues, government and activist groups' endorsement/criticism, local community supports/protests, and media's public opinion may also arm-twist the firm's environmental standing (Worthington 2013).

Resource-based view and O-PEB
Unlike institutional and stakeholder theories, resource-based view (RBV) turns focus to the internal competence of firms. According to Grant (1991), a firm's competences/capabilities to utilise valuable and inimitable assets/resources bring competitive advantage and superior performance. Quoting Russo and Fouts (1997: 536), "the resource-based view addresses the fit between what a firm has the ability to do and what it has the opportunity to do". Besides, RBV literature classifies resources into two types: tangible and intangible. Tangible resources refer to capitals and physical

resources like plant, equipment, and raw materials, whereas intangible resources include reputation, technology, culture, and human resources (Russo and Fouts 1997). It was argued that organisations, which endow valuable, rare, inimitable, and non-substitutable resources, can achieve competitive advantages over rivals (Barney 1991; Collis and Montgomery 1995; Grant 1991). Based on the RBV logic, Hart (1995) proposed an environmental win-win approach to competitive advantage generation, as social and environmental challenges can enhance the development of firms' intangible resources, which ultimately contribute to better performance.

Drivers of O-PEB
The three theoretical foundations in the management literature are often associated with three main motives underlying O-PEB. Institutional theory underlines the legitimation motive of O-PEB, which illustrates that organisations aim to achieve legitimacy via pro-environmental practices, and thus is identified as the first motive for O-PEB. Stakeholder theory suggests that organisations engage in PEB to cope with stakeholder pressures, which is identified as the second motive for O-PEB. Lastly, the resource-based view focuses on competitiveness, which is the third motive identified for O-PEB. Even though these three theories can be viewed in isolation, scholars sometimes use theories jointly to explain the motivations of engaging in O-PEB. For instance, the merging of stakeholder theory with the resource-based view proposes that environmental accountability leads to a competitive advantage because it helps to maintain reciprocal relationships with various stakeholders (Surroca et al. 2010).

In addition to the aforementioned three O-PEB motives, Bansal and Roth's (2000) model of ecological responsiveness identified a fourth driver of engaging in O-PEB, that is, ecological responsibility which acknowledges that decision-makers within organisations may truly care about the environment. Thus, in total, four motives to explain why companies go "green" have been identified, namely: legitimation, stakeholder pressure, competitiveness, and ecological responsibility.

According to the legitimation motive, organisations aim to improve the appropriateness of their behaviours within an established set of regulations, norms, values, and/or beliefs (Bansal and Roth 2000; Suchman 1995; Worthington 2013). Failure to keep up with environmental regulations will embroil companies in lawsuits and cause potential losses. Therefore, O-PEB that have occurred from this consideration are normally due to passive compliance with external constraints. In other words, O-PEB is not a representation of proactive efforts, instead it is a reactive defence for survival.

Stakeholder pressure is another strong force for corporate greening (Buysse and Verbeke 2003; Clarkson 1995; Worthington 2013), especially coming from primary stakeholders (e.g. shareholder, employees, customer, supplier) because of their importance, power, legitimacy, and leverage (Freeman 2010). For example, if shareholders are informed and alarmed by the company's unsatisfactory environmental performance, they can express their opposition to irresponsible behaviours via activism. In addition, organisations face pressures from internal stakeholders like employees, because employees have been known to blow the whistle when they cannot stand by the violation of environmental regulations (Dechant et al. 1994).

The competitiveness motive refers to the potential for environmental responsible behaviours to enhance long-term profitability (Bansal and Roth 2000; Dechant et al. 1994; Worthington 2013). This is consistent with the resource-based view, which believes that competitive positions can be strengthened through the possession of ecologically related sources and capabilities (Bansal 2005; Hart 1995). Companies with market orientation usually see environmental issues as business opportunities and engage in a proactive environmental strategy (Chen et al. 2015). However, O-PEB based on competitiveness have been criticised for being independent of ecological consequences because they target higher monetary returns (Bansal and Roth 2000), thus these behaviours may not be truly "green" in the sense of minimising environmental impacts and improving environmental performance.

Lastly, ecological responsibility is "a motivation that stems from the concern that a firm has for its social obligations and values" (Bansal and Roth 2000: 728). Ecological responsibility is different from other motives of O-PEB because it derives from the genuine concerns of a firm for the environment and a desire for social good (Bansal and Roth 2000; Takala and Pallab 2000; Worthington 2013; Wulfson 2001). Hence, the ecological responsibility motive is the sole driver of pure corporate greening with a more substantive component, compared to other drivers of O-PEB based on firm interests (Buchholz 1991).

Symbolism and O-PEB
To sum up, the reasons why organisations perform O-PEB are because: they are under regulative and/or stakeholder pressures; they regard O-PEB as a method to gain competitive advantage; and/or sometimes they believe it is "the right thing to do". Corporate greening based on these motives contains both symbolic and substantive components, or can be purely symbolic in extreme cases (Bowen 2014). Evidence for the latter can be found in cases such as the VW emission scandal introduced at the

beginning of the chapter and in academic studies that unmask the symbolic nature underneath those seemingly green organisational actions (e.g. Chen and Chang 2013; Forbes and Jermier 2012; Vidovic and Khanna 2012).

Scholars have discussed the reasons behind the symbolic nature of O-PEB through the construct of *symbolic corporate environmentalism*, which is discussed in detail in section 12.4 of this chapter. The motives of symbolic environmentalism at the organisational level are also extended to the employee level to propose a multi-level framework of symbolic environmental behaviour. However, before doing so, the motives of E-PEB need to be identified, first based on a review of the E-PEB literature.

12.3.2   Theoretical Foundations and Motives of E-PEB

In the management literature, the role of the employee tends to be downplayed in implementing CSR programmes including sustainability initiatives in organisations (Aguinis and Glavas 2012; Lamm et al. 2015). However, employees are an important stakeholder group and their behaviours largely affect the achievement of corporate sustainability and, therefore, should not be overlooked. As noted in the introduction of this chapter, E-PEB is distinguished from individual PEB in the household due to situational differences including economic constraints, social pressures, and opportunities to behave differently (Hines et al. 1987).

Although individuals may act differently at work, Rothbard (2001) suggested an enrichment process between the work role and the household role, which implies a consistency of behavioural patterns across the two different contexts. One possible explanation is that people want to maintain a holistic lifestyle by seeing their domestic and work selves as a continuum in respect to environmental attitudes and activities (Smith and O'Sullivan 2012). Support of this explanation can also be found through the view of cognitive dissonance reduction (Festinger 1957), which argues that people will try to reduce discomforts coming from the conflicts between their private and professional lives. So, if a person has a green lifestyle at home, to avoid cognitive dissonance, he/she is very likely to incorporate the green lifestyle into the workplace (Lamm et al. 2015). The environmental psychology literature also underscores this need for consistency in behaviour.

Employees' environmental actions can be explained by social psychological models that are mostly applied in the household context such as the Theory of Planned Behaviour (Ajzen 1991; Ajzen and Fishbein 1980), the Norm Activation model (Schwartz 1973), the Value-Belief-Norm Theory (Stern 2000), the Theory of Interpersonal Behaviour (Triandis 1977), and the Goal-framing Theory (Lindenberg and Steg 2007), among others. Even though all these models and theories can be used to explain motivational mechanisms behind individual and employee PEB, they fail to consider or tend to downplay the symbolic feature of PEB. Therefore, consistent with the goal of this chapter, only theories that can identify the drivers of E-PEB with a particular emphasis of symbolic aspect are reviewed here. The following sub-sections will introduce three theoretical foundations of E-PEB as well as discuss drivers to E-PEB focused on the symbolic nature of these behaviours within the workplace. Thus, from here onwards the term *employee* will be used instead of *individual* when referring to these theories even though the theories were initially proposed for individuals rather than employees.

Norms and E-PEB

In the environmental psychology literature, many studies have emphasised the influence of norms on PEB via different viewpoints. In general, employees tend to perform PEB because of their own personal standards (personal norms) and/or the need to comply with expectations of others (social norms). Multiple theories, such as the Theory of Planned Behaviour, the Norm Activation Model, the Value-Belief-Norm Theory and the Goal-framing Theory, identify norms as an important antecedent to PEB. For instance, the Theory of Planned Behaviour proposed that one of the antecedents of human action is subjective norms (Ajzen 1991). Employees are assumed to consider the degree of whether their ecological behaviours are normal, typical, average, and approved or disapproved by others. In other words, employees' environmental-related behaviours are subject to social norms in the workplace. Researchers have further distinguished two types of social norms: injunctive norms and descriptive norms. According to the Theory of Normative Conduct (Cialdini et al. 1990, 1991), people behave in a certain way by evaluating the extent to which an action is approved or disapproved of (injunctive norms) and the extent to which an action is perceived as common (descriptive norms).

Another two related theories, the Norm Activation Model and the Value-Belief-Norm Theory, regard behaviour, such as PEB, as an outcome of personal norms and therefore focus on the factors that influence the activation of personal norms. "Personal norm" is defined as the degree to which one feels morally obliged to perform a certain action (Schwartz 1973), and it reflects feelings of moral obligation to behave in an environmentally friendly way (Steg et al. 2012).

Additionally, Goal-framing Theory developed by Lindenberg and Steg (2007) also highlights the effect of norms on goal-directed actions. This theory suggests that behaviours derive from multiple goals, and therefore this theory can be used to explain why employees engage in PEB based on the impacts of different goal-frames. There are three distinctive goals that influence behaviour: the hedonic goal "to feel better right now," the gain goal "to guard and improve one's resources," and the normative goal "to act appropriately" (Lindenberg and Steg 2007: 119). When one of the goals becomes a focal goal, other goals become non-focal and secondary. Imagine an employee who wants to dispose of an empty bottle. He/she has a hedonic goal of throwing the bottle right away, a gain goal of saving time and effort to find a trash bin, and a normative goal of being civilised and environmentally friendly. If the person chooses to find a trash bin and put the bottle in the appropriate recycling division, then the normative goal becomes a focal goal, and is called a normative goal-frame in that situation. Several studies have confirmed that the normative goal-frame is a driver of PEB (Lindenberg and Steg 2007; Steg et al. 2014; Steg and Vlek 2009). To summarise, the normative motive plays an important role in urging PEB at the employee level, which spurs from the employee's own belief system and moral obligation to do the right thing, as well as others' expectations of doing something that is appropriate and commonly approved.

Symbolism and E-PEB
According to the Theory of the Meaning of Material Possessions (Dittmar 1992), material goods can fulfil individuals' needs not only through instrumental function but also symbolic and affective functions. In the same way, employee environmental activities can have a symbolic function.

The current PEB literature shows that the symbolism of PEB in the household context involves two key aspects: self-identity and status. Self-identity represents the label individuals use to describe themselves. Environmental self-identity is defined as "the extent to which you see yourself as a type of person who acts environmentally friendly" (Van der Werff et al. 2013a, 2013b). Additionally, the concept of identity similarity implies that there is a consistency between the characteristics an individual attributes to himself or herself and the type of behaviour the individual will have (Mannetti et al. 2002; Steg et al. 2012). It is argued that identity similarity accounts for reasons of environmentally friendly behaviour over and above other factors like attitude, perceived control, and subjective norms (Mannetti et al. 2002). Therefore, it is assumed that environmental self-identity can inherently spur pro-environmental intentions through the way of maintaining self-consistent image, that is, use PEB to express the type of person the employee is in the workplace.

Another feature is that individuals can seek to show their social status via pro-environmental actions. According to Griskevicius et al. (2010), status motive increases an individual's tendency to be more altruistic because such "altruism" signals one's ability and resources (e.g. time, money) to take self-sacrificing consequences (e.g. pay more money to buy green organic products compared to industrialised merchandise). This in turn showcases one's wealth and social status. The study confirms that individuals are more likely to choose green products when the price is higher than non-green products and when they are shopping and consuming in public. It reflects a possibility that employees are likely to consume green products to display their social status within the workplace setting (a public occasion).

Moreover, social identity theory, though not applied in the PEB literature yet, can be used to elaborate on employees' symbolic green actions particularly within the organisational setting. The theory suggests that individuals are inclined to classify themselves and others into different social categories (Tajfel and Turner 1985). The social identity construct encompasses individuals' perception of "oneness with and belongingness to some human aggregate" (Ashforth and Mael 1989: 21) and resembles the concept of group identification (Tolman 1943). Besides, social identification (i.e. social identity) is different from internalisation (i.e. self-identity or personal identity; Hogg and Turner 1987). The former refers to the process of identifying the self with a social category, whereas the latter refers to the process of incorporating values, beliefs, and attitudes within the self. According to Ashforth and Mael (1989), an employee's social identity can derive from the organisation, his or her work group, department, union, and age cohort, among others. The identification of the self within a particular group may create internalisation of group values and norms into the pool of personal values and norms. The adherence to, and homogeneity with, a group/social identity further engenders conformity to group norms (Ashforth and Mael 1989; Hogg and Turner 1987). Hence, employees within an organisation can identify themselves within a social category, and this self-stereotyping process will increase the likelihood of conformity to group norms and rules, such as being environmentally friendly. Therefore, an employee's social identity can also provoke symbolic PEB as this becomes part of the process of social/group identification. To sum up, the symbolism embedded in an employee's green activities may reflect the employee's self-identity, personal status, wealth, and social identity within the organisation.

Work environment and E-PEB

From the perspective of environmental management within organisations, employees' environmental-related activities are usually part of the organisation's whole management process and are a result of organisational procedures and requirements. For example, employee ecological behaviours are supposedly directed by ISO 14001 guidelines. However, this is not always the case. There is a large quantity of research, which studies employees' organisational citizenship towards the environment (e.g. Boiral 2009; Boiral and Paillé 2012; Lamm et al. 2015; Smith and O'Sullivan 2012; Temminck et al. 2015), defined as "individual and discretionary social behaviours that are not explicitly recognised by the formal reward system and that contribute to a more effective environmental management by organisations" (Boiral 2009: 223). For example, Boiral and Paillé (2012) identified three categories of these types of behaviours: eco-initiatives (i.e. employee-driven green initiatives), eco-civic engagement (i.e. contribution to and participation in the organisational environmental initiatives) and eco-helping (i.e. mutual assistance concerning environmental problems). This concept of employees' organisational citizenship behaviour towards the environment underlines the volunteering and self-giving nature of employee green behaviours, when PEB is not required by the work environment and is not included in work procedures.

Thus, a dichotomy of E-PEB emerges: required E-PEB and voluntary E-PEB (Norton et al. 2015). The former describes E-PEB that are mandatory and contribute to core business goals (i.e. task-related). This is particularly true in organisations with the adoption of an environmental management system. The latter emphasises employee green initiatives that go beyond organisational expectations and requirements, which is similar to the concept of employees' organisational citizenship behaviour towards the environment. Therefore, employees' environmentally friendly behaviours can be in-role, prescribed, and mandatory behaviours or extra-role, discretionary, and spontaneous actions. This dichotomy is important for identifying drivers of E-PEB, which is the focus of the next section.

Drivers of E-PEB

Based on the aforementioned theoretical foundations of E-PEB, four main drivers of E-PEB can be identified: the normative motive, the symbolic motive, the job requirement motive, and the ecological responsibility motive. The Theory of Planned Behaviour, the Norm Activation Model, the Value-Belief-Norm Theory and the Goal-framing Theory relate to the normative motive behind E-PEB. It shows that employees engage in PEB because they need to comply with external norms within their organisations or they feel morally obligated to perform pro-environmentally. Environmental self-identity, social identity, and social status usually explain the symbolic motive to E-PEB. That is, employees perform PEB to deliver symbolic messages of the type of person they are, the social category they identify with, and their social status and wealth. Complying with job requirements is a common reason for engaging in E-PEB, within organisations that adopt an environmental management system or establish environmental policies and standards. These E-PEB are compulsory for employees and restricted to external rules and work procedures. Finally, ecological responsibility is another source of E-PEB. Employees voluntarily initiate pro-environmental activities in the workplace simply because they feel the urge and responsibility to behave in an environmental way.

12.3.3 Discussion of Drivers of O-PEB and E-PEB

To conclude, so far this chapter has identified drivers of O-PEB and E-PEB based on prior theoretical grounding in the literature. In particular, organisations are motivated to engage in PEB due to legitimation restrictions, need for competitiveness, stakeholder pressures, and ecological responsibility. Employees are motivated to engage in PEB due to normative and symbolic reasons, job requirements and ecological responsibility. At each level (i.e. organisation and employee levels), the drivers of PEB pave the way for understanding the motivations of symbolic PEB, which is the focus of the next sub-section. For instance, the VW emission fraud introduced at the beginning of this chapter can be interpreted as a symbolic corporate practice to gain competitive advantage because the adoption of a greener engine would generate positive product image, expand the market and benefit the company with green subsidies. In that sense, the competitiveness motive to O-PEB helps to understand the reasons behind symbolic O-PEB. At the employee level, superficial employee green behaviours under the pressure of ISO 14001 can be attributed to job requirements, which serve as an important reason for engaging in symbolic E-PEB. Hence, drivers of PEB are key to identifying drivers of symbolic PEB at each level.

Additionally, previous discussion in this chapter reflects certain features of PEB shared across two levels. For example, the legitimation motive to O-PEB is similar to the job requirement reason of E-PEB, as environmental-related actions out of these two are both in essence driven by external restrictions. Besides, both organisations and employees can genuinely do good for the environment simply because they believe it is the right thing to do. However, organisations that genuinely care about the quality of environment tend to minimise the gap between their symbolic and substantive performance. The same applies to the employee level. Those who attempt to take ecological responsibilities will focus more on their actual impacts on the environment instead of ceremonial poses/ stands/actions that create false impressions. Therefore, the ecological responsibility motive across both levels is not relevant to understanding the drivers of symbolic environmental behaviours and thus is excluded in the discussions from here onwards. The commonalities and differences between motivations of PEB at two levels provide the possibility to bridge the different motives together, to integrate and transform them into a multi-level framework, which is the core aim of this chapter. The following section will present how the construct of symbolic environmentalism in both organisational and employee levels is built up via the lens of a multi-level perspective.

12.4 SYMBOLIC ENVIRONMENTALISM: AN INTEGRATED MULTI-LEVEL FRAMEWORK

12.4.1 Symbolic Environmentalism and its Drivers Across Organisational and Employee Levels

Both organisational and employee PEB literatures have noted the existence of symbolism embedded in ecological activities. Table 12.2 provides examples of studies in current literature that contribute to the construct

Table 12.2 Examples of studies on symbolic environmentalism across organisational and employee levels

	Study	Contribution to the construct of symbolic environmental behaviours (existence/motive/impact)
Organisational level	Bansal and Roth (2000)	Motive
	Boiral (2007)	Existence/impact
	Bowen (2014)	Existence/motive/impact
	Buysse and Verbeke (2003)	Motive
	Hart (1995)	Motive/impact
	Russo and Fouts (1997)	Motive
	Scott (1995)	Motive
	Washington and Zajac (2005)	Motive
Employee level	Boiral (2007)	Existence
	Griskevicius et al. (2010)	Motive/impact
	Lindenberg and Steg (2007)	Motive
	Mannetti et al. (2002)	Motive
	Noppers et al. (2014)	Motive
	Steg et al. (2012)	Motive
	Van der Werff et al. (2013a, 2013b)	Motive

of symbolic environmental behaviour. In general, the symbolism of environmental-related activities can be defined as the representation of pro-environmental behaviours with symbols or the symbolic meanings attributed to eco-friendly objects and actions. These activities come under the banner of *symbolic environmentalism*. Nevertheless, there is an imbalance between theoretical development of symbolic PEB at the organisational and the employee levels. A large number of studies disclose the symbolic nature of organisational greenings, focusing on symbolic corporate environmentalism (e.g. Boiral 2007; Bowen 2014; King et al. 2005), whereas similar studies focusing on the employee level are scant.

According to Bowen (2014), there are two theoretical traditions that explain motivations of symbolic corporate environmentalism. First, the conventional view stresses the economic and social benefits of acquiring social reputation and legitimacy, which organisations can gain by engaging in symbolic corporate environmentalism. This perspective is consistent with the legitimation, stakeholder pressure and competitiveness drivers of O-PEB as reviewed earlier in this chapter, because an illusion of environmental responsibility-taking does bring reputational resources and social legitimacy. Corporate practices portrayed as doing good for the environment are perceived as legitimate and appropriate, can serve as a method to reduce stakeholder pressures, and improve the competitiveness of the firm in the marketplace. This ultimately leads to social and economic benefits for the enterprise.

In contrast, the critical view emphasises that organisations may symbolically engage in corporate environmentalism actions to signal their status and authority (Bowen 2014). For example, an organisation may engage in symbolic environmental actions to reflect the organisation's power in controlling environmental issues/threats and to symbolise its leadership in green practices and standards. High-status actors within the field can signal environmental responsiveness to exhibit or maintain their authority.

These two perspectives are fundamentally different explanations for why companies engage in symbolic green practices (Bowen 2014). Symbolic corporate environmentalism is rooted in the information asymmetries problem within the conventional view, whereas it arises from the control problem within the critical view. Also, the conventional view is based on the economics of signalling and reputation, whereas the critical view is based on the power relations within institutional fields. To sum up, motives of symbolic corporate environmentalism partially overlap with drivers of O-PEB, but also include aspects of status and authority. This is important to note because the two perspectives give different insights and directions in terms of building a multi-level framework on drivers of symbolic PEB across employee and organisational levels.

On the other hand, the symbolism embedded in E-PEB has not been examined much in the workplace context even though researchers identify factors like self-identity, social identity, and social status in the household context (e.g. Griskevicius et al. 2010; Hogg and Turner 1987; Van der Werff et al. 2013a). For instance, employees may use green gestures to indicate the "environmental-caring type of person" they are due to the enrichment process between work and household roles. Hence, limited theoretical developments of symbolism embedded in household PEB lay the foundation for exploring symbolic environmentalism in the workplace context.

Based on the drivers identified in E-PEB literature, norms, symbolism of self-identity, social identity and social status, and job requirements can generate ceremonial green employee behaviours. To be more specific, social norms can motivate employees to perform environmental-friendly activities superficially if co-workers consider E-PEB appropriate and often engage in E-PEB at the workplace. Sometimes employees are also forced to engage in pro-environmental activities due to their job requirements. In this case, green work practices could be adopted for symbolic purposes to comply with the rules of the job (both external and internal). Also, symbolic meanings of self-identity, social identity and social status can be transmitted and received by others via green actions at work. For instance, frequent recycling leads to the impression of an environmental-caring type of person and also demonstrates belongingness to an environmental-caring group of members, while driving a high-tech emission-less vehicle (e.g. Tesla model S/model X) to work showcases the employee's status and wealth.

Thus, to sum up, symbolic environmental practices at the organisational level can be attributed to legitimation, stakeholder pressure, competitiveness, and status and authority motives, whereas symbolic environmental actions at the employee level are influenced by social norms, job requirements, self-identity, social identity, and social status.

12.4.2   A Multi-level Framework of Symbolic Environmentalism and its Drivers

The aforementioned symbolic O-PEB and symbolic E-PEB drivers share some commonalities. These commonalities serve as the way to merge drivers across the two levels into a single multi-level framework. Based on these commonalities three motivations – appropriateness, competitiveness, and status – that operate at both organisational and employee levels are identified.

First, the legitimation motive at the organisational level and the motives of social norms and job requirements at the employee level, are very much alike in the sense that they show compliance with external constraints to pursue legitimacy, appropriateness, and acceptance. These drivers are merged together under the label of "appropriateness" in this chapter's proposed multi-level framework. The rationale for rephrasing legitimation as a motive is because of the situational differences at the individual level. Specifically, for employees, their organisational environment may or may not require them to behave in an environmentally friendly way. Required behaviours are more connected to legitimation while voluntary ones are considered appropriate; at the organisational level legitimation implies required PEB. Thus, the term of appropriateness is more representative and comprehensive as it can cover both voluntary and required PEB across levels.

Second, the symbolic self-identity and social identity motive at the employee level shares commonalities with stakeholder pressures and competitive motives at the organisational level. Symbolic green behaviours may increase the behavioural actor's competitive power compared with their original state. These drivers are merged together under the label of "competitiveness" in this chapter's proposed multi-level framework. Moreover, the competitiveness motivation not only covers aforementioned motives in the current literature but also proposes feasible direction for further theoretical expansions. To be specific, it includes two dimensions: gaining scarce resources and being differentiated from others. At the organisational level, environmental friendliness reduces stakeholder pressures and is regarded as an important source of competitiveness, such as gaining a positive corporate reputation and better human resources, as per Hart's natural resource-based view (1995). Also, environmental friendliness can be seen as part of a brand's identity, which differentiates the organisation from its competitors. Although there are no theoretical and empirical studies regarding the relationship between environmental friendliness and competitiveness at the individual level, employees can take advantage of symbolic PEB through the two approaches at the organisational level (i.e. obtaining resources and differentiation). The competitiveness motivation with two dimensions serves as a more comprehensive and insightful description of motives that generate similar results at both levels.

Both appropriateness and competitiveness motivations in the proposed multi-level framework are supported by the conventional perspective of corporate symbolic environmentalism and are extended across the employee level. However, the critical perspective should not be neglected. Therefore, the status and authority motive as per the critical view, supported by the status and wealth driver of symbolic employee PEB,

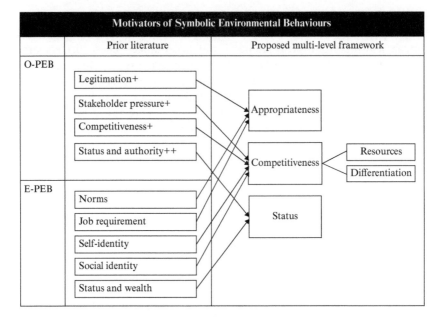

Notes: + labels motives of organisational symbolic environmental behaviours based on the conventional view; ++ labels motives of organisational symbolic environmental behaviours based on the critical view. Arrows do not infer causal relationships but guide the development of the multi-level framework proposed in this chapter.

Figure 12.1   *A multi-level framework of symbolic environmentalism in organisational and employee levels and its roots*

is proposed to be the third motivation of symbolic environmental behaviours across levels. In the proposed framework, this is termed "status" motivation.

Figure 12.1 illustrates the proposed three motives of PEB across organisational and employee levels, and their roots from O-PEB and E-PEB symbolic drives literature as well as reflective perspectives on symbolic corporate environmentalism literature. There are three motivations proposed in the multi-level framework: appropriateness, competitiveness (with two dimensions of resources and differentiation) and status. Appropriateness is built on prior literature on the legitimation motive at the organisational level; and norms and job requirement motives at the employee level. Competitiveness is built on prior literature on stakeholder pressures and competitiveness motives at the organisational level, and self-identity and social identity motives at the employee level. Status is built on prior literature on status and authority motives at the organisational level, and status and wealth motives at the employee level. The following sub-sections will explain each motivation in detail.

Appropriateness
The appropriateness motivation represents the organisation's and employee's intention to signal conformity with taken-for-granted norms or external regulations via symbolic environmental behaviour. Organisations and employees perceive symbolic environmental behaviour as a way of adjusting, improving and symbolising the propriety of environmental behaviours.

Institutional theorists used the legitimation motive to reflect the organisation's need to acquire legitimacy by engaging in pro-environmental behaviours. Legitimate organisational activities are appropriate behaviours. Organisational legitimacy (or appropriateness) can be obtained by means of symbolic environmental activities such as *greenwashing* if the nature of hypocrisy remains unquestioned. An example can be the superficial adoption of an environmental management system like ISO 14001, which "demonstrates compliance with current and future statutory and regulatory requirements" (ISO 2015). Legitimacy, or appropriateness, is by all means a major reason for organisations engaging into symbolic ecological actions.

At the individual level, employees pursue the appropriateness of their own environmental behaviours in response to external rules or social norms (e.g. peer pressures) at the workplaces. On the one hand, employees may engage in PEB superficially, as required by work, to show conformity to external constraints. For instance, the line workers at a factory under ISO 14001 may only engage in waste recycling and sewage treatments when encountering an environmental audit. On the other hand, employees may engage in symbolic environmental behaviours to show conformity to social norms: either to illustrate to people what others do (descriptive social norms) or what is commonly approved or disapproved (injunctive social norms). In the workplace, if being environmentally friendly is accepted as a part of the organisational culture, it is very likely for employees to superficially perform green actions because these are "approvable" and "appropriate". For instance, in order to fit in, an employee may fake his/her attendance of, or interests in, environmental protection activities in their social media pages simply because other co-workers have participated in this kind of activity.

Moreover, perceptions of appropriateness at the organisational and employee level interact with each other, based on bottom-up and top-down processes. That is, the relationship between organisational and employee appropriateness of PEB is bi-directional: one influences the other. First, appropriateness at the organisational level is composed of employees' subjective judgements towards what is legitimate, but aggregated and objectified at the collective level (Bitektine and Haack 2015). Based on the bottom-up influential logic, organisational appropriateness can be affected by employees' perceptions of what is an appropriate O-PEB and in turn these perceptions can influence managerial decisions on O-PEB. Second, an organisation's social norms are based on employee perceptions of the work climate. "Work climate" is defined as the perceptions of formal organisational policies, the procedures that translate policies into tacit guidelines, the practices that are rewarded or punished, as well as what is typically observed in the workplace (Norton et al. 2015). Based on the top-down influential logic, what is perceived to be appropriate among employees can be influenced by managerial practices such as environmental management policies or a rewards and punishment scheme. Therefore, the perceptions of appropriateness at organisational and employee levels interact with each other and are shaped by both parties.

Competitiveness
The competitiveness motivation refers to the organisation's and employee's intention to obtain a competitive superiority among rivals via symbolic environmentally friendly poses. There are two methods to achieving that goal: acquiring resources and being differentiated from others. The former tells how organisations and employees acquire competitiveness from external resources (e.g. reputation). The latter demonstrates how organisations and employees improve competitiveness through internal characterisation (e.g. identity).

Resources   Based on previous discussions, organisations may perform symbolic environmental behaviours to gain competitive power via acquiring a scarce resource. For instance, enterprises can attain a positive reputation via seemingly green activities, and thus temporarily improve a firm's competitiveness through strengthening relationships with stakeholders such as government, shareholder, and supplier (Fombrun and Shanley 1990; Surroca et al. 2010). In some cases, reputation can also lead to political resources (e.g. government support or tax exemptions) and human resources (e.g. a good reputation attracts and reserves better employees; Turban and Greening 1997) among others.

At the employee level, employees may engage in symbolic PEB to acquire, preserve, or enhance resources like personal reputation, and ultimately improve their personal competitiveness among other employees. Engaging in prosocial behaviours, especially pro-environmental actions, results in positive personal reputations (Semmann et al. 2005). An employee with a prosocial reputation is usually regarded as a more responsible, trustworthy, cooperative, and helpful group member (Griskevicius et al. 2010). These employees are also more desirable as friends, allies, and romantic partners (Cottrell et al. 2007). In addition, an employee may perform PEB symbolically to show his/her belongingness to a specific social category (i.e. social identity motive). It can be assumed that similarity, proximity, and shared values and norms in terms of the same group's identity can help the employee better manage interpersonal relationships with co-workers. Also, it is suggested that the identification of self within a social category can enhance self-esteem (Hogg and Turner 1985; Tajfel 1978). Hence, employees engaging in symbolic environmental behaviours can increase personal competitiveness because of a good reputation, a better interpersonal relationship with others, as well as a strengthened self-confidence.

Differentiation   Differentiation is a frequently applied marketing strategy that organisations use to promote a unique identity perceived by consumers (e.g. Dickson and Ginter 1987; Ghodeswar 2008; Smith 1956). Building a green corporate or brand image makes a firm differentiated from other competitors. Examples like The Body Shop and Wholefoods are typical enterprises that establish a green brand image and emphasise the pro-environmental feature of their products. However, it is also possible for organisations to enhance green brand image only through symbolic actions such as claims of future reforestation, and plans to decorate headquarters or offices with a "green" appearance. Thus, organisations can benefit from symbolic environmental behaviour since it helps to enhance the green brand image of the company identified by consumers.

At the individual level, employees can perform symbolic environmental behaviour to demonstrate a green self-identity perceived by others at work. As mentioned in a previous section of this chapter, performing symbolic PEB is a way for individuals to convey to others who they are, or from whom they are different. Employees could also engage in role-playing and fake a green identity via symbolic environmental behaviours to respond to identity threats at the personal, relational, or collective levels of identity in their organisational life, in exchange for self-gains (Leavitt and Sluss 2015).

In short, organisations and employees can be motivated to gain competitive advantages via symbolic environmentally friendly activities, which lead to reputational resources and differentiated identities. Additionally, the two methods of achieving competitiveness reinforce each other. For example, a featured green identity as part of the green marketing campaign usually leads to a green reputation and other beneficial resources from a strategic perspective (Chan et al. 2012). An enhanced green reputation will further consolidate the green identity of the behavioural actor perceived by others.

Status
Lastly, the status motivation refers to the organisation's and employee's intention to signal or strengthen their positions in social ranks via symbolic environmentally friendly actions. Status is defined as the "socially constructed, inter-subjectively agreed-upon and accepted ordering or ranking of individuals, groups, organisations or activities in a social system" (Washington and Zajac 2005: 284). Organisations and employees can particularly benefit from the social hierarchical system because higher status normally equals privilege or prestige (Bowen 2014).

Organisational symbolic environmental actions are driven by status according to the critical perspective of corporate environmentalism. A typical example is the Matthew effect, which means that the public is more likely to pay attention to, and overestimate the environmental performance of, higher socially ranked than lower socially ranked companies even if they are doing the same thing (Merton 1968). Besides, organisations with higher social status are often encouraged and granted the power to define green standards and codes. Therefore, a company can use symbolic environmental behaviour to showcase or improve its social status within the industry in exchange for privileges and other economic benefits.

At the employee level, employees may also seek to showcase their social status via engaging in symbolic environmental behaviours, such as displaying environmental-related material possessions. This is supported by the fact that consumers "go green" to show wealth and status and that higher prices attributed to being green increase the likelihood of purchase among consumers compared to lower priced alternatives as discussed previously (Griskevicius et al. 2010). The same could be applied to the workplace context, that is, what employees consume in front of others may embody a symbolic meaning. For instance, eating expensive organic foods or using high-tech eco-friendly products can showcase an employee's wealth and social status. This is an example of symbolic employee behaviour based on a status motive.

In conclusion, the multi-level framework proposed in this chapter identifies three motivations of symbolic environmental behaviour across organisational and employee levels: appropriateness, competitiveness (resource and differentiation), and status. Table 12.3 provides a summary of definitions and examples of the motives at each level according to

Table 12.3   A summary of the multi-level framework of symbolic environmentalism across organisational and employee levels

	Definitions	Examples	
		Organisational level	Employee level
Appropriateness	The organisation's and employee's need to signal conformity to the taken-for-granted set of norms or external regulations via symbolic environmental behaviour.	A company superficially adopts an environmental management system like ISO 14001.	Required: the line workers at a factory under ISO 14001 only engage in waste recycling and sewage treatments when encountering an environmental audit. Voluntary: an employee fakes his/her attendance of, or shows interest in, environmental protection activities on their social media pages.
Competitiveness	The organisation's and employee's need to obtain a competitive superiority among rivals via symbolic environmental behaviour.		

Table 12.3 (continued)

	Definitions	Examples	
		Organisational level	Employee level
Resources		A company obtains a positive reputation because it claims their products are environmentally friendly. A positive reputation helps the company further acquire more political resources (e.g. subsidies, government supports) or human resources (e.g. high quality employees).	An employee engaging in symbolic environmental behaviour to have a positive personal reputation at the workplace.
Differentiation		A company strengthens its green brand identity through symbolic actions such as claims of reforestation, plans to decorate headquarters or having offices with a "green" appearance.	An employee performing PEB to send a symbolic message to other employees of who he/she is, or whom he/she is different from.
Status	The organisation's and employee's need to signal or strengthen their positions in the social ranks via symbolic environmental behaviour.	A company uses symbolic environmental behaviour to express or reinforce its social status within the industry in exchange for privileges and other economic benefits.	An employee eats expensive organic foods or uses high-tech eco-friendly products to showcase his/her wealth and status.

the multi-level framework. Next, the implications of the framework and resulted insights for practice are discussed.

12.5   PRACTICAL IMPLICATIONS, FUTURE RESEARCH DIRECTIONS AND CONCLUSIONS

The symbolic nature of environmental activities in both organisational and employee levels is not a surprising finding, in most cases, researchers have explored it within one specific context such as the organisational context (e.g. Boiral 2007) or the household context (e.g. Griskevicius et al. 2010). The analysis of symbolic environmental-related activities is usually restricted to certain groups of behavioural actors and overlooks the possibility of bridging the motivational mechanisms across different levels. This chapter is the first systematic analysis of the drivers of symbolic environmental activities via a multi-level perspective, which explores the commonalities and differences among different motivators of PEB and provides theoretical insights into the symbolic nature of environmental activities. A multi-level model also provides a parsimonious overview of common motives of symbolic environmental behaviours across levels.

This framework of symbolic environmentalism introduced identifies three main motivators. First, organisations and employees engage in symbolic green activities to exhibit or improve the appropriateness of green behaviours. Second, organisations and employees perform symbolic environmental activities for competitiveness enhancement through two approaches: obtaining resources or differentiation. Lastly, symbolic environmental actions driven by status show the state of organisations and employees in a hierarchical system perceived by others. From a theoretical standpoint, the identification of three drivers clarify the connections among theoretical constructs at the organisational and employee levels and give future research directions in terms of exploring the commonalities and differences across the two levels.

From a practical standpoint, the multi-level framework proposed here, identifying the reasons why organisations and employees engage in symbolic environmental activities, provides valuable insights for government, organisations, managers, and employees. Specifically, for regulators or supervisors of employees, this multi-level framework of symbolic environmentalism illustrates the challenge of monitoring and evaluating organisations' and employees' substantive environmental performance, given that organisational and employee environmental practices can be based on self-interests, can be superficial, and can be symbolic in nature. Uncovering the motives of organisations' and employees' environmental behaviours is difficult and even if they are identified as symbolic in nature, the challenge still remains: how to motivate true green behaviours across organisation and employee levels; and how to reduce the symbolism within their PEB and instead translate it into truly green behaviours.

The problem of encouraging true PEB or transforming symbolic PEB into true PEB is that the line between the two kinds is blurred. For example, as discovered in the literature, organisational green solutions contain both symbolic and substantive components. There is no such assurance that greening practices will result in substantive performance only. When an organisation wants to truly do good for the environment, it tells something to the public, or is perceived as "telling a story" (e.g. as managing public relations or establishing a positive social image). Hence, the exhibition of symbolism is to some extent unavoidable for corporate greening practices. In terms of employee-level environmental-related activities, although those can be improvisational and superficial, motivating true PEB is less difficult to realise. One of the methods is to cultivate a habitual pattern of doing environmental-friendly actions arisen from those with symbolic purposes, that is, to turn symbolic PEB into truly green PEB. Habits guide pro-environmental behaviours via an automated rather than an elaborate cognitive process (Steg and Vlek 2009). The formation of habits depends on extensive repetition of behaviours (Aarts et al. 1998), and once formed, future behaviours are generated outside the realm of cognitions (e.g. attitudes, subjective norms, intentions, and perceived control) and affect (Gregory and Leo 2003; Ouellette and Wood 1998). Thus, it is possible that employees are highly likely to form a habit of engaging in pro-environmental activities in the workplace after first exhibiting symbolic green behaviours. Due to the enriching work-family interfaces (Rothbard 2001), employees are also likely to incorporate a habitual green behavioural pattern into the household context and thus develop a holistic true green lifestyle in general.

The discussions above raise another question of whether symbolic PEB should be advocated at all. Symbolic environmental activities can benefit the environment, even if originally this was not the intention of the organisation and/or employee. Symbolic gestures can also bring positive social and interpersonal gains. The superficial adoption of an environmental management system at least demonstrates the organisation's intention to control corporate environmental damages, and therefore depicts a positive social orientation to the public. For instance, according to Christensen et al. (2013), aspirational CSR *talk* is inevitable to the articulation of corporate reality and ideals, as opposed to the traditional perspective of CSR communications being superficial, hypocritical, and decoupled from material aspects of organisational practices. That is, talking about their

CSR plans, values, and ideals can be seen as "a transitional or preparatory stage towards a better organisation in which morally superior talk reflects virtuous behaviour" (Christensen et al. 2013: 384). Another example is that even though employees can consume expensive green products at work to showcase their status and wealth, they also set an example of being environmentally harmless and may consequently influence other co-workers' behavioural intentions to be greener. Thus, even though symbolic environmental activities are not true environmentalism they could lead to positive environmental improvements over time.

In addition, no matter if an individual green behaviour itself is true or symbolic, the meanings emerged from interactions between behavioural actors and perceivers are symbolic as per the symbolic interactionism theory (Blumer 1969; Denzin 1992; Fine 1993; Mead 1934; Shott 1976; Stryker 1980). This theory is a micro-scale-focused theoretical perspective in sociology that presents how society is created and operated through repeated interactions among individuals (Carter and Fuller 2015). Central to the perspective is the idea of people using language and important symbols to communicate with others. According to Blumer (1969), symbolic interactionism theory mainly proposed that (1) individuals behave based on the meanings objects have for them; (2) meanings are derived from interactions between individuals; (3) meanings are dynamic and changeable via interpretations during interactions with others. Therefore, to apply the view to previous discussions, both the green behavioural actor and perceivers of the green behaviour acquire symbolic meanings from the interactions between each other. For instance, the symbolic meaning of "recycling is an appropriate thing to do" can be assigned to the recycling behaviour via interactions between *me* and others (e.g. my supervisor says that what you did is right and rewardable). However, the symbolic interactionism theory is restricted to individual-level studies and has not yet considered collective interactions between a group of individuals with other groups, or between an organisation and other organisations etc.

Although the multi-level framework helps to specify relationships among theoretical constructs at different levels, it is not without limitations. The framework may overemphasise the commonalities and neglect the differences between the two levels. Future research could study the disparities and inconsistencies between drivers of symbolic PEB across the two levels. In addition, the framework is not empirically validated, and it should be evaluated in a practical setting. Especially, the most important step is to validate the extension of literature at the employee level since there are limited studies related to employee symbolic environmentalism. For instance, one way of testing symbolic environmental behaviours at the employee level is to set up scoreboards at work, which record the performance of each employee's environmental-related activities and accordingly give feedback to behavioural actors. A previous study of the efficacy of detailed private versus public information on conservation behaviours showed that public-disclosed information of students' energy consumption encourages electricity-saving behaviours due to the activation of social norms and reputation (Delmas and Lessem 2014). In the same way, it could be assumed that employees are likely to perform symbolic PEB in the workplace if their footprints are being tracked and displayed in public. Moreover, although this framework identifies three major reasons behind symbolic environmental behaviours, it does not specify the differences among them in terms of the efficacy (significant vs. non-significant) or constancy (short-run vs. long-run) of influences on the behavioural actors. The effectiveness of the motivational mechanism may differ among appropriateness, competitiveness, and status motives. For instance, symbolic green practices might be largely motivated by the competitiveness motive, whereas mildly encouraged by the status motive. Also, researchers could study the effectiveness of three motives through a longitudinal comparison. For example, the competitiveness motive may have a more long-lasting effect on the behavioural actor than the other two. Furthermore, although the framework clarifies the connections among theoretical constructs in organisational and employee levels, it underplays the dynamics between the two levels; future research could focus on the interactions between these levels (e.g. what is the impact of one level on the other). Hence, the framework should be theoretically extended in the future.

In conclusion, the multi-level framework of symbolic environmentalism fills in the research gap in the literature and opens the door to exploring the rhetorical and symbolic nature of environmental behaviours across different levels. It offers a new perspective of examining the motivational mechanism behind environmental symbolism, encourages thinking of how to see symbolic environmental activities in practice, and opens new opportunities for theoretical expansions in the future.

REFERENCES

Aarts, H., B. Verplanken and A. Knippenberg (1998), 'Predicting behavior from actions in the past: Repeated decision making or a matter of habit?', *Journal of Applied Social Psychology*, **28** (15), 1355–74.

Aguinis, H. and A. Glavas (2012), 'What we know and don't know about corporate social responsibility', *Journal of Management*, **38** (4), 932–68.

Ajzen, I. (1991), 'The theory of planned behavior', *Organizational Behavior and Human Decision Processes*, **50** (2), 179–211.

Ajzen, I. and M. Fishbein (1980), *Understanding Attitudes and Predicting Social Behavior*, Upper Saddle River, NJ: Prentice Hall.

Aldrich, H. E. and C. M. Fiol (2007), 'Fools rush in? The institutional context of industry creation', in *Entrepreneurship*, Berlin, Heidelberg: Springer Berlin Heidelberg, pp. 105–27.

Anderson, L. M. and T. S. Bateman (2000), 'Individual environmental initiative: Championing natural environmental issues in U.S. Business organizations', *Academy of Management Journal*, **43** (4), 548–70.

Ashforth, B. E. and F. Mael (1989), 'Social Identity theory and the organization', *The Academy of Management Review*, **14** (1), 20.

Bansal, P. (2005), 'Evolving sustainably: A longitudinal study of corporate sustainable development', *Strategic Management Journal*, **26** (3), 197–218.

Bansal, P. and K. Roth (2000), 'Why companies go green: A model of ecological responsiveness', *Academy of Management Journal*, **43** (4), 717–36.

Barney, J. (1991), 'Firm Resources and sustained competitive advantage', *Journal of Management*, **17** (1), 99–120.

Bitektine, A. and P. Haack (2015), 'The "macro" and the "micro" of legitimacy: Toward a Multilevel theory of the legitimacy process', *Academy of Management Review*, **40** (1), 49–75.

Blumer, H. (1969), *Symbolic Interactionis: Perspective and Method*, Berkeley, CA: University of California Press.

Boiral, O. (2007), 'Corporate Greening through ISO 14001: A Rational myth?', *Organization Science*, **18** (1), 127–46.

Boiral, O. (2009), 'Greening the corporation through organizational citizenship behaviors', *Journal of Business Ethics*, **87** (2), 221–36.

Boiral, O. and P. Paillé (2012), 'Organizational citizenship behaviour for the environment: Measurement and validation', *Journal of Business Ethics*, **109** (4), 431–45.

Bowen, F. (2014), *After Greenwashing*, Cambridge: Cambridge University Press.

Buchholz, R. A. (1991), 'Corporate responsibility and the good society: From economics to ecology; factors which influence corporate policy decisions', *Business Horizons*, **34** (4), 19–31.

Buysse, K. and A. Verbeke (2003), 'Proactive environmental strategies: A stakeholder management perspective', *Strategic Management Journal*, **24** (5), 453–70.

Campbell, J. L. (2007), 'Why would corporations behave in socially responsible ways? An institutional theory of corporate social responsibility', *Academy of Management Review*, **32** (3), 946–67.

Carter, M. J. and C. Fuller (2015), 'Sympolic interactionism', *Sociopedia.isa*, (1), 1–17.

Chan, H. K., H. He and W. Y. C. Wang (2012), 'Green marketing and its impact on supply chain management in industrial markets', *Industrial Marketing Management*, **41** (4), 557–62.

Chen, Y., G. Tang, J. Jin, J. Li and P. Paillé (2015), 'Linking market orientation and environmental performance: the influence of environmental strategy, employee's environmental involvement, and environmental product quality', *Journal of Business Ethics*, **127** (2), 479–500.

Chen, Y. S. and C. H. Chang (2013), 'Greenwash and green trust: The mediation effects of green consumer confusion and green perceived risk', *Journal of Business Ethics*, **114** (3), 489–500.

Christensen, L. T., M. Morsing and O. Thyssen (2013), 'CSR as aspirational talk', *Organization*, **20** (3), 372–93.

Cialdini, R. B., C. A. Kallgren and R. R. Reno (1991), 'A focus theory of normative conduct: A theoretical refinement and reevaluation of the role of norms in human behavior', *Advances in Experimental Social Psychology*, **24**, 201–34.

Cialdini, R. B., R. R. Reno and C. A. Kallgren (1990), 'A focus theory of normative conduct: Recycling the concept of norms to reduce littering in public places', *Journal of Personality and Social Psychology*, **58** (6), 1015–26.

Clarkson, M. E. (1995), 'A stakeholder framework for analyzing and evaluating corporate social performance', *Academy of Management Review*, **20** (1), 92–117.

Collis, D. J. and C. A. Montgomery (1995), 'Competing on resources: Strategy in the 1990s', *Harvard Business Review*, **73** (4), 118–28.

Cottrell, C. A., S. L. Neuberg and N. P. Li (2007), 'What do people desire in others? A sociofunctional perspective on the importance of different valued characteristics', *Journal of Personality and Social Psychology*, **92** (2), 208–31.

Dechant, K., B. Altman, R. M. Downing, T. Keeney, M. Mahoney, A. Swaine, R. A. Miller and J. Post (1994), 'Environmental leadership: From compliance to competitive advantage [and executive commentary]', *The Academy of Management Executive (1993–2005)*, **8** (3), 7–27.

Delmas, M. and N. Lessem (2014), 'Saving power to conserve your reputation? The effectiveness of private versus public information', *Journal of Environmental Economics and Management*, **67** (3), 353–70.

Denzin, N. (1992), *Symbolic Interactionism and Cultural Studies. The Politics of Interpretation*, Malden, MA: Blackwell.

Dickson, P. R. and J. L. Ginter (1987), 'Market segmentation, product differentiation, and marketing strategy', *Journal of Marketing*, **51** (1), accessed 19 June 2017 at http://anandahussein.lecture.ub.ac.id/files/2015/09/MPS2.pdf.

Dittmar, H. (1992), *The Social Psychology of Material Possessions: To Have Is to Be*, Hemel Hempstead: Harvester Wheatsheaf.

Doh, J., S. Howton and S. Howton (2010), 'Does the market respond to an endorsement of social responsibility? The role of institutions, information, and legitimacy', *Journal of Management*, **36** (6), 1461–85.

Festinger, L. (1957), *A Theory of Cognitive Dissonance*, Stanford, CA: Stanford University Press.

Fine, G. A. (1993), 'The sad demise, mysterious disappearance, and glorious triumph of symbolic interactionism', *Annual Review of Sociology*, **19** (1), 61–87.

Fombrun, C. and M. Shanley (1990), 'What's in a name? Reputation building and corporate strategy', *Academy of Management Journal*, **33** (2), 233–58.

Forbes, L. C. and J. M. Jermier (2012), 'The new corporate environmentalism and the symbolic management of organizational culture', in P. Bansal and A. J. Hoffman (eds), *The Oxford Handbook of Business and the Natural Environment*, Oxford: Oxford University Press, pp. 556–71.

Freeman, R. E. (2010), *Strategic Management: A Stakeholder Approach*, Cambridge: Cambridge University Press.

Galaskiewicz, J. (1991), 'Making corporate actors accountable: Institution-building in Minneapolis-St. Paul', in P. J. DiMaggio and W. W. Powell (eds), *The New Institutionalism in Organizational Analysis*, Chicago, IL: University of Chicago Press, pp. 293–310.

García-de-Frutos, N., J. M. Ortega-Egea and J. Martínez-del-Río (2016), 'Anti-consumption for environmental sustainability: Conceptualization, review, and multilevel research directions', *Journal of Business Ethics*, 1–25.

Ghodeswar, B. M. (2008), 'Building brand identity in competitive markets: A conceptual model', *Journal of Product and Brand Management*, **17** (1), 4–12.

Grant, R. M. (1991), 'The resource-based theory of competitive advantage: Implications for strategy formulation', *California Management Review*, **33** (3).

Gregory, G. D. and M. Di Leo (2003), 'Repeated behavior and environmental psychology: The role of personal involvement and habit formation in explaining water consumption', *Journal of Applied Social Psychology*, **33** (6), 1261–96.

Griskevicius, V., J. M. Tybur and B. Van den Bergh (2010), 'Going green to be seen: Status, reputation, and conspicuous conservation', *Journal of Personality and Social Psychology*, **98** (3), 392–404.

Hart, S. L. (1995), 'A natural-resource-based view of the firm', *Academy of Management Review*, **20** (4), 986–1014.

Hines, J. M., H. R. Hungerford and A. N. Tomera (1987), 'Analysis and synthesis of research on responsible environmental behavior: A meta-analysis', *The Journal of Environmental Education*, **18** (2), 1–8.

Hogg, M. A. and J. C. Turner (1985), 'Interpersonal attraction, social identification and psychological group formation', *European Journal of Social Psychology*, **15** (1), 51–66.

Hogg, M. A. and J. C. Turner (1987), 'Social identity and conformity: A theory of referent informational influence', *Current Issues in European Social Psychology*, **2**, 139–82.

Hotten, R. (2015), *Volkswagen: The Scandal Explained – BBC News*, accessed 19 June 2017 at http://www.bbc.co.uk/news/business-34324772.

ISO (2015), *ISO 14001: Key Benefits*, accessed 19 June 2017 at www.iso.org/iso/iso_14001_-_key_benefits.pdf.

Jääskeläinen, H. and M. K. Khair (2015), *Common Rail Fuel Injection*, accessed 19 June 2017 at www.dieselnet.com/tech/diesel_fi_common-rail.php.

Jepperson, R. L. (1991), 'Institutions, institutional effects, and institutionalism', in W. W. Powell and P. DiMaggio (eds), *The New Institutionalism in Organizational Analysis*, Chicago, IL: University of Chicago Press, pp. 143–63.

Kazdin, A. E. (2009), 'Psychological science's contributions to a sustainable environment: Extending our reach to a grand challenge of society', *American Psychologist*, **64** (5), 339–56.

King, A. A., M. J. Lenox and A. Terlaak (2005), 'The strategic use of decentralized institutions: Exploring certification with the ISO 14001 Management standard', *Academy of Management Journal*, **48** (6), 1091–106.

King, B. G. and D. A. Whetten (2008), 'Rethinking the relationship between reputation and legitimacy: A social actor conceptualization', *Corporate Reputation Review*, **11** (3), 192–207.

Kollmuss, A. and J. Agyeman (2002), 'Mind the gap: Why do people act environmentally and what are the barriers to pro-environmental behavior?', *Environmental Education Research*, **8** (3), 239–60.

Lamm, E., J. Tosti-Kharas and C. E. King (2015), 'Empowering employee sustainability: Perceived organizational support toward the environment', *Journal of Business Ethics*, **128** (1), 207–20.

Leavitt, K. and D. M. Sluss (2015), 'Lying for who we are: An identity-based model of workplace dishonesty', *Academy of Management Review*, **40** (4), 587–610.

Lindenberg, S. and L. Steg (2007), 'Normative, gain and hedonic goal frames guiding environmental behavior', *Journal of Social Issues*, **63** (1), 117–37.

Lyon, T. P. and J. W. Maxwell (2011), 'Greenwash: Corporate environmental disclosure under threat of audit', *Journal of Economics and Management Strategy*, **20** (1), 3–41.

Macey, S. M. and M. A. Brown (1983), 'Residential Energy conservation: The role of past experience in repetitive household behavior', *Environment and Behavior*, **15** (2), 123–41.

Manika, D., V. K. Wells, D. Gregory-Smith and M. Gentry (2015), 'The impact of individual attitudinal and organisational variables on workplace environmentally friendly behaviours', *Journal of Business Ethics*, **126** (4), 663–84.

Mannetti, L., A. Pierro and S. Livi (2002), 'Explaining consumer conduct: From planned to self-expressive behavior', *Journal of Applied Social Psychology*, **32** (7), 1431–51.

Mead, G. H. (1934), *Mind, Self, and Society: From the Standpoint of a Social Behaviorist*, Chicago, IL: University of Chicago Press.

Merton, R. (1968), 'The Matthew effect in science', *Science*, **159** (3810), 56–63.

Mesmer-Magnus, J., C. Viswesvaran and B. M. Wiernik (2012), 'The role of commitment in bridging the gap between organizational sustainability and environmental sustainability', in S. E. Jackson, D. S. Ones, and S. Dilchert (eds), *Managing Human Resources for Environmental Sustainability*, San Francisco, CA: Jossey-Bass/Wiley, pp. 155–86.

Noppers, E. H., K. Keizer, J. W. Bolderdijk and L. Steg (2014), 'The adoption of sustainable innovations: Driven by symbolic and environmental motives', *Global Environmental Change*, **25** (1), 52–62.

Norton, T. A., S. L. Parker, H. Zacher and N. M. Ashkanasy (2015), 'Employee green behavior: A theoretical framework, multilevel review, and future research agenda', *Organization & Environment*, **28** (1), 103–25.

Ones, D. S. and S. Dilchert (2012a), 'Employee green behaviours', in S. E. Jackson, D. S. Ones, and S. Dilchert (eds), *Managing Human Resources for Environmental Sustainability*, San Francisco, CA: Jossey-Bass/Wiley, pp. 85–116.

Ones, D. S. and S. Dilchert (2012b), 'Environmental Sustainability at work: A Call to action', *Industrial and Organizational Psychology*, **5** (4), 444–66.

Osbaldiston, R. and J. P. Schott (2012), 'Environmental sustainability and behavioral science: Meta-analysis of proenvironmental behavior experiments', *Environment and Behavior*, **44** (2), 257–99.

Ouellette, J. A. and W. Wood (1998), 'Habit and intention in everyday life: The multiple processes by which past behavior predicts future behavior', *Psychological Bulletin*, **124** (1), 54–74.

Ramus, C. A. and A. B. C. Killmer (2007), 'Corporate greening through prosocial extrarole behaviours? A conceptual framework for employee motivation', *Business Strategy and the Environment*, **16** (8), 554–70.

Randel, A. E. (2002), 'The maintenance of an organization? Socially responsible practice', *Business & Society*, **41** (1), 61–83.

Robertson, J. L. and J. Barling (eds) (2015), *The Psychology of Green Organizations*, Oxford: Oxford University Press.

Rothbard, N. P. (2001), 'Enriching or depleting? The dynamics of engagement in work and family roles', *Administrative Science Quarterly*, **46** (4), 655–84.

Russo, M. V. and P. A. Fouts (1997), 'A resource-based perspective on corporate environmental performance and profitability', *Academy of Management Journal*, **40** (3), 534–59.

Schwartz, S. H. (1973), 'Normative explanations of helping behavior: A critique, proposal, and empirical test', *Journal of Experimental Social Psychology*, **9** (4), 349–64.

Scott, W. R. (1995), *Institutions and Organisations*, Thousand Oaks, CA: Sage.

Semmann, D., H.-J. Krambeck and M. Milinski (2005), 'Reputation is valuable within and outside one's own social group', *Behavioral Ecology and Sociobiology*, **57** (6), 611–16.

Shott, S. (1976), 'Society, self, and mind in moral philosophy: The scottish moralists as precursors of symbolic interactionism', *Journal of the History of the Behavioral Sciences*, **12** (1), 39–46.

Smith, A. M. and T. O'Sullivan (2012), 'Environmentally responsible behaviour in the workplace: An internal social marketing approach', *Journal of Marketing Management*, **28** (3–4), 469–93.

Smith, W. R. (1956), 'Product differentiation and market segmentation as alternative marketing strategies', *Journal of Marketing*, **21** (1), 3–8.

Steg, L. and C. Vlek (2009), 'Encouraging pro-environmental behaviour: An integrative review and research agenda', *Journal of Environmental Psychology*, **29** (3), 309–17.

Steg, L., A. E. van den Berg and J. I. M. De Groot (eds) (2012), *Environmental Psychology: An Introduction*, Hoboken, NJ: Wiley-Blackwell.

Steg, L., J. W. Bolderdijk, K. Keizer and G. Perlaviciute (2014), 'An integrated framework for encouraging pro-environmental behaviour: The role of values, situational factors and goals', *Journal of Environmental Psychology*, **38**, 104–15.

Stern, P. C. (2000), 'New environmental theories: Toward a coherent theory of environmentally significant behavior', *Journal of Social Issues*, **56** (3), 407–24.

Stryker, S. (1980), *Symbolic Interactionism: A Social Structural Version*, Menlo Park, CA: Benjamin Cummings.

Suchman, M. C. (1995), 'Managing legitimacy: Strategic and institutional approaches', *Academy of Management Review*, **20** (3), 571–610.

Surroca, J., J. A. Tribó and S. Waddock (2010), 'Corporate responsibility and financial performance: The role of intangible resources', *Strategic Management Journal*, **31** (5), 463–90.

Tajfel, H. (1978), 'The achievement of group differentiation', in H. Tajfel (ed.), *Differentiation between Social Groups: Studies in the Social Psychology of Intergroup Relations*, London: Academic Press, pp. 77–98.

Tajfel, H. and J. C. Turner (1985), 'The social identity theory of intergroup behavior', in W. G. Austin and S. Worchel (eds), *Psychology of Intergroup Relations*, 2nd edn, Chicago, IL: Nelson-Hall, pp. 7–24.

Takala, T. and P. Pallab (2000), 'Individual, collective and social responsibility of the firm', *Business Ethics: A European Review*, **9** (2), 109–18.

Temminck, E., K. Mearns and L. Fruhen (2015), 'Motivating employees towards sustainable behaviour', *Business Strategy and the Environment*, **24** (6), 402–12.

Tilikidou, I. and A. Delistavrou (2008), 'Types and influential factors of consumers' non-purchasing ecological behaviors', *Business Strategy and the Environment*, **17** (1), 61–76.

Tolman, E. C. (1943), 'Identification and the postwar world', *Journal of Abnormal and Social Psychology*, **38** (2), 141–8.

Triandis, H. C. (1977), *Interpersonal Behaviour*, Monterey, CA: Brooks Cole.

Turban, D. B. and D. W. Greening (1997), 'Corporate social performance and organizational attractiveness to prospective employees', *Academy of Management Journal*, **40** (3), 658–72.

Van der Werff, E., L. Steg and K. Keizer (2013a), 'It is a moral issue: The relationship between environmental self-identity, obligation-based intrinsic motivation and pro-environmental behaviour', *Global Environmental Change*, **23** (5), 1258–65.

Van der Werff, E., L. Steg and K. Keizer (2013b), 'The value of environmental self-identity: The relationship between biospheric values, environmental self-identity and environmental preferences, intentions and behaviour', *Journal of Environmental Psychology*, **34**, 55–63.

Vidovic, M. and N. Khanna (2012), 'Is voluntary pollution abatement in the absence of a carrot or stick effective? Evidence from facility participation in the EPA's 33/50 program', *Environmental and Resource Economics*, **52** (3), 369–93.

Washington, M. and E. J. Zajac (2005), 'Status evolution and competition: Theory and evidence', *The Academy of Management Journal*, **48** (2), 282–96.

Whiteman, G., B. Walker and P. Perego (2013), 'Planetary boundaries: Ecological foundations for corporate sustainability', *Journal of Management Studies*, **50** (2), 307–36.

Worthington, I. (2013), *Greening Business: Research, Theory, and Practice*, Oxford: Oxford University Press.

Wulfson, M. (2001), 'The ethics of corporate social responsibility and philanthropic ventures', *Journal of Business Ethics*, **29** (1/2), 135–45.

PART III

EMPLOYEE ENVIRONMENTAL BEHAVIOUR, INTERVENTIONS, CAMPAIGNS AND MARKETING

13. Motivation towards "green" behaviour at the workplace: facilitating employee pro-environmental behaviour through participatory interventions
Paul C. Endrejat and Simone Kauffeld

13.1 THE (PSYCHOLOGICAL) REQUIREMENTS FOR PRO-ENVIRONMENTAL BEHAVIOUR IN THE WORKPLACE

One might say that all environmental problems have their roots in human behaviour (Schultz 2014). Enhancing pro-environmental behaviour (PEB), such as recycling, energy-saving, or ecological mobility/consumption, is a straightforward way to tackle these kinds of problems. More specifically, focusing on PEB within organisations uncovers much room for improvement, as this area is – in contrast to the household sector – underemphasised in research (Norton et al. 2015). This lack of research is astonishing because a workforce's behaviour contributes a great deal towards an organisation's environmental performance (Masoso and Grobler 2010). To fill this research gap, we show how Self-Determination Theory (SDT; Deci and Ryan 1985) could serve as the theoretical framework for raising employees' motivation to have *green* behaviour in their workplace. According to the SDT, the three psychological needs – relatedness, autonomy, and competence – are the basis for experiencing self-determination and facilitating a long-lasting behaviour change towards more PEB. To provide guidelines for how these requirements can be translated into organisational practices, we present participatory interventions (PIs) as a method for involving employees in the planning and decision process in which PEB is implemented in their workplace.

Change agents (i.e., the individuals who influence employees' behaviours in a desirable direction; Rogers 2003), who aim to enhance the motivation towards more PEB, are confronted with a challenging task: not only are individuals in general hesitant to change their behaviours (Gifford 2011), but also the organisational context itself generates various challenges that interfere with raising workers' PEB (Werner 2013). For instance, at work, individuals seldom take responsibility for their consumption. Within such a setting, individuals tend to maximise their own benefit and not care whether resources are depleted or used efficiently (Hardin 1968). Thus, for PEB to be effective, all members of a social unit need to change their behaviours (Gifford 2011). Accordingly, the inaction of colleagues decreases the likelihood for a single employee to show PEB (Darley and Latané 1968). Therefore, change agents should take the *relatedness* of employees into their social contexts and the pro-environmental norms within an organisation into account (Nielsen 2013).

Given the need for such a systemic perspective, raising PEB can also be understood as organisation development (Davis and Coan 2015). During such a change process, advising employees on how to behave fuels, rather than lowers, their resistance to the target behaviour (Brehm 1966; Klonek et al. 2015a). For instance, when employees are told to shut down their computers during lunch breaks, but that restarting them takes several minutes, employees' resistance would be a rational phenomenon. Moreover, employees' PEB cannot be sufficiently monitored, sanctioned, or rewarded. This makes it necessary for workers to embrace PEB with volition and self-determination. Hence, it is important to ensure employees' *autonomy* (Webb et al. 2013). Furthermore, telling employees how they should show more PEB not only undermines their autonomy, but also does not take different work settings into account (e.g., office vs. laboratory) that might require tailored behaviour modes to achieve the most effective PEB (Trianni and Cagno 2012). Thus, employees should experience their own *competence* in deciding which PEB is most suitable for their work context (Karjalainen 2016).

Considering these aspects, change agents need an approach that facilitates the workforce's involvement and considers employees' psychological needs for autonomy, relatedness, and competence (Ones and Dilchert 2013). This chapter contributes towards this goal by introducing PIs as a method for enhancing PEB. First, we give a definition and overview of PIs. Subsequently, we discuss the underlying psychological mechanisms that make PIs work. Hereby, we highlight the three basic psychological needs – autonomy, competency, and relatedness – as proposed by the SDT. Building on these needs, we provide several guidelines of how PIs can be conducted within an organisational context. More specifically, we discuss the required facilitation skills and present tools that can be applied during a PI, to establish a PEB fostering social norm. We also review studies using PIs within organisations and highlight how further research can help to understand the mechanisms that make PIs effective. This chapter concludes with recommendations for change agents as to how they could integrate PIs within their organisations.

13.2 PARTICIPATORY INTERVENTIONS AS A MEANS TO ENHANCE PEB WITHIN ORGANISATIONS

Participation is the process during which employees gain influence regarding information-processing, decision-making, or problem-solving (Wagner 1994). In this regard, a PI is not done *for* or *on*, but *with* employees (Heron and Reason 2001). Kurt Lewin (1947a) and his successors (e.g., Coch and French 1948) were among the first who systematically examined the effects of such an approach within organisations. These studies started a research tradition that is nowadays known as participatory action research (Lewin 1947b; Reason and Bradbury 2001) and has a strong impact on other subjects, such as job crafting (Wrzesniewski and Dutton 2001) and the organisational change literature (Pasmore and Fagans 1992). PIs have also been identified as a useful approach to raise users' acceptance for PEB (Rau et al. 2012; Staddon et al. 2016), and the 10th principle of the *Rio Declaration on Environment and Development* proclaims that "environmental issues are best handled with participation of all concerned citizens, at the relevant level" (Wheeler and Beatley 2014: 81). Surprisingly however, environmental psychologists tend to neglect participatory approaches to promote PEB (Gifford 2014).

PIs aim to involve employees and start a systematic inquiry about which PEBs are applicable at their workplace, thus increasing the feasibility of and the motivation for a behaviour change (Endrejat et al. 2015; Matthies and Krömker 2000). This involvement is necessary because raising PEB might be associated with disadvantages, such as comfort loss due to a change in transportation mode. In this regard, considering and valuing employees' opinions and perceptions throughout the change process, from planning to implementation, could enhance their acceptance for behaviour changes (Arnstein 1969; Nielsen and Randall 2013).

There are several concepts of PIs, such as websites to collect employees' suggestions or task forces to plan and implement new work routines. Within this chapter, we refer to PIs as workshops, during which employees of one department get together to elaborate on possibilities about how to raise the level of their PEB. Hereby, no specifications about how the final agreed measures will look are predefined by the organisation. In contrast to skill training, which fosters learning and behaviour modelling, within a workshop change agents act rather as facilitators and experts of the process that leads to a desired outcome. As we will show in the next section, such a setting meets participants' psychological needs for relatedness, autonomy, and competence, and thereby promotes an internalisation of

PEB norms into employees' self-concepts (Bradley et al. 2018, Chapter 17, this volume; Deci and Ryan 2000).

13.3 THE (PSYCHOLOGICAL) MECHANISMS THAT MAKE PARTICIPATORY INTERVENTIONS WORK

Given that an individual's PEBs are difficult to control, the norms underlying the target behaviours should be internalised to enhance the chances that behaviours are shown intentionally and autonomously (Norton et al. 2015). The SDT proposes that the fulfilment of the three psychological needs – autonomy, relatedness, and competency – are the precondition for the internalisation of green behaviours (Osbaldiston and Sheldon 2003). Thus, we discuss how PIs need to meet the requirements in order to promote norm internalisation (Endrejat and Kauffeld in press).

13.3.1 Autonomy: Consider Employees' Free Will

Individuals want to hold the belief that the self is the origin or driving force behind behaviour (Deci and Ryan 2000). In this vein, when employees hear themselves argue for more PEB, they will also adapt their attitude towards this (verbal) behaviour (Bem 1967). This is especially effective for individuals who have not yet achieved a steady environmental attitude (Chaiken and Baldwin 1981). Moreover, change agents should acknowledge that individuals can differ in their motivation and readiness to change their behaviours (Bamberg 2013). That is, some individuals might already plan to engage in more PEB, whereas other employees have not yet thought about these aspects (Prochaska et al. 1992). Thus, top-down communication, such as information campaigns, neglects these different stages of change readiness, which might explain their limited effectiveness (Delmas et al. 2013; Gifford 2014). Additionally, one can assume that the average Western employee was already exposed to several information cues aimed at enhancing PEB. Thus, environmental knowledge seems to be a necessary, but not a sufficient, requisite for PEB (Pelletier et al. 1998). Also advising employees individually can undermine their motivation to show more PEB (Klonek et al. 2015a; Reich and Robertson 1979). This is because when people feel pressured to change their behaviour, they tend to respond with rebellion against these directions (Brehm 1966).

Given that it is unlikely to persuade employees to change their behaviour, it might be most promising to provide them with autonomy and let them name the reasons for a behaviour change themselves (Miller and Rollnick 2013). Such a procedure is also legitimated by the fact that there exists *equifinality* towards PEB, meaning that having greener behaviour can be achieved in several ways. Equifinality offers the opportunity for employees to connect PEB goals with personal goals that might be unrelated to the environment (Unsworth and McNeill 2017). For instance, shutting down the computer at the end of a work day might help an employee to detach from work during leisure time (personal goal) and thereby also reduces energy-consumption (environmental goal). For such a connection to take place, it is important to provide an autonomy-supportive condition that leads individuals to engage in more informative and constructive statements (Oliver et al. 2008). As already mentioned, such self-expressed pro-environmental statements, in turn, enhance an individual's pro-environmental attitude (Bem 1967).

Nonetheless, also in an autonomy-supportive environment, it is important to acknowledge negative consequences that are associated with a behaviour change (Reeve et al. 1999). For instance, reducing the heating might make it necessary to wear some extra clothing, thus reducing the experienced comfort. Neglecting such potential objections voiced by those who are supposed to change their behaviour increases the chances of evoking their resistance (Dent and Goldberg 1999). Thus, PEB should be perceived as acceptable and applicable for integration into work routines. In other words, employees need to feel competent to show more PEB.

13.3.2   Competency: Employees Need to Have the Capabilities to Engage in PEB

Competence is associated with an internal locus of control and the belief in one's capabilities to act in a greener fashion, which subsequently also leads to more PEB (De Young 1996). Thus, competence includes the feeling that one can handle the environmental demands and has the capacity to affect outcomes (Bandura 1997). Without such behavioural control, it is unlikely that the intention to show more PEB is formed (Ajzen et al. 2011). Therefore, environments that do not provide employees with the possibility to interact or exert control (e.g., when the heating system is controlled by facility management), undermine employees' motivation for more PEB (Karjalainen 2016; Pelletier et al. 1999). Accordingly, the agreed measures for PEB should match the capabilities of the respective group and be aligned to the work routine and organisational structures (Senge 2010; Trianni and Cagno 2012). One way to ensure competence is collective or participative goal setting because it prevents under- or over-challenge

(Norton et al. 2015). Research regarding goal setting has also shown that employees who are involved in goal setting tend to set higher goals and show higher performance levels than those who received assigned goals (Locke and Latham 2002).

Nonetheless, even when employees have the competence to show more PEB, they might hesitate to show these because such a behaviour change exceeds their dedication (Kaiser et al. 2010). And even when their dedication is high, they might forget their intentions (Kollmuss and Agyeman 2002). This misremembering or low dedication is due to the fact that PEB remains on the surface of one's self-concept. A promising way to facilitate the required internalisation is to use social influence.

13.3.3   Relatedness: PEB at Work Takes Place in a Social Environment

The SDT proposes that individuals need to have satisfying and supportive social relationships, and to experience connectedness with others (Deci and Ryan 1985). Moreover, the social context can have a powerful impact on how individuals behave and what they regard as appropriate behaviour. Thus, interventions should consider that organisations are complex systems and employees' behaviours do not occur in a vacuum (Werner 2013). Consequently, there is the chance that employees' intentions to show PEB rise when they perceive a positive green climate within their organisation (Norton et al. in press). Descriptive norms (i.e., what individuals see their colleagues do, for example, whether they recycle or not) are part of these perceptions. Therefore, in a first step, it is necessary to enhance the descriptive norms (i.e., raise the percentage of colleagues that recycle).

However, when employees realise that they already show more PEB than their colleagues, descriptive norms could undermine PEB due to moral licensing. According to the moral licensing effect, people tend to strive for moral equilibrium, that is, individuals are concerned with not being too altruistic (Sachdeva et al. 2009). Therefore, for employees showing much PEB already, a low group norm might act as a restraining force to further increase their PEB (Lewin 1947a). To counter this effect, change agents should also introduce *injunctive norms* (e.g., recycling is necessary; Goldstein et al. 2008) to highlight that PEBs are favourably seen by others. Injunctive norms also emphasise the social consequences (approval/disapproval) for participating or ignoring PEB, respectively (Norton et al. in press). In the following section, we elaborate how change agents could channel this potential influence towards increasing PEB.

13.4 CONDUCTING PIs TO RAISE EMPLOYEES' PEB: THE ESSENTIAL ELEMENTS

A PI, in the tradition of action research (Lewin 1947b), is usually based on the following three stages: a *detection phase*, a *decision phase*, and an *implementation phase* (Pelletier and Sharp 2008; for a detailed sequence plan of a two-hour workshop, see Endrejat et al. 2017). In the detection phase, the facilitator engages with participants and provides information when requested. During this phase, the group develops potential opportunities for showing more PEB. From this collection of ideas, the group moves on to the decision phase, in which it decides which topics they want to elaborate further. For the chosen topics, strategies are developed for how the impact of factors that inhibit PEB can be reduced and the impact of factors that support PEB enhanced, respectively. Finally, the implementation phase highlights how the behaviours are translated into organisational structures.

We use this three-step sequence to structure the essential elements for successful PIs and to show how these elements relate to psychological needs (see Figure 13.1). Within the detection phase, change agents should provide an open and autonomy-supportive atmosphere and make clear that they understand employees' perspectives. In the decision phase, change agents should apply instruments to identify the reasons for and against PEB and develop strategies of how to overcome hindrances towards PEB. Finally, by using social influence, PEB fostering norms help to embed green behaviours into the organisational culture.

Naturally, this categorisation is made to reduce complexity and is not as distinct as Figure 13.1 might suggest. For instance, a change agent should pay attention to establishing an autonomy-supportive atmosphere throughout the workshop. In the following sections, we discuss how change agents could consider these elements while conducting a PI.

13.4.1 The Necessary Facilitation Skills to Ensure an Autonomy-supportive Atmosphere

The facilitation of PIs requires neutrality and specific communication skills to fulfil employees' need to experience autonomy (Endrejat et al. 2015). We therefore suggest the change agent should have a consultant status to avoid being pressured by performance specifications. An outside change agent also allows supervisors to participate in the workshop and add their perspectives, which might differ from the points of view voiced by their subordinates.

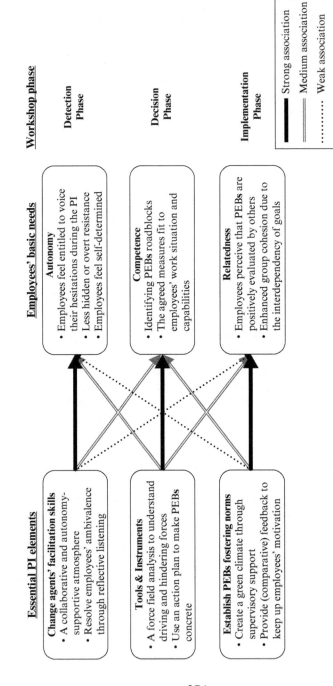

Figure 13.1   How participatory interventions (PIs) meet employees' psychological needs

Establishing a collaborative and autonomy-supportive atmosphere
Appropriate communication is among the most important determinants for behaviour change (Elving 2005). Giving orders, commands, or using coercion can be understood as roadblocks to efficient communication (Klonek et al. 2015a). Accordingly, trying to persuade employees to raise their PEB with the help of rational logic, is prone to failure (Brehm 1966). Moreover, such a communication style enhances the chances that employees remain quiet and do not voice their concerns during the PIs, which could be understood as hidden resistance (Meinecke et al. 2016). The problem associated with hidden resistance is that employees might not name the factors that prevent them from showing more PEB, so that no solutions of how these hindrances could be circumvented are generated during the workshop.

Instead, autonomy-supportive communication enhances acceptance by change recipients (Gagné et al. 2000), and an autonomy-supportive instructor is also able to increase users' subsequent PEB (Osbaldiston and Schott 2012). Such an atmosphere is generated when change agents are accepting and show empathy for employees' perspectives. Instead of commands, the change agent seeks collaboration with employees and establishes a focus towards desired outcomes (Forsberg et al. 2014). An effective technique for this purpose is reflective listening (Miller and Rollnick 2013).

Resolving employees' ambivalence with reflective listening
Change agents should explore employees' feelings and attitudes in order to understand the motives and reasons of their hesitation regarding the adoption of new behaviours (Oreg 2003). Moreover, employees need to hear that their concerns are understood (Miller and Rollnick 2013). Thus, acknowledging that employees might have second thoughts about the behaviour change is already an effective way to lower their resistance against new behaviours (Knowles and Riner 2007). Reflective listeners use paraphrasing or restate what a conversational partner has said, with a focus on the meaning of the statement and/or concomitant feelings (Bodie et al. 2016). Such communication helps to establish a shared perspective, and helps the change agent to understand what causes employees' reluctance to show more PEB.

Reflective listening is also effective to affirm employees' ambivalence with regards to a behaviour change (Piderit 2000): on the one hand, they might not want to produce waste or use resources inefficiently, and on the other hand, they prefer that PEB does not interfere with their work routines. Reflective listening can resolve ambivalence and foster motivation towards more PEB by developing discrepancies between employees' values (e.g., saving resources) and their current behaviour (e.g., wasting energy). Humans have a natural need to hold consistent attitudes and behaviours because discrepancy causes discomfort (Festinger 1957). As a result, individuals who find themselves being competent of changing their behaviour (e.g., "at home, I always turn out the light when leaving the room") should also think that they have the corresponding attitude (e.g., "saving money and/or energy seems to be important for me"). Accordingly, the need for consistency between attitudes and behaviours can be utilised to encourage PEB (Forsberg et al. 2014).

13.4.2   Tools and Techniques to Raise Employees' PEB Competencies

To explore employees' readiness to show more PEB, it is necessary to understand their reasons and behavioural intentions for and against PEB (Bamberg 2013). For instance, when change agents suggest PEB that are out of reach for employees, they undermine their motivation towards acting pro-environmentally (Pelletier et al. 1999). Therefore, we present the force field analysis as a tool to highlight the most relevant pro and contra arguments for increasing PEB, and subsequently discuss how an action plan strengthens the belief that the agreed measures are implementable.

A force field analysis: Understanding the driving and restraining forces that act on employees

According to Lewin (1947a), employees' current levels of PEB could be understood as being in equilibria between forces that foster PEB (i.e., *driving forces*, such as a good conscience) and oppose PEB (i.e., *restraining forces*, such as interference with work processes). For any change towards more PEB to take place, a change agent has to upset this equilibrium, either by reducing the impact of restraining forces or by strengthening the impact of driving forces (Lewin 1947a). To approach this task systematically, Lewin (1947a) suggested conducting a force field analysis.

Whether it is more effective to focus on reinforcing driving forces or reducing hindering forces should be decided by the employees. From a solution-focused perspective (e.g., de Shazer and Dolan 2007), it is recommended to neglect hindering forces. However, especially in the group context, an emphasis on the reasons for the status quo, understanding employees' concerns and perceived barriers is recommended (Gaspar 2013; Gifford 2011; Wagner and Ingersoll 2013). Also Lewin (1947a) recommended focusing on restraining forces. For him, individuals are usually already aware of the benefits associated with showing more target behaviours. Therefore, adding more driving forces might only increase the tension within employees.

Upon listing all driving and hindering forces, employees decide which forces have the strongest impact on their behaviours. To ensure autonomy, change agents should not prescribe whether these are driving or restraining forces. The goal of this procedure is for employees to develop strategies for how the effect of the most distinctive restraining forces could be reduced and the motivational effects of the driving forces enhanced, respectively. For instance, the driving force "monetary savings due to reduced energy consumption" could be enhanced by agreeing that half of the savings are invested to improve the next department party.

Using an action plan to make PEB concrete
To bridge the chasm between intention and actual behaviours, the strategies of how more PEB could be integrated into employees' work routine need to be translated into scalable and concrete behaviours (Ones and Dilchert 2013). This translation can be achieved with the help of an action plan that specifies *what* is done *when*, and by *whom* (Gollwitzer 1999). Such a definition also establishes clear accountabilities and thus inhibits a diffusion of responsibility (Darley and Latané 1968). Furthermore, the specification of an action plan also considers that the PEBs fit to the readiness and capability of employees, and are aligned to organisational structures (Bamberg 2013; Senge 2010). The positive effects of an action plan can be further enhanced through public commitment making (Lokhorst et al. 2013). A possible form of commitment making would be to ask employees to sign the action plan at the end of the workshop.

13.4.3   Establish PEB Fostering Norms to Take Account of the Need for Relatedness

To be successful, interventions aimed at enhancing employees' PEB should not be a one-time fix, but need to be interwoven into work routines (Werner 2013). To stabilise employee PEB on the enhanced level beyond the workshop, it is essential that PEB are internalised into self-concepts. To achieve this, the role of supervisors and group processes among colleagues is crucial (Norton et al. 2018, Chapter 11, this volume).

Creating a green climate through supervisory support
As employees overtly commit themselves to PEB measures, they lay the foundation for PEB fostering norms. However, to strengthen this effect, supervisors should attend the workshop because doing so signals organisational support and helps to establish an injunctive norm towards PEB (Norton et al. in press). Moreover, supervisors also act as role models and

make the descriptive norm salient. Accordingly, their green behaviours directly influence the green behaviours of their subordinates (Kim et al. 2014).

Providing (comparative) group feedback to keep up employees' motivation
Due to the organisational setting (e.g., only one meter reader for the whole building), employees usually do not receive feedback regarding the measurable effects (e.g., how much energy has been saved) caused by their behaviour changes. However, to foster employees' motivation, their actions and the corresponding results should be causally linked (Stern and Gardner 1981). To account for this requirement, change agents can embrace the fact that they can provide no individual, but only group feedback, as an opportunity: due to the interdependency of goals (i.e., the success of energy savings depends on everyone), employees might experience an enhanced group cohesion that positively affects PEB norms (Nielsen 2013). This cohesion effect can be enhanced using comparative feedback. During a comparative feedback intervention, two or more units compete with each other, which can show most PEBs. The evaluation is based on objective data (i.e., electric meters). There is evidence that such an intervention by itself is an effective way to enhance organisational members' PEB (e.g., Dixon et al. 2015), and further research might combine comparative feedback with PIs.

13.5   THE EFFECTIVENESS OF PIs TO ENHANCE PEB WITHIN THE ORGANISATIONAL CONTEXT

The majority of evaluation studies regarding PIs are conducted within the health or education context (e.g., Mikkelsen et al. 2000), whereas research that examines participatory approaches that are aimed to raise PEB within the organisations is sparse (Gifford 2014). Nonetheless, several studies support the notion that these interventions are effective. For instance, Endrejat and Kauffeld (in press) found that a three-hour workshop leads to an internalisation of energy-saving norms of organisational members. With regards to measurable, objective data, Griesel (2004) showed that workshops can cause a long-term energy reduction by 10 per cent. Similarly, Endrejat et al. (2017), who applied a force field analysis and ended their workshop with an action plan, report not only an increase of energy-saving norms and self-rated behaviours, but also reduced district heating and power usage by 11 per cent and 7 per cent respectively.

Furthermore, there is evidence that the necessary communication skills for change agents can be learned within two days (e.g., Klonek and Kauffeld 2015).

13.6 FURTHER RESEARCH TO BETTER UNDERSTAND HOW PIs CAN BE IMPROVED

To gain a better understanding of how PIs can be applied more efficiently, we suggest that future research should combine self-reported data with objective measures, examine what happens within workshops from a process perspective, and take employees' characteristics into account.

13.6.1 Combining Self-report Data with Objective Measures

As self-reports (i.e., questionnaires) are inexpensive, applicable for a plethora of situations, and suitable for quantitative data analysis, they are still the primary data collection method used to evaluate interventions aimed at enhancing PEB (Steg and Vlek 2009). However, to estimate the objective effectiveness of these interventions, self-reports are not sufficient (Gifford 2014). For instance, the attendance at a workshop might be effective when evaluated by questionnaire data, but not when the actual energy conversation of participants is examined (Geller 1981). Moreover, individuals tend to overestimate the environmental friendliness of their lifestyles, and thus they usually indicate more PEB than they engage in (Chao and Lam 2010; Corral-Verdugo 2002). As PEB are scalable (e.g., the percentage of recycled waste), researchers could use these data as dependent variables in addition to self-rated behaviour to evaluate the *real* effectiveness of PIs (Ones and Dilchert 2013).

13.6.2 Enhancing the Understanding of What Happens Within PIs

Although we have focused on one particular type of PI (i.e., workshops), there are still various ways for how these workshops are conducted (e.g., regarding length, involvement of participants, sequence plans, etc.). Next to examining which procedures are superior to others, it is also important to include participants' opinion regarding whether they are satisfied with the intervention and how they behaved during the workshop (Arnstein 1969). A promising approach towards opening this black box would be the usage of interaction analyses (Klonek et al. 2015b). Such an approach requires that PIs are recorded and analysed by coding the change agent's and participants' behaviours. By using this data for sequence analyses, researchers can draw causal conclusions of which behaviours of change agents lead to more self-committing statements of employees towards PEB, and whether the amount of these statements is eventually related to objective PEB.

13.6.3 Employee Characteristics that Impact the Influence of PIs

Next to individual factors, such as demographics (Wiernik et al. 2016) that have a direct effect on employees' PEB, within the context of PIs, one should also note that some employees are more interested in being involved in the change processes than others (Brown and Cregan 2008). Individual characteristics can also have an impact on how the communication with employees should be delivered. For instance, some individuals could be motivated to recycle when the attention is directed towards positive goals (e.g., being the greenest department within the organisation), other individuals, however, are more vigilant to change their behaviour if negative outcomes are highlighted (e.g., being considered as the *litterbugs* of the organisation; Higgins 1997). It would significantly enhance our understanding of how change agents should behave during PIs if further research could deepen the knowledge regarding this interplay.

13.7   RECOMMENDATIONS FOR PRACTITIONERS ON HOW TO CONDUCT PIs

Motivating employees to behave pro-environmentally is a complex issue and requires solid psychological knowledge. In this vein, models such as the SDT (Deci and Ryan 1985) help to understand why top-down communication (e.g., informational campaigns or persuasion) is unlikely to motivate employees to behave more *greenly*. In many cases, change agents' communication could even be the source of employees' resistance (Ford et al. 2008). However, also in an autonomy-supportive workshop employees might oppose PEB not because of bad will, but because they have comprehensible reasons to be hesitant. This means that many PEB are indeed associated with disadvantages, such as thermal comfort loss when the heating is lowered. Thus, change agents should bear the following proverb in mind: "You can't make an omelette without breaking eggs." This phrase should remind them that perceiving employees as stubborn is not likely to result in an intervention that raises employees' volitional PEB. Instead, change agents should understand employees' arguments against PEB as *reasoned resistance* (Dent and Goldberg 1999; Endrejat and Kauffeld in press) that needs to be resolved (Knowles and

Riner 2007). One method that change agents can apply to do so is a force field analysis. In a first step, the group identifies the most important driving and restraining forces. In a second step, change agents lead through a discussion of how the impact of the driving forces could be enhanced and the impact of restraining forces reduced, respectively. Although the development of such strategies might seem to be sufficient to raise employees' PEB, we strongly recommend that change agents also develop an action plan to solidify behaviour changes and let employees publicly commit to these actions or *if–then* plans (e.g., *"when we are in a meeting that takes more than an hour, we will use our computers' energy-saving mode"*).

Finally, we suggest that trained change agents, who possess communication skills that ensure an autonomy-supportive atmosphere, facilitate the workshops and supervisors attend as participants. In addition to the fact that supervisors can add their viewpoints or opinions that might differ from the perspectives of their employees, their participation at the intervention signals an organisation's commitment towards acting greener, and fosters PEB norms. If a supervisor's full attendance is not possible due to time constraints, they can at least authorise the group to develop solutions and only attend the formulation of an action (Kauffeld 2001).

13.8 CONCLUSION

Since employees' PEB can only be insufficiently monitored, it is important that workers show these behaviours with volition and self-determination. In this chapter, we have shown how PIs contribute towards this goal. During a workshop, employees view the energy-saving measures as their own results, and responsibility is ascribed to them of how these measures are implemented into their work routines. Although empowering employees might appear more effortful compared to advising them to show more PEBs, PIs are, in our opinion, the most promising way to promote employees' self-determination, encourage social processes that foster energy-saving behaviours, and enable an optimal fit between demands and employees' willingness, as well as their abilities to show more PEB in their workplace.

REFERENCES

Ajzen, I., N. Joyce, S. Sheikh, and N. G. Cote (2011), 'Knowledge and the prediction of behavior: The role of information accuracy in the theory of planned behavior', *Basic and Applied Social Psychology*, **33** (2), 101–17.

Arnstein, S. R. (1969), 'A ladder of citizen participation', *Journal of the American Institute of Planners*, **35** (4), 216–24.
Bamberg, S. (2013), 'Applying the stage model of self-regulated behavioral change in a car use reduction intervention', *Journal of Environmental Psychology*, **33**, 68–75.
Bandura, A. (1997), *Self-efficacy. The Exercise of Control*, New York: W. H. Freeman.
Bem, D. J. (1967), 'Self-perception: An alternative interpretation of cognitive dissonance phenomena', *Psychological Review*, **74** (3), 183–200.
Bodie, G. D., K. E. Cannava, and A. J. Vickery (2016), 'Supportive communication and the adequate paraphrase', *Communication Research Reports*, **33** (2), 166–72.
Bradley, P., S. Fudge and M. Leach (2018), 'The role of social norms in incentivising energy reduction in organisations', in V. K. Wells, D. Gregory-Smith and D. Manika (eds), *Research Handbook on Employee Pro-environmental Behaviour*, Cheltenham, UK and Northampton, MA, USA: Edward Elgar Publishing.
Brehm, J. W. (1966), *A Theory of Psychological Reactance*, New York: Academic Press.
Brown, M. and C. Cregan (2008), 'Organizational change cynicism: The role of employee involvement', *Human Resource Management*, **47** (4), 667–86.
Chaiken, S. and M. W. Baldwin (1981), 'Affective-cognitive consistency and the effect of salient behavioral information on the self-perception of attitudes', *Journal of Personality and Social Psychology*, **41** (1), 1–12.
Chao, Y.-L. and S.-P. Lam (2010), 'Measuring responsible environmental behavior: Self-reported and other-reported measures and their differences in testing a behavioral model', *Environment and Behavior*, **43** (1), 53–71.
Coch, L. and J. R. P. French (1948), 'Overcoming resistance to change', *Human Relations*, **1** (4), 512–32.
Corral-Verdugo, V. (2002), 'A structural model of proenvironmental competency', *Environment and Behavior*, **34** (4), 531–49.
Darley, J. M. and B. Latané (1968), 'Bystander intervention in emergencies: Diffusion of responsibility', *Journal of Personality and Social Psychology*, **8** (4), 377–83.
Davis, M. C. and P. Coan (2015), 'Organizational change', in J. Barling and J. Robertson (eds), *The Psychology of Green Organizations*, New York: Oxford University Press, pp. 244–74.
Deci, E. L. and R. M. Ryan (1985), *Intrinsic Motivation and Self-determination in Human Behavior*, New York: Plenum.
Deci, E. L. and R. M. Ryan (2000), 'The "What" and "Why" of goal pursuits: Human needs and the self-determination of behavior', *Psychological Inquiry*, **11** (4), 227–68.
Delmas, M. A., M. Fischlein, and O. I. Asensio (2013), 'Information strategies and energy conservation behavior: A meta-analysis of experimental studies from 1975 to 2012', *Energy Policy*, **61**, 729–39.
Dent, E. B. and S. G. Goldberg (1999), 'Challenging "resistance to change"', *The Journal of Applied Behavioral Science*, **35** (1), 25–41.
De Young, R. (1996), 'Some psychological aspects of reduced consumption behavior: The role of intrinsic satisfaction and competence motivation', *Environment and Behavior*, **28** (3), 358–409.
Dixon, G. N., M. B. Deline, K. McComas, L. Chambliss, and M. Hoffmann (2015), 'Using comparative feedback to influence workplace energy conservation', *Environment and Behavior*, **47** (6), 667–93.
Elving, Wim J. (2005), 'The role of communication in organisational change', *Corporate Communications: An International Journal*, **10** (2), 129–38.
Endrejat, P. C. and S. Kauffeld (in press), 'From "I should" to "I want": Increasing the internalization of employees' energy-saving motivation through participatory interventions', *Umweltpsychologie*.
Endrejat, P. C., F. Baumgarten, and S. Kauffeld (2017), 'When theory meets practice: Combining Lewin's ideas about change with motivational interviewing to increase energy-saving behaviours within organisations', *Journal of Change Management*, **17** (2), 101–20.
Endrejat, P. C., F. E. Klonek, and S. Kauffeld (2015), 'A psychology perspective of energy

consumption in organisations: The value of participatory interventions', *Indoor and Built Environment*, **24** (7), 937–49.

Festinger, L. (1957), *A Theory of Cognitive Dissonance*, Stanford, CA: Stanford University Press.

Ford, J. D., L. W. Ford, and A. D'Amelio (2008), 'Resistance to change: The rest of the story', *Academy of Management Review*, **33** (2), 362–77.

Forsberg, L., H. Wickström, and H. Källmén (2014), 'Motivational interviewing may facilitate professional interactions with inspectees during environmental inspections and enforcement conversations', *Peer Journal*, **2**, e508.

Gagné, M., R. Koestner, and M. Zuckerman (2000), 'Facilitating acceptance of organizational change: The importance of self-determination', *Journal of Applied Social Psychology*, **30** (9), 1843–52.

Gaspar, R. (2013), 'Understanding the reasons for behavioral failure: A process view of psychosocial barriers and constraints to pro-ecological behavior', *Sustainability*, **5** (7), 2960–75.

Geller, E. S. (1981), 'Evaluating energy conservation programs: Is verbal report enough?', *Journal of Consumer Research*, **8** (3), 331–35.

Gifford, R. (2011), 'The dragons of inaction. Psychological barriers that limit climate change mitigation and adoption', *American Psychologist*, **66** (4), 290–302.

Gifford, R. (2014), 'Environmental psychology matters', *Annual Review of Psychology*, **65**, 541–79.

Goldstein, N. J., R. B. Cialdini, and V. Griskevicius (2008), 'A room with a viewpoint: Using social norms to motivate environmental conservation in Hotels', *Journal of Consumer Research*, **35** (3), 472–82.

Gollwitzer, P. M. (1999), 'Implementation intentions: Strong effects of simple plans', *American Psychologist*, **54** (7), 493–503.

Griesel, C. (2004), 'Nachhaltigkeit im Bürokontext eine partizipative Intervention zur optimierten Stromnutzung' ['Sustainability in an office context – a participative intervention for an optimal use of energy'], *Umweltpsychologie*, **8** (1), 30–48.

Hardin, G. (1968), 'The tragedy of the commons', *Science*, **162** (3859), 1243–48.

Heron, J. and P. Reason (2001), 'The practice of co-operative inquiry: Research "with" rather than "on" people', in P. Reason and H. Bradbury (eds), *Handbook of Action Research: Participative Inquiry and Practice*, London: Sage, pp. 144–54.

Higgins, E. T. (1997), 'Beyond pleasure and pain', *American Psychologist*, **52** (12), 1280–300.

Kaiser, F. G., K. Byrka and T. Hartig (2010), 'Reviving Campbell's paradigm for attitude research', *Personality and Social Psychology Review*, **14** (4), 351–67.

Karjalainen, S. (2016), 'Should we design buildings that are less sensitive to occupant behaviour? A simulation study of effects of behaviour and design on office energy consumption', *Energy Efficiency*, **9** (6), 1257–70.

Kauffeld, S. (2001), *Teamdiagnose* [Team diagnosis], Göttingen, Germany: Hogrefe.

Kim, A., Y. Kim, K. Han, S. E. Jackson, and R. E. Ployhart (2014), 'Multilevel influences on voluntary workplace green behavior: Individual differences, leader behavior, and coworker advocacy', *Journal of Management*, **43** (5), 1335–58.

Klonek, F. E. and S. Kauffeld (2015), 'Providing engineers with OARS and EARS: Effects of a skills-based vocational training in motivational interviewing for engineers in higher education', *Higher Education, Skills and Work-Based Learning*, **5** (2), 117–34.

Klonek, F. E., A. V. Güntner, N. K. Lehmann-Willenbrock, and S. Kauffeld (2015a), 'Using motivational interviewing to reduce threats in conversations about environmental behavior', *Frontiers in Psychology*, **6**, 1015.

Klonek, F. E., V. Quera, and S. Kauffeld (2015b), 'Coding interactions in motivational interviewing with computer-software: What are the advantages for process researchers?', *Computers in Human Behavior*, **44**, 284–92.

Knowles, E. S. and D. D. Riner (2007), 'Omega approaches to persuasion: Overcoming resistance', in A. R. Pratkanis (ed.), *The Science of Social Influence*, New York: Psychology Press, pp. 83–114.

Kollmuss, A. and J. Agyeman (2012), 'Mind the gap: Why do people act environmentally and what are the barriers to proenvironmental behavior?', *Environmental Education Research*, **8** (3), 239–60.

Lewin, K. (1947a), 'Frontiers in group dynamics: Concept, method and reality in social science, social equilibria and social change', *Human Relations*, **1** (1), 5–41.

Lewin, K. (1947b), 'Frontiers in group dynamics: II. Channels of group life; social planning and action research', *Human Relations*, **1** (2), 143–53.

Locke, E. A. and G. P. Latham (2002), 'Building a practically useful theory of goal setting and task motivation: A 35-year odyssey', *American Psychologist*, **57** (9), 705–17.

Lokhorst, A. M., C. Werner, H. Staats, E. van Dijk, and J. L. Gale (2013), 'Commitment and behavior change: A meta-analysis and critical review of commitment-making strategies in environmental research', *Environment and Behavior*, **45** (1), 3–34.

Masoso, O. T. and L. J. Grobler (2010), 'The dark side of occupants' behaviour on building energy use', *Energy and Buildings*, **42** (2), 173–77.

Matthies, E. and D. Krömker (2000), 'Participatory planning: A heuristic for adjusting interventions to the context', *Journal of Environmental Psychology*, **20** (1), 65–74.

Meinecke, A. L., F. E. Klonek, and S. Kauffeld (2016), 'Using observational research methods to study voice and silence in organizations', *German Journal of Human Resource Management*, **30** (3–4), 195–24.

Mikkelsen, A., P. Ø. Saksvik and P. Landsbergis (2000), 'The impact of a participatory organizational intervention on job stress in community health care institutions', *Work and Stress*, **14** (2), 156–70.

Miller, W. R. and S. Rollnick (2013), *Motivational Interviewing. Helping People Change* (3rd edn), New York: Guilford Press.

Nielsen, K. (2013), 'How can we make organizational interventions work? Employees and line managers as actively crafting interventions', *Human Relations*, **66** (8), 1029–50.

Nielsen, K. and R. Randall (2013), 'Opening the black box: Presenting a model for evaluating organizational-level interventions', *European Journal of Work and Organizational Psychology*, **22** (5), 601–17.

Norton, T. A., S. L. Parker, H. Zacher, and N. M. Ashkanasy (2015), 'Employee green behavior: A theoretical framework, multilevel review, and future research agenda', *Organization and Environment*, **28** (1), 103–25.

Norton, T. A., H. Zacher, S. L. Parker, and N. M. Ashkanasy (in press), 'Bridging the gap between green behavioral intentions and employee green behavior: The role of green psychological climate', *Journal of Organizational Behavior*.

Norton, T. A., S. L. Parker, M. C. Davis, S. V. Russell and N. M. Ashkanasy (2018), 'A virtuous cycle: How green companies grow green employees (and vice versa)', in V. K. Wells, D. Gregory-Smith and D. Manika (eds), *Research Handbook on Employee Pro-environmental Behaviour*, Cheltenham, UK and Northampton, MA, USA: Edward Elgar Publishing, pp. 210–28.

Oliver, E. J., D. Markland, J. Hardy, and C. M. Petherick (2008), 'The effects of autonomy-supportive versus controlling environments on self-talk', *Motivation and Emotion*, **32** (3), 200–12.

Ones, D. S. and S. Dilchert (2013), 'Measuring, understanding, and influencing employee green behaviors', in A. H. Huffman and S. R. Klein (eds), *Green Organizations: Driving Change with IO Psychology*, New York: Routledge, pp. 115–48.

Oreg, S. (2003), 'Resistance to change: Developing an individual differences measure', *Journal of Applied Psychology*, **88** (4), 680–93.

Osbaldiston, R. and J. P. Schott (2012), 'Environmental sustainability and behavioral science: Meta-analysis of proenvironmental behavior experiments', *Environment and Behavior*, **44** (2), 257–99.

Osbaldiston, R. and K. M. Sheldon (2003), 'Promoting internalized motivation for environmentally responsible behavior: A prospective study of environmental goals', *Journal of Environmental Psychology*, **23** (4), 349–57.

Pasmore, W. A. and M. R. Fagans (1992), 'Participation, individual development, and organizational change: A review and synthesis', *Journal of Management*, **18** (2), 375–97.

Pelletier, L. G., S. Dion, K. M. Tuson, and I. Green-Demers (1999), 'Why do people fail to adopt environmental protective behaviors? Toward a taxonomy of environmental amotivation', *Journal of Applied Social Psychology*, **29** (12), 2481–504.

Pelletier, L. G. and E. Sharp (2008), 'Persuasive communication and proenvironmental behaviours: How message tailoring and message framing can improve the integration of behaviours through self-determined motivation', *Canadian Psychology/Psychologie Canadienne*, **49** (3), 210–17.

Pelletier, L. G., K. M. Tuson, I. Green-Demers, K. Noels, and A. M. Beaton (1998), 'Why are you doing things for the environment? The motivation toward the environment scale (MTES)', *Journal of Applied Social Psychology*, **28** (5), 437–68.

Piderit, S. K. (2000), 'Rethinking resistance and recognizing ambivalence: A multidimensional view of attitudes toward an organizational change', *Academy of Management Review*, **25** (4), 783–94.

Prochaska, J. O., C. C. DiClemente, and J. C. Norcross (1992), 'In search of how people change: Applications to addictive behaviors', *American Psychologist*, **47** (9), 1102–14.

Rau, I., P. Schweizer-Ries, and J. Hildebrand (2012), 'Participation strategies – the silver bullet for public acceptance?', in S. Kabisch, A. Kunath, P. Schweizer-Ries, and A. Steinführer (eds), *Vulnerability, Risks, and Complexity. Impacts of Global Change on Human Habitats*, Göttingen, Germany: Hogrefe, pp. 177–92.

Reason, P. and H. Bradbury (eds) (2001), *Handbook of Action Research: Participative Inquiry and Practice*, London: Sage.

Reeve, J., E. Bolt, and Y. Cai (1999), 'Autonomy-supportive teachers: How they teach and motivate students', *Journal of Educational Psychology*, **91** (3), 537–48.

Reich, J. W. and J. L. Robertson (1979), 'Reactance and norm appeal in anti-littering messages', *Journal of Applied Social Psychology*, **9** (1), 91–101.

Rogers, E. M. (2003), *Diffusion of Innovations* (5th edn), New York: Free Press.

Sachdeva, S., R. Iliev, and D. L. Medin (2009), 'Sinning saints and saintly sinners: The paradox of moral self-regulation', *Psychological Science*, **20** (4), 523–8.

Schultz, P. W. (2014), 'Strategies for promoting proenvironmental behavior', *European Psychologist*, **19** (2), 107–17.

Senge, P. M. (2010), *The Necessary Revolution. How Individuals and Organizations Are Working Together to Create a Sustainable World*, London: Nicholas Brealey.

Shazer, S. de and Y. M. Dolan (2007), *More than Miracles: The State of the Art of Solution-focused Brief Therapy*, New York: Haworth Press.

Staddon, S. C., C. Cycil, M. Goulden, C. Leygue, and A. Spence (2016), 'Intervening to change behaviour and save energy in the workplace. A systematic review of available evidence', *Energy Research and Social Science*, **17**, 30–51.

Steg, L. and C. Vlek (2009), 'Encouraging pro-environmental behaviour: An integrative review and research agenda', *Journal of Environmental Psychology*, **29** (3), 309–17.

Stern, P. C. and G. T. Gardner (1981), 'Psychological research and energy policy', *American Psychologist*, **36** (4), 329–42.

Trianni, A. and E. Cagno (2012), 'Dealing with barriers to energy efficiency and SMEs. Some empirical evidences', *Energy*, **37** (1), 494–504.

Unsworth, K. L. and I. M. McNeill (2017), 'Increasing pro-environmental behaviors by increasing self-concordance: Testing an intervention', *The Journal of Applied Psychology*, **102** (1), 88–103.

Wagner, C. C. and K. S. Ingersoll (2013), *Motivational Interviewing in Groups*, New York: Guilford Press.

Wagner, J. A. (1994), 'Participation's effects on performance and satisfaction: A reconsideration of research evidence', *Academy of Management Review*, **19** (2), 312–30.

Webb, D., G. N. Soutar, T. Mazzarol, and P. Saldaris (2013), 'Self-determination theory and consumer behavioural change: Evidence from a household energy-saving behaviour study', *Journal of Environmental Psychology*, **35**, 59–66.

Werner, C. M. (2013), 'Designing interventions that encourage permanent changes in behavior', in A. H. Huffman and S. R. Klein (eds), *Green Organizations. Driving Change with I-O Psychology*, New York: Routledge, pp. 208–30.

Wheeler, S. and T. Beatley (2014), *The Sustainable Urban Development Reader* (3rd edn), London: Routledge, Taylor and Francis Group.

Wiernik, B. M., S. Dilchert, and D. S. Ones (2016), 'Age and employee green behaviors: A meta-analysis', *Frontiers in Psychology*, 7, 194.

Wrzesniewski, A. and J. E. Dutton (2001), 'Crafting a job: Revisioning employees as active crafters of their work', *Academy of Management Review*, **26** (2), 179–201.

14. A socio-motivational perspective on energy conservation in the workplace: the potential of motivational interviewing

Amelie V. Güntner, Florian E. Klonek and Simone Kauffeld

14.1 INTRODUCTION

In contributing to the overall reduction of greenhouse gas emissions, activities that help improve energy efficiency are recognised as promising. Promoting investments in energy infrastructures, for example applying energy-saving building technology, is one line of strategy to tackle this challenge. At the same time, the potential of energy consumption-reducing investments can only partially be exploited if the people sitting inside the building behave in such a way that less energy is wasted (Janda 2011). This issue brings up the question of how employees (i.e., people in buildings) can be motivated to reduce their energy conservations in a sustainable long-lasting manner (Siero et al. 1996). While private households offer several possibilities to conserve energy, this can be challenging in the workplace (Endrejat et al. 2015). As a result, energy-saving interventions in organisations should focus on building up employees' motivation towards energy conservation before they are asked to change their behaviours (Matthies 2013). The present chapter addresses the challenge of motivating employees regarding energy conservation, by providing a socio-motivational and micro-interactional perspective on energy conservations in the workplace. First, we build on change management research to highlight the socio-relational and motivational dynamics between energy managers and employees in conversations about energy-related behaviour change. Second, we introduce Motivational Interviewing (MI) as a socio-relational approach that offers potential to help energy managers in discussing energy savings with employees. Third, we will outline how introductory training in MI for energy managers can be designed, give detailed information on procedures, and present methodological approaches to evaluate these types of interventions. Finally, we provide a detailed analysis of conversational dynamics between an energy manager and an employee that we evaluated as part of a training evaluation study.

14.2   A CHANGE MANAGEMENT MICRO-COMMUNICATION PERSPECTIVE ON RESISTANCE TO ENERGY CONSERVATION

Embedding environmental sustainability into an organisation often represents a challenge to those who have the task to communicate and implement the change measures. This task is often carried out by organisational change agents (Benn et al. 2014) – that is, individuals who are in charge of communicating and promoting the aspired change (Rogers 2003). In the case of energy conservation, change agents are usually energy managers who are working on steering the organisational members through the adaptations that come along with changes in the consumption of energy. At the same time, employees who consume energy can be described as change recipients because they have to carry out a change measure, that is, saving energy (Ford et al. 2008; Kanter et al. 1992).

Previous research has pointed to the negative effects of poor communication by change agents on the successful implementation of behaviour change (see e.g., Gilley et al. 2009; Klonek et al. 2014). From a relational perspective (Cowan and Presbury 2000; Ford et al. 2008), resistance towards change is considered an interactive process (Dent and Goldberg 1999). That is, resistance is regarded to be not merely an attitude the change recipient has developed within himself, but also to be a phenomenon that emerges between the micro-interactions of the change agent and the change recipient (Cowan and Presbury 2000; Ford et al. 2008; Klonek et al. 2014). That said, previous research has argued that the definition of the term 'resistance' must incorporate a much broader scope, and reformulated resistance as *ambivalence* (e.g., Engle and Arkowitz 2008). Ambivalence is described as a state in which individuals have two simultaneously concurring motivations (Miller and Rollnick 2013). In terms of pro-environmental behaviour this involves, for example, that people struggle with the inconvenient yet positive outcomes that a requested change of their environmental behaviour might involve (Castro et al. 2009; Chang 2011; Ojala 2008). In light of this challenge to organisations, we propose the need for training for energy managers to help them deal with resistance (i.e., ambivalence) and better motivate employees to engage in energy-saving behaviour.

14.3   THE BASIC TENETS OF MOTIVATIONAL INTERVIEWING (MI)

In addressing the challenge of motivating employees to save energy at work, we present the potential of MI. MI offers energy managers or environmental inspectors a new perspective on how to communicate energy conservation behaviour. That is, MI can provide valuable support in light of employee resistance towards change. MI is defined as a 'collaborative conversation style for strengthening a person's own motivation and commitment to change' (Miller and Rollnick 2013: 12). By means of resolving the change recipient's ambivalence and strengthening their intrinsic motivation, MI aims to motivate a person to reach a change-related goal (Miller and Rollnick 2013).

MI originates from clinical psychology and was developed as a way to motivate participants for drug and alcohol treatment or for a change of consumption behaviour (Miller and Rollnick 2013). Within the clinical setting, numerous meta-analyses have established MI as an evidence-based intervention method for behaviour change (e.g., Hettema et al. 2005; Lundahl et al. 2010; Magill et al. 2014). Besides recent studies that have proposed MI within the organisational context, for example, to improve team meetings (Klonek et al. 2015b), in career counselling or coaching (Klonek et al. 2016; Passmore 2007; Stoltz and Young 2013), another line of research has further proposed MI as a means to reduce energy consumption in organisations (Endrejat et al. 2015; Forsberg et al. 2014; Klonek and Kauffeld 2015), or as an approach in change management (Klonek et al. 2014).

MI can be directly contrasted to confrontational and autonomy-restrictive approaches, that is, it focuses on a generally empathetic person-centred style (Miller and Rose 2009). A core idea in MI is that people are almost never solely resistant towards change but rather they often express ambivalence towards change (Miller and Rollnick 2013). This mindset affects how change agents who employ an MI approach listen to what their change recipient tells them. MI suggests that individuals who are ambivalent possess a voice that speaks in favour of change (i.e., change talk) and a voice that argues against change (i.e., sustain talk; Miller and Rollnick 2013). Accordingly, paying attention to employees' verbal expressions within change-related conversations can provide information about their readiness and their resistance to change (Klonek et al. 2015b). When it comes to energy conservation in the workplace, employees may be ruminating whether saving energy will pay off, without being able to make a clear commitment to take actions. When employees are granted autonomy, they are likely to react with enhanced self-motivation towards behaviour change (Osbaldiston and Sheldon 2003; Ryan and Deci 2000). This indicates that autonomy-supportive communication with employees plays a critical role. However, the idea to motivate others for behaviour change is often tied to what is called 'the righting reflex' (Miller and Rollnick 2013). It occurs from the belief that one 'must convince or persuade the other [person] to do the right thing' (Miller and Rollnick 2013: 10), and describes behaviours such as persuading ('I would suggest you start printing less papers'), confronting/warning ('Think about the negative consequences for the environment'), or directing/preaching ('You should not use others as an excuse'). Unfortunately, the righting reflex is in direct contrast to autonomy-supportive behaviours and can increase levels of resistance towards behaviour change (Miller and Rollnick 2013). For these reasons, MI explicitly argues to abstain from behaviours like confronting, preaching, and persuading.

To create circumstances that fulfil people's need for autonomy and help individuals strengthen their intrinsic motivation, MI combines relational (e.g., empathy and respect for client autonomy) with technical (e.g., open questions, affirmations, reflections) components (Magill et al. 2014; see Figure 14.1). A conversation that follows an MI approach has two main phases: in the initial phase, the change agent seeks to evoke intrinsic motivation to change the target behaviour – that is, in the case of energy conservation at work – 'conserving energy at the workplace'. The change agent would enter the second phase only when the employee has expressed increased motivation to save energy. In that case, the change agent will focus on eliciting verbal commitments (e.g., 'I will switch off the lights, every time I leave the room') or action plans ('These are four steps that will help me to conserve energy in the future . . .') and discuss behaviour change goals (i.e., saving more energy). The overall MI approach is build on four processes: *engaging, focusing, evoking,* and *planning*. These processes are put into practice through a set of specific micro-behaviours (Figure 14.1 only depicts a selection).

In the following, we will provide a brief overview of the most important verbal micro-behaviours that are often part of MI. In short, the person-centred communication approach in MI is covered by the basic micro-behaviours while the directive and goal-oriented approach is realised by using the complex micro-behaviours (cf., Figure 14.1). The purely person-centred micro-behaviours are often summarised by the acronym OARS (Miller and Rollnick 2013): Open-ended questions, Affirmations, Reflective listening, and Summaries. The acronym OARS serves as a metaphor that illustrates how basic MI micro-behaviours constitute oars of a skiff when going through wild waters, that is, having a dynamic interaction with another person in which the verbal interaction constitutes a 'stream' that is often unpredictable (Klonek and Kauffeld 2015). The change agent needs the oars of the skiff as basic tools to manage through the wild waters. Table 14.1 presents examples of the basic micro-behaviours (OARS).

In our experience of providing introductory MI training for energy managers, trainers should focus on using OARS in order to help them

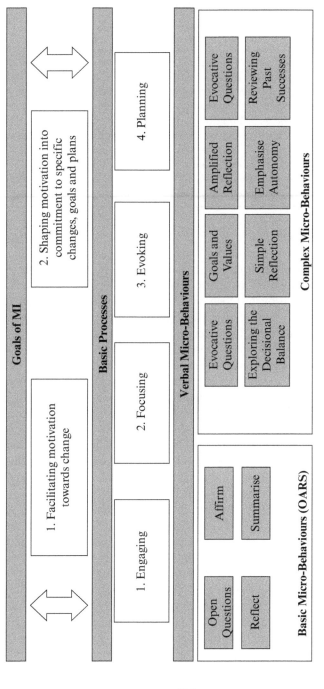

Source: Based on Klonek and Kauffeld (2012); Miller and Rollnick (2013).

Figure 14.1 Overview of the components of MI

Table 14.1   Person-centred micro-behaviours of MI (OARS)

Micro-Behaviour	Example Phrase
Open question	'What would help you remember to do this, every time you leave the office?'
Affirmation	'You have come up with a lot of great ideas.'
Reflective listening	*Employee*: 'We cannot just turn off the ventilation around here . . . You cannot interrupt our operating processes!' *Energy Manager*: 'You would prefer the implementation of energy-saving measures that do not interrupt your work.'
Summarising	'Let's go over what we have talked about so far. You said you will call the facility manager and ask him to install a motion detector in your department . . .'

establish an atmosphere of empathy and rapport in which employees can reflect on their own behaviour.

Both open-ended questions and reflective listening, as part of the four OARS micro-behaviours, originate from Rogers' (1951) person-centred communication approach. Open-ended questions provide a broad base for eliciting employees' reasons for behaviour change and exploring opportunities to increase their energy-saving behaviour. In using open-ended questions, in contrast to closed-ended questions, energy managers can promote a flowing conversation with the employee. Next to asking specific questions, energy managers can make use of reflective listening to encourage mutual understanding. Reflections, meaning repeating or paraphrasing what a change recipient said (Rogers 1951), serve as a means for energy managers to express their empathy towards employees. Furthermore, in using reflections, energy managers have the option to steer the conversation in a desired direction towards behaviour change. That is, if the employee gets caught in a spiral of arguments against change (i.e., sustain talk), the energy manager can choose to emphasise and strengthen primarily the statements that are in favour of change. Furthermore, the 'A' in OARS represents the skill of using affirmation statements in order to acknowledge employees' past steps in energy conservation and to build employees' self-efficacy regarding further energy-saving measures. Finally, the OARS are completed by the skill of summarising, a form of reflective listening, which can be used to review the conversation at the end or to move from one topic to another within the conversation.

While we have presented the basic tenets and conversational approach of MI, the next part introduces how organisations, which wish to conserve energy or other environmental resources, can implement the intervention.

14.4   IMPLEMENTING MI INTO ORGANISATIONS: SOME THOUGHTS ABOUT TRAINING DESIGN AND MODES OF DELIVERY

We have introduced MI as a new socio-motivational approach to foster sustainable energy conservation in organisations. MI brings in a new perspective on change conversations by training autonomy-supportive behaviours (e.g., affirming or emphasising the change recipient's control) and to restrain from autonomy-restrictive behaviours (e.g., confronting or persuading without permission). Accordingly, we argue that the knowledge transfer of adequate employee communication should feature MI skills prominently in communication training for energy managers. Since MI is a complex conversational skill, it requires training in order to be carried out in a way that provides adherence to the original concept. From a practical point of view, Human Resource managers and training agencies may need some guidance when advising organisations on how much training is necessary to properly implement MI into an organisation. In the following, we will provide some rough overview about the effects of MI training studies and discuss their impact in the context of organisational energy conservation.

14.4.1   Does MI Training Even Make a Difference?

Since MI has a long evidence-based research tradition, there is a substantial amount of training studies that have evaluated the impact of MI training on trainee conversational skills (de Roten et al. 2013). Most studies originate from the helping professions and show that even relatively short communication training in MI can have a measurable impact on the communication skills of those who apply it (Catley et al. 2006; Opheim et al. 2009; Tollison et al. 2008). For example, in a study by Opheim et al. (2009), medical students who received only 4 hours of an MI introductory training asked their conversational partner significantly more open-ended questions than did participants from a control group with no training. A meta-analysis on MI training studies in the clinical context (de Roten et al. 2013) showed that a 2-day training has on average an overall positive effect on verbal skills. Additional post-training coaching and individualised feedback even led to slightly higher effect sizes. There are only a few studies that evaluated MI training in the context of environmental conservation (Forsberg et al. 2014; Klonek and Kauffeld 2015, 2016). For example, Forsberg et al. (2014) trained environmental inspectors in Sweden and reported that it helped to improve their reflective listening skills. A study by Klonek and Kauffeld (2015) showed that trainees, namely engineering students, significantly increased their verbal skills in MI after a 2-day training. The authors also reported that the expressed motivation of their respective conversational partners was higher compared to the motivation of partners in the pre-training condition. The study further provides a transcribed post-training conversation in which the trainee discussed waste separation with his conversational partner in order to illustrate some basic concepts of MI. Further studies that apply MI in the environmental context, for instance, with regard to waste sorting and radiation, are currently in preparation (Herzing et al. in prep.; Wickström et al. in prep.).

14.4.2   How do Organisations Evaluate the Impact of MI Training?

Since the application of MI in the context of pro-environmental strategies is still relatively new, organisational developers may want to evaluate the impact of training and ongoing developmental measures themselves (e.g., coaching for trainees, feedback). To give readers a better understanding about measuring MI skills, we will use the next section to present details on the evaluation of MI in practice.

When it comes to evaluating individuals' MI skills, for example, as part of a pre-training skills screening or post-training evaluation, researchers and practitioners have a variety of options. Building on the evaluation model of Kirkpatrick (1996) that comprises: *reaction* (1), *learning* (2), *behaviour* (3), and *results* (4), training evaluation measures in MI can be ordered along these four levels. The four levels describe the criteria that need to be analysed step by step in order to derive meaningful results about the effectiveness and the return on investment of training measures.

The reactional level (1) is used to measure how trainees have responded to the training itself, meaning whether the trainees were satisfied with the training which is a prerequisite for the training's effectiveness (Kirkpatrick, 1996). These evaluations can be based on self-ratings about interest in the MI approach and its principles and specific skills.

The measurement at the learning level (2) can be used to determine whether the training helped in improving trainees' knowledge and complemented their skills (Kirkpatrick 1996). There is a variety of MI knowledge tests that allow to measure if trainees can recognise or even name specific MI concepts. With respect to reflective listening, one of the key skills in MI, organisations and scholars can use an adapted version of the original Helpful Response Questionnaire (original version from Miller et al. 1991), which was specifically designed to assess skills in reflective listening for energy managers (HRQ-E; Endrejat et al. 2015, 2017). Because the skill of reflective listening is crucial to the use of MI, previous research has frequently used the HRQ to assess individuals' skills in MI (see e.g., Madson et al. 2009). The HRQ-E is a multiple choice instrument comprising seven statements (= items) from employees who are yet unwilling to change their behaviour towards more energy-saving behaviour (Endrejat et al. 2015, 2017). These statements were based on a qualitative study by Murtagh et al. (2013) who categorised 'reasons not to switch off'. These are, for example, *inconvenience/speed, savings are too small*, or *political* (cf., Murtagh et al. 2013: 723). With each statement, four answering alternatives are presented and trainees (i.e., energy managers) are asked to select the response they think they would most likely give in that hypothetical situation. Of these answering alternatives, one option is reflective listening, and the remaining three options are fillers. Trainees who choose the reflective listening response achieve a higher score.

The behavioural level (3) evaluates whether the trainees can apply acquired skills in practice and, thus, transfer it into their workplace (Kirkpatrick 1996). In order to do this with respect to MI, researchers need to collect (or record) a behaviour change conversation between an energy manager and an employee. A variety of objective rating and coding instruments is available to be used to evaluate MI consistent communication skills. One of the most common is the *Motivational Interviewing Treatment Integrity Code* (MITI 4.2.1; Moyers et al. 2014). The MITI was originally designed as an economical instrument to assess adherence to the intervention of MI. This is of particular importance for evidence-based intervention research, that is, when testing the effectiveness of an MI intervention for a specific behaviour change context (e.g., energy conservation). The MITI provides behavioural counts that indicate the extent of behaviours that are consistent and inconsistent with an MI approach (Klonek et al. 2015c). Further information on the specific codes defined in the MITI will be presented later as part of a coded transcript from a change interaction. Moreover, Moyers et al. (2014) have proposed MI benchmarks in order to assess the proficiency levels of MI. These benchmarks consist of several verbal dimensions, such as the relative amount of open-ended questions, the rate of reflective listening, and specific MI consistent behaviours (persuading with permission, affirming). These benchmarks could to a certain extent also be applied to energy managers' communication skills in environmental conversations.

At the result level (4), we can measure the effectiveness of the training, that is, it evaluates whether the training has created added value for the organisation as a whole (Kirkpatrick 1996). In the context of energy conservation, it could be argued that the effectiveness of the MI training should be reflected in a decrease of energy consumption. Research to date fails to provide indicators in support of this, for instance, lower energy costs as a result of MI training for energy managers. However, the context of change in the workplace provides an additional way of measuring the effectiveness of MI training for energy managers – that is, measuring whether the training helped to increase employee motivation for a change in their energy consumption. Previous research from the clinical field points to the advantages of observational measures in assessing motivation for and against change, such as the elimination of self-representation bias (Westra 2011). Likewise, this is also evident when individuals are asked to self-report on their energy conservation, they tend to overestimate the degree to which they actually engage in energy-saving behaviour (Corral-Verdugo 2002).

An alternative solution is provided by using recorded conversations between an energy manager and an employee to assess the motivational language of the employee. One relatively simple observational instrument is the Client Language Easy Rating (CLEAR) Coding System (Glynn and Moyers 2012). It allows researchers to assess the motivational response of the change recipient within a behaviour change conversation. The coding system differentiates between change talk (i.e., statements with a positive inclination towards energy conservation), sustain talk (i.e., statements with negative inclination towards energy conservation), and neutral responses (i.e., statements unrelated to energy conservation). The results of coding employee communication can also be used to map the verbally expressed motivation of an employee over the course of a conversation in a dynamic motivation curve (Klonek et al. 2015b). For this, a so-called Readiness/Resistance-curve can be calculated that captures the verbally expressed willingness (change talk) or resistance (sustain talk) over the entire interaction. Interactive video examples which demonstrate the dynamic course of R-curves in the context of energy consumption are available as free online material (cf., Klonek and Kauffeld 2015).

14.5   AN EXAMPLE/CASE STUDY OF MI TRAINING FOR ENERGY MANAGERS

To assist practitioners and researchers rolling out MI training that aims to foster environmental conservation, we will present a training design that we developed as part of an energy-saving project for non-residential buildings.

14.5.1   Designing MI Training for Energy Managers

The overall goal of the training was to give energy managers an introduction to MI and let them get an idea of the application of MI. That said, we wanted energy managers to not only get familiar with the fundamental principles of MI and learn the basic micro-behaviours but also to have direct practice and experience with an MI approach. In order to do so, we took existing MI training formats from the Motivational Interviewing Network of Trainers (MINT Network of Trainers 2014) and adjusted them to create introductory MI training specifically for energy managers. In structuring our training intervention, we also followed the eight stages in learning MI (Miller and Moyers 2006). The authors propose a set of eight stages of MI proficiency that come along with specific skills and learning steps. Because our intervention should serve as introductory training, we designed our training on the basis of stage 1–5 (see Table 14.2 for a detailed training schedule).

14.5.2   What Skills did MI Training Cover?

The first of the two training parts covers content on the learning stages 1 to 4, that is, *the spirit of MI* (1), *OARS-Skills* (2), *recognising and reinforcing change talk* (3), as well as *eliciting and strengthening change talk* (4). In that part, trainers focus on the introduction of MI and its idea of a person-centred communication approach. This includes not only theoretical input by the trainer, but mostly the trainer goes into exchange with the energy managers and encourages them to self-reflect on their personal experiences with employees at their workplace. Additionally, energy managers have the opportunity to practice the skills they learned, for instance, using open-ended questions and reflections. In doing so, the first part covers MI principles and the basic micro-behaviours (OARS; cf., Figure 14.1). To evaluate training effectiveness, we start training sessions by asking energy managers to go into groups and motivate the conversational partner for energy conservation and to record the conversation (see Table 14.2).

The second part of the training introduces stage 5, that is, *rolling with resistance*. It covers complex micro-behaviours that can be used in realising a more directive and goal-oriented approach (cf., Figure 14.1). Besides teaching energy managers to use behaviours that adhere with an MI approach, it is equally important to emphasise the potential harmful effect of autonomy-restrictive communication (i.e., MI non-adherent behaviours) on employees' motivation to change. Autonomy-restrictive behaviours (e.g., persuading without permission, confronting, criticising, directing, arguing) are supposed to weaken the intrinsic motivation of change recipients and arouse reactance (Brehm and Brehm 2013; Miller and Rollnick 2013). Because energy managers are experts in the area of energy savings, we expect them to particularly rely on the righting reflex, that is, for them to show autonomy-restrictive behaviours. Therefore, we

Table 14.2   Overview of the introductory MI training for energy managers

Content	Aim	Facilitation	Learning Stage in MI[a]
Part I: learning MI principles and basic skills (OARS)			
Welcome: introduction and overview of training	Getting to know each other; give participants an idea about the content and process	Flip chart welcome; flip chart trainer profile; flip chart schedule day 1 and 2	
Eliciting expectations: What outcomes do trainees *desire* from the training? What *skills* do they already possess to discuss energy savings at work?	Stimulating trainees' change talk to increase motivation for training, listening for trainees' abilities, experience and background	'Tree of expectation'; Using two evocative questions that stimulate change talk: Pin board; pin board cards (green = skills; red = desire)	
MI competence screening (pre): Trainees have a conversation about behaviour change in groups of two. Role play: One change agent, one change recipient. Two turns with swapping roles. 25 mins. time for each conversation + buffer **Debriefing:** – How did the conversation go? – What was difficult? – What may help?	Assessing trainees' MI competence; have trainees record their conversations so they can receive individual feedback Hearing about trainees' self-perception in the role of change agent and recipient, experiences, and encourage them to self-reflect	Hand out role play instructions; tape recorders; optional: questionnaire for recipients to fill out	
Input MI (MI spirit and basic principles): Introduce the elements of MI spirit and main MI principles	Transferring knowledge about the background of MI and its key components	Pin board; pin cards with MI elements to create an overview of MI (cf. Figure 14.1)	**Stage 1:** MI Spirit

298

Micro-behaviour I – Open questions: identify and formulate open questions	Trainees learn the difference between open and closed questions; increase awareness for person-centred communication	Handout with examples of open and closed questions	**Stage 2:** OARS-Skills
Evocative questions: motivating vs. demotivating open questions; trainees formulate questions that evoke change talk and sustain talk	Trainees learn to recognise and elicit change talk	Pin board with table for motivating vs. demotivating questions; pin cards	**Stage 2:** OARS-Skills **Stage 3:** recognising and reinforcing change talk **Stage 4:** eliciting and strengthening change talk
Micro-behaviour II – Affirmation: Input on the effect of affirmations and 'break task': What does it mean for you to be appreciated by s.o.?	Transferring knowledge about the effect of affirmations in human interactions; encourage trainees to reflect on authentic affirmations		**Stage 2:** OARS-Skills **Stage 4:** eliciting and strengthening change talk
Break			
Micro-behaviour III – Reflective listening: Input on active listening (communication model Thomas Gordon[b]); input on MI non-adherent behaviour	Transferring knowledge about empathic behaviour; trainees expand their knowledge on evoking and strengthening change talk	Flipchart Thomas Gordon model; flipchart MI non-adherence	**Stage 2:** OARS-Skills **Stage 4:** eliciting and strengthening change talk
Written exercise: how to formulate reflections	In-depth practice of reflective listening (strengthening change talk)	Handout with statements of employees (based on Murtagh et al. 2013)	**Stage 2:** OARS-Skills **Stage 3:** recognising and reinforcing change talk

Table 14.2 (continued)

Content	Aim	Facilitation	Learning Stage in MI[a]
Exercise: hold a conversation with a partner using solely open questions and reflections (teams of three: change agent, change recipient, and observer; 5 min per conversation)	Introducing open questions and reflections in an ongoing conversation	Handout with instructions; observer sheet	**Stage 4:** eliciting and strengthening change talk
Micro-behaviour IV – Summarise: Input trainer	Transferring knowledge and discussing the application in energy-related conversations	Handout with example of a good summary	**Stage 2:** OARS-Skills **Stage 3:** recognising and reinforcing change talk **Stage 4:** eliciting and strengthening change talk
Reflection and conclusion: Let trainees line up on a scale from 1 to 10, regarding:	Let trainees reflect on their insights on day 1 and gather suggestions on how to improve the next training day	Flip chart with reflection questions (see also Readiness Ruler Line-up;	**Stage 2:** OARS-Skills **Stage 3:** recognising and reinforcing change talk **Stage 4:** eliciting and strengthening change talk

300

			TNT Manual, MINT 2014, p. 19)
– How great was your personal gain in knowledge? – How confident are you that you will use the micro-behaviours you learned? Optional: 'What needs to happen to increase your knowledge/confidence on the next training day?'			
Part II: learning to roll with the resistance **Welcome:** recapitulation of day 1 and overview of the schedule of day 2; reflecting trainees' experiences with MI in their daily work – What worked well? – What is still difficult?	Giving an overview on the training content; hearing participants' experiences using the confidence balance	Flip chart welcome; flip chart schedule day 1 and 2; flip chart reflection questions	
Feedback on trainees' first conversation practice: Explain the coding scheme and procedure; hand out two feedback sheets: one for MI competence, one for employee motivation (R-index)	Giving trainees feedback on their MI competence from first training day	Individual feedback sheets for each trainee	
8 micro-behaviours – Rolling with resistance:[c] Introduction; reflection questions: – How do people express resistance? – How can I strengthen resistance? – How can I soften resistance?	Evoking trainees own behavioural strategies in dealing with resistance (in a good or bad way)	Flip chart with table and three reflection questions	**Stage 5:** rolling with resistance

Table 14.2 (continued)

Content	Aim	Facilitation	Learning Stage in MI[a]
Trainer collects answers on flip chart 8 micro-behaviours to roll with resistance: Distribute handout and go through 8 micro-behaviours with all trainees; add pin cards on MI chart	Transferring knowledge and discussing the application in energy-related conversations	Handout rolling with resistance; pin cards with 8 micro-behaviours	**Stage 5:** rolling with resistance
Written exercise: trainees write down a typical statement of employee resistance (personal experience); trainees respond to this statement using each from the 8 micro-behaviours	Practising responding appropriately to resistance on paper	Handout responding to resistance	**Stage 5:** rolling with resistance
Break			
8 micro-behaviours – Develop discrepancy: Recap of the meaning of change and sustain talk; distribute handout and go through the 8 micro-behaviours with all trainees; add pin cards on MI chart; distribute handout	Transferring knowledge and discussing the application in energy-related conversations	Handout developing discrepancy; pin cards with 8 micro-behaviours	**Stage 3:** recognising and reinforcing change talk **Stage 4:** eliciting and strengthening change talk

Demo tape energy manager A (negative example): Play demo tape from a conversation with MI non-adherent communication; ask participants what comes to their attention; debrief showing R-index	Transferring knowledge and creating awareness for negative conversational dynamics	Laptop; projector; speakers; demo tape energy manager A	**Stage 3**: recognising and reinforcing change talk
Demo energy manager[d] B (positive example): Play demo tape from a conversation with MI consistent communication; ask participants what comes to their attention; debrief showing R-index	Transferring knowledge and presenting a positive example for an MI conversation	Laptop; projector; speakers; demo tape energy manager B	**Stage 3**: recognising and reinforcing change talk
MI competence screening (post): HRQ-E[e] Trainees fill out the HRQ-E	Assessing trainees' MI competence	Handout HRQ-E	**Stage 2:** OARS-Skills **Stage 3**: recognising and reinforcing change talk **Stage 4**: eliciting and strengthening change talk

Notes:
a Miller and Moyers (2006).
b MINT (2014: 71),
c MINT (2014: 155 ff.).
d Klonek and Kauffeld 2015; demonstration tapes can be downloaded without charge from https://doi.org/10.3389/fpsyg.2015.00252.
e Endrejat et al. (2015, 2017).

provide energy managers with detailed feedback about their autonomy-restrictive behaviours that occurred within their recorded conversation from the beginning of the training. Alternatively, energy managers can be asked to submit a recorded energy-saving conversation before training. Furthermore, we incorporate exercises in the training that illustrate the harm of autonomy-restrictive communication (cf., Klonek and Kauffeld 2015; see also Table 14.2). The training is wrapped up by asking energy managers to fill out the HRQ-E (Endrejat et al. 2015).

14.5.3   Pre-training Evaluation of Energy Managers' Communication Skills

At the beginning of training, we conduct a pre-training screening (MINT 2014). This can be used to give trainees feedback about their communication strengths and possibilities for improvement. While a range of options for pre-training screening exists, we use an observation-based approach, that is, we code audio-tapes of trainees who discuss energy conservation with a change recipient (i.e., an employee). Even though this approach substantially increases the workload for the trainer (in contrast to using self-reported skill measures), we use it, as it is common practice within the research tradition of MI to analyse audiotaped work samples with validated coding schemes. Therefore, we either ask energy managers prior to the training to send us an audiotaped conversation in which they motivated another person to show energy-saving behaviour or, alternatively, we put this as a first exercise at the beginning of the training. We analyse the conversations using INTERACT (Mangold 2010), a software that can substantially economise coding efforts (e.g., Klonek et al. 2015c) and provides a time-sensitive annotation of the interactional stream. To better depict the conversational dynamics of these conversations, we took an excerpt from one of these conversations, transcribed it, and assigned the relevant behaviour codes from both MITI (Moyers et al. 2014) and CLEAR (Glynn and Moyers 2012) (see Table 14.3). The most recent version of the MITI differentiates between ten codes that are intended to capture communication skills in MI: (a) Giving Information, (b) Persuade, (c) Persuade with Permission, (d) Question, (e) Simple Reflection, (f) Complex Reflection, (g) Affirm, (h) Seeking Collaboration, (i) Emphasising Autonomy, and (j) Confront. The MITI is not an exhaustive coding system, that is, some utterances are not coded at all (e.g., structure statements, greetings, off-topic material).

When the energy manager starts outlining the purpose of the conversation, the employee agrees that there is still space for improving her energy consumption. Instead of appreciating her willingness (i.e., recommended from an MI perspective), the energy manager confronts her by pointing out that she is not acting in a very environmentally friendly manner. On top of this, he tries to persuade her by getting her onto the 'right track'. As this likely threatens her autonomy, she resists change by clarifying that she might not agree with his plans. When the energy manager continues referring to the questionnaire about her energy-saving behaviour, he asks demotivating open questions, that is, he asks what prevents her from switching off her laptop – a question that likely evokes sustain talk (a positive evocative question would ask her what would help her to switch off the laptop). In the following, the energy manager expresses understanding in the first place, but then he persuades the employee to try the standby function. While the employee agrees to give it some thought, the energy manager misses the opportunity to affirm the employee's willingness but instead follows up on her laptop use and insists that it would be better if she switches off her laptop. He tries to persuade her to get help from their computer specialists – even when she keeps naming reasons against doing it. What we can observe at this point are negative conversational dynamics, typically elicited due to the righting reflex. Because the energy manager hears the employee arguing against energy conservation, he feels the need to increase the pressure to get her on the 'right track'. Most likely, he does so with the best intentions, for instance, doing good towards the environment, but his confrontations encourage the employee to justify her actions, resulting in sustain talk. In the course of the conversation that follows, the energy manager keeps being trapped into this reflex, for example, when the employee does not agree with switching the light off when leaving a room. Furthermore, he misses the chance to evoke change talk, e.g., through asking for her personal benefits envisaged when saving energy. Overall, the energy manager is not empathic, indicated by the low use of reflections. In sum, this transcript illustrates the confronting and autonomy-restrictive style that can be used by energy managers when they have the task to motivate employees to be more energy-efficient. Our experiences and observations with energy managers at a University of Technology in Germany are in line with previous research in that field (e.g., Klonek et al. 2015a).

14.6   RECOMMENDATIONS FOR PRACTITIONERS

In sum, the current chapter presented a socio-motivational perspective on increasing employees' energy-saving behaviour. We highlighted the need for preserving employees' autonomy and provided a micro-communication perspective from change management on employees'

Table 14.3 *Example transcript from a coded conversation between an energy manager and an employee*

Speaker	Transcript	Code
Energy manager	[Mrs. Smith, now that I've got your evaluation sheet here, I would like to have a look at the aspects where you still have potential to be more energy-efficient. Especially in the sense of our environment.]	No Code
Employee	[Probably still quite some potential, I guess.]	Change Talk
Energy manager	[Because saving energy is not only about the money, but I personally think it is important that we act sustainably to protect the environment.] [And then I see that you are not acting as strictly as I do.] [But perhaps I can get you onto the right track.]	Persuade Confront Persuade
Employee	[Well, if I want to be set onto the 'right track.']	Sustain Talk
Energy manager	[For example, let us take a look around here, I will call it a bit of an outlier, where you say: 'I never switch off electronic devices, for example laptop, in longer breaks.'] [Why do you not switch it off, for example, when you go for lunch? What is stopping you?]	Giving Information Question
Employee	[Because I find it annoying to start my laptop again after lunch break. Until the laptop is ready to use, already five minutes have passed and I find this quite annoying.] [And I am also not sure whether switching my laptop off for half an hour actually has an effect.]	Sustain Talk Sustain Talk
Energy manager	[Yes, I can understand that.] [But you know this function CTRL + Alt + Delete?] [This is the stand-by button, which means your laptop only uses less energy. And if you turn it on again, you only have to log in and all programs are back up immediately.] [So you could just try it and if you are not exactly sure, you could ask a colleague for help.]	No Code Question Giving Information Persuade
Employee	[Okay, I might think about it.]	Change Talk
Energy manager	[How did you do it this morning before seeing me?]	Question
Employee	[This morning, I just got up from my seat and left.]	Sustain Talk
Energy manager	[So, and you are saying that you got up and left.] [Of course, it would be desirable that you switch your laptop off during such long	Simple Reflection Persuade

Table 14.3   (continued)

Speaker	Transcript	Code
	breaks. That really helps. So if you leave your desk for four hours, it really has an effect on your energy consumption, if you switch off your laptop during that time.]	
Employee	[Well, yes, I can see that it makes sense to completely turn off my laptop when I am away from my desk for such a long time.] [It is just I am not aware of it at that exact moment.]	Change Talk Sustain Talk
Energy manager	[I think it might help, if you watch yourself more closely and think about where you can perhaps use a stand-by function. Perhaps there is also a possibility that you get another laptop that boots faster.]	Persuade
Employee	[No, I cannot use that as an excuse. I just got a new laptop.]	Sustain Talk
Energy manager	[Then you really should talk with your computer specialists and ask them to change the settings of your stand-by function accordingly. You could just check again what is possible in terms of saving energy.] [Now, next topic: what about the light? Is it turned on in a room even when it is not used by someone?]	Persuade Open Question
Employee	[That depends.] [If it is a room that I share with others, then the light remains on, because I can assume five minutes later someone comes back and turns on the light again.]	Change Talk Sustain Talk
Energy manager	[Ok, and why would that be a problem?] [Because actually, I think this is nothing bad.]	Question Confront
Employee	[I do not know exactly, but it may also consume additional energy, if the lamp is constantly switched on and off. And perhaps it breaks relatively easily.]	Sustain Talk
Energy manager	[Yes, that probably depends on the light bulbs you use.] [You could get some information about that.]	Giving Information Persuade
Employee	[Well, it is not my job to take care of this, really. I do not climb onto my seat to check the light bulbs. This is more the matter of the facility manager or someone like him.]	Sustain Talk
Energy manager	[Yes, you might be right, that is true.] [When it comes to your overall energy-saving behaviour	No Code Question

Table 14.3   (continued)

Speaker	Transcript	Code
	at work, do you think that there is room for improvement?]	
Employee	[Yes, this is the only thing I can think of.] [Other than that, I am relatively restricted. The printer must be on during the whole day, because many colleagues need to access it, too. I cannot just turn it off. Same thing with the light.]	Change Talk Sustain Talk
Energy manager	[And how is that when you air the room? Is it intermittent ventilation or do you permanently tip the windows?]	Question
Employee	[At work, we air relatively little, because we have a ventilation system.] [And at home, I usually ventilate intensively. So I turn the heating off, open the windows for ten minutes and then close the windows again and turn the heating back on.]	Neutral Following Change Talk
Energy manager	[Right, this is already very energy-saving. Because when you tip the window and the heating remains on, nothing of the heat remains.]	Giving Information
Employee	[Yes, exactly. I mean, it is not like I am a polluter or anything.] [But there are some things I just need to feel comfortable at home. I would like to relax there and therefore I just need my home to be warm. And I always wash my hands with warm water, even in summer, because that just relaxes me.] [And I just want to grant this to myself.] [I do not have a car.] [So I find, I have quite some 'bonus' already.]	Change Talk Sustain Talk Sustain Talk Change Talk Sustain Talk
Energy manager	[Yes, I also find the overall impression of your energy consumption, which may not be that excellent, is actually quite alright when you consider the fact that you are in an environment where there are simply many electrical devices. And you are also aware of the aspects where you can save energy.]	Affirm

resistance to energy conservation. Based on that, we introduced MI as a socio-interactional intervention that can be used by organisations to tackle energy conservation in the workplace. Readers learned about MI training and HR departments, training agencies, and researchers were provided with best-practice guidelines for implementation of MI training in organisations. We have argued that organisations should consider offering qualifications in MI to qualify energy managers and any organisational members who are responsible to monitor and control sustainable behaviour (e.g., supervisors, members of an organisational sustainability group[1]). The training and evaluation concept we illustrated, including the MI approach as a whole, is not restricted to energy conservation, but can be applied in other areas of pro-environmental behaviours, such as recycling behaviour, water usage, or sustainable mobility.

Deriving from our personal experiences with energy managers in MI training, we advise practitioners to be flexible with the handling of their planned training schedules. We found that energy managers regard this kind of training format as useful not only in terms of skill acquisition, but also for meeting with other energy managers and exchanging best practices on how to motivate employees for energy conservation.

Furthermore, we highly encourage trainers to make use of modelling a change-related conversation in MI style during training. If training is delivered by trainers who either have no practical experience in MI or are not skilful in using it, trainers can present trainees with interactive video examples that model MI micro-behaviours in the context of conversation about energy conservation (see also supplementary material in Klonek and Kauffeld 2015; see also demo tape energy manager in Table 14.2).

Moreover, to ensure a sustainable success of training, individual supervision/coaching sessions could be offered to trainees before, during and after the training intervention (see also Forsberg et al. 2014). In doing so, it is recommended to use conversations recorded by the trainee as a basis for individual feedback.

NOTE

1. For example, www.energysavingtrust.org.uk/about-us/corporate-social-responsibility.

REFERENCES

Benn, S., D. Dunphy and A. Griffiths (2014), *Organizational Change for Corporate Sustainability*, Abingdon: Routledge.

Brehm, S.S. and J.W. Brehm (2013), *Psychological Reactance: A Theory of Freedom and Control*, New York: Academic Press.

Castro, P., M. Garrido, E. Reis and J. Menezes (2009), 'Ambivalence and conservation behaviour: An exploratory study on the recycling of metal cans', *Journal of Environmental Psychology*, **29** (1), 24–33.

Catley, D., K.J. Harris, M.S. Mayo, S. Hall, K.S. Okuyemi, T. Boardman and J.S. Ahluwalia (2006), 'Adherence to principles of motivational interviewing and client within-session behavior', *Behavioural and Cognitive Psychotherapy*, **34** (1), 43–56.

Chang, C. (2011), 'Feeling ambivalent about going green', *Journal of Advertising*, **40** (4), 19–32.

Corral-Verdugo, V. (2002), 'A structural model of proenvironmental competency', *Environment and Behavior*, **34** (4), 531–549.

Cowan, E.W. and J.H. Presbury (2000), 'Meeting resistance and reactance with reverence', *Journal of Counseling and Development*, **78** (4), 411–419.

Dent, E.B. and S.G. Goldberg (1999), 'Challenging "resistance to change"', *The Journal of Applied Behavioral Science*, **35** (1), 25–41.

Endrejat, P.C., F.E. Klonek and S. Kauffeld (2015), 'A psychology perspective of energy consumption in organisations: The value of participatory interventions', *Indoor and Built Environment*, **24** (7), 937–949.

Endrejat, P.C., L. Müller-Frommeyer, F.E. Klonek, and S. Kauffeld (2017, August), How to Respond to Resistance to Change? An Analysis of Change Agents' Communication Behaviors, *Academy of Management Meeting*, Atlanta, United States.

Engle, D. and H. Arkowitz (2008), 'Resistance as ambivalence: Integrative strategies for working with resistant ambivalence', *Journal of Humanistic Psychology*, **48** (3), 389–412.

Ford, J.D., L.W. Ford and A. D'Amelio (2008), 'Resistance to change: The rest of the story', *Academy of Management Review*, **33** (2), 362–377.

Forsberg, L., H. Wickström and H. Källmén (2014), 'Motivational interviewing may facilitate professional interactions with inspectees during environmental inspections and enforcement conversations', *Peer Journal*, **2**, e508.

Gilley, A., J.W. Gilley and H.S. McMillan (2009), 'Organizational change: Motivation, communication, and leadership effectiveness', *Performance Improvement Quarterly*, **21** (4), 75–94.

Glynn, L.H. and T.B. Moyers (2012), 'Manual for the Client Language Easy Rating (CLEAR) coding system: Formerly Motivational Interviewing Skill Code (MISC) 1.1', [Online publication], accessed 12 January 2017 at http://casaa.unm.edu/download/CLEAR.pdf.

Herzing, M., H. Wickström, H. Källmén, L. Forsberg, and A. Jacobsson (manuscript in preparation), *Applying Motivational Interviewing to Induce Radon Gas Radiation Measurements by Property Owners*.

Hettema, J., J. Steele and W.R. Miller (2005), 'Motivational Interviewing', *Annual Review of Clinical Psychology*, **1** (1), 91–111.

Janda, K.B. (2011), 'Buildings don't use energy: People do', *Architectural Science Review*, **54** (1), 15–22.

Kanter, R.M., B. Stein and T. Jick (1992), *The Challenge of Organizational Change: How Companies Experience It and Leaders Guide It*, New York: Free Press.

Kirkpatrick, D.L. (1996), 'Great ideas revisited', *Training and Development*, **50** (1), 54–59.

Klonek, F.E. and S. Kauffeld (2012), '"Muss, kann . . . oder will ich was verändern?" Welche Chancen bietet die Motivierende Gesprächsführung in Organisationen' ['"Do I need to, am I able to . . . and do I even want to change?" Which potential does Motivational Interviewing offer for organisations'], *Wirtschaftspsychologie*, **4**, 58–71.

Klonek, F.E. and S. Kauffeld (2015), 'Providing engineers with OARS and EARS: Effects of a skills-based vocational training in Motivational Interviewing for engineers in higher education', *Higher Education, Skills and Work-Based Learning*, **5** (2), 117–134.

Klonek, F.E. and S. Kauffeld (2016), 'Watch your language! Analyzing active ingredients of client speech in a Motivational Interviewing Intervention for Environmental Behavior Change', *Umweltpsychologie*, **20** (1), 62–84.

Klonek, F.E., A.V. Güntner, N.K. Lehmann-Willenbrock and S. Kauffeld (2015a), 'Using Motivational Interviewing to reduce threats in conversations about environmental behavior', *Frontiers in Psychology*, **6**, 1015.

Klonek, F.E., N.K. Lehmann-Willenbrock, and S. Kauffeld (2014), 'Dynamics of resistance to change: A sequential analysis of change agents in action', *Journal of Change Management*, **14** (3), 334–360.

Klonek, F.E., H. Paulsen and S. Kauffeld (2015b), 'They meet, they talk . . . but nothing changes: Meetings as a focal context for studying change processes', in J.A. Allen, N. Lehmann-Willenbrock and S.G. Rogelberg (eds), *The Cambridge Handbook of Meeting Science*, New York: Cambridge University Press.

Klonek, F.E., V. Quera and S. Kauffeld (2015c), 'Computer-supported coded interactions in Motivational Interviewing with computer-software: What are the advantages for process researchers?', *Computers in Human Behavior*, **44**, 284–292.

Klonek, F.E., E. Wunderlich, D. Spurk and S. Kauffeld (2016), 'Career counseling meets Motivational Interviewing: Sequential analysis of dynamic counselor-client interactions', *Journal of Vocational Behavior*, **94**, 28–38.

Lundahl, B.W., C. Kunz, C. Brownell, D. Tollefson and B.L. Burke (2010), 'A meta analysis of Motivational Interviewing: Twenty-five years of empirical studies', *Research on Social Work Practice*, **20** (2), 137–160.

Madson, M.B., A.C. Loignon and C. Lane (2009), 'Training in motivational interviewing: A systematic review', *Journal of Substance Abuse Treatment*, **36** (1), 101–109.

Magill, M., J. Gaume, T.R. Apodaca, J. Walthers, N.R. Mastroleo, B. Borsari and R. Longabaugh (2014), 'The technical hypothesis of motivational interviewing: A meta-analysis of MI's key causal model', *Journal of Consulting and Clinical Psychology*, **82** (6), 973–983.

Mangold, P. (2010), *INTERACT quick start manual V2.4 [Computer Software]: Mangold International GmbH*, accessed 12 January 2017 at http://www.mangold-international.com.

Matthies, E. (2013), 'Nutzerverhalten im Energiesystem. Erkenntnisse und forschungsfragen aus der psychologie', *Technikfolgenabschätzung–Theorie und Praxis*, **22** (2), 36–42.

Miller, W.R. and T.B. Moyers (2006), 'Eight stages in learning motivational interviewing', *Journal of Teaching in the Addictions*, **5** (1), 3–17.

Miller, W.R. and S. Rollnick (2013), *Motivational Interviewing. Helping People Change* (3rd edn), New York: Guilford Press.

Miller, W.R. and G.S. Rose (2009), 'Toward a theory of motivational interviewing', *American Psychologist*, **64** (6), 527–537.

Miller, W.R., K.E. Hedrick and D.R. Orlofsky (1991), 'The helpful responses questionnaire: A procedure for measuring therapeutic empathy', *Journal of Clinical Psychology*, **47** (3), 444–448.

Motivational Interviewing Network of Trainers (MINT) (2014), *Motivational Interviewing: Training for New Trainers Manual. Resources for Trainers*, accessed 12 January 2017 at http://www.motivationalinterviewing.org/sites/default/files/tnt_manual_2014_d10_2015 0205.pdf.

Moyers, T.B., J.K. Manuel and D. Ernst (2014), *Motivational Interviewing Treatment Integrity Coding Manual 4.2.1*, Unpublished manual, accessed 12 January 2017 at http://casaa.unm.edu/download/MITI4_2.pdf.

Murtagh, N., M. Nati, W.R. Headley, B. Gatersleben, A. Gluhak, M.A. Imran and D. Uzzell (2013), 'Individual energy use and feedback in an office setting: A field trial', *Energy Policy*, **62**, 717–728.

Ojala, M. (2008), 'Recycling and ambivalence: Quantitative and qualitative analyses of household recycling among young adults', *Environment and Behavior*, **40** (6), 777–797.

Opheim, A., S. Andreasson, A.B. Eklund and P. Prescott (2009), 'The effects of training medical students in motivational interviewing', *Health Education Journal*, **68** (3), 170–178.

Osbaldiston, R. and K.M. Sheldon (2003), 'Promoting internalized motivation for environmentally responsible behavior: A prospective study of environmental goals', *Journal of Environmental Psychology*, **23** (4), 349–357.

Passmore, J. (2007), 'Addressing deficit performance through coaching – using motivational interviewing for performance improvement at work', *International Coaching Psychology Review*, **2** (3), 265–275.

Rogers, C.R. (1951), *Client-centered Therapy: Its Current Practice, Implications and Theory*, London: Constable.

Rogers, E.M. (2003), *Diffusion of Innovations* (5th ed.), New York: Free Press.

Roten, Y. de, G. Zimmermann, D. Ortega, and J.N. Despland (2013), 'Meta-analysis of the effects of MI training on clinicians' behavior', *Journal of Substance Abuse Treatment*, **45** (2), 155–162.

Ryan, R.M. and E.L. Deci (2000), 'Self-determination theory and the facilitation of intrinsic motivation, social development, and well-being', *American Psychologist*, **55** (1), 68–78.

Siero, F.W., A.B. Bakker, G.B. Dekker and M.T. Van den Burg (1996), 'Changing organizational energy consumption behaviour through comparative feedback', *Journal of Environmental Psychology*, **16** (3), 235–246.

Stoltz, K.B. and T.L. Young (2013), 'Applications of motivational interviewing in career counseling facilitating career transition', *Journal of Career Development*, **90** (4), 329–346.

Tollison, S.J., C.M. Lee, C. Neighbors, T.A. Neil, N.D. Olson and M.E. Larimer (2008), 'Questions and reflections. The use of Motivational Interviewing microskills in a peer-led brief alcohol intervention for college students', *Behavior Therapy*, **39** (2), 183–194.

Westra, H.A. (2011), 'Comparing the predictive capacity of observed in-session resistance to self-reported motivation in cognitive behavioral therapy', *Behaviour Research and Therapy*, **49** (2), 106–113.

Wickström, H.M. Herzing, H. Källmén, L. Forsberg and A. Jacobsson (manuscript in preparation), *Can Motivational Interviewing Enhance Compliance with Waste Sorting Regulations?*

15. Enabling employees and breaking down barriers: behavioural infrastructure for pro-environmental behaviour

Simon Lockrey,* Linda Brennan, Karli Verghese, Warren Staples and Wayne Binney

15.1 INTRODUCTION

This chapter addresses the development of environmental sustainability strategies in organisations. Ongoing problems are evident as organisations continue to seek environmentally sustainable outcomes (Wittneben et al. 2012). The strategies that organisations apply to environmental concerns involve employee behaviours and their interactions with social structures that facilitate or inhibit employee actions (Lockrey 2016). Social structures incorporate resources (i.e. infrastructure and technologies); and rules (i.e. policies and procedures), that affect employees when they think and act (Giddens 1984). Understanding the interplay between employees and the structures they encounter is crucial to determining what strategic problems exist, and what we can do about them.

Research has provided insights into the structural issues at play when organisations strategise for environmental sustainability. Resource-based theory (Wernerfelt 1984), institutional theory (DiMaggio 1988) and stakeholder theory (Freeman 1984) provide explanations of the structural problems organisations encounter. Resource-based challenges include: realigning processes for strategic efforts (Pullman et al. 2009); driving competitive advantage by resourcing stakeholder concerns (Markley and Davis 2007); or linking familiar performance measures (e.g. economic goals) (Zhu and Sarkis 2004) to environmental action. Institutional theory suggests that legitimisation requires: the navigation of strategy adoption (Campbell 2007); internal/external communications (Pérez-Batres et al. 2010); reporting (Jensen and Berg 2012); and innovation implementation (Aguilera-Caracuel and Ortiz-de-Mandojana 2013). Finally, stakeholders such as public policymakers (Doh and Guay 2006), communities (Kassinis and Vafeas 2006), markets (Preuss 2009), and investors (Neubaum and Zahra 2006) influence organisations seeking to reduce environmental impact. These macro perspectives have not examined employees and their behaviours within their (micro) organisational setting. Thus the link between employees and their structural influences is not well understood. We do not know how employee behaviours and social structures help or hinder organisational environmental impact reduction.

In this chapter we address organisational environmental sustainability by drawing on Giddens' (1984) structuration theory and the 'Nine Ps' framework by Brennan et al. (2015), to analyse two case studies. The case studies focus on the use of life cycle assessment (LCA) to develop and procure organisational sustainability strategy. LCA is a resource used in organisational processes aimed at reducing the environmental impacts of products, services, and systems (Baumann and Tillman 2004). As such, these cases provide a context where environmental impact reduction is a core strategic aim, revealing related, novel insights about employees, their behaviours, and the social structures in which they operate. We use structuration to determine if employees have the power to change organisational contexts for better environmental sustainability outcomes. By that we refer to Giddens' (1984) original notion of structuration being the reciprocal relationship between people, their actions, and the social structures in which they act. Power to change is necessary when employees are faced with barriers to action, or capitulation may result in light of the social structures they encounter. We explore whether employees establish agency by using resources and navigating rules to drive environmental sustainability within organisations. Based on the insights developed in the cases, the chapter concludes with how our conceptual model, built upon the link between agency and social structure, can be used by employees to identify and navigate barriers when implementing environmental sustainability within organisations.

15.2   EMPLOYEES AND ENVIRONMENTAL STRATEGIES

Reducing the environmental impact of organisational outcomes (e.g. products, services, and activities) requires planning and deployment of resources (i.e. strategy). Ideally, both strategic planning and implementation is undertaken to achieve common organisational goals (Varadarajan 2010). The goal of strategy for the environment is to protect the Earth's biosphere. However, we currently lack an understanding of the role of social structures in reducing environmental impact within organisations. Further, understanding the influence of employee actions on strategic outcomes is essential knowledge for those seeking to enhance organisational sustainability. As such, research has emerged focusing on employee attitudes (Davis et al. 2009) and intentions (Greaves et al. 2013). Likewise, the cognitive frames applied by employees (Hahn et al. 2014) and the identities they adopt (Wright et al. 2012) have been examined in relation to organisational sustainability. Each of these studies builds our understanding of employees, be that how they think, the personas they project, or the resources and power they employ in environmentally sustainable practice. However, individuals do not operate alone when it comes to organisations. They are intervolved in a system of actions and interactions. For example, while we know that an individual's attitudes are important, unless they have power when strategy is developed, their attitudes may be irrelevant. Additionally, the gap between attitudes and behaviours is well known, such as for purchasing behaviours related to sustainability (Deloitte 2009). As a consequence, it is critical to have a more comprehensive understanding of the barriers and facilitators of environmental sustainability within organisations.

There is an emerging strand of studies that links employee behaviour to institutional and structural considerations. Gond et al. (2015) found that behaviours that seem environmentally unsustainable to outside observers are considered reasonable by employees within the oil and gas industry. In Gond et al.'s research, employees believed that as leaders in their professional disciplines, their actions were legitimate[1] even when the result of their actions had a negative influence on curbing environmental impacts. Research into executive expectations has shown that employees can be at odds with the actions required in delivering environmental strategies. Petala et al. (2010) found that brand managers were not taking seriously environmental strategy directives from an executive level across product categories. Bocken et al. (2012) then show how that same organisation changed structures to enable environmental innovation in new product development. These studies highlight how employees and their behaviour have an influence on organisational sustainability, but that structural considerations shape their behaviour. However, work of this nature is sparse at this stage. New perspectives are required to develop the field.

In the next sections we explore structuration theory and the 'Nine Ps' framework that provides new ways of thinking about employee behaviour. In doing so we show how these concepts can also assist in linking back to structural aspects in an organisational and institutional context. Both aspects are imperative to consider if we are to stand a greater chance of addressing the environmental issues when strategic projects are enacted by employees within organisations.

15.3   ORGANISATIONAL STRUCTURE AND EMPLOYEE AGENCY

Giddens (1984) described the relationship between social structures and agency (see Figure 15.1). For organisational strategy, 'agency' is defined as the ability of the employee to act in support of the outcomes sought. The term 'structure' consists of systems of signification, legitimation, and domination.[2] Structure is made up of the various rules and resources that contribute to individuals' interpretations of communication as meaning, application of norms (descriptive and injunctive), and levels of power. Giddens (1984) proposed that social structures were twofold and consist of rules (e.g. policies) and resources (e.g. infrastructure and technologies). These structures are drawn upon by agents and applied using the agent's cognition. Thus, structures are instantiated when the agent acts. Further, a duality of structure is pertinent to determining the influence of employee thought and action in using rules and resources, and vice versa.

Employees within organisations (agents in Figure 15.1), have varying levels of agency. Consciously purposeful or not, these actions consist of: communication, moral sanctioning, or mastery over material resources and/or other people. In Figure 15.1 structure and agency is mediated by social modalities, which link employees and their actions to social structures when they utilise rules and resources embodied in these structures.

Employees reproduce social structures, or create/change structures through their actions. For instance, structures can either control employees and the outcomes they set out to achieve, or enable them in changing existing conditions. Structure is both the result of and medium of action, instantiated by employees' use, or encountering the effect, of rules and resources. This is represented by the double-ended arrows in Figure 15.1. By considering structuration in instances of strategising for environmental sustainability, we focus on whether employees can work toward beneficial outcomes, or are beholden to circumstances driving less than favourable environmental results. Structuration issues overarch investigations examining employees as 'agents for change' to influence strategic processes designed to increase environmental sustainability within organisations. It therefore provides a lens for considering whether organisational employees can (and do) behave in a way that can contribute to protecting Earth's ecology. The instruments required to examine structuration are well advanced since Giddens' proposal in 1984. However, implementation is not as well advanced. To this end, we propose the use of a practical toolkit: the 'Nine Ps' framework (Brennan et al. 2015) to assess behavioural infrastructures for sustainability within organisations.

Organisations/institutions

Source: Adapted from Giddens (1984: 29).

Figure 15.1   Structuration theory

15.4   STRUCTURE, EMPLOYEE AGENCY AND ENVIRONMENTAL STRATEGY

Brennan et al. (2015) assessed the performance of Australian Universities in tackling environmental sustainability and proposed a framework to explain the issues that exist in such contexts. This framework (see Figure 15.2) describes behavioural infrastructure and includes various elements of an agency–structure relationship (e.g. people, rules, and resources) relating to work practices associated with strategies for environmental sustainability. By applying the 'Nine Ps', we can demonstrate that the framework can be used to operationalise structuration based on an understanding of problems in relation to environmental strategies. We

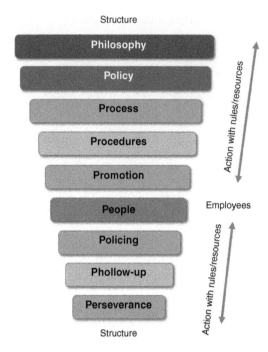

Source: Adapted from Brennan et al. (2015: 313).

Figure 15.2 *'Nine Ps' with structuration elements*

now describe how this can be achieved by linking the framework to key concepts from Giddens.

The 'Nine Ps' framework suggests that systems of social structure are underpinned by philosophy and policies that guide organisations in environmental sustainability strategies. These may be either formalised (e.g. written documents, explicit) or instantiated through employee memory traces (tacit). Brennan et al. (2015) describe a philosophy as the core set of beliefs guiding behaviour, and a policy as a statement of principles to guide decision-making, implemented using a process or procedure. These overarching organisational level rules set the conditions in which employees at all levels are expected to behave. Therefore, philosophy and policies relate to domination and control of employee behaviour, signification in terms of their related meaning to employees, as well as any sanctioning cultivated as employees seek legitimacy in strategic action. As such, explicit philosophies and policies are how the social structures of an organisation are arranged. These rules enable or constrain the actions of employees.

Employees may draw upon processes, procedures, and promotional activities as resources in strategising for environmental outcomes. Resources may limit effective action, or alternatively they may enable agency with resource use whilst navigating related rules. For instance, with the right strategic processes, employees have the tools to reduce the environmental impacts of organisations. Strategic processes are collections of related activities that are designed to achieve a goal (Brennan et al. 2015). Structures of domination can be reoriented to facilitate effective actions through these processes. Processes can again be both explicit and tacit. As such, more formal guidance may be required when it comes to enhancing strategic performance. Procedures, being the written guidance for navigating processes (Brennan et al. 2015), can help in ensuring that strategic actions are undertaken with effect. Procedures are approved documentation that communicates what needs to be done. Thus, procedures act in signifying legitimate action. If guidelines are aligned with favourable environmental outcomes, success comes easily when strategic action is taken.

Promotion refers to the communication of plans and actions and builds the signification structures that facilitate conditions in which favourable outcomes can occur. By communication we refer to any material conveyed to or by employees, by way of mediums such as verbal, audio-visual, email, print, and written, that they may interpret into meaning. As such, promotion can contribute to the series of internal marketing actions aimed at disseminating multi-level aspects to employees about what is being done, including how employees will benefit, and what (individual and group) contributions are necessary for achieving environmental sustainability. This planned effort using promotional activities can be considered a marketing approach to overcome resistance to change and to align, motivate and coordinate employee behaviours (Rafiq and Ahmed 2000). Internal marketing is useful in the co-creation of value (Russell-Bennett et al. 2013), where a range of stakeholders, including employees, is required to participate in tackling the issues at hand. The importance of co-creation in change settings is that outcomes are accepted by the participants as being shared decisions and not prescriptions by management. Transformative contexts, such as environmental sustainability strategies, are inherently caught up with power and domination structures, so co-creation can help to break associated tensions.

Promotion can also aid in legitimising strategic activities by making plans and actions visible to employees as endorsed by the organisation. The desired behaviours may then align to corporate and functional actions and be designed to deliver improved environmental outcomes. Power may also be enhanced for those involved in strategies when compelling arguments to act for environmental reasons are articulated. As such, promotion may be key to enabling employees' action, thereby creating the 'right' set of structural circumstances for enhanced environmental outcomes.

The central platform of behavioural infrastructure envisaged in the 'Nine Ps' is that of people within organisations. The agency of employees is pivotal to driving environmentally sustainable outcomes. This is represented by the action arrows in Figure 15.2, where actions emanate from employees or affects them by way of the actions of others and the social structure they encounter. In our conceptualisation, people include all participants in the organisation, regardless of profession, role, level, or status (e.g. service staff, management, customers).

Behaviour is explicitly embodied in the 'Nine Ps' framework through perseverance, policing and phollow-up[3] actions of employees. Perseverance comprises links to the inherent domination structures present, where employees either capitulate, or break through perceived barriers to environmental sustainability even in the face of adverse conditions. For the former they reproduce domination structures, for the latter they reimagine and contribute to structural realignment. Another component of the framework is that of policing, which creates a sanctioning context that either affects, or is affected by, legitimation structures. Where policing of the environmental sustainability strategy is weak, the status quo remains, even if it is a requirement of organisational philosophical and policy guidance. When policing is implemented effectively, action and behaviours are directed towards preferable environmental sustainability outcomes. What this means is that the behavioural infrastructure must include mechanisms by which behaviours are monitored and determined to be effective (or not) when it comes to achieving organisational goals. Policing, to be effective, must be evident to all actors in the system in terms of action and consequence (Moisander and Pesonen 2002). That is, any action, positive or negative, will have a consistently applied consequence associated with it.

A critical action-based element of the 'Nine Ps' is that of phollow-up, which is the organisational efforts designed to close the loop on, and provide continuous enhancement of, actions aimed at building environmental sustainability programmes. If phollow-up actions are present, the ability of employees to critically reflect either tacitly (practical consciousness) or knowingly (discursive consciousness) is facilitated (Giddens 1984). These reflective actions can determine what needs to remain the same, or be adjusted, in continually improving the performance of an organisation's approach to environmental sustainability. Without such thoughtful practice, the effectiveness of environmental strategies is at risk. Circumstances change and organisations need to be responsive, not reactive.

We have used the 'Nine Ps' to understand structural and agency-based issues of organisational strategy dealing with environmental sustainability. It can uncover structural problems in implementing environmental sustainability strategy through employee actions. The following section outlines the use of the framework as an analytical tool to explore planning and implementation of environmental sustainability strategy within two case study organisations.

15.5   CASE: PLANNING FOR SUSTAINABLE ACTION IN AGED CARE

The first case study examines a planning process for a context-specific environmental sustainability in a major aged care organisation in Australia, operating currently as Uniting Agewell (hereafter UA). UA is a network of facilities and personnel across Victoria and Tasmania that aims to support the health and well-being of older people through the services that they deliver (Uniting Agewell 2016). As part of that vision, the UA board planned an environmental impact reduction strategy (hereafter the strategy). The strategy was designed to maintain the well-being of residents, while addressing environmental impacts associated with service delivery. Streamlined LCAs and design-thinking processes, known as the Double Diamond method (Clune and Lockrey 2014) were employed to help UA to develop their strategy. LCAs helped benchmark the current aged care context in terms of environmental impacts. Design processes were used as tools by employees to conceptualise problems within aged care, and workshop solutions based on LCA data and cross-disciplinary experiences/expertise. LCA then helped verify if proposed changes would result in reduced environmental impacts. Hence, a range of conditions of action was evident.

UA employees from various disciplines at multiple levels within the organisation participated in an action research process (Swann 2002) over six months. Participants ranged from members of the executive, nurses, chefs, accountants, and operations managers, all working collaboratively with external experts and university academics (researchers) in developing a new strategic plan. The strategic plan was developed through a series of site visits; LCA modelling of current environmental impacts; stakeholder design workshops; and reporting of current and future scenarios. These actions resulted in the development of the strategy and revealed influential elements of structure and agency. The development of an environmental sustainability strategy was a new initiative for UA. As such we were able to consider the structural characteristics and actions associated from a low base, as well as any changes to this context over time as the strategy

developed. Data gathered from the case included: strategic reports, observations throughout the strategic planning process, field notes, researcher
insights, and publicly available organisational reports and websites. Data
were examined in relation to the 'Nine Ps' and structuration to generate
the results in relation to the strategy and the underlying processes (see
Appendix Table A15.1 for tabulated results).

The following three themes became apparent from our analysis of
strategic planning at UA:

1. Employees drew on key enabling rules and resources to enact the
    strategy;
2. Communication reduced resistance and enabled planning;
3. Employee 'buy-in' derived from co-creation and shared value.

15.5.1   Employees Drew on Key Enabling Rules and Resources to Enact the Strategy

In the pre-strategic planning context, formal environmental actions were not
evident at UA. Environmentally focused philosophies, policies, processes,
and procedures were not formalised, except for compliance reasons (e.g.
government regulations). A cross-disciplinary team within the organisation
progressed through the planning processes to formulate a strategy based on
their own unique perspectives and contributions. As such, UA demonstrated
how new rules and resources can represent opportunities for employees to
develop effective strategy. Technical, creative, and social processes helped
the team shape an emergent organisational philosophy for environmental
impact reduction. UA employees created a low environmental impact vision
for the organisation, thereby embracing new ways of working. Without seiz-
ing the opportunity to design such new rules and resources, that vision, and
the pathway to reach it, may not have been possible.

LCA was the process that enabled communication and promotion (i.e.
internal social marketing) of environmental opportunities to be exploited by
UA. Further, LCA communicated the benefits of the emerging strategy to a
range of stakeholders from various disciplines. LCA helped reveal environmental issues so that employees could contribute potential options to solve
them. Ultimately this helped the team to develop a common philosophical
goal of environmental impact reduction across organisational personnel
and departments, and a set of reoriented structures for this development.

Communication flowed throughout a series of workshops facilitated
by practitioners and academics. Employees engaged with signification
structures aimed at an open and discursive environment for all involved,
which included design processes such as (Clune and Lockrey 2014):

1. Brainstorming and mind maps of problems and practices;
2. A 'five whys' discussion (IDEO 2002) of current problems and practices;
3. Group sketching of barriers and options on UA site maps;
4. Discussion of 'world's best practice' in environmental sustainability;
5. Discussion of feasible interventions regarding current practices;
6. Back-casting solutions to map short-, medium- and long-term solutions;
7. Discussion of 'solutions as problems' to be solved.

These processes allowed a deep exploration of strategic options available in addressing the environmental problems revealed by LCA. The design processes represented resources that allowed for the navigation of complex and seemingly separate issues of food service and waste, as well as resident thermal comfort and general energy consumption across UA's sites. These nodes of environmental impact affected multiple UA employees and departments that traditionally did not have much contact with one another. As such, personnel had to interact with and reflect on different perspectives, agendas, values, and vocational experiences and their language of 'business'. Interaction and reflection was between and by traditionally powerful people (CEO, managers, etc.), and newly empowered employees (various departments). This meant that the planning was inclusive and participatory. Hence planning involved an opening of the domination structures to employees not necessarily used to being enabled with power.

15.5.2 Communication Reduced Resistance and Enabled Planning

Once employees considered the LCA data generated, planning occurred in spite of some structural resistance. Consistent with the 'Nine Ps' framework, resistance derived from some employees being concerned about participating in planning. Initially some employees had reservations about being questioned as a department in terms of their (lack of) addressing environmental issues highlighted by LCA. Planning prevailed and collective conversations tempered anxiety regarding stakeholder issues. These conversations continued throughout the process and concerns were eventually assuaged and participation enhanced. Importantly, concerns were settled at any point they emerged, as discussions progressed between various employees as to how developing strategies could work toward a 'shared value' model of impact reduction. These actions helped shape legitimation and signification structures between organisational personnel that enabled them to navigate tensions by communicating the options, working out any differences, and planning to address environmental issues together. Employees were required to consider their individual issues, listen to the perspectives of others, and then contribute to a collective strategy to lower energy use and greenhouse gases; for example, an early brainstorming session about the 'current context' for UA involved writing, sketching, and listening to each other's ideas. In this session, operations personnel described barriers to propositions of replacing infrastructure outside of the organisational procurement policies currently in place for electrical appliances. However, in listening to this, the financial representative suggested that, through a new set of replacement procedures currently under consideration, there could be an opportunity to create rules in a hire-purchasing list more informed by energy consumption. By creating this new set of rules and resources, superior environmental decisions could be made taking into account financial and operational perspectives. Without this open dialogue and reflection on multiple alternatives, opportunities may not have been revealed and exploited. Through engaging in this way, employees demonstrated perseverance in considering the options and negotiating solutions, even when some suggestions may have been at odds with their point of view. This also represented signification structures evolving to be inclusive, from being previously siloed. Without this structural shift, planning may not have garnered dialogue, negotiation, and resultant strategy.

In a session following the 'current context' brainstorm, employees were provided with a range of examples of global best practice environmental sustainability projects from outside the aged care industry. A 'round table' discussion between university participants, external consultants, and UA employees then developed. The group conceptualised 'what if' the best practice insights were applied to food, energy and thermal comfort at UA's sites. An example of one such discussion occurred when an interactive menu planning website was revealed, which prompted a discussion about the food practices of the organisation. What followed resembled the previous exchange between the operations and financial employees about electrical appliances, along with suggestions from participants:

- Food services personnel disclosed that they had direct discussion with residents and their families on what food would be provided, in planning for seasonal menus. This was a promotional opportunity for stakeholder engagement on environmental issues.
- Food services personnel had already conducted plate waste review processes and portioning meal-planning processes, and had produced procedures for both. This gave them existing rules and

resources to plan environmental impact reductions with the right people, on points such as meal portioning and ingredients, i.e. meat or vegetarian.

- Management employees felt that as different generations progressed into aged care, lower environmental impact cuisines would be easier to prepare. This opportunity derived from broader food experiences for those incoming generations.
- Nursing staff contributed the point that community gardening activities were popular with residents to create social interactions and a stronger connection to their food. From a thermal comfort perspective the physical component of gardening was favourable too, by way of residents exercising and keeping active.
- Operational staff noted that there was room to compost food waste, which was also seen as a way of dealing with a problem not completely addressed by better menu planning.

Strategic solutions such as the five described above required deliberation on current and future conditions, as connected to the environmental issues the team wished to solve. Through these types of multi-perspective discussions, the team collectively identified what rules and resources could work in the current UA structure, that is, people working with people to envisage new ways of being and creating new behavioural structures that achieve organisational goals. Further, participant suggestions led to what was feasible to change by realigning structural contexts over time. Discussions of this kind were repeated for other food, thermal comfort and energy issues throughout the strategising process, and linked back to the problems identified by the LCA process. In turn, employees mapped the solution because it could be put into effect through back-casting techniques, where the idealistic solution was visualised along with a pragmatic pathway to get there over time. They also inverted the proposed solutions into new problems to be solved. In this way they identified structural elements to exploit or be reoriented to enable the right behaviours to occur. For example, in food practices, current stakeholder engagement via promotion and meal planning and plate waste processes were to be retained and exploited as part of signification and domination structures for environmental purposes. Demographic shifts also meant that domination and legitimation structures could evolve naturally over time, enabling an opportunity for adjustment to less environmental impactful diets, as new generations became aged care residents. This happened as a result of favoured cuisines of growing stakeholder groups, such as Baby Boomers, eating recipes originating from Asian nations that consist of smaller portions of meat and higher portions of vegetables. Finally, infrastructure opportunities were viewed as possibilities to generate inter-est from employees and aged care residents in regard to gardening and food waste remediation initiatives. These new legitimation and significa-tion structures, in the form of the promotion of food as an environmental sustainability focus, could help enable employee and resident action for environmental impact reduction.

15.5.3   Employee 'Buy-in' Derived from Co-creation and Shared Value

Through the participative design processes, employees collectively helped shape the strategy with all their perspectives considered and embedded in the outcome. Key personnel used a suite of processes, including internal social marketing, to create a strategy for collective ownership, thus devel-oping a 'shared value'. This meant the strategy held meaning for, and could be actionable by, all involved. This was important in empowering as many employees through domination structures as were feasible. Important to this was collective empowerment through participation in strategy and planning; taking on a broad range of contributions from participants; and embedding ongoing actions in the strategic plan that was developed. An action plan emerged, sharing responsibility across departments, including:

- Finance managing a reinvestment model that worked in collabora-tion with operations, starting from a low economic base with early energy efficiency measures, using compounding monetary savings over time to fund for more expensive off-grid renewable energy over the long term;
- Residential care employees collectively managing local thermal comfort for residents, that is, heaters/fans/clothing/bedding/exercise (including gardening!), as well as improved spatial temperature zoning scenarios in collaboration with operations; and
- Food service personnel managing new purchasing options with finance, and meal planning practices by leveraging the existing relationships with residents and extended families on portioning and cuisine choice, with residential care employees.

These strategic actions incorporated economic, social, and environmental aspects, and cut across functional areas within UA. To help a wide range of employees persevere with the strategy, short-, medium-, and long-term goals were provided. Goals were considered feasible, in that the various employees who developed the solution deemed outcomes possible, had a role in its implementation, and a stake in the outcome. Investment support through a reinvestment-financing model acted as an incentive and was considered central to employees continuing with the strategy in achieving set goals. Thus the planning team believed that through these structural conditions proposed for the strategy, they would enable employees to persevere in achieving the goals.

One department acting alone could not have created the environmental strategy summarised above. If the existing domination structures were retained, only executive personnel would have strategised top-down; the result, therefore, would be devoid of the range of expertise that contributed. Instead, strategising progressed more inclusively, and with collective intelligence and power. This case could then be interpreted as a shift in the domination structures of the aged care organisation in helping to reduce the barriers traditionally present, so that more employees and their perspectives could contribute to the development of the strategy. The planning team persevered with multiple perspectives on the environmental issues raised, to plan actions toward a strategic outcome that catered for those perspectives and retained 'shared value' for all stakeholders. As a result, people, their beliefs, and their actions connected directly to the strategy through their participation, contribution, and ongoing actions that the strategy would require. Consequently a change in structural conditions enabled an organisational strategy to be developed that would be actionable by a greater range of employees and departments, in the hope to drive better environmental behaviour more broadly. Importantly, the 'Nine Ps' framework, while demonstrating that all Ps are required for environmental programme implementation, transformed throughout the action research process and different aspects reappeared at different stages. The dialogic nature of the process highlighted the need for phollow-up as the process of building a sustainable organisation is iterative. However, the case also demonstrates the benefit of starting an environmentally oriented philosophy, as well as taking the time to unearth tacit and explicit structures before designing any of the Ps for internal marketing purposes. Five of the Ps – people, processes, procedures, promotion and perseverance – were evident in employees being enabled to develop this strategy. Having a philosophical position on which to implement strategy for environmental impact reduction was viewed as important by participants moving forward.

15.6   CASE: IMPLEMENTING SUSTAINABLE ACTION IN ECO-DESIGN

In our second case, we investigated the next phases of environmental strategy, examining implementation and refinement for eco-design in a university educational setting – a university course (subject or unit of study) in a product design engineering (PDE) undergraduate programme. The course was delivered over four years to separate student cohorts. The eco-design case was selected as it involved people collaborating in a formally constructed but bounded setting where various interventions could be trialled and discarded or refined. The case participants were student designers and engineers, managing academic staff, and various industry partner (IP) employees from engineering and business (Lockrey and Bissett-Johnson 2013). Specific elements under examination related to operationalising a strategy for the design process, building the capacity of students with tools they used in the subsequent design process, engagement with industry, and designers being empowered as 'change agents' in the learning environment.

The course required students to work through a brief, using a number of design tools to produce outcomes that demonstrated environmental impact reduction. Students were educated in design and environmental sustainability skills. Interactions occurred between the employees from the IP and students, as well as within the university context where the engagement was mediated by academic staff. As such, the case provided a site to investigate employee agency with various structural influences (e.g. environmental, pedagogical, and commercial) in producing positive environmental outcomes from both a design and skills perspective. The case was also chosen as environmental sustainability strategy was an ongoing initiative, so we were able to consider structural characteristics and refinements as it evolved. Sources of data included design projects developed by the students; observations by researchers throughout the implementation process; formal collation of insights from academic staff; course surveys results from the students; and feedback from the IP. The data were reviewed for links to the 'Nine Ps' and structuration theory with information coded as it related to those concepts (see Appendix Table A15.2 for tabulated results).

The following three themes emerged from the analysis of the university eco-design strategy implementation and refinement:

1. Philosophy, policies, and procedures helped define rules and structural clarity;
2. Key resources enabled student reflection and eco-design agency;
3. Course reflection allowed strategic changes to better enable students.

15.6.1　Philosophy, Policies and Procedures Helped Define Rules and Structural Clarity

The case study reported that academic staff delivering the eco-design course developed and applied an overarching philosophy: environmental impact reduction is critical to business and the future of the planet. In doing so, they aligned course, university and IP philosophies to create a coherent platform from which other actions could be launched. Another key philosophical dimension was that of higher order student learning requirements for students to be both challenged and challenging: they should be challenged by the task and the learning environment and they should be able to challenge and redesign where and when required. IPs had to subscribe to those values in order to participate. Combining these philosophical dimensions contributed to legitimation structures in shaping the minds and actions of student designers, to be proficient in reducing environmental impacts through their design practice. With this philosophical position in place, a clear documented policy platform was devised by university staff, with student guidance on external regulatory requirements to be addressed; university requirements for learning outcomes and submission; IP expectations; and associated project actions.

A key component of these policies was to address environmental issues by producing designs with lower impact, required by fulfilling a design brief. A set of policies and procedures guided the actions intended to deliver university and IP expectations, deriving from university policy through to university and IP employee briefing of students. These included:

- University expectations for novelty of design outcomes;
- A timeline set for the project and associated tasks, as linked to the assessment schedule;
- A number of formal critical reviews;
- Final course assessment rubrics defining expectations of academic performance in key areas; and
- IP input, where they were provided with a design brief so they could understand the student tasks and their role in the learning process.

These rules were detailed in a number of resources, such as the design brief and course guides. As such, policy-based components of structure were explicit, easily understood and accessible by all participants. Hence, a clear structure helped define student expectations, supported by actions that policed their work throughout the course. Academic staff set domination and legitimation structures aimed at enabling student project and learning outcomes.

15.6.2 Key Resources Enabled Student Reflection and Eco-design Agency

Resources were drawn upon by multiple people throughout the course to navigate and, at times, transform the structure. For example, LCA tools and data provided by academics were made accessible to individual student designers in order to enact the set brief in implementing a design strategy. Students used LCA to identify environmental impact hot spots in their designs, and propose reduced impacts as they further refined their designs. Along with other tools, such as whole systems design and calculation of energy use, LCA was used through Sheppard's characterisation of 'what engineers do' (Dym et al. 2005), in scoping, generating, evaluating, and realising ideas. This meant that students reviewed their work so that their designs could be reflected on at multiple stages in the design process. These reflections were used to refine their designs to achieve an optimal environmental outcome.

Design processes enabled students to persevere, even when a particular option may not have succeeded, and improve design propositions as the eco-design strategy unfolded. Their perseverance was supported by ongoing feedback from academics, through in-class guidance and email correspondence. This helped in training students as to how they might use the resources provided to deliver superior environmental outcomes, contributing to their skill development and resilience in the face of barriers. It was also a form of reflective policing from both academic staff and students in determining what design decisions may be appropriate. Hence as processes were put to use, and support by staff continued over time, students further developed more compelling design outcomes as well as associated eco-design skills through the process. This resulted in students and academic staff maintaining key aspects of the domination structures present in addressing environmental issues. Importantly, the design iteration process permitted IPs, staff, and students to experiment and co-create preferable outcomes. Hence, while dominance structures were in place the locus of power shifted between participants throughout the design process.

Design and engineering processes were not the only tools used to enable the student designers. Students completing the course were regularly engaged in reflection about their eco-design efforts at key communication (promotion) points, including:

● University processes such as in-class consultation and critical reviews of their work, emails, online management portals, web forums, and content lectures;
● Student awards from the IP for the best final outcomes that drove

engagement. Monetary prizes were offered for some years of the IP awards;

- Reporting of successes and key learning through academic journals and conferences were provided as set readings; and
- Promoting benefits of undertaking the eco-design course to newer cohorts of students.

Industry participation with students has previously been explored as a key activity to heighten student engagement (Boks and Diehl 2006). Student survey data, assessment results, participation, design outcomes and IP feedback demonstrated that this, indeed, occurred. Promotion in turn contributed to signification structures that encouraged environmentally preferable designs by students, year on year.

15.6.3   Course Reflection Allowed Strategic Changes to Better Enable Students

When resources were restrictive, such as unwieldy tools used in the design process, students' power in designing environmentally focused outcomes noticeably diminished. This was until course refinement was enacted by academic staff to introduce better LCA tools, based on student and IP phollow-up, as resource-based problems became apparent. Students and the IP used phollow-up processes to suggest improvements to benefit future students in delivering preferable environmental outcomes. This feedback was also a resource drawn upon by staff to aid in course modification, effectively another layer of phollow-up agency. Changes included (Lockrey and Bissett-Johnson 2013):

- Scenario consolidation to create focus for the eco-design projects;
- Removal of design drawings, as they were covered in other courses;
- Room to review changes to aid IP and student collaboration and feedback;
- Identification of more time and new resources to support impact reductions; and
- Development of a marking rubric to make expectations clearer.

In terms of the new resources implemented, a user-friendly, streamlined LCA tool, Greenfly, was embedded in the course. This improvement replaced cumbersome hand calculations introduced at the inception of the course, which had been identified as problematic by students in efficiently delivering outcomes (i.e. too long spent on hand calculations). The new resource enabled student designs to be adapted effectively and quickly, leading to better managed and delivered enhanced environmental design propositions.

Policing and phollow-up processes were present, as dictated by policy. Course reflection by students was a university requirement designed to aid pedagogical improvements. In other words, the university level domination structure legitimised academic staff agency in changing the course for the better, based on student feedback. It also enhanced student agency as designers and IPs agency as co-creators of eco-design outcomes. As this occurred over a number of years of course delivery, the perseverance of university staff was evident. University employees accepted critical feedback from student designers, and acted to improve the eco-design learning outcomes.

Throughout this eco-design case, the importance of providing structural guidance to enable agency, and improving structures reflexively through agency over time is highlighted. Actions were bound in both practical and discursive consciousness (Giddens 1984), through the tacit expertise and considered reflection applied respectively by students. These two features are common elements of agency evident throughout the eco-design case, whether that be navigation of rules/structures, student mastery of resources, structural modifications initiated for improved student outcomes, or communicative interactions. Employees strategising for environmental sustainability may indeed need to keep these components of agency in mind. Expertise, reflection, or other combinations of knowledge, skill, and awareness may provide them with the agency to enact behaviours that reduce environmental impacts.

If behaviours demonstrated by students are retained beyond the learning process, in time the eco-design course could contribute to broader professional practice. It follows that the course has the potential to affect structures outside the course, as former students progress to contexts such as industry, government and civil society. In these roles their actions could make a significant difference to reducing environmental impacts in the projects with which they are involved.

15.7   CONCLUSIONS: BREAKING DOWN STRUCTURAL BARRIERS AND ENABLING OF EMPLOYEE ACTION

The two case studies have demonstrated important aspects of social structures that may enable employees and empower them to act in addressing environmental impacts within organisations.

The aged care case reveals that employees of different disciplines can draw on key enabling rules and resources to plan a strategy effectively. In this context, communication is pivotal in reducing barriers and resistance whilst fostering an environment where various options can be refined collectively from a multi-perspective view. A shared value approach ensures that employees have a stake in the strategy, by co-creating it and, in time, by co-managing it.

The eco-design case study demonstrates that, by setting up the right structures initially, strategies can run smoothly. This includes creating rules that guide employees to improve their approach to environmental problems, and in providing key resources that enable their reflection and agency. When the settings do not work, reflexivity was shown to be critical in ensuring ongoing strategic success over time. This relates to sensitivity to problems that are evident and responsiveness to feedback, leading to modifications to plans and actions.

Both cases illustrate that with appropriate and thoughtful design, organisations and stakeholders can co-create behavioural infrastructures to provide agency to participants that results in environmental outcomes. In future research, analytical frameworks such as the 'Nine Ps' could provide parameters to test for actionable change environments, rather than having large-scale problems that may remain unaddressed because of complexity. Second, structuration provides a theoretical lens by which we may view the development of strategy for environmentally sustainable outcomes. Understanding the interplay between social structures and employee applications of rules, resources, norms and their interpretive schemes in further applied research could allow internal marketers to design apposite behavioural infrastructures. Such infrastructures may enable people to actively co-create environmentally sound organisations. If patterns emerge through further research, scholars could then provide managers with confidence in the general rules to be applied to reach environmental goals. In other words, such research may provide a 'toolbox' for best practice success in environmental strategy. Creating organisational environments where human agency is welcomed, and exploited, means overcoming systemic barriers to action. This is the first step in the process of change to pivot to ongoing strategic success in addressing environmental impacts.

NOTES

*   The authors would like to acknowledge the assistance of the following people for their help in the formative stages of research and providing advice and support on the

case study components of this chapter: Kate Bissett-Johnson (Swinburne University), Stephen Clune (Lancaster University), Carol Fountain (Uniting Agewell) and Cedric Israelson (MicroHeat).
1. By legitimate, Gond et al. (2015) demonstrate that employees felt their actions were warranted based on beliefs drawn from institutions dictating their professional (engineering) discipline.
2. Systems of signification determine how people make sense of information and help them communicate; systems of legitimation determine socially accepted behaviours; and systems of domination determine how people wield power or are controlled (Giddens 1984).
3. By 'phollow-up' we mean 'follow up'. We phrase it as 'phollow-up' to fit with the 'P' convention of the 'Nine Ps'.

REFERENCES

Aguilera-Caracuel, J. and N. Ortiz-de-Mandojana (2013), 'Green innovation and financial performance: An institutional approach', *Organization & Environment*, **26** (4), 365–385.
Baumann, H. and A. Tillman (2004), *The Hitch Hiker's Guide to LCA. An orientation in life cycle assessment methodology and application.* Lund: Studentlitteratur.
Bocken, N., J. Allwood, A. Willey and J. King (2012), 'Development of a tool to rapidly assess implementation difficulty and emissions reduction benefits of innovations', *Technovation*, **32** (1), 19–31.
Boks, C. and J. Diehl (2006), 'Integration of sustainability in regular courses: experiences in industrial design engineering', *Journal of Cleaner Production*, **14** (9), 932–939.
Brennan, L., W. Binney, J. Hall and M. Hall (2015), 'Whose Job is that? Saving the biosphere starts at work', *Journal of Nonprofit & Public Sector Marketing*, **27** (3), 307–330.
Campbell, J. (2007), 'Why would corporations behave in socially responsible ways? An institutional theory of corporate social responsibility', *Academy of Management Review*, **32**, 946–967.
Clune, S. and S. Lockrey (2014), 'Developing environmental sustainability strategies, the Double Diamond method of LCA and design thinking: a case study from aged care', *Journal of Cleaner Production*, **85**, 67–82.
Davis, G., F. O'Callaghan and K. Knox (2009), 'Sustainable attitudes and behaviours amongst a sample of non-academic staff: A case study from an Information Services Department, Griffith University, Brisbane', *International Journal of Sustainability in Higher Education*, **10** (2), 136–151.
Deloitte (2009), 'Finding the green in today's shoppers: sustainability trends and new shopper insights, Report to the Grocery Manufacturers Association (GMA)'.
DiMaggio, P. (1988), 'Interest and agency in institutional theory', *Institutional Patterns and Organizations: Culture and Environment*, **1**, 3–22.
Doh, J. and T. Guay (2006), 'Corporate social responsibility, public policy, and NGO activism in Europe and the United States: An institutional-stakeholder perspective', *Journal of Management Studies*, **43** (1), 47–73.
Dym, C., A. Agogino, O. Eris, D. Frey and L. Leifer (2005), 'Engineering design thinking, teaching and learning', *Journal of Engineering Education*, **94** (1), 103–120.
Freeman, R. (1984), *Strategic Management: A Stakeholder Perspective.* Boston, MA: Pitman.
Giddens, A. (1984), *The Constitution of Society.* Cambridge: Polity Press.
Gond, J., L. Barin Cruz, E. Raufflet and M. Charron (2015), 'To frack or not to frack? The interaction of justification and power in a sustainability controversy', *Journal of Management Studies*, **53** (3), 330–363.
Greaves, M., L. Zibarras and C. Stride (2013), 'Using the theory of planned behavior to explore environmental behavioral intentions in the workplace', *Journal of Environmental Psychology*, **34**, 109–120.

Hahn, T., L. Preuss, J. Pinkse and F. Figge (2014), 'Cognitive frames in corporate sustainability: Managerial sensemaking with paradoxical and business case frames', *Academy of Management Review*, **39** (4), 463–487.

IDEO (2002), *IDEO Method Cards*. San Francisco, CA: William Stout Architectural Books.

Jensen, J. and N. Berg (2012), 'Determinants of traditional sustainability reporting versus integrated reporting. An institutionalist approach', *Business Strategy and the Environment*, **21** (5), 299–316.

Kassinis, G. and N. Vafeas (2006), 'Stakeholder pressures and environmental performance', *Academy of Management Journal*, **49** (1), 145–159.

Lockrey, S. (2016), 'Agents for sustainability: People and Structure in organizational strategy for ecology', *76th Annual Meeting of the Academy of Management*. Academy of Management, Anaheim, USA, Academy of Management, **1**.

Lockrey, S. and K. Bissett-Johnson (2013), 'Designing pedagogy with emerging sustainable technologies', *Journal of Cleaner Production*, **61**, 70–79.

Markley, M. and L. Davis (2007), 'Exploring future competitive advantage through sustainable supply chains', *International Journal of Physical Distribution & Logistics Management*, **37** (9), 763–774.

Moisander, J. and S. Pesonen (2002), 'Narratives of sustainable ways of living: Constructing the self and the other as a green consumer', *Management Decision*, **40** (4), 329–342.

Neubaum, D. and S. Zahra (2006), 'Institutional ownership and corporate social performance: The moderating effects of investment horizon, activism, and coordination', *Journal of Management Studies*, **32** (1), 108–131.

Pérez-Batres, L., V. Miller and M. Pisani (2010), 'CSR, sustainability and the meaning of global reporting for Latin American corporations', *Journal of Business Ethics*, **91**, 193–209.

Petala, E., R. Wever, C. Dutilh and H. Brezet (2010), 'The role of new product development briefs in implementing sustainability: A case study', *Journal of Engineering and Technology Management*, **27** (3), 172–182.

Preuss, L. (2009), 'Ethical sourcing codes of large UK-based corporations: Prevalence, content, limitations', *Journal of Business Ethics*, **88** (4), 735–747.

Pullman, M., M. Maloni and C. Carter (2009), 'Food for thought: social versus environmental sustainability practices and performance outcomes', *Journal of Supply Chain Management*, **45** (4), 38–54.

Rafiq, M. and P. Ahmed (2000), 'Advances in the internal marketing concept: Definition, synthesis and extension', *Journal of Services Marketing*, **14** (6), 449–462.

Russell-Bennett, R., M. Wood and J. Previte (2013), 'Fresh ideas: Services thinking for social marketing', *Journal of Social Marketing*, **3** (3), 223–238.

Swann, C. (2002), 'Action research and the practice of design', *Design Issues*, **18** (1), 49–61.

Uniting Agewell (2016), 'Uniting Agewell.' Retrieved 11/10/2016, from https://www.unitingagewell.org/.

Varadarajan, R. (2010), 'Strategic marketing and marketing strategy: Domain, definition, fundamental issues and foundational premises', *Journal of the Academy of Marketing Science*, **38** (2), 119–140.

Wernerfelt, B. (1984), 'A resource-based view of the firm', *Strategic Management Journal*, **5** (2), 171–180.

Wittneben, B., C. Okereke, S. Banerjee and D. Levy (2012), 'Climate change and the emergence of new organizational landscapes', *Organization Studies*, **33** (11), 1431–1450.

Wright, C., D. Nyberg and D. Grant (2012), 'Hippies on the third floor: Climate Change, Narrative Identity and the Micro-Politics of Corporate Environmentalism', *Organization Studies*, **33** (11), 1451–1475.

Zhu, Q. and J. Sarkis (2004), 'Relationships between operational practices and performance among early adopters of green supply chain management practices in Chinese manufacturing enterprises', *Journal of Operations Management*, **22** (3), 265–289.

APPENDIX

Table A15.1 Structure/agency characteristics of strategic planning aged care case data

'Nine Ps'*	'Nine Ps' and structural characteristics pre-strategic planning*	'Nine Ps' structural change/agency observed during strategic planning*
Philosophy	1.01 CEO committed to developing strategic environmental action. 1.02 Funding supplied for external experts/employee time for planning. 1.03 No philosophical statement was apparent publicly prior to strategic planning. 1.04 Domination/signification/legitimation structure did not aid environmental action.	1.05 Objectives to address energy/greenhouse gas reduction were made clear. 1.06 Employees generally approached planning as if environmental issues should be solved. 1.07 Techniques new to the organisation, namely LCA and design-thinking, were embraced in strategising. This helped reveal opportunities to exploit for better environmental outcomes.
Policy	2.01 Management demonstrated support by initiation of planning. 2.02 Planning was initiated to correct policy deficiencies guiding environmental action. 2.03 No apparent environmental policies/action plans (except regulatory compliance). 2.04 A lack of rules left structures for environmental action deficient.	2.05 Some employee/departmental concerns surfaced as to environmental action. 2.06 Internal/external teams collaborated to produce short/long-term actions. 2.07 Policy did not result from the planning process, so remains a structural deficiency that needs to be addressed as part of strategic implementation.
Process	3.01 Management, finance, risk assessment, operations, food service, care and stakeholder engagement processes existed, yet not focused on environmental impact.	3.04 Planning actions designed operational shifts for sustainable outcomes. 3.05 LCA revealed environmental hot spots and design-thinking methods revealed viable opportunities (contemplated risk/divergent design).

336

3.02 Operational practice, divergent innovation methods, risk-taking, measures of effectiveness, clear initiatives, and expected behaviours directly related to environmental issues were not previous organisational processes.

3.03 A lack of resources inhibited environmental action, with structural influences enabling other sorts of actions e.g. economic, resident needs, cultural.

3.06 Realigned resources were identified to drive strategic success e.g. procurement tendering for food/appliances, plate food waste studies, resident consultation, community gardening and space heating/cooling zoning.

3.07 New resources were identified to help strategic success, e.g. reinvestment of energy efficiency savings, and tools to measure environmental choices.

Procedure

4.01 Procedures were not apparent in relation to environmental sustainability.

4.02 An environmental management system e.g. set of processes and procedures, new staff environmental sustainability inductions, or sets of steps to achieve environmental outcomes were not apparent pre-planning.

4.03 Limited resources and rules again inhibited environmental action.

4.04 Employees planned clear steps/processes, designed to achieve environmental aims.

4.05 Collaboration helped reveal how policies/procedures may guide actions.

4.06 More needed to be done post-planning and in subsequent implementation in defining guiding procedures, for domination/signification/legitimation structures enabling action.

Promotion

5.01 Environmental sustainability was not broadly embedded in daily practices.

5.02 By reaching out to external experts the aged care organisation looked to professionals for support on this.

5.03 By communicating support for employee participation in planning, internal social marketing helped form the planning process.

5.06 Broad content that could be used for promotional activities in strategic implementation was developed in the planning process, regarding external and internal communications.

5.07 More work was needed in confirming the plan for: internal communication e.g. email, web, and e-news to staff, from philosophy down to initiatives; reporting initiatives to residents, regulators and broader community; and advertising success e.g. print, posters, and digital, in dealing with environmental issues.

Table A15.1 (continued)

'Nine Ps'*	'Nine Ps' and structural characteristics pre-strategic planning*	'Nine Ps' structural change/agency observed during strategic planning*
	5.04 Regular internal communication: external reporting, and advertising of the successes in dealing with environmental issues were not apparent pre-planning.	
	5.05 Signification/legitimation structures remained weak due to a lack of resources.	
People	6.01 The CEO drove strategic planning, a powerful central champion structurally.	6.08 Executive through to middle management engaged with the planning project, and supported lower-level employee involvement.
	6.02 A culture existed in supporting and rewarding savings in financial costs.	6.09 Actions for people were identified to drive strategic success, e.g. engagement processes with residents and families for thermal comfort and food outcomes.
	6.03 Individuals saving energy could be treated likewise, although being indirect environmental support, as it is economically focused.	6.10 Subsequent work on empowering mechanisms and related resources such as: rewards for individual action; positive activism; training; time off; or monetary reimbursement, is required for any implementation.
	6.04 Potentially important partnerships existed between key stakeholders such as departments, procurement partners, residents and their relatives.	
	6.05 No formal direct reward/recognition of individuals' environmental actions existed.	
	6.06 There were no empowering mechanisms for individual action for environmental outcomes, although the planning process could signify the inaugural one.	

6.07 Structures were subsequently limited in communications, enabling of power, and legitimisation of effective environmental actions by employees.

Policing

7.01 Policing extended only as far as environmental compliance e.g. waste and energy, to regulation prior to strategic planning.

7.02 Strong rules and resources to sanction employee behaviour counter environmental sustainability were not present.

7.03 Domination/legitimation structures did not provide deterrents to drive substantial environmental impact reduction.

7.04 Assessment through LCA for impact hot spots became strategically critical as employees worked through the pertinent issues.

7.05 Measureable goals/objectives were mapped in strategic planning.

7.06 Development of rules and resources such as: regular audits; enforcement of policy breaches; and employee complaint protection, were still required to guide policing action.

Phollow-up

8.01 Not previously initiated in connection to environmental sustainability strategy at the aged care organisation. As such, structure and agency in day-to-day practices at the organisation as related to environmental sustainability strategy and outcomes are insignificant.

8.02 Executive involvement in planning paved the way for closed-loop reporting e.g. issues addressed are reported to executive.

8.03 The reinvestment financing model for energy resolved to be iterative over time through planning actions.

8.04 Cross-disciplinary participation in strategic planning initiated organisational learning.

8.05 More work was required pre-strategic implementation to ensure: closed-loop reporting; strategic development from previous strategic outcomes; employee development; continuous improvement; and organisational learning.

8.06 Employee access of such resources, structures could be aligned to enable better environmental outcomes.

Table A15.1 (continued)

'Nine Ps'*	'Nine Ps' and structural characteristics pre-strategic planning*	'Nine Ps' structural change/agency observed during strategic planning*
Persevere	9.01 Not previously initiated in connection to an environmental sustainability strategy at the aged care organisation. As such, structure and agency in day-to-day practices at the organisation as related to environmental sustainability strategy and outcomes are insignificant.	9.02 Long-term (>5 years) goals and strategies in relation to environmental issues were developed through planning actions e.g. energy financing short to long term, relying on implementation. 9.03 The planning team persevered with multiple perspectives, to make pragmatic actions towards a strategic outcome that catered for those perspectives and retained 'shared value' for all stakeholders. 9.04 Investment was deemed central to strategic implementation. 9.05 Further work on: staff deployment, secondments, departmental budgets, and openness to prototype–failure–refinement cycles will allow resilient action.

Note: *Deriving from Brennan et al. (2015) 'Nine Ps' and Giddens' (1984) structuration.

Table A15.2 Structure/agency characteristics of eco-design strategic implementation case data

'Nine Ps'*	'Nine Ps' initial structural characteristics for strategic implementation*	'Nine Ps' structural change/agency observed during strategic implementation/refinement*
Philosophy	1.01 University/IP had executive/board support to address environmental issues. 1.02 Funding allowed external experts and employees time to deliver strategy. 1.03 Objectives to reduce energy use, greenhouse gas reduction, water and solid waste were the aim of the eco-design projects. 1.04 Philosophical statements existed for the university and IP during the design project. 1.05 As such, clear domination, signification, and legitimation structure in aiding environmental action was present.	1.06 Students approached strategic implementation in terms of reducing environmental impacts, as well as other design requirements. 1.07 New techniques for student design projects, namely whole systems design, engineering calculations and LCA and design-thinking, were used to help reveal opportunities to exploit, and whether designs achieved strategic success. 1.08 University staff used environmental impact savings as the overarching philosophy to create clear structural conditions for actions in eco-design projects.
Policy	2.01 University staff created a policy platform for the eco-design strategy, with regulatory/university/IP expectations, and associated projects. 2.02 Students accessed an easily understood/readily available project brief with relevant environmental/product issues, and pedagogical expectations in course outlines/assessment guidance. Clear project plans/actions accompanied the policy summary. 2.03 These rules set domination/legitimation structure for environmental action through design.	2.04 Students, university staff, and the IP used the design brief over time to produce eco-design outcomes. 2.05 Some student and IP concerns surfaced as to environmental action, based on some of the rules and resources included in the first few years of the course. 2.06 Policy refinement was actioned e.g. structures changed in light of shifting tasks, tools to be used, and outcome requirements written in the project brief.
Process	3.01 Clear processes were provided for the design of products through the strategy.	3.05 Streamlined LCA revealed environmental hot spots. 3.06 Engineering calculation/whole systems analysis tracked product performance.

Table A15.2 (continued)

'Nine Ps'*	'Nine Ps' initial structural characteristics for strategic implementation*	'Nine Ps' structural change/agency observed during strategic implementation/refinement*
Process	3.02 A clear set of processes for feedback on/refinement of the strategy over time existed. 3.03 Design/engineering practice; tools/methods; divergent innovation/risk-taking in design-thinking; measures of effectiveness through streamlined LCA; engineering calculation and critical design review sessions; and policies driving expected environmental outcomes were key processes drawn upon by student designers in a 'scaffolded learning' course structure. 3.04 Resources enabled action in creating structure central to environmental outcomes.	3.07 Design methods revealed opportunities for eco-design outcomes e.g. divergent design and contemplated risk, which were viable. 3.08 Feedback from IP and university staff during critical design reviews led students to refined eco-design outcomes over the eco-design project. 3.09 Feedback from IP and students led to impact assessment/design process changes, so domination structures shifted in order to better enable students to reduce the environmental impacts of their designs.
Procedures	4.01 Clear guidance/resources were provided to students, explaining how to use the design/environmental sustainability tools and methods they needed to fulfil the eco-design projects. 4.02 Clear guidance as to university expectations on academic conduct was available, distributed physically and reinforced verbally through marking rubrics, time management by way of key milestones, and progressive formative/summative assessment. 4.03 Project management, training in design/environmental sustainability concepts, and preferred actions for environmental outcomes were provided prior and throughout to students.	4.05 The strategy helped students work through a clear set of steps designed to reduce environmental impacts through a brief and online course management system. 4.06 Training was delivered through lectures and online resources. 4.07 In-class guidance, feedback, and ongoing email correspondence also helped form the real-time training and guidance. 4.08 Marking rubrics were developed in later years of the course for clarity of the task required for the course, which represented a shift in signification structures e.g. better visibility for students on what was required; and

domination structures e.g. more formalised requirements for action.

4.04 Guiding rules and resources enabled effective use of tools, even with structures also related to other actions e.g. user needs, manufacturability, robustness, or university policy.

Promotion	5.01 Environmental sustainability was embedded in practices involved in the eco-design course.	5.06 Students completing the course were regularly engaged as to benefits of eco-design, and key communication points with the IP.
	5.02 Through the IP, university staff pitched a real-world problem to be solved by students.	5.07 Student awards from the IP for the best student outcomes drove engagement.
	5.03 By promoting an authentic problem and participation/stake of the IP, student engagement was enhanced and internal social marketing dimension realised.	5.08 Reporting of successes/learning through academic journals/conferences were actioned by staff post course delivery. This added to the legitimacy of the techniques applied with peer review scrutiny and approval.
	5.04 Communication points between IP, staff, and students; student awards; external reporting; and promoting course benefits were resources used by staff to engage students.	5.09 Promoting benefits of the eco-design course to new cohorts of students was a practice initiated in time, strengthening signification structure.
	5.05 This had particular relevance in that signification and legitimation structures remained strong as these resources were utilised.	
People	6.01 University staff initiated eco-design strategy, a powerful position as central champions.	6.09 Staff managed the eco-design project to support student actions.
	6.02 Support and reward for student engagement in the eco-design strategy was evident.	6.10 Engagement processes for students were included throughout.
	6.03 Key partnerships were brokered between staff, IP personnel and students.	6.11 Student training in design methods, whole systems-thinking, LCA and energy calculations provided resources to shape designs/student skills.
	6.04 Direct reward and recognition of environmental actions taken by students were embedded in course	6.12 IP monetary prizes were dropped, as tangible feedback

Table A15.2 (continued)

'Nine Ps'**	'Nine Ps' initial structural characteristics for strategic implementation*	'Nine Ps' structural change/agency observed during strategic implementation/refinement*
People	marking structure. IP awards for the best outcomes were another reward. 6.05 Processes/tools empowering student action were explicitly part of the strategy. 6.06 Structures subsequently enabled communications, engendered power, and bore legitimacy for effective environmental actions by students. 6.07 Time was specifically allocated for student focus on environmental impact reduction. 6.08 Monetary prizes were offered for early years of the IP awards.	on commercial aspects of designs was considered more important. 6.13 Certainly the continued engagement of the IP added legitimacy to the course, based on verbal and written feedback from students. 6.14 In later years, more time was allocated for environmental impact reduction. Raised in student feedback, the change created enabling domination structures.
Policing	7.01 Policing was inherent in a timeline set for project tasks, linked to the marking schedule. 7.02 Rules to penalise outcomes counter environmental sustainability were in place. 7.03 Domination and legitimation structures were conducive to driving substantial environmental impact reduction through deterrent to not complying with the requirements of the course. 7.04 Task deadlines were clearly communicated in the project brief in order to signify the conditions for acceptable project management.	7.05 Policing actions were described in university/PDE policy and the course brief. 7.06 Measureable goals and objectives were in the course brief/assessment rubric. 7.07 LCA/engineering calculations allowed auditing/ environmental impact assessment. 7.08 Environmental impact reductions were checked in critical reviews/final marks. 7.09 A more understandable/readily available rubric helped student clarity on requirements, signification/domination structures for action on environmental impacts.
Phollow-up	8.01 A clear set of processes for feedback on, and refinement of, the strategy existed.	8.05 Ongoing IP relationship management by university staff facilitated IP feedback.

8.02 University policies in relation to course reflection/improvement enabled closed-loop reporting e.g. strategic issues reported by students/IP to university staff, and acted upon.
8.03 Strategy changes and continuous improvement from previous outcomes followed.
8.04 Formative/summative reflection within, and post, strategy enabled better outcomes.

8.06 Reflective tools during and in refining strategy enabled organisational learning.
8.07 Realigned and new resources were identified to drive further strategic success, thus adding to domination structures in enabling student action.

Persevere
9.01 Clear processes were provided for design refinement of products through the strategy.
9.02 A clear set of processes for the feedback on strategic implementation failure existed.
9.03 Lasting university/IP support (>12 months) was evident in commitment over years.
9.04 Time investment devoted to environmental issues and refinement of the course occurred.
9.05 Legitimation structures therefore enabled perseverance to flourish.

9.06 Long term (>5 years) product life-cycle goals developed through eco-design.
9.07 Design and engineering techniques allowed for prototype–failure–refinement, leading to better environmental outcomes, and student learning.
9.08 Strategic implementation concerns from IP/students led to strategy refinement over time to help improve components of the course.

Note: *Deriving from Brennan et al. (2015) 'Nine Ps' and Giddens' (1984) structuration.

PART IV

EMPLOYEE ENVIRONMENTAL BEHAVIOUR, FEEDBACK AND TECHNOLOGY

16. Workplace energy use feedback in context

Niamh Murtagh, Birgitta Gatersleben and David Uzzell

16.1 INTRODUCTION

Energy consumption in offices is particularly important amongst the environmentally impacting activities of office workers. A 2014–2015 study for the UK government reported that offices represent the highest sector for energy use of non-domestic buildings (DBEIS 2016a). Almost 70 per cent of this consumption is electricity, with information and computing technologies ranking third highest in usage after lighting and refrigeration (DBEIS 2016a). The study notes the high potential for reduction in consumption and this is supported by earlier evidence of wasted energy in offices from studies such as those described in the following. Almost two-thirds of workers in a US study left their PCs switched on at the end of the day (Webber 2006) but unused PCs still consume non-trivial amounts of energy, a so-called 'vampire' or 'phantom' load. A phantom load is defined as energy consumed by a device when it is not performing its primary function (Lawrence Berkeley Laboratory 2017) and is wasted energy. In a clear example of the potential size of the problem of phantom load, Masoso and Grobler (2010) found in an African study that 56 per cent of building energy was used during non-working hours. During the working day, unoccupied desks may consume about half the energy of occupied desks (Lobato et al. 2011), due to devices – especially PCs – left on but not in use. Kawamoto and colleagues (2004) estimated that utilisation of desktop equipment during the working day may be as low as 43 per cent. Interventions aimed at changing behaviour offer potential to reduce this wasted energy. For example, behaviour change programmes, in combination with energy management, could save up to 80 per cent of consumption in offices, according to Junnila (2007). Research interest in providing energy feedback to employees as part of behaviour change programmes has therefore burgeoned.

Although frequently included alongside other interventions, such as group comparison and energy information, a research question of interest is to what extent individual energy feedback in itself influences behaviour.

As a frequently challenging and costly intervention, as we will discuss below, it would be particularly useful to have empirical evidence which clearly points to its efficacy, before recommending that organisations embark on a programme of deployment of individual feedback. In this chapter, we review the research evidence on feedback on individual energy consumption at the work-desk. Factors beyond the individual will also have an influence and other perspectives may offer additional insights. However, our focus here is initially on the individual, based on extensive research evidence for the relationship between individual psychological factors and pro-environmental behaviours including energy use. The chapter begins with a brief review of research on feedback in residential settings (where much of the research on energy feedback has been conducted), before moving on to evidence from the workplace. An earlier study of ours which provided feedback to 80 workers over four months is described in detail, followed by more recent field research. The discussion then attempts to draw conclusions from the highly varied studies in the area; recommendations are provided for practitioners and researchers, and proposals are made on topics for the future research agenda.

16.2   ENERGY FEEDBACK IN RESIDENTIAL SETTINGS

Behaviour which results in energy consumption has critical environmental impacts, primarily through the emission of greenhouse gases when burning fossil fuels. However, energy use suffers from what Burgess and Nye (2008) describe as double invisibility: first, energy is an invisible force – we cannot see the electricity or gas that powers our workplaces and homes; second, energy use is embedded in daily actions – people come to work to do a job and the energy consumed in this activity is typically not visible to them, nor is the energy wasted by appliances left on while not in use. Feedback on energy use can render the invisible visible and quantified, and has therefore been assumed to be essential to counteract an 'information deficit' and to lead to more pro-environmental behaviour (Hargreaves et al. 2010).

Research on energy feedback in domestic settings is extensive. Three reviews in the past fifteen years examined over 100 published studies (Abrahamse et al. 2005; Faruqui et al. 2010; Ehrhardt-Martinez et al. 2010) and more have been published since. A major challenge noted by these review scholars has been the difficulty of comparison across different types of study. Domestic field studies have tended to combine different intervention techniques, such as feedback in monthly, weekly or (rarely) real-time via different media, alongside tariffing and dynamic pricing, provision of information, and group comparison, while dealing with different types of household in different geographic locations. From the perspective of psychological enquiry, this means that the effect of feedback is confounded with information, education, incentives and sociodemographics, amongst other variables. Further, sample sizes have been typically small, studies have been short in duration and little or no inferential statistical analysis has been undertaken for most studies. Limited use of control groups or adequate baseline behaviour means that the findings have lacked reliability for generalisability, and all of these factors may have contributed to very mixed results.

Ehrhardt-Martinez and colleagues (2010) noted that research has fallen into two eras: that of the energy crisis (1970–1980s) and that of climate change (starting in the late 1990s). Studies from the latter era are of more relevance now as public awareness as well as theoretical understanding of behaviour and technology have changed in the last three decades. Some of the larger and more rigorously designed studies from the 'climate change era' are now reviewed. In one of the earlier studies from this period, feedback was provided monthly for nine months to 120 households in Bath, a city in southern England (Brandon and Lewis 1999). Across a variety of intervention types aimed at reducing energy consumption, including individual and comparative feedback, financial and environmental information, and using different media, household energy use *increased* as well as decreased. Only one intervention type showed a statistically significant difference in households with reduced versus increased energy consumption (provision of computer-based feedback with historical comparative data and energy-saving information). In two US-based studies with military families aimed at reducing heating-related energy consumption (Study 1) and cooling-related energy consumption (Study 2) at two sites, energy use decreased in the heating-targeted sample but increased in the cooling-targeted sample (McMakin et al. 2002). A more recent and very extensive set of field trials in the UK concluded that real-time feedback through in-home displays had achieved an overall 3 per cent reduction in electricity use (Raw and Ross 2011). The report detailed four major trials with sample sizes between 1,300 and 7,100. However, the overall positive average hides a noticeable variation: one of the trials showed no positive effect of real-time displays and a second found no significant change for one intervention and increases of up to 14.1 per cent for three further interventions. In these studies, the only trial which measured how often participants accessed their feedback data – the first study to our knowledge which provided data on engagement with feedback – found that fewer than half of participant households checked their data more than twice over the duration of the trials. So wide variation in response to interventions using feedback has been found, including increased instead of reduced energy consumption.

More recent studies have moved beyond the provision of numeric feedback. Kim et al. (2010) compared a dashboard display of dials with a display that showed a colourful coral surrounded by fish becoming increasingly bleached with fewer fish as PC usage increased. Although participants reported greater energy use awareness for the more graphic feedback, little effect was found on energy behaviour and over a third of the coral display group requested more numeric information. Little behavioural impact was also noted in a study using EcoIsland, a highly sophisticated feedback application for households (Shiraishi et al. 2009). EcoIsland displayed a desert island with the participant family in residence, around which the water levels rose as energy use increased. It incorporated cooperative and competitive social goals, and affective and proxy economic rewards for energy reduction in the home. Again, despite self-report of increased energy awareness, no significant change was found in overall energy use. These two studies, which have been followed by many others exploring innovative means of feedback, illustrate an increasing research interest in gamification of feedback, with burgeoning cross-disciplinary collaboration, particularly with the computing disciplines with an interest in persuasive technology. However, more knowledge is needed to understand to what extent energy feedback in any form can be effective. In addition, we need to understand what psychological mechanisms underlie any success in behaviour change so that the effects can be reliably replicated across contexts.

16.3   ENERGY FEEDBACK IN THE WORKPLACE

Illustrating the potential improvements that can be accomplished in an office, Lobato and colleagues (2011) documented an extensive programme of interventions in the offices of a research facility. Availability of equipment was changed, with laptops replacing desktop computers, provision of centralised printing, withdrawal from the work-desks of all non-work appliances such as coffee makers, and power management equipment with automatic shut-down for selected power sockets after working hours to prevent phantom loads. A reduction of 47 per cent in plug load was achieved, through a combination of modification of the affordances of the physical environment and organisational change. Although individual feedback did not feature in the interventions, the study is nonetheless pertinent in demonstrating the energy savings that can be achieved in an office environment.

In contrast to domestic field trials, investigating the effect of feedback on energy behaviour in the workplace can offer several important methodological advantages. First, the work-desk may offer a less complex setting in which to examine individual behaviour (Carrico and Riemer 2011), whereas the effect of feedback in the home is confounded with household dynamics (Grønhoj and Thøgersen 2011). At the work-desk, the individual worker has full control over the devices and feedback can be targeted to the individual. Second, a limited set of appliances consume energy consumption at most work-desks. The primary energy behaviour is use of computing equipment, together with potentially a mobile phone charger, task light, personal heater or fan and miscellaneous personal appliances such as a kettle. Finally, although energy use of PCs and other desktop appliances is a relatively small proportion of overall building energy use, it is seen to contribute to the increasing total amount and share of electricity use in offices (US-EIA 2012). Thus providing feedback on energy use in the workplace not only addresses an environmentally important domain but can offer a field setting with the potential to avoid many of the confounds which have made findings from domestic feedback studies difficult to interpret. Although the devices at the work-desk are under the control of the individual employee, shared resources including lighting, heating and printing also consume energy in the workplace. In the studies we look at below, some studies have addressed a broad definition of energy use by the employee whilst others have focused on plug load or computer use. Our interest lies in the effect of individual feedback and so our focus is on actions under individual control.

Examining the extent of behavioural research in the work domain, Davis and Challenger (2009) calculated that only about 2 per cent of studies on pro-environmental behaviour were based in the workplace, and of these, most focused on waste and few were theoretically based. An early exception was that of Siero and colleagues (1996) who conducted a rigorously designed study based on theories of social identity and social comparison, in which they provided group-level feedback on energy use to two work teams, together with information and a target goal. The combination of information, goal setting and feedback resulted in energy savings for both groups. Attitudes and intention to save energy were measured. Interestingly, although psychological theory would predict that attitudes and intention influence behaviour, here behaviour change was recorded but attitudes and intentions did not change significantly.

In another study focusing on energy-related behaviour, Staats et al. (2000) selected two specific actions (keeping radiator vents clear and ensuring all radiators in a room were set to the same temperature) and ran a series of incremental interventions over two years. The interventions included information, communal feedback and individual feedback. In addition to finding changes in behaviour while individual feedback was being provided, at the end of the two years and after feedback had been withdrawn, a 6 per cent reduction in gas consumption was also recorded.

Arguing that the potential for energy conservation should be established before an intervention commences, Matthies et al. (2011) began with energy modelling to calculate that a 14 per cent reduction in electricity use by computing devices should be feasible. In 15 German university buildings housing over 2,000 office workers in total, they introduced an intervention based on an extended norm activation model (Klöckner and Matthies 2004), with communications (including posters, flyers and emails) and sticker prompts. Six out of eight buildings in the treatment group reduced their electricity consumption by a total of 7 per cent, although the variability of total consumption between buildings and the small number of buildings meant that the actual savings could not be calculated reliably. Psychological determinants of behaviour were not reported.

Also in university buildings, Carrico and Riemer (2011) compared the effects of group feedback, peer education, and combined group feedback and peer education against a control group. Feedback comprised a monthly email with graphs of building energy use. The intervention lasted four months and actual energy consumption was compared against consumption in the previous four months and against the same months in the previous year. Statistically significant reductions of 8 per cent for the combined intervention group, and 7 per cent for the feedback group were achieved. The peer education group achieved a non-significant decrease of 2 per cent.

In commercial offices with 200 employees, Owen et al. (2010) focused on lighting and provided public as well as individual feedback and incentives. They noted savings of 2.4 per cent for a feedback only condition. In another study in a commercial setting, Metzger et al. (2011) measured plug loads and implemented a series of four-week interventions at 126 desks. They provided feedback per six-person pod and encouraged inter-pod competition, achieving a 6 per cent saving. Handgraaf and colleagues (2013) combined feedback with incentives in an 83-participant study in the offices of an environmental consultancy firm, measuring computer energy use over a baseline two weeks, three weeks of intervention and a post-intervention eight weeks. Although the numbers per condition were small, they conducted an elegantly designed field experiment in which they found that social reward was more effective than financial incentives and that public rewards were more effective than private. The public, social reward condition resulted in the highest savings in contrast to the private, financial condition in which computer energy consumption increased (although not statistically significantly). Overall, the public and social rewards achieved a 6 per cent reduction in consumption, and reduced consumption in the effective conditions was maintained during post-intervention monitoring.

A common conclusion across these studies is that interventions in the workplace can contribute to behaviour change and reduction in energy consumption and, in particular, that feedback can be effective. However, the level of feedback that has been achieved in most workplace-based studies was limited by practical and technical issues. Although there is evidence that feedback is most effective when it is targeted to the individual and specific behaviour (Abrahamse et al. 2005; Daamen et al. 2001) and delivered as closely in time as possible to the relevant action (Midden et al. 1983), most earlier studies have provided monthly feedback, aggregated by building. More recent studies have begun to improve the timeliness and granularity of feedback. For example, Metzger and colleagues (2011) provided weekly feedback for workgroups of six employees. With technological development, it is now possible to provide real-time feedback to individual users at their work-desk. One of the first published studies to do so was our research conducted in 2012 which deployed state-of-the art technology at that time to monitor electricity consumption at individuals' work-desks and provide tailored feedback to individual workers. Published in Murtagh et al. (2013), this study is now described in detail to explore the effect of individual feedback over time, to examine psychological determinants of energy conservation at work and to discuss practical issues for consideration in providing feedback in the workplace.

16.4   INDIVIDUAL ENERGY FEEDBACK IN AN OFFICE SETTING: A FIELD TRIAL

The evidence discussed above suggests that feedback can lead to energy conservation but with wide variability. Individual psychological factors may play a part in this variation. Our research combined psychology and engineering approaches to examine individual energy behaviours. The study focused on three individual psychological factors and examined the relationship between these factors, personal near-real-time feedback and energy conservation. As other chapters in this *Handbook* discuss, there is extensive evidence for the influence of individual factors on pro-environmental behaviour, including energy use within and beyond the workplace. Meta-analysis has confirmed that environmental attitudes and beliefs contribute to 'green' behaviour (Bamberg and Möser 2007) and empirical evidence has demonstrated their influence on energy consumption

(Brandon and Lewis 1999). Research reviews have also found evidence for values as predictors of intention and actual pro-environmental behaviour (Dietz et al. 2005). In addition, self-identity has been linked to energy behaviour in the home (Whitmarsh and O'Neill 2010) as well as more general green behaviour (Gatersleben et al. 2012). Whereas attitudes offer the potential of plasticity, self-identity and values are more stable over time and more consistent across contexts (Gatersleben et al. 2012). Therefore, all three constructs – attitudes towards energy conservation, pro-environmental values and a green identity – offer different ways in which pro-environmental behaviour could be addressed.

The study was conducted in university offices in the UK, with approximately 80 workers (academic and administrative staff and doctoral research students). Pre- and post-intervention surveys were used to measure the psychological constructs; focus groups were held post-intervention; and energy use at individual work-desks was measured for a baseline four weeks, and then for 18 weeks during the intervention period. An energy monitoring device was installed at each work-desk, into which all desktop appliances were plugged. The device transmitted data to a central server which calculated daily and weekly totals. Although real-time data were available, monitoring at this level could constitute surveillance of individual workers as an individual's presence at, or absence from, their desk could be deduced from the energy consumption. Ethical considerations around protecting the interests of participants led to the design decision to provide visibility of energy aggregated to a minimum of an hour and viewed retrospectively by at least a day. Reliability tests were incorporated into the collection and aggregation of data, and the monitoring system was bedded in over a period of three months before data collection began for the baseline period. After measurement of data for the four-week baseline, the intervention commenced. The primary intervention was provision of a software application called MyEcoFootprint (MEF) developed for the study. This was installed on all workers' desktops or laptops and its design was based on the persuasive feedback literature (e.g. Ham and Midden 2010; Shiraishi et al. 2009). The front screen of MEF displayed a red/amber/green indicator summarising energy use in the previous week. The worker could then click to view more detail. Data were available both graphically and numerically, by hour, day and week and comparison to the average consumption across all participants in the trial. In addition, simple tips were given for saving energy, such as a reminder to switch off the computer screen when leaving the work-desk for a meeting. Security and privacy were protected through a robust password protocol. MEF was available to the participants for 18 weeks,

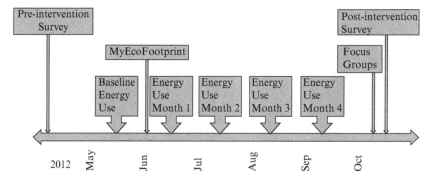

Figure 16.1 Data collection timeline

and a survey and focus groups were conducted after completion of the intervention period. Figure 16.1 shows the timeline for the study design.

Following the recommendations of Matthies and colleagues (2011) that research on energy conservation should estimate the reduction achievable, measures were initially taken of a typical personal computer (PC) and display screen configuration in minimal, typical and maximal usage over a 40-hour working week. In the baseline period, electricity use at 83 desks was measured and average energy consumption was found to be over three times the level measured as typical, and 45 per cent higher than the maximum level for a 40-hour week, adding to the findings of Kawamoto et al. (2004) and others on wasted energy at work-desks. This suggested considerable scope for reduction in consumption through behaviour change. Wide variation was noted between work-desks and relatively few workers appeared to switch off all devices on leaving work for the evening or at weekends.

The technology allowed measurement of engagement with feedback. Registration was required before usage in order to provide participants with secure access to their own data. The system was designed to minimise effort for registration (one click to begin, one-off entry of personal email address and cut-and-paste to enter a password) and for access (one click to use). Of the workers in the study, 59 per cent registered and used the system at least once. With two-fifths of participants not using the system once, despite reminders through emails, flyers and a promotional mug and coaster, provided at intervals in the first half of the intervention period, the implication was that a substantial minority appeared to be insufficiently interested in their energy usage to engage with feedback, a finding which also emerged in the focus groups, discussed below.

A pattern of reducing energy use was found over the intervention period (see Figure 16.2), resulting in reductions of 10.3 per cent and 12.7 per cent in the final two four-week periods, respectively.

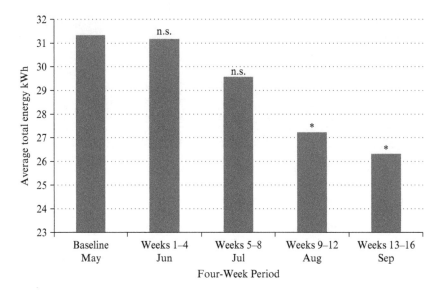

Notes: * indicates statistically significant difference from baseline; n.s. non-significant.

Figure 16.2   Average energy consumption over 20 weeks

Although reduction in the first two four-week periods was not statistically significant, the latter two four-week periods showed a significant fall in usage. There was a moderate negative correlation between the number and duration of accesses to MEF and energy consumption across the sample, in the first four weeks only, but not in the periods in which significant reduction was achieved. That is, there was a very limited relationship between use of the feedback and energy use. With respect to psychological determinants, correlation was observed between energy usage and attitudes to energy conservation ($r = -.46$) but not with values or environmental identity or intention to use MEF. That is, of the three psychological factors investigated (attitudes, values and environmental identity), only attitudes to energy saving were related to conservation across the trial and none of the three correlated with the use of feedback or with behaviour change (energy reduction). Self-reported pro-environmental behaviour was not related to energy use, before or after the intervention.

A clear implication of these findings is that actual behaviour may show a different pattern of influences than intention or self-reported behaviour, and this carries important empirical and theoretical implications. Empirically, it suggests that actual behaviour should be measured wherever possible. Technological advances make this increasingly feasible and practical for energy behaviours. Theoretically, it suggests the need for further development. Of particular interest here is the lack of a relationship between the use of feedback and behaviour change, despite an overall pattern of energy reduction. It is possible that external factors, especially those relating to workload, may have driven down energy consumption in the later periods of the intervention although none were identified. It is feasible that provision of feedback in itself raised awareness of energy usage. The reminders to use the system may have prompted increased awareness and that in itself led to reduced consumption.

There is evidence elsewhere that merely informing households that they were part of an energy-related trial resulted in lower energy consumption (Schwartz et al. 2013). Within the workplace, awareness that an intervention is underway may lead to the Hawthorne effect found by Schwartz and colleagues. Further research is needed to test these hypotheses, that increased awareness of energy consumption is a proximal determinant of energy conservation and that, although provision of feedback contributes to increased awareness, other mechanisms, such as reminders, may also generate awareness.

Two focus groups were conducted with study participants in our field trial, one of which comprised workers who had not made use of their personalised feedback. The discussions demonstrated wide awareness of energy wastage at work but a general lack of concern about energy conservation. Twelve different subthemes related to reasons why not to attempt to reduce energy use (such as inconvenience and the savings being too small) with a further three subthemes around attempting to save energy but failing (such as habit). The analysis noted that, although the subthemes individually appeared rational and logical, taken together they could be seen as a 'syndrome of reasons' which implied an underlying issue. This issue was argued to be a lack of motivation: the workers were not driven to, that is, they did not *want* to, reduce their energy consumption and ably provided a range of logically consistent reasons when questioned. The analysis pointed to a conclusion that behaviour change requires motivation – a goal or meaning which drives action. Feedback in itself cannot provide motivation but can be effective within a context or intervention that provides it.

16.5   RECENT STUDIES

More recent work has continued to apply varied and innovative means to investigate energy behaviour in offices, although a number of studies remain beset by dependence on self-reported behaviour and small sample sizes. Relying on self-reported behaviour, Russo and Buchanan (2016) used Mechanical Turk and showed that provision of information increased knowledge and awareness but not did not affect behavioural intention significantly. In a local authority office setting, Lokhorst and colleagues (2015) found that feedback, alongside commitment to reduce energy consumption for some participants, was unrelated to self-reported behaviour. Spence and colleagues (2016) conducted a small-scale office study (n=10) and noted that workers perceived a lack of control over their electricity use at work. In a large organisational study in the Netherlands, although they did not provide feedback to employees, Lo and colleagues (2014) found that attitudes were the strongest predictor of intention to switch off lights and reduce printing but habit affected lighting behaviour more than printing. Measuring actual behaviour and providing motivation through targets and group feedback, Mulville and colleagues (2014) monitored 90 office workstations for 16 weeks, and conducted sequential interventions which included fortnightly group feedback and a target reduction level, followed by individual versus group feedback. Energy use increased initially and then decreased and a substantial reduction of almost 20 per cent was achieved.

Goal setting was also introduced in the research of Kamilaris et al. (2015). They examined the energy consumption of computers used by administrative staff in a university setting. The sample size however was very small (n=18). The intervention ran for five weeks and provided general information and comparison with others in addition to goal setting. Although the interventions were designed to target psychological factors such as self-efficacy and beliefs, no measures of psychological determinants were presented. Interestingly, the study found non-significant reduction in energy use during the intervention but a significant reduction in the post-intervention monitoring, a pattern similar to that in our study above, and a reduction was maintained three months after the intervention. The authors suggested that the changed behaviour may have required time to take effect. An alternative explanation may lie in the argument proposed by Anderson and colleagues (2014). Based on their agent-based modelling, they suggested that the type and structure of the social network may influence the time required for a behavioural intervention to take effect and to reach a state of equilibrium.

Nilsson et al. (2015) provided group-level feedback on plug load to 93 employees of a Swedish construction company. Although the groups receiving weekly feedback plus information and tips for energy saving showed a 5.5–6 per cent reduction in energy use, the control group which received general information only reduced consumption by 13 per cent. This would suggest that individual feedback may be less effective than general awareness or a Hawthorne effect. In contrast, an extensive trial by Yun et al. (2015) with 61–80 office workers for a 13-week intervention found that the feedback condition resulted in a 13 per cent reduction of energy use. Further, they noted a moderate-to-strong correlation between access to the dashboard application and energy conservation (r=.53, n=45, p <.001), in contrast to our study.

16.6 DISCUSSION

Since publication of our study in 2013, research interest in energy consumption and monitoring in workplaces has increased rapidly. In the UK, this may be attributable in part to the five-year BuildTEDDI programme funded by Research Councils UK which started in 2012. This has facilitated the development of a vibrant, multidisciplinary research community which held a symposium on energy feedback in Edinburgh in 2016, with a special issue of the journal *Building Research and Information* published in April 2018, amongst many other activities. The current chapter is therefore a snapshot in time of a rapidly developing field.

Having reviewed research studies from the 1990s onwards seeking insight into whether feedback can effect change in energy behaviours in the workplace, and if so what psychological mechanisms are involved, what can we say are the main findings? Clearly, despite a rapidly growing empirical base, definitive findings remain elusive. Publication bias would suggest that the studies reviewed above are among the more successful. Published studies vary across a range of energy and other behaviours. Where feedback is provided, it may be at individual or group level or both and is typically combined with other interventions. Control of confounding variables is particularly challenging in field trials. Monitoring workers' whereabouts and attributing changes in energy consumption to behaviour change rather than contextual change is difficult. Many trials are too small for statistical significance. Despite these challenges, we attempt to summarise our conclusions.

Feedback in the workplace can be effective but behaviour change requires motivation beyond the provision of information. Thus the effect of feedback at work is likely to be greater when combined with other interventions that provide motivation or meaning, such as group and historical comparison, public notification of progress and increased control over appliances. Automation, such as powering down PCs when not used for a period of time, may be more effective than behaviour change (Staddon et al. 2016). During an intervention, it may take time for behaviour to change and results may not be immediate. More evidence is needed on the relative efficacy of group versus individual feedback. Individual feedback may only be appropriate for the devices that the individual controls. Group feedback may require less resource (energy monitoring at sub-meters rather than individual desks, for example) but there is as yet little robust evidence comparing individual feedback with that of a salient group. Existing evidence with group feedback makes little attempt to identify the basis for grouping or to establish levels of group identification, which can be essential for the mechanisms of group influence (Haslam 2004).

16.6.1 Collective and Participatory Approaches to Energy Saving in the Workplace

The approach of individual feedback in the workplace can appear as a reductionist perspective, in which the problem of energy conservation is the personal responsibility of individual employees. But energy at work is consumed in a collective endeavour with workers collaborating to achieve common goals. Rather than trying to change individual workers' incidental energy behaviour, significant savings are more likely to be achieved not by provision of information but by involving workers in energy-saving strategies. Workers who are directly involved in production processes will know their working practices and technology better than anyone (Stern 2000). Such a strategy may not only be more effective in leading to energy reduction, but it may also lead to a more engaged and satisfied workforce, who begin to feel a collective ownership for the climate crisis we face, giving meaning to changed behaviour. A collective and participatory approach is required in which a culture of engagement and trust is developed so that workers are treated as partners who are concerned to produce a quality product within an environment that is not physically damaging either to themselves or the wider community. Structural barriers (e.g. in communication, influence and environmental control) need to be removed in order to encourage ground-up initiatives drawing on workers' knowledge and skills for creating low-carbon production processes and thus, green workplaces.

There are some excellent examples of initiatives where public and private sector organisations have drawn on workers' knowledge and skills by organising working groups or working with trade unions to find ways of reducing the organisational environmental impact. For example, the ABVV union in the steel company Ellimetal (Belgium) reduced heat loss and oil bills, and improved the comfort of workers, after forklift truck drivers suggested that they should have control of automatic gates. The SEIU cleaners' union (USA) negotiated cleaning shifts to take place during the day; this not only reduced the need for night-time lighting but meant that these workers could spend the evenings with their families (ETUC 2013). In the UK, BT plc involved their workforce in a ground-up approach to carbon impact assessments covering energy, water and waste. The water services company, United Utilities, identified low/no cost energy-saving efficiency options through workshops with staff (TUC 2010). The efforts by the Lucas Aerospace workforce to convert production in their company from weapons to socially and environmentally sustainable and useful products have been cited in debates on creating low-carbon societies (Räthzel et al. 2010).

There are many occasions when individuals could and would do more but the conditions in which they work and live do not enable them to act more sustainably. Those responsible for company environmental policies and actions should try to ensure that they recognise when it is the inherent conditions and established structures, policies and processes that prevent change, rather than individual resistance. Company practices should be critically questioned to ensure that outdated management structures in the workplace (such as hierarchies that prevent bottom-up communication) do not prevent collective actions to improve the environmental impact of production processes, products and workplace behaviour.

16.6.2   Future Research Challenges for Workplace Feedback

The time for feedback aimed simply at energy reduction is gone. As economies shift towards lower carbon, the issue is no longer one of less energy use but shifting energy use to renewable sources as well as reducing waste. Beyond the double invisibility described by Burgess and Nye (2008), we suggest a third layer of invisibility: with an energy mix that is increasingly complex, including primarily gas, renewables, nuclear and coal in the UK (DBEIS 2016b), the relationship between energy and environmental impact is increasingly unclear to the typical employee. A growing number of workplaces are deploying photovoltaic panels, wind turbines, biomass or other technologies for renewable energy generation and will want to discourage working during gaps in self-generation when energy will cost them more. In terms of feedback, it will no longer be sufficient simply to provide consumption totals. Information displays will need to identify energy sources, or at least indicate 'good' versus 'bad' energy use, in order to contribute to changing behaviour to align with potentially intermittent generation. As the problem of energy behaviour and energy efficiency becomes increasingly complex, requiring more educated consumers, workplaces are particularly well-placed to provide that education, and to consider feedback and other interventions as part of a holistic energy strategy that begins with the sources of energy and harnesses collective action amongst employees.

The psychological mechanisms by which feedback may work are still unknown. The widely varying outcomes of research on feedback demonstrate that information deficit alone is insufficient as an explanation. The most promising constructs to explore further are motivation and meaning, awareness (even though we know that raised awareness in itself does not necessarily result in changed behaviour) and self-efficacy. A combination of experimental and field studies may serve better to identify the relative strengths of different psychological and social psychological factors. Within field studies, energy consumption may be a poor measure of behaviour: technology (e.g. faulty equipment) and context (e.g. outside temperature, workload) are also major determinants of total energy consumption. Contextual factors are still insufficiently explored. Although some work has considered social norms, the work context is a complex environment in which employees may identify with different social groups (Haslam 2004); organisational cultural norms may vary with respect to pro-environmental behaviour and in their alignment with mission and values; and the goal-oriented nature of work tasks combined with work pressure may dominate in determining individual behaviour. Internal structural constraints on communication with management may reduce workers' identification with their employing organisations and thus their interest in developing solutions to reduce the organisation's environmental impact.

16.7   RECOMMENDATIONS FOR PRACTITIONERS

The research reviewed above raised several practical issues which serve as learning points for future work on feedback in the workplace. First, as noted above, real-time monitoring of energy consumption can be used as surveillance of employees and this carries with it ethical implications (Coleman et al. 2013; Murtagh et al. 2013). As almost all enterprise at the office work-desk is now computer based, the ability to monitor energy consumption is effectively equivalent to monitoring activity at a worker's desk. If energy is being measured for research purposes or behaviour change, intervention designers should recognise that supervisors could use such information to the detriment of the employee. The ethical implications should be discussed openly and, in line with sound ethical practice, at a minimum, participants should be allowed to opt out. We would recommend that real-time monitoring is not made available to managers and supervisors and that retrospective and aggregated data only are accessible to participants and third parties.

Collection of (near-)real-time energy consumption entails very large volumes of data. Adequate design is needed for the collection, storage and analysis infrastructure. Collection at multiple points such as all work-desks in an office requires deployment of multiple items of sensing equipment. Appropriate processes are required to ensure the reliability of each item of equipment, to monitor ongoing reliability, for rapid replacement of faulty technology, for removal of data from analysis for any equipment reported as faulty and for robustness of analysis to allow for failures. Consideration also needs to be given to the risk of central failure, such as backing up data in raw and/or aggregated form – the loss of data and unreliability of equipment has detracted from previous studies (Gandhi and Brager 2016). Security of the data is very important and system design needs to ensure that individuals can access only their own data and that aggregated data is safe from hacking.

Within the workplace, staff churn is to be expected, that is, the departure of staff, arrival of newcomers and changing desks. More generally, this is an issue facing any longitudinal study which includes energy users. System design needs to incorporate the relationship between the individual and the work-desk, the ability to modify this relationship, and the processes for monitoring staff movement (subject to the ethical concerns mentioned previously) and updating the energy measurement system accordingly. Without rigorous monitoring of people and equipment, any energy savings cannot be reliably attributed to behaviour change as Gandhi and Brager (2016) noted. Finally, patterns of attendance and work require close attention. Holidays, staff awaydays, conferences, project deadlines and other work-related factors may have a substantial effect on energy consumption and studies of energy use need to be aware of external factors.

The discussion above leads to the conclusion that while behaviour change leading to energy conservation in the workplace is possible and worth pursuing, the role of individual feedback in behaviour change programmes is not proven. When it comes to designing programmes to reduce employee energy consumption in offices, the challenges, cost and effort of deploying individual feedback should be weighed against alternative interventions that may offer equivalent results more rapidly and cheaply.

REFERENCES

Abrahamse, W., L. Steg, C. Vlek and T. Rothengatter (2005), 'A review of intervention studies aimed at household energy conservation', *Journal of Environmental Psychology*, **25**, 273–291.

Anderson, K., S. Lee and C. Menassa (2014), 'Impact of social network type and structure on modeling normative energy use behavior interventions', *Journal of Computing in Civil Engineering*, **28**, 30–39.

Bamberg, S. and G. Möser (2007), 'Twenty years after Hines, Hungerford, and Tomera: A new meta-analysis of psycho-social determinants of pro-environmental behaviour', *Journal of Environmental Psychology*, **27**, 14–25.

Brandon, G. and A. Lewis (1999), 'Reducing household energy consumption: A qualitative and quantitative field study', *Journal of Environmental Psychology*, **19**, 75–85.

Burgess, J. and M. Nye (2008), 'Re-materialising energy use through transparent monitoring systems', *Energy Policy*, 36, 4454–4459.

Carrico, A. R. and M. Riemer (2011), 'Motivating energy conservation in the workplace: An evaluation of the use of group-level feedback and peer education', *Journal of Environmental Psychology*, **31**, 1–13.

Coleman, M. J., K. N. Irvine, M. Lemon and L. Shao (2013), 'Promoting behavioural change through personalized feedback in offices', *Building Research and Information*, **41**, 637–651.

Daamen, D. D. L., H. Staats, H. A. M. Wilke and M. Engelen (2001), 'Improving environmental behavior in companies', *Environment and Behavior*, **33**, 229–248.

Davis, M. C. and R. Challenger (2009), 'Climate challenge – warming to the task', *The Psychologist*, **22**, 112–115.

DBEIS (2016a), *Building Energy Efficiency Survey*, accessed 5 January 2017 at https://www.gov.uk/government/publications/building-energy-efficiency-survey-bees.

DBEIS (2016b), *Fuel Mix Disclosure Data Table*, accessed 13 October 2016 at https://www.gov.uk/government/publications/fuel-mix-disclosure-data-table.

Dietz, T., A. Fitzgerald and R. Shwom (2005), 'Environmental values', *Annual Review of Environmental Resources*, **30**, 335–372.

Ehrhardt-Martinez, K., K. A. Donnelly and J. A. Laitner (2010), 'Advanced metering initiatives and residential feedback programs: A meta-review for household electricity saving opportunities', Washington, DC: American Council for an Energy-efficient Economy.

ETUC (2013), 'Green workplaces: A guide for union representatives', Brussels: European Trade Union Confederation.

Faruqui, A., S. Sergici and A. Sharif (2010), 'The impact of informational feedback on energy consumption – a survey of the experimental evidence', *Energy*, **35**, 1598–1608.

Gandhi, P. and G. S. Brager (2016), 'Commercial office plug load energy consumption trends and the role of occupant behavior', *Energy and Buildings*, **125**, 1–8.

Gatersleben, B., N. Murtagh and W. Abrahamse (2012), 'Values, identity and pro-environmental behaviour', *Contemporary Social Science*, iFirst, 1–19.

Grønhoj, A. and J. Thøgersen (2011), 'Feedback on household electricity consumption: Learning and social influence processes', *International Journal of Consumer Studies*, **35**, 138–145.

Ham, J. and C. Midden (2010), 'Ambient persuasive technology needs little cognitive effort: The differential effects of cognitive load on lighting feedback versus factual feedback', *Persuasive Technology, Proceedings*, **6137**, 132–142.

Handgraaf, M. J. J., M. A. Van Lidth De Jeude and K. C. Appelt (2013), 'Public praise vs. private pay: effects of rewards on energy conservation in the workplace', *Ecological Economics*, **86**, 86–92.

Hargreaves, T., M. Nye and J. Burgess (2010), 'Making energy visible: A qualitative field study of how householders interact with feedback from smart energy monitors', *Energy Policy*, **38**, 6111–6119.

Haslam, S. A. (2004), *Psychology in Organizations*, London: Sage.

Junnila, S. (2007), 'The potential effect of end-users on energy conservation in office buildings', *Facilities*, **25**, 329–339.

Kamilaris, A., J. Neovino, S. Kondepudi and B. Kalluri (2015), 'A case study on the individual energy use of personal computers in an office setting and assessment of various feedback types toward energy savings', *Energy Build*, **104**, 73–86.

Kawamoto, K., Y. Shimoda and M. Mizuno (2004), 'Energy saving potential of office equipment power management', *Energy and Buildings*, **36**, 915–923.

Kim, T., H. Hong and B. Magerko (2010), 'Designing for persuasion: Toward ambient eco-visualization for awareness', *Persuasive Technology, Proceedings*, **6137**, 106–116.

Klöckner, C. A. and E. Matthies (2004), 'How habits interfere with norm directed behaviour: A normative decision-making model for travel mode choice', *Journal of Environmental Psychology*, **24**, 319–327.

Lawrence Berkeley Laboratory (2017), *Standby FAQ*, accessed 20 January 2017 at www.lbl.gov.

Lobato, C., S. Pless, M. Sheppy and P. Torcelli (2011), 'Reducing plug and process loads for a large scale, low energy office building: NREL's research support facility', ASHRAE Winter Conference, Las Vegas, US, 29 January to 2 February 2011.

Lokhorst, A. M., H. Staats and J. Van Iterson (2015), 'Energy saving in office buildings: Are feedback and commitment-making useful instruments to trigger change?', *Human Ecology*, **43**, 759–768.

Masoso, O. T. and L. J. Grobler (2010), 'The dark side of occupants' behaviour on building energy use', *Energy and Buildings*, **42**, 173–177.

Matthies, E., I. Kastner, A. Klesse and H.-J. Wagner (2011), 'High reduction potentials for energy user behaviour in public buildings: How much can psychology-based interventions achieve?', *Journal of Environmental Studies and Sciences*, **1**, 241–255.

McMakin, A. H., E. L. Malone and R. E. Lundgren (2002), 'Motivating residents to conserve energy without financial incentives', *Environment and Behavior*, **34** (6), 848–863.

Metzger, I., A. Kandt and O. Van Geet (2011), *Plug Load Behavioral Change Demonstration Project*, Golden, Colorado: National Renewable Energy Lab.

Midden, C. H., J. F. Meter, M. H. Weenig and H. J. A. Zieverink (1983), 'Using feedback, reinforcement and information to reduce energy consumption in households: A field experiment', *Journal of Economic Psychology*, **3**, 65–86.

Mulville, M., K. Jones and G. Huebner (2014), 'The potential for energy reduction in UK commercial offices through effective management and behaviour change', *Architectural Engineering and Design Management*, **10**, 79–90.

Murtagh, N., M. Nati, W. R. Headley, B. Gatersleben, A. Gluhak, M. A. Imran and D. Uzzell (2013), 'Individual energy use and feedback in an office setting: A field trial', *Energy Policy*, **62**, 717–727.

Nilsson, A., K. Andersson and C. J. Bergstad (2015), 'Energy behaviors at the office: An intervention study on the use of equipment', *Applied Energy*, **146**, 434–441.

Owen, T., A. Pape-Salmon and B. McMurchy (2010), 'Employee engagement and energy information software supporting carbon neutrality', *ACEEE Summer Study on Energy Efficiency in Buildings*, **7**, 233–244.

Räthzel, N., D. Uzzell and D. Elliott (2010), 'Can trade unions become environmental innovators?', *Soundings*, **45**, 76–87.

Raw, G. J. and D. I. Ross (2011), *Energy Demand Research Project: Final Analysis*, St Albans, Herts: Ofgem.

Russo, R. and K. Buchanan (2016), 'Vanquishing energy vampires: The failure of feedback', in K. Buchanan and S. Staddon (eds), *Feedback in Energy Demand Reduction: Examining Evidence and Exploring Opportunities*, Edinburgh: ECEEE/TEDDINET.

Schwartz, D., B. Fischhoff, T. Krishnamurti and F. Sowell (2013), 'The Hawthorne effect and energy awareness', *Proceedings of the National Academy of Sciences*, **110**, 15242–15246.

Shiraishi, M., Y. Washio, C. Takayama, V. Lehdonvirta, H. Kimura and T. Nakajima (2009), 'Using individual, social and economic persuasion techniques to reduce CO_2 emissions in a family setting', 4th International Conference on Persuasive Technology, ACM.

Siero, F. W., A. B. Bakker, G. B. Dekker and M. T. C. Van Den Burg (1996), 'Changing organizational energy consumption behaviour through comparative feedback', *Journal of Environmental Psychology*, **16**, 235–246.

Spence, A., N. Banks, B. Bedwell, E. Constanza, E. Ferguson, M. Goulden, M. Jewell and C. Leygue (2016), 'GENIE (Goal-setting and ENergy Information Engagement) in the workplace', in K. Buchanan and S. Staddon (eds), *Feedback in Energy Demand Reduction: Examining Evidence and Exploring Opportunities*, Edinburgh: ECEEE/TEDDINET.

Staats, H., E. Van Leeuwen and A. Wit (2000), 'A longitudinal study of informational interventions to save energy in an office building', *Journal of Applied Behavioral Analysis*, **33**, 101–104.

Staddon, S. C., C. Cycil, M. Goulden, C. Leygue and A. Spence (2016), 'Intervening to change behaviour and save energy in the workplace: A systematic review of available evidence', *Energy Research and Social Science*, **17**, 30–51.

Stern, P. C. (2000), 'Toward a coherent theory of environmentally significant behavior', *Journal of Social Issues*, **56**, 407–424.

TUC (2010), *GreenWorks: TUC Green Workplaces Project Report 2008–2010*, London: Trade Union Congress.

US-EIA (2012), 'AEO2013 Early Release Overview', US Energy Information Administration.

Webber, C. (2006), 'After-hours power status of office equipment in the USA', *Energy*, **31**, 2823–2838.

Whitmarsh, L. and S. O'Neill (2010), 'Green identity, green living? The role of pro-environmental self-identity in determining consistency across diverse pro-environmental behaviours', *Journal of Environmental Psychology*, **30**, 305–314.

Yun, R., A. Aziz, P. Scupelli, B. Lasternas, C. Zhang and V. Loftness (2015), 'Beyond eco-feedback: Adding online manual and automated controls to promote workplace sustainability', *CHI*, Seoul, Korea.

17. The role of social norms in incentivising energy reduction in organisations
Peter Bradley, Shane Fudge and Matthew Leach

17.1 INTRODUCTION

Around the world there is strong interest in the use of energy feedback via smart metering technology as an option for businesses to reduce their energy use and mitigate greenhouse gases (GHGs). In order to bring about such energy reductions in this way, the feedback provided needs to motivate changes in energy behaviours and practices within organisations. The chapter explores the impact of a real-life smart metering intervention and its impact on the emergence and diffusion of energy-related social norms and the link between these and energy use. The chapter begins by looking at early organisation and energy conservation studies (mainly feedback-based), before moving on to organisational and social norms studies, and concluding with those most relevant to the current chapter. We first briefly define what we mean by social norms. Cialdini et al. (1991) argue that social norms can be defined as either injunctive (characterised by perception of what most people approve or disapprove of) or descriptive (characterised by what most people do). According to this argument, injunctive norms incentivise action by promising social rewards and punishments (informal sanctions) for it (and therefore enjoin behaviour). According to Cialdini et al. (1991) these constitute the moral rules of a group. Descriptive norms, on the other hand, inform behaviour, and incentivise action, by providing evidence of what are likely to be effective and adaptive steps to take based on what others do (Cialdini et al. 1991). The 'focus theory' of Cialdini et al. (1991) stipulates that this differentiation of social norms is critical to a full understanding of their influence on human behaviour.

17.1.1 Organisational Energy Studies

There are three broad findings from the review of previous organisational studies for this section: first, the vast majority (all but one of the studies looked at here) rely on self-reporting of energy use when examining individual-level energy behaviours. Second, few studies investigate the role of social norms in influencing energy use within organisations. Finally, most studies that do look at social norms and energy (or environmental sustainability-related behaviours) tend to only pick up on the role of injunctive (subjective) social norms and not descriptive social norms. However, these studies provide a useful background for more detailed exploration of the different norms. This section now provides an overview of these studies.

There have been a number of different studies of the use of feedback on energy consumption behaviour. Siero et al. (1996) explored the effect of two different types of feedback on energy consumption behaviour within a metallurgical company. Two different groups of employees were given different types of feedback: one received information about their energy conservation and personal performance and were set a conservation goal; the other group received the same but also comparative feedback about the other group. It was notable that more energy was saved when comparative feedback was provided, even half a year after the intervention, and this took place with little change in attitudes or intentions. The study recorded energy wastage around key energy consumption objects, drilling and assembly lines etc. Records were sometimes not based on actual energy data (for feedback). Behaviour change of the groups from the interventions were based on self-reports.

Gustafson and Longland (2008), on the other hand, measured whole-building electricity consumption on a monthly basis and applied a wide variety of initiatives and interventions with employees in order to encourage energy conservation. Benchmark and end of year surveys provided a comparison of employees' stated behaviours, environmental perceptions and impacts. However, whilst at the end of the first year the initiative achieved a 5 per cent reduction in electricity consumption, it was difficult to unpick the influences underpinning this change because effects could not be attributed to any one intervention and interventions were not set out in a transparent way.

Another study was carried out by Schwartz et al. (2010) who conducted participatory action research studies in an organisation, which included: small-scale interviews, workshops and smart metering of offices before and after workshops. A larger survey was also conducted. This more bottom-up approach allowed the study to be reflexive and provide depth of insight on the engagement of participants in energy reduction, beyond the impact of just putting the technology in place. Energy use measurement took place at the office level.

Finally, Carrico and Riemer (2011) conducted three intervention studies in a workplace setting. One provided group-level feedback, presented monthly to employees via email. The second involved peer educators to disseminate information and encourage reductions in energy use by colleagues, the third involved peer education and feedback. Feedback and energy-monitoring was provided at the building level and energy use during the interventions was compared to energy use during the bench-mark. Feedback and peer education resulted in reductions in energy use of 7 per cent and 4 per cent, respectively. Surveys were also conducted to provide additional data at the individual level but were not correlated with individuals' energy use. Energy was measured at the building level, but individual energy-use estimates were based on self-reports.

17.1.2 Organisational and Social Norms Studies

A number of studies that investigate energy feedback in organisations pointed to the potential for normative influence from one's peers in bring-ing about energy reductions. Cordano and Frieze (2000) looked at percep-tions of norms for environmental regulation – they focused on descriptive norms of environmental managers; other employees were not included. Also focusing on managers, Flannery and May (2000) investigated the individual and contextual influences shaping the environmental and ethical decision intentions in the US metal-finishing industry. They found that the magnitude of consequences and a dimension of moral intensity moderated the relationships between subjective (injunctive) norms and managers' environmental and ethical decision intentions.

Looking more broadly, Ramus and Killmer (2007) provided a con-ceptual framework to look at prosocial extra role behaviours and their relationship to employee motivation. Within their framework, they picked up on the role of social norms within an organisation, as well as outside the organisation on environmental behaviours. They did not, however, provide any differentiation between injunctive and descriptive norms, nor were salience of norms and empirical analysis conducted.

A useful study by Goldstein et al. (2008) undertook two field experi-ments in the Hospitality sector to investigate the effectiveness of signs (on room doors) that asked hotel guests to conduct actions that result in energy conservation (i.e. not requesting towels to be washed every day). They found that messages employing descriptive norms ('the majority of guests reuse their towels') proved more effective than widely used messages that focus on environmental conservation.

Vazquez Brust and Liston-Heyes (2010) presented a model that investi-gates the extent to which environmental behaviour intentions are explained by managers' core values, beliefs and basic assumptions; individual and socio-cognitive frames; contextual factors; and principles of governance. In the paper they identified the importance of social norms, but they did not recognise different types of social norms and did not actually look at social norms when applying their model in a regression analysis with survey data. A key limitation of their approach was that they focused on just managers and not employees.

Papagiannakis and Lioukas (2012) specified and tested a model of corporate environmental responsiveness, by adapting a version of the theory of planned behaviour and the value–belief–norm theory. They found that subjective norms (injunctive norms) expressing stakeholder expectations affected corporate environmental responsiveness.

Ture and Ganesh (2014) reviewed employee-centric sustainability literature in management, pro-environmental areas of psychology and sociology disciplines. Similar to quite a number of other studies, they only picked up on injunctive social norms in their review (subjective norms) and not descriptive norms.

In relation to the study of social norms and energy feedback in organisations, five highly relevant studies for the current intervention were found: Siero et al. (1996), Carrico and Riemer (2011), Lo et al. (2014), Dixon et al. (2014) and Chen and Knight (2014). These most relevant studies are now summarised, focusing primarily on approaches.

In their intervention, Siero et al. (1996) measured changes in social norms. They did not, however, explicitly classify in terms of descriptive and injunctive norms. They defined social norms in terms of normative belief and motivation to comply following Ajzen and Fishbein (1980). Social norms about shutting off machines and switching off lights revealed only an effect of the intervention on behavioural beliefs that these habits resulted in energy saving.

In their study, Carrico and Riemer (2011) examined whether their interventions changed the levels of descriptive and injunctive norms around energy services. They found that the intervention increased both. There was, however, no effect on energy conservation behaviour (which was based on self-reports).

Lo et al. (2014) investigated the effect of social norms (descriptive and injunctive) on energy-saving behaviours. The office energy behaviours measured however, were only a select few and based on self-reports not actual energy use. In the study, the perceived norm was a significant predictor of printing intentions and intention to switch off monitors, but not intention to switch off lights. The study was not an intervention study, but a regression analysis based on survey data.

Dixon et al. (2014) undertook a comparative feedback study where individual and collective progress on energy reduction is fed back to participants. The individual-level data generated, however, is based on self-reports of energy conservation behaviours (building-level data is actual, not reported). Surveys were conducted before and after the intervention to measure the extent to which the comparative feedback campaign influenced subjective norms as well as self-reported energy behaviours amongst other variables. The measures of injunctive and descriptive norms applied were broadly the same as used in the current study. Results showed that descriptive norms increased after the intervention. Injunctive norms did not change. No link between changes in norms and changes in energy behaviours was explored.

Chen and Knight (2014), as part of their analysis looked at the effect of injunctive norms on energy preserving intentions for 564 employees of nine state-owned electric power companies. The study came up with their own questions for measuring injunctive norms; what is surprising, however, is that some of the questions related to recycling, reusable materials and protecting the environment, which do not seem necessarily salient or directly correspond with energy use. Energy-saving intentions were self-reported. The study found that injunctive norms have a direct, positive and strong effect on energy conservation intentions.

17.1.3 Social Norms and the Environmental Psychology Literature

Abrahamse and Steg (2013), from an extensive review of the literature on social influence approaches to encourage resource conservation (including energy), identified that more empirical research linking social influence mechanisms to behaviour change was needed. They found that relatively few field studies have looked at social norms and social comparison as part of effective measures. They also stated that emphasis on intervention studies had predominantly focused on looking at whether a social influence approach was successful, not on why it was successful.

Social norms have been systematically researched in the environmental psychology literature. In this literature, analysis tends to focus on examining the effect of social norms on behaviour. There is little work that quantitatively and qualitatively examines the emergence of social norms, a finding in line with Abrahamse and Steg (2013). The main aim of the study upon which this chapter is focused was to investigate and provide empirical evidence on the emergence and diffusion of social norms in relation to energy services from energy feedback provided by smart metering technology, measuring individuals' actual energy use. We use the 'focus theory of normative conduct' (Cialdini et al. 1991) as the starting point to guide this investigation.

17.2   SOCIAL NORMS

17.2.1   Theory and Empirical Evidence in Relation to Norm Emergence within Organisations

There are a number of processes that lead to the development of social norms and changes in behaviour, these are as follows: (1) norm *emergence*, (2) norm *diffusion* and (3) *translation* into behaviour. Norm diffusion involves the spread of social norms (injunctive and descriptive). The emergence process and the diffusion processes involve social construction (Lyndhurst 2009) and social comparison (Vishwanath 2006). The social construction and social comparison processes occur for both descriptive and injunctive norms and are informed from other referent individuals.[1] Social construction is the theory that norms, beliefs and attitudes are constructed through a process of social interaction (Lyndhurst 2009). Burr (2003) identifies the major influence of Berger and Luckmann (1991) on the development of social constructionism, who, in turn, acknowledge earlier influential work on their thinking, in particular that of Mead, Marx, Schultz and Durkheim (as seen in Andrews 2012).

For social comparison, individuals compare with what others do/how they respond to a given situation. In this regard, Snyder and Swann (1978) as seen in Flynn and Chatman (2003), assert that 'Emergent norm formation is an inherently social psychological process. People form impressions of others in their social environments by interpreting information gathered from observation of an interpersonal interaction with the focal individual and similar others.'

17.2.2   Translating Social Norms into Actions and Behaviour

A refinement that needs to be applied before the use of normative explanations can be confidently established is whether people's attention is focused on that particular norm in any given situation. This is an important consideration as whether the norm will influence behaviour will depend on whether attention is focused on it, and on its activation. This is important as social norms motivate and direct action primarily when they are activated (said to be made more salient or otherwise focused upon). Social norms have to be activated to influence behaviour (Cialdini et al. 1991).

Rimal and Real (2005) have extended the work of Cialdini et al. (1991) to present a theory of normative social behaviour. The theory/model has three variables/parameters that effect the translation of social norms into behaviour. They state that social identity, norm interaction (injunctive norms in their model), and outcome expectations moderate the influence of descriptive norms on behaviour, that is, if you share identity, you are more likely to follow the descriptive norm. The theory of social identity was developed by Tajfel (1974), and group identity comes from this. In the current project, we restrict our concept and discussion of group identity to the workplace of the relevant department within which the trial was run. The work of Rimal and Real (2005) is a useful extension of the work of Cialdini et al. (1991) as these authors start to incorporate influencing factors in their model of translating norms into behaviour. They identify that the translation of a descriptive norm into behaviour is moderated by the existence of injunctive norms relevant to the behaviour, outcome expectations and group identity. If you believe in, and have alignment with, outcomes you are more likely to enact the norm into behaviour, and if there are injunctive norms against not doing the action you are more likely to enact the descriptive norm into behaviour; also, if you share a group identity with others who have and enact the norm you are also more likely to do the same.

17.2.3   Questions and Gaps

Significantly, the focus theory of Cialdini et al. (1991) only looks at norm activation and translation into behaviour, it does not look at the emergence and diffusion of social norms. The same can be said of Rimal and Real (2005). Both Cialdini et al. (1991) and Rimal and Real (2005) focus on the translation of norms into behaviour; for example, the work of Cialdini et al. (1991) typically attempts to invoke a particular norm and then measure behaviour change. Although a useful and valid approach, such research provides no information on the pre-stages of social norm emergence and social norm diffusion. In this study, emergence refers to the arising of norms in participants, which can occur through social interaction (and social learning) and other forms of communication, amongst others. Norm diffusion is used to refer to the extent to which norms (via social interaction/visual observation etc.) become prevalent amongst participants. Rimal and Real (2005) identify group identity and outcome expectations as being important in determining the translation of social norms into behaviour. However, there is little testing of whether group identity and outcome expectations actually affect the emergence of group norms in the first place; this is the focus of the current study. Additionally, we seek to investigate social construction and social comparison processes occurring during the study (via interview data) to provide added insight and depth on these processes, as they are important to norm emergence and diffusion.

17.3   METHODS

17.3.1   Context and Overview

This study was part of a larger project that ran a longitudinal energy feedback intervention in an organisational setting. The intervention was to put in place a smart meter energy feedback system where an energy footprint tool called MyEcoFootprint (MEF) which measures desk-based energy use and provides feedback to users (via a web-based interface) was provided to participants.

The participants were from a higher education sector organisation, made up of predominantly lecturers, researchers and students. The department was chosen based on availability and access. The larger project (Murtagh et al. 2013) applied an opt-out policy to recruit participants for the project as literature indicated that this was the most effective recruitment policy: participants were provided with smart metering equipment and included in the project unless they identified to the project team that they did not want to participate.

A flow chart for benchmark and intervention periods is provided in Figure 17.1 showing key timings; it also identifies at what stages surveys and interviews were conducted. Interviews were carried out with the aim of understanding and exploring participants' experience of the intervention, to explore the social context, and to gain insight and depth on social construction and social comparisons occurring during the intervention. The interview approach was believed to be the most suitable method to collect such data, as previous studies such as Schwartz et al. (2010) indicated suitability and validity for the context and workshops were

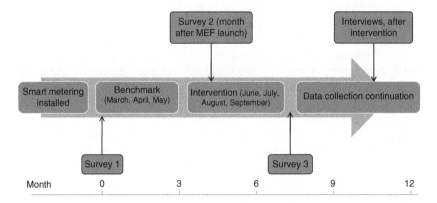

Figure 17.1   A timeline of activities for the study

considered, but it was felt that the presence of third parties may inhibit or influence data attained. Surveys were conducted to primarily pick up on factors identified in Rimal and Real (2005) and other relevant information, as identified in section 17.3.3. Most studies that look to measure social norms in organisational energy study contexts apply the survey approach, as seen towards the end of section 17.1.2. Three surveys were deployed to participants (paper and online formats via email) as well as interviews as set out in Figure 17.1 and further discussed in section 17.3.3. Interview participants were also requested via email, the response to both surveys and interviews are provided below in section 17.3.2.

The benchmark and the intervention lasted seven months. Detail on the smart metering deployment is in Murtagh et al. (2013) and a summary is provided here. Desk-based electricity (plug-based) and presence data were collected for the benchmark for each participant. After the benchmark data collection, the MyEcoFootprint tool was provided to each participant to provide them with energy feedback information.[2] The energy feedback information from MEF was available for the four-month intervention period; energy and presence data was again collected during this time. The smart metering technology implemented during the study measured both energy use and energy use while present (providing a measure of efficient energy use).

17.3.2 Response to Surveys and Interviews

Survey 1 was sent to the 83 intervention participants and received a response of 40 (31 in the intervention group and that group had energy data), survey 2 received a response of 37 out of 83 (19 that used MEF and filled out the survey) and survey 3 received a response of 29 out of 83 (19 filled out surveys 1 and 3, of these 17 provided data for all relevant variables tested). The sample was based on a case study university academic department that was willing to be involved in the study. Of those in the university who were approached to participate, eight people took part in interviews. The interviews were conducted with two academics, three researchers, two PhD students and one administrator. All interview participants were in the intervention group; of the eight, six had used the MEF tool.

17.3.3 Surveys

A key approach adopted by the study was to apply and measure the change in social norms and efficient energy use via a longitudinal study. Measurement of desk-based energy use was captured above. To pick up on the processes of social norm emergence and diffusion in relation to energy, the study made use of surveys as well as interviews. Measurement of social norms was conducted via surveys. The surveys allowed quantification and significance testing of the emergence of social norms in relation to energy, but also quantitative testing of relationships between social norm emergence, group identity, outcome expectations and injunctive norms (in line with factors identified as important by Rimal and Real (2005)). The questions were informed and developed based on reviews of previous studies looking at similar issues and through dialogue and discussion with researchers (where previous questions and measures were not available in the literature). For social norms measurement, the authors found robust previous survey questions for these and the factors identified above, as outlined in the next paragraph. Quantitative data for a few other variables to understand social construction was also included in survey 1, these questions were constructed in debate and dialogue by the current authors to ensure strong questions. When measuring actual energy behaviours, measuring energy took place at the desk of the occupant, where they received feedback from the smart metering on energy use as well as normative information; this ensured salience to the relevant energy behaviour. Survey 1 was carried out at the beginning of the benchmark. The most important measurement was the benchmark of injunctive and descriptive norms around energy use. Specific questions on these (in Table 17.1) are adapted from Ohtomo and Hirose's (2007) measure of injunctive and descriptive norms for recycling, which have been shown to be a reliable and valid measure of these concepts. They use a 5-point Likert scale. Questions for collective outcome expectancy are from Carrico (2009) as were questions on group identity. With regards to group identity, these are originally from Mael and Ashforth (1992).

Survey 2 was designed primarily to measure quantitative variables relevant to social construction and social comparison processes; the questions (in Table 17.2) were developed by the current authors in order to deliver information relevant to the current study: the extent of discussion, socialising and communication around MEF and energy use, individual cost and gain, and effort required in relation to using MEF and reducing electricity. Feelings of 'duty' and also 'pressure' in relation to using MEF were also measured.

Survey 3 was carried out four months after the intervention period after MEF implementation and measured changes in injunctive and descriptive norms (so it used the same questions as survey 1).

17.3.4   Interviews

Interview participants were recruited based on an email request (to) and response (from) the intervention group. Interviews ranged from between just

Table 17.1   Survey 1 questions

Factor	Questions	Answer
Group identity	I am very interested in what others think about the department When I talk about the department, I usually say 'we' rather than 'they' When someone praises the department, it feels like a personal compliment	7-point Likert scale from strongly disagree (1) to strongly agree (7)
Outcome expectations	By changing our behaviour, employees and students like me can reduce the department's energy use The department should do more to save energy I am concerned about the amount of energy that the department uses Energy conservation should **not** be a priority for the department now	
Descriptive norms	How many people in your department: turn off office or lab equipment when they are finished using it? How many people in your department: turn off their computers before leaving work for the day? How many people in your department: turn off their monitors before leaving work for the day? How many people in your department: turn off the lights at their desk/office before leaving work?	5-point Likert scale: very few (1), 25%, 50%, 75%, Nearly everyone (5)
Injunctive norms	If the other people in your department saw that a computer was left on when the user was not at work, they would: If the other people in your department saw that a monitor was left on when the user was not at work, they would: If the other people in your department saw that an individual's lights were left on when he/she was not at work, they would: If the other people in your department saw that office or lab equipment had been left on when it was not in use, they would:	5-point Likert scale: Strongly disapprove (1), Disapprove somewhat, Neither approve nor disapprove, Approve somewhat, Strongly approve (5)

under one to up to two hours depending on the interviewee. Interviews provided more depth and exploration (via qualitative data) of emergence and diffusion processes, by providing insight and examples of the sorts of social construction and social comparison processes occurring during the intervention. The questions were developed after reviewing the range of factors

Table 17.2   Survey 2 questions

Factor	Questions	Answer
Communication and social interaction	I discussed energy use with colleagues I discussed MyEcoFootprint with colleagues Such opportunities for discussion encouraged my use of MyEcoFootprint Discussion with colleagues about MyEcoFootprint helped me reduce my energy use I encouraged my colleagues to use MyEcoFootprint I use MyEcoFootprint because my colleagues use it Because I used MyEcoFootprint I now know more colleagues Because I used MyEcoFootprint I now talk to more colleagues Because I used MyEcoFootprint I now know my colleagues better	7-point Likert scale from strongly disagree to strongly agree
Duty	I felt a duty to department managers to use MyEcoFootprint I felt a duty to my colleagues to use MyEcoFootprint I felt a duty to the team who developed MyEcoFootprint	7-point Likert scale from strongly disagree to strongly agree
Pressure	I felt pressure from my managers in the department to use MyEcoFootprint I felt pressure from my colleagues to use MyEcoFootprint I felt pressure from the team who developed MyEcoFootprint	

that can influence the emergence, diffusion and translation of social norms into behaviour; the review was provided in a working paper (Bradley et al. 2014). Again, in order to ensure effective questions, the current researchers revised and debated the questions and also piloted them. The questions helped shed light on the social context in which the intervention took place and the emergence and diffusion of social norms. The full interview schedule is provided in the working paper for this study, the main questions are provided in Table A17.1 in the Appendix. Each interview was designed to be first unstructured in order to capture the essentially qualitative nature of this part of the study (Kleining 1998). The second part of the interview was more semi-structured and focused, in order to pick up relevant findings to compare across participants. Based on the review of social science research methods, this was felt to be the strongest approach to attain interview data for the current study. In analysing the interview data, all interviews were transcribed and the data was coded and key themes drawn out.

17.4 RESULTS

17.4.1 Benchmark and Intervention

Descriptive and injunctive norms for energy services in the benchmark period
It was found that both descriptive and injunctive norms were much stronger for practices around lighting and office and lab equipment than for those around computers and monitors. Differences in the mean values around different energy services are provided in Table 17.3 (key values are highlighted in grey).

Significant difference was found for injunctive and descriptive norms for office and lab equipment and lights, compared to computers (see Bradley et al. 2014 for details).

Table 17.3   Descriptive statistics for descriptive and injunctive norms for energy services

	Observations	Index (mean)	Standard deviation	Minimum	Maximum
Descriptive_norm_ computers	31	2.5	1.03	1	4
Descriptive_norm_ office_or_lab_ equipment	31	3.2	1.04	1	5
Descriptive_norm_ monitors	31	2.5	1.31	1	5
Descriptive_norm_lights	31	4.1	1.22	1	5
Injunctive_norm_ computer	31	2.9	0.67	1	4
Injunctive_norm_ office_or_lab_ equipment	31	2.5	0.96	1	5
Injuntive_norm_ monitor	31	2.9	0.65	1	4
Injuntive_norm_lights	31	2.5	0.93	1	5

Some of the reasons for differences between computers and lighting were explored in the interviews; often it emerged that participants could see differences in the attributes of behaviour around particular energy services that would affect norms. A range of factors, however, including cultural influences, was mentioned. The current study applies a broad definition of culture, following Kapp (2011).[3] As one participant put it:

> 'turn the lights off', 'keep off the grass' – you see signs like this everywhere. Yeah, but 'turn off your monitor', 'turn off your computer' ... this is very recent. People are not used to that, eh, culture. There is a culture of turning off the light. There is no culture for turning off the computer.

Changes in descriptive and injunctive between the benchmark and intervention

There was a significant change (increase) in descriptive norms for computers and monitors going from the benchmark to the intervention period (but not for lighting and office and lab equipment) (see Tables 17.4 and 17.5). This is an interesting finding, as these are the very energy services that the energy intervention was set up to explore. Significant change was not observed for injunctive norms. Due to being related samples the observation number (17) is enough to test for significance in changes for this test.

Table 17.4   Descriptive statistics comparison for the benchmark and intervention period

	Observations	Mean (Index)	Minimum	Maximum
Descriptive_norm_computer_ (Benchmark)	17	2.3	1	4
Descriptive_norm_monitor_ (Benchmark)	17	2.4	1	5
Descriptive_norm_computer_ (Intervention)	17	2.8	1	5
Descriptive_norm_monitor_ (Intervention)	17	3.1	2	5
Injunctive_norm_computer_ (Benchmark)	17	3.1	2	4
Injunctive_norm_monitor_ (Benchmark)	17	2.9	2	4
Injunctive_norm_computer_ (Intervention)	17	2.6	1	4
Injunctive_norm_monitor_ (Intervention)	17	2.8	1	4

Table 17.5   Significance of changes in injunctive and descriptive norms

	Significance Des_office_ lab_(Int) – Des_office_ lab_(Bench)	Significance Des_ computer_ (Int) – Des_ computer_ (Bench)	Significance Des_ monitor_ (Int) – Des_ monitor_ (Bench)	Significance Des_ lights_(Int) – Des_lights_ (Bench)
The median difference between the benchmark and intervention	0.688	0.048	0.04	0.417
	Significance Inj_ office_ lab_(Int) – Inj_office_ lab_(Bench)	Significance Inj_ computer_ (Int) – Inj_ computer_ (Bench)	Significance Inj_ monitor_ (Int) – Inj_monitor_ (Bench)	Significance Inj_lights_ (Int) – Inj_lights_ (Bench)
The median difference between the benchmark and intervention	0.346	0.07	0.45	0.717
	Related-Samples Wilcoxon Signed Ranks Test			

The two cells highlighted in grey are significant because they are less than 0.05 (applying a 95 per cent confidence interval). Given the significance of changes in descriptive norms, next the relationship between descriptive norms and energy use was tested.

Testing the relationship between descriptive norms and efficient energy use
A cross tabulation and chi-squared test was run to observe whether there was a significant relationship between descriptive norms for computers[4] and energy efficiency ratios (energy use while present/overall energy use). In order to test this, the descriptive norms category data was put into one of two groups: low descriptive norms (*LOW*) (score 1 to 2.9); and moderate to high descriptive norms (*MODERATE TO HIGH*) (score 3 to 5). Results from cross tabulation with the energy efficiency ratio are provided in Table 17.6 below. It was possible to conduct this for the 25 participants who had both filled out survey 3 and who had energy data.

Table 17.6 Cross tabulation of descriptive norms (computers) against energy efficiency

Des_norm_computers		0.00	0.10	0.20	0.30	0.40	Total
LOW	Count	7	4	0	0	1	12
	Expected Count	3.4	4.8	1	1	1.9	12
	Std. Residual	2	-0.4	-1	-1	-0.7	
MODERATE TO HIGH	Count	0	6	2	2	3	13
	Expected Count	3.6	5.2	1	1	2.1	13
	Std. Residual	-1.9	0.4	0.9	0.9	0.6	
TOTAL	Count	7	10	2	2	4	25
	Expected Count	7	10	2	2	4	25

Table 17.7   Significance of the cross tabulations provided in Table 17.6

	Value	df	Asymp. Sig. (2-sided)	Exact Sig. (2-sided)	Exact Sig. (1-sided)	Point Probability
Pearson Chi-Square		4	0.015	0.005		
Likelihood Ratio	16.7	4	0.002	0.004		
Fisher's Exact Test	11.9			0.005		
Linear-by-Linear Association		1	0.009	0.005	0.002	0.000
No. of Valid Cases	25					

Note: 9 cells (90%) have expected count less than 5. The minimum expected count is .96. The standardised statistic is 2.623.

It was apparent that those with moderate to high scores for descriptive norms for computers (at which the intervention was primarily targeted), tended to have higher values for energy efficiency (meaning they are more energy efficient). The significance of this finding is identified in Table 17.7.

The Fisher's Exact Test is an appropriate test statistic to use when the sample size is lower, as it is here (but still high enough to robustly test significance). It can be seen that the Fisher's Exact Test provided a value for exact significance (two-sided) at 0.005, which is highly significant as 0.05 is the threshold for testing significance (applying a 95 per cent confidence interval).

Group identity, group outcome expectations, and descriptive norm changes
As identified in section 17.2, Rimal and Real (2005) identify group identity and outcome expectations as being important in determining the translation of social norms into behaviour. However, there is little testing of whether group identity and outcome expectations actually effect the emergence of group norms in the first place; this is the focus of the current study. From testing with a chi-squared test, for the benchmark, group identity was found to have a significant relationship with descriptive norms for computers (those with higher group identity tended to have higher descriptive norms around computers). For monitors, a significant link was not found. This result can only be said to be indicative and not conclusive, however, as although the Fisher's Exact Test is designed for small sample sizes, sensitivity testing revealed that the result is somewhat unstable due to the particular sample size (17); see full details and results in Bradley et al. (2014).

For collective outcome expectancy: The relationship between collective outcome expectancy and descriptive norms was investigated. Significance of a relationship was not proven in the benchmark or the intervention period; see full results and details in Bradley et al. (2014).

For norm interaction: Although the significance of changes in injunctive norms could not be proven, the mean index scores indicate a strengthening of these norms (lower score) from the benchmark to the intervention. It was perhaps not surprising that change was not significant as the emergence and diffusion of injunctive norms tend to follow some time after descriptive norms.

Social context around MEF and energy use

Survey data also presented quantitative evidence of social construction and social comparison in relation to the use of MEF and energy. Interestingly, this showed roughly an even split between participants who discussed MEF with colleagues and those who did not, as can be seen in Bradley et al. (2014).

For at least six of the participants, such discussion encouraged their use of feedback. In this way, social interaction played a role in incentivising and motivating people to use the feedback tool.

17.4.2   Social Construction, Social Comparison and Social Norms

In this section, the main findings relevant to social construction and social comparisons and the development of social norms are presented. Findings are developed below under key themes that emerged: views and attitudes (and others' views and feelings); social distance and interaction; and referents proximity and location. A summary table of responses for the full range of questions is provided in Table A17.1 in the Appendix. In general, attitudes and experience were generally positive for participants 1, 4, 5 and 8; participants 2, 3, 6 and 7 seemed to share a somewhat less positive experience.

Before interview findings are presented, measured changes in descriptive norms for participants are presented (results from survey).

Changes in Table 17.8 show that participants 1, 3, 5 and 8 primarily experienced increases in descriptive and injunctive norms. This was based on comparing relevant scores for questions before and after the intervention. Results for descriptive norms for other participants were mixed.

View and attitudes

Views towards the project at the start and participation: From the top two questions in Table A17.1 in the Appendix ('What were your experiences of the beginning of the project?'; 'What kinds of things encouraged you

Table 17.8   Change in descriptive and injunctive norms (benchmark to intervention) for participants 1 to 8

Interview participant	Change in descriptive norms	Change in injunctive norms
Interview participant 1 (researcher)	Increase (apart from office and lab equipment)	Increase (all categories)
Interview participant 2 (PhD student)	*No data (but view informed from interview)*	
Interview participant 3 (admin)	All increased by 1	No change in injunctive norms (neutral)
Interview participant 4 (researcher)	Increase for lights, others remain the same	Decrease for lab equipment and lights
Interview participant 5 (academic)	Increase all categories	Increase all categories
Interview participant 6 (PhD student)	Increase for 2 of the 4, decrease for 1 of the 4	Increase for 1 of the 4, decrease for 1 of the 4
Interview participant 7 (academic)	*No data – but did not use MEF*	
Interview participant 8 (researcher)	Increase for 3 of the 4 categories	Decrease for 2, increase for 1

to use MEF?'), participants 1 (researcher), 4 (researcher), 5 (academic) and 8 (researcher) held fairly positive attitudes towards the project and the MEF tool from the start. All four participants signalled that they felt comfortable/could not see any problem with taking part/were interested in the project (questions 5 and 7).

Participant 2 (PhD student), had a less positive attitude towards the project and the MEF tool, stating: 'I don't see any gain from turning off my computer etc.' Participants 2 (PhD student) and 3 (admin) did use MEF but were not that positive about participating. Participant 7 (academic) did not use MEF and had not experienced much. Participants 6 (PhD student) and 7 (academic) did not use MEF. Participant 6 (PhD student) had an initial experience at the beginning of the project that was somewhat negative: 'Having these devices next to you at the beginning might be a bit uncomfortable, we don't know exactly what they are there for. But afterwards, once we understand that they are not recording the discussion, you don't care about it'.[5] The latter comment 'flags up' participants' early concerns around privacy. This project, as well as others such as Bolderdijk et al. (2013), identifies privacy to be a significant issue for businesses attempting to introduce smart metering.

Others' views and feelings: With regards to how others felt about participating (question 4), participant 1 was positive. Participants 2, 3, 5, 7 and 8 were rather more neutral.[6]

In terms of feelings and opinions of others in the department towards the project, participant 8 identified (question 3) that: 'he had not heard any complaint about it, I don't think they felt bad'. Interestingly, participant 5 (lecturer) identified that they had noticed some discussion/reaction when people were getting access to online information, and that the general feeling that came out was that they would have to turn off their computers all the time (response to question 3).

Participants 3, 4, and 6 were somewhat more negative. Participant 4 states (question 3): 'Compared to my office mates, I was more interested in it, I think. Because I was taking a look at it and they were not very interested at all, so really, yeah.' Question 17 provided additional information, he stated: 'So they had a positive attitude towards it, but using it was entirely the choice of the Department, as they feel it, I think.' For question 4, he identified that some people might have some privacy concerns.

> I just felt it. People never talked about that. I just thought that, well . . . I was thinking like what privacy issues could it be, possibly, but eh . . . perhaps like they might think there is . . . I don't know, a microphone inside listening to them or . . . So they are not present there when they are supposed to be and then.

This shows clearly the perceptions of others' views that participant 4 had observed. When asked whether they were aware of the feelings and opinions of others in the department about the project (question 3), participant 6 expressed similar observations:

> In the office that we were like . . . five or six students having these devices, some were more concerned about privacy and what's that for, eh, but I haven't talked to them to learn more about that.

This interview data suggests that privacy concerns were an issue for at least some participants. Question 6 and further discussion is quite revealing about perceptions of how the project was introduced, and views on participating:

> There wasn't any em . . . like . . . eh . . . self em . . . motivation about doing something with that, so, eh, these were told to us, okay, we will install these devices in your office, if you have any problem, then . . . any concerns talk with us, otherwise they will be there. That's how they introduced it to us. (Participant 6)

This resonates strongly with participant 4's perception from the observation of others. When further asked if the introduction was appropriate or could it have been done better, participant 6 stated: 'It could have been done on a voluntary basis. If they didn't have enough volunteers, then they could [employ] non-volunteers.'

Somewhat similar views were reflected by participant 3 (before direct questions), about how the project was introduced and the opt-out policy. This is interesting as it shows how making a policy decision on opt-out versus opt-in can affect the social context and the social construction of attitudes towards the project. Further interview data from participant 3 (non-academic) identified that the management's announcement and introduction about the project did not feel particularly encouraging. This highlights the unknown and influential factor of how well management will implement such technologies in organisations and industry,[7] the effect that this can have on perception and the social construction of attitudes and views that emerge in groups, and how this can affect the norms that emerge; the above data from participants 4 and 6 also hint towards effects on motivation. Participants 3 and 7 had fairly neutral responses to question 3.[8] From their review, Bolderdijk et al. (2013) provide light on the underlying roots of privacy concerns in smart metering, and suggest that employee privacy concerns may be tracked back to a lack of apparent positive personal consequence. The findings of the current chapter indicate that it also relates to how the project is implemented and later data suggests that the cultural background of participants also influences privacy concerns.

Social distance and interaction in shaping norm emergence and diffusion
It was clear from responses to question 3 that participant 5 gleaned information (intentionally or non-intentionally) about others' participation via discussions on such things as technical issues. Participant 5 was also asked about the situations or circumstances where he was able to discuss the project with others (question 8), where he gave the following response: 'you know, corridor chats when you're getting a coffee or doing a fire drill (laughing)'.

This is important as it signals the ability for discussion to provide information on referents outside of one's immediate office environment. In terms of the people that participant 5 interacts with in such discussions, the following is informative: 'people passing do catch me for a quick chat, so I sort of do interact with . . . usually the academics and senior researchers'. This referent selection reflects organisational structure, as participant 5 is also an academic.

Participants 2 and 4 also discussed the project (although participant 2 rarely).[9] With regards to what was discussed, participant 4 states:

> Perhaps about the reasons the project is run. Perhaps about confidentiality, privacy, are we being tracked or not? How successful it will be in reducing energy use. Speculated about how it may affect wellbeing of the centre.

These concerns have resonance with the literature and show that extensive monitoring of employees bears the risk of decreasing employee satisfaction and possible detachment from the process (see review in Bolderdijk et al. 2013).

Although participant 4 was generally positive about the project, it was clear that they encountered differing views and concerns relating to confidentiality, privacy and the project, which informed a particular perception of others' views. Neither participants 2 nor 4 identified that their discussion encouraged their use of MEF (unlike participant 5). It is clear that discussion and social context amongst participants and subgroups on a project like this can have a positive or neutral (even perhaps negative) effect in encouraging engagement and motivation to use the MEF tool. This is in line with quantitative findings from the survey, which showed that for some, discussion encouraged the use of MEF but for others it did not. It is clear from the discussions of participant 4 (and other participants) that concerns and negative perceptions about the intervention can be shared through discussion (and in this way, can be socially constructed) as well as more positive perceptions. In this way, attitudes and perceptions as well as norms can be socially constructed within groups. Social distance (taken to be frequency and intensity of social interaction) and interaction affect the emergence and diffusion of descriptive norms because they increase the amount of information available about others' views and what they are doing. Gächter and Fehr (1999) state that social distance and familiarity are important to injunctive norms, as repeated interaction is positively correlated with the importance of approval incentives; and repeated interaction is also likely to increase costs from non-compliance.

Proximity, location and referents in shaping norm emergence and diffusion
This section demonstrates the role of proximity and location on referent selection, as well as observational data available for social comparison. From the above section, it would seem that the information that participant 5 gained from discussion was mainly the views of other academics. Given that participant 5 is in a single office, their main referents for verbal information are therefore other outside academics.

For participant 1 the situation is quite different, as environment, proximity and location play the main role in shaping his perception of others' use of MEF. When asked question 15, he stated that definitely everybody in his office used MEF. It is further identified that they are researchers (equivalent in terms of organisational structure). Importantly, information was not communicated verbally (identified from findings for questions 8 and 17), therefore it must have been based on observation. Such observations about others' engagement with energy reduction (via MEF) would not be readily available in a single office. Therefore, this highlights a role for environment and proximity and location in determining referents' available and observational information (and therefore informing social norms via social comparison). It is also clear that this was the case for participant 8, when asked about his office colleagues' use of MEF (question 16) he states: 'they seemed to check their electricity usage on their computer screens.' This participant tended to 'hang out' with his office colleagues (researchers), so they will have been his main referents. Participant 4 also only knew of his roommates' use of MEF, again indicating the role of proximity and location in determining referents and observational information. Gartel (1982) identifies the importance of proximity in relation to awareness of others and social comparison processes, Goodman and Haisley (2007) further discuss. Goldstein et al. (2008) identify that: 'it is typically beneficial to follow the norms that most closely match one's immediate settings, situations, and circumstances' (p. 8, line 34).

Continuing on this theme, when asked 'Do people [in the department] use MEF that you are aware of?', it is interesting to note that participants 1, 4, 5 and 8 all identified awareness of participants, and all of these participants showed increases in descriptive norms as identified in Table 17.8. For participants 2, 3, 6 and 7 none of these participants identified knowledge of others using MEF. Following this, the norm in these latter participants' surroundings (and their 'social context') was to not use MEF, either this, or these participants were generally not interested to know of their referents' use of MEF (but this would go against the strong evidence that there was a general shift in social norms from the benchmark to the intervention). Goodman and Haisley (2007) identify from earlier studies that the perceived relevance of referents determines selection and that relevance and attractiveness of referents is affected by ease of access to the referent and appropriateness of the referent in addressing the person's needs of concern. Individuals will gravitate towards referents that are appropriate and computationally easy to assess.

Culture
Goodman and Haisley (2007) identify culture as playing an important role in social comparison processes. Drawing on Bourdieu's (1984) ideas around the influence of 'cultural capital', they suggest that the background of workers can be important in determining perception (and therefore also

shaping evaluation) in an organisational environment. Perceptions can sometimes differ between workers from the culture in which the organisation exists as compared to those from outside cultures. Therefore, the international mix is an organisational variable that can influence perceptions within an organisation, probably in many different ways.[10] Hechter and Opp (2002) in their review relating to social norms, express surprise that many authors do not explicitly note the importance of culture and history and the current context in restricting the set of norms that are able to arise and that are available to be adopted at any given time. We now look at relevant interview findings and where appropriate, discuss in relation to social construction and social comparison processes.

Question 21 asked: 'How would you best describe the culture in the department?' Participant 4 (researcher) identified the culture as work orientated and that people are tolerant and respectful of others and reasonable, also that the department is well organised. Participant 5 described the culture as very international, but quite fragmented and very focused on what it's got to do. Participant 8 stated: 'There are many projects [in the department] and people work hard'. He further identified that the department works like an enterprise. Participant 2 (PhD student) identified the department as a sociable place. Participant 3 (admin) identified that she felt the department could be a bit isolating, with pressure from the UK's Research Excellence Framework (a national scheme which assesses the strength of research of each researcher and of their research group as a whole) and a focus on income. Participant 7 (academic) identified that the department works like an enterprise. Participant 6 (PhD student) identified the following:

> the department has researchers from all around the world, eh, mainly, eh, Asia, eh . . . The culture is a bit different from Europeans and the Western world. So, there is a . . . a different approach in . . . cultures about things, for like privacy.

Interviewer: Okay.
Participant 6:

> So, eh, their . . . the use of the tool and this project raised more concerns from that . . . from those guys than average.

The interviewee was later asked if they had any idea as to why this is? The interviewee answered as follows: 'I think it's their culture and I don't know if . . . it's rights perhaps.' The interviewer then asked about specific countries as opposed to Asia and participant 6 identified China, Iran and Pakistan and such areas. This latter dialogue from participant 6 indicates the influence that an international culture may have in determining people's attitudes to technologies such as smart metering. The participants' data suggests that this can influence how the intervention is perceived and socially constructed and, therefore, the social context and norms (as the literature suggests) that emerge.

17.5   DISCUSSION

This study set out to explore the role of social norms in energy conservation within organisations. Social norms around specific office-based energy services were measured before and after an energy intervention to observe changes. Changes in energy for each participant were also captured. Factors identified in Rimal and Real's (2005) model for determining whether social norms affect behaviour were explored in the current study, but with regards to norm emergence as opposed to translation into behaviour. Social construction and social comparison processes are important in determining the norms that emerge and diffuse within a group. Interviews were applied to provide insight on the social construction and social comparison processes occurring within the group during the intervention. The main findings from the paper are now discussed.

Descriptive and injunctive norms measured in survey 1 (benchmark), were much stronger for lighting and office and lab equipment than for computers and monitors. Some of the reasons for differences between computers and lighting were explored in the interviews, where often it emerged that participants could see differences in the attributes of behaviour around particular energy services that would affect norms. A range of factors however, including culture, was also mentioned.

Change in descriptive and injunctive norms between the benchmark and intervention period was then examined. There was a significant change (increase) in descriptive norms for computers and monitors going from the benchmark to the intervention period (but not for lighting and office and lab equipment). This is an important finding, as these are the very energy services that the energy intervention was focused on. Also, a significant relationship was found between descriptive norms and energy efficiency ratios for participants, after the intervention – those who displayed higher descriptive norms tended to be more efficient in their energy use.

Chi-square tests were then applied to explore the relationship between group identity and descriptive norms, and collective outcome expectations and descriptive norms. A significant relationship was found to exist between group identity and descriptive norms for computers during the benchmark period; further testing is, however, advised to confirm this as sensitivity testing suggested instability due to the low number of observations in the case of this particular result. The preliminary result identifies to companies that group identity is important in determining the emergence of pro-energy conservation norms.

With regards to social construction and social comparison processes occurring during the intervention, roughly an even split was seen between participants who discussed MEF and those who did not (from survey data). It is clear that for at least six of the participants, discussion encouraged their use of feedback. The implication for businesses is that social interaction and discussion of such interventions, can incentivise and motivate people to use the feedback tool for some. However, interview data suggests that in some situations, discussion may discourage the use of MEF.

17.5.1   The Role of the Physical Environment, Proximity and Location in Shaping Norm Emergence and Diffusion

The interviews in this research highlight how the physical environment, proximity and location can affect the referents available and the accessibility of observational data as well as the environment of social construction (and resulting social context) within which participants find themselves and therefore the normative information available. This will shape the social norms that emerge around energy and their diffusion. For participants interviewed, available referents (those with whom people tended to hang out or share a room) often reflected the position held by the participant (organisational structure), for example, whether a lecturer, researcher or PhD student etc. and/or location. The literature shows that people on the same level (in terms of organisation) provide attractive referents for attaining normative information. The implications of these findings for businesses are that having multiple occupant offices can increase the number of referents and observational/comparative data (visual and social interaction) available, and in this way can increase the emergence and diffusion of social norms and, potentially, energy reduction due to the relationship between strength of energy-related descriptive norms and energy efficiency, as earlier demonstrated.

17.5.2   The Role of Management, Policy and Culture in Shaping Social Context and Norms

The findings discussed in this chapter highlight a deep interaction between technology, social context, norms and policy; this interaction has the potential to affect the success of energy reduction from smart metering.

From the interviews, it was clear that both the introduction to the

REDUCE intervention as well as policy decisions taken to make the project one of opt-out as opposed to opt-in influenced the development of attitudes and views for most of those interview participants who had a less positive view/experience of the project. It is interesting to note that of those who had a less positive view/experience (participants 2, 3, 6 and 7), none were aware of their office mates/colleagues' use of MEF. For those who had a more positive view/experience (participants 1, 4, 5 and 8), however, all were aware of at least some colleagues' use of MEF. This is an interesting observation and, when taken in conjunction with findings of the impact that management's implementation and opt-out policy has on the experience of participants, would indicate that, with respect to the development of descriptive norms, policy as well as communication are important factors in smart metering due to influencing the social context of participants and social construction and comparison. This has real relevance as it is clear from our study that there is a significant link between the development of descriptive norms around energy services and actual energy behaviours.

Some of the interview data indicated that the cultural background of participants can affect their experience, perception and views and attitudes around privacy and acceptability of the technologies applied and the intervention. Attitudes and views can affect the social context, discussion and norms that emerge. Given such findings and the need for energy interventions and smart metering to have a positive as opposed to negative impact on organisations, the design and implementation of interventions and technologies used should take account of how a particular technology and intervention design may be acceptable/unacceptable as a result of cultural background or the mix of participants. Such considerations are highly relevant in the UK, which is culturally quite mixed and currently rolling out smart metering to small- and medium-sized businesses (as well as households) on a large scale, and future research should further investigate this issue. One participant identified discussions about how such interventions affect well-being within the department and it is important to note this, as well as the number of concerns around privacy, as this indicates that such high-resolution technology interventions do generate anxieties.

17.6 CONCLUSIONS

This research demonstrates the difficulties of getting people to change behaviour in relation to environmental responsibility in relation to energy. Environmental psychology has been good at pinpointing the influence of norms (descriptive and injunctive), but less convincing in explaining their emergence. More recent research has considered the significance of social and cultural settings in encouraging and influencing the activation of social norms. As with more recent policies designed to encourage more environmentally responsible behaviour in individuals in households, energy use in the workplace may become more important for future environmental targets. As the study used as the focus of this chapter shows, however, institutional settings are a critical factor in developing effective interventions of this kind – particularly the existing organisational structure, which may prioritise the social norms that conflict with the intervention that is being implemented.

17.7 RECOMMENDATIONS FOR PRACTITIONERS

The implication of the findings of this chapter for businesses is that smart metering feedback-based interventions can impact social norms, and evidence suggests that this impacts efficient energy use within an organisation. Organisations should attempt to foster descriptive norms that encourage energy conservation/efficiency if implementing smart metering. This study found that the opt-out policy will increase initial levels of participation, but can reduce motivation to engage with feedback and energy reduction. We recommend that businesses take care when deciding on whether to employ smart metering and involve their employees with any intervention and with how it is introduced, in order to increase acceptability, and avoid negative perceptions and social interaction/construction that may hinder motivation to engage with the project. Decisions on the level of resolution of energy-monitoring are a key consideration, as on the one hand they determine the level of feedback that participants receive, but on the other hand, over-monitoring of employees' behaviour risks decreasing worker satisfaction and performance, as seen in the review by Bolderdijk et al. (2013). Care and consultation is required to come up with the optimum balance here that is acceptable to employees, if smart metering is being considered.

We recommend involving participants in decisions and consultation/workshops to design the intervention and formulate the decisions on smart metering as this is likely to help increasing acceptability, trust, reducing privacy concerns and clarify benefits as well as the positive personal consequences for participants that should result.

NOTES

1. Goodman and Haisley (2007) identify that there are a number of ways to classify social comparison processes. They identify: initiation, selection of referents and an evaluation process as important.
2. For more detail on the feedback tool (MEF), please see Murtagh et al. (2013).
3. '[T]he sum total of a complex of institutions and interrelated habitual models of thinking, acting, and feeling (including the corresponding valuations, norms, and interpretations of the world of a particular epoch) – thus comprises the man-made learned and transmitted adaptive tools which form the prerequisites of human life and survival. In order to survive and exist, each individual must learn and master the system of institutionalized behaviour patterns that his group or society transmits to him in the process of enculturation.'
4. This was chosen as opposed to monitors as computers use significantly more energy than do monitors.
5. Participant 3 also recalled a negative perception of the start of the project and how it was introduced.
6. Participant 1 identified that there was a positive attitude. Participant 1 further identified common agreement on taking part in his office (question 6). Participant 5 identified that he did not know of anyone refusing to take part, or joking/procrastinating, but identified that it may happen (question 6). The response from participant 8 to question 4 was: 'It was not bad'.
7. The introduction made by the management was an unplanned impromptu face-to-face introduction to the project for participants (beyond that made by electronic communication).
8. When asked question 3, participant 3 responded: 'The academics thought it was very important.' Question 6 was not answered directly by participant 3. Participant 7 gave the following account for question 3: 'Have not heard much, but think it has just become a part of things. I don't think people were very enthusiastic about it, and I have not seen much concern about it.' And question 4: 'Initially, there was not much enthusiasm. After some time, people were willing.'
9. Participant 2 (PhD student) and 4 (researcher) tend to 'hang out' with other researchers within their department.
10. The current authors identify that it may affect referent selection and evaluation processes in social comparison.

REFERENCES

Abrahamse, W. and L. Steg (2013), 'Social influence approaches to encourage resource conservation: A meta-analysis', *Global Environmental Change*, **23**, 1773–1785.

Ajzen, I. and M. Fishbein (1980), *Understanding Attitudes and Predicting Social Behavior*, Englewood Cliffs, NJ: Prentice-Hall.

Andrews, T. (2012), 'What is social constructionism?', *Grounded Theory Review: An International Journal*, **1** (11).

Berger, P. and T. Luckmann (1991), *The Social Construction of Reality*, London: Penguin Books.

Bolderdijk, J., L. Steg and T. Postmes (2013), 'Fostering support for work floor energy conservation policies: Accounting for privacy concerns', *Journal of Organizational Behavior*, **34**, 195–210.

Bourdieu, P. (1984), *Distinction: A Social Critique of the Judgement of Taste*, Cambridge, MA: Harvard University Press.

Bradley, P., S. Fudge and M. Leach (2014), 'The role of social norms in incentivising energy reduction in organisations', *Economics Working Paper Series* 1404, University of the West of England.

Burr, V. (2003), *Social Constructionism* (2nd edn), London: Routledge.

Carrico, A.R. (2009), 'Motivating pro-environmental behaviour: The use of feedback and peer education to promote energy conservation in an organisation setting', *Dissertation submitted to the Faculty of the Graduate School of Vanderbilt University in partial fulfilment of the requirements for the degree of Doctor in Philosophy in Psychology,* accessed on 4 January 2014, available at: http://etd.library.vanderbilt.edu/available/etd-07202009-180058/unrestricted/Carrico20May09.pdf.

Carrico, A.R. and M. Riemer (2011), 'Motivating energy conservation in the workplace: An evaluation of the use of group-level feedback and peer education', *Journal of Environmental Psychology*, **31** (1), 1–13.

Chen, C. and K. Knight (2014), 'Energy at work: Social psychological factors affecting energy conservation intentions within Chinese electric power companies', *Energy Research and Social Science*, **4**, 23–31.

Cialdini, R.B., C.A. Kallgren and R.R. Reno (1991), 'A focus theory of normative conduct: A theoretical refinement and re-evaluation of the role of norms in human behavior', *Advances in Experimental Social Psychology*, **24** (20), 201–243.

Cordano, M. and I. H. Frieze (2000), 'Pollution reduction preferences in of U.S. environmental managers: Applying Ajzen's theory of planned behaviour', *Academy of Management Journal*, **43**, 627–641.

Dixon, G.N., M.B. Deline, K. McComas, L. Chambliss and M. Hoffmann (2014), 'Using comparative feedback to influence workplace energy conservation: A case study of a university campaign', *Environment and Behavior*, 1–27.

Flannery, B.L. and D.R. May (2000), 'Environmental ethical decision making in the U.S. metal-finishing industry', *Academy of Management Journal*, **43**, 642–662.

Flynn, F.J. and J.A. Chatman (2003), '"What's the norm here?" Social categorisation as a basis for group norm development', in Jeffrey Polzer (ed.), *Identity Issues in Groups (Research on Managing Groups and Teams)*, vol. 5, Bingley: Emerald Group Publishing Limited, pp. 135–160.

Gächter, S. and E. Fehr (1999), 'Collective action as a social exchange', *Journal of Economic Behaviour and Organisation*, **39**, 341–369.

Gartrell, C.D. (1982), 'On the visibility of wage referents', *The Canadian Journal of Sociology*, **7** (2), 117–143.

Goldstein, N.J., R.B. Cialdini and V. Griskevicius (2008), 'A room with a viewpoint: Using social norms to motivate environmental conservation in hotels', *Journal of Consumer Research*, **35** (3), 472–482.

Goodman, P. and E. Haisley (2007) 'Social comparison processes in an organizational context: New directions', *Organizational Behavior and Human Decision Processes*, **102** (1), 109–125.

Gustafson, C. and M. Longland (2008), 'Engaging employees in conservation leadership', presented at American Council for an Energy Efficient Economy (ACEEE) Summer Study on Energy Efficiency in Buildings, Asilomar, 17–22 August.

Hechter, M. and K.D. Opp (2002), 'On the emergence of social norms', *Contemporary Sociology*, **31** (6), 638–640.

Kapp, K.W. (2011), *The Foundations of Institutional Economics*. Edited by S. Berger and R. Steppacher, London and New York: Routledge, Taylor & Francis Group.

Kleining, G. (1998), *Das Rezeptive Interview*, Bielefeld: University of Bielefeld.

Lo, S.H., G.Y. Peters, G.J.P. van Breukelen, and G. Kok (2014), 'Only reasoned action? An interorganizational study of energy-saving behaviors in office buildings', *Energy Efficiency*, **7**, 761–775.

Lyndhurst, B. (2009), *A Report for the Department for Environment, Food and Rural Affairs*, Defra: London.

Mael, F. and Ashforth, B.E. (1992), 'Alumni and their alma mater: A partial test of the reformulated model of organizational identification', *Journal of Organizational Behavior*, **13**, 103–123.

Murtagh, N., M. Nati, W.R. Headley, B. Gatersleben, A. Gluhak, M.A. Imran, and D. Uzzell (2013), 'Individual energy use and feedback in an office setting: A field trial', *Energy Policy*, **62**, 717–728.

Ohtomo, S. and Y. Hirose (2007), 'The dual-process of reactive and intentional decision making involved in eco-friendly behavior', *Journal of Environmental Psychology*, **27**, 117–125.

Papagiannakis, G. and S. Lioukas (2012), 'Values, attitudes and perceptions of managers as predictors of corporate environmental responsiveness', *Journal of Environmental Management*, **100**, 41–51.

Ramus, C.A. and A.B.C. Killmer (2007), 'Corporate greening through prosocial extrarole behaviours – a conceptual framework for employee motivation', *Business Strategy and the Environment*, **16**, 554–570.

Rimal, R.N. and K. Real (2005), 'How behaviors are influenced by perceived norms: A test of the theory of normative social behavior', *Communication Research*, **32** (3), 389–414.

Schwartz, T., M. Betz, L. Ramirez and G. Stevens (2010), 'Sustainable energy practices at work: Understanding the role of workers in energy conservation', proceedings of the Nordic Conference on Human-Computer Interaction, October 16–20.

Siero, F., W.A.B. Bakker, G.B. Dekker and M.T.C. Van Den Burg (1996), 'Changing organizational energy consumption behaviour through comparative feedback', *Journal of Environmental Psychology*, **16** (3), 235–246.

Tajfel, H. (1974), 'Social identity and intergroup behaviour', *Social Science Information*, **13**, 65–93.

Ture, R.S. and M.P. Ganesh (2014), 'Understanding pro-environmental behaviours at the workplace: Proposal of a model', *Asia-Pacific Journal of Management Research and Innovation*, **10** (2), 137–145.

Vazquez Brust, D.A. and C. Liston-Heyes (2010), 'Environmental management intentions: An empirical investigation of Argentina's polluting firms', *Journal of Environmental Management*, **91**, 1111–1122.

Vishwanath, A. (2006), 'The effect of the number of opinion seekers and leaders on technology attitudes and choices', *Human Communication Research*, **32** (3), 322–350.

APPENDIX

Table A17.1 Summary table

QUESTION	Participant 1 (researcher)	Participant 2 (PhD student)	Participant 3 (admin)	Participant 4 (researcher)	Participant 5 (academic)	Participant 6 (PhD student)	Participant 7 (academic)	Participant 8 (researcher – emailing answers)
1. What were your experiences of the beginning of the project?	Technology implementation went smoothly.	Concern – I don't see any gain from turning off my computer etc.	A negative perception of how the project was introduced and early experience of being told off. Problem with accessing MEF.	Not very clear experiences as I used MEF from time to time, sometimes I would click and look. Forgot/ ignored from time to time, becomes part of the screen.	Good, but was not aware of a comparison with the average.	Having these devices next to you at the beginning might be a bit uncomfortable, we don't know exactly what they are there for. But afterwards, once we understand that they are not recording discussion, you don't care about it.	I have not installed MEF or used MEF, so have not experienced much.	I wanted know the project and the technology used in it.

2. What kinds of things encouraged you to use MEF?	Good to see facts and compare.	At the beginning, curious to see my energy behaviour.	I did look at a couple of times, but it did not tell me how I could do anything about it.	I liked monitoring my usage.	When my computer brings up the screen and the emails.	Did not use MEF.	na	I was interested in the project and I wanted to consider my next research referring to this project.
3. Were you aware of the feelings and opinions of others in the department of the project?		I don't know, but my guess is that they are thinking the same.	The academics thought it was very important.	No – can say that he was more interested than office mates.	Noticed some discussion, more the reaction when people were getting access to their online information. Interpretation from some was that I have to turn my computer off all the time. And I think that was the feeling that came out.	In the office that we were like … five or six students having these devices, some were more concerned about privacy and what's that for, eh, but I haven't talked to them to learn more about that.	Have not heard much, but think it has just become a part of things. I don't think people were very enthusiastic about it, and I have not seen much concern about it. Later discussion	No, I wasn't. Because I hadn't had a discussion about it. Second answer provided: As I hadn't heard any complaint about it, I don't think they felt bad.

Table A17.1 (continued)

QUESTION	Participant 1 (researcher)	Participant 2 (PhD student)	Participant 3 (admin)	Participant 4 (researcher)	Participant 5 (academic)	Participant 6 (PhD student)	Participant 7 (academic)	Participant 8 (researcher – emailing answers)
							signals there may have been some concern at the start – privacy concerns.	
4. How did people feel about partici-pating?	There was a positive attitude.	I don't think there are people resentful to participate.	Some early discussion around lack of choice in participating.	Yea, some people might have some privacy concerns.	Not asked.	States that there wasn't any self motivation about doing something with partici-pating, he indicates that it was mainly department led.	Initially, there was not much enthusiasm. After some time, people were willing.	It was not bad.
5. Were there any reasons why you	Felt comfortable with.	No, I don't think.	Yes. You would have felt like	Would have felt bad for	Could not see a problem as was not dealing	If there was surveillance, i.e. When you	No	No, there weren't.

Respondent	might have felt uncomfortable by not participating in the MEF project?	6. Were you aware of others' viewpoints on taking part/not taking part in using MEF?
1	you were not really helping.	Common agreement at least in my office, taking part.
2	environmental reasons.	Yes some, but just from a general point of view. They simply don't care in my opinion.
3	with personal information.	Did not directly answer.
4	come to the office and leave and reducing pay/salary. This was not the case. If I would have perhaps, had to announce in public. But if I had to just sign, perhaps I might not be that uncomfortable.	Just a feeling, that some had privacy concerns. I think some people just said … "okay just install it I don't mind" but they were not really interested.
5		Did not know of anyone refusing to take part, or joking/ procrastinating, but it may happen.
6		Yes some.
7	No	No

Table A17.1 (continued)

QUESTION	Participant 1 (researcher)	Participant 2 (PhD student)	Participant 3 (admin)	Participant 4 (researcher)	Participant 5 (academic)	Participant 6 (PhD student)	Participant 7 (academic)	Participant 8 (researcher – emailing answers)
7. What was your view about taking part in using MEF?	Positive	Could not see any gain from.	Early discussion signals that they wanted to take part.	Positive	Positive	He did not use MEF, but was a participant in the project.	Did not take part.	I was interested in the project itself and how the sensors worked.
8. Were there situations or circumstances where you were able to discuss the project with others?	No (yes for the other project).	Yes	Not really.	Might have been, maybe lunch breaks.	Yes	The specific project, I don't think so.	No	No
9. Did you have such discussions often? What did you discuss?	na	Rarely	na	Now and again. Perhaps about the reason the project is run. Perhaps about confidentiality, privacy, are we	Often enough.	Quite irregular. Discussion was about potential applications and how we can use	na	No

404

			being tracked or not? How successful it will be in reducing energy use. Speculated about how it may effect wellbeing of the centre.	sensors to get information and smart-cities, smart offices etc.			
10. Were such discussions before or after using MEF?	na	After	After	After, once you start seeing things online.	Not asked.	na	na
11. Did such discussions encourage/ discourage your MEF use?	na	I don't think they changed my ideas.	No	Yeah, it certainly didn't discourage me.	na	na	na
12. In what ways was the project a shared experience do you think?	Because I know some colleagues also using – common interest from a technical view.	I suppose the department involvement, if there is some sort of campus wide, or national	Maybe. On a scale of 1–100, I would say 20/25.	Shared in the sense of other research projects that I'm linked to.	It could be a shared experience, if when results are published, whether people in the same	Maybe, everyone working to reduce energy, could be as shared.	I don't think the project was shared with participants.

Table A17.1 (continued)

QUESTION	Participant 1 (researcher)	Participant 2 (PhD student)	Participant 3 (admin)	Participant 4 (researcher)	Participant 5 (academic)	Participant 6 (PhD student)	Participant 7 (academic)	Participant 8 (researcher – emailing answers)
			interest, then you could feel you are partici-pating. Yes, I suppose you could feel shared ownership but . . .			office have similar results, something like that.		
13. Was this experience positive or negative?	Positive		Fairly positive, I guess.	Can't say positive or negative.	Positive	Neutral	Did not directly answer.	It was positive. To reduce our electricity is very important for the environment.
14. In what ways was this not a shared experience?	You can see a comparison performer, but you don't know		Early discussions identified some issues.	Some discussion but not long lasting.	I don't think so really, as I'm some one who gets out and about and	It was not, because each individual has his own information	Not a shared experience in that not enough face to face	I hadn't had any discussion about it with

	(continuation)				(continuation)	(continuation)	(continuation)
	who's in your group.				talks to a lot of people.	and they did not interact with each other.	meetings, only emails which people delete. other people.
15. Do other people in CCSR use MEF that you are aware of? Do they tend to be lecturers, researchers or students?	Definitely everybody in my office, researchers.	No	I don't know.	I just know about my room mates. Researchers.	Aware of one or two others that actively use it. Probably the others I would expect use it, or at least every so often, but may not take further. Certainly the ones he knows that use are academics.	I am not aware, but I guess there will be.	Yes, researchers.
16. What about your office colleagues use?	na	na		" "	I have my own office.	No I don't know. Probably, they don't.	They seemed to check their electricity usage on their computer screens.

Table A17.1 (continued)

QUESTION	Participant 1 (researcher)	Participant 2 (PhD student)	Participant 3 (admin)	Participant 4 (researcher)	Participant 5 (academic)	Participant 6 (PhD student)	Participant 7 (academic)	Participant 8 (researcher – emailing answers)
17. Of those using MEF, why do you think they used MEF?	I'm not aware, we have not discussed.	na	I don't know why they would, I suppose it's because their interested in ecology/ saving energy/ the research aspect.	Probably because it is being installed, rather than them choosing to use it.	I think it's because they are keen to know how the project is working and what exactly it's doing.	They would use if it was related to their research.		I think they were asked to use MEF.
18. Who do you tend to 'hang out' with within your department when you have time to catch up?	My corridor (and a few on the ground floor).	Mainly researchers (particularly one he works with). Other friends from outside as well, sometimes meets his supervisor.	Admin	Researchers	Academics	Office mates and a couple of others from CCSR.	All of them.	Persons in the same room.

19. Do such colleagues feel a strong connection with CCSR?	Did not ask.	I don't know.	Not necessarily, no.	Yes, at least the ones I know.	Yes	Yes, some of them. Students, not so much, because they are here just a few years and see as a way to a job. Others like fellows and lecturers, feel more close.	Friendlier in a previous department.	I think so.
20. How do you feel about your role in CCSR?	Positive		Okay, don't get much input or influence into anything that's going on.	Does not directly address, but later states he feels comfortable and likes.	Sees his role as important.	My role as a student is to produce a research programme and papers. I find it an interesting place to also make friends and work and a community.		As a visitor, I hadn't felt that I had some role in CCSR.

409

Table A17.1 (continued)

QUESTION	Participant 1 (researcher)	Participant 2 (PhD student)	Participant 3 (admin)	Participant 4 (researcher)	Participant 5 (academic)	Participant 6 (PhD student)	Participant 7 (academic)	Participant 8 (researcher) – emailing answers
21. How would you best describe the culture in CCSR?		Sociable place.	Can be a bit isolating. Pressure from the REF and focus on income.	Work orientated, people are tolerant of each other and respect. People are reasonable. Well organised.	Very international, fragmented, because of how we are positioned and size, and pressure. Very focused with what we have got to do.	International, e.g. Asia etc. and the culture is a bit different from European and the western world. There is a different approach in cultures about things, for like privacy.	It works like an enterprise.	There are many projects and people work hard.
22. Is there a team atmosphere in the group?	Not really, with the people you directly work with, maybe there is. Not a team in the sense that you don't know everyone.		Not really.	Within individual projects, yes – who you are working with.	Not entirely, a bit short on, because were large probably.	Yes, but whether it's a happy team or not, I'm not sure.		Yes

PART V

EMPLOYEE ENVIRONMENTAL BEHAVIOUR IN CONTEXT

18. Embedding pro-environmental behaviour change in large organisations: perspectives on the complexity of the challenge
Terry Tudor and Cleber Dutra

18.1 ORGANISATIONS

18.1.1 What is an Organisation?

According to management theorists, an organisation is the coordination (usually planned) between two or more people or groups to achieve a common goal or objective (Robbins and Judge 2014; Mullins 2010). Hence, three key elements are embodied in the definition of an organisation. First, *two or more people*, second, a *coordinated working effort* towards the third and final element, which is *some common goal*. Mullins (2010) notes that these goals or objectives can be either 'formal' or 'informal'. Robbins (2000) explains that the 'formal' organisation is characterised by formal roles that define and shape the behaviour of its employees, primary goals and functions. The informal organisation is concerned with meeting the personal and social needs and wants of staff. Within the informal organisation, interactions take place on the basis of status and personal characteristics, rather than the formal duties in the formal organisation. As outlined by both Robbins and Judge (2014) and Mullins (2010) the study of organisational behaviour examines what individuals and groups, and structures do within organisations, and how these impact upon its effectiveness and efficiency. The study of organisational behaviour is therefore multidisciplinary in nature, taking account of a number of work-related factors such as the individual, groups, the organisation itself, as well as its environment, and is grounded in various disciplines including psychology, anthropology and sociology.

18.1.2 Historical Perspectives on Organisational Behaviour

Early research into human behaviours tended to view the goal or objective of the behaviour as 'economic optimisation'. These theories were based on the classic works of economic geographical theorists such as von Thunen, Christaller and Losch. Decision-making was viewed in terms of 'economic rationality' and led to the creation of an 'economic man' or 'Homo economicus' derived from the 'marginalist revolution' in economic theory in the late nineteenth century. *Economic rationality* was therefore considered to be the only driver for behaviours.

However, these perceptions shifted over time. For example, the work of E. L. Thorndike and John Watson, and later B. F. Skinner on instructional design and other early applications of what was then termed 'behaviour modification to clinical populations', showed that human behaviour could be changed for the better with the use of operant principles (Bucklin et al. 2000). Research beginning in the 1950s and 1960s on human responses to environmental hazards demonstrated that it was possible to empirically test behaviours. These works included Kates' (1962) study of the incorporation of risks and opportunities into individuals' decision-making about resource management and Wolpert's (1964) work on decision-making by farmers in Sweden. Fincham and Rhodes (2005) make mention of studies in industrial psychology after the Second World War, that attempted to determine what factors influenced the productivity of workers and how the link between the employee and the job could be improved. Beal and Bohlen (1955) developed a model to initiate and support behavioural change. There were other complementary theories of behavioural change, including Prochaska and DiClemente's (1986) Transtheoretical Model that focused on how interventions could be used to promote changes in health behaviours, particularly addictive behaviours.

The outcomes of these various studies led to the realisation that the answers lay not only with 'environmental' factors such as job design, but also subjective factors, including employee attitudes to work and job satisfaction. The importance of a range of cognitive and decision-making variables, and the work that it spawned, led to the development and growth of the field of 'behavioural geography'. This shift in thinking saw the increasing significance of the study of 'people–environment' variables as behavioural antecedents. According to Robinson (1998) both the physical and social aspects of the environment were considered. These included variables such as the role of culture, social and political systems and institutions, as well as the intervening psychological processes on people's perception of their environment and their subsequent behaviours.

Hence, recent research on organisational behaviour has progressed from previous approaches such as the classical approach (organisations without people) and the human relations approach (people without organisations) of the early twentieth century (Mullins 2010), to one which takes account of a range of organisational and employee-focused constructs.

18.2   FACTORS INFLUENCING ORGANISATIONAL PRACTICES

Several management theorists note that the *structure* of an organisation affects its performance (Fincham and Rhodes 2005; Child 2005; Mullins 2010). Structure influences not only productivity and economic efficiency, but also morale and job satisfaction (Mullins 2010; Williams et al. 1994). For example, if the organisation's priorities are entrepreneurial it is more likely to have a less formal structure, with greater individual freedom. Werkman (2009) notes that in more 'organic' organisations with less formal structures, staff are more positive about work, and view leadership and culture more favourably. These entities tend to use participative change approaches, and are generally smaller and more innovative and flexible in the manner in which they work.

Closely linked to structure, various writers (e.g. Burns and Stalker 1994; Ostroff and Schmitt 1993; Knights and Willmott 2007), argue that *bureaucracy* leads to a number of limitations in the functioning of organisations. These limitations include increased red tape, discouragement of innovation or individuality, and more coordination and control (Haveman 1993). However, bureaucracy also discourages arbitrary decision-making, and is effective for managing large-scale complex, but routine tasks (Asch and Salaman 2002). Thus, bureaucracy serves both as a disadvantage and an advantage in shaping organisational behaviour.

The late 1970s and early 1980s saw a shift in the study of *leadership*, as it was argued that there was limited guidance on how to approach leadership in an environment of continuous and significant change (Hunt 1999; Mintzber 1982). It was in this climate that the 'new paradigm' approaches to leadership emerged (Bryman 1992; Bass 1998; Kotter 1990; Leonard et al. 2013). These comprised the 'visionary' (Sashkin 1988), 'charismatic' (House 1977; Conger and Kanungo 1998) and 'transformational' models (Bass 1990; Tichy and Devanna 1986). Psychologists in the field of leadership research argue for the link between leadership and organisational culture. For example, Schein (2010) described them as 'two sides of the same coin'. Leaders are responsible for setting the overarching vision and strategy of the organisation (Kotter 1990; Porter 2003). This vision is then operationalised by *managers.*

Organisational *culture* (shared systems of meaning and values) can be viewed as a means of improving corporate performance (Kotter and Heskett 1992) or to describe and explain social phenomena in organisations (Willmott 1993). It affects the decisions made, the goals and standards set and the pattern and manner of behaviour. According to Asch and Salaman (2002) when employees are committed to their organisation and its purposes, they energetically and enthusiastically carry out their work because they identify with it and share the purposes to which it is directed. Staff do not have to be told what to do or when to do it because they see what needs to be done and want it done well. Mullins (2010) states that organisational culture develops over many years from a range of factors including the organisation's history (philosophy and values of why originally formed), its primary function and technology, its goals and objectives, size (larger companies tend to have more formalised structures and culture) and location. It is usually perpetuated through a combination of dominant personalities, positive reinforcement and by the strategies of the founders. Williams et al. (1994) concluded that it is learnt, impacted on and impacts on the organisation, commonly held rather than shared and heterogeneous (i.e. most organisations have a dominant culture and various subcultures).

Opinions differ on the exact nature of the relationship between employee *attitudes* and organisational behaviour. While one group states that attitudes impact directly on behaviour (Roberts and Hunt 1991; Robbins and Judge 2014), other researchers point out that there has been no clear causal link found between the two (Chaiken and Stanford 1987; Williams et al. 1994). For those that believe there is a link, they posit that it is due to three groups of factors: cognitive, affective or behavioural (Katz and Stotland 1959; Robbins and Judge 2014; Weddfelt et al. 2016), even though some view these three as affective only (Ajzen 2005). The cognitive factors refer to the properties of the object, event, action, etc. (e.g. a job may be viewed as challenging). The affective component relates to how much an individual likes an object, event, action etc. (e.g. a person may have certain beliefs about the qualities of an object). Their attitude to the object then depends on whether they view these qualities positively or negatively (for example, how the employee feels about the job). Alternatively, those who argue that there is no clear causal link indicate the need to take into account 'moderating contingency variables' (Williams et al. 1994). Attitudes (including values) and subsequent behaviour are thought to depend on sets of *beliefs*. Each group of factors can have a different set of underlying beliefs, hence there is not always an overlap. Consequently, there are differences between what is said (attitudes and values) and what is done (behaviour). Robbins and Judge (2014) claim that when staff internalise the values of the organisation they are more likely to engage in cooperative behaviour. The behaviour is self-reinforcing, and reward and control become less important.

Finally, *identity* also plays a key role in organisational behaviour. Indeed, Mead's (1934) Identity Theory asserts that the roles played by individuals have a major impact on what skills they learn and how they identify themselves. Roles serve as a framework for identifying how staff view themselves. This range and number of antecedents to behaviour point to the inherent challenges and complexity involved in attempting to effect behaviour change amongst staff in organisations.

18.3   PRO-ENVIRONMENTAL BEHAVIOUR CHANGE IN ORGANISATIONS

In the previous section a number of different factors that impact upon organisational behaviour were identified, including organisational culture, leadership and management, organisational structure and attitudes. This section will outline examples of case studies that have sought to utilise these factors in changing pro-environmental behaviours (PEBs) in organisations.

18.3.1   Pro-environmental Behaviours

Kollmuss and Agyeman (2002: 240) define PEB as 'behavior that consciously seeks to minimise the negative impact of one's actions on the natural and built world'. Employees can exhibit a number of PEBs (e.g. recycling, sustainable procurement, and energy and water conservation) (Greaves et al. 2013; Zhang et al. 2013; Thøgersen 2005; Homburg and Stolberg 2006). PEBs may be direct (direct gestures to enhance the environment – e.g. conserving water) or indirect (motivating other staff to engage in direct gestures) (Homburg and Stolberg 2006). According to Ones and Dilchert (2012), PEBs may fall into one of five categories, namely: (1) conserving (use, reuse, recycling and repurposing); (2) working sustainably (e.g. changing how work is done); (3) avoiding harm (prevention pollution); (4) influencing others (encouraging and supporting others); and (5) taking initiatives (initiating programmes and policies). Much of the work in this field has utilised social marketing: the application of marketing to achieve specific behavioural goals for a social good (e.g. Wilhelm-Rechmann 2007; Barr and Shaw 2016). Defra (2008) notes that common motivators for PEBs include: the 'feel good factor'; the social norm; individual benefits (e.g. health, financial outlay); ease; and being part of something, while key barriers include: external constraints (infrastructure, cost, working patterns, demands on time); habit; scepticism; and disempowerment.

18.3.2   Change Management Approaches

As noted earlier, factors influencing organisational behaviour can be placed into various categories. Based on Armenakis and Bedeian (1999), the psycho-sociological approaches to be discussed here are grouped into three broad categories of characteristics, namely: (1) organisational (e.g. the organisational culture or focus); (2) change processes (i.e. change approaches and the management of change); and (3) contextual (i.e. the conditions in which the organisation is operating).

Organisational perspectives
Rusly et al. (2012) argue that for change to be successful, there are four elements that the organisation should put in place, namely: (1) *communication*, in order to change beliefs and motivate staff to make decisions regarding the implementation of new ideas (Abdolvand et al. 2008; Rogers 2003; Helfrich et al. 2009; Jones et al. 2016). Within this context, provision of feedback on progress is also important. For example, Siero et al. (1996) and Dixon et al. (2015) found that energy conservation initiatives were more successful when employees were given feedback on their performance; (2) employee *participation*, with regards to the extent to which the culture and structure of the organisations gives them the opportunity to contribute to the change initiative (Holt et al. 2007; Leonard et al. 2013). If employees are of the view that they are being involved in the decision-making, then they are more likely to change. For example, according to Paillé and Mejía-Morelos (2014), organisational support has an indirect effect on PEBs through employee commitment to the organisation. Staff who identify strongly with the organisation and are more committed are more likely to engage in PEBs; (3) *opportunities for learning* created through various forms of training and development, as this creates new knowledge (Akipieyi et al. 2015); and (4) *clarity of vision*. If the change initiatives can be clearly linked to the organisational vision, this will enhance employees' involvement in, and contribution to, the implementation of the initiatives (Gold et al. 2001; Kotter 1996; Lehman et al. 2002). Indeed, authority figures (e.g. a senior manager or government agencies), can positively influence environmental values. For example, government agencies can create legislation to regulate large-scale environmental pollution, while leaders can influence staff to recycle or conserve water at work (Turnbull and Newell 2012). Indeed, Newhouse (2009) contended that signage using an image of (former US) President Obama recycling had a far more significant impact than signs simply asking individuals to recycle. The role of the *group* is also an important consideration. Change is based on shared beliefs and feelings (Eby et al. 2000; Laurens 2012). There are

two key elements that enhance confidence to undertake change, namely collective commitment and *collective efficacy* (Holt et al. 2009). Collective commitment refers to shared determination to implement change initiatives, based on the shared feelings of the capabilities of the group (Holt et al. 2009; Weiner 2009). Therefore, stakeholders commonly seek to act in a manner similar to the group's members (Herscovitch and Meyer 2002; Holt et al. 2007; Jimmieson et al. 2008). Collective efficacy is a measure of how confident employees are that they can perform well, based on their shared capabilities, despite the proposed changes (Holt et al. 2009; Weiner 2009). For example, Cojuharenco et al. (2016) found that when individuals possessed a sense of being connected to others they were more likely to engage in PEBs and socially responsible behaviours (e.g. giving donations to charity).

Change perspectives

One of the most well-known change theories is that of Lewin (1951), which argued for change using *Force Fields Analysis*. The concept of 'forces' represented the perceptions of staff towards a particular factor and its influence. Driving forces are those that affect a situation and which are attempting to push it in a particular direction and thus tend to initiate change or keep it going. However, increasing these forces results in an increase in the resisting forces. As a result, there is no change to the equilibrium, as it is simply under increased tension. Restraining forces act to restrain or decrease the driving forces. Focusing on the restraining forces is therefore a more favourable approach, as it reduces tension. Change is viewed as a three-stage process, involving:

- Unfreezing the existing organisational practices. This can be achieved by either outlining the differences between the beliefs of employees and reality, or their actual and espoused values. Strategically, it is important to target current values and behaviours, or pre-existing values and behaviours;
- Moving to a new position;
- Refreezing in a new equilibrium position.

According to Steg and Vlek (2009), in many cases, behaviour is habitual and guided by automated cognitive processes, rather than being preceded by elaborate reasoning. Thus James (2010) advocates employing situational change in order to 'unfreeze' existing practices and effect PEB change amongst staff. For example, this change could be effected through the use of monetary incentives (e.g. free bus passes and rewards for low energy use) and non-monetary incentives (car-pooling and competitions to reduce energy use), as a means of making environmental behaviour less costly and more desirable. In addition, based on the 'choice architecture' concepts of libertarian paternalism (Thaler and Sunstein 2008), the default option (i.e. everyday practices), should be changed. For example, setting the printer to double-sided printing will refreeze behaviour to a new equilibrium and reduce consumption of paper.

The University of Cambridge faced a challenge of high energy consumption and subsequently, high bills (Pema 2015). One of the options identified was to reduce its printing. It sought to achieve this through a combination of: technological solutions (e.g. replacing small individual printers in offices with larger communal printers, using display screens rather than paper-based notices and providing staff with iPads), and raising awareness of energy costs amongst staff.

Fujii and Gärling (2003) found that temporarily forcing car drivers to use alternative travel modes induced long-term reductions in car use. The impacts of such temporary changes were particularly strong for habitual car drivers. The authors indicate that this suggests that habitual drivers have inaccurate and modifiable perceptions of the pros and cons of alternative transport modes. Understanding how habits are formed, reinforced and sustained is therefore crucial to determining how best to overcome them.

Santos and van der Linden (2016) report on an initiative to change the norms of new students at Princeton University, towards decreased use of disposable bottled water consumption on campus. The initiative provided all new students with reusable water bottles. Those who received the reusable Drink Local bottles upon arrival were found to be significantly less likely to drink disposable bottled water and more likely to support a campus-wide bottled water ban. By giving the students a water bottle from the outset, an 'unfreezing' of any previous wasteful practices had taken place, and these had been replaced by new habits.

Contextual perspectives
Contextual factors such as physical infrastructure, technical facilities, the availability of products, and product characteristics, can play a key role in staff engagement with PEBs (Steg and Vlek 2009). These factors may in some cases facilitate or constrain PEBs and influence individual practices (Stern 1999; Thøgersen 2005; Van Raaij 2002). For example, the availability of recycling facilities, the availability of resources and their costs can serve to influence staff engagement with PEBs (Santos 2008; Van Diepen and Voogd 2001; Vining and Ebreo 1992). Steg and Vlek (2009) contend that contextual factors can affect PEBs in four main ways, namely: (1) directly, for example, through the availability of recycling facilities; (2)

through mediation by psycho-sociological constructs such as attitudes and beliefs. For example, the introduction of recycling might result in increased use; (3) the factors may be the mediating factors between the psycho-sociological constructs. For example, the introduction of recycling may only result in increased recycling amongst those with strong existing environmental values; and (4) based on Goal-Framing Theory, the factors influence which type of motivation is most important for undertaking the PEB. For example, normative behaviours may be strongest if the recycling service is frequent.

Crucially, PEBs at work can spill over into the home (Voydanoff 2001; Shultz et al. 2007; Tudor et al. 2007). Thus improved PEBs at work can also potentially lead to enhanced practices at home and vice versa. For example, Tudor et al. (2007) demonstrated that staff who recycled or conserved materials at work were also likely to practice similar PEBs at home.

18.4   BEYOND PSYCHOLOGICAL CONTRUCTS: TRANSITION PERSPECTIVES

A number of studies have demonstrated that organisational and individual employee factors are strongly *interrelated*. One of the earliest studies to illustrate the interrelated nature of behaviour by Heider (1958), contended that behaviour is determined both by perceived internal forces (personality attributes such as skill, effort and fatigue) and external forces (organisational rules and policies, etc.). This has been confirmed in subsequent research by a number of noted writers (e.g. Bennett 1975; Elbing 1978; Weiner 1986; Locke 1991; Drucker 2007), suggesting the need for holistic approaches to embedded corporate PEBs. Indeed, various writers (e.g. Tudor et al. 2008; Greaves et al. 2013; Blok et al. 2015) are of the view that this interrelatedness introduces a degree of complexity both in the range and types of interactions between factors which should be taken into consideration when examining how best to effect changes in PEBs within organisations. For example, Tudor et al. (2008) found that the sustainable waste management practices of staff were influenced both by organisational factors (e.g. the organisational culture and structure), and personal factors (e.g. environmental attitudes, job satisfaction and environmental beliefs). This complexity is further compounded in large organisations which, for example, have additional layers of bureaucracy and formalised structures.

As a result of this complexity and the limitations in focusing solely on psycho-sociological constructs, attempts to formulate more effective approaches to examine the embedding of PEBs in large organisations have

422   *Research handbook on employee pro-environmental behaviour*

fostered the emergence of *Transition concepts*. These concepts have been
primarily represented by the *multi-level perspective* (MLP) and *social practices'* (SPs) affiliates (e.g. Elzen and Wieczorek 2005; Geels 2004, 2005,
2010; Shove et al. 2012; Shove and Walker 2010; Walker and Shove 2007).
These multifaceted theoretical developments offer improved possibilities
to best manage the complex tasks of encompassing multiple dimensions,
elements, and factors involved in extended PEB change processes. They
offer advanced alternatives to examine social phenomena beyond the
polarity established by traditional streams between structure and agency,
positioning themselves as an intermediate lens which bridges both angles
of analysis. The MLP regards contributions of networks of varied
stakeholders as multiple agents influencing the change process (having
'actors' as an analytical category). However, social practice streams that
focus on sustainable Transitions emphasise the option of minimising the
individuals' role as an analytical imperative. Therefore, although both
approaches offer wide possibilities to analyse structural influences, the
MLP articulates clearly their relationship with agency aspects.

According to the MLP, innovations would 'diffuse' from the micro-
level of occurrences (in Niches) into meso-levels of societal patterns of
use/consumption/behaviour (Regime), benefiting from macro-level influences which destabilise well-established competitor patterns in the market
(Landscape). Thus, human and non-human factors, formal and informal
regulatory processes, socio-economic issues, technological aspects, infrastructures, and other determinants could influence the emergence of new
patterns of PEBs in a social system. SPs approaches regard the roles that
diverse elements (shared meanings, competences, social norms, teleo-affec-
tive structures, material components, amongst others) play in establishing/
discontinuing practices adopted by a particular society. Such extended
analytical capacity strengthens research possibilities aimed at understanding change mechanisms, contributing to PEB shifts in large organisational
settings. It is important to note, however, that both sustainable Transition
perspectives (i.e. multi-level perspectives and social practices), bear limitations of studying cases in retrospect, and explaining events with the benefit
of hindsight. Their shortcomings in terms of supporting change interventions have been noted as having only a propositional/speculative character
(Hargreaves et al. 2013; Spurling et al. 2013).

Despite these limitations, initiatives to resolve the explanatory constraints addressed as mutual criticism by representatives from both
streams (Shove and Walker 2007, 2008; Rotmans and Kemp 2008;
Geels 2011) open up possibilities to enhance their contributions to
intervention purposes (Birtchnell 2012; Smith et al. 2010; Watson 2012).
Indeed, the integration of theories, approaches and methods opens up a

promising avenue towards an in-depth understanding of PEB changes in large organisational settings. This integrated approach, however, raises demanding paradigmatic shifts and corresponding challenges, including the complexity of their methodological features (Dutra and Tudor 2016).

Integrated studies on societal transformations towards PEBs within the context of large system change (LSC) offer valuable insights into how to tackle the challenges associated with embedding PEBs in large organisations. Indeed, these perspectives could contribute to an improved understanding of how to change employees' PEB, both at their workplace and during their external societal roles/activities. In order to effectively promote more sustainable realities, in which organisations 'engage and contribute' (rather than 'react') to changes in their environment, organisational change management must consider its role within an integrated network of multiple institutions and organisations (Waddock et al. 2015). In this context, Waddock et al. (2015) propose a framework for supporting effective LSC solutions, underpinning their concepts by a literature review on complexity perspectives. Similar arguments are proposed as prospective paths for the integration of sustainable Transition approaches, benefiting from advanced concepts for complexity from Edgar Morin's perspectives (Dutra and Tudor 2016). It would be sensible to consider that, if progress in the research on changing PEBs in large organisations demands paradigmatic shifts, more comprehensive conceptual foundations amongst complexity streams should be assigned to such challenging endeavours. Initiatives to truly embed PEBs within large organisations would profit by going beyond a focus solely on psycho-sociological factors, to underpinning their efforts with advanced complexity paradigms.

18.5   RECOMMENDATIONS FOR PRACTITIONERS

Practitioners should adopt a participative, rather than a unilateral approach to change. A participative approach that seeks to involve staff in the processes, explains what is happening and why, is more likely to engage them. Greater engagement and ownership would mean that the change is more likely to succeed. Strategies for participation might take various forms. For example (Jones et al. 2016): (1) the use of association (e.g. with likeable people or activities); (2) modelling (i.e. using social proof to demonstrate an image, for example someone else conserving water); (3) providing feedback behaviour (e.g. on recycling); (4) through reciprocation of a 'favour'; (5) using monetary or non-monetary incentives; and (6) outlining the potential disadvantages of not engaging.

Staff should be provided with strong leadership, as well as a clearly outlined vision, messages and timeframes for what is expected. If employees are provided with a clearly defined path and milestones, as well as mechanisms for feedback, learning and support, they are more likely to come on board with the change.

Given the complex nature of large organisations and the number of influencing factors, organisational change will not be linear and there will be several challenges. It is important therefore for those managing the change to anticipate potential sources (e.g. from groups of employees) and types of challenges, and to be prepared with strategies for overcoming resistance to change. Overcoming resistance may involve utilising incentives. These incentives should focus especially on intrinsic motivators for change, if they are to be successful. The targeting of specific segments of staff should be employed, with particular focus on those who are willing to engage, but require assistance (Defra 2008; Steg and Vlek 2009).

It is important that change be thought through and planned in a step by step, phased and iterative manner. This approach is especially crucial when attempting significant change, for example within large organisations or in the case of changing the focus of an organisation. Steg and Vlek (2009) argue that in identifying which PEBs to target, the choice should be those PEBs with the highest potential negative environmental impacts. For example, focusing on sustainable procurement will have a greater impact than recycling or reuse. However, the feasibility of the actions should also be taken into consideration.

Finally, given the complexity of the change processes, no one strategy will work for all organisations. Thus, change agents should develop holistic, but bespoke approaches that take account of the specific considerations of the organisation, its employees, as well as its internal and external environments. The strategy should be flexible and be modified in response to changes in the contexts. Processes for monitoring and evaluation, as well as for feedback to inform effective execution, should also be built into the change processes.

REFERENCES

Abdolvand, N., A. Albadvi and Z. Ferdowsi (2008), 'Assessing readiness for business process reengineering', *Business Process Management Journal*, **14** (4), 497–551.
Ajzen, I. (2005), *Attitudes, Personality and Behaviour* (2nd edn), Open University Press, Berkshire: McGraw-Hill Education.
Akipieyi, A., T.L. Tudor and C. Dutra (2015), 'The utilisation of risk-based frameworks for managing healthcare waste: A case study of the National Health Service in London', *Safety Science*, **72**, 127–132.
Armenakis, A.A. and A. Bedeian (1999), 'Organisational change: A review of theory and research in the 1990s', *Journal of Management*, **25** (3), 293–315.

Asch, D. and G. Salaman (2002), 'The challenge of change', *European Business Journal*, 3rd quarter, **14** (3), 133–144.

Barr, S. and G. Shaw (2016), 'Knowledge co-production and behavioural change, collaborative approaches for promoting low carbon mobility', in D. Hopkins and J. Higham (eds), *Low Carbon Mobility Transitions*, Oxford: Goodfellow Publishers.

Bass, B.M. (1990), 'From transactional to transformational leadership: Learning to share the vision', *Organizational Dynamics*, **18** (3), 19–31.

Bass, B.M. (1998), *Transformational Leadership: Industrial, Military, and Educational Impact*, Mahwah, NJ: Lawrence Erlbaum Associates.

Beal, G.M. and J.M. Bohlen (1955), 'How farm people accept new ideas', Cooperative Extension Service Report 15, Ames, IA: Department of Agriculture.

Bennett, C. (1975), 'Up the hierarchy', *Journal of Extension*, **13** (2), 7–12.

Birtchnell, T. (2012), 'Elites, elements and events: Practice theory and scale', *Journal of Transport Geography*, **24**, 497–502.

Bryman, A. (1992), *Charisma and Leadership in Organizations*, London: Sage.

Bucklin, B.R., A. Alvero, A. Dickinson, J. Austin, and A. Jackson (2000), 'Industrial-organizational psychology and organizational behavior management: An objective comparison', *Journal of Organizational Behavior Management*, **20**, 27–75.

Burns, T. and G.M. Stalker (1994), *The Management of Innovation*, Oxford: Oxford University Press.

Chaiken, S. and C. Stanford (1987), 'Attitudes and attitude change', in M. Rosenzweig and L.W. Porter (eds), *Annual Review of Psychology*, **38**, 211–226.

Child, J. (2005), *Contemporary Principles and Practices*, Oxford: Blackwell Publishing.

Cojuharenco, I., G. Cornelissen and N. Karelaia (2016), 'Yes, I can: Feeling connected to others increases perceived effectiveness and socially responsible behaviour', *Journal of Environmental Psychology*, **48**, 75–86.

Conger, J.A. and R.N. Kanungo (1998), *Charismatic Leadership in Organizations*, Thousand Oaks, CA: SAGE Publications.

Defra (2008), *A Framework for Pro-environmental Behaviours*, London: Defra.

Dixon, G., M. Deline, K. McComas, L. Chambliss and M. Hoffmann (2015), 'Using comparative feedback to influence workplace energy conservation: A case study of a university campaign', *Environment & Behavior*, **47**, 667–693.

Drucker, P.F. (2007), *Management Challenges for the 21st Century*, New York: Routledge.

Dutra, C.J.C. and T.L. Tudor (2016), 'Challenges to advancements in transition research on paradigmatic grounds', paper presented at the 7th International Sustainability Transitions (IST) Conference, Wuppertal, Germany.

Eby, L.T., D.M. Adams, J.E.A. Russel and S.H. Gaby (2000), 'Perceptions of organisational readiness for change: Factors related to employees' reactions to the implementation of team based selling', *Human Relations*, **53** (3), 419–442.

Elbing, A. (1978), *Behavioural Decisions in Organizations*, Glenview, IL: Scott, Foresman and Company.

Elzen, B. and A. Wieczorek (2005), 'Transitions towards sustainability through system innovation', *Technological Forecasting & Social Change*, **72** (6), 651–661.

Fincham, R. and P.S. Rhodes (2005), *Principles of Organizational Behaviour* (4th edn), Oxford: Oxford University Press.

Fujii, S. and T. Gärling (2003), 'Development of script-based travel mode choice after forced change', *Transportation Research F*, **6**, 117–124.

Geels, F.W. (2004), 'From sectoral systems of innovation to socio-technical systems: Insights about dynamics and change from sociology and institutional theory', *Research Policy*, **33** (6), 897–920.

Geels, F.W. (2005), 'Processes and patterns in transitions and system innovations: Refining the coevolutionary multi-level perspective', *Technological Forecasting & Social Change*, **72** (6), 681–696.

Geels, F.W. (2010), 'Ontologies, socio-technical transitions (to sustainability), and the multi-level perspective', *Research Policy*, **39** (4), 495–510.

Geels, F.W. (2011), 'The multi-level perspective on sustainability transitions: Responses to seven criticisms', *Environmental Innovation and Societal Transitions*, **1** (1), 24–40.

Gold, A.H., A. Malhotra and A.H. Segars (2001), 'Knowledge management: An organisational capabilities perspective', *Journal of Management Information Systems*, **18** (1), 185–214.

Greaves, M., L. Zibarras, and C. Stride (2013), 'Using the theory of planned behaviour to explore environmental behavioural intentions in the workplace', *Journal of Environmental Psychology*, **34**, 109–120.

Hargreaves, T., N. Longhurst and G. Seyfang (2013), 'Up, down, round and round: Connecting regimes and practices in innovation for sustainability', *Environment and Planning A*, **45** (2), 402–420.

Haveman, H.A. (1993), 'Organizational size and change: Diversification in the savings and loan industry after deregulation', *Administrative Science Quarterly*, **38**, 20–50.

Heider, F. (1958), *The Psychology of Interpersonal Relations*, New York: John Wiley and Sons.

Helfrich, C.D., Y.F. Li, N.D. Sharp and A.E. Sales (2009), 'Organisational readiness to change assessment (ORCA): Development of an instrument based on the promoting action on research in health services (PARIHS) framework', *Implementation Science*, **4** (1), 38.

Herscovitch, L. and J.P. Meyer (2002), 'Commitment to organisational change: Extension of a three-component model', *Journal of Applied Psychology*, **87** (3), 474–487.

Holt, D.T., A.A. Armenakis, H.S. Feild and S.C. Harris (2007), 'Readiness for organisational change: The systematic development of a scale', *Journal of Applied Behavioural Science*, **43** (2), 232–255.

Holt, D.T., C.D. Helfrich, C.G. Hall and B.J. Weiner (2009), 'Are you ready? How health professionals can comprehensively conceptualize readiness for change', *Journal of General Internal Medicine*, **25** (1), 50–55.

Homburg, A. and A. Stolberg (2006), 'Explaining pro-environmental behaviour with cognitive theory of stress', *Journal of Environmental Psychology*, **26** (1), 1–14.

House, R.J. (1977), 'A 1976 theory of charismatic leadership', in J.G. Hunt and L.L. Larson (eds), *Leadership: The Cutting Edge*, Carbondale, IL: Southern Illinois University Press, pp. 189–207.

Hunt, J.G. (1999), 'Transformation/charismatic leadership's transformation of the field: An historical essay', *Leadership Quarterly*, **10**, 129–144.

James, R. (2010), 'Promoting sustainable behaviour: a guide to successful communication', accessed 12 June 2017 at http://www.sustainability.berkeley.edu/sites/default/files/Promoting_Sustain_Behavior_Primer.pdf.

Jimmieson, N.L., M. Peach and K.M. White (2008), 'Utilizing the theory of planned behaviour to inform change management: An investigation of employee intentions to support organisational change', *Journal of Applied Behavioural Science*, **44** (2), 237–262.

Jones, J., J. Jackson, M.P. Bates and T.L. Tudor (2016), 'Factors influencing corporate pro-environmental behaviour – a case study from the UK construction sector', *International Journal of Environment and Sustainable Development*, **15** (1), 1–15.

Kates, R.W. (1962), 'Hazard and choice perception in flood plain management', research paper no. 78, Department of Geography. University of Chicago.

Katz, D. and E. Stotland (1959), 'A preliminary statement to the Theory of Attitude Structure and Change', in S. Koch (ed.), *Psychology: A Study of Science*, New York: McGraw-Hill.

Knights, D. and H. Willmott (2007), *Introducing Organizational Behaviour*, London: Thompson Learning.

Kollmuss, A. and J. Agyeman (2002), 'Mind the gap: Why do people act environmentally and what are the barriers to pro-environmental behavior?', *Environmental Education Research*, **8** (3), 239–260.

Kotter, J.P. (1990), *A Force for Change*, London: The Free Press.

Kotter, J.P. (1996), *Leading Change*, Boston, MA: Harvard Business School Press.

Kotter, J.P. and J.L. Heskett (1992), *Corporate Culture and Performance*, New York: The Free Press.

Laurens, J.M. (2012), 'Changing behavior and environment in a community-based program of the Riverside Community', *Procedia-Social and Behavioral Sciences*, **36**, 372–382.

Lehman, W.E.K., J.M. Greener and D.D. Simpson (2002), 'Assessing organisational readiness for change', *Journal of Substance Abuse Treatment*, **22** (4), 197–209.

Leonard, H.S., R. Lewis, A.M. Freedman and J. Passmore (2013), *The Wiley-Blackwell Handbook of the Psychology of Leadership, Change and Organisational Development*, Chichester: Wiley-Blackwell.

Lewin, K. (1951), *Field Theory in Social Science*, New York: Harper and Row.

Locke, E.A. (1991), 'The motivation sequence, the motivation hub and the motivation core', *Organisational Behaviour and Human Decision Processes*, **50**, 288–299.

Mead, G.H. (1934), *Mind, Self, and Society*, Chicago, IL: University of Chicago Press.

Mintzberg, H. (1982), 'If you're not serving Bill or Barbara, then you're not serving leadership', in J.G. Hunt, U. Sekaran and C.A. Schriesheim (eds), *Leadership Beyond Establishment Views*, Carbondale: Southern Illinois University Press, pp. 239–259.

Mullins, L.J. (2010), *Management and Organisational Behaviour* (9th edn), London: Pearson Education Ltd.

Newhouse, R. (2009), 'Psychology and social science inform climate campaigns', *ClimateEdu*, 11 August, accessed on 14 June 2017 at http://www.nwf.org/campusecology/climateedu/articleView.cfm?iArticleID=95.

Ones, D. and S. Dilchert (2012), 'Employee green behaviors', in S.E. Jackson, D.S. Ones and S. Dilchert (eds), *Managing Human Resource for Environmental Sustainability*, San Francisco, CA: Jossey-Bass, pp. 85–116.

Ostroff, C. and N. Schmitt (1993), 'Configurations of organizational effectiveness and efficiency', *Academy of Management Journal*, **36** (6), 1345–1361.

Paillé, P. and J.H. Mejía-Morelos (2014), 'Antecedents of pro-environmental behaviours at work: The moderating influence of psychological contract breach', *Journal of Environmental Psychology*, **38**, 124–131.

Pema, J. (2015), 'Helping staff to think before they print: The Faculty of Education', accessed on 14 June 2017 at http://www.environment.admin.cam.ac.uk/resource-bank/case-studies/behaviour-change/helping-staff-think-they-print-faculty-education.

Porter, M.E. (2003), *The Competitive Strategy*, Canada: Simon and Schuster.

Prochaska, J.O. and C.C. DiClemente (1986), 'Toward a comprehensive model of change', in W.R. Miller and N. Heather (eds), *Treating Addictive Behaviors: Processes of Change*, New York: Plenum, pp. 3–28.

Robbins, S.P. (2000), *Essentials of Organizational Behaviour*, Upper Saddle River, NJ: Prentice Hall.

Robbins, S.P. and T.A. Judge (2014), *Organizational Behaviour* (15th edn), New York: Pearson Education Ltd.

Roberts, K.H. and D.M. Hunt (1991), *Organisational Behaviour*, Boston: PWS-Kent Publishing Company.

Robinson, G.M. (1998), *Methods and Techniques in Human Geography*, Chichester and New York: John Wiley and Sons.

Rogers, E.M. (2003), *Diffusion of Innovations* (5th edn), New York: Free Press.

Rotmans, J. and R. Kemp (2008), 'Detour ahead. A response to Shove and Walker about the perilous road of transition management', *Environment and Planning A*, **40**, 1006–1014.

Rusly, F.H., J. Corner and P.Y.T. Sun (2012), 'Positioning change readiness in knowledge management research', *Journal of Knowledge Management*, **16** (2), 329–355.

Santos, G. (2008), 'The London experience', in E. Verhoef, B. Van Wee, L. Steg and M. Bliemer (eds), *Pricing in Road Transport: A Multi-Disciplinary Perspective*, Cheltenham, UK and Northampton, MA, USA: Edward Elgar Publishing, pp. 273–292.

Santos, J.M. and S. van der Linden (2016), 'Environmental reviews and case studies: Changing norms by changing behavior: The Princeton Drink Local Program', *Environmental Practice*, **18** (2), 116–122.

Schein, E.H. (2010), *Organizational Culture and Leadership* (4th edn), San Francisco, CA: John Wiley and Sons.

Shove, E. and G. Walker (2007), 'CAUTION! Transitions ahead: Politics, practice, and sustainable transition management', *Environment and Planning A*, **39** (4), 763–770.

Shove, E. and G. Walker (2008), 'Transition Management (TM) and the politics of shape shifting', *Environment and Planning A*, **40** (4), 1012–1014.

Shove, E. and G. Walker (2010), 'Governing transitions in the sustainability of everyday life', *Research Policy*, **39** (4), 471–476.

Shove, E., M. Pantzar and M. Watson (2012), *The Dynamics of Social Practice: Everyday Life and How It Changes*, London: Sage.

Siero, F., A. Bakker, G. Dekker and M. Van Den Burg (1996), 'Changing organizational energy consumption behavior through comparative feedback', *Journal of Environmental Psychology*, **16**, 235–246.

Smith, A., J.-P. Voß, and J. Grin (2010), 'Innovation studies and sustainability transitions: The allure of the multilevel perspective and its challenges', *Research Policy*, **39** (4), 435–448.

Spurling, N., A. McMeekin, E. Shove, D. Southerton and D. Welch (2013), 'Interventions in practice: Re-framing policy approaches to consumer behaviour', Social Practices Research Group, accessed 14 June 2017 at http://www.sprg.ac.uk/uploads/sprg-report-sept-2013.pdf.

Steg, L. and C. Vlek (2009), 'Encouraging pro-environmental behaviour: An integrative review and research agenda', *Journal of Environmental Psychology*, **29** (3), 309–317.

Stern, P.C. (1999), 'Information, incentives, and proenvironmental consumer behaviour', *Journal of Consumer Policy*, **22**, 461–478.

Thaler, R.H. and C.R. Sunstein (2008), *Nudge: Improving Decisions about Health, Wealth, and Happiness*, London: Penguin Books Ltd.

Thøgersen, J. (2005), 'How may consumer policy empower consumers for sustainable lifestyles?', *Journal of Consumer Policy*, **28**, 143–178.

Tichy, N. and M. Devanna (1986), *Transformational Leadership*, New York: Wiley.

Tudor, T., S. Barr and A. Gilg (2007), 'A tale of two locational settings: Is there a link between pro-environmental behaviour at work and at home?', *Local Environment: The International Journal of Justice and Sustainability*, **12** (4), 409–421.

Tudor, T., S. Barr and A. Gilg (2008), 'A novel conceptual framework for examining environmental behaviour in large organisations: A case study of the Cornwall National Health Service (NHS) in the UK', *Environment and Behavior*, **40** (3), 426–450.

Turnbull, D. and R. Newell (2012), 'Interactive case studies in sustainable community development', accessed 14 June 2017 at https://crcresearch.org/community-research-connections/crc-case-studies/pro-environmental-behaviours-workplace-driving-socia.

Van Diepen, A. and H. Voogd (2001), 'Sustainability and planning: Does urban form matter?', *International Journal of Sustainable Development*, **4**, 59–74.

Van Raaij, W.F. (2002), 'Stages of behavioural change: motivation, ability and opportunity', in G. Bartels and W. Nelissen (eds), *Marketing for Sustainability: Towards Transactional Policy-making*, Amsterdam, The Netherlands: IOS Press, pp. 321–333.

Vining, J. and A. Ebreo (1992), 'Predicting recycling behavior form global and specific environmental attitudes and changes in recycling opportunities', *Journal of Applied Social Psychology*, **22**, 1580–1607.

Voydanoff, P. (2001), 'Incorporating community into work and family research: A review of basic relationships', *Human Relations*, **54** (12), 1609–1637.

Waddock, S., G.M. Meszoely, S. Waddell and D. Dentoni (2015), 'The complexity of wicked problems in large scale change', *Journal of Organizational Change Management*, **28** (6), 993–1012.

Walker, G. and E. Shove (2007), 'Ambivalence, sustainability and the governance of sociotechnical transitions', *Journal of Environmental Policy and Planning*, **9** (3–4), 213–225.

Watson, M. (2012), 'How theories of practice can inform transition to a decarbonised transport system', *Journal of Transport Geography*, **24**, 488–496.

Weddfelt, E., M. Vaccari and T.L. Tudor (2016), 'The development of environmental visions and strategies at the municipal level: Case studies from the county of Östergötland in Sweden', *Journal of Environmental Management*, **179** (1), 76–82.

Weiner, B. (1986), *An Attributional Theory of Motivation*, New York: Springer.

Weiner, B.J. (2009), 'A theory of organisational readiness for change', *Implementation Science*, **4** (67), 1–9.

Werkman, R.A. (2009), 'Understanding failure to change: A pluralistic approach and five patterns', *Leadership & Organization Development Journal*, **30** (7), 664–668.

Wilhelm-Rechmann, A. (2007), 'Social marketing: More than just "advertising" for the environment', *Society for Conservation Biology Newsletter*, **14** (4), 10–11.

Williams, A., P. Dobson and M. Walters (1994), *Changing Culture: New Organizational Approaches*, Wiltshire: Cromwell Press.

Willmott, H. (1993), 'Strength is ignorance: Slavery is freedom: Managing culture in modern organisations', *Journal of Management Studies*, **30** (4), 515–552.

Wolpert, J. (1964), 'The decision process in spatial context', *Annals of the Association of American Geographers*, **65**, 24–35.

Zhang, Y., Z. Wang and G. Zhou (2013), 'Antecedents of employee electricity saving behaviour in organizations: An empirical study based on norm activation model', *Energy Policy*, **62**, 1120–1127.

19. Measuring and tracking pro-environmental behaviour amongst university employees
John Callewaert and Robert W. Marans

19.1 INTRODUCTION

Universities throughout the world are actively trying to become more sustainable, in part to reduce their operating costs but also to instil in their students and employees an understanding of the meaning of sustainability, its importance in a local and global context, and the need for individuals to adapt a more pro-environmental way of life. As part of this effort, universities are initiating programmes aimed at conserving energy and reducing their carbon emissions, reducing the amount of material and food wastes, educating employees as well as students and, both implicitly and explicitly, changing the culture of sustainability on their campuses. But few universities are undertaking systematic approaches to evaluating the effectiveness of these various initiatives other than tracking operating costs or compiling other hard data such as measures of waste tonnage, energy use, bus ridership and so forth.

Institutions of higher education play a pivotal role in addressing the more difficult yet powerful part of the sustainability transition. That role is in creating and maintaining a "culture of sustainability" among members of the university community. A culture of sustainability has been defined as "a culture in which individuals are aware of major environmental (and social/economic) challenges, are behaving in sustainable ways, and are committed to a sustainable lifestyle for both the present and future" (Marans et al. 2010; Marans et al. 2014). To achieve this ideal state within institutions of higher education, Sharp (2002) calls for a rethinking of organisational action and actors that questions the prevailing assumptions of organisational rationality that stay within the confines of the current systems. Similarly, Senge (2000) stresses the importance of cultivating a "learning organisation," rather than a "knowing organisation" since change at higher education institutions is a "complex learning and unlearning process for all concerned" (Scott 2004). Therefore, nothing less than a paradigmatic shift in organisational thinking is needed for colleges and universities to promote cultural transformation.

This organisational transformation is needed in all sectors of society. Yet institutions of higher education can and should be at the forefront with the collective mission of fostering sustainability, given their role of cultivating future sustainability leaders. To date, however, most campus sustainability efforts stop either at "greening" or at the level of institutional commitments to eco-efficiency, climate and waste mitigation, and increasing environmental education. Though calls for institutional and cultural transformation are multiplying at a rapid rate, rarely do institutions address the deeper cultural change necessary to transform into sustainable organisations which empower citizens with a sustainability perspective; instead, focus is often on implementing many individual projects, isolated initiatives, or broad commitments (Sharp 2002, 2009). This is partly attributable to the lack of guidance for institutions attempting to follow this more uncertain and uncomfortable path. However, it should be noted that the Association for the Advancement of Sustainability in Higher Education (AASHE) is doing much to support these efforts through their Sustainability Tracking, Assessment & Rating System (STARS) which is used by hundreds of institutions. The 2.1 version of STARS asks institutions to report on both their sustainability literacy assessment efforts and assess a culture of sustainability (Association for the Advancement of Sustainability in Higher Education 2016). In addition, the works of Bartlett and Chase (2004, 2013) have done much to chronicle institutional sustainability transformation efforts.

The Sustainability Cultural Indicators Program (SCIP) is a multi-year project designed to measure and track the *culture of sustainability* on the University of Michigan's (U-M) Ann Arbor campus. To date, more than 20,000 U-M students, faculty and staff have completed SCIP questionnaires over the past 4 years. Fifteen key cultural sustainability indicators were developed to measure and track change over time for a range of campus sustainability topics. With respect to employee behaviour programmes, U-M offers two unique efforts to support the development of a culture of sustainability – the Planet Blue Ambassadors programme and the Sustainable Workplace Certification programme. This chapter provides an overview of these programmes along with an analysis of how SCIP results for programme participants compare to the general campus population. The chapter concludes with a summary of future plans for SCIP, opportunities for collaboration and a set of recommendations for practitioners.

19.2   THE UNIVERSITY OF MICHIGAN

The University of Michigan (U-M) has been engaged in efforts to create a culture of sustainability for more than a decade. In October 2009, former U-M President Mary Sue Coleman elevated the University's commitment to sustainability in teaching, research, operations, and engagement by creating the U-M Environmental Sustainability Executive Council.[1] One of the first actions of the Council was endorsing a Campus Sustainability Integrated Assessment (CSIA) to analyse U-M's sustainability efforts to date, benchmark against other institutions, and chart a course for the future through identifying long-term goals for sustainable operations on U-M's Ann Arbor campus, including the Athletic Department and the Health System. The CSIA was built on a long history of sustainability commitments in U-M campus operations, such as implementing cogeneration technology at the Central Power Plant in the 1960s, adopting the EPA Green Lights and Energy Star programmes in the 1990s, and more recently establishing LEED (Leadership in Energy and Environmental Design) Silver certification as the standard for new non-clinical construction projects where the construction value exceeds US$10M.

The geographic scope of the CSIA spanned the five Ann Arbor campuses (South, Central, Medical, North and East Medical), which currently includes over 3 million square metres of teaching, research, health care, athletics and administrative building space. In 2014, these buildings served more than 80,000 occupants – students, faculty and staff (University of Michigan 2015) – and generated over 700,000 metric tons of carbon dioxide emissions (University of Michigan Office of Campus Sustainability 2014). Additional information on sustainability at the University of Michigan can be found on the Planet Blue website – the main sustainability portal for academic, research, and operations initiatives.[2] The magnitude of U-M campus operations suggests that aggressive sustainability goals for University campus operations could have significant positive environmental, fiscal, and health impacts.

The final CSIA report outlined four high-level themes – *Climate Action, Waste Prevention, Healthy Environments*, and *Community Awareness*. Accompanying the themes are Guiding Principles to direct U-M's long-range strategy and 2025 Goals that are time bound and quantifiable.[3] Table 19.1 provides an overview of U-M's 2025 Sustainability Goals.

Table 19.1   CSIA themes, guiding principles and 2025 goals

Theme	Guiding Principle	2025 Goals
Climate Action	We will pursue energy efficiency and fiscally-responsible energy sourcing strategies to reduce greenhouse gas emissions towards long-term carbon neutrality.	Reduce greenhouse gas emissions *(scopes 1 and 2)* by 25% below 2006 levels. Decrease carbon intensity of passenger trips on U-M transportation options by 30% below 2006 levels.
Waste Prevention	We will pursue purchasing, reuse, recycling, and composting strategies towards long-term waste eradication.	Reduce waste tonnage diverted to disposal facilities by 40% below 2006 levels.
Healthy Environ- ments	We will pursue land and water management, built environment, and product-sourcing strategies towards improving the health of ecosystems and communities.	Purchase 20% of U-M food from sustainable sources. Protect Huron River water quality by: • minimising runoff from impervious surfaces *(outperform uncontrolled surfaces by 30%)*, and • reducing the volume of land management chemicals used on campus by 40%.
Community Awareness	We will pursue stakeholder engagement, education, and evaluation strategies towards a campus-wide ethic of sustainability.	*There is no goal recommendation for this theme. However, the report recommends investments in multiple actions to educate our community, track behaviour, and report progress over time.*

19.3   PROGRAMMES PROMOTING A CULTURE OF SUSTAINABILITY FOR EMPLOYEES

One of the most direct efforts to create a culture of sustainability at universities can be found in "eco-rep" type programmes (Erickson 2010). These programmes usually rely on peer-to-peer methods and use social media and marketing to promote sustainable lifestyles and practices. U-M supports two such programmes, the Planet Blue Ambassadors Certification (PBAC) programme and the Sustainable Workplace Certification (SWC) programme.[4]

Launched in 2013, the PBAC programme fosters environmentally and socially responsible thinking and action to advance a campus-wise culture of sustainability through an online training tool consisting of five modules directly related to U-M's sustainability goals. The training involves an individual's commitment of 30–60 minutes and includes a dynamic and interactive learning platform with elements of online gaming. Once completed, the new "Ambassadors" have access to a personalised online dashboard to pledge actions, access resources, and track their personal progress. To date, over 2000 employees have completed the training. Perhaps the best measure of success is that over 80 per cent of the people who start a module complete the entire training. Related efforts include a monthly e-newsletter focused on a targeted action such as using sustainable power settings on computers or increasing proper e-waste disposal. Important components of the e-newsletters are resources for encouraging others to take action, additional impact information, news, and special events or training opportunities. Additionally, a series of online and in-person events are periodically hosted that strive to build community and skills, including a "Healthy Holidays" open house, local foods dinner, and a green computer webinar (Marans and Shriberg 2012; Marans et al. 2014).

Whereas the PBAC programme focuses on individual behaviour change and action, the SWC programme encourages U-M employees to join in working together towards a more sustainable university through participation in an informal inventory of their office practices, identification of gaps, and taking action to implement best practices. By engaging employees in a voluntary programme, the programme promotes both sustainable behaviour across the campus and progress towards U-M's sustainability goals.

Offices or departments interested in the SWC programme first complete an online self-assessment of current office conditions and practices. The assessment should preferably be completed by someone in the unit willing to assume leadership and move the process forward. Once the assessment is submitted, a staff member from U-M's Office of Campus Sustainability (OCS) meets with the unit to review the checklist and answer questions. Areas in which there is room for improvement will receive special attention in order to overcome any barriers and develop an action plan for improvement.

Based on the points earned, the unit will be given a rating to determine if they qualify for being a Sustainable Workplace. OCS provides recommendations and technical assistance to help implement best practices and make the largest positive environmental impact feasible. The unit receives a packet of resources including informational handouts and signage for use throughout the office workspace. In addition to ongoing technical assistance, units committed to reducing their environmental footprint through the Sustainable Workplace programme are recognised with the award of a certificate, a Sustainable Workplace digital logo for web and print use, and placement on the Sustainable Workplace webpage. More than 100 U-M units or workplaces are participating in the SWC programme with more than half having received the highest certification rating – platinum (University of Michigan Office of Campus Sustainability 2017).

19.3.1   The Sustainability Cultural Indicators Program

U-M cultural change initiatives stem from the principles outlined under the CSIA theme of Community Awareness and include efforts that not only offer targeted programming initiatives such as the PBAC and SWC programme but also scientifically measure and report progress and behaviour as a community. The evaluation strategies involve a ground-breaking programme for monitoring U-M's progress in moving towards a culture of sustainability. Progress is determined by an annual survey of students and employees regarding sustainability awareness and behaviour, and tracking changes over time.

To create the surveys, a small group closely involved with the CSIA met for over a year working on what came to be known as SCIP. The group started by examining the recommendations from the CSIA Culture Team report (Marans et al. 2010), reviewed related literature, spoke to key national leaders working on similar efforts, ran focus groups with students and staff to determine current understandings of sustainability, and analysed more than thirty existing campus surveys from numerous institutions (including U-M) about topics such as recycling, transportation, etc.

SCIP is intended to inform U-M administrators and others responsible for day-to-day operations of the University including its academic programmes. Furthermore, it is intended to serve as a model demonstrating how behavioural research can be used to address critical environmental issues within universities generally and in other organisational settings.

SCIP involves annual web surveys of large samples of employees as well as students. SCIP uses two questionnaires – one for staff and faculty (university employees), and one for students. In the US context, "staff" refers to employees who focus on administrative and programmatic activities whereas "faculty" refers to employees who focus on teaching and research. While many of the questions are similar, different time frames and sequences are used in the two versions. For example, while the employee survey questions are primarily set within a time frame of the past year, students are often asked to answer questions based on their experiences since the start of the fall semester. Also, students are asked several demographic questions at the start of the survey, such as whether they live in campus housing or not, in order to skip certain questions which do not apply to students living in campus housing. Staff and faculty demographic questions are asked at the end of the survey.

The sample design during the first year (2012) targeted 1000 faculty and 1000 staff employees and 4400 students (1000 from each undergraduate class and 400 graduate students). In subsequent years, the design called for 750 faculty, 750 staff, and 2400 students. Targeted numbers of faculty and staff were reached or exceeded with response rates averaging around 40 per cent for faculty and 45 per cent for staff. During the first year, over 4000 students responded with a 40.6 per cent response that averaged about 22 per cent in subsequent years. The surveys ask questions about awareness, commitment, engagement and actions or behaviours dealing with the University's goals of Climate Action, Waste Prevention, and Healthy Environments. Responses to individual questions are combined to create 15 diverse indicators that deal with awareness, behaviours, degrees of commitment, and levels of sustainability engagement (Callewaert and Marans 2016; Graham Sustainability Institute 2017). The average time to complete the online survey is about 15 minutes. Table 19.2 offers an example of a SCIP question.

Table 19.3 offers an overview of the question type and modules. In total, the questionnaires each contain approximately 242 questions although respondents can skip any question they did not want to answer and responses to some questions generate a skip sequence for subsequent questions. A limited number of modifications have been made to the questionnaires each year – adding questions, deleting questions, or clarifying questions – with the goal of as little modification as possible to avoid

Table 19.2   SCIP question example

How much do you know about the following at U-M?	A lot	A fair amount	A little	Not much/ nothing
a. Recycling glass	○	○	○	○
b. Recycling plastic	○	○	○	○
c. Recycling paper	○	○	○	○
d. Recycling electronic waste (i.e. computers, cell phones)	○	○	○	○
e. Property disposition services	○	○	○	○
f. Composting	○	○	○	○

Table 19.3   SCIP survey questions by module and question type

Survey Module	Question Type					
	Knowledge	Disposition	Behaviour	Other	Demographics	Total
Transportation	9	10	21	1	0	41
Conservation	5	5	33	1	0	44
Environment	4	2	9	1	0	16
Food	7	6	19	2	0	34
Climate	1	2	0	2	0	5
Sustainability (general)	0	20	13	3	0	36
U-M efforts	8	0	8	8	0	24
Demographics	0	0	0	0	42	42
TOTAL	34	45	103	18	42	242

increasing the amount of time required by respondents to complete the survey and to allow for as much longitudinal analysis as possible.

19.3.2   Analysis of Results: 2012–2015

Table 19.4 presents employee characteristics for the staff and faculty who responded to the 2015 survey. More than half of the former indicated they were in professional, administrative, or managerial positions and 1 in 5 said they were either a nurse or member of the medical staff. Somewhat more than a third of the staff respondents (36 per cent) had worked at U-M for more than 10 years and a quarter (25 per cent) had been employed by U-M for 2 years or less.

Among the faculty respondents, nearly half were affiliated with the University for more than a decade whereas 17 per cent had been employed for 2 years or less. About a third identified themselves as teaching faculty although a number also mentioned their role as researchers. An additional 1 in 5 were clinical instructors and 8 per cent of the faculty respondents were lecturers. Thirty-five per cent of them said they were primarily researchers and nearly 4 in 10 faculty respondents were tenured.

As noted above, during the initial year of SCIP (2012) indicators or indices were created that combined responses to closely related questions about a common idea, concept, or action. In many instances, responses were statistically correlated. Weakly correlated responses that reflect different dimensions of the same idea, concept, or action were nevertheless combined to create a desired indicator.[5, 6]

For most of the indices, the number of response categories to their respective questions was identical.[7] Numerical values were assigned to

Table 19.4   Staff/faculty employee characteristics

2015 (percentage distribution)*	Staff	Faculty
Type of Staff		
Professional	26	
Managerial	10	
Administrative	20	
Research	14	
Medical, Nursing	20	
Service	5	
Other	5	
Total	100	
Type of Faculty		
Teaching-Tenured		20
Teaching-Non-tenured		10
Research-Tenured		14
Research-Non-tenured		21
Clinical instructional-Tenured		3
Clinical instructional-Non-tenured		19
Lecturer		8
Other		5
Total		100
Years at U-M		
Less than a year	10	7
1–2 years	15	10
3–5 years	20	16
6–10 years	19	21
11–20 years	21	24
More than 20 years	15	22
Total	100	100

The minimum number of respondents for faculty
and staff is shown below.

	Staff	Faculty
Number of respondents	850	873

Note: * Percentage distributions are based on the weighted number of respondents to each question. The actual number differs since not all questions were answered by all respondents.

responses such that higher values represented the most sustainable forms of behaviour or the highest levels of awareness, while the lower values represented the least sustainable behaviours or lowest levels of awareness. For example, for responses to the question, "During the past year, how often did you turn off lights when leaving the room", "always/most of the time" was coded 4, "sometimes" was coded 3, "rarely" was coded 2, and "never" was coded 1. Together with three other questions, the maximum summary score for any respondent would be 16 and the minimum score would be 4. The distribution of summary scores for all student and staff/ faculty respondents was then tabulated.

Respondents who said "don't know" or "not applicable" to questions used in developing selected indicators were not included when building those indicators. That is, index scores were not calculated for these respondents. On occasion, some of the remaining respondents skipped one of the questions comprising the index. Rather than eliminating these respondents from the analysis and thus reducing the sample size, the modal value of all other respondents to the question was assigned to the non-response item. These respondents were then retained in the sample. The operational rule for dealing with missing values was as follows. For indicators consisting of one or two items, participants with one or two non-responses were excluded from the analysis. For indicators consisting of three items, respondents with one non-response were assigned the modal value to that item. For indicators using four or more than four items, participants who had more than two non-responses were eliminated from the analysis. Those with one or two non-response items were assigned the modal value of all responses to those items.

The second step involved the creation of a common metric or scale for all indicators. This was necessary since the range of scores for each indicator varied. Some varied from 1 to 4 while others varied from 8 to 32. In order to make the indicators comparable and easier to understand, all the indicators were converted to common metric or a zero-to-ten scale. For instance, the summed Waste Prevention Behaviour Index for participants ranged from 4 to 16. In this case, the minimum value (4) was subtracted from the maximum value (16) resulting in a scale ranging from 0 to 12. Each value was then divided by the new maximum value (12), so that the new index score would be between 0 to 1. That score was then multiplied by 10, resulting in a value ranging from 0 to 10. SPSS Complex Samples was then used to determine the distributions and the mean scores of indicators.[8] Table 19.5 provides the results for all the indices for staff and faculty between 2012 and 2015.

In general, findings from 4 years of data collection (2012–2015) indicate that U-M has made progress with waste prevention, in promoting sustain-

Table 19.5   *Change in sustainability cultural indicators for staff and faculty, 2012–15*

INDICES (mean scores)	STAFF				FACULTY			
	2012	2013	2014	2015	2012	2013	2014	2015
PRIMARY								
Climate Action								
Conservation Behaviour	6.6	6.7	6.5	6.5	6.9	6.9	7.0	7.0
Travel Behaviour	1.6	1.4	1.6	1.5	2.2	2.0	1.8⬇	2.3 ▲
Waste Prevention								
Waste Prevention Behaviour	7.0	7.0	7.0	7.1 ⬆	7.3	7.3	7.4⬆△	7.6⬆
Healthy Environments								
Sustainable Food Purchases	5.7	5.8	5.8⬆	5.9⬆	6.3	6.2	6.3	6.4
Protecting the Natural Environment	6.5	6.4	6.6	6.7	6.1	6.1	6.4△	6.6⬆
Community Awareness								
Sustainable Travel & Transportation	3.0	3.0	3.1	3.1	3.4	3.3	3.3	3.5
Waste Prevention	5.0	5.1	5.0	4.9	5.1	5.4⬆	5.5⬆	5.3
Natural Environment Protection	4.1	4.3⬆	4.3⬆	4.2	4.3	4.6⬆	4.6⬆	4.5
Sustainable Foods	4.7	5.1⬆	5.0⬆	5.2⬆	5.6	5.7	5.7	6.0⬆△
U-M Sustainability Initiatives	5.4	5.6	5.3	5.3	4.9	5.1⬆	5.0	5.1
SECONDARY								
Sustainability Engagement at U-M	0.9	0.7	0.7	1.1⬆▲	0.7	0.7	0.7	1.2⬆▲
Sustainability Engagement Generally	1.9	1.9	1.8	1.8	3.0	2.9	3.0	2.7⬇▼
Sustainability Commitment	6.3	6.4	6.4	6.4	7.0	7.2⬆	7.1	7.2
Sustainability Disposition	2.9	2.6⬇	2.5⬇	2.5⬇	5.3	4.7⬇	4.9⬇	4.8⬇
Rating U-M Sustainability Initiatives	6.7	6.8	6.6▼	6.7	6.4	6.5	6.4	6.5

Table 19.5 (continued)

⬆ significant change from 2012 (p<.001)
⬆ significant change from 2012 (p<.01)
⬆ significant change from 2012 (p<.05)
▲ significant change from previous year (p<.001)
▲ significant change from previous year (p<.01)
▲ significant change from previous year (p<.05)

able food, and engaging the campus community through efforts such as the PBAC programme. Additional results indicate that more efforts are needed to promote sustainable transportation options, energy conservation initiatives, and ways to expand involvement in U-M sustainability activities. In addition, several key items can be identified when the indicators for 2015 are compared against the results from 2012.

First, there is considerable room for improvements in the pro-environment behaviours, levels of awareness, degrees of engagement, and expressions of commitment to sustainability among members of the University community. Second, faculty are more engaged in pro-environmental behaviours than staff outside the University. These activities include conserving energy, preventing waste, and purchasing sustainable foods. Faculty members also express a higher degree of commitment to sustainability than staff or students. Third, staff tend to know more about U-M's sustainability initiatives than faculty. Yet both groups have become more engaged in sustainability activities on campus over the four-year period. Finally, both groups express high levels of commitment to sustainability.

19.3.3 Impact of Engagement Programmes

In an attempt to see if participation in the PBAC and SWC programmes has had any impact on individual behaviours and levels of awareness and engagement, the 2015 data covering faculty and staff were examined. Staff and faculty who reported being part of either programme had significantly higher index scores for many of the cultural indicators than those who had never participated in the programmes. For instance, staff in the PBAC programme were more likely to conserve energy, reduce their waste, and purchase sustainable foods than those who were not in the programme. Similarly, they were also more likely to understand all aspects of sustainability, know more about U-M's sustainability efforts, rate those efforts higher, and be more committed to sustainability than those who were not PBAC programme participants. Faculty in the PBAC programme were also more knowledgeable, more engaged in sustainability activities off- as well as on-campus, and more committed than faculty who have not participated in the programme.

The SWC programme has had a similar impact on both staff and faculty understanding of sustainability generally and what U-M was doing to promote it. Not surprisingly, programme participants from both groups were more engaged and more committed than those who were not certified. And for faculty who participated in the programme, they were more likely to purchase sustainable foods and prevent waste than faculty members who were not certified.

Table 19.6 provides the results for all the indicators. Although participating in the two outreach programmes resulted in significantly higher scores for most indicators, participation had no effect on respondents' mode of travel to and from campus, nor on their maintenance of their lawns and gardens. The similarities in indicator scores for Travel Behaviour and behaviour with respect to Protecting the Natural Environment are possibly due to other factors. In the case of travel, many faculty and staff live far from campus in neighbourhoods having limited or no public transportation and therefore, their involvement with U-M's sustainability programmes would have no bearing on their mode of travel to campus. In the case of protecting the natural environment, a significant number of staff and faculty live in apartments or condominiums where opportunities for self-directed lawn/garden care are limited. With additional waves of data collection, we will be able to determine if programme participants might have already been relatively engaged/committed to sustainability before starting the programme or if programme participation expanded their pro-environmental behaviours.

Overall, the PBAC and SWC programmes represent two of U-M's most significant efforts to build a culture of sustainability within the campus community – specifically U-M employees. The SCIP results indicate that these programmes have been successful to date and that the participants are clearly sustainability champions.

19.3.4 Application of SCIP Results

The relatively large numbers of respondents each year enable the production of index scores for each of Ann Arbor's campuses, regions, and subregions of the most populated regions. The regions are based on similar regions developed by U-M's energy management teams (see Figure 19.1). These different geographic areas present opportunities to conduct experiments or trial programmes in some places and not in others in order to determine the impact of new initiatives – particularly when combined with the sustainability commitments of PBAC and SWC programme

Table 19.6 Difference in sustainability cultural indicators for staff and faculty by participation, 2015

| INDICES | PBAC PROGRAMME – 2015 | | | | | | SWC PROGRAMME – 2015 | | | | | |
| | FACULTY | | | STAFF | | | FACULTY | | | STAFF | | |
(mean scores)	Yes	No	sig.	Yes	No	sig.	Yes	No	sig.	Yes	No	sig.
PRIMARY												
Climate Action												
Conservation Behaviour	7.5	7.0	p<.01	7.3	6.4	p<.001	7.5	7.0	n/a	7.1	6.5	n/a
Number of respondents	118	993		117	634		67	1049		62	695	
Travel Behaviour	2.2	2.3	n/a	1.0	1.5	p<.05	2.0	2.3	n/a	1.5	1.5	n/a
Number of respondents	118	1008		120	663		67	293		64	726	
Waste Prevention												
Waste Prevention Behaviour	8.1	7.5	p<.001	7.9	7.0	p<.001	8.2	7.5	p<.01	7.8	7.1	p<.001
Number of respondents	119	1008		119	662		67	1065		64	724	
Healthy Environments												
Sustainable Food Purchases	6.6	6.4	n/a	6.3	5.9	p<.05	6.9	6.4	p<.05	6.4	5.9	n/a
Number of respondents	116	983		120	637		67	1037		64	699	

Table 19.6 (continued)

INDICES (mean scores)	PBAC PROGRAMME – 2015						SWC PROGRAMME – 2015					
	FACULTY			STAFF			FACULTY			STAFF		
	Yes	No	sig.	Yes	No	sig.	Yes	No	sig.	Yes	No	sig.
Protecting the Natural Environment	6.7	6.7	n/a	6.8	6.7	n/a	6.7	6.7	n/a	6.8	6.7	n/a
Number of respondents	101	850		106	523		55	900		58	577	
Community Awareness												
Sustainable Travel & Transportation	4.5	3.4	p<.001	3.7	3.1	p<.05	4.0	3.4	n/a	3.7	3.1	n/a
Number of respondents	119	1007		119	660		67	1063		64	721	
Waste Prevention	6.9	5.1	p<.001	6.5	4.7	p<.001	7.3	5.1	p<.001	6.5	4.8	p<.001
Number of respondents	119	1007		120	663		67	1064		64	726	
Natural Environment Protection	5.4	4.4	p<.001	5.4	4.0	p<.001	6.1	4.4	p<.001	5.1	4.2	p<.01
Number of respondents	119	1007		120	662		67	1064		64	725	
Sustainable Foods	6.6	5.9	p<.01	6.0	5.1	p<.01	7.2	5.8	p<.001	6.2	5.1	p<.01
Number of respondents	119	1008		120	663		67	1065		64	726	

Measure	Mean	Mean	Sig.	Mean	Mean	Sig.	Mean	Mean	Sig.	Mean	Mean	Sig.
U-M Sustainability Initiatives	**6.5**	**4.9**	**p<.001**	**6.8**	**5.0**	**p<.001**	**6.9**	**5.0**	**p<.001**	**6.8**	**5.2**	**p<.001**
Number of respondents	118	1006		120	662		66	1062		64	725	
SECONDARY												
Sustainability Engagement at U-M	**1.8**	**0.4**	**p<.001**	**2.4**	**0.2**	**p<.001**	**1.6**	**0.5**	**p<.01**	**2.9**	**0.4**	**p<.001**
Number of respondents	117	1002		117	660		65	1060		61	719	
Sustainability Engagement Generally	**3.5**	**2.6**	**p<.01**	**3.2**	**1.6**	**p<.001**	**3.3**	**2.6**	**p<.05**	**2.9**	**1.7**	**p<.01**
Number of respondents	118	1006		118	660		67	1062		63	722	
Sustainability Commitment	**7.7**	**7.1**	**p<.01**	**7.2**	**6.2**	**p<.001**	**8.1**	**7.1**	**p<.001**	**7.0**	**6.4**	**p<.05**
Number of respondents	119	1005		120	661		67	1062		64	724	
Sustainability Disposition	**5.6**	**4.7**	**p<.05**	**3.3**	**2.4**	**p<.01**	**6.2**	**4.7**	**p<.01**	**3.1**	**2.5**	**n/a**
Number of respondents	117	989		119	650		65	1045		64	712	
Rating U-M Sustainability Initiatives	**6.8**	**6.5**	**p<.05**	**7.0**	**6.7**	**p<.05**	**7.0**	**6.5**	**p<.05**	**7.2**	**6.7**	**p<.05**
Number of respondents	106	780		111	482		61	770		58	540	

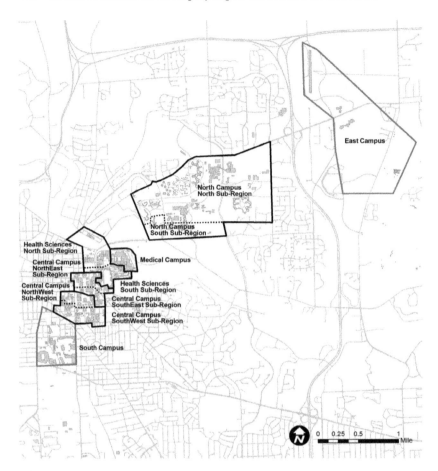

Figure 19.1   Campus regions and subregions

participants. An example of the mapping work which can be done based on these regions is provided in Figure 19.2.[9] Catalysing the commitments of programme participants in areas which fall below the mean deviation for a particular indicator has the potential to accelerate progress towards institutional sustainability goals. Similarly, focusing efforts and awareness of the PBAC and SWC programmes in these areas has the potential to build a cohort of sustainability leaders where they are most needed.

Current regional outreach efforts by U-M's Energy Management Group and an assessment and recommendations regarding "barriers to recycling" are examples of how SCIP data is being used to gauge impact and guide programming. Such efforts are examined in more detail in a related paper

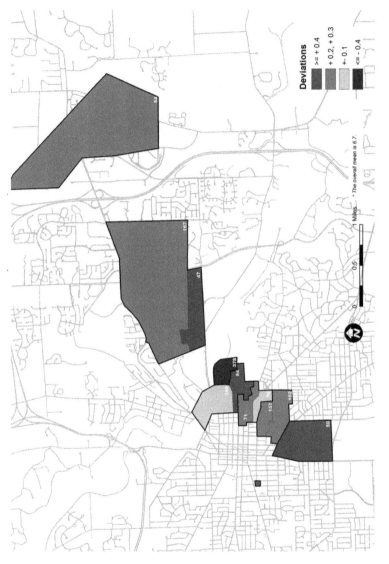

Figure 19.2   Staff and Faculty Conservation Behaviour Index Mean Deviation (2013) by campus region and subregion (numbers in regions show number of respondents)

(Marans and Callewaert 2016). In addition, we have begun to examine SCIP data in relation to contextual or environmental data derived from other sources such as metrics for campus energy use and recycling rates.[10] Furthermore, a graduate level course is utilising SCIP data to develop programming interventions to support greater pro-environmental behaviour, and for subsequent cohorts of students to test hypotheses based on SCIP data collected in the future.

19.4   CONCLUSION AND NEXT STEPS

This chapter has provided an overview of the efforts of the University of Michigan that focus on creating a culture of sustainability and pro-environmental behaviour among faculty and staff. Key programmes include the Planet Blue Ambassadors Certificate programme and the Sustainable Workplace Certification programme. The Sustainability Cultural Indicators Program works in parallel to these other programmes to measure and track impact over time. A key finding is that employees who participate in the PBAC and SWC programmes report higher levels of pro-environmental and sustainability commitments than employees who do not participate in these programmes. SCIP provides not only a valuable tool for measuring impact and validating resources committed to the PBAC and SWC programmes but can also help determine where to focus efforts and how best to catalyse key staff members to advance sustainability goals.

Because of the ground-breaking nature of SCIP, its relationship to the many U-M initiatives designed to promote sustainability throughout the University and its importance in addressing cultural issues and behavioural change when dealing with complex and pressing environmental problems, we are eager to see the programme replicated elsewhere. We believe that such efforts will be beneficial to other universities and colleges as well as to other types of institutions, corporations, and cities where movements towards a more sustainable future are taking place. It is our belief that, in order for those movements to be successful, consideration needs to be given to shifting towards a culture of sustainability. The University of Michigan is doing so as part of its overall sustainability initiative and SCIP is the vehicle for measuring that change and assessing its impacts.

19.5   RECOMMENDATIONS FOR PRACTITIONERS

- Start with securing institutional support
  While the important work of campus sustainability and pro-envi-

ronmental employee behaviour initiatives often rely on the dedicated efforts of a few key individuals, it is critically important to secure institutional support for your efforts. Having the support of the U-M president and a unit-spanning group like the Environmental Sustainability Executive Council was critical for gaining traction at the start of U-M's efforts and for ongoing work to improve and modify efforts. This support needs to be accompanied by financial resources.

- Develop goals to guide actions

It has been our experience that specific, quantifiable goals are very important for providing employees or administrators with action-able targets. Saying we want our employees to be "more sustain-able" is a start, but setting that within the context of specific climate action or waste prevention goals provides an important direction and also serves as a transparent metric for whether we are making progress or not.

- Take a longitudinal approach

Meaningful efforts require a long-term perspective. Changing the culture of sustainability is a slow-moving process that often requires new initiatives, some of which have short-term impacts while others take time. Still others may be terminated. Developing a monitoring programme such as SCIP can be used to assess the impact of new initiatives and suggest programme modifications and opportunities for organisational learning.

- Create opportunities for engagement

Sometimes some of the most significant institutional sustainability efforts are done behind the scenes, for example, automated energy conservation efforts and higher efficiency systems. That said, it is important to also develop opportunities for employees to under-stand institutional efforts and to take an active role in supporting and advancing those efforts. One strategy for this is to use the campus or work environment as a living-learning lab, providing opportunities for employees or community members to investi-gate systems and identify options for improvement. One student group at U-M recently completed a basic analysis of one of the newer, energy efficient buildings on campus and proposed changes which resulted in savings of US$160,000 per year (McIntyre et al. 2015).

- Strive for multi-approach initiatives

One of the areas where U-M has made the most progress towards sustainability is promoting sustainable foods (both awareness of and participation in programmes such as campus farmers' markets at several locations around campus). We believe one of the reasons for this success is that there are multiple efforts focused on sustainable foods (faculty cluster hires in sustainable foods, the Sustainable Food Systems Initiative, a recently developed campus farm, and several faculty-led research initiatives).

- Seek creative collaborations
  Look for ways to create opportunities for synergies across efforts. For example, U-M has a very well-developed employee health programme – MHealthy.[11] Having more employees walking or biking to work is something both programmes can support and promote. There have been several programme links developed between MHealthy and the Planet Blue Ambassadors programme such as the campus famers' markets noted above.

ACKNOWLEDGEMENTS

The SCIP analytical work would not have been possible without the assistance of Will Chan, Minako Edgar, Leonard Ang, and Mary Hirt. We also acknowledge the statistical guidance provided by Brady West from ISR's Programme in Survey Methodology, and Dan Zahs, Heather Schroeder, as well as the expert survey administration efforts of Cheryl Wiese and Andrew Hupp from Survey Research Operations (SRO) of ISR's Survey Research Centre. Finally, sincere appreciation must be extended to key leaders at the University of Michigan whose support makes SCIP possible – in particular, the Office of the President, the Office of the Provost, the Institute for Social Research, and the Graham Sustainability Institute.

NOTES

1. The Council comprises the University President, the Provost and Executive Vice President for Student Affairs, the Vice Presidents for Research, Student Affairs, Development, and Global Communications & Strategic Initiatives, the Executive Vice President for Medical Affairs, and the Executive Vice President and Chief Financial Officer. Accessed 1 June 2017.
2. The Planet Blue website can be found at: http://sustainability.umich.edu/. Accessed 1 June 2017.
3. More information on the CSIA process, outcomes, and evaluation can be found at: http://graham.umich.edu/knowledge/ia/campus. Information on progress towards the 2025 Climate Action, Waste Prevention, and Healthy Environments goals can be found at: http://www.ocs.umich.edu/goals.html. Accessed 1 June 2017.
4. More information can be found on the programme websites: http://sustainability.umich.edu/pba, http://sustainability.umich.edu/ocs/workplace. Accessed 1 June 2017.

5. Exploratory factor analysis with a Cronbach Alpha was employed to assess associations and the internal consistency in a set of responses. The alphas for the indices used in the 2012 SCIP survey vary from .32 to .94. The alphas are shown in Table D1 in the 2012 SCIP report available at: http://graham.umich.edu/campus/scip/materials. Accessed 1 June 2017.
6. The complete list of questions used to generate the indices can be found in Appendix D of the Year 4 Report, available at: http://graham.umich.edu/campus/scip. Accessed 1 June 2017.
7. The exception was the Sustainability Food Purchase Index, where one question had five response options while the other two questions had four. These three variables could not be added up immediately. They were first normalised and after normalising, were added together.
8. SPSS Complex Samples gives more accurate statistical estimates than Base SPSS.
9. Additional regional analyses can be found in the SCIP Annual Reports available at: http://graham.umich.edu/campus/scip/materials. Accessed 1 June 2017.
10. Initial results from this work can be found in the Year 3 and Year 4 reports found at: http://graham.umich.edu/campus/scip/materials. Accessed 1 June 2017.
11. Information on MHealthy can be found at: https://hr.umich.edu/benefits-wellness/health/mhealthy. Accessed 1 June 2017.

REFERENCES

Association for the Advancement of Sustainability in Higher Education (AASHE) (2016), *Sustainability, Tracking, Assessment & Rating System (STARS) 2.1 Technical Manual*, accessed 19 March 2016 at https://stars.aashe.org/pages/about/technical-manual.html.
Bartlett, P. F. and G. W. Chase (2004), *Sustainability on Campus: Stories and Strategies for Change*, Cambridge: MIT Press.
Bartlett, P. F. and G. W. Chase (2013), *Sustainability in Higher Education: Stories and Strategies for Transformation*, Cambridge: MIT Press.
Callewaert, J. and R. W. Marans (2016), 'Measuring progress over time: The sustainability cultural indicators programme at the University of Michigan', in W. Leal (ed.), *Handbook of Theory and Practice of Sustainable Development in Higher Education*, vol. 2, Springer International Publishing, pp. 173–187.
Erickson, C. (2010), *Peer to Peer Sustainability Outreach Programs: The Interface of Education and Behavior Change*, Vermont, VT: University of Vermont.
Graham Sustainability Institute (2017), *Sustainability Cultural Indicators Programme*, accessed 26 January 2017 at http://graham.umich.edu/campus/scip.
Marans, R. W. and J. Callewaert (2016), 'Evaluating sustainability initiatives on university campuses: Examples from the University of Michigan's sustainability cultural indicators programme', in W. Leal (ed.), *Handbook of Theory and Practice of Sustainable Development in Higher Education*, vol. 2, Springer International Publishing, pp. 189–199.
Marans, R. W. and M. Shriberg (2012), 'Creating and assessing a campus culture of sustainability: The University of Michigan Experience', in *Sustainable Development at Universities*, Frankfurt: Peter Lang.
Marans, R. W., J. Callewaert and M. Shriberg (2014), 'Enhancing and monitoring sustainability culture at the University of Michigan', in W. Leal Filho, N. Muthu, G. Edwin and M. Sima (eds), *Implementing Campus Greening Initiatives: Approaches, Methods and Perspectives*, Frankfurt: Peter Lang, pp. 165–179.
Marans, R. W., B. Levy, B. Bridges, K. Keeler, T. Avrahami, J. Bennett, K. Davidson, L. Goodman, B. Holdstein and R. Smith (2010), *Campus Sustainability Integrated Assessment: Culture Team Phase I Report*, University of Michigan, accessed 14 January 2017 at http://www.graham.umich.edu/pdf/culture-phase1.pdf.
McIntyre, A., H. Price, D. Sheehan, J. Buchsbaum (2015), *Programmatic Heat Optimization:*

    A Case Study on Reducing Excess Heating in the Biomedical Science Research Building and other Campus Buildings, accessed 1 June 2017 at http://graham.umich.edu/media/files/391-W15-Overheating-Buildings.pdf.
Scott, G. (2004), *Change Matters: Making a Difference in Higher Education*, accessed 21 March 2016 at http://www.eua.be/eua/jsp/en/upload/Unive%20Tech%20final%20paper.107668938 3316.pdf.
Senge, P. (2000), *The Fifth Discipline: The Art and Science of the Learning Organisation*, New York: Crown Business.
Sharp, L. (2002), 'Green campuses: The road from little victories to systemic transformation', *International Journal of Sustainability in Higher Education*, **3**, 128–45.
Sharp, L. (2009), 'Higher education: The quest for a sustainable campus', *Sustainability: Science, Practice and Policy*, **5**, 1–8.
University of Michigan (2015), *University of Michigan STARS Report*, accessed 19 March 2016 at https://stars.aashe.org/institutions/university-of-michigan-mi/report/2015-06-30/.
University of Michigan Office of Campus Sustainability (2014), *Sustainability Goals, Climate Action: Greenhouse Gas*, accessed 19 March 2017 at http://sustainability.umich.edu/ocs/goals/ghg.
University of Michigan Office of Campus Sustainability (2017), *Sustainable Workplace Certification Programme*, accessed 26 January 2017 at http://sustainability.umich.edu/ocs/certified-workplaces.

PART VI

OTHER PERSPECTIVES ON PRO-ENVIRONMENTAL EMPLOYEE BEHAVIOUR

20. Spillover of pro-environmental behaviour
Caroline Verfuerth and Diana Gregory-Smith

20.1 INTRODUCTION TO THE SPILLOVER EFFECT

The aim of this chapter is threefold. First, the chapter aims to introduce the term 'spillover' and its different conceptualisations, as well as providing an overview of current research developments. This chapter will overall provide the reader with a broad understanding of the different concepts of the spillover effect alongside its implications for environmentally friendly behaviours in the workplace. Second, the chapter aims to give an overview of underlying factors that influence spillover and a discussion of how the spillover effects might influence social marketing campaigns and behavioural change programmes that promote pro-environmental behaviours in organisations. Finally, the chapter aims to assess the methodological approaches used to investigate spillover effects, inclusive of quantitative, qualitative and mixed methods.

The psychological concept of spillover could be simply understood as the flow and propulsion of cognitive thoughts, emotions or actions from one area to another. In relation to the latter aspect, Nilsson et al. (2016: 1) consider that 'the spillover effect proposes that engaging in one behavior affects the probability of engagement or disengaging in a second behavior'. The idea of the spillover effect is not new and has been applied in a number of areas such as knowledge (Acs et al. 2009), emotional conflicts between the workplace and the family (Grunberg et al. 1998; Westman 2002) and health behaviour (Dolan and Galizzi 2014). More recently, research in the fields of ethical marketing and environmental psychology has been investigating the spillover phenomenon in the context of sustainable lifestyles; here an increasing interest in understanding the secondary behaviour effects of pro-environmental behaviours on other behaviours has emerged. In this area, the concept of spillover has been used to explore the link between different pro-environmental behaviours and between pro-environmental behaviours in different contexts. For example, a positive spillover has been found between individuals' energy saving at home and openness to more generic low-carbon policies such as infrastructural changes and subsidies for reducing household carbon emissions (Steinhorst and Matthies 2016).

Following the same line of thinking, three approaches to conceptualising spillover of pro-environmental behaviour have emerged. One strand of research conceptualises spillover as the effect that past pro-environmental behaviour has on the likelihood of an individual engaging in other future pro-environmental behaviours (e.g. Lauren et al. 2016; van der Werff et al. 2014a). For instance, an employee who always cycles to work and has done so in the past might also try to save energy at work by switching off his/her computer at the end of the working day. Another strand of research conceptualises spillover as the effect a behaviour change intervention may have on pro-environmental behaviours that were not the specific target of a given intervention (Truelove et al. 2014). For example, when an energy-saving programme encourages employees to conserve energy at work, a spillover effect occurs if the increased energy-saving behaviour of the employees has a knock-on effect on other pro-environmental behaviours such as commuting to work or recycling. This conceptualisation of spillover presumes that a behaviour change intervention is needed to trigger spillover. A third strand of spillover research suggests that the commonly used conceptualisations of spillover fall short of acknowledging individual agency, that is individuals' active choice to engage in a behaviour (Uzzell and Räthzel 2013). Uzzell and Räthzel (2013) argue that individuals actively shape, adjust and negotiate their behaviours and social environments, and they are also shaped by their environments. This view is contrary to the other conceptualisations of spillover that often imply an 'automatic' spillover of a pro-environmental behaviour to other pro-environmental behaviours or settings. As a consequence, Uzzell and Räthzel (2013) prefer the term 'border-crossing', which particularly refers to spillover effects between social contexts (e.g. work and home); for more details see section 20.3.1.

Some researchers also suggest that a distinction should be made between behavioural spillover, contextual spillover and temporal spillover (Nilsson et al. 2016). Behavioural spillover describes spillover effects across behaviours (Nilsson et al. 2016); for example, from energy-conserving behaviours to waste management behaviours. Contextual spillover – sometimes referred to as spillover between settings (Littleford et al. 2014) – refers to spillover effects of pro-environmental behaviours between different social and physical contexts or settings (e.g. between work and home). Temporal spillover incorporates the time component and refers to the effect a pro-environmental behaviour at time T1 has on a pro-environmental behaviour at a later time T2 (Nilsson et al. 2016).

Previous research has mostly focused on behavioural spillover with the aim to understand and explain how pro-environmental behaviours are connected and future behaviours might be promoted (Dolan and Galizzi 2015; Truelove et al. 2014). However, temporal and behavioural spillover are often not differentiated. Cross-contextual spillover research, on the other hand, aims to understand how a pro-environmental behaviour in one context, such as the workplace, may spill over to other settings like the home or leisure. People spend a large amount of their day-to-day time within these settings (Klade et al. 2013) and this is why cross-contextual spillover, in addition to behavioural spillover, can provide implications for promoting sustainable lifestyles.

20.1.1   Positive Spillover and Negative Spillover

Spillover of pro-environmental behaviour can broadly be divided into two types: positive spillover and negative spillover (Thøgersen 1999). Positive spillover describes the positive effect a pro-environmental behaviour has on other pro-environmental behaviours (Thøgersen and Ölander 2003) or environmental attitudes (Lacasse 2016). This includes pro-environmental behaviours and attitudes in a different context or at a different time point, and may be triggered by a behaviour change intervention or occur organically. For example, when a person purchases organic food he/she might subsequently purchase products with less packaging. This instance would be described as positive spillover. Conversely, negative spillover refers to subsequent behaviour that is contrary to previous pro-environmental behaviours (Truelove et al. 2014; Thøgersen and Ölander 2003). Thus, negative spillover describes instances when a pro-environmental behaviour can be linked to a decrease in other pro-environmental behaviours or an increase in environmentally damaging behaviours. An example could be a situation when a person's decision to switch to organic food might lead subsequently to an increase in their water consumption. Some studies suggest that positive and negative spillover may occur simultaneously (Klöckner et al. 2013; Lacasse 2016), which leads to an observed 'no net' spillover, that is, when positive and negative spillover average out. For instance, a recent study by Lacasse (2016) found that when people were reminded of their past pro-environmental behaviours a very small total spillover effect occurred. This effect was mediated by environmental self-identity and guilt, which explained a positive and a negative spillover path, respectively (Lacasse 2016). Thus, Lacasse's (2016) findings indicate that both positive and negative spillover occur simultaneously, but – in sum – averaged out to a small spillover effect.

The effect described above as positive spillover can be found in the literature under a variety of terms such as catalyst behaviour (Austin et al. 2011), virtuous escalator effect (Thøgersen and Crompton 2009), foot-in-the-door effect (Thøgersen and Noblet 2012), or carryover effect (Lerner et al. 2004; Dolan and Galizzi 2015). The idea of catalyst behaviour is that certain environmentally friendly behaviours have a knock-on effect and may cause broader behaviour change (Austin et al. 2011). The virtuous escalator effect refers to the assertion that one small environmentally friendly behaviour can spill over to other, more ambitious and environmentally significant behaviours (Thøgersen and Crompton 2009). Similarly, the foot-in-the-door effect (Burger 1999) is based on the idea that an easy behaviour increases the chances that people will also perform a second, more difficult behaviour. For example, a campaign promoting simple behaviours such as switching off lights in offices would then have a positive spillover effect on other, more difficult pro-environmental behaviours such as reducing the temperature in offices in the winter or commuting to work by public transport instead of by car. The carryover effect, on the other hand, describes emotional spillover that occurs long after the initial behaviour took place and which affects a subsequent behaviour (Lerner et al. 2004).

The negative spillover effect, or special cases of it, can be found under terms such as rebound effect (for an overview see Sorrell et al. 2009) or single action bias (Dolan and Galizzi 2015). The rebound effect describes an increase of energy demand after energy efficiency was improved (e.g. increase in distances travelled after purchase of a fuel-efficient car) which means the savings that could be achieved are not realised in full (Peters et al. 2012). The rebound effect is specific to energy behaviours and often discussed in relation to the introduction of an energy-efficient technology while only addressing energy demand, not pro-environmental behaviours in general. The single action bias refers to the phenomenon that people change one – often relatively insignificant – behaviour but do not take on any further behaviours (Truelove et al. 2014). Taking on a single action reduces people's feeling of worry; as a result of this, individuals do not take on any further pro-environmental actions (Weber 2006) or compensate for their behaviours (Gregory-Smith et al. 2015).

20.1.2   Psychological Theories Explaining the Spillover Effect

Both positive and negative spillover effects are frequently explained with a number of psychological theories. While these theories have been established in different contexts, they are frequently used to explain spillover of pro-environmental behaviours. Two of the most commonly used psychological theories to explain positive spillover are the cognitive dissonance theory (Festinger 1957) and the self-perception theory (Bem 1972). Negative spillover is often explained with moral licensing (Truelove et al. 2014), compensatory green beliefs (CGBs; Kaklamanou et al. 2013), and neutralisation theory (Sykes and Matza 1957).

Cognitive dissonance and self-perception theory

According to cognitive dissonance theory (Festinger 1957) people experience discomfort when holding two contrasting cognitions and are motivated to reduce the psychological uneasiness they experience. This can be achieved in a number of ways, including changing attitudes or behaviours, externalising responsibility or reducing the importance of dissonant elements (Gregory-Smith et al. 2013). In the pro-environmental context, this means a person holding pro-environmental views but acting unsustainably will experience a psychological discomfort. This may be reduced by acting in an environmentally friendly way (Thøgersen 2004). Therefore, the need for consistency might lead to positive spillover between environmentally friendly behaviours and between settings. Inconsistent pro-environmental behaviours (sometimes referred to as the attitude behaviour gap; Kollmuss and Agyeman 2002) are often explained with the neutralisation theory (Sykes and Matza 1957). For instance, negative spillover and a lack of positive spillover can arise when a person aims to overcome cognitive dissonance by using neutralisation techniques, including denial and justification (Chatzidakis et al. 2006) or CGBs (Kaklamanou et al. 2013). On the other hand, self-perception theory (Bem 1972) posits that people infer their identities and attitudes from past behaviours. According to this, people align their cognitions (e.g. attitudes, values, identity) with their observed past behaviour, particularly in ambiguous situations (Austin et al. 2011). Hence, acting pro-environmentally leads people to reaffirm their 'green' identity, which subsequently motivates them to act in line with their identity and cognitions in the future. Self-perception theory (Bem 1972) suggests that past pro-environmental behaviours lead to more pro-environmental behaviours which are connected through one's self-perception; hence, positive spillover can occur (van der Werff et al. 2014a).

Moral licensing and compensatory green beliefs

Moral licensing describes the effect by which people, who initially behaved morally (e.g. environmentally friendly), subsequently display immoral behaviours as a result of feeling licensed to do so (through their previously moral behaviour) or vice versa (Blanken et al. 2015). A quasi-experimental field study showed that donating to a charity subsequently led to lower environmental intentions (Meijers et al. 2015). Similarly, negative spillover in an environmental context can be explained by CGBs (Kaklamanou et al. 2013). CGBs refer in particular to people's belief that pro-environmental behaviour can compensate for more negative environmental behaviour; for example, purchasing organic food as a compensation for flying abroad on holidays (Gregory-Smith et al. 2013; Kaklamanou et al. 2013). In a qualitative study, Hope et al. (2017) found that people experienced psychological benefits from holding CGBs as it reduced their negative feeling (e.g. guilt) towards negative environmental behaviour. This in turn made them feel more positive about their overall environmental impact (Hope et al. 2017). These findings indicate that CGBs are sometimes used to justify a person's environmentally damaging behaviour.

Emotional carryover effect

The concept of carryover or spillover of emotions and their influence has originated in the psychology literature. Han et al. (2007: 158) have developed the appraisal-tendency framework, which illustrates 'how and why specific emotions carry over from past situations to colour future judgments and choices'. The framework distinguishes between integral emotions (i.e. emotions relevant to present decisions) and incidental emotions (i.e. emotions irrelevant to present choices but which influence them). It is precisely the latter category that has a carryover effect, mostly unconscious, into decisions and contexts other than where they originated. For example, sadness experienced in a personal context could influence one's shopping or eating behaviours.

While the emotional spillover effect has been examined in contexts such as economic decisions (e.g. buying decisions, assessment of risk – Lerner et al. 2004) and in relation to negative emotions (e.g. sadness, disgust, anger – Winterich et al. 2010), this concept is under-researched in the pro-environmental literature. This has happened despite some studies pointing out the influence integral emotions have on individuals' pro-environmental decisions (e.g. Carrus et al. 2008; Gregory-Smith et al. 2013; Lacasse 2016). Evidence for this potential spillover of emotions across contexts, including pro-environmental behaviours, comes from the field of organisational psychology where research has identified a spillover of behaviours and emotions between the work and home (e.g. happiness – Rodríguez-Muñoz et al. 2014; aggression and conflicts – Sanz-Vergel et al. 2015; exhaustion and satisfaction – Lee et al. 2016).

Similarly, a stream of research looking at ethics and morality hints at the potential negative spillover of emotions. Particularly, it is believed that moral behaviours will generate positive emotions, that in some cases and for some individuals, will influence negatively other decisions with a moral valence; that is, they will reduce the negative emotions that might be anticipated or arise from engaging in an immoral behaviour (Merritt et al. 2010). A similar line of thought could be applied to pro-environmental behaviours for those individuals who perceive these behaviours as having a moral dimension. Alternatively, research has pointed out that positive moral behaviours such as altruism can also carry over from one domain to another. For example, Laury and Taylor (2008) have demonstrated altruism spillover across contexts; in particular, they showed that altruism in the laboratory setting can spread to decisions related to naturally occurring public goods.

20.2   SPILLOVER IN THE WORKPLACE

Organisations show an increasing interest in sustainability, which is driven both by cost and corporate social responsibility considerations (Young et al. 2013). However, unlike at home, at work employees face additional barriers towards acting pro-environmentally (e.g. sharing electronic devices with colleagues when trying to conserve energy) and financial interests to save energy or water may differ (Carrico and Riemer 2011). While antecedents and motivators for pro-environmental household behaviours have been widely investigated (e.g. Abrahamse et al. 2005; Steg and Vlek 2009), more recently, research aims to understand and promote pro-environmental behaviour at work (e.g. Gregory-Smith et al. 2015). In addition to the home, the workplace is one of the main 'microenvironments' where people spend most of their day-to-day time (Cox et al. 2012), which is why the workplace is an important setting for promoting sustainable lifestyles. Thus, potential spillover effects between behaviours at home and work as well as spillover between the two settings has recently started to attract research interest (Muster 2011). Nonetheless, spillover effects both between behaviours and between settings are under-researched and need further understanding as this would help promote sustainable lifestyles within and across people's life-domains.

20.2.1   Spillover Between Pro-environmental Behaviours in the Workplace

There is a growing interest in employees' pro-environmental behaviour (e.g. recycling, energy saving), which can be defined as 'scalable actions and behaviours that employees engage in that are linked with and contribute to or detract from environmental sustainability' (Ones and Dilchert 2012: 87). Work in this area has led to the development of a classification of employee green behaviour, called the 'Green Five taxonomy' (Ones and Dilchert 2012). This classification includes five meta-categories of employee green behaviour: (1) avoiding harm, (2) conserving, (3) working sustainably, (4) influencing others, and (5) taking initiative.

According to Ones and Dilchert's (2012) taxonomy (see taxonomy details in Chapter 2 in this *Handbook*), spillover of pro-environmental behaviour at work can occur within a specific category (e.g. spillover from reusing to recycling in the 'conserving' category) or between categories (e.g. from the 'conserving' category to the 'taking initiative' category). For instance, reducing energy use at work by switching off electrical devices instead of standby, which would be in the category 'conserving', might have a spillover effect on recycling behaviour, also in the category 'conserving'. In line with this, in a study investigating the effect of feedback on residential water, Tiefenbeck et al. (2013) found that while people reduced their water consumption, they also increased their electricity consumption. This suggests a negative spillover effect within the 'conserving' category. Although the study was conducted in the residential and not the work context, it is possible that similar effects occur in the workplace context between and within behaviour categories. For instance, reducing energy use at work might have a positive spillover effect on encouraging and supporting others from the category 'influencing others' or it might have a negative spillover effect on recycling behaviour.

Similarities between behaviours in the workplace
An important aspect of the spillover between the home and workplace contexts is the (lack of) similarities between behaviours. Empirical evidence suggests that spillover is more likely between behaviours that are perceived as being similar as opposed to dissimilar (Margetts and Kashima 2017; Littleford et al. 2014). Likewise, in relation to workplace spillover, it can be assumed that perceived similarity of pairs of pro-environmental behaviours (e.g. taking public transport to work and buying environmentally labelled brands) increases the consistency of engaging in these activities (Thøgersen 2004), leading to positive spillover between similar behaviours. Littleford et al. (2014) investigated spillover between office and household settings and found correlations between behaviours that shared the same type of equipment (i.e. computer) or the same triggers or behaviour settings (i.e. leaving the room). Despite not finding evidence to support the existence of positive spillover across settings, they concluded that spillover across settings would be most likely when categories such as the type of equipment or the behavioural trigger were similar (Littleford et al. 2014). Likewise, Margetts and Kashima (2017) found that pro-environmental behaviours that require the same resources (e.g. money or time) are also perceived as more similar and thus more likely to spillover. These studies suggest that perceived similarity between pro-environmental behaviours is a relevant aspect to consider when researching spillovers in relation to the workplace context but it is also a complex aspect to investigate.

Additionally, Lanzini and Thøgersen (2014) differentiate between functional and symbolic similarities, in the context of spillover from 'green' purchasing behaviour to other pro-environmental behaviours. Lanzini and Thøgersen (2014) propose that symbolic similarities of behaviours might have an effect on consistency-based spillover, whereas functional similarities between behaviours might have an effect on knowledge-based spillover. Although their study does not focus on the workplace setting, the differentiation between functional and symbolic similarities also has implications for spillover of pro-environmental behaviours in the workplace. Similarities can act either as drivers or as barriers to positive spillover between behaviours. For instance, the relevance of similarities of behaviours is somewhat reflected in Ones and Dilchert's (2012) classification of employee green behaviour. Specifically, for employee pro-environmental behaviours this means that positive spillover is more likely to occur between categories of behaviours such as 'conserving' and 'working sustainably' or between 'influencing others' and 'taking initiatives'; and between specific behaviours that are perceived similar, such as turning off lights and turning off electric devices (rather than between behaviours perceived as dissimilar such as recycling and reducing meat consumption).

Easy and difficult behaviours in the workplace
Spillover from 'easy' to 'difficult' pro-environmental behaviours and vice-versa is often discussed as a potential direction for positive spillover. According to the foot-in-the-door effect (Burger 1999), 'simple and painless' behaviours might open the door to more difficult pro-environmental behaviours (Thøgersen and Crompton 2009). In support of this, a study on water-conserving behaviours suggests that foot-in-the-door effects may occur from easy to more difficult pro-environmental behaviours but only when people's self-efficacy to perform such behaviours is high (Lauren et al. 2016). The foot-in-the-door effect (Burger 1999) and people's preference for consistent behaviour (Cialdini et al. 1995) can have relevant implications for promoting pro-environmental behaviours in the workplace. For instance, encouraging employees to conserve energy in their workplace may lead to a higher acceptance of more radical 'green' policy changes in the organisation. Empirical support for this was found by a number of studies suggesting that encouraging people to engage in pro-environmental behaviours leads to a greater acceptance of green policies (low-carbon policy acceptability – Steinhorst and Matthies 2016; acceptance of wind power – Thøgersen and Noblet 2012). On the contrary, some studies also found that easy and costless behaviours (e.g. recycling) lead to a decreased acceptance of green policies and negative spillover (Truelove 2016; Gneezy et al. 2012). Nonetheless, the assumption that positive spillover will occur simply by nudging people to engage in simple and easy pro-environmental behaviours is often implicitly made by campaigners and policymakers in the hopes that campaigns and policies that promote easy behaviours spill over to encourage more difficult and

environmentally significant behaviours (Defra 2008). Thus, although some empirical evidence suggests that a positive spillover effect from easy to more difficult pro-environmental behaviours may occur, this needs to be treated with caution (for an overview of the limitations of spillover in environmental campaigning see Thøgersen and Crompton 2009).

20.2.2   Theoretical Frameworks of Behavioural Spillover in the Workplace

To gain a better and more comprehensive understanding of positive, negative but also a lack of spillover, theoretical frameworks have been developed. In contrast to the theories that are used to explain spillover effects, these theoretical frameworks have been developed to explain spillover effects between pro-environmental behaviours, taking into account previous empirical findings and theoretical considerations.

Decision mode and behavioural characteristics in the workplace context
Truelove et al. (2014) proposed a conceptual framework for spillover that focuses on the decision-making processes involved when acting environmentally friendly. They define spillover as the effect of an intervention on a secondary behaviour, which was not targeted by the intervention (Truelove et al. 2014; see also conceptualisations of spillover in section 20.1). Truelove et al. (2014) propose that the direction of the spillover effect is based on the decision-making style which leads to different paths of secondary pro-environmental behaviours; that is, positive, negative or no net spillover. Positive spillover occurs when a pro-environmental behaviour increases the likelihood of performing another pro-environmental behaviour, while negative spillover occurs when the initial pro-environmental behaviour leads to a reduction of pro-environmental behaviours (Truelove et al. 2014). No net spillover refers to an instance when positive and negative spillover average out, which means that overall no spillover occurs (Truelove et al. 2014). The framework identifies two main factors that influence spillover: (1) decision mode (different ways of decision-making) and (2) attribution of one's behaviour after the decision process (Truelove et al. 2014). Three types of decision-making are proposed: calculation-based, negative affect-based and role-based; the first leads to no net spillover, the second leads to negative spillover, and the latter leads to positive spillover (Truelove et al. 2014).

According to the framework, a calculation-based decision leads to no net spillover that is influenced by external attribution (e.g. incentive for previous pro-environmental behaviour) or difficulty of the behaviour, which would increase the likelihood of negative spillover (Truelove et al.

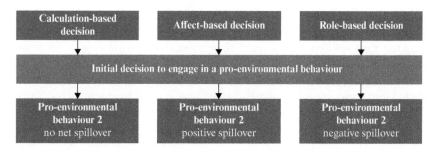

Source: Adapted from Truelove et al. (2014).

Figure 20.1 *Theoretical framework illustrating simplified decisions modes*
on spillover

2014). An affect-based decision is more likely to lead to negative spillover
mediated by reduced negative affect (e.g. fear, guilt; Truelove et al. 2014).
The link between negative affect-based decision-making and negative
spillover draws on moral licensing theory (Blanken et al. 2015) and single
action bias (Dolan and Galizzi 2015). Role-based decision-making, on
the other hand, has a positive effect on identity reinforcement, which
then increases the likelihood for positive spillover (Truelove et al. 2014).
A decision made based on a role enhances the identification with the role
and the social identity that is associated with it, for example, a decision
made in the role of a factory worker reinforces the identity as a factory
worker as well, which is here called identity reinforcement (Truelove et al.
2014). Identity reinforcement can be amplified with internal and external
attribution and difficulty of the behaviour (Truelove et al. 2014). For
example, if an employee attributes her/his energy-saving behaviour at
work to her/his abilities of being a pro-environmental person (internal
attribution) this will reinforce the employee's environmental identity
(Truelove et al. 2014). On the other hand, if an employee attributes her/his
energy-saving behaviour at work to external factors (external attribution),
such as financial incentives that the employer provides for their staff to
save energy, this decreases the employee's intrinsic motivation and the
perception of her/him being a pro-environmental person (Truelove et al.
2014). When the financial incentive is then taken away, the employee is
no longer likely to engage in the energy-saving behaviour and potentially
any other pro-environmental behaviours at work and negative spillover
occurs (Truelove et al. 2014). The link between identity reinforcement and
positive spillover is amplified when the subsequent behaviour is similar to
the previous behaviour, but weakened when the subsequent behaviour is
difficult (Truelove et al. 2014). See Figure 20.1 for a simplified illustration.

Promoting, permitting and purging strategies in the workplace

Similar to Truelove et al.'s (2014) framework, Dolan and Galizzi (2015) suggest that spillover links an initial pro-environmental behaviour with a subsequent pro-environmental behaviour. More specifically, Dolan and Galizzi (2015) propose that pro-environmental behaviour A (initial behaviour) and pro-environmental behaviour B (subsequent behaviour) can be linked in three ways: promoting, permitting, and purging – processes that lead to positive spillover, negative spillover, and neutralisation of spillover (Dolan and Galizzi 2015). They suggest that underlying motives link the behaviours at an unconscious or conscious level and build their framework based on existing mechanisms that are associated with spillover (Dolan and Galizzi 2015). Thus, the 'promoting' strategy can be explained with cognitive dissonance theory (Festinger 1957), foot-in-the-door effect (Burger 1999), emotion carryover (Dolan and Galizzi 2015) and other theories, and will lead to positive spillover. The 'permitting' strategy can be explained with ego-depletion (Baumeister et al. 1998), moral licensing (Blanken et al. 2015), single action bias (Weber 2006) and other theories and leads to negative spillover. The 'purging' strategy assumes an environmentally unfriendly behaviour, which then leads to a pro-environmental behaviour through moral cleansing (Sachdeva et al. 2009) and other processes.

To summarise, both theoretical frameworks aim to explain spillover effects between different pro-environmental behaviours, which can be positive, negative or not occur at all. Although the frameworks proposed by Truelove et al. (2014) and Dolan and Galizzi (2015) differ, both have implications for spillover of pro-environmental behaviour in the workplace as they outline processes that may lead to spillover effects. The framework proposed by Truelove et al. (2014) can inform strategies and techniques of behaviour change interventions in workplaces. However, Dolan and Galizzi's (2015) framework uncovers some of the mechanisms that may lead to pro-environmental behaviours in line with a behaviour change programme in an organisation (i.e. positive spillover), which is of interest for people designing effective behaviour-change programmes in the workplace. Further research is needed to investigate the pathways that lead to spillover of pro-environmental behaviours as proposed by Truelove et al. (2014) and Dolan and Galizzi (2015).

20.3   CONTEXTUAL SPILLOVER

As mentioned before, Nilsson et al. (2016) distinguish between behavioural spillover, contextual spillover and temporal spillover. Contextual spillover – sometimes also found under the concept of border-crossing (Uzzell and Räthzel 2013) – describes spillover of pro-environmental behaviours between different settings, for example, between home and work, or between work and home settings. A spillover effect between settings occurs when a pro-environmental behaviour in one context has a 'knock-on' effect on pro-environmental behaviours in another context (Littleford et al. 2014; Margetts and Kashima 2017). For instance, when energy-saving behaviour at home is subsequently followed by increased energy-saving behaviours at work this is described as positive spillover between settings. Similar to spillover between behaviours, spillover between settings can also be negative, in which case the reverse effect occurs, that is, when energy-saving behaviour at home leads to a decrease in energy-saving behaviour at work.

20.3.1 Spillover Between the Home and the Workplace Settings

Spillover effects between the workplace and the home settings have been investigated for a number of years. However, most studies have been focusing on work flexibility and stress (Hyland and Prottas 2016), happiness and well-being (Rodríguez-Muñoz et al. 2014) and work–family conflict (Sanz-Vergel et al. 2015), but to a lesser extent for pro-environmental behaviours. More recently, emerging research has been examining potential spillover effects of pro-environmental behaviours and attitudes between the work and home settings. People spend a large amount of their time within their homes and workplaces (Klade et al. 2013), which is why understanding the potential for spillover between these contexts plays an important role in promoting more sustainable lifestyles.

A number of studies have researched predictors of 'green' employee behaviour in organisations and found that pro-environmental behaviour at home explains a reasonable share of pro-environmental behaviour at work (for a literature review of predictors of employee pro-environmental behaviour see Young et al. 2013 and Lo et al. 2012). For instance, Tudor et al. (2008) found that pro-environmental behaviours of employees at home determined their sustainable waste management behaviour which indicates a spillover effect from the home setting to the workplace. Thus, employees who already engage in pro-environmental behaviours at home are likely to also bring these behaviours to their workplace. In fact, research in human resource management even suggests that the organisation's environmental reputation plays an increasingly important role for jobseekers (Renwick et al. 2013). This impels organisations to increase their efforts to provide environmentally friendly workplaces for their employees. However, very little research has been done to investigate the effects that an environmentally friendly workplace or behaviour change programmes at work have on employees' pro-environmental behaviour at home. To date, most research focuses on pro-environmental behaviour at home as a predictor of pro-environmental behaviour at work, but spillover effects can occur in both directions, that is, from home to work and from work to home.

A study by Rashid and Mohammad (2011) found that employees, who were involved in the implementation of an environmental management system in their workplace, were also more likely to be involved in pro-environmental behaviours at home. In their study, the positive spillover effect between the workplace and the home was positively influenced by the employee's identification with the organisation (Rashid and Mohammad 2011). Similarly, environmental education programmes in organisations can also have an effect beyond pro-environmental behaviours at work. A case study analysis by the Scottish Government showed that exposure to environmental education at work and employees' commitment to the organisation's environmental values were key drivers of spillover from the workplace to other areas of life (Cox et al. 2012). On the other hand, employees' engagement in pro-environmental behaviours does not always have positive spillover effects on pro-environmental behaviours at home. Cox et al. (2012) report that some employees who complied with pro-environmental behaviours at work were less likely to engage in similar activities at home, thus, negative spillover occurred. According to Cox et al. (2012), these findings were more typical in larger organisations and when the employees agreed less with the organisation's corporate values.

Border-crossing
An alternative approach to cross-contextual spillover is the concept of 'border-crossing' (Uzzell and Räthzel 2013). The term 'border-crossing' is proposed to describe the transfer of pro-environmental practices, in particular from one setting (e.g. the workplace) to another setting (e.g. the home; Uzzell and Räthzel 2013). According to Uzzell and Räthzel (2013: 19), 'border-crossing takes into account that people are active agents, who negotiate their relations within and between the different areas in different ways at different times and places'. They argue that, in contrast to the spillover concept that suggests employees will copy behaviour from one setting (e.g. the workplace) to another setting (e.g. the home), the concept of border-crossing recognises that employees understand a behaviour (e.g. at work) and then transfer it to another setting (e.g. the home) (Uzzell and Räthzel 2013). In two case studies with organisations from the oil and car manufacturing industry they investigated the concept of border-crossing and identified several characteristics of (e.g. physical border-crossing, temporal border-crossing, psychological border-crossing, and social and

organisational border-crossing) and barriers to (e.g. disempowerment, conflicts, lack of influence, and identity) border-crossing (for a full report on the case studies see Uzzell and Räthzel 2013). Although spillover between settings or cross-contextual spillover is currently the dominant conceptualisation, the concept of border-crossing constitutes an alternative view to the way employees 'transfer' pro-environmental behaviours from work to other life settings and vice versa, which takes people's agency into account.

A theoretical framework of spillover between the workplace and home
Nik Ramli and Naja (2012) propose a framework of positive spillover from the workplace to the home setting. Drawing from social identity theory, place attachment theory and cognitive dissonance theory, they suggest that spillover of pro-environmental behaviours goes through three stages: (1) formation of attitude and behaviour in the workplace; (2) the need to maintain one's behaviour consistent with one's attitudes and norms; and (3) performance of pro-environmental behaviour as a responsible community member (Nik Ramli and Naja 2012). This model is mainly underpinned by the consistency theory that posits that 'attitude, values and norms are what make the whole person – no matter where he or she is' (p. 1068) and complemented by factors such as management support and employees' organisational identification (Nik Ramli and Naja 2012).

20.3.2   Spillover Between the Home and Tourism/Travelling Settings

Spillover between the home setting and tourism (e.g. holidays) or travelling settings is also a type of contextual spillover but it is less researched than spillovers between the work and home and vice versa (Nilsson et al. 2016). In the context of holiday decision-making, Schütte and Gregory-Smith (2015) found a lack of spillover between the home and holiday settings when people were using neutralisation and mental accounting techniques to justify their unethical behaviour and to manage their negative emotions.

The above findings about negative spillover are consistent with those of Barr et al. (2010) and Hares et al. (2010). Barr et al. (2010) have identified distinct clusters of consumers who displayed different levels of greener lifestyles and (lack of) spillover between home and travel/holiday settings. This points out that spillover between these two domains is not straightforward due to various influencing factors such as values, attitudes, habits, disposable time and income. Overall, the potential spillover between home-based and tourism/travel-based environmental behaviours remains largely under-researched. Although Schütte and Gregory-Smith (2015) and Barr et al. (2010) investigated spillover effects between the home and leisure travelling, their findings could have implications for business travel as well. However, to our knowledge, spillover effects between the home or workplace to the business travel setting have not been investigated yet.

20.4 FACTORS INFLUENCING SPILLOVER INVOLVING A WORKPLACE CONTEXT

The occurrence of spillover effects both positive and negative, as well as between behaviours and between settings is influenced by a number of factors. More recently, research has been focusing on identifying underlying factors of spillover effects. The aim is to gain a better understanding of what influences both positive and negative spillover effects. In the organisational context, the factors that influence spillover effects can have implications for the communication of pro-environmental behaviours and for the design and implementation of behaviour change programmes. In particular, a greater knowledge about factors that influence spillover effects can help promote positive spillover effects in order to create a greater impact of, for instance, behaviour change programmes in organisations. On the other hand, knowing about factors that make negative spillover more likely or prevent a positive spillover effect can help to recognise the limitations that certain behaviour change campaigns might have (Thøgersen and Crompton 2009).

20.4.1 Values, Personal Norms and Self-efficacy

Drawing from theories explaining pro-environmental behaviours (e.g. theory of planned behaviour by Ajzen 1991; value–belief–norm theory by Stern 2000), several studies indicate that values, personal norms and self-efficacy influence spillover, both between behaviours and settings. For instance, in a three-wave-panel study with Danish consumers Thøgersen and Ölander (2003) found a moderating effect of individual values and personal norms for positive spillover. They found that the likelihood of positive spillover was higher when people had a high priority for Schwartz's 'universalism' values (Thøgersen and Ölander 2003). Similarly, Steinhorst and Matthies (2016) identified personal norms as a predictor and moderator of positive spillover from energy-saving behaviour to acceptability of policies. In another study, they found that positive spillover is mediated by personal norms and self-efficacy (Steinhorst et al. 2015). In line with this, a high personal norm for pro-environmental behaviour was found to have a moderating effect on the likelihood of spillover between similar pro-environmental behaviours (Thøgersen

2004). Overall, these findings indicate that self-transcendent values moderate positive spillover whereas self-interest values inhibit positive spillover or might even lead to negative spillover. Although the studies above are not workplace specific, the findings can be transferred to the workplace context. Making employees' 'universalism' values and personal norms salient or promoting employees' self-efficacy could increase positive spillover effects between pro-environmental behaviours at work and from the workplace into the home setting.

20.4.2   Organisational Values

Employees' identification with organisational values also influences the occurrence of spillover effects, both between behaviours in the workplace and between the work setting and other areas of life. An overlap between the employee's and the organisation's values can promote positive spillover whereas incongruity can lead to negative spillover. In a case study analysis for the Scottish Government, Cox and colleagues (2012) found that shared values between organisations and employees and employees' commitment to 'green' organisational values leads to positive spillover, whereas a lack of shared values and commitment to the organisation's green values can lead to a lack of spillover or even negative spillover. Thus, the employee–organisation–value fit, as well as the organisation's communication and realisation of pro-environmental values, can lead to positive spillover effects and promote sustainable lifestyles at work and beyond the workplace.

20.4.3   Framing of Behaviour and Communication

The way pro-environmental behaviours are framed and communicated also has a great impact on potential spillover effects. When promoting pro-environmental behaviours, monetary rewards are a popular tool (Abrahamse et al. 2005). However, financial framing of pro-environmental behaviour makes self-interest values more salient, whereas environmental framing makes self-transcendent values – which are associated with pro-environmental values – more salient (Evans et al. 2012). For instance, when self-interest was prompted right after self-transcendent motives had been used, environmental effect was neutralised and no spillover effect was detected (Evans et al. 2012). Steinhorst and Matthies (2016), for example, found a spillover effect only in the environmental framing condition and not in the financial framing condition. Consequently, it is important to consider potential spillover effects that the framing of a social marketing campaign in an organisation or for a wider context can have. Although financial framing might often seem to be the easiest and most promising way to encourage environmentally friendly behaviours among employees, the studies suggest that there is a downside. Thus, communications using environmental framing might have more positive effects on employees' pro-environmental behaviour in the long run in comparison to financial framing.

20.4.4   Environmental Identity

'Who am I?' – If the answer is 'an environmentally sustainable person', positive spillover effects between behaviours and across contexts is more likely compared to people who do not see environmental sustainability as part of their identity (Whitmarsh and O'Neill 2010). Environmental identity is a determinant for pro-environmental behaviour in general but also for positive spillover effects (Whitmarsh and O'Neill 2010). For instance, van der Werff et al. (2014a, 2014b) showed in several studies that environmental identity acts as an antecedent of pro-environmental behaviours while also being influenced by past pro-environmental behaviour. In line with this, Lacasse (2016) showed past pro-environmental behaviour strengthens people's environmental self-identity, which then leads to greater concern for climate change. This indicates that environmental identity is an underlying factor of spillover, which is in line with self-perception theory. An experimental study among US students on recycling behaviour found that environmental identity mediated spillover between recycling behaviour and support for a green fund (Truelove et al. 2016). In the organisational context, the values–identity–personal norms (VIP) model integrates identity theory with value and personal norm theories to explain pro-environmental behaviour at work (Ruepert et al. 2016). In a study with 618 employees, Ruepert et al. (2016) found that environmental identity mediated biospheric values and personal norms which in turn affected pro-environmental behaviour at work. Hence, environmental identity plays an important role for facilitating positive spillover. These findings can be utilised for communication and social marketing campaigns in organisations. Based on Lacasse's (2016) findings it could be inferred that labelling people as being 'environmentalists' would enhance their environmental identity and that this would, thus, have a positive effect on the intention to act pro-environmentally in the future.

20.5   METHODOLOGICAL APPROACHES TO RESEARCHING SPILLOVER

The spillover phenomenon has been investigated so far drawing on a rich array of methods inclusive of quantitative, qualitative and mixed methods.

The choice of the most appropriate method should be based on the assessment of key assumptions of the spillover effect: (1) the spillover effect presumes a change in one behaviour leads to changes in other behaviours; and (2) the spillover effect occurs in a timely order as the initial behaviour influences other behaviours at a later point. Thus, the relationship of pro-environmental behaviours – between different behaviours, over time, or between different settings – should always be paramount to the chosen methodological approach.

20.5.1 Quantitative Methods Approach

Quantitative methods are most commonly used to investigate the spillover effect and they mainly include correlational, longitudinal cross-lagged designs and experimental and quasi-experimental approaches. A correlational approach is reflected in a research design that collects data on people's pro-behaviours at one time point (e.g. through a survey) and then investigates the relationship between these behaviours. For example, in a survey with US residents Thøgersen and Noblet (2012) investigated the correlation between 'every-day green behaviours' and the acceptance of wind power. Similarly, a survey by Lauren et al. (2016) investigated the correlation between easy and difficult water-saving behaviours while also examining the mediating effect of self-efficacy of these behaviours. A survey conducted by Littleford et al. (2014) with employees of local government organisations examined how energy-saving behaviours at home and at work are correlated. Although correlational studies are popular and the research design is low in cost, one might critique that correlational data is not as meaningful to investigate spillover as timely data collection (e.g. longitudinal studies) or experimental designs. While correlational data can provide initial indications of types of spillover effects or potential underlying factors influencing spillover, experimental and longitudinal data collection should be the preferred approach when using quantitative methods.

Longitudinal studies observe behaviour over a period of time. For instance, studies using a longitudinal cross-lagged design measure the 'organic' development of pro-environmental behaviours over time. In most cases, the focus is on the observation of the influence of an initial behaviour (e.g. recycling at work) on a second behaviour (e.g. energy use at work) at a later time point. If the second behaviour increases, this is interpreted as positive spillover, whereas if it decreases, a negative spillover effect occurs. If there is no relationship between behaviours over time, this indicates a lack of spillover or no net spillover. A study using this methodological approach was conducted by Thøgersen and Ölander

(2003). By using a three-wave cross-lagged panel, they investigated how pro-environmental behaviours (i.e. organic consumption, recycling and transport behaviour) would influence each other over a period of two years. Another approach for using a longitudinal design is by observing the effect a behaviour change intervention or a policy change has on pro-environmental behaviours compared to behaviour prior to the intervention. For instance, Thomas et al. (2016) analysed longitudinal data from a nationally representative sample (n = 17,636; Wales, England, and Scotland) to investigate spillover effects from the single-use carrier bag charge in Wales to six other pro-environmental behaviours. Over the course of three years they found that the use of own shopping bags increased in Wales compared to Scotland and England after the introduction of the charge and that it was also linked to the increase of six other pro-environmental behaviours (Thomas et al. 2016); which is interpreted as a positive spillover effect. However, the increase of three of the pro-environmental behaviours was weaker in Wales than in England and Scotland (Thomas et al. 2016). But there was a significant increase in pro-environmental attitudes, which indicates a positive spillover effect to pro-environmental attitudes, from the increased own bag use due to the carrier bag charge (Thomas et al. 2016).

Lastly, spillover has been investigated through studies employing experimental and quasi-experimental designs, which focus on the causal effects between independent and dependent variables. For example, Evans et al. (2012) investigated the cause–effect relationship between information provided by an intervention and its effect on behavioural spillover. The information given to participants (independent variable) was manipulated so that one group received environmental information about car-sharing and the other group received financial information about car-sharing (Evans et al. 2012). Ultimately, the former group showed higher recycling behaviour (dependent variable), which was interpreted as positive spillover, compared to the group that received financial information (Evans et al. 2012). Based on these findings, Evans et al. (2012) conclude that environmental framing of a message makes self-transcendent values salient which then leads to positive spillover. While this example concurs that cause–effect relationships could be explored via experimental designs (ensuring a high internal validity), they cannot capture the multitude and complexity of all the factors that influence environmental spillover in the 'real world'. Steinhorst and Matthies (2016) conducted a longitudinal field experiment in order to account for both cause–effect relationships and 'real-world' complexity. In their online survey, clients of a German energy provider were either randomly assigned to receive financially or environmentally framed energy-saving tips or randomly assigned to a control group, which did not receive any information (Steinhorst and Matthies 2016). In line with Evans et al.'s (2012) findings, the study showed people in the environmental framing condition increased their energy-saving behaviour and also increased their acceptance towards low-carbon policies, which is interpreted as a positive spillover effect (Steinhorst and Matthies 2016). People in the financial framing condition, on the other hand, showed an increase in their energy-saving behaviour but not in their acceptance towards low-carbon policies (Steinhorst and Matthies 2016).

Overall, quantitative methods are currently the most commonly used approach to examine spillover effects. And, as shown above, there are a number of approaches to measure spillover effects with quantitative data, which differ in costs (time and resources), causality assessment, and consideration of 'real-world' complexity. Although correlational studies are a suitable way to test initial ideas and directions for further research, future research should focus on longitudinal data and integration of experimental designs in order to measure spillover (Lanzini and Thøgersen 2014; Wells et al. 2016; Dolan and Galizzi 2015; Poortinga et al. 2013). Furthermore, the integration of qualitative and quantitative methods into mixed-methods designs could be informative for a more in-depth understanding of spillover and particularly motivations and other factors that influence spillover effects.

20.5.2 Qualitative Methods Approach

Qualitative methods have also been used as an alternative to quantitative approaches, to explore pro-environmental behaviours and their (lack of) spillover. For example, Schütte and Gregory-Smith (2015) have examined the cognitive and emotional processes related to lack of spillover between sustainable behaviours at home and holiday-related behaviours using semi-structured interviews. Other studies have employed a multi-method qualitative approach such as Dumitru et al.'s (2016) study that used documents, interviews and focus groups. Their comparison of two organisations (i.e. a green energy company and a university) revealed only a spillover of values from the green energy company to its employees; this was not noticed in the case of the employees of a public university organisation (Dumitru et al. 2016).

An alternative qualitative approach is that of Uzzell and Räthzel (2013) who applied an integrative ethnographic and interpretative method to explore contextual spillover between the workplace and home, which they refer to as 'border-crossing'. Their study used life-history interviews with employees, which implied interviewees acting 'as an independent narrator of her/his life trajectory and personal subjectivity' (Uzzell and Räthzel

2013: 11). Overall, while qualitative methods have been used both to probe and gain a more in-depth understanding of environmental behaviours and spillover, their use alone is not sufficient to capture accurately actual behaviour and longitudinal aspects of spillover. Therefore, a more comprehensive approach to researching spillover would use a mixed-methods approach.

20.5.3 Mixed Methods

Mixed-methods designs allow the collection of diverse perspectives on the research topic by using both quantitative and qualitative data (Teddlie and Tashakkori 2003). Mixed methods in spillover research are rare, partly because it is a very time-consuming approach.

An example of a mixed-methods study was conducted by Barr et al. (2010), who looked at the spillover between pro-environmental behaviours at home and away/on holiday. They used an on-street survey that led to a clustering of consumers' lifestyles, followed by focus group discussions with each of the identified consumer clusters (Barr et al. 2010). Another example is a study on the introduction of the plastic bag charge in Wales and its spillover into other pro-environmental behaviours (Poortinga et al. 2016). Using a mixed-methods and longitudinal approach, Poortinga et al. (2016) examined attitudinal and behaviour changes following the English plastic bag charge that was introduced in 2015. They integrated a longitudinal survey, a longitudinal diary-interview study, and a longitudinal supermarket observation study conducted in three countries (England, Wales and Scotland) to uncover potential spillover effects from the introduction of the plastic bag charge (Poortinga et al. 2016). The findings showed people became more supportive of the plastic bag charge as well as of other charges to reduce waste; which is interpreted as a positive spillover effect (Poortinga et al. 2016). Poortinga et al. (2016) also concluded that, using a mixed-methods and longitudinal approach, the findings constitute a comprehensive and robust evaluation of attitudinal and behavioural impact of a policy change such as the plastic bag charge in England.

20.6   POLICY AND MANAGERIAL IMPLICATIONS

Researchers and policymakers have been particularly interested in the idea of accelerating sustainable lifestyles by campaigning for simple and low impact environmental behaviours, which could have a 'knock-on' effect on other potentially more difficult pro-environmental behaviours.

However, encouraging spillover across various aspects of one's life, particularly with regards to more difficult and complex behaviours, is not an easy task to achieve (Thøgersen and Crompton 2009). Despite various challenges, measures could be taken to increase the likelihood of spillover. For example, past research (Bratt 1999; Thøgersen 2004) has shown that spillover is more likely to happen between similar (or perceived to be similar) behaviours. Thus, both governmental campaigns targeting the general public and organisation-based interventions targeting employees should focus on making clear-cut links between the behaviours that they would target and expect to engender spillover (Thøgersen 2004).

In relation to environmental communications, Thøgersen and Crompton (2009) consider that contextual spillover is more likely to be generated by the use of communications or interventions that allude to individuals' environmental values and concerns rather than financial rewards and status signalling. These findings are complemented by those of Steinhorst and Matthies (2016) who examined the long-term spillover effects of electricity saving behaviour. Following the study results, they recommended that information campaigns targeting individuals with strong personal ecological norms should use environmental framing (CO_2) rather than monetary framing (money) (Steinhorst and Matthies 2016). This will encourage positive spillover into the acceptance of other environmental policy measures. However, for the individuals with weak personal ecological norms, the environmental framing had a negative effect and thus further research is needed in terms of effective design and communications for this group of people (Steinhorst and Matthies 2016).

Moreover, Thøgersen and Noblet's (2012) study on consumers' acceptance of spillover to wind power concluded that information should be provided via social marketing campaigns to increase environmental awareness and concern. Particularly, they consider the focus should be on encouraging individuals to perform 'regular' or 'more familiar' green behaviours, and in time this action-based learning could lead to positive spillover in other environmental contexts and behaviours (Thøgersen and Noblet 2012).

Another avenue for potentially achieving spillover of environmental behaviour is the appeal to, and development of, one's environmental identity. A study among US students on recycling behaviour found that environmental identity mediated spillover between recycling behaviour and support for a green fund (Truelove et al. 2016). However, this relationship and the influence of identity, in general, can be quite complex and at times unfavourable. For example, Truelove et al. (2016) also uncovered that for the Democrats in their study (who are expected to support pro-environmental behaviour as part of their political identity) recycling behaviour had a negative effect on environmental identity (i.e. lower environmental identity), which in turn decreased support for a green fund, indicating negative spillover. Therefore, caution should be exerted when developing social marketing interventions and communications based on the 'environmental identity' psychological concept.

While in section 4 a range of individual and organisational factors that can foster environmental spillover were mentioned, some researchers caution that these might not be always effective in practice. For example, it is considered that social norms are expected to have a positive impact but such an approach would be 'only useful when a majority of the target population actually performs the desired pro-environmental behaviour, which is often not the case for the more difficult' (Thøgersen and Crompton 2009: 156) and hence spillover is less likely to occur. Therefore, emphasising the exceptional behaviour rather than the normative existent behaviour is needed. Thus, overall, a range of communications and behaviour change approaches could be used in relation to engendering spillover between the home and workplace settings, but these should be carefully assessed in relation to its audience, targeted behaviours and contexts.

Implications for the organisational context include suggestions for communicating pro-environmental behaviours in the organisation and the framing of messages. In line with findings from Steinhorst and Matthies' (2016) and Evans et al.'s (2012) studies, organisations should be cautious to use financial framing and rewards to promote pro-environmental behaviours among their employees as these are likely to lead to no or negative spillover. Furthermore, in the organisational context a number of organisational factors can influence both positive and negative spillover. For instance, factors such as organisational culture, management support, and the employees' identification with the organisation can promote positive spillover between pro-environmental behaviours at work (Lo et al. 2012; Cox et al. 2012). A case study by the Scottish Government found that employees' commitment to ecological organisational values led to positive spillover between pro-environmental behaviours in the workplace but also between work and home (e.g. fuel-efficient driving and recycling) (Cox et al. 2012). On the other hand, a lack of employees' commitment to the organisation's green values led to a lack of or even negative spillover (Cox et al. 2012).

Additionally, one of the biggest policymakers' challenges in normalising spillover, both within and across contexts, is individuals' choice of lifestyles. As Barr et al. (2010) pointed out, the motivations and behavioural spillover predisposition of some individuals will differ according to their lifestyle choices. Therefore, generic interventions and marketing communications approaches might require some levels of tailoring according to the context and behaviours targeted for spillover. Moreover, Barr et al.

(2010) concluded that certain contexts, such as holidays and travelling, are less likely to witness spillover because of hedonism, convenience preferences and neutralisation tendencies. This suggests that additional research is needed to understand how these psychological mechanisms can be counteracted and future findings might inform practice, both at policy and organisational levels.

The present chapter has discussed the concept of spillover in pro-environmental behaviour research. More particularly, it provided an overview of the current spillover literature and its relevance to environmentally friendly behaviours and the workplace. Additionally, this chapter also critically examined methodological approaches to investigate spillover effects both between behaviours and between settings. Lastly, it considered the implications of both positive and negative spillover effects for social marketing campaigns and behaviour change programmes that promote pro-environmental behaviours in organisations. As outlined throughout the chapter, there are a number of individual factors (e.g. identity, norms) as well as contextual and behavioural factors (e.g. similarity between behaviours and/or settings) that influence spillover effects. For organisations that want to promote pro-environmental behaviours among their employees, it is important to consider these factors as they may endorse or inhibit behaviour change programmes and the organisation's environmental impact. Organisations that aim to promote pro-environmental behaviours among their employees might, therefore, prefer to promote those behaviours which are similar to behaviours already performed by their employees at home.

REFERENCES

Abrahamse, W., L. Steg, C. Vlek and T. Rothengatter (2005), 'A review of intervention studies aimed at household energy conservation', *Journal of Environmental Psychology*, **25** (3), 273–291.

Acs, Z. J., D. B. Audretsch and E. E. Lehmann (2009), 'The knowledge spillover theory of entrepreneurship', *Small Business Economics*, **32**, 15–30.

Ajzen, I. (1991), 'The theory of planned behavior', *Organizational Behavior and Human Decision Processes*, **50** (2), 179–211.

Austin, A., J. Cox, J. Barnett and C. Thomas (2011), 'Exploring catalyst behaviours: Full Report', a report to the Department for Environment, Food and Rural Affairs, Brook Lyndhurst for Defra, London, accessed 21 May 2017 at http://randd.defra.gov.uk/Default. aspx?Module=More&Location=None&ProjectID=16324.

Barr, S., G. Shaw, T. Coles and J. Prillwitz (2010), 'A holiday is a holiday: Practicing sustainability, home and away', *Journal of Transport Geography*, **18** (3), 474–481.

Baumeister, R. F., E. Bratslavsky, M. Muraven and D. M. Tice (1998), 'Ego depletion: Is the active self a limited resource?', *Journal of Personality and Social Psychology*, **74** (5), 1252–1265.

Bem, D. J. (1972), 'Self-perception theory', *Advances in Experimental Social Psychology*, **6**, 1–62.

Blanken, I., N. van de Ven and M. Zeelenberg (2015), 'A meta-analytic review of moral licensing', *Personality and Social Psychology Bulletin*, **41** (4), 540–558.

Bratt, C. (1999), 'Consumers environmental behavior: Generalized, sector-based, or compensatory?', *Environment and Behavior*, **31**, 28–44.

Burger, J. M. (1999), 'The foot-in-the-door compliance procedure: a multiple-process analysis and review', *Personality and Social Psychology Review*, **3** (4), 303–325.

Carrico, A. R. and M. Riemer (2011), 'Motivating energy conservation in the workplace: An evaluation of the use of group-level feedback and peer education', *Journal of Environmental Psychology*, **31** (1), 1–13.

Carrus, G., P. Passafaro and M. Bonnes (2008), 'Emotions, habits and rational choices in ecological behaviours: The case of recycling and use of public transportation', *Journal of Environmental Psychology*, **28** (1), 51–62.

Chatzidakis, A., A. Smith and S. Hibbert (2006), '"Ethically concerned, yet unethically behaved": Towards an updated understanding of consumer's (un) ethical decision making', *ACR North American Advances*.

Cialdini, R. B., M. R. Trost and J. T. Newsom (1995), 'Preferences for consistency: The development of a valid measure and the discovery of surprising behavioural implications', *Journal of Personality and Social Psychology*, **69** (2), 318–328.

Cox, A., T. Higgins, R. Gloster, B. Foley and A. Darnton (2012), 'The impact of workplace initiatives on low carbon behaviours', a report to the Scottish Government. Accessed 21 May 2017 at www.scotland.gov.uk/socialresearch.

Defra (2008), 'Framework for pro-environmental behaviours', report for the Department for Environment, Food and Rural Affairs. Accessed 21 May 2017 at https://www.gov.uk/government/uploads/system/uploads/attachment_data/file/69277/pb13574-behaviours-report-080110.pdf.

Dolan, P. and M. M. Galizzi (2014), 'Because I'm worth it: A lab-field experiment on the spillover effects of incentives in health', *CEP Discussion Papers*. Accessed 21 May 2017 at http://ideas.repec.org/p/cep/cepdps/dp1286.html.

Dolan, P. and M. M. Galizzi (2015), 'Like ripples on a pond: Behavioral spillovers and their implications for research and policy', *Journal of Economic Psychology*, **47**, 1–16.

Dumitru, A., E. De Gregorio, M. Bonnes, M. Bonaiuto, G. Carrus, R. Garcia-Mira and F. Maricchiolo (2016), 'Low carbon energy behaviors in the workplace: A qualitative study in Italy and Spain', *Energy Research & Social Science*, **13**, 49–59.

Evans, L., G. R. Maio, A. Corner, C. J. Hodgetts, S. Ahmed and U. Hahn (2012), 'Self-interest and pro-environmental behaviour', *Nature Climate Change*, **3** (2), 122–125.

Festinger, L. (1957), *A Theory of Cognitive Dissonance*, Stanford, CA: Stanford University Press.

Gneezy, A., A. Imas, A. Brown, L. D. Nelson and M. I. Norton (2012), 'Paying to be nice: Consistency and costly prosocial behavior', *Management Science*, **58** (1), 179–187.

Gregory-Smith, D., A. Smith and H. Winklhofer (2013), 'Emotions and dissonance in "ethical" consumption choices', *Journal of Marketing Management*, **29** (11–12), 1201–1223.

Gregory-Smith, D., V. K. Wells, D. Manika, and S. Graham (2015), 'An environmental social marketing intervention among employees: Assessing attitude and behaviour change', *Journal of Marketing Management*, **31** (3–4), 336–377.

Grunberg, L., S. Moore and E. Greenberg (1998), 'Work stress and problem alcohol behavior: A test of the spillover model', *Journal of Organizational Behavior*, **19** (5), 487–502.

Han, S., J. S. Lerner and D. Keltner (2007), 'Feelings and consumer decision making: The appraisal-tendency framework', *Journal of Consumer Psychology*, **17** (3), 158–168.

Hares, A., J. Dickinson and K. Wilkes (2010), 'Climate change and the air travel decisions of UK tourists', *Journal of Transport Geography*, **18** (3), 466–473.

Hope, A. L., C. R. Jones, T. L. Webb, M. T. Watson and D. Kaklamanou (2017), 'The role of compensatory beliefs in rationalizing environmentally detrimental behaviors', *Environment and Behavior*, accessed at http://journals.sagepub.com/doi/full/10.1177/0013916517706730.

Hyland, M. and D. Prottas (2016), 'Looking at spillover from both sides: An examination of work and home flexibility and permeability', *Community, Work & Family*, **8803** (June), 1–20.

Kaklamanou, D., C. R. Jones, T. L. Webb and S. R. Walker (2013), 'Using public transport can make up for flying abroad on holiday: Compensatory green beliefs and environmentally significant behavior', *Environment and Behavior*, **47** (2), 184–204.

Klade, M., W. Mert, U. Seebacher and I. Schultz (2013), 'Sustainable behaviour at work and in private life: The contribution of enterprises', *International Journal of Innovation and Sustainable Development (IJISD)*, **7** (4), 321–332.

Klöckner, C. A., A. Nayum and M. Mehmetoglu (2013), 'Positive and negative spillover effects from electric car purchase to car use', *Transportation Research Part D: Transport and Environment*, **21**, 32–38.

Lacasse, K. (2016), 'Don't be satisfied, identify! Strengthening positive spillover by connecting pro-environmental behaviors to an "environmentalist" label', *Journal of Environmental Psychology*, **48**, 149–158.

Lanzini, P. and J. Thøgersen (2014), 'Behavioural spillover in the environmental domain: An intervention study', *Journal of Environmental Psychology*, **40**, 381–390.

Lauren, N., K. S. Fielding, L. Smith and W. Louis (2016), 'You did, so you can and you will: Self-efficacy as a mediator of spillover from easy to more difficult pro-environmental behaviour', *Journal of Environmental Psychology*, **48**, 191–199.

Laury, S. K. and L. O. Taylor (2008), 'Altruism spillovers: Are behaviors in context-free experiments predictive of altruism toward a naturally occurring public good?', *Journal of Economic Behavior & Organization*, **65** (1), 9–29.

Lee, S., K. D. Davis, C. Neuendorf, A. Grandey, C. B. Lam and D. M. Almeida (2016), 'Individual- and organization-level work-to-family spillover are uniquely associated with hotel managers' work exhaustion and satisfaction', *Frontiers in Psychology*, **7**.

Lerner, J. S., D. A. Small and G. Loewenstein (2004), 'Heart strings and purse strings carryover effects of emotions on economic decisions', *Psychological Science*, **15** (5), 337–341.

Littleford, C., T. J. Ryley and S. K. Firth (2014), 'Context, control and the spillover of energy use behaviours between office and home settings', *Journal of Environmental Psychology*, **40**, 157–166.

Lo, S. H., G.-J. Y. Peters and G. Kok (2012), 'A review of determinants of and interventions for proenvironmental behaviors in organizations', *Journal of Applied Social Psychology*, **42** (12), 2933–2967.

Margetts, E. A. and Y. Kashima (2017), 'Spillover between pro-environmental behaviours: The role of resources and perceived similarity', *Journal of Environmental Psychology*, **49**, 30–42.

Meijers, M. H. C., P. W. J. Verlegh, M. K. Noordewier and E. G. Smit (2015), 'The dark side of donating: How donating may license environmentally unfriendly behavior', *Social Influence*, **10** (4), 250–263.

Merritt, A. C., D. A. Effron and B. Monin (2010), 'Moral self-licensing: When being good frees us to be bad', *Social and Personality Psychology Compass*, **4** (5), 344–357.

Muster, V. (2011), 'Companies promoting sustainable consumption of employees', *Journal of Consumer Policy*, **34** (1), 161–174.

Nik Ramli, N. A. R. and M. Naja (2012), 'A discussion of underlying theories explaining the spillover of environmentally friendly behavior phenomenon', *Procedia – Social and Behavioral Sciences*, **50** (July), 1061–1072.

Nilsson, A., M. Bergquist and W. P. Schultz (2016), 'Spillover effects in environmental behaviors, across time and context: A review and research agenda', *Environmental Education Research*, **4622** (November), 1–17.

Ones, D. S. and S. Dilchert (2012), 'Employee green behaviours', in S. E. Jackson, D. S. Ones and S. Dilchert (eds), *Managing Human Resources for Environmental Sustainability*, San Francisco, CA: Jossey-Bass, pp. 191–202.

Peters, A., M. Sonnberger, E. Dütschke and J. Deuschle (2012), 'Theoretical perspective on rebound effects from a social science point of view', Working paper Sustainability and Innovation S2/2012, Karlsruhe: Fraunhofer ISI.

Poortinga, W., E. Sautkina, G. O. Thomas and E. Wolstenholme (2016), 'The English plastic bag charge: Changes in attitudes and behaviour', Cardiff: Welsh School of

Architecture/ School of Psychology, Cardiff University. Accessed 29 June 2017 at http://orca.cf.ac.uk/94652/1/Cardiff_University_Plastic_Bag_Report_A4%20(final%20proof).pdf.

Poortinga, W., L. Whitmarsh, and C. Suffolk (2013), 'The introduction of a single-use carrier bag charge in Wales: Attitude change and behavioural spillover effects', *Journal of Environmental Psychology*, **36**, 240–247.

Rashid, N. R. N. and N. Mohammad (2011), 'Spillover of environmentally friendly behaviour phenomenon: The mediating effect of employee organizational identification', *OIDA International Journal of Sustainable Development*, **2** (12), 29–42.

Renwick, D. W. S., T. Redman and S. Maguire (2013), 'Green human resource management: A review and research agenda', *International Journal of Management Reviews*, **15** (1), 1–14.

Rodríguez-Muñoz, A., A. I. Sanz-Vergel, E. Demerouti and A. B. Bakker (2014), 'Engaged at work and happy at home: A spillover–crossover model', *Journal of Happiness Studies*, **15** (2), 271–283.

Ruepert, A., K. Keizer, L. Steg, F. Maricchiolo, G. Carrus, A. Dumitru, ... D. Moza (2016), 'Environmental considerations in the organizational context: A pathway to pro-environmental behaviour at work', *Energy Research and Social Science*, **17**, 59–70.

Sachdeva, S., R. Iliev and D. L. Medin (2009), 'Sinning saints and saintly sinners: The paradox of moral self-regulation', *Psychological Science*, **20** (4), 523–528.

Sanz-Vergel, A. I., A. Rodríguez-Muñoz and K. Nielsen (2015), 'The thin line between work and home: The spillover and crossover of daily conflicts', *Journal of Occupational and Organizational Psychology*, **88** (1), 1–18.

Schütte, L. and D. Gregory-Smith (2015), 'Neutralisation and mental accounting in ethical consumption: The case of sustainable holidays', *Sustainability*, **7**, 1–14.

Sorrell, S., J. Dimitropoulos and M. Sommerville (2009), 'Empirical estimates of the direct rebound effect: A review', *Energy Policy*, **37** (4), 1356–1371.

Steg, L. and C. Vlek (2009), 'Encouraging pro-environmental behaviour: An integrative review and research agenda', *Journal of Environmental Psychology*, **29** (3), 309–317.

Steinhorst, J. and E. Matthies (2016), 'Monetary or environmental appeals for saving electricity? – Potentials for spillover on low carbon policy acceptability', *Energy Policy*, **93**, 335–344.

Steinhorst, J., C. A. Klöckner and E. Matthies (2015), 'Saving electricity – For the money or the environment? Risks of limiting pro-environmental spillover when using monetary framing', *Journal of Environmental Psychology*, **43**, 125–135.

Stern, P. C. (2000), 'New environmental theories: Toward a coherent theory of environmentally significant behavior', *Journal of Social Issues*, **56** (3), 407–424.

Sykes, G. M. and D. Matza (1957), 'Techniques of neutralization: A theory of delinquency', *American Sociological Review*, **22** (6), 664–670.

Teddlie, C. and A. Tashakkori (2003), 'Major issues and controversies in the use of mixed methods in the social and behavioural sciences', in A. Tashakkori and C. Teddlie (eds), *Handbook of Mixed Methods in Social & Behavioural Research*, 2nd edn, London: SAGE Publications Ltd, pp. 3–50.

Thøgersen, J. (1999), 'Spillover processes in the development of a sustainable consumption pattern', *Journal of Economic Psychology*, **20** (1), 53–81.

Thøgersen, J. (2004), 'A cognitive dissonance interpretation of consistencies and inconsistencies in environmentally responsible behavior', *Journal of Environmental Psychology*, **24** (1), 93–103.

Thøgersen, J. and T. Crompton (2009), 'Simple and painless? The limitations of spillover in environmental campaigning', *Journal of Consumer Policy*, **32** (2), 141–163.

Thøgersen, J. and C. Noblet (2012), 'Does green consumerism increase the acceptance of wind power?', *Energy Policy*, **51**, 854–862.

Thøgersen, J. and F. Ölander (2003), 'Spillover of environment-friendly consumer behaviour', *Journal of Environmental Psychology*, **23** (3), 225–236.

Thomas, G. O., W. Poortinga and E. Sautkina (2016), 'The Welsh single-use carrier bag charge and behavioural spillover', *Journal of Environmental Psychology*, **47**, 126–135.

Tiefenbeck, V., T. Staake, K. Roth and O. Sachs (2013), 'For better or for worse? Empirical evidence of moral licensing in a behavioral energy conservation campaign', *Energy Policy*, **57**, 160–171.

Truelove, H. B., A. R. Carrico, E. U. Weber, K. T. Raimi and M. P. Vandenbergh (2014), 'Positive and negative spillover of pro-environmental behavior: An integrative review and theoretical framework', *Global Environmental Change*, **29**, 127–138.

Truelove, H. B., K. L. Yeung, A. R. Carrico, A. J. Gillis and K. T. Raimi (2016), 'From plastic bottles to policy support: An experimental test of pro-environmental spillover', *Journal of Environmental Psychology*, **46**, 55–66.

Tudor, T. L., S. W. Barr and A. W. Gilg (2008), 'A novel conceptual framework for examining environmental behavior in large organizations: A case study of the Cornwall National Health Service (NHS) in the United Kingdom', *Environment and Behavior*, **40** (3), 426–450.

Uzzell, D. and N. Räthzel (2013), 'Modelling agents and organisations to achieve transition to a low carbon Europe', D5.3: Final Report on the study of Everyday Environmental Strategies and Practices in Shell UK Ltd and AB Volvo, Umeå, Sweden.

van der Werff, E., L. Steg and K. Keizer (2014a), 'Follow the signal: When past pro-environmental actions signal who you are', *Journal of Environmental Psychology*, **40**, 273–282.

van der Werff, E., L. Steg and K. Keizer (2014b), 'I am what I am, by looking past the present: The influence of biospheric values and past behavior on environmental self-identity', *Environment and Behavior*, **46** (5), 626–657.

Weber, E. U. (2006), 'Experience-based and description-based perceptions of long-term risk: Why global warming does not scare us (yet)', *Climatic Change*, **77** (1–2), 103–120.

Wells, V. K., B. Taheri, D. Gregory-Smith and D. Manika (2016), 'The role of generativity and attitudes on employees home and workplace water and energy saving behaviours', *Tourism Management*, **56**, 63–74.

Westman, M. (2002), 'Crossover of stress and strain in the family and in the workplace', in P. L. Perrewe and D. Ganster (eds), *Research in Occupational Stress and Well-being*, 2nd edn, JAI Press/Elsevier Science, pp. 143–118.

Whitmarsh, L. and S. O'Neill (2010), 'Green identity, green living? The role of pro-environmental self-identity in determining consistency across diverse pro-environmental behaviours', *Journal of Environmental Psychology*, **30** (3), 305–314.

Winterich, K. P., S. Han and J. S. Lerner (2010), 'Now that I'm sad, it's hard to be mad: The role of cognitive appraisals in emotional blunting', *Personality and Social Psychology Bulletin*, **36** (11), 1467–1483.

Young, C. W., M. Davis, I. M. McNeill, B. Malhotra, S. Russell, K. Unsworth and C. W. Clegg (2013), 'Changing behaviour: Successful environmental programmes in the workplace', *Business Strategy and the Environment*, **24**, 689–703.

Index

488   *Research handbook on employee pro-environmental behaviour*